POLITICS IN
THE AMERICAN STATES

POLITICS IN
THE AMERICAN STATES

A Comparative Analysis

SECOND EDITION

EDITED BY

Herbert Jacob *Northwestern University*

Kenneth N. Vines *State University of New York at Buffalo*

LITTLE, BROWN AND COMPANY *Boston*

LIBRARY OF CONGRESS CATALOG CARD NUMBER: 78–160698

FOURTH PRINTING

Published simultaneously in Canada
by Little, Brown & Company (Canada) Limited

PRINTED IN THE UNITED STATES OF AMERICA

Preface to the Second Edition

Since the first edition of this work was published, the comparative study of state politics has developed rapidly. New aspects of state politics have been investigated and existing lines of investigation have been broadened and analyzed in more sophisticated ways. In this second edition we present many of the most important findings by scholars who have been in the forefront of the movement.

Whereas in the first edition we strongly advocated the utility of comparative studies in state politics, we find now that comparative analysis has become the predominant mode of investigation. We formerly hypothesized that state politics should be in the main stream of political science; we find now that such studies of the states are among the more advanced instances of theoretical development and empirical testing. Indeed, measured by explicit comparative criteria, state politics has generated more theory by means of comparative study and conducted more analytical tests through comparative analysis than cross-national studies. In many respects, the study of state politics has become the seedbed of comparative analysis in political science.

Successful experiences in comparative analysis impose a responsibility on state politics scholars. Much remains to be done. In many vital areas there is a poverty of data (i.e., the lack of indicators of state parties); aspects of state politics have not been examined (i.e., the lack of studies on regulation policies). The modest degree of analytical success merely emphasizes the need for more sophisticated techniques of comparison.

In the epilogue of this volume we describe the limitations of our study of state politics and speculate on directions that successful development might take. Scholars in state politics have accomplished much in a short time and we hope that our present writings will stimulate even greater development in the field.

As in the first edition, we would like to thank several members of the staff of Little, Brown and Company. Donald R. Hammonds gave us his enthusiastic support and made this edition financially possible; Alfred Browne gave additional encouragement and guided the publication to completion. Jeannine Laverty worked with us in dedicated fashion to make our work more readable and presentable.

Herbert Jacob
Kenneth N. Vines

Preface to the First Edition

This text seeks to bring contemporary political science concepts and techniques to the general study of state politics. It examines the states comparatively; it is systematically empirical; it limits itself to state politics. Each of these features is incorporated through the experience of leading experts.

The principal feature of this volume is that it undertakes a comparative analysis of politics in the fifty states. It has always seemed anomalous to us that "comparative government" is a phrase used to describe the study of foreign governments. Comparative analysis is even more appropriate to the study of domestic institutions like the states since they are enough alike to make comparative analysis plausible, but different enough to produce valuable insights into the conditions that affect political institutions and the behavior of citizens and officials. Furthermore, comparative analysis of state politics reveals those features of the political process that are common not only to the states but also to political phenomena in general. It emphasizes the extent to which the study of state politics is not an insulated specialization, but in the mainstream of political science.

A second characteristic of this book is that it is empirical and analytic. Our collaborators have sought to describe by keeping close to the facts, and to analyze by examining those empirical relationships they actually found. As there are only fifty states, they have always sought to account for each of them. All too often in the literature of state politics one or another state has been selected to illustrate a point; this allows colorful description but it introduces biases into the analysis, for such casual selections can hardly serve as a valid basis for generalizations. Either the whole "universe" must be described, or the limits of generalization must be carefully specified. We have examined political practices in all fifty states wherever possible; where this was not feasible, we have tried to limit our conclusions accordingly.

Empirical analysis has been enriched in the last decade by the development of new political science techniques. Our authors make frequent use of these advances. Their data, for example, are sometimes based on sample surveys, as well as upon official government sources. Quantitative techniques that have been employed include percentage distributions, averages, cross tabulations, and correlation coefficients. These are used when appropriate to describe, analyze, and simplify the complexities of state politics. In addition, measurements are used because some features of state politics lend themselves to quite precise measurement — for example, voter turnout. Other concepts are less precise. The degree of party competition, the amount of interest group activity, the degree of legislative cohesion, and the power of a governor do not allow the same degree of precision as the number of votes cast at an election. Yet each of these important phenomena are measurable and have been tabulated by our authors. For instance, the degree of party competition can yield an ordinal scale that shows where each state stands in relation to every other state.

The third distinctive feature of this book is that it limits its attention to state politics. Most texts combine state politics with local politics. We have not done so because we felt that local political systems cannot be examined thoroughly when combined with state politics. Local political systems involve different participants, different institutions, and different stakes. Moreover, local politics flourishes in many forms; no simple generalizations do justice to the variety of local political systems that exist in the United States. As a consequence, we felt it unwise to attempt an analysis of local politics here.

Emphasis on comparative analysis of empirical data about state politics has yielded a text rich in description and explicit in its analysis. Rather than summarize and digest the process of analysis for the student, we allow him to see for himself the methods by which conclusions are reached and the process by which the descriptions and analyses are made.

The idea for this book originated in correspondence between the Editors concerning the possibility of a more effective text for teaching state politics. Given the increase in information about the states and the important advances in the methodology and theory of political studies in recent years, we felt the time had come to depart from traditional ways of presenting the subject.

The conception of a comparative study of state politics is not new. The Social Science Research Council encouraged this type of state study through its publications and fellowship programs after World War II. V. O. Key, Jr., in his pioneering *Southern Politics* and *American State Politics* undertook the comparative examination of several aspects of state political experience; a few others have also looked at different geographical regions along these lines. Yet, after hopeful beginnings, no systematic treatment of state politics emerged.

The character of state politics indicated that successful study could best be achieved by a collaborative project. The amount of literature and the effort required for research and analysis make it difficult for one or two scholars, no matter how experienced, to cope with the variety of phenomena and the complexities encompassed. On the other hand, a team of scholars — each highly qualified in some area of state politics — could command the resources necessary for a thorough treatment. Therefore, the Editors invited scholars who had published in various fields to participate, and found them enthusiastic about the idea.

Although written by separate experts, the chapters form a unified study, for each is set within a common frame of reference. Each encompasses:

1. A comparative analysis in which variations and similarities of state politics are systematically described, examined, and then related to other features of the political and social environment of the states;

2. An analysis that utilizes modern methods and theoretical conceptions to clarify the operation and functions of state political systems.

Through correspondence and conversations, the Editors and authors discussed the problems of comparison, and in some cases worked together toward the solution of difficulties in data collection and analysis. The Editors commented on rough drafts of the texts. Each chapter, however, is the product of its author.

Although this volume is as definitive as present available knowledge allows us to make it, throughout the book our authors point to gaps in the data — areas about which we do not know enough to make even tentative generalizations. This is part of the challenge of state politics. We hope this volume does not lull the reader into complacence; on the contrary, we hope it generates disagreement, controversy, and productive new research.

We are more than usually indebted to several members of the staff of Little, Brown and Company. Donald R. Hammonds gave us his enthusiastic support and made the project financially possible. Ronald Q. Lewton, Freda Alexander, and their assistants rounded off many rough edges that inevitably appear in such a collaborative work.

We dedicate this volume to the memory of V. O. Key, Jr., whose research in state politics marked the path we have tried to follow.

Herbert Jacob
Kenneth N. Vines

About the Authors

RICHARD E. DAWSON is Associate Professor of Political Science at Washington University in St. Louis. He has authored or coauthored several articles on welfare politics and state policy outputs. He has coauthored a book on political socialization.

THOMAS R. DYE is Professor and Chairman of the Department of Government at Florida State University. He has taught at the universities of Georgia and Wisconsin. He is the author or coauthor of a number of books and articles on American politics, state and local government, and public policy, including *Suburban Differences and Metropolitan Policies* (1965), *Politics, Economics, and the Public* (1966), *Politics in States and Communities* (1969), *The Irony of Democracy* (1970), and *The Politics of Equality* (1971).

ROBERT S. FRIEDMAN is Professor and Head of the Department of Political Science at Pennsylvania State University. He has been on the faculties of the University of Michigan, Louisiana State University, and the University of Maryland. Publications he has authored are: *State and Local Relations in Highway Finance in Louisiana* (1961), *The Michigan Constitutional Convention and Administrative Organization: A Case Study in the Politics of Constitution-Making* (1963), *The Maryland County Unit System and Urban-Rural Politics,* and *Professionalism: Expertise and Policy-Making* (1971). He is coauthor of *Local Government in Maryland* (1958), *Government in Metropolitan New Orleans* (1960), and *Political Leadership and the School Desegregation Crisis in New Orleans* (1963). He has contributed to numerous professional journals.

VIRGINIA GRAY is Assistant Professor of Political Science at the University of Kentucky. She has published previously in the *Journal of American History*.

RICHARD I. HOFFERBERT is Associate Professor of Political Science at the University of Michigan and Executive Director of the Interuniversity Consortium for Political Research. He previously taught political science at Cornell University for three years and at Williams College for five years. He is coeditor (with Ira Sharkansky) of *State and Urban Politics* (1971). He has contributed articles to several professional journals and symposia.

HERBERT JACOB is Professor of Political Science at Northwestern University. Earlier he was a member of the faculty of Tulane University and at the University of Wisconsin in Madison. He is author of *German Administration Since Bismarck* (1963), *Justice in America* (1965, 1972), *Debtors in Court* (1969), and coauthored *Studies in Judicial Politics* (1963) and *Elementary Political Analysis* (1970). He has written articles for several professional journals and symposia.

LESTER W. MILBRATH is Professor of Political Science at State University of New York at Buffalo, where he is also Associate Provost of the Faculty of Social Sciences and Administration, Director of the Social Science Research Institute, and Director of the Social Science Measurement Center. Before this, he was on the faculty of Northwestern University, Duke University, and the University of Tennessee. He wrote *The Washington Lobbyists* (1963), *Political Participation* (1965), and has contributed to a number of professional journals.

CLARA PENNIMAN is Professor of Political Science at the University of Wisconsin and Director, Center for Public Policy and Administration. She is the author of *Science and State Government in Wisconsin* (1956) and *Wisconsin's State and Local Tax Burden* (1959); she coauthored *The Minnesota Department of Taxation* (1955), *State Income Tax Administration* (1959), and *Government in the Fifty States* (1960). She has published many articles on taxation in professional journals.

AUSTIN RANNEY is Professor of Political Science at the University of Wisconsin. His published works include *The Doctrine of Responsible Party Government* (1954), *The Governing of Men* (1958, 1966, 1971), *Illinois Politics* (1960), and *Pathways to Parliament* (1965). He is also coauthor of *Democracy and the American Party System* (1956), and editor of *Essays on the Behavioral Study of Politics* (1962) and *Political Science and Public Policy* (1968). He has also contributed numerous articles to professional journals, and from 1965–1971 served as managing editor of the *American Political Science Review*.

ROBERT H. SALISBURY is Professor of Political Science and Chairman of the Department at Washington University in St. Louis. He is the author of *Interest Group Politics in America* (1970) and coauthor of *American Government and the Mid-Twentieth Century* (1959, 1965), *Democracy and the Mid-Twentieth Century* (1960), and *State Politics and the Public Schools* (1964). He has contributed numerous papers to symposia and professional journals.

JOSEPH A. SCHLESINGER is Professor of Political Science at Michigan State University. He has also served on the faculties of Boston University, Wesleyan University, and the University of California at Berkeley. In addition to *How They Became Governor* (1957), and *Ambition and Politics* (1966), he has written many articles for professional journals.

IRA SHARKANSKY is Professor of Political Science at the University of Wisconsin. His books are *Spending in the American States* (1968), *The Politics of Taxing and Spending* (1969), *Regionalism in American Politics* (1970), *The Routines of Politics* (1970), *Public Administration: Policy-Making in Government Agencies* (1970), *Policy Analysis in Political Science* (1970), *Urban Politics and Public Policy* (with Robert L. Lineberry, 1971), and *State and Urban Politics: Readings in Comparative Public Policy* (with Richard I. Hofferbert, 1971). His newest book, currently in press, is *The Maligned States: Policy Accomplishments, Problems and Opportunities*. He also has written for numerous professional journals and symposia.

HENDRIK VAN DALEN is completing his Doctorate in Political Science at the University of Oregon, where he has been a research assistant at the Center for the Advanced Study of Educational Administration since September, 1969.

KENNETH N. VINES is Professor of Political Science at the State University of New York at Buffalo. He is coauthor of *Theory and Practice of American Foreign Policy* (1955), *Studies in Judicial Politics* (1963), *The Politics of the Federal Courts* (1970), *Research in American Politics: Laboratory Workbook* (1971), and author of *Republicanism in New Orleans* (1956) and *Two Parties for Shreveport* (1958). His newest book, written with Henry Glick and still in press, is *State Courts*. Besides these he has contributed numerous articles to professional journals and symposia.

JACK L. WALKER is Associate Professor of Political Science and Research Associate in the Institute of Public Policy Studies at the University of Michigan. He is the author of numerous articles and monographs on state and urban politics, and is coauthor of the forthcoming *Race and the Urban Political Community* (1972).

L. HARMON ZEIGLER is Professor of Political Science at the University of Oregon. He is the author of *Interest Groups in American Society* (1964), *The Political Life of American Teachers* (1967), *Lobbying* (with Michael Baer, 1969), and *The Irony of Democracy: An Uncommon Introduction to American Politics,* (1970). He was a Ford Foundation Fellow in 1969 and a Guggenheim Foundation Fellow in 1970.

Contents

xv

List of Tables and Figures

TABLES

CHAPTER THREE

CHAPTER FOUR

FIGURES

POLITICS IN
THE AMERICAN STATES

PART ONE

INTRODUCTION

CHAPTER ONE

The Study of State Politics

Herbert Jacob and Kenneth N. Vines

The roll call of state capitals — learned perhaps only by schoolchildren who want to earn a dollar from a friendly uncle — is like a list of America's forgotten cities. Although it includes a few well-known metropolitan areas such as Boston, Honolulu, and Denver, it is dominated by cities such as Dover, Boise, Topeka, Helena, Carson City, Augusta, Montpelier, Olympia, and Cheyenne. Yet most of the vital decisions affecting the health, education, safety, and welfare of all Americans are made in state capitals. Abortions are legalized and narcotics laws are tightened there. In the legislative halls and office buildings of administrative agencies in each state capital, officials determine the number of students who may go to state colleges and set the amount of money to be sent to local schools. Other officials determine the living standards of those on welfare, the fate of urban transit systems, and the routes of highways and expressways. State supreme courts settle complex questions of law and justice, and regulatory agencies determine how much consumers can be charged for telephone service, electricity, and natural gas.

Partly because many of these decisions are made in small, relatively unknown cities, the news media neglect to cover them as they do Washington or the international scene. Occasionally, a particularly colorful state politician such as Lester Maddox attracts nationwide attention, but the daily political struggle that occurs in state legislatures, administrative agencies, and courts remains veiled from most of the public. The stakes of this struggle are enormous, for billions of dollars are allocated and millions of citizens derive benefits or disadvantages from actions of state officials.

Outwardly state politics appears very much the same throughout the

3

United States. Each state has the same set of governmental institutions, grapples with many of the same problems, and operates in the same national environment.

Such appearances are entirely misleading, for state politics varies tremendously from state to state. Contrast the sedate election campaigns of Vermont with the swashbuckling campaigns in Tennessee, replete with hillbilly bands. Compare the $165 million that Massachusetts spent in 1969 on state colleges and universities with the $368 million that smaller, less wealthy Wisconsin spent.[1]* The state of Louisiana collects three-fourths of all state and local taxes; South Dakota collects less than two-fifths of these taxes.[2] Illinois is actively involved in pollution control; Alaskan leaders exploit the natural resources of their state.

Why do such differences occur? Why do Vermont and Tennessee politicians campaign so differently? Why does Massachusetts spend so little on its public colleges and Wisconsin so much? Why are some state governments more powerful than others?

The state political process is complex. Elections and politicking for office are only a small part of it. Interest groups, such as the Food Retailers Association and the Concrete Contractors Association, seek benefits outside the electoral process. In fact, most decisions in state politics are made without direct reference to elections by appointed officials who work in the bureaucracy and respond to demands made on them. Every use of a government service is an occasion for partaking in the political process.

We can examine the political process in many ways. We can study the nature of electoral participation and classify governments as democratic or undemocratic. We can examine how decisions are made and categorize governments as presidential or parliamentary. We can question the scope of governmental activity and list some governments as totalitarian and others as laissez-faire. Finally, we can consider the ideology of the ruling elite and categorize governments as communist, socialist, Maoist, or libertarian.

We need still another kind of classification to explain how and why variations exist in the political processes of the states. We are less interested in applying labels than in learning why the governor dominates in some states, legislators in others, and why services and taxes vary from state to state.

We need to clarify three elements of our study: (1) the focus on American states, (2) the conceptual framework of systems theory, and (3) the logic of analysis.

* [See pp. 563–564 for notes to this chapter. — Eds.]

THE STATES AS POLITICAL UNITS

The states as political units have many distinctive features. Their peculiar middle position in the American political system makes them less than sovereign nations but more than administrative districts. They share a common national tradition that limits their options for experimentation. They also cluster into regional groupings with common traditions and practices. The gyrations of our national economy affect all of them.

The States as Middlemen

The Constitution restricts the scope of state activity. Since it requires that foreign affairs be conducted by the national government, the states have no role in making or executing foreign policy. Although each state may keep a militia, the high cost of war and its close association with foreign policy has meant that the states have little role in national defense. The only soldiers under direct state control are those in the National Guard, a weekend force that is authorized, equipped, and subsidized by the national government and subject to its call in any national emergency.

Consequently, the governmental functions of the states are restricted entirely to the domestic arena. Even in domestic politics, the Constitution limits state activity and places it under the supervision of the national government. Originally the Constitution prohibited state interference with interstate commerce and the national currency system, but amendments and new interpretations of old provisions have further restricted the states. Now states may not discriminate against citizens on the basis of race, color, or previous servitude. The Constitution protects many of the political rights of citizens, such as voting and the right to counsel in criminal cases, from violation by the states.

The states must also contend with their political subdivisions — the cities, towns, and counties that actually deliver most governmental services. In most states, large cities struggle to dominate the state's government; the smaller cities, suburbs, and rural areas resist this domination. Many residents of large cities are poorer than those who live in other parts of the state. The cost of governing large cities is higher than the cost of governing smaller towns because the large cities have a greater portion of crime, welfare needs, health problems, and old housing. School systems are often exceptionally expensive in large cities, since they have many pupils from poor families whose educational needs are often costlier than those of pupils from middle-class families. All these characteristics mean that residents of large cities make greater demands on state politics than residents of small towns. Moreover, the financial assistance they seek would restrict state expenditures in suburban and rural areas. In many states, the conflict of these demands is intensified because representatives from the largest cities are not the majority in either legislative house, and sometimes they are also divided against each other. Frustrated by the conflict within their states, many large city mayors look to Washington rather than to the state capital for assistance.

Nevertheless, the states provide many important services and are the link between federal and local governments. On their own, states sponsor most of the college and university education available in the United States. With federal contributions they construct highways, provide hospital care for the mentally ill, and administer most welfare programs. They provide courts and a legal system for judicial resolution of conflict, and they operate extensive prison systems for incarcerating and rehabilitating criminals. In many portions of the country, states collect much of the money to run the public schools. As Table 1 indicates, the states spend much of the money expended for domestic programs in the United States. But their role is more important than the raw statistics suggest because they supervise much of the local government spending and make many of the most important distributive decisions. Thus, the states set the level of welfare payments even though they channel much of the federal money from Washington

TABLE 1

Expenditures by Federal, State, and Local Governments, 1968

	Amount (millions of dollars)		
Function	*Federal*	*State*	*Local*
National defense and international relations	83,874	–	–
Space research and technology	4,645	–	–
Postal service	6,485	–	–
Interest on general debt	11,607	1,128	2,138
Education	7,184	24,279	30,237
Highways	4,464	11,848	4,713
Natural resources	7,001	2,005	522
Health and hospitals	3,751	4,203	3,806
Public welfare	6,794	8,649	4,828
Housing and urban renewal	1,995	103	1,614
Air transportation	917	96	448
Social insurance administration	1,363	606	–
Other and combined	11,909	7,478	16,087

Source: United States Bureau of the Census, *Statistical Abstract of the United States, 1970* (Washington, D.C.: United States Government Printing Office, 1970), 407.

to local welfare departments; they allocate much of the federal money for improving police departments and decide which localities will receive funds and for what purposes they may be used, although the money is actually spent at the local level. In addition, many of the most important regulatory actions — such as setting rates for utility companies — are made by state agencies, although the importance of these decisions is not reflected in the minute sums spent by the states on regulatory agencies.

The intermediate position of the states has many consequences for their political processes. It limits the financial resources of some states and benefits others. It makes them vulnerable to "end runs" when interests that do not receive favorable action in the state capital seek to obtain it at the national level. It increases states' dependence on other units of the political system.

Common National and Regional Traditions

The Constitution is part of the common historical tradition of the American people. This common experience has defined a range of values and political institutions for state political systems. They all pay obeisance to the ideology of the American Revolution: constitutionalism guaranteeing life, liberty, and the pursuit of happiness. Every state has a constitution: some constitutions are more than a century old; a few have been drafted in recent decades. Although they vary in length and content, they are fundamentally alike. Each has a bill of rights that includes many of the freedoms guaranteed by the federal Bill of Rights. Each constitution establishes a framework of state governmental institutions that resembles the national framework. Only Nebraska has broken with the general pattern by specifying a unicameral legislature that has one house instead of the traditional two. Other details such as the size of the legislature, the length of legislators' terms, the length of the governor's term, the number of other elective offices, and the degree of detail regarding administrative structure and fiscal policy vary, but the range of variation is remarkably small. No state for instance, has a parliamentary system, and no state has a judiciary that is responsible to a ministry of justice.

Matters that are usually not prescribed by state constitutions, such as the party system, are also remarkably alike among the states. The Democratic and Republican parties operate in all states and in many they compete closely with each other. No state has a true single-party system; only a few have supported third parties for long. No state has a multi-party system based on proportional representation.

The legal systems of the states also have many similarities. With the exception of Louisiana, which retained for many years elements of the Napoleonic Code originally introduced by the French, each state has a legal system based on the Anglo-American common law tradition. Although laws on particular subjects — divorce, abortion, auto accident liability — differ in detail from state to state, their fundamental assumptions are generally alike. In addition, states have almost identical statutes on many subjects because of explicit attempts to make state laws uniform.

In addition to the national characteristics that restrict the variation among state political systems, regional characteristics also set groups of states apart from others. Regional patterns are not as pervasive as the national characteristics, and they often affect only a portion of the political system. In addition, they are receding in significance as many Americans move from one region to another and as the national media smother regional peculiarities. Nevertheless, some regional differences persist.[3] The South — usually defined as the states of the Confederacy [4] — is one such region. It is distinguished by a historical tradition that included slavery, the Civil War, and Reconstruction.[5] Until recently it was the area with the heaviest concentration of Negroes, the least industry, and the most poverty. The South has changed greatly in the last generation and is still changing. Many blacks have left and northern whites have moved in. The economy has become industrialized and agriculture has become mechanized. As in other regions of the country, urban areas have grown rapidly and now have larger populations than the rural hinterlands. Although portions of the South are still very poor, other portions are as rich as any other part of the country. Nevertheless, the tradition of segregation and discrimination against Negroes persists more openly in the South than in many other areas.

The Northeast is another recognizable region. It, too, is marked by a unique ethnic blend, the result of many immigrants from Ireland, Italy, and the Slavic countries who settled in the northeastern states after entering the country in the late nineteenth and early twentieth centuries. This region had early and intense industrialization, although many of the first industries declined in the middle of the twentieth century, leading to a period of economic decline in the Northeast. It is also an area of intense urbanization, containing the nation's first megalopolis, which extends from Boston to Washington, D.C. The Northeast, especially New England, is more heavily Catholic than many other areas of the country.

The third distinctive region is the Far West, the nation's last frontier. Much of its population has lived there less than a generation and came predominantly from other parts of the United States rather than from foreign countries. Although western institutions are often more than a century old, the recent arrival of most of its population means that its political traditions and ways of life are less settled than in other parts of the country. Hence, both political innovation and sudden seemingly erratic turns to traditionalism are commonplace.

Other areas of the country form less distinct regions. For instance, Middle West is a frequently used label but it is applied to a widely varying group of states. The designation Border States is almost equally uncertain.

The effect of national and regional traditions is subtle but pervasive. They limit the range of experimentation not by formal restrictions but by limiting the imagination of reformers. No state constitutional convention has seriously considered adopting a parliamentary government because it seems "un-American" to most people. Reformers look to other states rather than to foreign nations for their inspiration, and often they look only as far as neighboring states because they consider regional experiences more relevant than those in some more distant part of the nation.

National Economy and National Events

State politics are also affected by the national economy. No state can escape the effect of an inflation or depression, although one region or state may be more or less affected by national economic trends than others. The condition of the economy manifests itself in demands for programs and in the use of available resources to meet those demands. Recessions increase the welfare load, which is partially borne by the states, and may lead to demands for laws to make evictions more difficult or to delay foreclosure sales of property. Since the yield of state taxes declines during a recession, the states often find themselves with increased demands but diminished resources. During periods of economic growth and inflation, costs and tax yields both rise. During controlled growth, tax revenues may increase so substantially that new programs can be added without costly fights about raising tax rates.

Like national and regional characteristics and the economy, social trends are not isolated in one state or region. When narcotics abuse is a problem in one area, it rapidly becomes a national problem. Unrest on university campuses originated at a few large campuses but it spread rapidly to colleges throughout the nation. Pollution of air and water cannot be stopped at state boundaries: sewage dumped into Lake Michigan in Milwaukee causes Chicago suburbs to close their beaches; clouds of smoke from the steel mills of Indiana choke the residents of Illinois as well. The decision to refuse electric utilities permission to construct large generating plants in one state may cause a brownout in another because electricity is marketed beyond state boundaries. None of these problems remains enclosed by a single state's boundaries because of the mutual interdependence of the states. Problems spread quickly because the nation has a communications and transportation network that carries troublesome ideas and issues with the same ease as it transports beneficial goods and cheerful messages.

THE CONCEPTUAL FRAMEWORK

To probe deeply into the nature of political life in the American states, we shall use a conceptual framework that broadly defines American political life. This framework is called systems theory and its best-known exponent in political science is David Easton.[6] He thinks of all political life as a system, a series of interdependent events. A systems framework rests on a limited number of concepts including *politics, inputs, conversion processes, outputs, outcomes, feedback, community, regime, and authorities.*

Politics is much more than elections, party activity, or even governmental activity. It includes all activities that contribute to the authoritative allocation of values. Thus, actions that result in value distributions that people considered legitimate or rightfully backed by the force of the state are political. For example, political activity allocates much money to highway construction, schools, and welfare. But it also distributes well-being, learning, safety, power, and rectitude. Some of these values are material, such as money or skills taught in public schools. Others are symbolic, such as the honor accorded to heroes and symbolized by their medals, the respect given to judges and other high officials, and the recognition accorded individuals and groups through public statements by officials. Most political activity has some relation to government; it is either action by a government official or agency or activity directed at them. Some political activity is indirectly related to government: closing parochial schools is a political act because it places a greater burden on public schools and may, in fact, put pressure on public officials to provide tax support for parochial schools. Likewise, the struggle to control an interest group such as the American Medical Association is political since it affects the direction of the group's activities that influence public policies.

First in the series of activities that define a political system are *inputs.* Inputs are demands made on the system or support given to the system. Political demands may be made in several ways. Most commonly, demands are made by individuals or groups through speeches, demonstrations, letters to officials, or advertisements. Demands may be made less obtrusively through public services. For instance, the demand for public schooling is in part made by sending children to school. The schools, in turn, generally measure the demand for their services by counting the children they expect to be enrolled. Similarly, the demand for highways is indicated by the number of vehicles following a given route. Demands may originate from partisan groups such as the Democratic and Republican parties and from avowedly political groups such as the American Civil Liberties Union or the John Birch Society. Demands may also come from groups and individuals who are not principally engaged in politics but who enter the political system occasionally. The American Legion is mainly a social group but it makes political demands when it supports partisan causes and seeks to improve the services that government agencies provide for Legion members.

Support, the other input to the political system, may be both positive and negative. It may help maintain the system or it may undermine its stability. Examples of positive support include the pride some people have about their state, a willingness to pay taxes, a recognition of the need to serve in the armed forces, and a desire to participate in "normal politics." Examples of negative support include rejecting the symbols of the system by refusing to salute the flag or rise for a judge, resisting taxation and service in the armed forces, and withdrawing from the rituals of the political system such as voting or the observance of national holidays and ceremonies. Support, like demands, may originate from avowedly partisan groups and public officials or from groups and individuals who are only occasionally involved in political activity. Each instance of demand or support activity, however, links its originator to the political system. It does not matter whether the demand is met or the support recognized. Even if the activity is habitual — singing the national anthem at athletic events — it links the person and the political system.

Consequently, we may compare political systems by considering the proportion of people involved with politics as a result of their demand and support activities and the characteristics of these people. Until the last decade in southern states, for instance, most Negroes were systematically excluded from many input activities. The poor are still as systematically limited in many northern cities. Such groups can make few demands although they can display support. Regional or class distinctions in input activities are among the standard variables that explain differences in political systems among states and nations.

Inputs are combined and compromised to produce government decisions and policies by *conversion processes*. Most conversion occurs within governmental agencies from all three branches of government. Conversion is most visible in legislatures because they are elective bodies with a tradition of working in full public view. The introduction of bills (one form of demand), the holding of open hearings (where other demands are voiced), the compromise in committee, the debate during which amendments are proposed and adopted, and the final adoption of a bill are all parts of the conversion process. Even in the legislature not all phases of conversion are public, since much bargaining is carried on in private and many legislatures divide themselves into committees that meet in executive (secret) sessions. Less of the conversion process is visible to the public in executive and judicial agencies, but the same activities occur. Both inputs and the form of the decision differ throughout the agencies. Many political scientists study the work of these organs under the rubric of decision-making theory. Such theory focuses on the conversion process alone, taking it out of the context of the political system of which it is a part, but it is the same kind of activity that systems theory is concerned with.

In studying the conversion processes, we shall be concerned with the conditions associated with each process and how structural differences are reflected in the decisions themselves. In addition, we shall be concerned with the manner in which inputs flow to the conversion processes: the kind of personnel involved, the interest groups that are associated with particular processes, the structure of intelligence and information services, and the decision rules that govern the operation of each conversion agency. Each of these variables affects the selection of inputs to which attention is paid and influences the decisions that each of these bodies make.[7]

Outputs are decisions made by governmental agencies that distribute values among various elements of the population. One frequently used output indicator is the level of government expenditure for various programs, since each expenditure reflects a financial value judgment made by legislatures and executive agencies. Many decisions involve no expenditures — for instance, the decision to honor a group by proclaiming one day in its behalf. The work of public officials is a constant flow of decisions. Some of these decisions may be negative in the sense that they prevent the allocation of values to some individual or group, but even negative decisions are outputs.

Concern with outputs takes many forms. We can divide outputs into various functional areas — education, welfare, transportation. Or, we may prefer to concentrate on major decisions, usually called policy decisions, that require many subsequent implemental (administrative) decisions. The level of governmental attention to particular problems may be measured by the frequency of these decisions. Alternatively we can study the distribution of outputs among various segments of the population and ask who benefits from welfare, education, transportation, and conservation decisions.

Outcomes are the consequences of outputs when they interact with the social and physical environment; they are the results of governmental decisions. A government may decide to build an expressway to revive the downtown shopping area of a city. Such a decision may mean that downtown neighborhoods are destroyed by the expressway and that the downtown shopping area becomes unsafe and remains unattractive to shoppers and businesses. The output was the decision to build the expressway. The consequence of the decision, its outcome, was increased deterioration in the downtown shopping area. Some outcomes are congruent with the intentions of policy makers: they may hope to improve education by deciding to spend more on teacher salaries, and education subsequently improves. Other outcomes are unanticipated and contrary to the intentions of policy makers. A welfare program that is adopted with the intention of assisting the poor may actually anchor them more firmly into the culture of poverty.

Outcomes require different measures than outputs. Whereas expenditures per pupil is an indicator of outputs, the income differential between high school dropouts and high school graduates is an indicator of outcomes. Likewise, we may use the number of miles of expressway as an output indicator; but the number of people who die in traffic accidents is an index of an outcome.

Outcomes are what people are ultimately concerned with. They formulate demands, provide support, seek to manipulate the conversion processes, seek outputs — all in order to achieve desired outcomes. But outcomes are not entirely the product of government decisions. They are partly the result of individual citizens' decisions. By using government services and environmental conditions, individual citizens can affect the distribution of outputs within a population. No description of a political system is complete without a consideration of outcomes, although they have been the least studied political concept and are often the most difficult one to measure — in part, because there are relatively few official indicators of outcomes whereas official data about outputs are abundant.

The conceptual framework outlined above operates in a time sequence. Demands precede decisions, which precede outcomes. Systems theory is not static; it assumes that the system is constantly adapting to the environment, to new demands, and to participants' perceptions of the consequences of past decisions. The way in which past decisions and outcomes generate new inputs in the form of additional demands and support is called the *feed-*

back process. Like a physical system that has feedback — for instance, a thermostat that turns the heating on when the temperature falls below a specified level and turns it off again after the temperature has climbed to the desired level — the political system reacts to changes in its environment. It may become attentive to new demands, it may formulate new decisions, or its conversion processes may adopt new decision rules. Many kinds of changes may occur within the system as the result of feedback.

A political system operates wherever there is an authoritative allocation of values. Political activity, however, exists at several different levels. At the level of the political *community,* it involves all the people who identify with common symbols. At the level of the *regime,* it involves structures of government such as the federal government, the fifty state governments, or municipal governments. At the level of *authorities,* it involves particular decision makers such as governors, legislators, or judges.

In this book the regime and authorities of the fifty states will receive most of the analysis. Each state is considered a subsystem of the national political system. Each has demands and supports directed toward its conversion processes and each produces a multitude of outputs that have many outcomes.

THE LOGIC OF ANALYSIS

The following chapters provide detailed analyses of inputs, conversion processes, outputs, and outcomes. The analyses rely on several techniques to display evidence for the reader and to permit him to understand the reasoning underlying the authors' conclusions. First the analyses seek to establish a measure for the phenomena that are being observed. Then they seek to discover the association of one phenomenon with others, exposing theoretically significant or causal relationships. Such relationships are further analyzed by intensive examination of typical and deviant cases.

The Measurement of Variables in State Politics

All measurement is based on comparison. Even simple description requires putting like items into categories. We then attach labels to each set. If we are describing public officials, we may put those who are elected into one category and those who are appointed into another. Or if we are describing states, we may put those bordering on an ocean in the category of coastal states and place the remainder in the category of interior states.

Here we simply compare items according to characteristics that appear relevant and categorize them accordingly.

The characteristics that should be used to describe politics are not always obvious. Which characteristics we choose usually make a substantial difference as to whether our description is useful. We may describe a group of people by physical characteristics (height, weight, skin color, head size), social characteristics (educational attainment, income, occupation, associational membership), psychological traits derived from psychological tests (IQ, degree of neurosis, degree of psychosis, degree of depression), or political characteristics (party identification, regularity of voting, size of campaign contribution, knowledge of politics). All of these ways of categorizing people are valid but they lead to vastly different conclusions. We may be able to draw interesting political implications from a description of people according to their political or social characteristics, but we could not usually infer political consequences from physical traits.

Thus, one critical element of measurement is the choice of characteristics to be used in making comparisons. The systems framework provides some of the categories: inputs, conversion processes, outputs, outcomes, and feedback. We may describe state political systems according to any of these categories.

In addition to choosing relevant characteristics, an analyst must find indicators that will provide reliable results when he attempts to sort through the phenomena he is studying. He must be sure that he can recognize the difference between elected and appointed officials if he seeks to categorize public officials on this basis. When categories hinge simply on the presence or absence of some characteristic (such as elected or not elected) the measurement is usually reliable because it is easy to detect the absence or presence of gross traits. But often we want to measure the quantity of some characteristic: whether certain states are wealthier than others, whether governors are more powerful in some states than others, whether some states are more innovative than their neighbors. We try to assign numbers that reflect the amount of the characteristic present. These kinds of measurements provide many opportunities for error.

Some errors are imbedded in the source of our data. We can obtain listings of elected officials from organizations such as the Council of State Governments. If their listing is incorrect, their errors will be incorporated in the analysis. Even official sources of data may be unreliable. For example, each year the FBI measures crime in the United States in "The Uniform Crime Report." The name and source of the report might lead us to believe that it encompasses a reliable measure of crime in the United States.

But the footnotes and headings to the table indicate that the report is simply a compilation of reports sent to the FBI by local police departments. The classification of a crime — whether it is an assault or a rape, for instance — is the work of the local police department. Since efficient departments are likely to report more crimes than inefficient departments, cities that report high crime rates may have more crimes or they may simply have more efficient departments.[8] Another potentially unreliable official source is the United States census, which tries to count all people living in the United States on April 1 at the beginning of every decade. Because poor people and blacks are more difficult to locate than white middle-income householders, the census usually distinctly underestimates the number of poor, especially black poor.[9]

We must also ask whether a measure accurately indicates the phenomena we want to examine. In physics, temperature is a valid indicator of the presence or absence of heat. But in political science, a man's past voting record is a less than perfect indicator of his political commitments. We can count the number of Democratic and Republican voters in a state at the time of an election but we cannot be certain that these people consider themselves members of distinct political parties. Some are highly committed whereas others are merely casual voters. In studying state politics we are often concerned with phenomena that cannot be directly observed, such as the attitudes of the people, the power of governors, the innovation rates of states, or the burden of taxation. Usually we must infer the presence or absence of such phenomena and their level of intensity from substitute indicators that are imperfectly related to the concepts we are really interested in. Thus, governors with some characteristics are classified as stronger than governors who lack these characteristics, and a state in which the Republican or Democratic party has won most elections is categorized as a one-party dominant state.

In order to make measures as accurate as possible, we often try to base them on several indicators. The wealth of a state should be measured not only by the per capita income of its inhabitants, but also by the value of real property, the number of motor vehicles, the number of telephones, and the general level of education. A statistical technique called *factor analysis* enables us to determine whether such indicators cohere along a single dimension or indicate several dimensions. If indicators cohere along a single dimension, factor analysis also allows us to construct a composite measure of wealth that includes all the individual indicators. Such composite measures are generally more reliable than single indicators.

Discovering Patterns of Association

Once we have derived reliable and valid measures, we can proceed with the analysis. Our objective, explaining political phenomena in the states, requires the discovery of regular patterns of association so that whenever we observe one variable, we can predict the presence of others. Thus, if we know the economic resources of a state, we are able to predict to some degree the level of its public services because past research has uncovered a direct relationship between these variables. With further research, we may even be able to state that one phenomena causes another, although the complexity of political phenomena usually prevents political scientists from identifying causal patterns in the political process.

Comparative analysis is used to discover patterns of association or causation.[10] The comparative method is fundamentally simple and familiar. We examine a phenomenon and inquire what other phenomena occur with it. In analyzing why some states have larger public expenditures than others, we first examine the relationship between population and expenditures. We find that, in general, the most populous states spend the most, and the least inhabited spend the least. This is such a strong and obvious relationship that we will substitute per capita expenditures in order to remove the effect of population size. Another variable we may wish to examine is the previous expenditure of the states. We could suppose that state expenditures would remain stable in the short run because expenditure commitments are difficult to terminate. Once a state university has been established, it is almost impossible to cease its operation. Therefore, the expenditures for a past year should be closely related to expenditures for the present year. When we examine the data, we find this supposition to be true. The relationship is not perfect, however, and some states spend a little more or less than we would predict on the basis of their previous record.[11]

Comparisons can be made in several ways. We may list the past and current per capita expenditures of the fifty states. Comparing these two lists would give us a gross idea of whether a relationship existed between these expenditures. Such lists are awkward and time-consuming to compile and do not provide a firm measure. An improvement on the lists is crosstabulating two variables. If, for example, we arbitrarily classify the states by the quartile in which they fall in past expenditures and current expenditures, we can obtain a clearer picture of the relationship between these expenditures. Table 2 presents these data. It shows that a relationship exists, but

TABLE 2
Per Capita State Expenditures for 1969 by 1968 Per Capita
Expenditures

States by quartiles of 1968 expenditures	States by quartile of 1969 expenditures			
	Bottom quartile	Second quartile	Third quartile	Top quartile
Bottom quartile	91%	14%	–	–
Second quartile	–	79	8%	–
Third quartile	–	7	85	8%
Top quartile	9	–	8	92
	100%	100%	101%[a]	100%

[a]Rounding error.
Source: United States Bureau of the Census, *State Government Finances, 1968* (Washington, D.C.: United States Government Printing Office), 14; *State Government Finances in 1969* (Washington, D.C.: United States Government Printing Office), 13.

again, it fails to provide us with a summary statistic by which we could compare the relationship between per capita expenditures for 1968 and 1969 with other relationships. The association can also be shown by a graphical representation. In Figure 1, which is a scatter diagram, each dot represents one state's expenditures in 1968 and 1969. The line indicates the points at which 1969 expenditures would equal those of 1968. The graph shows a close relationship between expenditures of the two years although most states spent more in 1969 than in 1968. Graphs are good visual devices for showing relationships but also do not measure the relationship for us.

The most common measure for summarizing and measuring relationships between two variables is the correlation coefficient.[12] If two variables are perfectly related, the correlation coefficient will have a value of +1 or −1. A value of +1 indicates that as one variable increases, the other also increases. That is true in our example, since as 1968 expenditures increase, 1969 expenditures also increase. A value of −1 indicates an inverse relationship in which one variable increases as the other decreases. For instance, as poverty increases, state expenditures decrease. When no relationship exists, the correlation coefficient has a value of 0. In most research situations, correlation coefficients rarely reach either +1 or −1 but instead range somewhere in between. When the coefficient is relatively close to +1 or −1, we can say that the two variables are closely related; when the coefficient is close to 0, we can say that the relationship is negligible. For the data in Table 2 and Figure 1, the correlation coefficient is .94.

Usually we wish to consider more than two variables at a time, but when we examine just two variables, we use zero-order correlations. When

FIGURE 1
1969 Per Capita Expenditures for the States by 1968 Per Capita Expenditures

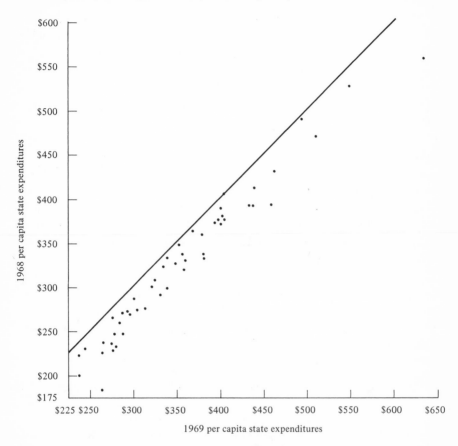

1969 per capita state expenditures

we control for other variables, such as urbanization and education when examining the relationship between wealth and expenditures, we use partial correlation coefficients that show how closely two variables are associated with one another when others are held constant. Such analysis enables us to untangle the complex relationships in political life. Politics is never so simple that nothing intervenes between the relationship of two variables. Usually, an event occurs because many phenomena have coalesced. Spending for highways is associated with dense traffic, urbanization, industrialization, wealth, and distance between cities. If we want to determine whether competition between the Republican and Democratic parties is related to highway spending, we must hold all the other variables for highway spending constant by calculating partial correlation coefficients. Using this method, Robert Friedman shows in Table 13.6 that this relationship does exist.

Finally, we may determine the total relationship between expenditures, social and economic indicators, and political variables by using a multiple correlation coefficient that indicates the strength of the total relationship. The multiple correlation coefficient has only positive values from 0 to 1. When the value is close to 1, the relationship between the set of variables and the phenomena we are trying to understand is close; when the coefficient's value approaches 0, the relationship is minimal.

Each of these statistical techniques is simply a device to summarize information and assist us in making inferences about the political questions we ask. The logic of comparative analysis leads us from observations about single states to generalizations about relationships in all the states. For instance, we may discover from our description of each state's politics that New York and Connecticut have stiff competition between the two major parties, whereas Mississippi and North Dakota are essentially one-party states. We may also find that New York and Connecticut are very urban and Mississippi and North Dakota are not. Such comparisons made systematically over all fifty states permit us to generalize that urbanization is closely associated with party competition. The generalization transcends the description of individual states; now we can determine the level of party competition from the level of urbanization, even if we lack other knowledge.

Examining Typical and Deviant Cases

Statistical analysis helps us identify states that are typical of a general set of relationships. If all relationships were perfect — if there were no exceptions to the association between two phenomena — our analysis would be complete. However, political phenomena are so complex that few explanations are complete. Every statistical analysis of the states produces a residual of states that do not follow the typical pattern of relationships. Both the typical and the deviant states often require more intensive examination before we can complete the analysis.

Statistical analysis identifies both typical and deviant states. Then we must continue our search for associations that may help explain the imperfect relationships already established. Thus, the general relationship between the wealth of states, their political processes, and welfare expenditures is well known but far from perfectly understood. Measures of the political process seemed to add little to the explanation until further intensive analysis suggested that the relationship might be different for the several welfare programs. Cnudde and McCrone discovered that for unemployment compensation and aid to dependent children, political phenomena were far more significant than had previously been recognized; for old age assistance, the relationship remained weak.[13]

Deviant cases are readily identifiable through correlation analysis, because the explanation that works for most states does not work for them. Intensive examination may reveal a variable absent in other states, or it may reveal that phenomena interact with one another in peculiar ways in the presence of a third variable. Many researchers have shown that voting turnout is strongly related to education and income. In some states, however, the presence of large numbers of Negroes has spurred the turnout of low-incomes whites. In the presence of well-organized Negro groups, low-income blacks may also turn out on election day in unusually high numbers.[14]

The search for additional relationships and for peculiar interactions between phenomena cannot be conducted entirely by statistical methods. It requires a thorough understanding of the context of state politics. Such an understanding can be gained only by intensive case analyses of typical and deviant states. Several such analyses are provided in the following chapters.

COMPARATIVE POLITICS AND THE STATES

These comparative techniques are not new to political science, but they have been employed more systematically in the study of state politics than elsewhere. The study of foreign governments — often called comparative politics — does not employ comparative techniques with the same success. The study of single nations or single institutions may be implicitly comparative, but because only a single phenomenon is under examination, more universal relationships cannot be discovered. Comparative techniques can be used with good reason in the study of state politics. Data are readily available and the complexity of political processes can be reduced by discovering characteristics that the states share.

The Data Base

Information about the American states is plentiful and within the reach of anyone near a public library. The census bureau and many other federal agencies publish extensive information about many phases of state government each year. These sources of data extend back for at least twenty years in many instances and longer in others.[15] The information is relatively reliable and uniformly collected. Where the data are in monetary terms, the monetary unit is the same for all fifty states. When census or other governmental information does not suffice, news services and private research make further information available with relative ease. In addition to information about governmental activities, the census bureau and many other agencies routinely publish information about social and economic phenomena for every state. These data permit us to examine the relationships among political activities and between politics and socioeconomic phenomena.

The data for analysis of politics in the American states are far better than those for the study of politics in other areas. Such a range of information is not available even for American cities because city boundaries are constantly changing and many agencies use either larger or smaller geographic units in collecting and publishing their data. Even less information is available for foreign countries, and much of the data that are published are of variable reliability. Thus, the states provide readily accessible laboratories for analyzing political phenomena. Many different political activities take place within them, permitting systematic comparative analysis and the discovery of relationships that apply to specified conditions.

The Analytic Effect of Common Characteristics

Comparative analysis is also aided by the characteristics the states share that have been described earlier. In studying politics in the American states, we are holding constant many variables that confound analysis of foreign nations. All the states share an attachment to constitutionalism, both as a set of governmental institutions and as a set of values restricting government interference with private life. In studying the conversion of demands into outputs through the legislative process, we do not have to account for differences imposed by parliamentary legislatures or totalitarian systems, for such differences are not represented among the states. Similarly, we do not have to account for varying national traditions of tribal society, of a feudal background, or of strong religious divisions.

The opportunity to disregard some of the phenomena that determine political events because they do not vary in the states allows the investigator to concentrate on others that have a more immediate effect. Yet, the greater simplicity of research in American state politics limits the generalizations that can be discovered. We may learn more about politics by studying the American states systematically, but we cannot extend our findings to conditions that do not exist in the states. The relationships discovered in state politics may not hold true in Europe, Africa, or Latin America. Nevertheless, relationships that are valid among the American states at least provide effective starting points for the study of other political systems.

CONCLUSION

We have discussed three elements of the analyses that will follow: the concentration on state politics; the use of a systems framework; and the use of systematic comparative techniques in examining the ways in which political phenomena work in the several states. Each of these elements involves simplifying assumptions that make the analysis more manageable but also limit the generality of our conclusions.

The emphasis on *state* politics means that we are not dealing with the entire range of political phenomena. For instance, we do not discuss foreign policy, and we do not examine data beyond the American experience. But intensive examination of state politics not only permits us to learn a great deal about an important element of the American political system but also allows us to examine political phenomena more intensively than would generally be possible in a study of national or local politics.

The use of a systems framework provides a convenient paradigm or diagram that helps us classify events and their relationships. It is not the only way to examine politics, but besides aiding the analysis of political events, it may help the analyst decide whether a particular remedy would actually produce the results he wants. It does not automatically formulate remedies for failings that become apparent to the reader when he compares what he finds with what he would like to see happen. Before remedies can be formulated, the failures must be identified and the conditions that brought them about must be discovered. Inappropriate remedies may be as objectionable as uncorrected shortcomings. The following chapters rarely suggest remedies, but they may lead to sufficient understanding so that political activists can advocate appropriate prescriptions for the infirmities of the political process.

PART TWO

PARTICIPATION
IN STATE POLITICS

CHAPTER TWO

Individuals and Government

Lester W. Milbrath

Over the centuries man has learned what governments can do for him and how they can oppress him. His objective is to design a government that will enable him to live in peace and order with his fellow men and yet not be oppressive or tyrannical. The relationships that are worked out between people and their government are essential to the happiness and security of all the individuals in a society. That these relationships are not always felicitously established is apparent from the many conflicts and expressions of dissatisfaction with governmental performance that so pervade our lives today. Many people are apparently very unhappy with what their governments do for them. This unhappiness influences the kinds of inputs people make to their government. Hundreds of political philosophers have theoretically analyzed the design of "the best" government. Curiously, in spite of all this philosophical discussion of the problem, very little empirical investigation has been made of the relationships between people and their government. To understand these relationships we must empirically investigate both the inputs that individuals make to a political system and the things they take from that system.

In the first chapter of this book the editors distinguished the *outputs* of a political system — legislative bills, executive orders, judicial decisions — from the *outcomes,* pervasive societal conditions such as employment rates, numbers of persons educated, roads built, and medical patients cured. I would extend the idea of outcomes by adding the dimension of individual satisfaction with governmental performance. In addition to knowing how many houses or roads have been built, how many people have been educated or cured, how many cases have been processed through the courts,

we must also know how satisfied people are with these levels of performance. Satisfactions cannot be counted simply as the number of service
units that governments put out because satisfactions are related to expectations and responsibilities that citizens assign to government. Rather than
talk about the things individuals receive from the government as outputs or
outcomes, I suggest that we talk about them as *outtakes* to make it clear
that we are speaking about the individual and what he takes out of the
political system.

The individual inputs to the political system discussed in this chapter
differ from group or institutional inputs to the system, such as political
parties or pressure groups. Group or institutional inputs to a political system are very important in understanding how government functions, and
they have been so recognized in teaching and research for many years.
We should enlarge our understanding of the functioning of the political
system, however, by incorporating individual inputs and outtakes. We
should look for different patterns of inputs from state to state, for example, and then attempt to relate these patterns to the way government functions in those states. These different patterns of governmental functioning
should, in turn, be related to the kinds of satisfactions that individuals receive from their government. Careful examination of these patterns across
many states, and over time, should lead to much more adequate theories of
governmental functioning.

DIMENSIONS OF INPUTS AND OUTTAKES

Political behavior, whether measured as an input or an outtake, has several
dimensions that make the prospect of action attractive or unattractive to a
potential participant. A scholar who wants to understand a political action
might find it helpful to characterize the action according to one of the
following dimensions.

The Active-Inactive Dimension

People act politically in an active, passive, or inactive manner. Every
person participates at least passively in the political system in which he
lives. Mere compliance gives support to the existing regime and is therefore
political behavior. Other essentially passive responses to the political system

include obeying laws, paying taxes, and experiencing order and security. These passive behaviors must be distinguished from the inactive counterparts to political action such as not voting, not contributing, or not attending.

Activity generally can be graded into quantities: some people may engage in an activity with greater frequency or regularity than others, they may contribute more hours or more money, or they may participate in a wider repertoire of activities. Some people are almost totally inactive politically; some are active in one behavior but not in others; some are active in a wide variety of behaviors. Inactivity may be considered a zero or base point from which quantities of actions can be measured.

The Instrumental-Expressive Dimension

Expressive political action manipulates symbols; mere participation in the behavior is satisfying or drive-reducing. Instrumental action, in contrast, is oriented primarily toward manipulating and changing things. Actions are classified as instrumental or expressive according to the situation and motivation of the actor. Consequently, it is difficult to classify specific acts as expressive or instrumental in every case. Casting a vote, for example, may be primarily expressive in one situation or for one person but primarily instrumental for another situation or person.

A person who behaves politically to satisfy expressive needs seems to consume his experience. As his needs are satisfied by engaging in an action, his drive reduces, and his behavior ceases until a new need for expressive consumption arises. Participating in a demonstration, shouting a protest, engaging in political argument, and pledging allegiance are examples of specific acts that in most situations are expressive. The classification is one of motivation and emphasis since the same acts also may have instrumental consequences.

Instrumental action follows through a long chain of events and intermediary goals leading to a final goal. Although participation in the action may be immediately satisfying to the actor, mere participation is not a sufficient reward to produce the action; rather, reaching the goal is the source of drive reduction. Participating in a campaign, collecting information, or volunteering for a job are acts that are primarily instrumental in orientation and emphasis, even though their performance may provide expressive rewards as well.[1] *

* [See pp. 564–566 for notes to this chapter. — Eds.]

The Overt-Covert Dimension

Some political actions are taken in full public view with exposure to the possibility of criticism and acclaim, while others are essentially private. An act, for example, writing a letter, may be private in one context (writing to a friend) and public in another (writing to an editor). A discussion about politics with friends in a private home is quite different from a discussion of the same subject before the public media. The overt action usually has higher costs than the covert action, and thus requires higher rewards before people engage in it.

The Autonomous-Compliant Dimension

All action is a response to a stimulus of some sort, but there is an important difference between a response to an inner or general environmental stimulus, for example, an awareness that a campaign is in progress, and a response to solicitation. Action taken in response to a request is certainly action rather than inaction, but it has passive overtones when compared to an autonomous action. Furthermore, if a request is virtually irresistible, such as a governmental order to pay taxes, action in compliance with it is more passive than efforts to avoid compliance. It also is possible for a person to receive a request not to take an action; inaction, in this case, becomes compliance. Although the boundary between autonomy and compliance may be indistinct, there is an important difference in emphasis. Most often, compliant behavior is the route of least cost and greatest reward.

The Approaching-Avoiding Dimension

Approaching behavior is characterized by a positive valence between actor and object; avoiding behavior is characterized by a negative valence between actor and object. A valence is a reaction of either attraction or repulsion to a stimulus. If a person likes ice cream, for example, he has a positive valence toward it. If he hates giving speeches, he has a negative valence toward the action. A valence is a property characterizing the actor and must have an object referent of which the actor is aware. Absence of action is not necessarily avoidance; an actor must withdraw or consciously abstain from an object or action before his behavior can be characterized as avoidance. For example, a person who does not make a political contribution because he is unaware that anyone wants him to contribute is not avoiding, although a person who does not contribute when he is requested to do so is. Avoiding behavior flows from an anticipation of high costs, whereas approaching behavior follows the anticipation of high rewards.

The Episodic-Continuous Dimension

Some political action, such as voting, takes place only at specified times. The decision to act usually is conscious and often is preceded by a build-up period such as a campaign. Other actions, such as contacting a politician, holding office, or supporting a party, can be taken up at any moment and may last for extended periods. Actions that can be continuous often become part of living patterns and may take on a routine character with little conscious decision from the actor. Continuous action generally has higher costs than episodic action. A significant reward structure, preferably built in (a salary), is needed to ensure performance. When measuring quantities or magnitudes of political action, we must ascertain the episodic or continuous character of the action.

The Verbal-Nonverbal Dimension

Most political acts require the use of verbal symbols, but some, such as discussing politics, writing letters, or making speeches demand much more verbal ability than others such as stuffing envelopes or marching in parades. A person who does not possess verbal skill faces a barrier to verbal participation that may be so great that he avoids or withdraws from verbal activities.

The Social-Nonsocial Dimension

This dimension of action is closely related to the verbal-nonverbal dimension, but they are not identical. Writing a letter or a speech, for example, is highly verbal but does not require social interaction. Nearly all political acts entail some minimal kind of social interaction, but it is useful to distinguish the amount required. Soliciting political funds or campaigning from door to door requires much more social interaction than voting, attending a meeting, joining a party, or making a monetary contribution. The cost of participating in activities requiring a good deal of social interaction is very high for people who are unskilled or ill at ease socially. In contrast, people with a strong need for social interaction may find sociable political activities very rewarding.

SUMMARIZING BEHAVIORAL DIMENSIONS

Since the political analyst would like to consider political behavior in all of its richness, some means must be found for summarizing or classifying the above dimensions. Classifications alert us to the ways specific acts are similar or different and thus facilitate the search for variables that explain the occurrence of acts.

If one is concerned with only two or three dimensions of specific political acts, we show a way of summarizing these dimensions in Figure 1, where the input-outtake distinction is modified by the active-passive dimension and the instrumental-expressive dimension. The six-celled table or abstract map shown in Figure 1 suggests pigeonholes into which political behavior might be classified for certain analytical purposes. We will see later in this chapter how this approach was operationalized in a study of political behavior conducted in Buffalo, New York, in the late 1960s. The acts shown in the various cells of the figure are not analytically exclusive, having been classified from the perspective of an individual actor, not the political system. An act — a vote, a protest, a contribution — may be primarily expressive in one setting or for one individual but may be primarily instrumental in another setting or for another individual. Similarly, other specific acts may be primarily passive in one setting and primarily active in another.

The summarizing methods illustrated in Figure 1 alert us to dimensions that may be overlooked in research. As we look at state-by-state data on political participation we will discover that many dimensions have been overlooked in research to date. Most previous research on political behavior has studied a single active input: voting. Almost no attention has been given to outtakes. We will look first at state-by-state data on voting turnout and registration; later we will look at data from a specific study that demonstrates how the analytical framework shown in Figure 1 can enrich the acquisition and analysis of data on political behavior.

COMPARING PARTICIPATION ACROSS STATES

A major reason that we do not have state-by-state comparative data on rates of participation in a variety of political actions is that no national polling or survey research organization draws random samples state by state. This data gap is not likely to be corrected in the near future because state-by-state samples would require polling about 500 respondents in each

FIGURE 1

Abstract Map of an Individual's Political Behavior.[a] The political acts shown in the various cells are illustrative for a hypothetical individual; for another individual, certain specific acts might appear in different cells.

		Inputs to the system by individuals	Outtakes from the system by individuals
Active	Instrumental	Leader selection (vote) Party activity Contributing money Keeping informed Volunteering Disobedience	Stewardship Communication opportunities Services Economic opportunities Conflict resolution Justice
	Expressive	Allegiance Demonstrations Protests (vote) Political argument	National symbols Sense of identification Governmental protests Sense of superiority
Passive		Obedience Compliance Conscription Paying taxes Indifference	Public order Security

[a] I am indebted to Professor David W. Minar, Northwestern University, for suggesting an earlier version of this figure. Reprinted with permission from Lester W. Milbrath, *Political Participation* (Chicago: Rand McNally, 1965).

state, creating a total national sample of 25,000, more than ten times as large as most of the national polling samples today.[2] Some national survey organizations do draw regional samples, however, and we can obtain region-by-region figures for several types of political participation.

The Survey Research Center of the University of Michigan has conducted surveys of national elections since 1948. In several of these studies they asked questions about participation in the seven political acts listed in Table 1. The table shows the percentages of the sample who participated in each of these activities, arranged in order from the most to the least popular, in the 1956 and the 1964 elections in the Northeast, the Midwest, the Far West, and the South.[3] The similarities across the regions in the percentages participating in each activity are immediately obvious, although the South, especially in 1956, showed a somewhat lower than average participation rate for several activities (voting, proselytizing, displaying preference, and contributing money). The percentage for attending political meetings, joining a club, and working for a party was about the same as that observed in other regions. By 1964, the rate of participation in the

TABLE 1

Percentages of Respondents in 1956 and 1964 Nationwide
Election Studies Who Performed Each Type of Political Act—by Region

	Northeast		Midwest		Far West		South	
	1956	1964	1956	1964	1956	1964	1956	1964
Vote	85	86	81	81	80	80	57	67
Talk others into voting a certain way	28	30	30	30	30	37	25	31
Wear a button or put sticker on car	18	13	17	16	17	14	10	21
Give money to candidate or party	13	8	10	12	10	13	6	10
Attend political meetings	7	7	8	9	5	10	6	8
Join political club	4	4	3	5	2	6	1.7	2.5
Work for a party	3	4	4	6	1.7	8	2.5	4

Source: Data drawn from the 1956 and 1964 election studies of the Survey Research Center, University of Michigan. Percentages total more than 100 because some individuals performed more than one act.

South was, for nearly all of these activities, equivalent to that in other sections of the country. The rate of voting turnout continues to be lower in the South than in other regions, but even here the percentage gained from 1956 to 1964 is significant. Table 1 also shows that in the Far West the rate of participation in activities other than voting increased slightly from 1956 to 1964. The Goldwater campaign of 1964 was remarkable partly because it enlisted the enthusiastic energies of many ordinary citizens. Since Goldwater ran strongest in the South and in the Far West the increase in these activities shown for these regions may result from his campaign.

The data in Table 1 show that a very small proportion of the population becomes active in party and campaign work. How reliable are these estimates from a national sample? Voting turnout is the only behavior for which we can get reliable official figures to compare with percentages obtained from sample surveys. Table 2 shows nationwide turnout figures for several recent presidential elections. The nationwide percentage in the 1956 presidential election was 60.1, yet Table 1 shows turnout percentages in three regions of 80 per cent and above. Similarly, the nationwide presidential turnout in 1964 was 62.8 per cent, yet most of the figures shown in Table 1 for 1964 are well above that amount.

The turnout figures for the sample survey are somewhat inflated for several reasons. The most important is that it is extremely difficult to include certain groups, mostly nonparticipants in politics, in random samples: people living in institutions, resident aliens, the "floating population" and mental incompetents. The Survey Research Center estimates that these excluded people account for 6 per cent of the difference between their figures and the national percentage. A second factor is that although about 2 per

TABLE 2

Voter Participation Figures. Turnout in Elections for President and House of Representatives (Vote as a percentage of the civilian population of voting age)

| Year | 1920-1968 | |
	President	Representatives
1968	61.0	54.8
1966	–	45.6
1964	62.8	57.8
1962	–	48.9
1960	63.8	59.4
1958	–	43.4
1956	60.1	56.6
1954	–	42.2
1952	62.0	58.2
1950	–	41.6
1948	51.5	48.6
1946	–	37.6
1944	56.3	53.0
1942	–	32.7
1940	59.7	56.2
1938	–	44.5
1936	57.5	54.0
1934	–	41.8
1932	52.9	50.2
1930	–	34.1
1928	52.3	48.2
1926	–	30.1
1924	44.3	41.0
1922	–	32.4
1920	44.2	41.4

Source: United States Bureau of the Census, *Statistical Abstract of the United States: 1962,* eighty-third edition, Washington: 1962. Reproduced and updated from the Report of the President's Commission on Registration and Voting Participation (Washington, D.C.: United States Government Printing Office, November, 1963).

cent of the ballots cast in an election are invalidated and not counted in the turnout totals, these 2 per cent still report to the survey that they voted. A third factor is that those who faithfully turn out to vote are somewhat easier to locate and more willing to consent to an interview than those who are disinclined to vote. A final factor is the tendency for some people to report to an interviewer that they have voted when, in fact, they have not. This number is not large, but it may be as high as 3 to 4 per cent.[4]

Because of these factors we can be confident that percentages shown for the seven types of political acts in Table 1 are more likely to be a slight exaggeration of the true figure than an underestimation. The percentage of people who get out and work in a given election for a party or in a campaign for an individual may be only a few per cent and probably not any higher than 5 per cent. The percentage of Americans who have at one time or another in their life worked in a campaign, however, is much higher, probably around 25 per cent.[5] The best estimate of participation is that three-quarters of the adult American population has never done any party or campaign work, and the percentage of nonvoters in many elections, especially local elections, may be as high as 70 or 80 per cent. The inescapable conclusion is that a very large percentage of citizens are almost completely unconcerned with becoming active in politics.

Table 2 demonstrates that invariably the percentage of votes cast in representative elections is less than the percentage cast in presidential elections. Turnout in state elections is closely comparable to turnout in representative elections. If the state or representative election occurs in a nonpresidential year, the turnout is likely to be significantly lower. Table 3 shows the state-by-state average turnout in nonpresidential election years from 1952 to 1960 for gubernatorial and senatorial elections. If we compare

TABLE 3
Forty-Eight States Ranked by Their Average Turnout in Gubernatorial and Senatorial Elections in Nonpresidential Years 1952-1960, and Percentage Turnout

Rank	State	Average percentage turnout[a]		Rank	State	Average percentage turnout[a]
1	Idaho	64.6		25	Michigan	51.2
2	Utah	64.3		26	Vermont	51.0
3	Connecticut	63.4		27.5	Iowa	50.9
4	Indiana	63.1		27.5	New York	50.9
5	Rhode Island	62.7		29	New Jersey	49.9
6	South Dakota	62.5		30	Nebraska	48.7
7	Delaware	61.4		31	Maine	45.7
8	Wyoming	60.5		32	New Mexico	44.4
9	Montana	59.6		33	Kentucky	44.0
10.5	Minnesota	58.8	Border	34	Missouri	43.7
10.5	Massachusetts	58.8	States	35	Arizona	43.5
12	North Dakota	56.5		36	Maryland	42.6
13	Oregon	55.9		37	Oklahoma	40.9
14	Nevada	55.7		38	Arkansas	29.0
15.5	Illinois	55.3	Middle	39	North Carolina	25.1
15.5	West Virginia	55.3	South	40	Virginia	21.4
17	New Hampshire	55.0		41	Tennessee	18.5
18	Pennsylvania	54.6		42	Florida	17.4
19	Colorado	54.3		43	Alabama	16.7
20	California	53.4		44	Texas	13.6
21	Kansas	52.7	Deep	45	Louisiana	12.3
22	Washington	52.6	South	46	South Carolina	11.9
23	Ohio	52.3		47	Georgia	10.7
24	Wisconsin	51.3		48	Mississippi	4.2

[a]Alaska and Hawaii did not become the 49th and 50th states of the union until after the 1956 election and thus could not be included in the table.

the percentage turnout in these state elections with presidential turnouts for comparable years (1956 and 1960) shown in Table 4, we see turnout figures for the state elections that average 15 to 20 per cent below the presidential turnout figures.

Table 4 suggests that voting is habitual or patterned behavior. The percentage turning out in each state is fairly constant across the elections; drastic shifts in percentage turnout from election to election are extremely rare. The elections shown in Table 4 were selected from a much larger table going back to 1824, and the generalization just stated would also apply across the greater span of that table. The 1948 election, generally considered unexciting, is a slight exception to this generalization, as Figure 2 shows. Most states show a slight gradual rise in turnout from the 1920s up to about 1952, when turnout levels off for three regions in the country. In the South the turnout rate has continued to rise. Tables 2 and 4 and Figure 2 indicate this overall trend. The cause of this gradual rise in turnout in the South is not known for certain. We can speculate that it is due to improvements in economic well-being, education, transportation, and communication. We know from other studies that improvements in these conditions are associated with increasing political participation. This interpretation is given credence by the figures in Table 4 and the slope of the lines in Figure 2. They show a rise in turnout in the southern region of the country that corresponds with its postwar period of swift industrialization.

The consistency of state-by-state voting turnout is striking. If the states are ranked by turnout for different years and for different types of elections, marked similarities appear.

Table 5 shows a correlation matrix for five types of turnout rankings; the very high correlation coefficients indicate how similar those rankings are. Table 5 also shows that correlations with the turnout ranking that does not include presidential elections (the same ranking as that shown in Table 3) are a little lower than the other correlations in the matrix, suggesting that somewhat different factors induce people to vote in presidential elections than in state or local elections.

The strikingly lower turnout figures for the South have been discussed above. We can seek further explanation for this difference by examining several social and economic factors that are likely to be related to political participation. The data in Tables 3 and 4 and the curves in Figure 2 demonstrate that the low turnout characteristics of the South go back three or four decades at least. More extensive tables suggest that the decline began shortly before the turn of the century.

Close study of Table 3 shows that the state-by-state ranking on turn-

TABLE 4

Percentage of Voter Turnout in Selected Presidential Elections 1920-1968

State[a]	1968	1964	1960	1956	1944	1932	1920
Utah	76.9	76.9	80.1	75.2	76.2	75.1	63.8
Idaho	72.8	75.8	80.7	77.6	76.3	73.4	57.9
Minnesota	71.8	76.8	77.0	67.7	70.2	62.7	53.3
Delaware	71.7	71.1	73.6	72.1	68.9	72.8	69.5
Iowa	71.6	72.3	76.5	73.2	72.0	67.8	62.7
Indiana	71.5	74.0	76.9	71.8	76.2	76.4	71.0
New Hampshire	70.9	72.3	79.4	75.2	78.1	68.5	56.6
South Dakota	70.8	72.6	78.3	73.5	70.8	73.4	52.8
Colorado	70.2	68.0	71.4	67.6	76.2	71.5	51.7
West Virginia	70.0	75.2	77.3	75.2	74.1	78.5	67.8
Illinois	69.3	74.0	75.7	73.2	79.4	68.6	53.1
Wyoming	69.3	73.2	74.0	67.8	75.6	71.3	45.4
Connecticut	68.5	71.8	76.8	76.6	70.2	58.3	43.6
Rhode Island	68.2	68.7	75.1	73.7	65.3	62.9	47.3
Wisconsin	68.0	70.8	73.4	67.4	71.2	60.7	45.9
Massachusetts	67.8	71.3	76.1	75.7	73.0	58.0	41.2
Maine	67.5	65.6	72.6	62.8	60.5	60.2	41.6
North Dakota	65.5	72.2	78.5	70.6	71.0	71.4	63.7
Vermont	65.5	68.0	72.5	67.4	63.6	62.0	41.4
New Jersey	65.1	68.6	71.8	69.0	70.9	62.3	48.0
Washington	65.0	71.5	72.3	70.8	65.6	59.9	46.5
Montana	65.0	69.8	71.4	71.0	70.8	67.4	55.8
Michigan	64.9	68.9	72.4	68.1	63.7	56.6	47.3
Oregon	64.4	69.6	72.3	68.2	59.7	57.5	48.2
Ohio	63.6	66.6	71.3	65.0	69.5	61.3	56.8
Kansas	63.5	64.8	70.3	67.2	68.3	68.9	55.7
New Mexico	63.3	63.9	62.1	59.6	59.0	66.2	56.9
Pennsylvania	63.2	68.1	70.5	65.7	64.1	48.8	36.7

Missouri	63.1	67.4	71.8	67.8	68.9	68.7	65.4
Oklahoma	62.9	62.5	63.8	63.6	62.0	53.7	47.6
Hawaii	62.7	52.5	51.3	–	–	–	–
California	61.0	64.7	67.4	63.8	62.9	55.9	40.7
Nebraska	59.9	66.6	71.4	67.1	75.9	69.1	51.8
Florida	58.2	52.7	50.0	45.9	36.3	30.2	36.0
Maryland	57.7	56.0	57.2	54.5	47.5	49.1	49.7
New York	57.3	63.2	67.0	66.0	74.1	56.0	44.5
Alaska	56.4	48.7	45.5	–	–	–	–
Louisiana	55.6	47.3	44.8	36.4	26.3	22.5	13.6
North Carolina	54.7	51.8	53.5	48.2	43.1	43.7	44.5
Nevada	54.2	55.5	61.2	62.8	62.3	63.7	52.1
Virginia	53.1	41.0	33.4	33.5	23.9	21.7	19.1
Tennessee	53.0	51.1	50.3	46.3	31.0	26.1	35.3
Arkansas	52.5	49.9	41.1	39.9	22.0	22.5	21.2
Texas	51.6	44.4	41.8	37.9	30.5	25.8	19.8
Mississippi	51.6	32.9	25.5	21.7	16.8	13.8	9.4
Alabama	51.5	36.0	31.1	28.3	16.4	17.6	20.8
South Carolina	48.0	38.0	30.5	25.2	11.0	12.1	8.6
Kentucky	46.8	52.9	59.2	58.8	59.7	67.4	71.2
Arizona	43.6	54.7	54.5	50.8	43.4	46.6	35.4
Georgia	41.6	44.9	30.4	29.7	18.2	16.4	10.4
District of Columbia	33.5	40.2	–	–	–	–	–
Average for U.S.	60.6	61.8	63.8	60.1	56.3	52.9	44.2

aStates are ranked by percentage turnout in the 1968 election and the vote is a percentage of the civilian population of voting age.

Sources: United States Bureau of the Census, *Statistical Abstract of the United States: 1962*, 83d ed. (Washington D.C.: United States Government Printing Office, 1962) for civilian population of voting age figures, 1920, 1940, 1960; Population Division, United States Bureau of the Census for estimates of civilian population of voting age, 1924-1936, 1944-1956; Richard M. Scammon (ed.), *America Votes*, Vol. IV (Pittsburgh: University of Pittsburgh Press, 1962), for votes cast in presidential elections, 1948-1960; *Statistics of Presidential and Congressional Elections, 1920-1958*, compiled under direction of Clerk of House of Representatives, for votes cast in presidential elections, 1920-1944. Reproduced from the Report of the President's Commission on Registration and Voting Participation, November, 1963. Figures for 1964 and 1968 were compiled by Walter Dean Burnham and taken from a table in "That All May Vote," a report by The Freedom to Vote Task Force of the Democratic National Committee, December, 1969.

FIGURE 2
Average Voting Turnout in Presidential Elections by Regions from 1920 to 1968

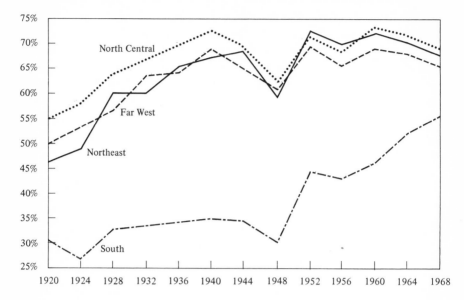

Source: The data were derived from Table 4. For each election the turnout percentages for the states in a region were averaged. Regional definitions are those used by the United States Bureau of the Census; see *Statistical Abstract, 1963*, p. xii, for details.

out assumes a North-South gradient pattern. The states with the lowest turnout ranking are the deep South states; the next lowest are the middle South states; and the next lowest are the border states. This North-South gradient pattern still persists in the latest figures although southern turnout is increasing. Among states ranking high on turnout is a preponderance of

TABLE 5
Rank-Order Correlation Matrix for Five Different Measures of Voting Turnout

	Average presidential turnout 1940-1948	*Average presidential turnout 1952-1960*	*Presidential turnout 1960*	*Average gubernatorial turnout 1952-1960*
Average presidential turnout 1952-1960	.93			
Presidential turnout 1960	.88	.96		
Average gubernatorial turnout 1952-1960	.89	.92	.89	
Average turnout for governor or senator in nonpresidential years 1952-1960	.84	.88	.86	.87

northern plains and mountain states. These are sparsely populated and largely agricultural states. The few exceptions to this generalization — Connecticut, Indiana, Rhode Island, Delaware — suggest that regional characteristics cannot solely explain voting turnout. The heavily industrialized states, with large metropolitan complexes, fall in the middle of the distribution.

It is often argued that since the Democratic party dominates state and local elections in the South and predetermines their outcome, citizens have little incentive to turn out and vote in general elections. The argument often suggests that turnout is much higher in party primary elections where different factions within the party contest vigorously to nominate their man on the Democratic ticket. Voting turnout is somewhat higher for primary elections than for general elections in the South, but the overall difference is relatively slight. Primary election turnout figures were substituted for general election turnout figures for southern states in some of the rankings used in this study. This substitution of primary turnout figures made almost no change in the state-by-state ranking; southern states still held the bottom of the list. The pattern of low voting turnout seems to be a general cultural factor in the South that continues no matter what the type of election is. This finding lends additional credence to the point that voting or not voting is patterned or habitual behavior.

What cultural factors depress turnout in the South? Some of them are social, some are economic, and some are political. Politically, the lack of interparty competition influences state and local elections, but presidential elections have been very closely contested in southern states for the past two decades. Several studies have shown that the more vigorous the competition between parties, the greater the interest of citizens in the election and the larger the turnout.[6] Dawson and Robinson developed a rank order of the states according to party competition.[7] Their measure included: (1) the percentage of popular vote for governor; (2) the percentage of seats in the Senate held by the major party; and (3) the percentage of seats in the House held by the major party. It covered the years from 1938 to 1958. This measure showed a Spearman rank-order correlation of .807 with the ranking on turnout reported in Table 3: the more vigorous the party competition, the greater the turnout. This measure showed a positive correlation with all the other rankings of turnout developed here. Furthermore, Dawson and Robinson developed six other measures of party competition, some based on competition in presidential elections, some on competition in both presidential and state elections, and others on evaluations of the party system in the state. Five of these measures had a positive, significant correlation with each of the measures of turnout (forty-six correlations in all).

The one exception among these measures of party competition was based on the extent to which the two-party vote differed from 50 per cent in recent presidential elections. In these elections there has been much more competition between the parties in the South. Some southern states have moved up to the middle competitive ranks; others, to the most competitive. For example, in 1960 Arkansas ranked 6th in competition whereas in the 1940–1948 period she ranked 44th; Louisiana ranked 8th in 1960 but 45.5 in 1940–1948; Texas ranked 9th in 1960 but tied with Louisiana at 45.5 in 1940–1948; South Carolina ranked 3rd in 1952–1960 but 47th in 1940–1948; North Carolina ranked 6.5 in 1952–1960 but 43rd in 1940–1948; Tennessee ranked 1.5 in 1952–1960 but 40.5 in 1940–1948; Mississippi ranked 6.5 in 1952–1960 but 48th in 1940–1948. The tendency is clear: the South is now very competitive in presidential elections, although party competition for state and local elections continues to be relatively low. The increase in party competition for presidential elections seems to have had only a minor effect on turnout, as Table 4 shows. Southern states continue to rank lowest on turnout, even in presidential elections, suggesting that other factors as well as party competition contribute to low southern turnout.

The racial problem of the South contributes to low turnout. Using 1960 census data to rank states by their percentage of Negroes, shows a negative correlation ($-.67$) with the turnout ranking shown in Table 3. Generally, higher percentages of blacks in an area mean lower turnout. Early studies of political participation also showed that blacks were less likely to vote than whites.[8] The interpretation that there is some biological characteristic of race that depresses black turnout, however, has been proven false since some studies show that in cities where blacks are given free opportunity and encouragement to participate they are as likely, or even more likely, to turn out than whites.[9] We shall soon see data from a recent study of Buffalo that show that blacks are somewhat more likely than whites to be active in politics in both conventional and unconventional ways.

The depressed turnout of blacks in the South is more likely due to systematic pressures, both social and political, than to lack of interest.[10] Generally, the higher the percentage of blacks in an area, the greater the local pressure to prevent them from voting, especially in the rural South. Some of these pressures are legal regulations, such as stringent registration requirements. Due to the intervention of the federal government some of these requirements have been made more reasonable, dramatically increasing black registration. Some of these pressures are social, such as ostracism and verbal abuse. Some take the form of economic reprisals, such as being fired from a job or evicted from rented quarters. Some pressures are unabashedly violent, such as beatings and killings.[11] These pressures inescapably depress turnout.

Another possible contribution to low turnout in the South is its low socioeconomic condition. Ranking the states for several economic variables, based on 1960 census data, shows a positive correlation with turnout rankings: average weekly unemployment benefits, .55; median family income, .52; per capita tax revenue, .55; median school years completed, .52; per pupil expenditures on education, .51. On all of these variables the South ranks lower than the rest of the nation. Although the correlation is clear, the influence of economic factors on turnout is difficult to assess. Is the correlation between turnout and these economic variables mere coincidence of the rankings or is there some causative relationship? It may be mere coincidence that southern states rank low on turnout and that they also rank somewhat lower on economic advancement. A variety of studies in at least six countries, however, have shown that persons of lower socioeconomic status (SES) are less likely to participate in politics than those of higher SES.[12] Keep in mind that socioeconomic status alone cannot cause any social behavior. We can speak of SES causing behavior only as experience affects personality, beliefs, and attitudes and, through these factors, behavior. As education and prosperity levels in the South increase we can anticipate that levels of political participation will increase as well. Table 1 and Figure 2 suggest that this probably is happening already.

Although turnout and other types of political participation may increase for a period as the overall economic level increases, the rise of political participation lags considerably behind the rise of economic levels. In recent years the Deep South has shown the greatest percentage rise on several prosperity indices: the percentage increase in per capita income from 1950 to 1960, the percentage increase in median family income from 1949 to 1959; and the percentage increase in urban population from 1950 to 1960. These rankings of states on prosperity increase are negatively related to turnout rankings for the years 1950 to 1960: the greater the percentage rise in prosperity, the more the likelihood of a low ranking on turnout. These data do not suggest that greater prosperity produces lower turnout but rather that habits of political participation change less rapidly than levels of prosperity.

Does the economic condition of a state affect its rates of political participation? The data available at this time do not enable us to give a clear-cut answer to this question. Minimal levels of education, economic well-being, communication facilities, and ease of getting around the community are important in facilitating political participation. Beyond these, the economic level of a state seems to have little relationship to its level of political participation.

Other possible factors producing lower turnout in the South are legal restrictions on the franchise. Many of these were adopted to make it more difficult for blacks to vote, but they have the side effect of making it slightly more difficult for some whites to vote too.

PARTICIPATION AND THE POLITICO-LEGAL SETTING

The political and legal characteristics of a state may confine or depress political participation but they also may facilitate it. Under the United States Constitution, the states, rather than the national government, are given the power to define legally who is eligible to participate in elections. However, the federal government limits that power: those eligible to vote for members of the most numerous house of the state legislature are eligible to vote in federal elections, and no one can be denied the franchise because of sex, race, color, or previous condition of servitude. Because of these laws, and other conventions, general suffrage requirements are fairly uniform across the states. Uniformities in laws, however, do not necessarily result in uniformities in practices. In fact, the same laws may be administered rather differently to exclude certain persons from participating in politics. These discriminatory practices have been on the decline during the decade of the sixties, and the federal government has taken vigorous action to insure that the franchise is not denied to citizens because of sex, race, or color.

In recent years vigorous political campaigns have been launched in many states to lower the voting age to eighteen or nineteen. Only four of these efforts succeeded. In June, 1970, however, Congress renewed the Voting Rights Act of 1965 and also passed a rider that lowered the voting age in all states to eighteen. A subsequent Supreme Court decision limited its applicability to elections for federal office. In March 1971 Congress passed a constitutional amendment that lowers the voting age to eighteen for all elections, including state and local. It has been submitted to the states for ratification.

The federal government added another uniformity in the suffrage laws by forbidding the poll tax in elections for national office in the Twenty-fourth Amendment to the Constitution. This action eliminated the poll tax as a significant factor in determining turnout. Other differences in state laws do seem significant to turnout. Table 6 presents a state-by-state summary, as of 1963, of the more important of these laws. The states are ranked in order of their average turnout in the presidential election of 1960. The presence of a star in a column means that the election law tends to facilitate turnout. A quick study of the patterning of the table shows that states ranking high in turnout tend to have more facilitative laws than states ranking low in turnout. The clustering of southern states at the bottom of the ranking and the relative infrequency of facilitative laws for those states is also evident.

Registration Requirements

Registration can be administered either to facilitate or to hinder voting. Many countries have what is called official or automatic registration whereby no initiative by the potential voter is required to get his name on the list of eligibles since the responsibility for keeping the list up to date lies with registration officials. Some studies suggest that turnout for voting is higher under automatic registration.[13] Certain states in the United States use a registration system that is akin to automatic registration. Idaho, which ranks near the top in turnout in the country, selects and pays a deputy registrar in each precinct to canvass door-to-door and keep registration rolls up to date. California law authorizes the appointment of deputy registrars and door-to-door canvassing.[14] Canada uses teams of enumerators to canvass residences prior to each parliamentary election.[15] In urban districts enumerators work in pairs, each representing a specific political interest. Only one enumerator is required in rural districts. Preliminary lists are posted so that any voter may protest the inclusion or omission of any name. A proposal is currently before the United States Congress to establish a Universal Voter Enrollment Plan for the entire United States.[16]

In many localities the act of registration is much more inconvenient than the act of voting. Some states require a trip to the county court house, usually during working hours. To alleviate this inconvenience, more than half of the states have adopted precinct or mobile registration on designated days preceding elections (See Table 6). On these days the voter makes only a short trip in his immediate neighborhood. There does not seem to be any pattern in turnout rankings, however, for states permitting precinct registration.

TABLE 6

*Voting Turnout and Election Law. Vote in Presidential Elections as a Percentage of Civilian Population of Voting Age, by State, with Provisions of Election Laws Facilitating Participation. Key: * = statewide, † = some areas only.*ᵃ

	Turnout		State	Residence in state under 1 year	No literacy test	Permanent registration	General civilian absentee registration permitted	Precinct registration	Registration closes within 1 month of election	Civilian absentee vote	Mere absence a ground for absentee vote	Absentee ballot application by mail	Polls open 12 hours or longer	Presidential voting by new residents	Presidential voting by former residents
1920	1940	1960													
57.9	75.1	80.7	Idaho	*	*	*	*	*	*	*	*	*	*	*	—
63.8	80.3	80.1	Utah	—	*	*	*	*	*	*	*	*	*	—	—
56.6	72.4	79.4	New Hampshire	*	—	*	—	—	*	*	*	*	†-*	—	—
63.7	75.2	78.5	North Dakota	—	*	b	b	b	b	*	*	*	*	—	—
52.8	79.5	78.3	South Dakota	—	*	*	*	—	b	*	*	*	*	—	—
67.8	81.4	77.3	West Virginia	*	*	*	*	*	*	*	—	*	*	—	—
53.3	69.6	77.0	Minnesota	*	*	†-*	—	—	—	*	*	*	*	—	—
71.0	79.8	76.9	Indiana	—	*	*	*	—	*	*	—	*	*	*	*
43.6	67.4	76.8	Connecticut	*	—	†-*	—	—	*	*	*	*	*	—	—
62.7	74.1	76.5	Iowa	—	*	*	*	*	*	*	—	*	*	*	—
41.2	69.5	76.1	Massachusetts	—	*	*	—	*	*	*	*	*	*	*	—
53.1	78.4	75.7	Illinois	—	—	†-*	—	†-*	—	*	*	*	†-*	—	*
47.3	67.4	75.1	Rhode Island	—	—	†-*	—	*	*	*	*	*	†-*	—	—
45.4	72.2	74.0	Wyoming	—	*	*	*	*	—	*	*	*	—	*	—
69.5	76.8	73.6	Delaware	—	*	—	—	—	*	*	*	*	*	*	*
45.9	69.6	73.4	Wisconsin	—	—	†-*	*	—	*	*	*	*	†-*	—	—
41.6	60.2	72.6	Maine	*	*	—	—	—	*	*	—	*	—	—	*
41.4	62.7	72.5	Vermont	—	*	*	—	—	*	*	*	*	†-*	*	—
47.3	61.8	72.4	Michigan	*	*	—	*	—	*	*	*	*	†-*	—	—

State													
Washington	46.5	66.5	72.3	—	—	*	*	*	*	—	—	—	—
Oregon	48.2	64.3	72.3	—	*	*	*	*	*	*	*	*	*
New Jersey	48.0	69.6	71.8	*	*	*	*	*	—	—	*	*	*
Missouri	65.4	73.3	71.8	—	*	†	*	*	*	—	†	†	†
Colorado	51.7	76.9	71.4	—	*	†	*	*	*	*	—	†	†
Nebraska	51.8	73.6	71.4	—	*	†*	*	*	*	*	*	†	*
Montana	55.8	69.6	71.4	—	—	†	*	*	—	*	*	†	†
Ohio	56.8	72.4	71.3	—	*	†*	*	*	—	*	*	†*	†
Pennsylvania	36.7	64.2	70.5	—	—	†	*	*	*	*	*	†	†
Kansas	55.7	74.0	70.3	*	*	†*	*	*	*	*	*	†	*
California	40.7	66.9	67.4	—	—	—	*	*	*	*	—	—	—
New York	44.5	67.4	67.0	—	*	†	*	*	†	†*	*	†*	†
Oklahoma	47.6	60.3	63.8	—	—	†*	*	*	†	†*	†	†	—
New Mexico	56.9	64.4	62.1	—	*	†*	*	*	*	*	*	*	*
Nevada	52.1	70.6	61.2	*	—	*	*	—	—	*	*	*	*
Kentucky	71.2	59.3	59.2	*	*	†	*	*	—	—	*	*	*
Maryland	49.7	55.7	57.2	—	—	†	*	*	—	—	*	†	*
Arizona	35.4	52.0	54.5	—	—	*	*	*	*	*	*	†	*
North Carolina	44.5	42.6	53.5	—	*	*	*	*	*	*	*	†	*
Hawaii			51.3	—	—	—	—	—	—	—	—	—	—
Tennessee	35.3	30.6	50.3	—	—	*	*	*	*	*	—	†	*
Florida	36.0	39.8	50.0	—	—	†	*	*	b	b	b	†	b
Alaska			45.5	—	*	b	*	*	b	b	b	b	*
Louisiana	13.6	27.1	44.8	—	—	†	—	*	—	b	—	†	*
Texas	19.8	27.0	41.8	—	*	b	*	*	b	b	b	b	*
Arkansas	21.2	18.2	41.1	—	*	b	*	*	b	b	b	b	*
Virginia	19.1	22.0	33.4	—	*	*	*	*	—	*	—	*	*
Alabama	20.8	18.9	31.1	—	—	*	*	*	*	*	—	—	*
South Carolina	8.6	10.1	30.5	—	—	—	*	*	*	*	—	*	—
Georgia	10.1	17.6	30.4	—	*	*	—	—	—	*	—	*	*
Mississippi	9.4	14.7	25.5	—	—	—	*	*	*	—	—	—	—

[a]The information in this chart has been checked with responsible officials in every state. In certain instances, it has not been feasible to show in detail specific exceptions to general provisions.

[b]No registration in this state.

Source: Reproduced from *Report of the President's Commission on Registration and Voting Participation, November, 1963.* The states are ranked by percentage turnout in the 1960 presidential election.

In some states, again mainly in the South, registration is more than inconvenient, it is difficult. Registration forms are deliberately complicated. Some jurisdictions require witnesses to testify to the identity and residence of the applicant. Literacy tests in many jurisdictions are extremely difficult and, if the applicant is black, letter-perfect accuracy often is required to pass. Such a literacy test was administered by a political science professor at a good southern university to his class of white students; a majority of the class would have failed to qualify to vote under the test.

Responding to strong national pressure to correct this situation, Congress passed the Voting Rights Act of 1965, banning literacy and other discriminatory voter registration tests and requirements wherever less than 50 per cent of the voting age residents were registered or where less than 50 per cent voted in the November, 1964, presidential election. Federal action has also provided federal registrars to register voters for federal elections where local registrars could not be counted on to facilitate registration. A close comparison of rates of registration before and after the passage of the act shows that registration of blacks increased considerably in counties that previously had restricted registration (usually those with the highest black concentration). Prior to the act there had been a negative correlation in the $-.40$ to $-.50$ range between the percentage of registered blacks and the percentage of blacks in the county. After the act went into effect this negative correlation was reduced to about $-.22$. In many states black registration rates no longer differed between counties with a relatively small proportion of blacks and counties with a very high proportion of blacks. As expected, the counties that had been more restrictive of registration showed the greatest overall increase in black registration. This change was most pronounced for Alabama, Louisiana, and South Carolina. Only in Georgia did counties continue to show a clear negative correlation between black registration and black concentration, but even in Georgia registration percentages shifted up about 20 per cent.[17] The Federal Voting Rights Act of 1965 can be regarded as a natural political experiment since it is possible to trace rather clearly the changes in registration rates that derive from the act. These changes were so dramatic that we must view ease of registration as a major contributor to increasing turnout rates.[18] This clear rise in registration may also contribute to the recent rise in participation levels for the South.

Nearly all states permit some type of permanent registration so that citizens do not need to reregister before each election. Seventeen states also permit absentee registration, which shows a significant, positive relationship with turnout ranking. It also facilitates registration if the registration books can be kept open reasonably close to the election. This objective must be balanced against the registrar's practical task of preparing precinct lists of eligibles by election day. Most states close registration within one month of the election (See Table 6). Only four states have no registration system. This arrangement seems to be practical only in sparsely populated areas.

Residence Requirements

The United States Census Bureau revealed that 20 million American adults changed their residence in 1961. In a society with a highly mobile population, requiring lengthy periods of residence before allowing a citizen to vote can be a significant barrier to turnout. Using census data for 1960, states were ranked by the percentage of their citizens who changed residence after 1958; this ranking was correlated against the state-by-state turnout rankings. It shows a negative correlation with all of the turnout measures; the greater the mobility the lower the turnout. As we might expect, since the ranking is for persons who moved after 1958, it shows the highest negative correlation ($-.515$) with turnout in the 1960 presidential election. Table 6 shows that only twelve states have residence requirements of less than one year. The lowest turnout states, those ranking toward the bottom of that table, uniformly require a year or more of residence. The President's Commission on Registration and Voting Participation (hereafter called the President's Commission) estimated that 4 million persons were disfranchised by residence requirements in 1950, 5 million in 1954, and 8 million in 1960. The commission recommended that state residence requirements should not exceed six months and that local residence requirements should not exceed a period of thirty days.

The Commission also recommended that new state residents should be allowed to vote for president even if not for state and local offices. Table 6 shows that in 1963, fifteen states granted this privilege; some additional states have added this option since then. This characteristic was correlated with the turnout rankings; the correlation was not significant for turnout in state elections but was significantly related to turnout in presidential elections. Table 6 also indicates that several states allow former residents to vote for president even though they have moved away.

Absentee Ballot

All states except Mississippi, New Mexico, and South Carolina provide some form of absentee balloting for their non-military citizens. Table 6 shows that thirty-four states provide absentee privileges for anyone who expects to be away from home on election day. In other states, a person must be unavoidably absent or have some special status, such as a business-man on a regular trip or a student at an accredited college or university in order to be able to vote by absentee ballot. Although there is a slight trend in the data for states that have easy absentee voting procedures to rank high in turnout, there are enough exceptions to suggest that the trend is not significant.

Voting Hours

The President's Commission recommended that polling places should be kept open all day and remain open until 9 P.M. Ten states in 1963 kept their polls open for less than twelve hours. Six of these ten states are southern and rank low in turnout. Thus, there is a significant correlation between length of time the polls are open and state rank on turnout. The original justification for closing polls early was to give election officials time to count the ballots, but widespread use of voting machines makes this plea seem less and less valid.

Scholars at the Survey Research Center of the University of Michigan examined several of the above legal requirements and grouped states into a two-category measure as having restrictive suffrage laws or moderate suffrage laws.[19] They concluded from their analysis that restrictive suffrage requirements inhibit turnout the most in the South. This inhibition was most pronounced for southern blacks and was highest in areas where the per-centage of blacks was close enough to the percentage of whites to constitute a threat to white political dominance. They also concluded that informal, extralegal barriers — not state legislation — account for much of the vari-ability in turnout of southern blacks.

The Political Party Setting

If party activity is vigorous, and especially if party competition is in-tense, turnout is likely to be high. Several related mechanisms seem to be operating here. When parties and candidates compete vigorously, they make news and are given much attention by the mass media. This provides more political stimuli in the environment for citizens to pick up, which in turn, generates greater interest in the contest. If the contest seems to be close and citizens believe that their vote is likely to be important, they are more likely to turn out and cast it. It is also true that in a close contest the party workers on both sides get out and work more vigorously trying to per-suade people to their point of view and to get them out to vote.[20]

A similar point was made by Campbell when he classified elections into high stimulus and low stimulus elections.[21] In a high stimulus election people generally perceive that the vote will be close and, therefore, that their votes will count; they think the office being decided is important; they see a clear choice between alternative candidates or parties; the candidates are attractive; campaign propaganda abounds. High stimulus elections bring out a comparatively high turnout. People living in a state with vigorous party competition are more likely to experience high stimulus elections than those living in states dominated by one party.

INPUT AND OUTTAKE ANALYSIS

Figure 1 showed how three dimensions of activity could be summarized in an abstract map. Inputs to and outtakes from the political system by individuals were modified by the active-passive dimension and then by the instrumental-expressive dimension. This abstract map provided some ideas for a much richer examination of the relationships between individuals and their government than had been attempted in previous studies. A three-year project investigating the political behavior of individuals in the Buffalo, New York, metropolitan area during the years 1966 through 1968 provided an opportunity to try out the approach contained in Figure 1 in an actual project. Two waves of interviews were conducted for this study. About half of the respondents were part of a panel and were interviewed on both waves. A major focus of this study was on the relationship of the individual to his government. The study sought these basic kinds of information about this relationship: (1) how frequently respondents made certain kinds of inputs to the political system; (2) how much responsibility they had to make each of these inputs; (3) how effective government had been in performing certain kinds of services for them; and (4) how much responsibility the government had to perform each of these services. Some of the basic findings on inputs and outtakes from this study are presented here in order to illustrate the kinds of questions that one can ask to derive a more adequate understanding of state politics. Unfortunately, we do not have data of this type for even one state, much less data that might be compared across the various states. The Buffalo data are presented in the hope that these ideas may be picked up for a comparative state study in the future.

The Buffalo data are neither idiosyncratic nor unique and thus should provide some insight into the basic postures that American citizens take toward their government at this time in their history. With a judicious

choice of questions a researcher can develop a thorough and complex statement of the relationship between an individual and his government. It is
my belief that thorough data of this sort are needed before we can fully
understand governmental effectiveness and the complex processes that go to
make up governments.

In order that the reader may fully understand the data that follow, it
will be necessary to describe briefly the method used for collection of the
data. We wished to facilitate comparison of specific acts, to compare the
respondent's judgment about what actually takes place with what he felt
ought to take place, and finally, to study change in these beliefs over time.
A card sorting method seemed most apt to facilitate these comparisons. A
general question was read to the respondent, and a placement board showing the categories of response was put before him. Then he was presented
with a deck of numbered stimulus cards, each containing different content,
and was asked to sort the cards into one or another of the response boxes
shown on the placement board. If this were a deck of input cards it contained simple items such as "Vote in elections," "Engage in political discussion," or "Join in public street demonstrations." If it were a deck of
outtake cards, it contained items such as "Provide justice," "Build urban renewal projects," or "Take actions that make me proud of my country."

The respondent was asked to sort the cards first according to how frequently he performed the activity. Once the cards were sorted into those
categories, the interviewer picked them up, shuffled them, and asked the
respondent to sort them again according to his responsibility to do each of
these things. Another deck of cards and other placement boards were used
for things that people take out of the political system. The respondents
were asked first to sort the cards according to how effectively government
performed each function. Once sorted, the cards were shuffled and sorted
again by the respondent, but this time according to the responsibility the
government had to carry out the function.[22]

We wished to see if the conceptual classification set forth in Figure 1
came close to reflecting the classification that was in the minds of our respondents as they sorted these input and outtake cards. The responses to all
of these items, both input and outtake, were factor analyzed to find out how
they clustered. The clustering was used to group items in the following
tables. The categorization shown in Figure 1 is reasonably reflective of the
reality we found. Before discussing those clusters of items, it would be helpful to clarify the kind of data reported in the table for each item.

Each card could be sorted into one of four boxes. If the respondent
placed it in the box saying he *never* did the activity, that response was

scored as 1; if he *seldom* did it, it was scored as 2; if he did it *fairly often,* it was scored as 3; and if he did it *regularly,* it was scored as 4. The figure reported in the table is a mean or average score for the entire sample of either blacks or whites.[23] Race was such a significant variable in the Buffalo study that separate scores are reported for blacks and whites on all the tables. A similar method of scoring was used for the sorting on "Responsibility to take the action." If a person said he had *no* responsibility, he was given a 1; if he had *some* responsibility, he was given a 2; if he had an *important* responsibility, he was given a 3; and if he said he had an *essential* responsibility to do it, he was given a 4. Again, mean scores were calculated for both blacks and whites. The same card sorting method and the same method of scoring were used on both waves of interviews. The mean scores on the input items were very similar on both waves of interviews; thus, the tables reporting mean input scores will only report the second wave findings. Respondents did react somewhat differently on the two waves when sorting the outtake items, and several of the tables reporting outtake items will show figures from both waves.

If the mean responsibility score for an item is higher than the mean frequency score, as is usually the case, it is an indication that respondents generally assign themselves a greater responsibility to carry out the action than they fulfill. When we conducted the second wave of interviews we decided to find out if respondents believed it was wrong to perform some of these activities. Thus, at the conclusion of the sorting on responsibility, we asked respondents to take those cards which they had sorted into the "No responsibility" box and to indicate to us any activities that they felt should not be done. The last two columns of the input tables indicate the percentages of blacks and whites who believe that it is wrong to carry out each of these actions.

Table 7 shows the mean scores for party and campaign activity inputs to the political system. Most respondents said that they seldom did these activities although they indicated that they had some responsibility to do them. Blacks reported a higher level of responsibility to perform these acts than whites and their levels of performance were slightly higher than those of whites. Several of these items had appeared on the first wave. The data showed a slight increase in responsibility to perform these activities by blacks from the first to the second wave. Whites stayed at approximately the same level on both waves. This high level of political activity by blacks contrasts sharply with findings from previous studies that showed whites considerably more active than blacks. Events in the decade of the sixties, however, have taught blacks to be active in politics in both conventional and unconventional ways. In the conventional ways reported in Table 7, we find older blacks more likely to be active than younger blacks. Only small percentages of either race believe it is wrong to take most of these actions. A slight exception is the item "Give money to help a party and candidate," where 8 per cent of each race believed it is wrong to do so.

Even more striking are the sizable percentages, 29 per cent for blacks and 38 per cent for whites, who believed that it is wrong to try to convince people to vote their way. Apparently, nearly one-third of the people in Buffalo believed that people should make up their minds how they are going to vote without being influenced in any way by other persons around them. Data from other studies suggest that Buffalonians are not unique in this respect. There seems to be a societal norm that is accepted by a sizable portion of people to avoid trying to influence another on how he should vote. This aversion to influencing other people in their voting is reflected in the mean scores for both responsibility and performance. Few people try to convince others on how they should vote and, in contrast to other items, the responsibility for performing the activity is lower than the actual performance for both blacks and whites. A similarly low responsibility level was shown on the first wave for an item (not reported on the table) that read "Be a candidate for public office." Most respondents said they had no responsibility to do this; even more reported never having done so.

The Buffalo study confirmed the finding from many previous studies that people who are involved in community groups are more likely to become active in party and campaign work. The item that read "Join groups working to improve community life" correlated so highly with the other items in Table 7 that it is included here as part of this grouping. The respondents, especially blacks, indicated a high responsibility to be active in community groups, and almost none of them thought this activity was wrong. The second highest responsibility shown in the table is for the item "Join and support a political party." Both of these activities were considered relatively effective for trying to influence what government does.

One would expect a relationship between the responsibility a person feels to carry out a political action and the actual carrying out of that action. The strength of this relationship is shown on these input tables under the column heading "Correlation of responsibility and frequency." Generally these correlations are in a range from .40 to .60, confirming our supposition that people who feel a responsibility to take an action are more likely to follow through by carrying out the action. On Table 7 you can see that for the item "Try to convince people to vote your way" the correlation between responsibility and the frequency of carrying out the action is

TABLE 7
Party and Campaign Activity Inputs (Mean scores by race, second interview wave, 1968)

	Blacks[a]		Whites[a]		Correlation of responsibility and frequency		Percentage who believe it is wrong to take the action	
	Frequency of activity	Responsibility to do it	Frequency of activity	Responsibility to do it	Blacks	Whites	Blacks	Whites
Take an active part in a political campaign	1.80	2.33	1.54	2.00	.44	.47	4	2
Give money to help a party or candidate	1.79	2.07	1.49	1.70	.54	.59	8	8
Work to get people registered to vote	2.02	2.61	1.64	2.23	.46	.46	3	2
Join and support a political party	2.20	2.66	2.11	2.46	.44	.55	2	2
Try to convince people to vote your way	1.69	1.67	1.61	1.48	.61	.61	29	38
Join groups working to improve community life	2.52	3.29	1.99	2.75	.29	.42	1	0

[a]The N for blacks is approximately 300; the N for whites is approximately 1,000.

exceptionally high, .61 for both races. We saw a moment ago that many respondents believe they have no responsibility to do this. Those who do feel a responsibility to try to convince others are clearly more likely to carry out the action. The item "Join groups working to improve community life" is striking for the lowness of the correlations, especially for blacks. This suggests that in the black community persons are likely to get involved in community groups whether or not they feel a high responsibility to do so.

Table 8 shows communication and information inputs that people can make to a political system. Most respondents believed that it is relatively important to keep informed about politics, and most of them reported that they do a reasonably adequate job of keeping informed. (This should not be taken as the author's judgment of adequacy, rather that most respondents believe that they are adequately informed.) Slightly less responsibility was evidenced for sending messages to political leaders, but most respondents indicated that they have at least some responsibility to do this. Apparently, most people have a barrier to composing and transmitting messages since performance lags considerably behind responsibility for these activities, especially if the message is one of protest. This effect can also be seen on the correlations between frequency and responsibility. The correlations for the three items that involve composing messages are considerably lower, especially for blacks. Presumably, lack of education and confidence among blacks inhibits the framing of messages even though they feel a responsibility to do so. Also, 7 per cent of blacks and 11 per cent of whites believed it wrong to send protest messages to political leaders.

Performance levels for engaging in political discussion were considerably higher. For whites, the overall levels of performance were slightly above the level of responsibility that they acknowledged. It is very easy to get involved in a political discussion whether one wishes to do so or not, and that situation is reflected in these figures. Responsibility to inform others in one's community about politics was relatively low, although it was somewhat higher for blacks than for whites. Blacks also showed a slightly higher performance level than whites. The relatively low responsibility levels are reflected in the 5 per cent of each race who believe that it is wrong to do this. It is interesting that respondents show relatively little responsibility to write letters to the editors of newspapers and very few of them have done so.

All the items in this table, with the exception of "Keep informed about politics," were assigned only moderate levels of responsibility and respondents' performance levels are fairly low. Our data show that younger people, who are presumably better educated than their elders, participate a little

TABLE 8
Communication and Information Inputs (Mean scores by race, second interview wave, 1968)

	Blacks		Whites		Correlation of responsibility and frequency		Percentage who believe it is wrong to take the action	
	Frequency of activity	Responsibility to do it	Frequency of activity	Responsibility to do it	Blacks	Whites	Blacks	Whites
Keep informed about politics	2.61	3.00	2.91	3.04	.52	.54	2	5
Send protest messages to political leaders when they are doing badly	1.64	2.41	1.48	2.07	.34	.45	7	11
Engage in political discussion	2.20	2.29	2.28	2.19	.64	.55	4	4
Inform others in my community about politics	1.95	2.29	1.84	2.01	.57	.52	5	5
Make my views known to public officials	2.10	2.76	1.88	2.43	.33	.44	3	2
Write letters to the editors of newspapers	1.50	2.17	1.41	1.90	.33	.47	4	4

more readily in these communication activities. This statement is more true of young whites than young blacks. We will see in the next section that young blacks place more emphasis on protest and demonstration activities than do their elders, who emphasize party and campaign activity inputs.

Although in recent years the frequency of protest and demonstration inputs has risen sharply, the data in Table 9 also show that, nevertheless, most respondents felt relatively little responsibility to engage in these activities. As a matter of fact, sizable percentages of both blacks and whites believed that it is wrong to protest and demonstrate. The percentage feeling it is wrong is much greater among whites than blacks, and older blacks are more likely to feel it is wrong than young blacks. The racial contrast is particularly striking for the item "Join in a protest march": 52 per cent of whites but only 14 per cent of blacks believed it is wrong to do this.

Not surprisingly, 83 per cent of whites and 62 per cent of blacks believed it is wrong to riot in order to correct political wrongs. The mean responsibility scores here are the lowest of any item and the proportion of people who have ever done this is also the lowest of any item. The responsibility-frequency correlation is very low for whites but relatively high for blacks, suggesting that rioting is a possibility for blacks but not whites. On another question respondents ranked this item as the lowest in effectiveness of any of the input items. Slightly higher proportions have joined in public street demonstrations, but here, too, the responsibility levels are fairly low, especially for whites. Twenty-one per cent of blacks believed it wrong to do this compared with 62 per cent of whites. The items in this table have the lowest responsibility levels and the lowest performance levels of all of the input items. They were also considered least effective by our respondents. In Figure 1, protests and demonstrations were classified as expressive-active inputs, and that classification seems to fit well the activities shown in Table 9.

In contrast to the protest and demonstration inputs, another set of expressive-active inputs was assigned a very high responsibility by our respondents; these are the patriotism and love of country inputs shown in Table 10. Almost no one in our sample believed it wrong to do these things. Particularly high responsibilities were shown for loving one's country, paying all taxes (this item appeared only on the first wave and is not shown in the table), and respecting the police. These three items contrast with the general pattern in that the performance levels exceed the responsibility levels for both blacks and whites.

An interesting finding of our study is that voting in elections clustered into this group of inputs rather than in the party and campaign activity in-

TABLE 9

Protest and Demonstration Inputs (Mean scores by race, second interview wave, 1968)

	Blacks		Whites		Correlation of responsibility and frequency		Percentage who believe it is wrong to take the action	
	Frequency of activity	Responsibility to do it	Frequency of activity	Responsibility to do it	Blacks	Whites	Blacks	Whites
Join in public street demonstrations	1.35	1.63	1.09	1.14	.45	.52	21	62
Riot if necessary to get public officials to correct political wrongs	1.24	1.30	1.06	1.13	.60	.30	62	83
Attend protest meetings	1.71	2.15	1.20	1.41	.44	.44	8	29
Join in a protest march	1.48	1.84	1.10	1.21	.52	.50	14	52
Refuse to obey unjust laws	1.80	1.91	1.52	1.68	.45	.42	21	41

TABLE 10

Patriotism and Love of Country Inputs (Mean scores by race, second interview wave, 1968)

	Blacks		Whites		Correlation of responsibility and frequency		Percentage who believe it is wrong to take the action	
	Frequency of activity	Responsibility to do it	Frequency of activity	Responsibility to do it	Blacks	Whites	Blacks	Whites
Love my country	3.73	3.61	3.89	3.79	.65	.47	0	0
Show my patriotism by flying the flag, attending parades, or in some other way	2.69	2.98	3.12	3.28	.57	.60	3	1
Vote in elections	3.42	3.66	3.31	3.63	.37	.51	1	0
Respect the police	3.71	3.48	3.83	3.72	.56	.53	0	0
Support my country in wars that I don't agree with	2.24	2.30	2.91	2.79	.67	.66	19	9

puts shown in Table 7. For many people the act of voting is as much or more an act of patriotism as it is an act designed to achieve a specific political end. Our respondents assigned themselves a high responsibility to vote; it was the highest responsibility item for blacks and the third highest for whites. The relatively low frequency-responsibility correlation for blacks (.37) suggests that many of them find it difficult to vote as frequently as they believe they ought to. Voting was also believed to be highest in effectiveness for influencing government by both blacks and whites.

The last item in Table 10, which reads "Support my country in wars that I don't agree with," was given only a moderately high level of responsibility. The performance levels slightly exceeded the responsibility levels for whites and the two levels were fairly even for blacks. Nineteen per cent of blacks and 9 per cent of whites believed it wrong to do this. Performance is strongly affected by responsibility for this activity as evidenced by the high correlation shown for both blacks and whites. The item dealing with conscription and the item from the first wave dealing with paying taxes might be viewed as passive inputs (see Figure 1). It is interesting that respondents assign relatively high responsibilities to doing things they really have very little choice about. As noted above, the rest of the items in Table 10 may be viewed as expressive-active inputs. Generally the performance levels are equal to or higher than the responsibility levels. There is a slight exception for voting and showing patriotism, where performance lags slightly behind responsibility. Psychological theory suggests that when something is considered as important as these activities, a person must believe that he performs the activity reasonably well.

Our second wave of interviews was conducted in the spring and summer of 1968 when the law-and-order issue was a major factor in the 1968 election campaign. To investigate this issue, the three items shown in Table 11 were included in our second wave of interviews. Many of our respondents, especially the whites, clearly believed that they had an important responsibility to support officials as they tried to keep order during a disturbance. This input was also rated as quite effective by both blacks and whites, ranking fifth in overall effectiveness for blacks and fourth for whites. The proportion of blacks supporting law and order was as great as that for whites on this first item but considerably fewer blacks supported police when they cracked down on demonstrators or when they shot looters. Blacks ranked the effectiveness of these items as very low, twenty-first rank for the "demonstrators" item and twenty-sixth for the "shoot looters" item. In contrast, whites gave them ranks of five and nine respectively. Many more blacks than whites also thought it wrong to support public officials when

TABLE 11
Support Law and Order Inputs (Mean scores by race, second interview wave, 1968)

	Blacks		Whites		Correlation of responsibility and frequency		Percentage who believe it is wrong to take the action	
	Frequency of activity	*Responsibility to do it*	*Frequency of activity*	*Responsibility to do it*	*Blacks*	*Whites*	*Blacks*	*Whites*
Support community leaders when they are trying to keep order during a disturbance	2.91	3.23	2.92	3.24	.43	.47	1	1
Support public officials when they crack down on demonstrators	1.81	2.05	2.68	2.89	.45	.58	19	3
Support police when they shoot looters	1.69	1.71	2.74	2.79	.67	.63	38	9

they do these things. Nineteen per cent considered it wrong for officials to crack down on demonstrators and 38 per cent considered it wrong for police to shoot looters. The corresponding percentages for whites were much less, 3 on the "demonstrate" item and 9 on the "shoot looters" item. The high responsibility-frequency correlations for the "shoot looters" item suggests that performance closely follows responsibility for this item.

Table 12 shows three items dealing with child-training inputs that we included in our first wave of interviews. Both blacks and whites showed a high responsibility to teach children about democracy and citizenship. The responsibility-frequency correlations were especially high for blacks for these items. Less emphasis was placed upon teaching children to participate in politics beyond voting, but most respondents indicated a moderate level of responsibility even for this activity. The frequency of teaching children to be active in politics was also lower than for the other items.

The input items just reviewed in Tables 7 through 12 list some of the kinds of inputs that individuals can make to a political system. The activities covered in our studies are by no means exhaustive. Other scholars will add to the list, and as other items are used in future studies, the clustering shown here may shift as new kinds of inputs are considered. My purpose

TABLE 12
Child-Training Inputs (Mean scores by race, first interview wave only, 1966-1967)

	Blacks		Whites		Correlation of responsibility and frequency	
	Frequency of activity	Responsibility to do it	Frequency of activity	Responsibility to do it	Blacks	Whites
Teach my children the importance of give and take in the democratic way of life	3.11	3.24	3.09	3.38	.61	.47
Teach my children to participate in politics beyond voting	2.15	2.59	2.05	2.65	.48	.50
Personally see to it that my children understand and accept the responsibility of citizenship	3.14	3.36	3.15	3.49	.57	.40

was to illustrate the variety of ways that individuals can contribute to the functioning of a political system. In addition, I strongly recommend that future studies of state politics incorporate many of these ways of making inputs to a political system into their research design. Only by investigating what people give to a political system can we trace the connection between these inputs and the way that system functions.

What responses were obtained regarding outputs? What do individuals take *from* a political system? Again the ideas for items were drawn from the abstract map shown in Figure 1. The same card sorting method used to investigate inputs was used to investigate outtakes. Respondents were asked to rate first the effectiveness of the government as it performed the function and then, in the second card sort, they were asked to assign responsibility to government to perform the function. The response category "very effective" was scored as a 4, "moderately effective" as a 3, "not very effective" as a 2, and "ineffective" as a 1. On the "responsibility" sort the category of "essential responsibility" was given a 4, "important responsibility" was given a 3, "some responsibility" was given a 2, and "things the government should not attempt to do at all" was given a 1.

Many of the outtake items showed a change from the first to the second wave. Thus, in Tables 13 through 17, mean scores for blacks and whites will be reported either for the first or the second wave or both. As with the input items, we wanted to see if the conceptual categorization in Figure 1 would be reflected in the clusterings that factor analysis would disclose. The clustering of the outtake items was not so clear-cut as for the input items. Some items could as well have fallen into one categorization as another. The general clustering that is shown in Tables 13 through 17 is derived mainly from the factor analysis. These clusterings seem to reflect the political ideology of groups of people as they differ in how they would assign responsibility to government to perform the functions listed.

In the outtake data, people generally assign a higher responsibility to government than they rate it as being effective. If the responsibility level is higher than the effectiveness level we can say that the government is deficient on that function, or we can say that there is a deficiency gap. A gap of two or more positions is a serious deficiency. For example, if a respondent assigns an essential responsibility to government to perform a function but says that it is performed not very effectively or ineffectively that may be characterized as a serious deficiency. The last two columns of the outtake tables report the percentages of black and white respondents who see a serious deficiency in governmental performance on a function.

A sizable group of our respondents thought about governmental responsibilities in very traditional terms. The functions to which they assigned a very high responsibility are shown in Table 13. The responsibility for "providing justice for all" is assigned the highest priority by both blacks and whites for both waves of interviews. There was a slight decline in governmental effectiveness in providing justice as seen by both races from the first to the second wave. This seemed to be especially true for the young and better-educated respondents. Forty-one per cent of blacks and 19 per cent of whites saw a serious deficiency by government for this function.

Other high priority items on this table, especially for whites, are "Providing protection and security," "Being careful in using public money and trust," and "Providing strong leadership." The item on providing protection and security, which appeared on both waves, shows a sharp decline, especially for higher-educated people, in the effectiveness rating for both blacks and whites from the first to the second wave. By the second wave 27 per cent of blacks and 23 per cent of whites saw a serious deficiency by government on this item. On the first wave both blacks and whites, but especially whites, saw a very large deficiency in "Being careful in using public money and trust." The deficiency in "Providing strong leadership" as measured on the first wave was moderate. On the second wave the overall levels of effectiveness and responsibility were somewhat lower when the item was changed to ask about local leadership. The deficiency gap was about the same as was noted for the first wave for the more general item. More than one-fourth of both blacks and whites saw a serious deficiency in local leadership.

Taking actions that make a person proud of his country or city are classified as expressive outtakes in Figure 1. Our respondents assigned very high responsibility levels to government to fulfill these needs, yet fairly large deficiency gaps occur between performance and responsibility for both items, for both races, on both waves. On the second wave, more than one-fourth of blacks see a serious deficiency for both the country and the city in this respect, as do sizable percentages of whites. Curiously, the higher the socioeconomic status of the respondent, the more likely he was to see a deficiency. Young people were more likely to see a deficiency on these matters than older people. For blacks there was a considerable decline from the first to the second wave in the effectiveness of government in making citizens proud.

The last three items in the table deal with general law-and-order functions of government. The responsibilities assigned to government here are quite high, especially for whites. Both races see a very serious deficiency in keeping neighborhoods safe and in providing ways to control riots. Furthermore, blacks are just as concerned about these problems as whites, with

TABLE 13
Traditional Outtakes From Government (Mean scores by race, and by interview wave)

	First wave, 1966-1967				Second wave, 1968				Percentage seeing serious deficiency, second wave	
	Blacks		Whites		Blacks		Whites			
	Effectiveness	Responsibility	Effectiveness	Responsibility	Effectiveness	Responsibility	Effectiveness	Responsibility	Blacks	Whites
Providing protection and security	3.12	3.62	3.19	3.69	2.64	3.55	2.87	3.67	27	23
Providing justice for all	2.69	3.76	3.14	3.81	2.49	3.71	3.03	3.78	41	19
Taking actions that make me proud of my country	3.09	3.35	3.28	3.61	2.68	3.50	3.12	3.66	28	14
Taking actions that make me proud of my city	2.75	3.21	2.84	3.37	2.58	3.42	2.75	3.44	29	23
Being careful in using public money and trust	2.57	3.52	2.49	3.69						
Making it possible for a person to have some say in his government					2.85	3.38	3.01	3.36	14	12
Providing public order; e.g., traffic regulations	3.16	3.29	3.22	3.38						
Providing courts for resolving conflicts between private parties	3.08	3.17	3.14	3.19						
Providing strong leadership	3.12	3.66	3.15	3.66						
Providing strong local leadership to deal with community problems					2.46	3.38	2.65	3.34	29	24
Keeping neighborhoods safe					2.14	3.45	2.40	3.64	47	41
Making sure criminals get punished					2.66	3.44	2.64	3.62	26	34
Providing ways to control riots					2.32	3.51	2.42	3.66	43	42

more than 40 per cent of both races believing that government is seriously deficient on both functions. Republican blacks were more likely to see a deficiency on these functions than were Democratic blacks, however. It has often been noted that lower-educated whites were very concerned about this issue in 1968, and our data show that lower-educated whites were more likely to see a deficiency here than those that were better educated. On the item that deals with making sure that criminals get punished, whites were more likely to see a serious deficiency than were blacks. A larger percentage of blacks than whites saw a serious deficiency on most of the other items.

In the general pattern of response for whites regarding the traditional items in Table 13, Republicans saw greater deficiencies than did Democrats. On many other clusters of items, for example, "civil rights and integration" or "openness and opportunity," Democrats were more likely to see deficiencies than were Republicans.

Although protecting civil rights is certainly a traditional governmental function, a group of items clustered on Table 14, called "Civil Rights and Integration Outtakes," seems to be somewhat set aside from the items shown in Table 13. Probably these functions are strongly related to the aspirations of blacks for full civil rights and integration. In Table 14 blacks assign higher responsibility to perform most of these functions than do whites. At the same time, they judge government effectiveness in carrying out these functions lower than whites. Thus, the gap between performance and responsibility is generally much larger for blacks than for whites. This can also be seen in the percentage of black and white respondents who see a serious deficiency by government on these functions. The black percentage seeing a serious deficiency is generally around 40; the white percentage is between 10 and 20. For both races the young and the better-educated respondents were more likely to see a deficiency. They were especially likely to see a decline in effectiveness from the first to the second wave of interviews. In contrast to the large deficiency gaps seen by blacks regarding open housing and integrated education, the table indicates that whites think the government is doing all they want it to do. These mean scores mask a split in views on these topics in the white community, however. Sizable percentages of whites believe that the government is doing too much for open housing and integrated education, and many other whites believe that the government is doing much too little. For the function of protecting the rights of persons accused of crime, both races indicated that they considered the government reasonably effective.

Table 15 shows a group of governmental functions that I have labelled "Openness and Opportunity." Persons assign government the re-

TABLE 14

Civil Rights and Integration Outtakes From Government (Mean scores by race, and by interview wave)

| | First wave, 1966-1967 | | | | Second wave, 1968 | | | | Percentage seeing serious deficiency, second wave | |
| | Blacks | | Whites | | Blacks | | Whites | | | |
	Effec- tiveness	Respon- sibility	Effec- tiveness	Respon- sibility	Effec- tiveness	Respon- sibility	Effec- tiveness	Respon- sibility	Blacks	Whites
Securing civil rights and liberties for all	2.62	3.72	3.06	3.54	2.47	3.72	2.98	3.53	41	18
Making it possible for a person with the means to live where he wishes to live	2.31	3.37	3.06	2.97	2.44	3.59	2.97	3.01	39	11
Providing education in the same schools for blacks and whites					2.36	3.65	2.82	2.76	47	11
Insuring fair treatment of citizens by the police					2.30	3.58	3.10	3.56	47	13
Protecting the rights of persons accused of crime					2.74	3.28	3.24	3.33	18	7
Intervening to stop an individual or group from persecuting another individual or group	2.69	3.29	2.69	3.16						
Keeping the people from persecuting each other					2.23	3.24	2.48	3.11	34	22

sponsibility to structure the environment so that an individual has a chance to make a good life for himself: to find a job, to obtain an education, and to live where he chooses. Blacks generally assign a higher responsibility to government to do these things than whites, but whites too believe these are important responsibilities of government. Very large deficiency gaps are shown for blacks for "Seeing to it that every man who wants a job can have a job" and "Seeing to it that people can get better jobs and places to live without any restrictions." Forty to 50 per cent of blacks think the government is seriously deficient on these items, in contrast with about 15 per cent of whites. The deficiency is a bit less for "providing a chance to make a good living." On both waves, whites in general felt that the government was doing all that it should and blacks saw a moderate deficiency gap. High-status whites were more likely to see the government as doing too much here, whereas high-status blacks saw the government as deficient on this function. On the second wave, blacks, especially the better educated, tended to assign a higher responsibility for government to provide a chance to make a good living than they did on the first wave, but at the same time they saw a decline in the effectiveness of government in carrying out this function.

On the first wave, whites tended to see the government as doing a bit too much in "Trying to even out differences in wealth," while blacks saw a slight deficiency. On the second wave, blacks assigned a higher responsibility to government, whereas the responsibility assigned by whites declined. Estimates of governmental effectiveness declined sharply for both blacks and whites, producing by the second wave a serious deficiency gap for blacks and a tiny one for whites. Thirty-two per cent of blacks saw a serious deficiency here in contrast to 12 per cent of whites. The items dealing with education also show sizable deficiency gaps for blacks, with 25 per cent seeing a serious deficiency in university education and 31 per cent seeing deficiency for general education. Blacks considered the provision of education one of the most important responsibilities of government. Democrats were more likely to see governmental deficiency than Republicans for all the items in Table 15.

It is theoretically important that the items on Table 15, which deal with openness and opportunity, cluster separately from the items on Table 16, which deal mainly with welfare. Popular thinking about governmental functions has not always distinguished governmental care of people from governmental creation of opportunities to enable people to take care of themselves, yet our respondents indicated by their sorting of cards that they do make such a distinction. The first item on Table 16 is especially interest-

TABLE 15

Openness and Opportunity Outtakes from Government (Mean scores by race, and by interview wave)

| | First wave, 1966-1967 | | | | Second wave, 1968 | | | | Percentage seeing serious deficiency, second wave | |
| | Blacks | | Whites | | Blacks | | Whites | | | |
	Effec- tiveness	Respon- sibility	Effec- tiveness	Respon- sibility	Effec- tiveness	Respon- sibility	Effec- tiveness	Respon- sibility	Blacks	Whites
Providing a chance to make a good living	2.92	3.41	3.21	3.15	2.64	3.50	3.11	3.14	27	9
Seeing to it that every man who wants a job can have a job	2.39	3.40	2.80	3.27	2.38	3.54	2.77	3.14	40	16
Seeing to it that people can get better jobs and places to live without any restrictions					2.34	3.65	2.74	2.95	47	14
Trying to even out differences in wealth	2.11	2.50	2.33	2.22	1.77	2.70	1.97	2.02	32	12
Providing free university education for all who can qualify					2.44	3.15	2.59	2.91	25	18
Providing a good educa- tion for all	2.51	3.11	2.74	3.08	2.65	3.65	3.13	3.48	31	13

ing in this regard. The item was answered very similarly by both blacks and whites on both waves of interviews. (Table 16 only shows the second wave data.) The mean scores show that the respondents evaluated the government as providing welfare services at about the same level as the responsibility that they assigned to it. Blacks were a little more likely to see a deficiency at the second wave than they were on the first wave. These mean scores cover up considerable disagreement, however. Blacks especially were very split on this item, some thinking the government was doing too much in the way of providing welfare and others thinking it was doing too little. For both races, Republicans were more likely to see the government as doing too much. Only 11 per cent of blacks and 6 per cent of whites saw a serious deficiency by government on this item.

The above data should be contrasted with the second item, which asks the government to make sure that nobody lives in poverty. Both black and white respondents assigned a high importance to government to perform this function and they judged the government as performing it rather ineffectively. This is especially true for blacks since 64 per cent saw a serious deficiency by government; 34 per cent of whites saw a serious deficiency. The gap between performance and responsibility for blacks on this item is the largest of any shown in our data. Nearly as large a deficiency was seen on the responsibility to provide decent housing for the poor; 54 per cent of blacks saw a serious deficiency here in contrast to 23 per cent of whites. Curiously, both black and white respondents saw the government as doing a reasonably good job of providing medical care for the poor.

Obviously many functions already discussed deal with services that the government performs. Table 17 shows some additional services that do

TABLE 16
*Welfare Outtakes from Government (Mean scores by race,
second interview wave, 1968)*

	Blacks		Whites		Percentage seeing serious deficiency	
	Effec-tiveness	Respon-sibility	Effec-tiveness	Respon-sibility	Blacks	Whites
Providing welfare services	3.08	3.22	3.17	2.97	11	6
Making sure than nobody lives in poverty	1.77	3.44	2.20	3.09	64	34
Providing decent housing for the poor	2.01	3.51	2.50	3.13	54	23
Providing medical care for the poor	3.03	3.52	3.22	3.36	14	10

TABLE 17

Service Outtakes from Government (Mean scores by race, second interview wave, 1968)

	Blacks		Whites		Percentage seeing serious deficiency	
	Effec- tiveness	Respon- sibility	Effec- tiveness	Respon- sibility	Blacks	Whites
Providing parks and recreation	2.57	3.41	3.11	3.26	32	9
Providing public transpor- tation	2.81	3.04	2.87	2.75	11	7
Providing garbage collection	2.77	3.32	3.30	3.32	19	9

not cluster into the previous tables. For these three services, blacks and whites assigned moderately important responsibilities to the government and did not differ significantly in the responsibilities they assigned. The races differ, however, in the ratings of the effectiveness of government in performing these services. Blacks considered the government considerably more deficient than whites. Higher percentages of blacks saw a serious deficiency as indicated in the right-hand columns of the table. The difference is especially marked for providing parks and recreation; nearly one-third of blacks saw a serious deficiency here in contrast to only 9 per cent of whites.

One way of trying to summarize some of the main findings from this study would be to present five items considered most important and least important for both inputs and outtakes, for both races, for both waves of interviews. These data are set forth in Tables 18 through 21.

Looking in Tables 18 and 19 at the important inputs as seen by respondents on both waves, we notice the very high responsibility respondents assigned themselves for making expressive inputs. Love of country ranks first or second for both waves of interviews for both races. It was exceeded only by the passive input of paying all taxes on the first wave, a responsibility that few seriously considered shirking. We noted earlier that "Vote in elections" is seen as an expressive input by many respondents, and it, too was given great importance by both races on both waves of interviews.

Support of law and order, which was inquired into more on the second wave of interviews, also received considerable prominence from both races, with slightly greater emphasis from whites. Working in community organizations also was assigned considerable responsibility by both races, somewhat more by blacks than by whites. It is apparent that both races see that they have a duty to keep informed about politics and to teach their children the responsibilities of citizenship and democracy. Upon only one item,

TABLE 18

Possible Inputs to the Political System (First wave, 1966-1967)

Blacks	Mean response	Mean response	Whites
Most responsibility to perform			
Pay all taxes[a]	3.69	3.79	Pay all taxes[a]
Have undivided loyalty and love for my country	3.59	3.70	Have undivided loyalty and love for my country
Vote in elections	3.59	3.68	Vote in elections
Personally see to it that my children understand and accept the responsibility of citizenship[a]	3.36	3.49	Personally see to it that my children understand and accept the responsibility of citizenship[a]
Teach my children the importance of give and take in the democratic way of life[a]	3.24	3.38	Teach my children the importance of give and take in the democratic way of life[a]
Keep informed about politics	2.96	3.14	Keep informed about politics
Actively support community organizations	2.96	2.76	Actively support community organizations
Least responsibility to perform			
			Participate in a political party between elections as well as at election time
Take an active part in political campaigns	2.20	2.06	
Send protest messages to political leaders when they are doing badly	2.19	1.99	Take an active part in political campaigns
Join in public street demonstrations	1.56	1.42	Be a candidate for public office
Be a candidate for public office	1.44	1.21	Join in public street demonstrations
Riot if necessary to get public officials to correct political wrongs	1.43	1.19	Riot if necessary to get public officials to correct political wrongs

[a]These items appeared only on the first wave; two additional items are ranked to facilitate comparison with the second wave.

showing patriotism, do the whites and blacks differ; whites believe they have greater responsibility to do this.

The two races assigned the least important input responsibilities in many similar and some different ways. Both placed a very low emphasis on "Riot if necessary to get public officials to correct political wrongs" and "Join in

TABLE 19

Possible Inputs to the Political System (Second wave, 1968)

Blacks	Mean response	Mean response	Whites
Most responsibility to perform			
Vote in elections	3.66	3.79	Love my country
Love my country	3.61	3.72	Respect the police
Respect the police	3.48	3.63	Vote in elections
			Show my patriotism by
Join groups working			flying the flag, attending
to improve community			parades, or in some other
life	3.29	3.28	way
Support community			Support community
leaders when they are			leaders when they are
trying to keep order			trying to keep order
during a disturbance	3.23	3.24	during a disturbance
Least responsibility to perform			
			Try to convince people
Join in a protest march	1.84	1.48	to vote your way
Support police when			
they shoot looters	1.71	1.41	Attend protest meetings
Try to convince people			
to vote your way	1.67	1.21	Join in a protest march
Join in public street			Join in public street
demonstrations	1.63	1.14	demonstrations
Riot if necessary to get			Riot if necessary to get
public officials to			public officials to
correct political			correct political
wrongs	1.30	1.13	wrongs

public street demonstrations." On the first wave they also placed a very low emphasis on being a candidate for public office. On the second wave a different item, "Try to convince people to vote your way" also received little sense of responsibility. On the first wave, "Take an active part in political campaigns" received little sense of responsibility.

The races differed in their perspective on protest activities. Whites placed a very low emphasis on "Join a protest march" and "Attend protest meetings." Blacks, in contrast to whites, placed a very low emphasis on "Support police when they shoot looters." These tables indicate a general pattern for blacks to assign themselves a higher responsibility on most inputs than whites. This is mainly true for inputs that are less than unanimously considered important.

Blacks and whites were not in such close agreement about the most and least important responsibilities (outtakes) of government as they were concerning inputs (see Tables 20 and 21). Both races agreed on both waves that providing justice for all is a very important responsibility; it ranked first or second in all instances. For blacks, securing civil rights and

TABLE 20
Possible Outtakes from the Political System (First wave, 1966-1967)

Blacks	Mean response	Mean response	Whites
Most responsibility of government			
Providing justice for all	3.76	3.81	Providing justice for all
Securing civil rights and			Providing protection and
liberties for all	3.72	3.69	security
			Being careful in using
Providing strong leadership	3.66	3.69	public money and trust
Providing protection and			
security	3.62	3.66	Providing strong leadership
Being careful in using			Taking actions that make
public money and trust	3.52	3.61	me proud of my country
Least responsibility of government			
Making it possible for a			Making it possible for a
person to be heard when			person with the means
he feels he has some-			to live where he wishes
thing to say	3.10	2.97	to live
Arranging things so it is			Providing stability in
easy for citizens to move			society even if it means
from place to place, job			slowing down the rate
to job, class to class	2.84	2.68	of progress
			Arranging things so it is
Trying to even out dif-			easy for citizens to move
ferences in wealth and			from place to place, job
prestige	2.50	2.65	to job, class to class
Providing stability in			
society even if it means			
slowing down the rate			Arranging things so that
of progress	2.45	2.52	business is left alone
			Trying to even out dif-
Arranging things so that			ferences in wealth and
business is left alone	2.17	2.22	prestige

liberties for all was equally important, but for whites it did not even fall in the first five important items on either wave. The responsibility to provide protection and security was considered second most important for whites on both waves but for blacks it was fourth on the first wave and did not fall in the first five on the second wave.

The general pattern for whites on both waves was to emphasize justice, law and order, and expressive outtakes such as "Taking actions that make me proud of my country" or "Providing strong leadership." Blacks, in contrast, want civil rights, integration, and the opportunity for a good education as well as justice. The responsibility for the government to be careful in using public money and trust, which appeared only on the first wave, was considered very important by both races.

Clearly both races on both waves want the government to do very little

TABLE 21

Possible Outtakes from the Political System (Second wave, 1968)

Blacks	Mean response	Mean response	Whites
Most responsibility of government			
Securing civil rights and liberties for all	3.72	3.78	Providing justice for all
Providing justice for all	3.71	3.67	Providing protection and security
Seeing to it that people can get better jobs and places to live without any restrictions	3.65	3.66	Taking actions that make me proud of my country
Providing education in the same schools for blacks and whites	3.65	3.66	Providing ways to control riots
Providing a good education for all	3.65	3.64	Keeping neighborhoods safe
Least responsibility of government			
Keeping the people from persecuting each other	3.24	2.91	Providing free university education for all who can qualify
Providing free university education for all who can qualify	3.15	2.84	Fighting the war in Vietnam
Providing public transportation	3.04	2.76	Providing education in the same schools for blacks and whites
Trying to even out differences in wealth	2.70	2.75	Providing public transportation
Fighting the war in Vietnam	2.36	2.02	Trying to even out differences in wealth

about trying to even out differences in wealth. On the first wave they indicated they were not eager to have government avoid regulating business affairs. They also were not eager to have the government slow down the rate of progress just to provide stability. On the first wave whites were not eager to have the government provide open housing, although blacks placed greater responsibility on that function. On the second wave both races assigned little responsibility to government to provide public transportation, to provide free university education for all those who could qualify, or to fight the war in Vietnam. They differed, however, in that many whites did not want the government to provide integrated education but blacks did.

A great deal of additional data could be presented about these inputs and outtakes but that would take us far afield from the major purpose of this chapter, which has been to demonstrate that we need detailed information of this type on the inputs that individuals make to a political system and on the levels of satisfaction that individuals derive from what they take out of the system. If we could obtain these kinds of data for each state, or even for a sample of states, we could develop more adequate theories for structuring government and society so that the people who live in those societies will be pleased with their lives.

INDIVIDUALS AND THE OPEN SOCIETY

Having seen many ways that an individual may make inputs to a political system or take things from a political system, we still cannot answer the question "Do state-by-state differences in patterns and levels of political participation produce differences in the functioning of government and in citizen satisfaction with government?" Very likely they do, but only a state-by-state study that uses input and outtake information, such as that just examined, will enable us to be more specific. The problem of sorting out cause from effect also makes it difficult to say whether differences in participation produce differences in the governmental system or vice versa. For example, we noted that weak party competition is associated with low levels of participation. Which is cause and which is effect?

Some theories suggest that people who participate in a political process are more content with the decisions that come from it than those who don't participate. On the other hand, some theories suggest that those who are very dissatisfied with governmental decisions will participate more vigorously in order to try to change them than those who are more satisfied with government. The results of the Buffalo study showed very little relationship between levels of satisfaction with government and the pattern of inputs that people made to the political system. Apparently the relationship is more complex than we supposed, and comparative state studies would help to unravel the mystery. The data hint that people are taught to take basic postures toward the political system that include both inputs and outtakes. For example, we discovered that people who confine their inputs to rather traditional activities, such as voting, keeping informed, or being patriotic, are likely to hold the government responsible only for fairly traditional outtakes such as those shown on Table 13. In contrast, the black community of Buffalo, very active in conventional and unconventional politics, places very high responsibilities on government to perform a great variety of functions. Without comparative data it is pointless to speculate further on the solidity of the evidence or the ramifications of the meaning of these suggestive findings.

Whether input and outtake postures can shape the structure and direction of government depends on the openness or closedness of the political system. If a system is to be sensitive to the needs and desires of its citizens it must be kept open so that a large influx of new participants will be possible if inactive citizens desire to enter politics. People who cannot enter the competition for public office, even if they should wish to, can more safely be ignored. We have seen important state differences in the openness of politics. Some of these differences are regulatory as shown in Table 6. Registration and voting are much easier in some states than in others, and some political parties are more open to new recruits and to easy advancement than others.

Differences in openness derive also from environmental differences. Citizens who are well educated and who know the political system find it easier to enter and to participate than those who do not know what to do. People growing up in a community where participation is normal and expected have fewer inhibitions toward participation than those reared where participation is almost unknown. In some communities a citizen pays a price for becoming active in politics. This price could be loss of respect, certainly loss of time and money, and in more severe cases, loss of a livelihood. Openness, then, includes community willingness to accept differences and willingness to respect political action by one's neighbors. In general, the openness or closedness of the system rather than the mere fact of participation or nonparticipation most affects the likelihood that the government will serve all the people.

What do groups do when they find the ordinary channels of participation and political redress closed to them? History suggests that for a time they wait patiently to see if the system will open and respond to their wishes. But history also suggests that frustrated persons eventually lose patience and turn to extraordinary methods of participation to circumvent the barriers thrown up by the dominant political group. There are increasingly frequent examples of this phenomenon in state politics. Blacks who were systematically excluded from participation in politics in the South have used several extraordinary methods to participate politically. First, they took their grievances to the federal government, bypassing the state governments that were closed to them. Second, they went to the federal courts rather than to the presumably more responsive Congress that was prevented from acting by a determined southern minority. Eventually, they took their grievances to the streets in mass demonstrations, sit-ins, boycotts, and even riots. The increased political pressures from frustrated and angry blacks, as well as from many sympathetic whites, eventually forced Congress to pass new legislation and support civil rights enforcement by federal officials, thus opening many areas of political participation that were formerly closed to blacks. This experience has taught a new disruptive pattern of political participation to many citizens of the United States, but especially to blacks, as evidenced by the data from the Buffalo study.

Although the fight of blacks for access to the political and social system is the most dramatic political struggle of our time, other groups have used extraordinary methods to bypass closed channels in state politics. For a half century urban elements in many states tried to get reapportionment of state legislatures in order to represent better the growing population of urban centers. Rural elements, which controlled most state legislatures, steadfastly refused to reapportion despite, in many states, specific constitutional provisions requiring them to do so. Normal political access in the form of equality of the vote was blocked. The first attempts to use the extraordinary method of appeal to the Supreme Court failed when the court declared that reapportionment was not a justiciable question, and that redress should be sought by political action.[24] Repeated political efforts — election of legislators — produced no substantial change, however, and the problem was brought again to the Supreme Court, which had had a turnover of justices. This time the Court decided the problem was justiciable and in succeeding cases ordered reapportionment of both the house and the senate in each state on the basis of population.[25] This reapportionment is known popularly as the "one-man one-vote principle."

Another attempt to obtain political access occurred earlier in the twentieth century. Labor unions had been frustrated in their attempts in many states to achieve collective bargaining rights. Anti-labor elements dominated most state legislatures, and urban underrepresentation prevented removal of these elements by normal channels of electoral state politics. Labor groups shifted their drive to the federal government where urban elements were not seriously underrepresented. Political action aimed at the Congress, the presidency, and the Supreme Court finally produced the passage of the Wagner Act in 1935 and a favorable verdict on its constitutionality in 1937.[26]

In recent years college students have turned to extraordinary political action to force the political system to respond to their needs. They have used strikes, demonstrations, marches, and riots as well as more conventional political inputs such as votes, letters, and lobbying. College youth have not yet seen their political wishes realized in governmental decisions. Many youths claim that the political system will never respond in satisfactory ways to their needs, and they plan to do everything they can to overthrow it. Others seem content to work within the system, hoping to change some of the rules (lowering the voting age, for instance) so that young people can more effectively make inputs.

One lesson seems clear. Extraordinary political means and alternative political arenas may be sought by people who are shut out of normal political participation. The fact that the percentages of persons participating generally is low does not mean, in and of itself, that democracy is in danger. It may, as a matter of fact, be a sign that the political system is functioning reasonably satisfactorily for most people. Governments can function quite adequately and responsibly even if the mass of people give them very little attention and take very little political action. It is much more important to make sure that the political system is kept open so that all elements of society that seek to enter can do so. The frustrated actions of those who do not have access are a greater danger to democracy than a low rate of political participation by a disinterested citizenry.[27]

SELECTED BIBLIOGRAPHY

Almond, Gabriel, and Sidney Verba. *The Civic Culture*. Princeton: Princeton University Press, 1963. This is a report of a cross-national survey conducted in the United States, Mexico, Great Britain, Germany, and Italy. A good deal of attention is devoted to explaining political participation, especially as it varies from nation to nation.

Barber, James David. *Citizen Politics*. Chicago: Markham Publishing Co., 1969. This book is an introduction to political behavior and deals with many of the topics discussed in this chapter.

Campbell, Argus, Phillip Converse, Warren Miller, and Donald Stokes. *The American Voter*. New York: John Wiley and Sons, 1960. This report of the 1956 Presidential election in the United States is the best and most comprehensive book on American voting behavior. Chapter V deals with voting turnout. Another book by the same authors, *Elections and the Political Order*, New York: John Wiley & Sons, 1966, compiles many of the articles written by this research team on their voting studies which now cover two decades.

Key, V. O., Jr. *Southern Politics in State and Nation*. New York: Alfred A. Knopf, 1949. This book, a recognized classic in political science, is based on empirical studies of politics in eleven Southern states. It is especially good on the problems of Negro participation in politics.

————. *Public Opinion and American Democracy*. New York: Alfred A. Knopf, 1961. This leading text on public opinion does a good job of relating public opinion to the functioning of the political system. Much of the empirical evidence presented is drawn from the voting studies conducted by the Survey Research Center of the University of Michigan. (See Campbell, et al., above).

Lane, Robert E. *Political Life: Why People Get Involved in Politics.* Glencoe, Ill.: The Free Press, 1959. This is the most comprehensive book dealing strictly with political participation. It is not a research report but is based on many previous studies.

————. *Political Thinking and Consciousness: The Private Life of the Political Mind.* Chicago: Markham Publishing Co., 1969. This book goes into greater depth on the psychology of political postures and helps us to understand how people think politically.

Lipset, Seymour Martin. *Political Man: The Social Bases of Politics.* Garden City, N.Y.: Doubleday and Co., 1960. This book takes a sociological perspective on political behavior. It is not a report of original research, but materials are drawn from many countries in addition to the United States.

Matthews, Donald M. and James W. Prothro. *Negroes and the New Southern Politics.* New York: Harcourt, Brace & World, 1966. This is a major study of political participation in the eleven southeastern states. It is especially useful in describing the transition of American blacks from a relatively inactive political minority to a well-organized and active political group.

Milbrath, Lester W. *Political Participation.* Chicago: Rand McNally, 1965. This short book summarized all that was known up to 1963 about why individuals became involved in politics. Findings are drawn from many studies and linked together in a theoretical structure.

————, Everett F. Cataldo, Lyman A. Kellstedt, and Richard M. Johnson. *Final Report on a Study of Change Processes in Buffalo, N.Y.* submitted to the Office of Research, Plans, Programs, and Evaluations of the United States Office of Economic Opportunity, July, 1969.

President's Commission on Registration and Voting Participation, Report of. Washington, D.C.: United States Government Printing Office, November, 1963. This report focuses on participation in presidential elections. In addition to reporting state-by-state data, it argues for reforms to stimulate voting turnout.

Rokkan, Stein. "The Comparative Study of Political Participation: Notes Toward a Perspective on Current Research," in Austin Ranney (ed.), *Essays on the Behavioral Study of Politics.* Urbana: University of Illinois Press, 1962. He argues for the use of historical and ecological data as well as survey findings. Rokkan is one of the leading scholars of political participation and has been in the forefront of comparatively studying nations. Most of his wirtings have recently been compiled in *Citizens, Elections, Parties.* New York: David McKay Co., 1970.

Woodward, Julian L., and Elmo Roper. "The Political Activity of American Citizens," *American Political Science Review,* 44 (December, 1950): 872–885. This article is based on a nationwide sample of 8,000 cases. It was the first article to give nationwide percentages for participation in a variety of political activities.

CHAPTER THREE

Parties in State Politics

Austin Ranney

"The rise of political parties is indubitably one of the principal distinguishing marks of modern government. . . . Modern democracy is unthinkable save in terms of the parties. As a matter of fact, *the condition of the parties is the best possible evidence of the nature of any regime.*" [1] * So begins one of the more influential books in modern political science; and the italicized affirmation will serve as the major premise of this chapter.

In all democratic polities, parties are, first and foremost, organizations formed to make nominations and contest elections. Consequently, wherever the constitutional-legal structure decrees that important elections be held — parliamentary constituencies, congressional districts, cities, and the like — political parties organize to win those elections.

In the United States elections are regulated and administered mainly by the fifty states, not by the national government. The national Constitution and Congress, to be sure, exercise some control over their timing and conduct. But, for the most part, the questions of who can get on the ballot and how, who can and cannot vote, and how the votes shall be cast and counted and the winners identified are determined by the states.

Accordingly, the Democratic and Republican parties in each of the states are in no sense merely local representatives of national firms. Many commentators, indeed, regard the national parties as little more than coalitions of state parties formed intermittently to capture the presidency. However that may be, we can be sure that in the states — as in any modern democracy — parties, in Schattschneider's words, "are not merely append-

* [See pp. 566–571 for notes to this chapter. — Eds.]

ages of modern government; they are in the center of it and play a determinative and creative role in it." [2]

LEGAL FORMS AND POLITICAL REALITIES

In most democratic countries political parties are largely or wholly outside the law. Written constitutions and statutes do not mention them, and no governmental agency has the legal power to regulate their recruitment of members, organization, or selection of leaders so long as they do not transgress general prohibitions against conspiracy, subversion, and the like. Hence most political parties are considered to be purely private associations, like Freemasons or Rotarians, and they transact their internal business privately.

So it was in the United States until after the Civil War. However, the steady parade of political scandals, bribery, and "boss rule" in the postwar decades convinced respectable people that the parties had become dangerously corrupt. Acting in the characteristic American conviction that the best way to prevent an evil is to pass a law against it, one state legislature after another wrote statutes regulating the parties. Consequently, in our time each of the states fences its parties with elaborate legal rules intended to keep them within proper bounds. The principal matters regulated are: [3]

1. *Access to the Ballot.* Each state specifies the conditions an organization must meet to qualify as a political party and thus get its candidates' names printed on election ballots.
2. *Membership.* Each state stipulates the qualifications for membership in a party — that is, how one acquires the right to vote in the party's primary elections.
3. *Organization.* Each state prescribes the number, composition, selection, and functions of the various officials, committees, and conventions that constitute the parties' legal organizations.
4. *Nominating Procedures.* The state, not the parties, decides how official candidates for public office shall be formally selected. Most states require that most nominations be made publicly by direct primaries rather than privately by party caucuses or conventions.
5. *Party Finance.* All the states except Alaska, Delaware, Illinois, Nevada, and Rhode Island regulate one or more aspect of party finance: how much a party may spend in election campaigns, who may and may not contribute to party funds, what public reports of receipts and expenditures should be filed, and so on.

In each of the states, in short, political parties are legally defined public organizations required to transact their most important business in public. Their high legal visibility may well elicit the often-heard remark that the United States has not two major parties but one hundred and two: the national Democrats and Republicans and their namesakes in each of the states. It may also underlie the view of some political scientists that our national parties are "loose alliances to win the stakes of power embodied in the presidency" or "ghost parties" with neither the commanders nor the discipline of *real* parties, and that the loci of effective party power and discipline are in the state and local parties.[4]

Whether or not these characterizations of the national parties are accurate, the most casual glance at state politics shows that the orderly structures erected by the statutes mask a wide variety of political realities. For example, in Georgia the legal structure of the Democratic party is no more than a neutral arena for a kaleidoscopic interplay of forming and re-forming factions and appearing and disappearing personalities striving for place and perquisites.[5] In Wisconsin, the legal Democratic organization is a shell inhabited and animated by an entirely extralegal band of dues-paying enthusiasts.[6] In Connecticut the legal Democratic committees and conventions come close to matching the unity, discipline, and "responsibility" some commentators insist our national parties should have.[7]

In short, by no means all state political parties are highly organized, well disciplined, and strongly led political "armies."[8] Like most other aspects of state government discussed in this book they vary widely from one state to another. The present chapter is intended to describe some of the principal variations and their causes and consequences for state politics.

INTER-PARTY COMPETITION

Of all the variables analyzed in the study of state party politics, the one receiving the most attention from political scientists has been inter-party competition, conceived as the usual or "normal" distribution of popular votes and elective offices between Democrats and Republicans. The analysts who pioneered the study of state politics declared that the different degrees of inter-party competition among the states are significantly related to other variations in the nature of their parties, politics, and policy outputs. The parties in the most competitive states, they observed, are likely to have the most centralized control of nominations and the highest cohesion in the legislatures and in gubernatorial-legislative relations. Consequently, they are likely to be the most effective and responsible governing agencies.[9]

More recently, however, some political scientists have disputed these generalizations. They have correlated the states' rankings in inter-party competition with their rankings on per capita expenditures on such social welfare measures as education, old age assistance, and unemployment compensation. Their correlations show that a state's level of welfare expenditures is only weakly — in a statistical sense — related to its degree of inter-party competition and very strongly related to its level of wealth and resources.[10]

Still more recently, a third group of political scientists, using different measures of outputs and different analytical techniques, have concluded that high levels of competition are significantly related to high levels of social welfare expenditures, though they are by no means the only factor stimulating full social welfare programs.[11]

In any case, most political scientists continue to think that a state's level of inter-party competition has a major impact on the organization and activities of its political parties. Accordingly, we begin our analysis of state parties by categorizing the states according to their degrees of competition.

Dimensions and Measurement

In recent years several political scientists have developed ways of measuring inter-party competition in the states.[12] Each measure differs somewhat from the others in time period covered, offices for which elections are tabulated, and definitions of categories. All who try to measure interparty competition, however, agree with Richard Dawson and James Robinson that it has at least three basic dimensions:

> *Proportion of Success:* the percentage of the votes won by each party for statewide offices and the percentage of seats in the legislature held by each.
> *Duration of Success:* the length of time each party has controlled the statewide offices and/or the legislature.
> *Frequency of Divided Control:* the proportion of time in which control of the governorship and legislature has been divided between the parties.

The purposes of this chapter seem best served by an adaptation of the Dawson-Robinson measure, which we have used as follows: *
For each state we first tabulated the percentages of the two-party

* Since this book is concerned exclusively with state government and politics, we have examined only state offices; and we have chosen the governors and state legislators because they are the states' most powerful elected officers. The period from 1956 to 1970 takes account of the fact that postwar state politics have differed significantly from prewar politics, yet still gives a long enough period in which to absorb temporary surges or declines for particular parties in particular states (for obvious reasons, Alaska and Hawaii were covered only from 1958 to 1970).

popular vote for governor received by each party in each election, and the percentages of the seats in each house of the legislature held by each party in each legislative session.* From these tables we computed four basic figures: (1) the average percentage of the popular vote won by Democratic gubernatorial candidates; (2) the average percentage of the seats in the state senate held by the Democrats; (3) the average percentage of the seats in the state house of representatives held by the Democrats; and (4) the percentage of all terms for governor, senate, and house in which the Democrats had control.

For each state we then averaged together all four percentages to produce an "index of competitiveness" carried to four decimal places. It has a possible range of .0000 (total Republican success) to 1.0000 (total Democratic success), with .5000 representing absolutely even two-party competition.

Finally, we listed the states in descending order of index numbers, and the resulting clusters suggested the following categories and definitions:

.8500 or higher: one-party Democratic
.7000 to .8499: modified one-party Democratic
.3500 to .6999: two-party
.1500 to .3499: modified one-party Republican
.0000 to .1499: one-party Republican

No state qualified as one-party Republican by these criteria. The states' distribution among the other four categories is given in Table 1, and their geographical distribution is shown in the map in Figure 1.

Some Warnings

The classifications in Table 1 and Figure 1 are likely to hold some surprises for most readers: for example, Arizona, the home of Barry Goldwater, is classified as modified two-party as are Nebraska and Wisconsin. Our classifications will raise fewer eyebrows if we bear in mind two warnings about what they mean.

First, they are based wholly on state offices. Hence, while Arizona twice elected Goldwater senator and voted for the Republican candidate for president in five of the six elections from 1948 to 1968, the Republicans until 1966 seldom held more than 25 per cent of the seats in the upper house or over 31 per cent of the seats in the lower house of the state legis-

---

* Since Minnesota and Nebraska have formally nonpartisan legislatures, only their gubernatorial elections have been used to measure inter-party competition.

TABLE 1

The Fifty States Classified According to Degree of Inter-Party Competition, 1956-1970

One-party Democratic	Modified one-party Democratic	Two-party		Modified one-party Republican
Louisiana (.9877)	North Carolina (.8332)	Hawaii (.6870)	New Jersey (.5122)	North Dakota (.3305)
Alabama (.9685)	Virginia (.8235)	Rhode Island (.6590)	Pennsylvania (.4800)	Kansas (.3297)
Mississippi (.9407)	Florida (.8052)	Massachusetts (.6430)	Colorado (.4725)	New Hampshire (.3282)
South Carolina (.9292)	Tennessee (.7942)	Alaska (.6383)	Michigan (.4622)	South Dakota (.3142)
Texas (.9132)	Maryland (.7905)	California (.6150)	Utah (.4565)	Vermont (.2822)
Georgia (.9080)	Oklahoma (.7792)	Nebraska (.6065)	Indiana (.4450)	
Arkansas (.8850)	Missouri (.7415)	Washington (.6047)	Illinois (.4235)	
	Kentucky (.7170)	Minnesota (.5910)	Wisconsin (.4102)	
	West Virginia (.7152)	Nevada (.5742)	Idaho (.4077)	
	New Mexico (.7150)	Connecticut (.5732)	Iowa (.3965)	
		Delaware (.5687)	Ohio (.3837)	
		Arizona (.5663)	New York (.3835)	
		Montana (.5480)	Maine (.3820)	
		Oregon (.5387)	Wyoming (.3537)	

lature. Wisconsin, which at the present writing has a Democratic governor and two Democratic U.S. senators, has seen Democratic control of either legislative house only twice in twenty-six opportunities in this period, and Democratic governors only four of twelve terms. Florida voted for the Republican presidential candidate in 1952, 1956, 1960, and 1968 and elected two Republican U.S. representatives in 1962; but the Republicans won the governorship only once and until 1966 never held more than 7 per cent of the seats in either house of the legislature. These examples show that a state that has been highly competitive for some national offices may have been much less so for state offices; and the latter are our primary concern here.

Second, any measurement such as ours is a snapshot of an object moving in time and hence does not always capture changes that may be occurring when the measurement is taken. Thus, Wisconsin and South Dakota

FIGURE 1
The State Party Systems

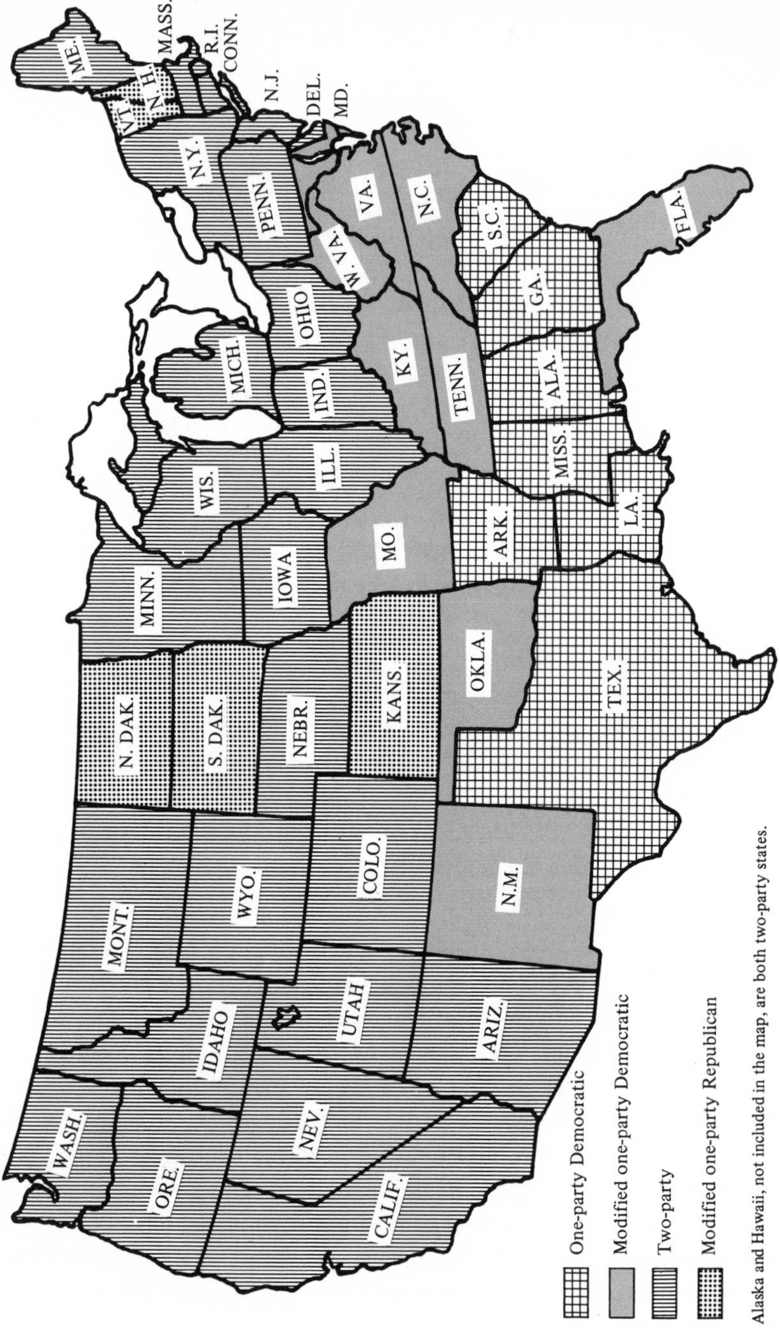

One-party Democratic

Modified one-party Democratic

Two-party

Modified one-party Republican

Alaska and Hawaii, not included in the map, are both two-party states.

are becoming more Democratic and Arizona and Florida more Republican; another measurement taken a decade from now may well change the classifications of all four states. All our present classification does is indicate the relative competitiveness of the fifty states in the two decades after World War II.

Our next task, then, is to see whether the differences shown in Table 1 are significantly related to any other characteristics of the states in each category.

Correlates of Competitiveness

Most of the one-party and modified one-party states of both parties have had their present political colorations ever since the Civil War. All eight Democratic one-party states were members of the Confederacy; and, of the nine modified Democratic one-party states, North Carolina, Tennessee, and Virginia were Confederate; West Virginia was the Unionist rump of Virginia; Kentucky and Maryland were border states (i.e., states that allowed slavery but remained in the Union), and Arizona, New Mexico, and Oklahoma were originally settled mainly by immigrants from the South. Of the eight Republican modified one-party states, on the other hand, Iowa, Kansas, Maine, New Hampshire, Vermont, and Wisconsin all fought on the Union side, and the two Dakotas were settled mainly by immigrants from Union states.

It is not surprising that the deepest political trauma of American history left its mark on state politics. The Republican party, after all, was founded in 1854 specifically to resist the further spread of slavery and to secure its eventual abolition. A Republican president wrote the Emancipation Proclamation and led the Union to victory over the Confederacy. A Republican Congress launched the Thirteenth, Fourteenth, and Fifteenth Amendments to the national Constitution and adopted the Reconstruction Acts. Most leading Confederates were Democrats before the war, and Southern resistance to Reconstruction was led by Democrats. For both sides, accordingly, party identification and patriotism were closely intertwined, and for a long time after Appomattox a familiar electioneering slogan for both parties was "Vote as You Shot!" When the federal occupation troops left the South after 1876, the southern whites determined to restore and maintain racial segregation and white supremacy by the one-party system and by excluding Negroes from participation in that one party.[13]

But the Civil War ended a century ago; how can it influence the party loyalties of so many voters in the 1970s? The answer seems to lie in the essential nature of party identification. The leading studies of voting behavior emphasize that the typical American acquires his party preference early in life, and that it grows stronger the longer he holds it. Moreover, it is reinforced and activated by the similar preferences of his parents, his wife, and his friends and work associates. Also, living in a one-party atmosphere tends to corrode the loyalties of the few who identify with the minority party.[14] Although a few individuals switch parties, perhaps because they move to new communities or change their socioeconomic positions, *massive* switches take place only under such apocalyptic circumstances as the Civil War or the Great Depression of the early 1930s.[15]

The self-renewing and self-intensifying nature of party identification, then, means that it is not surprising that the deepest political cleavage in our history remains the basic source of party predominance in half our states. It is more surprising that the other half have two-party systems. After all, no fewer than seventeen fought for the Union in the war, one (Missouri) was a border state, and most of the others were settled by immigrants from the North. Why are they not also one-party or modified one-party Republican? Some of the answers are suggested by the data in Table 2.

TABLE 2

*Social and Economic Characteristics of States by Degree of
Competitiveness*

Characteristic	One-party Democratic	Modified one-party Democratic	Two-party	Modified one-party Republican
Number of states	7	10	28	5
Percentage of population urban	53	57	68	46.5
Percentage of population living in cities of over 100,000	17	20	22	5
Percentage of blacks in population	29	14.5	4	1
Percentage of foreign stock in population	3	6	23	22
Percentage of Roman Catholics among church members	16	21	44	42
Median income	$3884	$4764	$5999	$4920
Percentage of labor force in agriculture	11	8	7	17
Percentage of labor force in manufacturing	20'	19	22.5	17

Source: Congressional District Data Book (Washington, D.C.: Bureau of the Census, 1963).

The most striking contrast evident in Table 2 is the fact that the two-party states are substantially more urbanized than the states in the other three categories. All the nation's cities with populations of over one million (New York, Chicago, Los Angeles, Philadelphia, and Detroit) are located in these states. The two-party states also have to a higher degree than the others the characteristics usually associated with urbanization: they have the highest median income, the highest percentage of the labor force engaged in manufacturing and the lowest in agriculture, and the highest proportion of "foreign stock" (i.e., immigrants or children of immigrants).

When we compare the two-party states with the two groups of Democratic-dominated states we see that the former have a much smaller proportion of Negroes,* and a larger proportion of foreign stock and Roman Catholics. A more suggestive comparison, however, is that between the two-party states and the modified one-party Republican states; for if the Civil War were the sole source of present-day political loyalties, the two groups of states should be very similar. However, in certain respects they are at opposite extremes: the two-party states are the most urban and the Republican states the least; the two-party states are the least agricultural and the Republican states, the most.

All these comparisons are consistent with the general pattern of distribution of party strength *outside the South* noted by most commentators. Democratic support generally tends to be concentrated in big cities, for the minority ethnic groups and trade unionists who vote predominantly Democratic constitute the bulk of the big cities' populations. Republican voting strength tends to be concentrated in smaller towns and cities (i.e., those with populations from 2,500 to 100,000), for the "WASPs" (white, Anglo-Saxon Protestants) who vote predominantly Republican constitute the bulk of the small town populations.† And the northern rural farm areas are the most likely to switch back and forth between the two parties depending upon whether farms are prosperous (vote Republican) or depressed (vote Democratic).[16]

The states' differences in inter-party competition, then, are related to their differences in certain social and economic traits and in historical experiences and traditions. But what does it matter? In what, if any, significant respects do parties in the one-party states differ from those in the two-party states?

---

* The percentage of Negroes declines sharply as we pass from the most Democratic to the least Democratic states.

† The "WASPs" also constitute the bulk of the small town population in the South, of course, but for the reasons noted earlier they vote Democratic.

PARTY ORGANIZATION

Legal Structure

We noted earlier that in most states political parties are elaborately regulated by statute. Significantly, the only major exceptions are six southern states: five (Alabama, Arkansas, Georgia, North Carolina, and Virginia) in which the laws affecting parties have always been substantially looser than elsewhere; and South Carolina, which, after the U.S. Supreme Court outlawed the "white primary" in 1944,[17] repealed all laws regulating parties to give its Democrats the best possible chance of evading regulation by the federal courts.[18]

Statutes in each of the other forty-four states prescribe the number, composition, powers, and duties of the committees, conventions, and caucuses that constitute the parties' legal skeletons. They vary widely in detail, of course, but most state legislatures evidently regard parties as primarily agencies for making nominations and contesting elections; hence they have established party organizations at every level significant for the conduct of elections. Every state has precinct or ward "committeemen" or "captains," county "central committees" and county chairmen, and state "central committees" and state chairmen. Many states also prescribe party committees and/or conventions for congressional districts and cities.

The committees' members are officially selected in various ways, but the most common are: selection by party activists in local caucuses, election by party registrants in direct primaries, election by delegates to party conventions, or ex officio membership by virtue of holding posts in lower party committees.[19]

It is difficult to generalize about the number, composition, and selection of legal party committees, caucuses, and conventions in all the states, but it is easy to generalize about the legal allocation of authority among them. In no state are the legal party units organized as a true hierarchy, with the lower levels legally controlled and removable by the upper. Most commonly the officers and committees at each level are chosen locally and cannot be removed by any higher party authority. In Illinois, for example, each precinct committeeman is elected by the registered party voters in his precinct and holds office for four years; he cannot be removed by the county or state central committees even if he campaigns for the opposition party (which some have actually done).[20] In Washington, as another example, each county central committee consists of all the precinct committeemen in the county and elects its own chairman; he, in turn, cannot be removed by his party's state central committee or even its national committee no matter what he does.[21]

So it is in most states. The result is that authority is not legally concentrated in any single statewide party agency; rather the law chops it into many small bundles and scatters them among the precinct, county, and district committeemen and committees.

Informal Allocation of Authority

In most states most of the time informal or "actual" authority is quite as decentralized as legal authority. To be sure, there have been a few statewide "machines" headed by state "bosses" who by effective use of patronage and persuasion controlled the selection and commanded the loyalties of most county and district committees and chairmen. Some, like the Huey Long organization in Louisiana in the 1920s and 1930s and the Harry Byrd organization in Virginia from the 1930s to the 1960s,[22] appeared in solid one-party states. Others, like the Thomas Dewey organization in New York in the 1940s and the Hubert Humphrey organization in Minnesota in the 1950s and 1960s,[23] have operated in two-party states. However, these few instances are highly exceptional, and the powerful sub-national "machines" that have received so much attention (and tongue-clucking) from political commentators and civic reformers have mostly been confined to particular metropolitan areas *within* states: e.g., Tammany Hall in New York City, the old William Green "machine" in Philadelphia, and Mayor Daley's "machine" in Chicago.[24]

Some political scientists have the impression that state party organizations tend to have more centralized authority where two-party competition is keenest.[25] But the tendency is slight at best, and both Republicans and Democrats are highly decentralized in many of our most competitive two-party states: e.g., Washington (with a competitiveness index of .6047), California (.6150), Illinois (.4235), and Indiana (.4450).

The most distinguished scholar of state parties summed it up thus:

> The party organization is sometimes regarded as a hierarchy based on the precinct executive and capped by the national committee, but it may be more accurately described as a system of layers of organization. Each successive layer — county or city, state, national — has an independent concern about elections in its geographical jurisdiction. Yet each higher level of organization, to accomplish its ends, must obtain the collaboration of the lower layer or layers of organization. That collaboration comes about, to the extent that it does

come about, through a sense of common cause rather than by the exercise of command.[26]

In a few states the legal organizations' feebleness and/or concentration upon dispensing patronage rather than advancing programs has led some party activists to form "clubs" to ginger or take over or bypass the official structures.[27] The earliest instance was "The Republican Party of Wisconsin," an extralegal organization founded by conservative Republican activists in 1925 to take the party's machinery and nominations away from the LaFollette progressive wing. They were so successful that in the 1930s the LaFollette faction broke away entirely to form a third party. In 1948 Democratic activists formed "The Democratic Party of Wisconsin" to breathe some life into their moribund formal organization. Since then both parties' legal structures have been controlled entirely by their extralegal "clubs." [28]

In 1934 a progressive faction among California Republicans created "The California Republican Assembly" to revive the party after its disastrous defeat of 1932. California Democratic enthusiasts established "The California Democratic Council" in 1953, and since then both organizations have played key roles in their parties' affairs, although neither has dominated the regular organization to quite the same degree as in Wisconsin.[29]

In New York City after 1952 a number of local anti-Tammany Democratic "reform clubs" were formed under the leadership of such distinguished party activists as Mrs. Eleanor Roosevelt, former governor and senator Herbert Lehman, and former secretary of the air force Thomas Finletter. These clubs have, with varying degrees of success, fought Tammany's domination of the party's official organization and nominations.[30]

Despite differences in ideology and partisan affiliation, these extralegal activist organizations have several features in common. Their members, like party members in western European nations, pay regular dues. They consist mainly of middle-class business and professional people who have no interest in patronage jobs and go into politics primarily to advance the political programs they believe in. They are usually organized into local clubs that federate for county and state purposes. One of their main objectives is getting the right kind of candidate nominated (all but the Wisconsin Democrats publicly endorse particular candidates in primaries). They do most of their parties' grass-roots campaigning and fund raising. And they have generally had considerable success in rebuilding and invigorating moribund legal organizations (as in Wisconsin and California) or in weakening the hold of patronage-oriented professionals over the official structures (as in New York City).

Only a few comparable movements have been launched elsewhere, however, and most of them have failed.[31] Yet, there is some reason to believe that the "clubs" are the wave of the future in American state politics, although they are developing slowly. Accordingly, it seems likely that for some time to come the party organizations in most states — legal *and* informal — will remain congeries of sporadically active state and local caucuses, committees, and conventions supplemented by ad hoc organizations formed to support particular candidates. In a word, *decentralization* is likely to continue to be as characteristic of American state parties as national.

NOMINATIONS

Legal Procedures

Every state except Connecticut * legally requires that party candidates for some or all public offices be nominated by "direct primaries." Thirty-nine states require it for both parties for all major offices; three southern states (Alabama, Georgia, and South Carolina) require it for the Democrats, but allow the Republicans to use conventions if they wish (as they usually do); and seven states require it for some offices and allow party conventions to choose nominees for others.[32]

All direct primaries have several features in common: they require that nominations be made directly by ordinary voters rather than indirectly by the voters' representatives in party conventions; they are regulated by state law, not by party rules; they are administered by state-appointed officials, not by extralegal party officers; and, as in general elections, the secrecy of the ballot is legally protected.

However, a few variations deserve brief notice. Seven states (Alaska, Michigan, Minnesota, Montana, North Dakota, Utah, and Wisconsin) use some version of the "open primary," in which the person may vote in whichever party's primary he chooses without public disclosure of his

---

* Under its unique "challenge primary" law adopted in 1955, Connecticut provides that all party candidates be nominated by party conventions. However, anyone who receives at least 20 per cent of a convention's votes but loses the nomination may petition the authorities to hold a primary election in which he "challenges" the convention-nominated candidate. A regular closed primary is then held, and whoever wins a majority of the votes becomes the official nominee. If no person challenges the convention's choice within fourteen days after the convention, he automatically becomes the official party nominee: see Duane Lockard, *Connecticut's Challenge Primary: A Study in Legislative Politics* (New York: Henry Holt and Co., 1959).

choice; Washington uses the "blanket primary," in which a voter may indicate preferences in both parties, but not two preferences for one office; and the remaining forty-two states use some version of the "closed primary," in which the voter must declare his party affiliation and vote only in that party's primary until he publicly changes his affiliation.

In addition, all eight southern one-party states and three modified one-party Democratic states (North Carolina, Oklahoma, and Virginia) provide for second or "run-off" primaries: if no candidate receives at least 50-per-cent-plus-one of the votes in the first primary, a second may be held in which only the two top candidates compete. This, of course, is a device to ensure that the Democratic nominee, who is in effect the elected official, has majority support.

Competition and Participation in Primary Elections

The direct primary was generally adopted in the "progressive era" from the early 1900s to the late 1920s with the avowed purpose of taking control of nominations away from the party "bosses," who were thought to manipulate party conventions in a disgracefully undemocratic manner, and restoring it to the party "rank-and-file." [33] But has it done the job?

A number of studies have been made of the degree of competition and voting turnout in primary elections.[34] Their findings generally agree on the following observations:

First, there are fewer contestants in primaries in which incumbents are seeking renomination than in those in which no incumbents are running. The reason for this is, of course, that an incumbent is hard to beat: he is usually far better known than his opponent(s); he usually has the best campaign organization and the best-stocked war chest; and the local party leaders are usually reluctant to surrender the benefits his legislative seniority brings the district. Thus, Key's study of primaries from 1920 to 1954 in which incumbent U.S. senators ran for renomination found that only 10 per cent were defeated. Significantly, however, only 2 per cent were defeated in the non-southern states, while 30 per cent lost in southern states.[35] Evidently, voters are more likely to defeat an incumbent in the primary if that is their only real shot at him than if they have another in the general election.

Second, the better a party's chances of winning the election, the more probable are its primaries to be contested, especially if no incumbent is running. Thus, at the Democratic extreme of our scale of competitiveness, Louisiana (.9877) and Alabama (.9685) are likely to have two or three contestants in Democratic primaries for most offices where there is no incumbent running, while the Republicans not only hold no primaries but are not likely to put up any candidate at all. At the Republican extreme, Vermont (.2822) and South Dakota (.3142) will usually have their Republican primaries contested and their Democratic primaries uncontested, although the Democrats will usually put up candidates. And in the middle, Nevada (.5742) and Colorado (.4725) are likely to have only one or two contestants in each party's primary, for each party knows it will have to have a united front to beat the opposition party in the general election. So, if at all possible, they will avoid intra-party primary fights that might leave bitterness and division.

Third, outside the South voting turnout is markedly lower in primaries than in general elections. The data in Table 3 show that only in the southern one-party Democratic states have turnouts for primary elections generally been higher than turnouts for general elections. Moreover, this appears to result from extremely low turnouts in general elections rather than unusually high turnouts in primaries. In the other three types of states, primary turnouts have averaged around 26.9 per cent while turnouts in general elections have averaged from 16.4 to 40.2 points higher.

Unfortunately, we lack sample-survey data on a national scale and over a long period of time to tell us *why* turnouts in primaries should generally be so much lower than in general elections. However, the general discussion of political participation in Chapter 2, and two sample-survey studies of voters and nonvoters in two Wisconsin primaries give us several clues. We know that in general elections the turnout rate is highest among the most "involved" voters — that is, those who care most who wins. This kind of involvement usually stems from strong party identifications: persons who are deeply attached to the Democratic or Republican party are likely to vote in November to make sure *their* side wins.[36] But a primary election is not a contest between one's own party and its opponents; it is a disagreement among different members of the same party. Hence, the party identification basis for involvement in general elections does not operate for primaries. The Wisconsin studies showed that people who voted in both the primary and general elections for governor in 1964 and 1966 differed from those who voted only in the general election in several respects: they were better educated, held more prestigious jobs, enjoyed higher incomes, and were more interested in and knowledgeable about public affairs. They were *not,* however, more strongly identified with their parties. Moreover, when the primary voters were asked *why* they had voted in the primaries, most replied that it was their duty as good citizens to do so, and only a

TABLE 3
Mean Voting Turnout in Primary and General Elections for Governor and U. S. Senator, 1962-1968

State groups	Percentage voting for governor			Percentage voting for U. S. senator		
	Primary election	General election	Difference	Primary election	General election	Difference
One-party Democratic	35.9	36.2	−0.3	28.1	33.4	-5.3
Modified one-party Democratic	33.5	49.9	-16.4	23.9	46.7	-22.8
Two-party	28.1	60.7	-32.6	26.4	61.3	-34.9
Modified one-party Republican	24.4	64.6	-40.2	19.5	58.6	-39.1

Source: Richard Scammon (ed.), *America Votes* (Pittsburgh: University of Pittsburgh Press, 1964; and Washington, D.C.: Governmental Affairs Institute, and Congressional Quarterly, Inc., 1966-1970).

minority said that it was because they wanted to help nominate a particular candidate.[37] We cannot yet say with any confidence whether Wisconsin primary voters and nonvoters are typical of their counterparts in the other states; but it seems clear that the all-in-the-family situation produced by the absence of competing party labels in a primary election makes it very different from the interparty competition of a general election.

Control of Nominations for Statewide Offices

The direct primary, in short, is intended to give "the people" power to control the parties' nominations; usually only about a quarter of those busy and bored worthies bother to use it. If they do not control the nominations, who does? The only accurate answer is that the patterns of control of nominations vary widely from one state to another and from one time to another within most states. The principal patterns appear to be the following:

Candidates for state senators and representatives are everywhere nominated by primaries or conventions in senatorial and representative districts. In almost all states almost all of the time these nominations are controlled locally. It is as rare for a statewide party "machine" to reach into a local district and determine its nominee as for the president or the national chairman to reach into a state or congressional district and control the nomination for U.S. senator or representative. It has happened on a few occassions, but in an overwhelming number of instances legislative nominations are locally controlled.[38]

In the few states in which nominations for statewide offices are made by state party conventions rather than primaries, the nominees are usually selected by negotiation among the leaders of the parties' principal factions; rarely does an "outsider" sweep the convention delegates against the leaders' wishes.

In Colorado and Massachusetts the law stipulates that state party conventions must meet before the primaries and ballot on nominees. In Colorado the winners are listed first for their respective offices on the primary ballots and, while anyone who receives over 20 per cent of the convention votes also goes on the ballot, the candidate preferred by the convention majority usually wins the primary.[39] In Massachusetts the same system is used, except that the convention winners are designated as such on the primary ballots and they, too, usually win the primaries.[40] In California and Wisconsin state conventions of the extralegal party activists meet before the primaries and (except for Wisconsin's Democrats) endorse candidates. No evidence of the endorsements appears on the primary ballots, and occassionally their choices lose (as when Glenn Davis lost the Wisconsin senatorial primary to incumbent Senator Alexander Wiley in 1956 despite having been endorsed by the Republican activists' convention); but usually they win.

In some states strong leaders of powerful statewide factions publicly endorse and support certain candidates in the primaries and regularly muster enough votes in the primaries to win. One well-known case in point is Mayor Daley's Cook County organization, which has played a decisive role in Illinois's statewide Democratic primaries since the mid-1950s.[41] In some southern one-party states, notably Louisiana and Virginia, the Democratic party is divided into two well-organized and durable factions, each of which regularly presents and support slates of candidates for all statewide offices in primary elections, and the result resembles — but is not identical with — two-party competition in general elections.[42]

In southern states such as Georgia and Mississippi and in some northern states as well, primary elections are usually contested by temporary, ad hoc factions that arise to support particular candidates and disappear when the primary is over. At the next primary some old factions try again, some drop out, and some new ones emerge. Thus, personalities, issues, and factions come and go so rapidly that the conflict over nominations is truly "patternless." [43]

For the most part, then, the control of nominations is not noticeably more centralized in American state politics than in national politics. In the states as in the nation this has a profound impact upon the conduct of elections and government.

ELECTIONS

Campaign Organization and Techniques

Daniel Ogden and Hugh Bone describe campaign organization in the state of Washington:

> Candidates are on their own in political campaigns in the state of Washington. Because of the independence of regular local party organizations, no candidate can be sure they will put forth the effort necessary to elect him. Thus every candidate, to some degree, creates his own campaign organization. . . . Candidates further illustrate their independence of party organization by running alone, rather than as part of a team. Their advertising is individual. Each candidate pictures himself as making the state stronger or doing a great job. Rarely will a popular candidate permit his name to appear on an ad or billboard with that of a much less known figure.[44]

This description fits most other two-party states as well. The decentralization it portrays results in part from the general decentralization of party organization reviewed earlier. It also stems from the fact that most states still retain the Jacksonian long ballot — that is, they select most major executive officers by independent election rather than by appointment by the governor.[45] Maine, New Hampshire, and New Jersey elect only the governor, who, like the president, appoints the other top executives. Alaska, Hawaii, and Tennessee elect the governor and one other executive. The remaining 45 states elect not only the governor and lieutenant governor, but also four to ten other executives — the most common being the secretary of state, treasurer, auditor, and attorney general.*

Not only are these officials elected independently, but it is by no means uncommon for a particularly popular incumbent to win re-election even when his fellow partisans are being defeated.† Such a man has every reason

---

* The champion is Oklahoma, which elects a governor, lieutenant governor, secretary of state, attorney general, treasurer, auditor, state examiner and inspector, superintendent of public instruction, chief mine inspector, commissioner of labor, commissioner of charities and corrections, commissioner of insurance, clerk of the supreme court and corporation commissioner!

† Among the better known of many examples are "Pat" Brown, whose success in winning the attorney generalship in California while the Republicans were sweeping the other offices in the early 1950s led to his nomination and election as governor in 1958; Republican John Chafee, who won re-election as Rhode Island's governor in 1964 while the rest of the state ticket went down to defeat; and Democrat Paul Powell, who was re-elected Illinois secretary of state despite the Republican sweep of 1968.

to play up his own experience and qualifications and play down his party connections with other candidates on the ticket. So usually only weak or little-known candidates talk much about the party ticket or seek joint campaign appearances with their fellow candidates. Thus does the long ballot contribute to the general decentralization of state parties and campaigns.

The years since 1945 have seen three main innovations in campaign techniques. First, parties and candidates have made increasing use of professional public relations firms to plan and conduct their campaigns rather than relying on regular party committees and workers in the traditional manner. Since such firms charge fees averaging 15 per cent of the total outlay and costs range in amount from $5,000 to $75,000, using them adds considerably to campaign costs. Nevertheless, more and more candidates seem to feel that the professionals do a far better job of "projecting the right image" than the old-line party faithful.[46]

Second, candidates and campaign managers are increasing use of privately hired and secretly reported public opinion polls to measure their appeals and the most effective allocation of their resources. This, too, has added considerably to campaign costs.

Third, while most candidates still devote considerable time and energy to personal appearances at party rallies and shaking hands on street corners, more and more — particularly those running for governor and other major offices — are placing their main reliance on televised spot announcements and speeches, "telethons," and the like. Some diehards still dispute the prevailing view that television provides the most effective exposure to the most voters, but no one disputes that the "televisation" of campaigns has, like the other two innovations, greatly increased campaign costs.

Campaign Costs

The nation's continuing economic inflation, the decreasing incidence of joint campaigning, and the increasing use of public relations firms, private polling, and television have steadily boosted the costs of political campaigns since 1945. In the 1950s and early 1960s, for example, it was estimated that the costs of campaigns in general elections for governor in populous two-party states ranged around $500,000 in Michigan, $600,000 in Illinois, $850,000 in California, and $1 million in New York. By the late 1960s, as Table 4 shows, the corresponding costs had become $1 million in Illinois and $5 million in New York, and other states showed comparable increases. Even campaigns for less visible offices with much smaller constitu-

encies became very costly. In California in 1964, for example, a candidate
for the state assembly spent $42,000, and a candidate for the state senate
spent $64,000. Furthermore, campaigns for primary elections increase
the total costs by a third or more. It has been estimated that in a large state
such as California or New York it costs around $2 million to mount a
serious campaign in a closely contested primary election for a gubernatorial
nomination.[47] There is every reason to believe that campaign costs in both
primary and general elections will continue to rise.

These facts of life mean that individuals or factions wishing to make
serious tries for statewide office must be able to raise a great deal of money.
Where do they get it? The general rule emphasized by students of campaign
finance is that however many individuals or groups may make contributions, most campaign funds for both parties come from large donations
by a few donors. In the two-party states the Republicans are financed
mainly by businessmen and the Democrats by labor unions, although it is
not unknown for both to contribute to both parties.[48] Undoubtedly there
also have been substantial contributions by underworld "syndicates" as
rewards for past favors and insurance against future prosecutions. Just how
much no one can say, though most would agree that any is too much.[49]

What campaign contributors *expect* to get for their contributions
ranges from a "generally favorable climate" for their interests to such
specific rewards as public works contracts, liquor licenses, utility franchises,
and tax favors. What they *actually* get is a topic discussed at several points
in this book.

TABLE 4
Representative Central Campaign Costs, Per Vote Cast in
Election: Selected Statewide Contests, 1962-1968

Type of campaign	Estimated costs, central campaign responsibility	Number of votes cast	Cents per vote cast
California, statewide election	$850,000	5,647,952	15¢
Michigan, statewide election	500,000	2,764,839	18
Illinois, statewide election	1,000,000	3,822,725	26
California, statewide primary	1,500,000	4,101,048	37
Connecticut, statewide election	550,000	1,206,537	45
New Jersey, statewide election	1,200,000	2,229,583	54
California, statewide election	3,617,000	7,041,821	51
California, statewide primary	2,270,000	3,776,256	60
New York, statewide election	5,000,000	6,031,585	83
Tennessee, statewide election	950,000	1,064,018	89
Indiana, statewide election	2,000,000	2,076,963	96

Source: Reports by the Citizens' Research Foundation, Princeton, New Jersey, Herbert E.
Alexander, Director.

A surprising number of people believe that money is an absolute weapon in state politics — that whoever mounts the most lavish campaign wins. If this were true, the Democrats, who rarely get or spend as much as the Republicans, would rarely win; yet, as we have seen, the Democrats have won more often than they have lost in twenty-four states, and only eight states are classified as modified one-party Republican. The leading students of the subject suggest a more balanced view. Money, they say, is only one of a number of factors affecting the outcome of elections. If most of these — e.g., traditional party identifications, recent political events, the candidates' personalities, and the level of prosperity — favor a particular party, the opposing one cannot win no matter how much more it may spend. But, if the other factors are evenly balanced, the party that out-spends and outcampaigns the other is likely to win.

Less widely discussed but probably more significant is the influence of money on nominations. Direct primaries make getting a nomination almost as expensive as winning an election; and there is little doubt that even an aspirant for nomination by a convention will receive substantial support if he has convinced the party's leaders that he and/or his backers are able and willing to contribute heavily to the party's war chest. These consider-ations rather than any ability to "buy" elections increasingly favor the well-to-do and/or the well-backed in state politics.[50]

Legal Regulations of Campaign Finance

We pointed out earlier that all states except Alaska, Delaware, Il-linois, Nevada, and Rhode Island have laws regulating one or more aspects of party finance. As in so many other matters, the details vary widely from state to state, but the principal forms of regulation are the following: limitations on total expenditures *by* a candidate (twenty-nine states) or, more stringently, on expenditures *in behalf of* a candidate (fifteen states); prohibitions against contributions by corporations (thirty-three states), labor unions (four states), and persons or firms holding state franchises, liquor licenses, and the like (eleven states); compulsory filing of public statements of receipts (thirty-seven states); and compulsory filing of public statements of expenditures (forty-five states).[51]

However, many commentators agree that most of these regulations are not only ineffective but actually damaging. The limits on expenditures, for example, were generally adopted decades ago and are far too low for the demands of modern campaigns. As a consequence, they are regularly evaded by such subterfuges as the proliferation of special campaign committees, each spending the legal limit, or the filing of reports containing something less than full accounts of receipts and expenditures. The prohibitions against contributions by corporations are evaded by "private" contributions by corporation executives and members of their families, and those against contributions by labor unions by the formation of "political education" organizations like the AFL-CIO's Committee on Political Education. The campaign finance laws have not controlled the use of money in state politics; they have only forced it to be collected and spent in an atmosphere of evasion, misrepresentation, and hypocrisy.

Accordingly, most political scientists now contend that the most the law can do is publicize the getting and spending of campaign money somewhat more effectively than at present, and that the real problem is finding ways of broadening the base of support by encouraging small contributors, perhaps by making political contributions tax deductible, and by instituting some form of direct public subsidy of campaigns.[52] To date, few steps have been taken in these directions by state legislatures, so it seems probable that the role of money in state politics will remain substantially the same for some time to come.

The Influence of National Politics
on State Elections

Many commentators contend that state elections should be as independent as possible of influence by national issues, personalities, and party loyalties. The states and the nation, they argue, are separate sovereignties with distinct powers and different problems. They think it makes no sense that elections for state officials should largely reflect the voters' feelings about national issues and parties.

One way of insulating state elections from national influences that some civic reformers have urged is holding state elections at times other than the dates of national elections. It is particularly important, they argue, to avoid holding state elections at the same time as presidential elections, when popular concentration on national affairs is at its highest. The following review of the scheduling of state gubernatorial elections shows that reformers have won their point in some states, but not all.

At present, only five states (Kentucky, Mississippi, Louisiana, New Jersey, and Virginia) have complete separation of elections. Four of them elect their governors for four-year terms in odd-numbered years (i.e., 1967, 1971, 1975) and their legislators for two- or four-year terms also in odd-numbered years. Mississippi elects its governor and both houses of its legislature for four-year terms in odd-numbered years. Four of these four states are one-party or modified one-party Democratic states.

Next closest to the separation ideal are the twenty-four states that elect their governors for four-year terms in off years (i.e., even-numbered years in which no presidential election is held). Of these, three (Alabama, Georgia, and South Carolina) are one-party Democratic, four (Florida, Maryland, Oklahoma, and Tennessee) are modified one-party Democratic, and the remaining seventeen are two-party.

Still further from the separation model are the eleven states that elect their governors for two-year terms in even-numbered years and, therefore, alternate between presidential and off years. Four of the five modified one-party Republican states are in this group, together with four two-party states, one-party Democratic Texas and Arkansas, and one modified one-party Democratic state (New Mexico).

Furthest away from separation are the eleven states that elect their governors for four-year terms in presidential years. They include six two-party states (Delaware, Illinois, Indiana, Montana, Utah, and Washington), one-party Democratic Louisiana, three modified one-party Democratic states (Missouri, North Carolina, and West Virginia), and modified one-party Republican North Dakota.[53]

Thus the device of formal separation of state from national elections has been fully adopted by only four states and largely rejected by eleven. Does this mean that state elections are unduly influenced by national factors? V. O. Key attempted to answer this question for the period 1932 to 1950, which was dominated by an unusually popular Democratic presidential candidate, Franklin D. Roosevelt. Key took the states electing governors every two years and compared the gubernatorial results in presidential years with those in off years. He found that the better the Democrats did in presidential elections, the more likely they were to win governorships in presidential years but not in off years, and he ascribed this to the power of Mr. Roosevelt's "coattails" in state politics.

I have extended Key's study to the period 1952 to 1970, the first part of which was dominated by an unusually popular Republican candidate, Dwight D. Eisenhower. The results, presented in Table 5, generally confirm Key's findings, showing that in the period 1952 to 1970 the Republicans generally did better in gubernatorial elections in presidential years than in off years.[54] However, it also shows that the general disparity between presidential and gubernatorial voting in the post-Eisenhower era was substantially greater than in the Roosevelt years. This is largely a result of the fact that in the period from 1948 to 1968 there were several southern and bor-

TABLE 5
Success of Republican Gubernatorial Candidates in Presidential Years and Off-Years according to Success of Democratic Presidential Candidates (for states with two-year gubernatorial terms, 1932-1970)

Democratic presidential percentage	1932-1950		1952-1962		1964-1970	
	Presidential years	Following off-years	Presidential years	Following off-years	Presidential years	Following off-years
Under 45	80.0%	80.0%	74.5%	51.5%	80.0%	20.0%
45-49	70.6	82.4	41.7	8.3	100	a
50-54	45.0	75.0	22.3	22.0	50.0	100
55-59	9.5	42.9	a	a	66.7	100
60 or more	6.7	20.0	a	a	28.6	28.6

[a]No states in these categories.

der state defections from Democratic presidential candidates. These defections are summarized in Table 6.

Table 6 shows that the southern states classified as one-party for state purposes defected from the Democratic presidential candidate twenty times out of forty-eight chances. The southern and border states classified as modified one-party defected twenty-six times out of fifty-four opportunities. Consequently, however "solid" the South may be in state and local elections, it has become much more competitive for national offices. We shall return to this development and its significance at the end of this chapter.

PARTY GOVERNMENT IN THE STATES

For almost a century several eminent political scientists, from Woodrow Wilson and Frank Goodnow in the 1890s to E. E. Schattschneider and James MacGregor Burns in the 1960s, have argued that the only way a modern mass society can have a government that is both effective and democratic is to establish "responsible party government." [55] By this they mean a situation in which two (and preferably only two) parties regularly present alternative programs in election campaigns, and a majority of the voters chooses one or the other to rule. The party winning a majority of the votes wins a majority of the public offices and all the governmental power it needs to write its program into law. During their terms in office the majority party's public officials act cohesively as a unit, not as isolated individuals. As a result, their party is *collectively* responsible for whether affairs have gone well or badly. At the end of its term the voters decide whether they approve of how the governing party has managed affairs; if a majority approve, they return it to power for another term; if they disapprove, they replace it with the opposition party.

Other political scientists believe that the responsible-parties model is neither practicable nor desirable for the special requirements of American society.[56] Without weighing the merits of either position, we need to know what role political parties actually do play in the governing processes of the states.

Structural Difficulties

DIVIDED PARTY CONTROL BETWEEN GOVERNOR AND LEGISLATURE. Two essential prerequisites for responsible party government in the states

TABLE 6
Southern and Border States in Post-War Presidential Elections

State	Presidential elections carried by			
	Democratic	*Republican*	*Third party*	*Other*
One-party Democratic				
Alabama	52, 56	64	48, 68	60[a]
Arkansas	48, 52, 56, 60, 64		68	
Georgia	48, 52, 56, 60	64	68	
Louisiana	52, 60	56, 64	48, 68	
Mississippi	52, 56	64	48, 68	60[a]
South Carolina	52, 56, 60	64, 68	48	
Texas	48, 60, 64, 68	52, 56		
Modified one-party Democratic				
Florida	48, 64	52, 56, 60, 68		
Kentucky	48, 52, 64	56, 60, 68		
Maryland	60, 64, 68	48, 52, 56		
Missouri	48, 56, 60, 64	52, 68		
North Carolina	48, 52, 56, 60, 64	68		
Oklahoma	48, 64	52, 56, 60, 68		
Tennessee	48, 64	52, 56, 60, 68		
Virginia	48, 64	52, 56, 60, 68		
West Virginia	48, 52, 60, 64, 68	56		

[a] In 1960 all of Mississippi's electors and six of Alabama's eleven voted for Senator Harry Byrd for president.

are: (1) the majority party must control both the governorship and the legislature at any given time, or else it cannot be collectively responsible for how the government is run; and (2) there must be strong two-party competition so that the majority party may be turned out at any time when the voters decide it is time for a change.

However, the separate elections of the governor and the two houses of the legislature endanger the first prerequisite, for they make it possible for the governor to be of one party and one or both houses of the legislature to be controlled by the other. This possibility, moreover, often becomes reality: from 1946 to 1970 in forty of the fifty states there was at least one period, and usually more, in which control of the governorship and legislature was divided between the two parties. The ten exceptions were nine southern one-party states and one border modified one-party state (Alabama, Georgia, Louisiana, Mississippi, Missouri, North Carolina, South Carolina, Tennessee, Texas, and Virginia). The two-party states, on the other hand, had united party control only about half of the time. The result: the states most likely to satisfy the second prerequisite of party government are *least* likely to fulfill the first!

V. O. Key found the same pattern of divided control in the period from 1931 to 1952, and suggested several reasons for it.[57] One is the apportionment of state legislatures, which, by overrepresenting rural areas and small towns and underrepresenting metropolitan areas, typically exaggerates Republican strength and understates Democratic. Dramatic evidence of this is provided by the fact that since World War II the Democrats have never controlled the upper house of the legislature in such competitive states as Pennsylvania, Wisconsin, and Wyoming. Therefore, if responsible party government were ever to operate in these states, the Republicans had to operate it, for the very structure of the state governments made it impossible for the Democrats to do so. The "apportionment revolution" growing from *Baker* v. *Carr* [58] may alter this situation somewhat in the Democrats' favor in the years ahead; but the concentration of Democratic votes in the metropolitan areas will probably sustain this anti-Democratic bias for a long time, and the resulting tendency for divided party control will persist.

A governor facing a legislature controlled by the opposition party does not invariably mean angry partisan wrangling and deadlock. If the governor carefully cultivates the opposition's legislative leaders, proposes a moderate program to which they have agreed, and in general plays down party politics and the independence of his office, the government may proceed about as smoothly as if all concerned were members of the same party. But men are not angels and politicians have to fight elections, so such cross-partisan harmony is rare. A more common story has been the bitter partisan conflict and resultant near-total deadlock, typically between Democratic governors and Republican legislators that marked such administrations as those of Otto Kerner in Illinois and John Reynolds in Wisconsin in the early 1960s. All resulted in deadlocks over such basic matters as taxation, legislative apportionment, and executive appointments; and for a good part of the time the governments of all three states were brought to nearly complete standstills. In short, separation of powers, rural overrepresentation in legislatures, and close statewide two-party competition sometimes make for inter-party deadlock rather than responsible party government.

DIVIDED PARTY CONTROL WITHIN THE EXECUTIVE. We noted earlier that forty-five states retain the "long ballot" by which from four to twelve executive officers in addition to the governor are independently elected. Not only does this encourage the decentralization of parties in campaigns, as we have seen, but it also enables divided party control *within* the executive branch to complicate the divisions between the executive and the legislature. How often does this actually happen and in what kinds of states? Key has given us our most complete answer in his study of the outcome of all executive elections in nine northern states from 1900 to 1952. His results are summarized in Table 7.

Table 7 shows that divided control within the executive follows the same general pattern as divided control between the governor and the legis-

TABLE 7

Relation Between Size of Gubernatorial Pluralities and Outcomes of Simultaneous Elections of Minor State Officials in Nine States, 1900-1952

		Results of simultaneous elections of minor officers					
Percentage of two-party vote for governor	*Number of gubernatorial elections*	*All from governor's party*		*All from opposition party*		*Divided between parties*	
		No.	%	No.	%	No.	%
50.1-52.4	58	32	55.2	12	20.7	14	24.1
52.5-54.9	49	30	61.2	5	10.2	14	28.6
55.0-57.4	40	35	87.5	0	0.0	5	12.5
57.5-59.9	23	23	100.0	0	0.0	0	0.0
60.0-62.4	18	18	100.0	0	0.0	0	0.0
62.5-64.9	8	8	100.0	0	0.0	0	0.0

Source: V. O. Key, Jr., *American State Politics,* 200, Table 27. (The nine states were: Illinois, Indiana, Iowa, Massachusetts, Michigan, Missouri, Ohio, Rhode Island, and Wisconsin.)

lature: the closer the competition for governor, the more likely it is that the governor and some other elected executives will be of different parties. When the governor was elected by less than 52 per cent of the vote, the chances were one in two that some of his fellow executives would be of the opposition party. When he won by less than 55 per cent, the chances were two in five. Only when he won by 57.5 per cent of the vote or more were his fellow executives always of his own party.

Here again, where political conditions create the keen inter-party competition that responsible party government requires, constitutional structures and ticket-splitting voters combine to work powerfully against the majority-party control the model also requires.

Party Organization in State Legislatures

Both parties in both houses of the United States Congress have elaborate arrays of caucuses, steering committees, floor leaders, whips, committees on committees, and other organizations purporting — though by no means always succeeding — to mobilize their legislators for coordinated action. In any legislative body such agencies would seem to be indispensable if the parties are to play significant roles; yet they are by no means universal in state legislatures.

The basic party organ in most legislatures is the "caucus" or "conference" — an assembly of all the party's members in the particular house. However, a survey of state legislatures conducted by the Committee on American Legislatures of the American Political Science Association in the early 1950s reported that the majority parties had no caucuses of any kind in fifteen senates and fourteen houses. Most of these, to be sure, were in the one-party states in which caucuses would simply be meetings of all or nearly all of the members of the entire assembly, and would therefore seem pointless. But, the committee's report adds, "in only thirteen states do majority caucuses meet frequently and exert or attempt to exert any significant control over their members or the program of the legislature." Significantly, all thirteen (Colorado, Connecticut, Delaware, Idaho, Indiana, Massachusetts, Nevada, New Jersey, New York, Pennsylvania, Rhode Island, Washington, and Wyoming) were two-party states. However, factional caucuses within the majority party were reported for three one-party states (Arkansas, Florida, and Georgia) and four modified one-party states (Arizona, Kansas, New Mexico, and North Dakota).[59]

Each party in each house of Congress has a "steering" or "policy" committee — a small group of leaders selected by the caucus to act as a sort of board of directors. These bodies have little influence and less power in Congress, and in many states the situation is the same. However, in a few states (e.g., Illinois, Maine, Rhode Island, and Wisconsin) the parties' leadership committees are considerably more powerful than their congressional counterparts.[60]

The dominant figures of party organization in Congress are the Speaker of the House and the minority leader, and the majority and minority leaders of the Senate. Their counterparts exist in most state legislatures, but legislative proceedings, particularly in the lower houses, are dominated more than in Congress by their presiding officers. Indeed, "in the typical state government the speaker's powers are very great, second only to those of the governor." [61] In all but two states the speaker of the lower house, unlike his Washington counterpart, personally appoints members of all legislative and party committees; and as he is largely unhampered by seniority rules, he has a free hand and typically puts on the most important committees legislators he can count on to "go along" with his program and strategy.[62]

Party Cohesion in State Legislatures

Another prerequisite of responsible party government is that the parties' legislators maintain high cohesion in their votes on legislative issues, for only in this way can the voters meaningfully hold the majority party — as opposed to individual legislators — responsible for what the legislature does or fails to do.

The varying degrees and conditions of party cohesion in state legislatures are discussed at length in Chapter 5. For present purposes the essential points to grasp are: that party cohesion is generally very low in the one-party and modified one-party states, and that it tends to be higher in the two-party states. Its general relation to party competitiveness is illustrated in Table 8, which classifies the states in each of the categories of competitiveness according to their degree of party cohesion as reported by the Committee on Legislatures.

Table 8 shows that more two-party states have strong cohesion than weak or moderate; more modified one-party states have weak cohesion than strong or moderate; and all eight one-party states have weak cohesion. So the degree of party competition is clearly one, but only one, factor affecting legislative cohesion.

Chapter 5 shows that the other factors have to do with the degree to which party divisions correspond with socioeconomic divisions. Generally speaking, where the basic political conflict is between metropolitan areas

TABLE 8
Legislative Party Cohesion and Inter-Party Competition

Cohesion in the two-party states			Cohesion in the modified one-party states			Cohesion in the one-party states		
Strong	Moderate	Weak	Strong	Moderate	Weak	Strong	Moderate	Weak
Colorado	Illinois	Arizona	Kansas	New Hampshire	Florida			Alabama
Connecticut	Montana	California	Maryland	South Dakota	Kentucky			Arkansas
Delaware	Nevada	Maine	Missouri	Vermont	North Dakota[c]			Georgia
Idaho	Ohio	Nebraska[b]	North Carolina		New Mexico			Louisiana
Indiana	Utah	Oregon	West Virginia		Oklahoma			Mississippi
Iowa	Washington				Tennessee			South Carolina
Massachusetts	Wyoming				Virginia			Texas
Michigan								
Minnesota[a]								
New Jersey								
New York								
Pennsylvania								
Rhode Island								
Wisconsin								

aStrong factional cohesion in nonpartisan legislature.
bWeak factional cohesion in nonpartisan legislature.
cStrong factional cohesion in dominant party.
Source: Adapted from Belle Zeller, ed., American State Legislatures, 190-191, Table 9. (Alaska and Hawaii not included).

and small towns, and where most Democratic legislators are elected from the former and most Republicans from the latter, cohesion in both legislative parties tends to be high. Where party divisions do not coincide with metropolitan–small town conflict, however, party cohesion tends to be lower even where party competition is close. Thus, in some state legislatures cohesion comes very close to the responsible-parties model, while in others it is considerably further away.

The Governor as Party Leader

Chapter 6 describes the general position of the governor as a legislative, executive, and administrative leader. Here we are concerned with his position as leader of his party and the extent to which it helps him in his other roles. We should begin by distinguishing between his "outside" and "inside" roles.

In most states, whether one-party or two-party, the governor is usually (though not invariably) the principal leader and spokesman for his party in its relations with other state parties and with the national party. One evidence of this is the fact that the dominant figures in state delegations to national party conventions are usually governors rather than U.S. senators, mayors, state chairmen, or other rivals.[63] The reason is plain enough: most state parties see many advantages in presenting a united front in their operations in national party affairs, for this is the way to maximize their power. The governor is usually the logical person to act as their spokesman and chief strategist. This fact has sometimes misled outsiders to assume that the governor must be just as much in charge back home as he is at national conventions. This is rarely the case.

We observed earlier that in some one-party and modified one-party states (e.g., Virginia, Louisiana, Vermont, and North Dakota) the dominant party is divided into two well-organized, relatively cohesive and durable factions. Where this is the case, the governor can usually count upon regular support only from his fellow factionalists in the legislature; and, while he cannot be said to be the leader of the whole party for state purposes, he certainly has as much control over the machinery of government as any governor of a two-party state. In other one-party and modified one-party states (e.g., Florida, Oklahoma, and Mississippi) there are no durable factions, and the coalition that elects the governor usually has little carry-over in the legislature. As a result, the governor of such a state is the leader of his party in only the most nominal sense, and he must negotiate with factions in the legislature on an issue-by-issue basis to accomplish whatever he wishes to accomplish.[64]

However, whether in a bifactional or multifactional state, the leadership of most governors in the one-party states is materially weakened by the fact that they are constitutionally prohibited from succeeding themselves: four of the seven one-party Democratic states have such prohibitions (only Louisiana and Texas do not), as well as six of the twelve modified one-party Democratic states. By contrast, only one two-party state (Indiana) has comparable prohibitions, but eight more (Alaska, Delaware, Maine, Nebraska, New Jersey, Ohio, Oregon, and Pennsylvania) limit their governors to two terms.[65]

Where the governor's term is limited, as it is in most of the Democratic states, whatever leadership he may have had over his party when first elected is likely to dissipate as he nears the end of his term; legislators and party chairmen alike know that he will soon be in a position to neither help nor hurt them very much.

A leading student of American governorship, Professor Coleman Ransone, sums up the party leadership of governors in the two-party states thus:

> It is primarily because we do not really have party government at the state level that the governor must continue to play the role of the politician even after his election. . . . The idea of disciplined parties in the legislature who work with the governor to execute a party program is largely a none-too-effective myth at the state level. The governor is elected in an atmosphere of factional politics and he continues to operate in that atmosphere in his dealings with the legislature, with his department heads, and with the other members of the executive branch.[66]

The principal reasons for this relative weakness of gubernatorial party leadership in the two-party states include: (1) the general decentralization of the state parties, which means that most county leaders and state legislators hold their positions by their own efforts and owe the governor nothing; (2) the frequency with which divided party control forces the governor to bargain with factions in the opposition party in the legislature and within the executive branch; (3) the fact that the use of his patronage and item-veto powers may well make at least as many enemies as friends. The upshot, Ransone concludes, is this:

> There are situations in the two-party states in which the governorship and the legislature are controlled by the same party and

where, given some party discipline, the governor may be able to make an appeal to the legislators on the basis of a party program. These situations, however, tend to be infrequent. . . . The American governor must concern himself with building legislative support from among clusters of legislative factions. In only a few states does the party actually play its traditional role.[67]

The New Vulnerability of the Governor

Traditionally the governorships of large northern two-party states such as New York, Ohio, Pennsylvania, and Illinois, have been ideal stepping-stones to the major parties' presidential nominations. However, in presidential elections from 1960 to 1968 none of the presidential, and only two of the six vice-presidential candidates of either party had ever been a governor. Why this sudden downgrading of gubernatorial office? Undoubtedly, part of the reason lies in the increasing importance of foreign policy issues and the need of a presidential candidate to have some experience and reputation in foreign affairs. But part also lies in the increasing political vulnerability of governors. In 1966, for example, twenty-six incumbent U.S. senators ran for reelection and only two were defeated; but of the twenty-four incumbent governors running in the same year, eight were beaten. In 1968, twenty-four incumbent senators ran, and only four lost; but of the thirteen incumbent governors running, four lost. So in these two elections 88 per cent of the incumbent senators survived, compared with only 67 per cent of the incumbent governors.

The reason for the new political vulnerability of governors is plain: most state governments, as this volume makes abundantly clear, now face enormously increased demands for more and better schools, highways, welfare, recreational facilities, and so on — but most face them armed with very inadequate revenue sources. Consequently, most large two-party states are in perpetual financial crisis: The governor is to a great extent the most visible state official and therefore the logical scapegoat for the state's apparent inability to solve its problems. It is he who must press for new taxes or announce the curtailment of services — neither of which encourages political popularity. Thus, when the voters wish to express their annoyance with high taxes or inadequate services, the governor is their natural target.

Most state politicians know this, and many are reluctant to tie their own fortunes to a man who might well be thrown out at the next election. Accordingly, the governors in the two-party states, as Ransone points out, are rarely both strong *and* durable party leaders. To get things done they must rely mainly on weapons other than their leadership of their parties, and they must often enlist the cooperation of at least some of the opposition party. As this becomes more and more common, governorships may well lose their traditional place as ideal stepping-stones to higher office.

CHANGING ELECTORAL PATTERNS IN STATE POLITICS

The Growth of Inter-Party Competition

We noted earlier that the Civil War hammered most states' party alignments into forms that long seemed permanent. Since 1945, however, a number of hitherto one-party states have seen their second parties mount major challenges to the dominant parties. As a result, the nation's political landscape has come to look much different since V-J Day from the way it appeared before Pearl Harbor.

Perhaps the most dramatic change has been the rise of Republican strength in several southern and border states. We have already observed its effects on presidential voting, but in some states it has operated in elections for other offices as well.

For example, in 1966 Arkansas and Florida elected their first Republican governors since the 1870s. South Carolina elected its first Republican senator in nearly a century, and Tennessee elected its first Republican senator ever. In 1968 Arkansas reelected its Republican governor, and Florida and Oklahoma elected their first Republican senators in history. In all, Republicans won a total of 31 seats out of a regional total of 119 in the national House of Representatives, their highest ever. They also made impressive gains in the state legislatures of Alabama, Florida, Kentucky, North Carolina, and Tennessee. There is little doubt that southern Republicans are stronger today than they have been since Reconstruction days, and they are very likely to grow stronger in the future.[68]

Less dramatic but equally significant has been the rise of Democratic strength in a number of formerly solid Republican states. For example, Democrats in Iowa and Maine have done so well in gubernatorial and legislative elections since the mid-1950s that we now classify Iowa and Maine as two-party states. Comparable movements seem to be taking place in many of the states we still classify as modified one-party Republican. Vermont, historically the most Republican state of all, elected its first Democratic governor in history in 1962, reelected him in 1964 and 1966, and gave the Democrats over 40 per cent of the seats in the state senate in

1964. Kansas elected a Democratic governor in 1966 and reelected him in 1968. New Hampshire had a three-term Democratic governor from 1962 to 1968 and reelected a Democratic senator in 1966. North Dakota elected a Democratic senator in 1964 and reelected its Democratic governor for a fourth term in 1968. It seems, then, that what the Democrats have lost in the South they have regained in the rural Midwest and Northeast.

We cannot now provide a complete and definitive explanation for these changes from traditional state political alignments. However, a major part of any such explanation will surely be interstate migration.[69] Americans have always moved about within their country frequently and in large numbers, and the post-1945 era has witnessed one of the greatest migrations since the Civil War: the Bureau of the Census found that 12 per cent of the population over five years of age in 1960 had moved from one state to another since 1955! [70]

Perhaps the most significant movement politically has been the parallel immigration of northern whites into the South and southern Negroes into the North. One effect has been to reduce the proportion of Negroes in the southern states' populations: in the decade from 1950 to 1960 the proportion of Negroes declined in all eight Democratic one-party states, the largest drops being from 27 to 18 per cent in Florida and from 43 to 35 per cent in South Carolina; the average drop for the eight states was 5.6 per cent.[71] The trend seems to have continued in the 1960s. This Negro exodus has "lightened" many of the South's "black belts," which, according to Key, have always constituted the nucleus of Southern one-party politics.[72] At the same time the influx of northern whites, about half of whom were Republicans in the North and have remained so after moving to the South, has not only given southern Republicans more votes; more significantly, it has greatly enlarged the pool of well-educated and active party supporters from which they can draw candidates for office and leaders of party organization. Both movements, accordingly, have encouraged a higher degree of interparty competition in the South.

The other main postwar interstate migration has been the massive movement to the Far West. The most spectacular instance, of course, is the growth of California from a population of 6,907,000 in 1940 to 15,717,000 in 1960, and a position as the most populous state in the Union by 1970. The Survey Research Center of the University of Michigan studied a sample of 588 western adults in 1956, and its findings tell us much about the postwar western immigrants and their impact on western politics. Slightly over twice as many came from the North as from the South. Those from the North were closely split between Democratic identifiers (39 per cent) and

Republican (34 per cent), while those from the South were heavily Democratic (57 per cent to 20 per cent Republican). From one point of view, the new effect has been to make the West somewhat more Democratic than before; from another, it has sustained two-party competition, for the northern immigrants have supplied large numbers of Republicans, enough indeed to keep the region from the two-to-one lead the Democrats would probably have if the western electorate consisted entirely of persons born in the region and immigrants from the South.[73]

CONCLUSIONS

We end where we began: in every state most elections are fought and most public offices are held by persons bearing the labels "Democratic" and "Republican"; but the meaning of "political parties" as applied to these aggregates varies considerably from one state to another. In the six southern one-party states "the Democratic party" is almost coterminous with the state itself; everyone is a Democrat; elections are not inter-party contests; and the Democratic party has as much "cohesion" and "responsibility" as the whole government, for they are one and the same.[74]

In the seventeen modified one-party states, the "political parties" are somewhat more meaningful entities. Although most voters identify with the dominant party, a noticeable minority identifies with the other. Both parties nominate candidates in most elections, which thereby become genuine choices between parties; and occasionally a candidate of the second party wins. Much political conflict is fought out in the primaries and committees of the dominant party, but the presence of an organized party opposition ready to take over in case of schism or scandal makes the context of intraparty conflict substantially different from that in the one-party states.[75]

In the two-party states each party musters a large segment of the population as its identifiers. Almost every election is contested by a Republican and a Democrat. In some two-party states there is high cohesion among both parties in the legislature and close cooperation between the governor and his fellow partisans. Such states, indeed, come closer than the national government to the responsible-party-government model. In other two-party states, however, the parties are little, if any, more cohesive than in the modified one-party states. We are as yet unable to say why two-party competition produces unified parties in some states but not in others.

Therefore, relatively even party competition seems to be a necessary — but not sufficient — condition for state parties to operate as unified governing agencies. Its postwar increase in many American states may help bring some of them nearer the responsible-parties ideal. But in other two-party states, two-party competition, because of its combination with separation of powers and some residual malapportionment of the legislatures, may serve instead to intensify the partisan political deadlock of governmental paralysis that constitutes one of the principal barriers to making states into more effective units of government. Inter-party competition, in short, does make a difference; but the kind of difference it makes depends upon the context in which it operates.

Whatever may be the future of inter-party competition, however, political parties will continue to be the states' principal agencies for making nominations, contesting elections, recruiting governmental leaders from the general population, and so providing the vital link between the people and their government that democracy demands. What Clinton Rossiter has said of the nation applies with equal force to each of the states:

> Our party system will continue to serve us well as long as we keep the old definition firmly in mind: Politics is the art of the possible. Whatever America finds necessary to do in the years to come, the politics of American democracy will surely make possible.[76]

SELECTED BIBLIOGRAPHY

Adamany, David. *Financing Politics: Recent Wisconsin Elections.* Madison: University of Wisconsin Press, 1969. The most authoritative analysis of campaign finance in a single state.

Crew, Robert E., Jr. (ed.). *State Politics.* Belmont, Calif.: Wadsworth Publishing Co., 1968. Useful paperback collection of leading articles on state parties and politics.

Epstein, Leon D. *Politics in Wisconsin.* Madison: University of Wisconsin Press, 1958. An application of Key's hypotheses and techniques to Wisconsin, supplemented by the author's interviews with state party leaders.

Fenton, John R. *Politics in the Border States.* New Orleans: The Hauser Press, 1957. Descriptions of politics in Kentucky, Maryland, Missouri, and West Virginia.

————. *Midwest Politics.* New York: Holt, Rinehart & Winston, 1966. Descriptions of politics in Illinois, Indiana, Michigan, Minnesota, and Wisconsin.

Herndon, James, Charles Press, and Oliver P. Williams (eds.). *A Selected Bibliography of Materials in State Government and Politics.* Lexington: Bureau of Government Research, University of Kentucky, 1963. The most complete state-by-state bibliography of state politics, though now somewhat outdated.

Jonas, Frank H. (ed.). *Politics in the American West.* Salt Lake City: University of Utah Press, 1969. Essays on the politics of Alaska, Arizona, California, Colorado, Hawaii, Idaho, Montana, Nevada, New Mexico, Oregon, Utah, Washington, and Wyoming.

Key, V. O., Jr. *American State Politics: An Introduction.* New York: Alfred A. Knopf, 1956. Pioneering and influential study of nonsouthern state politics resting almost entirely on statistical analysis of aggregate data.

————. *Southern Politics in State and Nation.* New York: Alfred A. Knopf, 1949. A classic of contemporary political science, somewhat outdated in detail, but still the most comprehensive and authoritative general analysis.

Lockard, Duane. *New England State Politics.* Princeton: Princeton University Press, 1959. Useful analysis of politics in Connecticut, Maine, Massachusetts, New Hampshire, Rhode Island, and Vermont, concentrating on inter-party competition and legislative politics.

Matthews, Donald R., and James W. Prothro. *Negroes and the New Southern Politics.* New York: Harcourt, Brace & World, 1966. Sophisticated study of changing political attitudes and behavior of southern Negroes, with many implications for the future of southern state politics.

Munger, Frank (ed.). *American State Politics: Readings for Comparative Analysis.* New York: Thomas Y. Crowell Company, 1966. Well-chosen and edited collection of articles on state parties and politics.

National Municipal League. *State Party Structures and Procedures: A State-by-State Compendium.* New York: National Municipal League, 1967. The most recent and most thorough collection of state laws and party rules governing the organization and procedures of political parties in each of the states.

Ransone, Coleman B., Jr. *The Office of Governor in the United States.* University, Ala.: University of Alabama Press, 1956. Comprehensive analysis of state politics focused on the office of governor.

Sindler, Allan P. *Huey Long's Louisiana: State Politics, 1920–1952.* Baltimore: The Johns Hopkins Press, 1956. The most scholarly account of a significant case in southern state politics.

Sorauf, Frank J. *Party and Representation: Legislative Politics in Pennsylvania.* New York: Atherton Press, 1963. A stimulating study of the selection of candidates and conduct of elections for the Pennsylvania legislature in 1958, used as a base for generalizing about interrelations among constituencies, local party organizations and leaders, and state organizations and leaders.

Wilson, James Q. *The Amateur Democrats.* Chicago: University of Chicago Press, 1956. The most complete account of the Democratic "club" movements in various states.

CHAPTER FOUR

Interest Groups in the States

L. Harmon Zeigler and Hendrik van Dalen

The ability of political parties to meet the demands of the electorate varies considerably from state to state. Where the political machinery capable of channeling these demands and translating them into policy is lacking or relatively inefficient, interest groups have grown in strength and number, and have come to be regarded as the principal alternative to parties or the major supplement to their activity.[1] *

In this chapter we will examine interest group activity, focusing in particular on lobbyists and their method of interacting with state legislators. Our first consideration is conceptual differences between state and national lobbying practices. Then we will discuss elements in the politico-economic setting that influence the strength and behavior of interest groups in the several states. The background of lobbyists and the manner in which they communicate demands will complete our analysis.

CURRENT CONCEPTIONS OF STATE VERSUS
NATIONAL INTEREST GROUPS:
THE CASE OF LOBBYING

A popular conception of lobbying is that, for the most part, lobbyists provide elaborate entertainment for legislators, offering bribes and, if all else

The authors wish to acknowledge the support of the Center for the Advanced Study of Educational Administration during a portion of the time they devoted to the preparation of this paper. CASEA is a national research and development center established under the Cooperative Research Program of the U.S. Office of Education. The research reported in this paper was conducted as part of the research and development program of the center.

* [See pp. 570–575 for notes to this chapter. — Eds.]

fails, threatening the recalcitrant legislator with defeat in the next election. Insofar as the national legislative process is concerned, recent research has fairly well dispelled this notion.[2] However, there does seem to be evidence that at the state level the high-handed methods of the past still persist. For instance, Robert Engler in discussing the techniques of oil lobbyists before state legislatures says, "The crude and more obvious practices commonly identified with lobbying are still familiar here." Engler refers to a remark by a Standard Oil executive to Rockefeller in the early days of the growth of refining companies that he had "arranged to kill two bills in the Maryland legislature at comparatively small expense." [3] Although he concedes that it is difficult to document such activity today, Engler gives the impression that unscrupulous lobbying is still the order of the day.

Further evidence of the belief in the crude nature of state lobbying techniques is provided by Lester Milbrath. In interviewing lobbyists and legislators in Washington, D.C., he found that they perceived state lobbying to be considerably more corrupt than national lobbying. Some of the comments of his respondents illustrate this belief:

> Lobbying is very different before state legislatures; it is much more individualistic. Maybe this is the reason they have more bribery in state legislatures than in Congress.
> In the state legislatures, lobbying is definitely on a lower plane. The lobbyists are loose and hand out money and favors quite freely.
> Lobbying at the state level is cruder, more basic, and more obvious.
> Lobbying at the state level is faster and more freewheeling and less visible; that is why it is more open to corruption.[4]

In theory, some characteristics of state legislatures and legislators contribute to more corrupt lobbying techniques. State legislatures meet less often and for shorter durations of time than does Congress; therefore an internalized set of formal and informal rules such as those of the Senate would be more difficult to develop. Such a system of internalized expectations of behavior would, perhaps, impose limits upon individual legislative behavior and thus restrict the operating limits of interest groups. Also contributing to the lack of internal systems of authority is the rapid turnover of state legislators. Since about half of these legislators are first-term members of their respective houses, their unfamiliarity with the legislature improves the general access of lobbyists. State legislators are less likely to be "professionals" and more likely to regard a legislative career as a secondary aspect of their lives. Finally, state legislators make less money than national legislators; since they usually do not reside in the state capital, they incur more expenses in relation to their income than national legislators.

In practice, however, crass lobbying techniques do not appear to be as widespread or as effective as some believe. Analyzing the responses to an intensive survey of lobbyists and legislators in Massachusetts, North Carolina, Oregon, and Utah, Zeigler and Baer found that "both groups rank bribery as the least effective method" of influence.[5] Entertainment wasn't ranked much better, although state lobbyists gave entertainment and parties higher scores than Washington lobbyists. In fact, Milbrath states that parties are so numerous in Washington that an invitation

> becomes a punishment instead of a reward. The decision maker, who is required by his position and role to attend a large number of functions, treasures most highly the freedom to spend an evening at home with his family. Such a situation is not characteristic of state legislators, who frequently are anxious to burn the candle at both ends. Since legislative sessions do not last very long, and since the social life in state capitols is considerably less developed than social life in Washington, state legislative sessions occasionally acquire the atmosphere of a long and extravagant house party.[6]

Entertainment, however, does not set the stage for a bribe or provide opportunities for applying pressure against a legislator. Rather, it facilitates communication between legislator and lobbyist.[7] A basic rule among lobbyists is that they do not discuss business at these sessions unless a legislator introduces the subject. As one lobbyist put it:

> We don't talk issues unless the legislator brings them up. The basic purpose is to get the legislator to call you by your first name. So much lobbying has to be done in a short span of time. You've got 30 seconds to talk to the guy and I don't want to spend any of this time introducing myself and telling him whom I represent.[8]

These findings should not be surprising, for interest groups function at the legislative level — state and national — by having their representatives communicate with legislators and transmit information to them, not by employing overt pressure and threats. Thus, if the legislator cannot get what he wants in the often hurried environment of the committee hearing [9] and lacks knowledge of, or contacts with, legislators "in the know," the lobbyist is close at hand.[10]

The information provided by the lobbyist is likely to be more technical and more precise with regard to the views and problems of a segment of the population than that obtained through channels connected to the political party apparatus.[11] Information supplied by party sources can be expected to contain a political bias geared toward success at forthcoming elections — a bias prone to overlooking the technical aspects of a bill and the areas that need attention but do not appear politically relevant at that time.

As a result, information from political parties tends to lag behind events. Popular issues such as pollution, the preservation of natural ecological relations, and the protection of the environment had to catch the public eye before both political parties jumped on the bandwagon they provided. These issues have been around for years, however, and much technical information already has been disseminated by conservationist organizations such as the Sierra Club and the Audubon Society.

Since people tend to communicate most readily with those who share similar views and backgrounds, it may be difficult for a lobbyist to gain access to a legislator who holds a key vote or can exert influence over the votes of other legislators if he possesses opposing beliefs and attitudes.[12] If the legislator's need for information is great, however, he will be more favorably disposed toward communication with lobbyists he differs with. Thus, the possibility of minimally disruptive change is facilitated as the legislator's need for information overcomes the inertia of closed communication nets based upon attitudinal and ideological similarity that tends to support the status quo.

Where such inertia is high, the lobbyist must initiate the attempts to break through it, for "the legislator has the power to vote; the lobbyist has an interest in that vote. Therefore, the lobbyist must seek to interact. Since the lobbyist has no formal power but is dependent upon one who does, interaction is a matter of necessity for him." [13] Thus, lobbyists keep open the communication channels between active sections of the community and the legislature, decreasing the chances that demands of important groups in the population will be ignored completely.

In sum, the lobbyist gains the ear of the legislator by providing information and assistance the legislator needs to carry out his obligations and responsibilities. The lobbyist may on occasion do research for the legislator and provide information about voting blocs and coalitions taking shape on bills coming before the legislature. Indeed,

> whatever their image of lobbyists, legislators are more likely to look on them as service agents than as opinion manipulators. . . . Typically, legislators utilize lobbyists as sources of influence in three ways: by calling upon lobbyists to influence other legislators, by calling upon lobbyists to help amass public opinion in favor of the legislator's position, and by including lobbyists in planning strategy in an effort to negotiate a bill through the legislature.[14]

In this context, entertainment is a meaningful activity, for it allows the legislator to "peruse the fields," and to become familiar with the area of expertise represented by the lobbyists he encounters.

Several factors create legislators' willingness to interact with lobbyists and to rely upon them as sources of assistance and information. Those peculiar to the political environment of state politics already have been mentioned as characteristics traditionally associated with strong interest group systems: short legislative sessions, frequent turnover, the amateur status of state politics, and the part-time nature of the job.[15] The strength of interest group representation and influence varies among the states, however, indicating that the need for lobbyists and the functions they perform are not constant across all states, but depend upon other variables, economic and social as well as political.

THE POLITICO-ECONOMIC SETTING

It is not difficult to establish that the economic and social systems of a society structure its political system, but it is more difficult to establish the manner in which these systems interact. If the socioeconomic structure of a state determines the behavior and importance of interest groups, it probably influences other components of the political system. Furthermore, the strength of the party system itself can inhibit or encourage interest groups. It has long been suggested that strong party cohesion in legislative voting contributes to interest groups. Yet, if we examine the causes of party voting, we find a relationship with great variation between legislative cohesion and party competition. If we probe deeper, we discover that both legislative cohesion and party competition are related to the industrialization and urbanization of a state. Accordingly, it is best to treat economic and political variables as components in a single system, rather than as independent or dependent variables.

Table 1 describes the strength of pressure groups in the American states in terms of three variables:[16] strength of party competition; legislative cohesion; and the socioeconomic variables of urban population, including per capita income, and percentage of the population employed in occupations other than agriculture, forestry, and fishing (industrialization index). Taken together, these economic factors indicate the existence or absence of a heterogeneous society with its corresponding increase or decrease in group tensions. A state that has a high per capita income, a high percentage of its population employed in industrial occupations, and a high proportion of its population living in urban areas should exhibit a strong and active group life, but not necessarily a strong pressure group system. This becomes clear if we examine the table. Pressure groups are strongest when political parties and legislative cohesion are weakest and when the socioeconomic variables are lowest. Two patterns emerge from the table. The first consists of strong pressure groups, weak parties (both electorally and legislatively), low urban population, low per capita income, and a larger proportion of the population engaged in nonindustrial occupations. The second consists of moderate or weak pressure groups, competitive parties, and an urban, industrial economy. In short, pressure politics, party politics, and socioeconomic structure are related.

Notable exceptions, however, occur in California and Michigan, which are hardly nonindustrial, nonurban states, yet they have strong pressure groups. Nevertheless, the pattern is clear enough that the deviant states do not destroy it. In the strong pressure group category we find every state in the South, where the economy is less developed and organizational memberships are the fewest. What produces a strong pressure group system in these states? The nonindustrial nature of the economy is not a fundamental cause, but rather the lack of diversity in such economies. That is, states with nonindustrial economies tend to be dominated by one type of enterprise, whereas industrial economies are keyed to a larger number of businesses and are less likely to be monopolized.

TABLE 1

The Strength of Pressure Groups in Varying Political and Economic Situations

	Types of pressure systems[a]		
Social Conditions	Strong[b] (24 states)	Moderate[c] (14 states)	Weak[d] (7 states)
Party competition			
One-party	33.3%	0%	0%
Modified one-party	37.5	42.8	0
Two-party	29.1	57.1	100.0
Cohesion of parties in legislature			
Weak cohesion	75.0	14.2	0
Moderate cohesion	12.5	35.7	14.2
Strong cohesion	12.5	50.0	85.7
Socioeconomic variables			
Urban population	58.6	65.1	73.3
Per capita income	$1,900	$2,335	$2,450
Industrialization index	88.8	92.8	94.0

[a]Alaska, Hawaii, Idaho, New Hampshire, and North Dakota are not classified or included.
[b]Alabama, Arizona, Arkansas, California, Florida, Georgia, Iowa, Kentucky, Louisiana, Maine, Michigan, Minnesota, Mississippi, Montana, Nebraska, New Mexico, North Carolina, Oklahoma, Oregon, South Carolina, Tennessee, Texas, Washington, Wisconsin.
[c]Delaware, Illinois, Kansas, Maryland, Massachusetts, Nevada, New York, Ohio, Pennsylvania, South Dakota, Utah, Vermont, Virginia, West Virginia.
[d]Colorado, Connecticut, Indiana, Missouri, New Jersey, Rhode Island, Wyoming.

Emerging Patterns of Group Conflict

The fact that interest groups thrive in nonindustrial states does not mean that there is a *single* pattern of group activity. Rather, four distinct patterns emerge from the strong pressure group category of states. First, there is the "typical" strong pressure group pattern consisting of a non-diversified economy, relatively noncompetitive party politics, and weak legislative cohesion. This pattern is descriptive of the southern states and of other states with similar economic and political systems, such as Maine. In these states the strength of interest groups is achieved by an *alliance of dominant groups*. The next pattern combines an equally nondiversified economy with two-party politics and moderate legislative cohesion, such as in Montana. Here we find that a *single dominant interest* strengthens the pressure system. The third pattern consists of a nondiversified industrial economy, two-party politics, and strong legislative cohesion. The best example of this pattern is Michigan, where there is a *conflict between two dominant groups*. Finally, California is an example of the fourth pattern, with a diversified economy, two-party politics, and weak legislative cohesion. A classic case of the free play of interest groups in a legislature unencumbered by demands originating from political parties, California illustrates the *triumph of many interests*. To understand how each system operates, we will explore them in some detail.

ALLIANCE OF DOMINANT GROUPS. A good example of the first pattern is Maine, of which Lockard writes: "In few American states are the reins of government more openly or completely in the hands of a few leaders of economic interest groups than in Maine." [17] Specifically, electric power, timber, and manufacturing — the "Big Three" — have been the catalysts for much of the political controversy in the state. Other interests occasionally voice demands, but the Big Three clearly outdistance any rivals in political activity and power. The key position of these interests in Maine's economy establishes their crucial position in state decision making. Over three-fourths of the state is woodland that is owned by a handful of timber companies and paper manufacturers. These interests, combined with power companies and textile and shoe manufacturers, are often able — insofar as their well-being is directly involved — to "control" Maine politics.

Maine, like other states with similar economic structures, went through a phase in which the dominant economic interests engaged in rather flamboyant lobbying techniques. Though more restrained today, the Big Three still are able to ensure that public policy is to their liking. Lockard points out that when Edmund Muskie was governor, he secured the passage of most of his legislative program but suffered the largest portion of his defeats on matters opposed by the Big Three. He was unable to establish an intrastate minimum wage, a state labor relations commission, a state income tax, and a corporate franchise tax. Perhaps most indicative of the power of economic interests in Maine was the defeat of a proposed water pollution law in 1955. In spite of a determined effort to convince the legislature that the prohibition of water pollution would not harm industry, the bill was defeated easily. The passage of strong anti-pollution legislation in the 1969–1970 session, however, indicates that the situation has changed somewhat.

Since nondiversified economies, weak parties, and strong pressure groups are a "normal" combination, it is not surprising that the political processes of Maine and the southern states — most of which display this combination — are quite similar. V. O. Key, Jr., for example, describes the politics of Alabama:

> The Extension Service — big farmer amalgam, which covers the entire state but is most potent in the black belt, usually teams up with the big money interests. . . . The "big mules" probably exert their strength far more effectively in the politics of legislation than in gubernatorial campaigns. And it is mainly in the legislature that questions of concern for them are settled: measures of taxation and regulation.[18]

At the time Key wrote this, Alabama had an urban population of 30.2 per cent. With an urban population of 54.8 per cent, according to the census of 1960, Alabama is no longer as noncompetitive a field of combat for the large farmer — "big mule" interests and labor organizations, for example, are becoming more active.

Increasing urbanization and industrialization do seem to countervail against formerly dominant economic power groups. For example, organizations lobbying in favor of state right-to-work laws have generally been successful in southern or midwestern states where union membership is low and union political organization weak. Right-to-work laws have been easily defeated in states with strong and active unions, such as California and Illinois, and have never been a serious issue in other heavily unionized states, such as New York and New Jersey.[19] The pressure for the enactment of this kind of legislation is concentrated in such states as Maine, New Hampshire, New Mexico, Vermont, Idaho, Kansas, and Delaware, few of which boast any appreciable union membership.[20] Also, in those states currently having right-to-work laws, there is some evidence of a counterrevolution as urbanization and industrialization increase. In Georgia, for example, labor leaders who remember the days when speaking favorably of organized labor on the floor of the General Assembly invited informal but severe censure have seen strong legislative support for improved workmen's compensation laws develop and have adopted the repeal of the state's right-to-work law as a long-range, but feasible, goal. One such leader said, "Things were different at the State Capitol this year. The atmosphere has changed. Labor was treated in a much different manner. Labor was respected. . . . We have our head in the door." [21]

SINGLE DOMINANT INTEREST.   In Montana, an example of the second system, the economy has become somewhat more diversified, the urban population has increased, and the dominant role of the Anaconda Company has been diminished by self-restraint and competition. In a state where mining is the major nonagricultural source of personal income, Anaconda is the largest employer. Although "the Company," as it is known in Montana, began its operations in mining for copper, it now owns mills, aluminum companies, railroads, fabricating plants, and forests. The enormity of the Anaconda empire is described by Thomas Payne:

> Its strength rests not only in its wealth and resources, but also in its elaborate network of relationships with key citizens, banks, legal firms, and business organizations throughout the state. Rare is that unit of local government — county, city, or school district — that does not have among its official family an associate, in some capacity, of the Anaconda Company.[22]

In addition, until 1959, Anaconda controlled a chain of newspapers with a combined circulation greater than that of all the other daily papers in the state.

In the turbulent frontier atmosphere of the West, Anaconda played the classic role of economic royalist, making frequent and extravagant forays into the electoral process. Politicians such as Burton K. Wheeler became legendary as courageous foes of the company in much the same manner that Senator Borah built a political career upon the crusade against the trusts. Much of Montana's political history reflects a basic division of the population: men were either for the Company, or, in the case of the unions and Farmer's Union, against it. In Wheeler's autobiography, the struggle against Anaconda is the major theme of the portions dealing with his career prior to becoming a senator. Conflict in the state seemed to be structured around the Company rather than the political parties. Wheeler writes that "in the 1911–1912 legislature the Democrats controlled the House, the

Republicans controlled the Senate, and the Company controlled the leaders of both." [23]

Public policy in Montana reflects the power of Anaconda, although it is hard to imagine that an elite could be as invulnerable as the Company is described by its enemies. Montana politics is not completely dominated by Anaconda; although the Company is a major actor that can claim success in many instances, it sometimes has been forced to accept defeat. For instance, its efforts to elect the "right" candidates have met with only moderate success. Wheeler was consistently supported by organized labor and enjoyed electoral success in spite of, perhaps because of, Anaconda's opposition.

The best example of the strength and weakness of Anaconda in Montana is the struggle to increase the taxation of mines. The mining companies had succeeded in including an extraordinary clause in the state constitution when Montana was admitted to the Union. The clause provided that mining claims could be taxed only "at the price paid the United States therefor" and that taxes could be levied on "net proceeds" only. In accordance with this constitutional provision, oil production, which grossed only one-sixth as much as mines, paid twice as much in taxes. Mines contributed less than 9 per cent of Montana's revenue while farms contributed 32 per cent. As early as 1916 the legislature had become aware of the inequities of this situation, and in 1918 a faculty member of the University of Montana began a study of the tax system, only to be dismissed by the chancellor. A book based on his research was published, however, and Anaconda's role in its suppression became apparent.[24] As a result of the furor over the author's dismissal, the state board of education reinstated him with back pay.

The next step in the taxation episode took place in 1920 when Wheeler — with his reputation as an enemy of the Company — ran as Democratic candidate for governor against Republican Joseph Dixon, who had the Company's support. Wheeler promised tax revision but was defeated by Dixon who promptly urged the legislature to figure out some way to increase the taxes on mines. His proposal for a license tax based on each ton of ore produced was defeated in the legislature with Anaconda lobbyists working vigorously against him. To overcome his lack of influence with the legislature, the governor submitted the tax revision to the voters in the form of a referendum in the 1924 election. Dixon, now the enemy of the Company, lost the election. The taxing proposal was approved, however, even though Anaconda maintained that "the mining industry cannot stand any additional tax load." [25]

Defeats such as this convinced the Company that its wisest course of action lay in more moderate demands. In the 1920s the Company press was vitriolic in its treatment of its opponents; in the 1930s the papers became less venomous and simply did not mention enemies or their activities. By the 1940s and early 1950s the papers began to print hostile speeches and their editorials took on a rather neutral flavor; in the late 1950s the Company disposed of its newspapers. In recent years Anaconda has remained as quiet as possible, confining itself to blocking adverse legislation and reducing its efforts to influence the electoral process.[26]

The experiences of Montana with the Anaconda Company in the thirties and forties seem roughly parallel to those of other states with a single dominant economic interest — such as oil in Texas or Du Pont in Delaware. In both of these states the reputation for absolute control is widespread. However, a difference between specific and generalized power can be suggested. Anaconda is probably capable of protecting or enhancing its interest in areas of specific concern, but success in a specific area can lead to misleading assumptions about generalized power, especially by those who use power as a symbol to be attacked. Thus, we might ask: do the timber, paper, power, and manufacturing interests control Maine or do they partially control public policy as it impinges upon their interests? Does Anaconda control Montana or is the company a significant and frequently decisive determinant of policy in its area of involvement? The same question could be asked in other states where policy disputes are bipolarized by the concentration of economic power.

For instance, the chairman of the Texas Democratic State Executive Committee once said: "It may not be a wholesome thing to say, but the oil industry today is in complete control of state politics and state government." [27] No one needs to be reminded of the loyalty of Texas politicians to the oil depletion allowance in the federal tax structure, but this matter directly and vitally affects the oil producers. A recent case study of the Texas legislature suggests that oil producers are indeed influential, but are opposed by equally influential competitors. The study covered the 1961 session of the Texas legislature, which, in attempting to pass a tax bill, had to decide between income and sales taxes. The governor, trying to avoid either solution, presented a program calling for, among other things, an increase in the severance tax on natural gas production. Manufacturing groups, led by the Texas Mid-Continent Oil and Gas Association, countered with the general sales tax proposal. The opposition to the governor was sufficient to ensure that the sales tax would be the final solution, but the legislature also supported a tax on the natural gas pipeline companies.[28]

Neither side enjoyed total victory, and neither group of protagonists controlled the outcome of this issue, much less the sum of the decisions reached by the state government.

The confusion between power and the potentiality for power occurs most frequently in bipolarized states. It is natural to presume that those with sources of influence will choose to maximize them, but this assumption is not always true. We have seen how Anaconda restricted its activities. Many other dominant economic interests have found it prudent to follow a similar course of action. In their study of American tariff policy, Raymond A. Bauer, Ithiel de Sola Pool, and Lewis A. Dexter found that large corporations were reluctant to speak openly of their views on foreign trade because of sensitivity about their public image. With so much weight to throw around, the giants were afraid of a public display of strength. In Delaware, for example, Du Pont is traditionally protectionist, but none of the elected officials from the state think that they are under pressure to oppose reciprocal trade. The authors explain: "A business can be too big to be politically effective along some lines." [29] This is not to say that large companies are always the "good guys." Rather, it means that unless such companies can operate within the processes of government that are relatively secure from direct public participation, the fear of public response is sufficient to restrain their actions. Perhaps this provides a partial explanation as to why right-to-work laws are usually approved by legislatures in nonindustrial states. In industrial states most large corporations are reluctant to attack labor unions directly.

The low-keyed approach to influence that is increasingly undertaken by apparently dominant interests of a state and the lack of "total victory" accompanying their efforts indicate that the increasing diversification of the American economy and the urbanization of society are reducing the power of single dominant interests. This reduction has been accelerated in recent years, for diversification and urbanization have brought an expansion of communications, an increasing awareness of economic and social interdependence. Issues that in the past have been of local or regional concern now arouse national interest. This dynamic widens the basis of potential support for groups opposing entrenched interests. Issues such as water and environmental pollution, the treatment of minorities, and auto safety could be successfully manipulated by strong local or regional interests as long as the issue interested only people and organizations within their sphere of influence. Attempts by powerful area-specific interests to control the situation are much less likely to achieve success when they must counter the efforts of individuals such as Ralph Nader and the late Dr. Martin

Luther King, who command attention from a broad and active spectrum of the population. It is even more difficult for powerful interests to engage in "low visibility" efforts to influence legislators when spectacular events such as riots, demonstrations, and leaking offshore oil platforms bring national attention to the issues in question and turn a spotlight on the actions of legislators at the moment when reaction to the event has unified opposition forces. As a result, the number of states in the single dominant interest pattern of the theoretical classification has been diminished.

Diminution has not been limited to single interests alone. For example, we saw how the Big Three in Maine were easily able to defeat legislation aimed at curbing water pollution in 1955, but were themselves defeated in 1969 and 1970.[30] Public opinion across the nation had come to favor such measures, and events such as uncontrolled oil leakage from an offshore platform in the Santa Barbara Channel had alerted voters in Maine to the magnitude of the problems posed by pollution.[31] The issues were further dramatized when, almost simultaneously with the passage of the legislation, a large oil tanker ran aground and broke up off the coast of Nova Scotia, endangering the livelihood of fishing and tourist interests in the area.[32] Under these conditions the Big Three were unable to turn the tide running against them.

CONFLICT BETWEEN TWO DOMINANT GROUPS. The states considered up to this point have had rather underdeveloped economies, that contribute to bipolarization of political conflicts. Michigan is an industrial, urban, competitive state with strong cohesion in legislative parties — a combination of factors sharply deviant from the normal strong pressure group pattern. Michigan is the only state in the strong pressure group category that contains no single characteristic in common with the other states in this category, at least insofar as the variables in Table 1 are concerned. However, Michigan's economy is perhaps less diversified than even that of Montana, since its economic life is strongly keyed to the activities of the automotive industry, a fact that has contributed to periodic crises that probably would not have occurred in a more diversified economy. A progressive diversification of the economy now is taking place. In 1951, automotive workers accounted for 22.7 per cent of all wage and salary workers in the state (excluding farm workers, railroad employees, and the self-employed), and 39.3 per cent of the manufacturing wage and salary workers; by 1968 these percentages had declined to 13.4 and 28.5 respectively.[33] Still, automobile manufacturers are the largest single employer.

These circumstances promote the conflict between union and management that has been a consistent theme in Michigan politics since industrialization.[34] The presence of many organized interests in Michigan, as in most urban states, substantiate the assumptions of a pluralistic theory of power. However, as in the other states examined so far, when matters of concern to powerful interest groups are raised, these groups become major determinants of public policy. As Joseph LaPalombara concludes, "No major issues of policy (taxation, social legislation, labor legislation, etc.) is [sic] likely to be decided in Michigan without the intervention, within their respective parties and before agencies of government, of automotive labor and automotive management." [35]

The major difference between Michigan and the other bipolarized states is the degree to which interest group cleavages have been mirrored and, hence, institutionalized in the structure of the political parties and the legislature. In Maine, the Big Three functioned to some extent within the Republican party, but the loose and sprawling nature of that organization made efforts at control hardly worth the effort since control of the party would not improve the chances of controlling the legislature. In Montana, Anaconda worked first with one party, then with another, finally showing slightly more interest in the Republicans. However, LaPalombara speaks of the intervention in Michigan of unions and management "within their respective parties." [36] This statement reflects the fact that the Michigan unions, especially the United Automobile Workers, are deeply involved in the affairs of the Democratic party while the automotive managers are equally involved in the Republican party. It would be an exaggeration to maintain that either of these two interests controls the party, but labor and management are surely the most active and influential components of "their" parties.[37]

Neither management nor labor makes much of an effort to extend its base of operations beyond the parties, for the cohesion of the legislative parties is strong. On matters of labor legislation, the Michigan legislature has revealed parties as cohesive as those of the House of Commons. For example, in the 1954 session of the legislature the indexes of cohesion on partisan roll calls were 77 for the house Democrats and 75 for the senate Democrats. However, on partisan roll calls involving labor legislation the index of cohesion for house and senate Democrats was 97.[38]

A recent study of issue conflict in the fifty states based upon a questionnaire administered to state legislators in 1963 indicates that the labor-management bifurcation still follows party lines. According to the analysis contained in Wayne L. Francis, *Legislative Issues in the Fifty States,* Michigan ranks sixth among the states in the amount of partisan conflict

perceived by a sample of legislators from that state and fourth in amount
of pressure group conflict perceived. Ranks on the nonparty (or cross-
party) categories of regional and factional conflicts, on the other hand, are
considerably lower, 13 and 47, respectively.[39] If interest group conflict were
not primarily related to party conflict, we would expect that the use of other
than party channels of influence by opposing interests would raise the rankings of regional or factional conflict to the point where they exceeded or at
least came close to the rank held by partisan conflict.

It would seem, then, that the coincidence of cleavage contributes to
an intensification of group conflict in Michigan. Rather than serving as
moderators of group conflict — as the national parties do — the Michigan
parties communicate interest group values to the electorate and to the governmental officeholders.[40] Still, the vigor of pressure groups does not mean
that the Michigan parties function as auxiliaries; if anything, the reverse is
true. Neither unions nor management are so cohesive as to avoid the
periodic squabbles that allow other interests to compete more effectively.
Further, if unions and management are the single largest contributors to
their respective parties, it is these parties that maintain the machinery
necessary for the contesting of elections. It would be hard to imagine the
United Automobile Workers deciding to withdraw support from the Democratic party.[41] Key's description of the pressure group as a "junior partner"
in the alliance with a party holds true even in Michigan.[42] The unions must
remain Democratic in order to maintain a viable bargaining position. If
the pressure group has little choice but to support party candidates, the
party usually assumes a position of dominance in the relationship.

TRIUMPH OF MANY INTERESTS.   The economic structure of California is more diversified than that of any state considered in this analysis.
Raw materials, which were primarily derived from forest land in Maine,
for example, are abundant and of considerable variety in California. Manufacturing enterprises range from cement to motion pictures, and agriculture
is far from a single-crop activity. Under these circumstances, although the
economic basis for strong pressures is apparent, the structure of economic
activity leads to a fragmentation of interest group activity. Indeed, the
diversification of the economy and the attendant competitiveness of politics
make it difficult to comprehend the strength that interest groups have been
able to develop in California.

At one point in California's history, a single interest — the railroads,
especially the Southern Pacific — did dominate both parties and the legislature.[43] However, the national reaction against the "trusts" that arose in the

early years of the twentieth century contributed to a wave of reformism in California, weakening the parties and, ironically, paving the way for pressure groups that, even when the most lurid and sensational exposés are discounted, were perhaps more powerful than those in any other state legislature. One feature of party-weakening reform was the introduction of cross-filing in elections. From 1917 until 1954 the election laws of California provided that a person could contest both the Democratic and Republican nominations without his party affiliation appearing on either ballot. After 1954 party labels were required, and in 1959 cross-filing was abolished. The system of cross-filing seriously weakened the ability of the party to assume any significance in the consciousness of the legislator. Further, the lack of any effective party organization left candidates for the state legislature on their own as they sought adequate funds for campaigning. As in the southern one-party states, the interest groups of California were willing and anxious to meet this need for capital.

The spectacular nature of California politics and lobbying attracted reporters and resulted in some extravagant statements concerning the nature and source of interest group strength in California.[44] Recently, California politics has come under the scrutiny of more systematic observers. In his superb study of the California legislature, William Buchanan looks carefully at interest groups in California and concludes that the sensationalism of journalism should not obscure the fact that, especially during the "lobby era" of 1942 to 1953, the initiation of public policy was largely the responsibility of organized groups.[45]

During the administration of Governor Earl Warren, the practice of cross-filing became quite common and the viability of parties diminished. Buchanan notes that "the advantage went to the candidate who best could obscure his party affiliation, attract or pay for attention in the press, and wrangle endorsements from editors and the local units for pressure groups." [46] Very few legislators could afford to meet the costs of such requirements and very few could resist the temptation of easy money from interest groups. The interest-dominated environment of California is well illustrated by the perceptions of legislators of their career patterns. Nine per cent of the California legislators referred to interest groups as sponsors of their careers as compared to 1 per cent in New Jersey and 2 per cent in Ohio. Only in Tennessee, where parties are less competitive than those in California, did legislators (16 per cent) refer to interest groups as sponsors more frequently.[47]

In one sense, the interest groups in California actually resemble political parties in organization. The most famous lobbyist, Artie Samish, expended a great amount of money and energy in the electoral process. Samish began his career as a lobbyist for bus companies in the 1930s but soon expanded his operations to include a host of other interests, including the California State Brewers' Institute, railroads, horse racing, gambling, motion pictures, and many others.[48] It is not unusual in the state legislatures for lobbyists to represent more than one client. Moreover, Samish was a successful agent for his numerous clients. In most cases legislators see relatively little of multi-group lobbyists because they are frequently responsible for a series of explicit and limited interests that are concerned with a small portion of the legislative output. There is little doubt, however, that Samish's influence with the California legislature was considerable. Buchanan maintains that Samish's influence was developed not from the fact that his clients were affluent but because he welded the diverse interests he represented into an organization that functioned as a political party in the individualized environment of California politics. The common denominator of these interests was that they were all industries new to the state when Samish began to recruit his organization in the 1930s. Samish's main effort was to prevent state taxation of these enterprises.

Other constellations of interest groups functioned simultaneously with the Samish organization but not necessarily in competition with it. For example, a "conservative lobby" of insurance companies, large farmers, and utilities were interested in preventing any departure from an antitax philosophy and found cooperation with the Samish organization useful. This collection of interest groups, essentially nonideological like a typical American political party, selected candidates to run for office and supplied them with the funds for effective campaigning. When campaign costs were high and parties unwilling to pull their share of the load, the Samish organization was the most significant factor in the life of the legislator. Of this situation, Buchanan writes:

> In the absence of adequate party machinery at the local level they [interest groups] took over what is ordinarily the party's function of financing and managing campaigns. Thus they came to restrict the potential candidate's route of access to legislative power. It is not difficult then to snatch from the limp hands of the party the privilege of organizing the legislative chambers. Once influential in legislative organization, lobbyists could make attractive offers of exchange of power inside the legislature.[49]

The California experience is somewhat special due to the unusual legal restrictions on partisan activity. However, it affords us an opportunity to speculate on the relationship of parties and pressure groups in a period of flux. The addition of party labels to the ballot in 1954 coincided with structural reforms in the legislature that gave political parties a part in organizing that body. During the same period the legislature, stung by national publicity surrounding the activities of lobbyists, passed a lobby control act. An embryonic partisanship — expressed first in the form of factional alignments — indicated that the legislature was moving away from lobby dominance and toward active participation by parties. In 1957, the year the California legislators were interviewed in connection with the preparation of *The Legislative System,* partisanship still had not developed to a degree comparable with other urban, competitive states. Three out of five legislators believed parties played little or no part in the legislative process, a proportion nearly as high as that of Tennessee, a weak minority party state. It is significant, however, that in this unsettled situation the Democratic party was judged to be more influential than the Republican party. While legislators did not perceive parties as influential, roll-call analysis indicated that party membership accounted for more divisions in voting than any other characteristic of the members. Party influence was growing and was more important than the members themselves believed.

Did emerging partisanship reduce the influence of interest groups? We should be cautious not to imply a single cause-effect relationship. After all, legislative salaries had increased to the point where it was possible to survive in Sacramento without the largess of lobbyists, and the exposés of Artie Samish had reduced the legitimacy of lobbying to some extent. Further, lobbying by the Samish organization had developed during the 1930s, a period that, by California standards, was partisan. Nevertheless, there does appear to be some inverse relationship between the strength of parties and interest groups. As the parties began to play some role, however small, in the legislative process, they also began to meet campaign costs, which reduced the necessity of interest groups. In terms of legislative output, the challenge to the interest groups by parties resulted in 1959 in the first significant increase in beer taxes, despite the prediction of the brewers, once the heart of the Samish organization, that the tax could be defeated.

CONTRASTING PATTERNS: STATES WITHOUT A DOMINANT PRESSURE SYSTEM. A strong party system contributes to a balancing of power between parties and interest groups or, in some cases, to a clear dominance of the parties. If the strength of parties produces a more balanced distribution of power, we can expect to find that interest groups are vigorous and active, but clearly dependent upon parties for access to governmental decision makers. Contributions are channeled to the candidate through the party organization, and the candidate owes fealty to the party. Further, each party tends to develop its own constellation of interests from which support can be expected. These interests rarely attempt to persuade individual legislators to cast a favorable vote on a specific issue but rather devote their attention exclusively to party leaders. In these situations it is clear that the party is in control. In Connecticut, for example, parties are able to punish an interest group if its demands become intolerable.

In contrast to this pattern of cooperation, Missouri is an example of a genuinely low pressure system. Salisbury has described the pressure system of Missouri as one of ad hoc rather than permanent alliances. He found that broad coalitions of groups in conflict with rival combinations do exist, but are a rare phenomenon.[50] The shifting, temporary issue-oriented alliances in Missouri cannot compete with the stable and competitive party system. Lacking a major economic cleavage, interest groups have not developed either the ability to work closely with a party as in Michigan or the power to circumvent and dominate the parties as in Maine or California. In fact, Missouri and California have similarly diverse economies. It is probable that, had California not undergone its unique historical development, its pressure system would have been as weak as Missouri's. Diffusion and fragmentation of power, a pluralistic situation endemic to most industrial, urban states, provides parties with the opportunity to function without severe competition from interest groups.

LOBBYING AS A COMMUNICATIONS PROCESS

In order to achieve success in state politics, an interest group must have access to key decision makers. Up to this point, factors within the political and socioeconomic system over which interest groups have no control have been described in terms of their influence upon the performance of groups. Such factors structure and limit the activities of interest groups and success or failure is probably more dependent upon the nature of the society than upon the skills or techniques of lobbyists. Nevertheless, it is within the power of interest groups to maximize whatever advantages accrue to them through their place in a social system. A high status manufacturers' organization might sacrifice its initial advantage by using lobbying techniques that offend the sensibilities of legislators or make it difficult for them to vote the way the organization would prefer. If, for example, such an organization publicly threatens to defeat all legislators who vote the "wrong" way, it may be necessary for these legislators to establish their independence by voting against the wishes of the organization. In Massachusetts, for example, 66 per cent of those who believed they were pressured by education lobbyists favored an increased education budget as opposed to 90 per cent who felt no pressure. The direction of the relationship was the same in the other states sampled, as Figure 1 shows. Access, then, does depend to some extent upon skills. In lobbying, as in any other profession, such skills are acquired by experience and practice. A pertinent question is: how experienced are state lobbyists?

The Characteristics of State Lobbying

The experience of lobbyists in relation to legislators varies widely. Although Patterson found that about 47 per cent of his sample of forty-three Oklahoma lobbyists were registered for their first term at the time of the interview,[51] Massachusetts, North Carolina, and Utah "had more 'freshmen' among legislators than lobbyists and more lobbyists than legislators who have been around for 25 years or more." [52] The lobbyists had also chalked up more mean years of experience than legislators, the differences ranging from 1.1 in Oregon to 7.3 in Utah.

To lament the amateurism of the legislators, however, is to forget that the lobbyist is often not any more of a professional. Walter DeVries's study of lobbying in Michigan, for example, points out that the majority of lobbyists are not very frequent visitors to Lansing; only a core of regulars

FIGURE 1
Relation between Legislators' Belief That They Were "Pressured" by Education Lobbyists and Their Attitude Toward Education Goals: Percentage Favoring Increased Education Budget

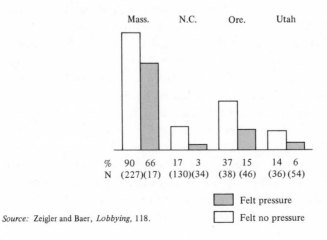

	Mass.	N.C.	Ore.	Utah
%	90 66	17 3	37 15	14 6
N	(227)(17)	(130)(34)	(38) (46)	(36)(54)

◼ Felt pressure
☐ Felt no pressure

Source: Zeigler and Baer, *Lobbying,* 118.

are really familiar with the vagaries of the legislative process. Of equal significance is the fact that not very many lobbyists spend their full time in lobbying during the session. Patterson found that over 60 per cent of the Oklahoma lobbyists spend half their time or less engaged in lobbying.[53] In Massachusetts, lobbyists spend an average of 2.5 hours a day on the job, in North Carolina 3.9, and in Utah 4.5. Only in Oregon, a weak party-strong lobby state, does the figure approach full-time proportions at 7.7.[54] Like legislative skills, lobbying skills develop with experience and practice; like state legislators, relatively few lobbyists possess such experience.

What kinds of backgrounds do state lobbyists have? One striking difference between state and national lobbyists is that few state lobbyists are lawyers. Milbrath found that most Washington lobbyists were lawyers, but this is not true in the states for which we have information. In Oklahoma, only four out of a sample of forty-three listed law as their occupation. The figures for Michigan, Massachusetts, Oregon, and Utah are 12, 21, 19, and 10 per cent respectively. However, in Virginia and North Carolina the respective percentages were 46 and 51.[55] Whether the higher proportion of lawyers as lobbyists in southern states is a coincidence or a reflection of the cultural or political structure of the South cannot be ascertained from so few cases. The largest single occupational category in both Oklahoma and North Carolina is that of full-time executive or employee of an association engaged in lobbying. In Virginia, association executives are second to lawyers. In Massachusetts, Oregon, and Utah professionals and managers, not lawyers, occupy the modal category. Beyond this, the occupational background of lobbyists has little pattern. The absence of lawyers in most states is worthy of attention because of the popularly held assumption that legal experience contributes to political effectiveness.

That legal experience may not always be necessary for effective lobbying is indicated by the relation between attitudinal similarity and interaction. In Massachusetts, North Carolina, Utah, and Oregon, legislators with high interaction rates are the most likely to perceive lobbyists as "intelligent and knowledgeable" [56] — an attitude conducive to further interaction. Since individuals coming from similar backgrounds are more likely to share similar attitudes and viewpoints than those with differing backgrounds, occupation can make a difference in attitude, especially in the crucial first few encounters when the lobbyist may have to break through a legislator's negative view of his purpose and function. Shared attitudes also contribute to lobbying effectiveness, for the greater the congruence in communicating, the less ambiguity is likely to be involved in the transaction. In a situation of greater congruence, the lobbyist is able to make his point clearly and the legislator finds out what he wanted to know. As a result of the communication, neither is likely to be surprised by the actions of the other, and mutual faith is reinforced. The same cannot be said of transactions involving considerable ambiguity.[57] In the strong lobby states of Oregon and Utah where "among legislators, professional and managerial personnel without legal training far outnumber lawyers," [58] the percentage of lobbyists who are lawyers is correspondingly low.

It would seem that interest groups would be anxious to employ people who had an intimate knowledge of the legislature, and that ex-legislators would be eagerly sought after. They may be sought, but relatively few ever become lobbyists. Zeller, Patterson, Epstein, and DeVries have called attention to this absence.[59] This does not mean that ex-legislators are not useful as lobbyists. DeVries's study suggests a significant relationship between any amount of legislative experience and lobbying effectiveness, but since so few ex-legislators become lobbyists, very few groups benefit from their experience.

The scarcity of ex-legislators acting as lobbyists could be partially explained by differences in career motivations and job orientation between legislators and lobbyists. Legislators tend to take an interest in politics fairly early in life. Over half the legislators in the Zeigler-Baer study recalled having an interest in politics before they were twenty years of age, as compared with slightly more than 10 per cent of the lobbyists interviewed. Similarly, one-third of the legislators but 85 per cent of the lobbyists stated they previously had nonpolitical occupations.[60] The legislator, generally a man moving upward, contrasts greatly with the laterally mobile lobbyist. While the former can enjoy the security of a relatively high status position, the latter faces considerable status insecurity — a fact reflected in his tendency to "drift into" the lobbying profession. The highest percentage of legislators in the four-state sample drifting into their position is 22, in North Carolina; the lowest percentage drifting into the job of lobbying is 79, in Oregon, a strong interest group state that views lobbyists favorably.[61]

On the other hand, quite a few lobbyists have had some form of governmental or political experience. Whereas the previous experience of legislators is likely to involve elected positions on the local level, lobbyists are much more likely to have occupied an appointed position on the state or national level. Figure 2 details these generalizations.

DeVries found no significant relationship between nonlegislative experience and lobbying effectiveness, confirming the supposition that legislative service provides the most desirable background for lobbying.[62]

Moreover, there is a significant relationship between length of government service and effectiveness: the longer the experience, the greater the effectiveness. The same relationship exists with regard to experience in a political party. Milbrath noted that the Washington lobbyists find it useful to avoid partisan activity and that "the party with which a man identifies appears to be relatively unimportant in lobbying." [63] The competitive nature of Congress would make open partisanship hazardous, but in states in which one party can be relied upon to control the legislature the risks are less and the advantages considerable. Although Patterson found that few Oklahoma lobbyists had held party positions, this condition did not hold for Michigan and North Carolina where more than half the lobbyists had been active in party affairs.[64] Membership in the dominant legislative party is an asset to lobbyists, who can use party ties as a means of access to legislators. Thus, in Michigan the lobbyists with a considerable number of years of experience in the Republican party were more effective than those lacking such experience. Certainly this would be true in a state in which the party greatly

FIGURE 2
Proportion of Legislators and Lobbyists Holding Previous Local, State, and National Government Office

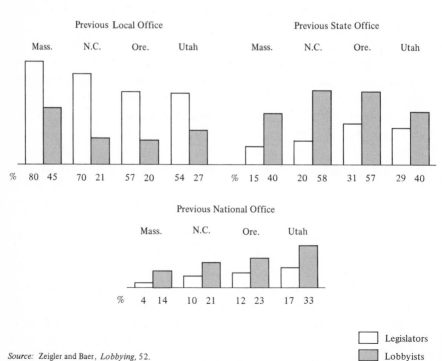

Source: Zeigler and Baer, *Lobbying,* 52.

influenced the determination of public policy. A strong party system does not necessarily mean the diminution of the influence of interest groups but may mean that pressure is put upon holders of party office rather than upon the party rank and file. This is the case in Michigan and Massachusetts, for example, where labor organizations serve frequently as auxiliaries to the parties.

No clear relationship between the governmental experience of lobbyists and the strength of interest groups appears in the four-state study, since the state with the largest percentage of lobbyists with such experience is North Carolina, a weak lobby state, and the state with the second highest percentage, Utah, is a strong lobby state.[65] Irregularities peculiar to the states concerned could account for this, however, and until data covering more states can be gathered for this particular variable the precise form of the relationship cannot be discerned. Nevertheless, the data highlight an area of difference between lobbyist and legislator. The former is likely to have become directly involved in the activities of interest groups while the latter, holding elective positions, has developed a different orientation. This adds another reason for the lack of occupational interchange between legislator and lobbyist.[66]

How Necessary for Access Is Money?

The use of money in establishing a satisfactory relationship with a group of legislators cannot be ignored, but it can be put in proper perspective. It is relatively easy for journalists to nod knowingly at the magic power of money and to assume that merely by uttering the word they have offered the insider's explanation of how legislation is enacted. But what does money buy? How is money spent? These questions are frequently left unanswered. Consider entertainment, for example. Reports on various states such as Wisconsin, Florida, and Michigan suggest that lobbyists at the state level do more entertaining than lobbyists in Washington.[67] State lobbyists do not rate entertaining as high as other techniques, however, and its role is probably exaggerated by popular accounts. In the four-state sample, committee hearings were the primary method of communication between lobbyist and legislator. The percentages listing "social gatherings" as a method of communication are small: 4 per cent in Massachusetts, 2 per cent in North Carolina and Oregon, and none in Utah.[68] Also, the style of entertaining is more circumspect than might be expected. Although some lobbyists maintain an open bar for legislators, most entertaining falls into the category of lunches for small groups or annual dinners for the entire legislature. As noted earlier, such affairs do more to create access than to provide a place for discussion of explicit legislation. A lobbyist who relied upon entertaining exclusively would not be very successful, although in Michigan, the more effective lobbyists spend more time entertaining than the less effective lobbyists.

We can exclude overt bribery from our consideration of state lobbying techniques because it is either extremely rare or impossible to substantiate. In addition, it is ineffective: in the four-state sample, both legislators and lobbyists rank it as the least effective of all methods of communication.[69] On the other hand, contributions to political campaigns can be an important part of group strategy. Realistically speaking, money does not win elections. If it did, Republicans would win oftener than they do. But money can create a relationship of gratitude and trust. Politicians seeking public office have basic campaign costs to meet, and those organizations willing to meet some or all of these costs certainly can be assured of at least formal access to decision makers. The Artie Samish organization in California was perhaps the prototype of the interest group using money for this purpose. More recent examples are equally useful because we can compare the use of campaign contributions in states with competitive and noncompetitive party systems. The basic difference seems to be that in the competitive systems the contributions are channeled to candidates through the party organization, while in one-party systems the contact between candidate and organization is not marred by an intermediary. Within the competitive systems, a distinction can be made between groups that contribute with a specific goal in mind and groups that make contributions because of general agreement with a political party.

Andrew Hacker's study of the conflict between railroads and truckers in Pennsylvania is instructive of interest groups that contribute with a specific goal in mind. The truckers, undertaking a long and arduous campaign to repeal a state law limiting the weight of trucks to 45,000 pounds, contributed heavily to the campaigns of state legislators. The specific goal was the repeal of the law; the partisan sympathies of the trucking companies did not matter. Therefore the $76,000 collected by the Pennsylvania Motor Truck Association was divided almost equally between the parties. Hacker writes that the organization expected to recoup this expenditure by revenue gained from a more favorable weight law: "Many of the men who voted for S.615 (to increase the permissible weight of trucks) knew that they were doing so to repay a campaign debt or in anticipation of future contributions. . . . They consciously made a bargain to limit their freedom in return for a payment." [70]

Such an unequivocal exchange is unlikely to take place in situations where groups with more continuing and long-range goals are giving the money. The best example is, of course, organized labor. Labor contributions usually flow through the offices of the Democratic party on a more or less permanent arrangement. Labor organizations, because of their relatively large membership, are also anxious to offer their services in the mobilization of voters for the Democratic party. Alexander Heard points out that the financial resources and potential voting strength of unions are concentrated in seventeen * states where the percentage of union members among persons of voting age equaled or exceeded the national percentage and where the percentage of nonagricultural employers was 30 or more.[71] In such states as Massachusetts and Michigan, the collaboration between the unions and the Democratic party is complete to the point where the unions serve as auxiliary parties and assume many of the responsibilities of the formal party organization. In Massachusetts, Lockard writes, "In some areas the Democratic party . . . will leave to labor almost the whole job of campaigning for state candidates, and in many campaigns the money labor gives is a very crucial factor in the Democratic effort." [72] In other states of the seventeen mentioned by Heard, the collaboration is less formal. In Washington, for example, the unions are friendly to the Democratic party but have not infiltrated to the extent that they have in Michigan and Massachusetts. These contributions are probably not accompanied by explicit expectations. Also, it is likely that, at least in Michigan and Massachusetts, less money filters down to candidates for the state legislature than ends up in the coffers of gubernatorial candidates.

In one-party states, the exchange between candidate and interest groups is more explicit because of the absence of a party organization. Joseph Bernd's investigation of contributions in Georgia shows that about 50 per cent of the money received by major candidates for governor came from liquor dealers and highway contractors, both of whom have clear and narrowly defined expectations.[73] Here again, the money flows past the legislature to the place where it is expected to do the most good.

While campaign contributions do form a part of the strategy of those groups in state politics able to afford it, it would be inaccurate to assume that more contributions are made at the state than the national level. The total amount of money spent at the state level is much lower, although a little money goes a longer way at the state level, where candidates are per-

* The states are New York, Pennsylvania, California, Illinois, Ohio, Michigan, New Jersey, Indiana, Massachusetts, Missouri, Wisconsin, Washington, Minnesota, West Virginia, Oregon, Montana, and Nevada.

sonally less well-off and generally of lower social status than candidates to
the national legislature.

There is some indication that the extent of campaign contributions
varies with the strength of the interest group system. "In the weak-lobby
states, less than a majority of legislators have received financial help in
their campaigns from interest groups (32 per cent of legislators in Massachusetts and 42 per cent of legislators in North Carolina)." In Oregon and
Utah the figures are 58 and 62.[74] The most visible result of such contributions appears as an increased rate of interaction between legislator and
lobbyist, indicated in Figure 3.

In terms of the strength of the interest group system, it would appear
that a dollar spent supporting legislators in weak-lobby states goes farther
than one spent in strong-lobby states where a favorable environment for
communication already exists, although Utah is an exception. In that state
the inexperience of the legislators and their consequent need for information rather than any special regard for lobbyists accounts for most of their
interaction. Thus, a campaign dollar spent in Utah is probably worth more
than one spent in Oregon.

Money may also be used in public relations campaigns, but, with a
few notable exceptions, state interest groups are not as concerned with the
"new lobby" technique of mass persuasion. Public relations campaigns usually occur when state interest groups have an affiliation with a national
organization that provides much of the propaganda. For instance, the
struggle over right-to-work laws has attracted national organizations that
supply state units or sympathetic but unaffiliated organizations with litera-

FIGURE 3
*Comparative Percentages of Legislators in the High Interaction Category Who
Did/Did Not Receive Campaign Support*

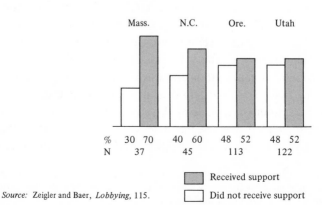

	Mass.	N.C.	Ore.	Utah
%	30 70	40 60	48 52	48 52
N	37	45	113	122

Received support
Did not receive support

Source: Zeigler and Baer, *Lobbying,* 115.

ture, arrange for public meetings, and the like. The perennial conflict between trucking companies and railroads has understandably interested the representatives of the respective national associations. The relatively slight use of public relations at the state level is not difficult to understand. The indirect communication of the mass media, for example, is not presumed to be as persuasive as personal communication. Since the state legislators are generally more accessible than their national counterparts, the use of indirect methods to create a favorable climate of opinion is not really necessary. Daily attendance at the state capitol, the cultivation of key legislators, the establishment of feelings of respect and confidence on the part of those legislators who have authority in the area of interest to the lobbyist and his organization — these are the preferred techniques of experienced lobbyists.

This preference is borne out by the lobbyists' perceptions of effectiveness. On a scale ranging from 0 (ineffective) to 8 (effective), lobbyists rated personal presentations of arguments highest, with public relations campaigns lower, but above the mean in all states (see Table 2). One factor against extensive use of public relations campaigns is their cost; it is simply cheaper to work directly with the legislature. However, the tactic remains in the repertoire of the lobbyist in case he needs to invoke the actions of a larger public.

The Advantage of the Defense

Groups whose basic goal is defensive, who are satisfied with the status quo and concern themselves primarily with maintaining it, have a better chance of success than those who try to alter the existing distribution of values. In Michigan, high-status groups such as manufacturers or professional associations have been able to play the role of policeman with con-

TABLE 2
*Lobbyists' Perception of the Effectiveness of Two Methods
of Communication on a Scale Ranging from 0 (Ineffective)
to 8 (Effective)*

	Massachusetts	*North Carolina*	*Oregon*	*Utah*
Personal presentation of arguments	6.6	6.7	6.9	6.4
Public relations campaign	3.7	4.6	4.0	4.6
Mean for all techniques of communication used	3.0	3.5	3.5	3.7

Source: Zeigler and Baer, *Lobbying,* 176.

siderable success, whereas groups such as labor unions that are struggling for social change think they are at a disadvantage. The coexistence of high-status groups and defensive posture is not coincidental, but it does not necessarily mean that labor unions will usually be attacking state legislatures. In Massachusetts, for example, the unions spend practically all their time in consciously defensive maneuvers to prevent the opposition from weakening existing labor laws. Of course, labor's most consistent defensive position has been against right-to-work laws. In states listed by Heard as having the greatest concentration of union membership, the union lobbyists act as policemen while business groups must induce the legislature to change the status quo.

Biemiller gives an excellent description of the policeman's job:

> One morning in late January the four-man legislative team of the Oregon A.F.L.–C.I.O. in Portland was scanning the batch of bills dropped into the hopper of the newly-convened legislature the previous day.
> This was a daily routine for the labor watchdog committee. An important part of the job was to read every bill introduced in the two branches of the legislature as a safeguard against reactionary attacks on the rights of working people in the states.[75]

He goes on to relate how the labor lobbyists discovered a "backdoor" right-to-work law hidden in legislation that seemed on the surface to be unrelated to labor-management relations. A civil rights bill introduced by a Republican legislator would have amended the Oregon Fair Employment Practices Act to provide that no person should be denied a job because of race, religion, color, or "membership or nonmembership in any organization of any kind." The quoted words were the extent of the proposed amendment. The discovery of this "sleeper" by the labor lobbyists and the subsequent death of the amendment in committee illustrate not only the value of the defense but also the necessity for full-time, rather than amateur, lobbyists.

Utah illustrates another dimension of the advantage of the defense. Like independent regulatory commissions that are "captured" by their clientele after associating closely with them and viewing their problems first hand, legislators and lobbyists tend to come from occupational and educational backgrounds that favor business and other status quo oriented interests more than civil rights, labor, or educational interests. This situation is disadvantageous to lobbyists who represent groups with interests or orientations that differ markedly from those of the legislator they seek to influence. For example, attempts by education lobbyists to interact with legislators whose views diverge from theirs lead to a vicious spiral in which the number of interaction attempts is not correlated with the amount of information transmitted or the likelihood of a successful transaction but with an increased probability that the legislator will believe he has been "pressured" by the lobbyist. The legislator will become hostile toward the lobbyist, and will be even more unwilling to assist in the pursuit of his goals. Under these conditions intensive lobbying is disfunctional. Instead of leading to change, it reinforces the status quo or, even worse, leads to reaction and the introduction of countermeasures against the organization. Thus, Utah has more education lobbyists on the job than any other state in the four-state sample, but legislators, especially Republicans, feel pressured. The result is that Utah ranks third in dollars expended per pupil: in 1966 Utah spent $351 per pupil, Oregon spent $518, Massachusetts spent $465, and North Carolina spent $296.[76]

This reaction need not be interpreted exclusively in direct causal terms. An initial unwillingness to meet the demands of a segment of the population can produce organization and an attempt to change the legislator's priorities. The best tactic is to reduce attitudinal discrepancies by working through intermediaries whose views are more consonant with those of the legislators involved. Campaign contributions might be used in a quiet attempt to build legislative obligation. Failing this, low key public relations campaigns, the publication of voting records, and petition drives may be necessary to change attitudes significantly. Since the line between efforts that result in success and efforts that result in reaction can be a thin one, the skill of the lobbyist counts heavily.

Lobbying Techniques

THE COMMUNICATION OF INFORMATION.   We cannot assume that because the more experienced lobbyists are more successful, their experience includes knowledge of the ways to manipulate legislators, to guide unpopular legislation through a series of hostile entrapments, and, in general, to utilize pressure. In practice, the duties of the skilled lobbyist are far less dramatic. Generally, his job is little more than that of an agent communicating the position of a group on an issue to someone he believes will have some control over the outcome.[77] Of course, it is also part of the lobbyist's job to communicate the notion of group power, but this is largely determined without the intervention of lobbying skills. Actually, the job of the lobbyist, communication, is quite an assignment, for he cannot automatically transmit information. To whom should communications be addressed? When is the proper time to approach a legislator? How should the argument be phrased? These questions are not answered the same way for every situation.

As the example of the education lobby in Utah indicates, communication directed at legislators who are unfavorable to the goals of an organization is likely to result in failure. Interaction and communication are more probable with a favorable attitude. In the four-state sample, 11 per cent of the legislators with negative attitudes toward lobbyists were high interactors, compared with 27 per cent with neutral attitudes, and 61 per cent with positive attitudes.[78]

Recent studies of Washington lobbying all have a similar result: lobbying is very rarely directed at legislators who have taken a position in opposition to the desired goals of the group employing the lobbyist. Most contact between lobbyist and legislator occurs between two partisans who are reinforcing agreement.[79] In this context, pressure is not very useful. In the legislature, as with the general public, pressure is a tactic only opponents engage in. If the legislator and lobbyist have similar goals, communication is likely to be perceived as the legitimate expression of a sound point of view. Consequently, if a legislator feels that the legislature is under considerable pressure, either the lobbyists are talking to the wrong people or the legislator "has heard" of great pressure on the part of his opponents. In all four states studied by Zeigler and Baer, for example, legislators "had heard" of education and labor exerting pressure. Because of the background and attitudinal differences between legislators and lobbyists representing such groups, "nothing more than hearsay evidence" was sufficient to make the rumor credible.[80]

A study of the Indiana legislature further illustrates the tendency for a legislator's perceptions of a group to accord with his background and predispositions, a factor militating against forces of change.[81] Once again a correlation was found between the occupation of the legislator and his attitudes toward specific interest groups. The clearest relationship is that of sympathetic identification between legislators and lobbyists from the same occupational category. Thus, legislators whose occupation is farming agreed with the goals of the Farm Bureau; businessmen agreed with the goals of business groups. Naturally, the attitudes of the legislator are related to his ranking of the legislative efficiency of various groups. Legislators who agreed generally with the goals of a particular organization ranked that organization somewhat higher in effectiveness than those groups with which they disagreed. Democrats ranked the AFL-CIO higher than the Farm Bureau, whereas Republicans reversed the order. However, the question that elicited this response was phrased so as to equate effectiveness with the group's skill in presenting its case to the legislature, a judgment that would be colored by the values of the legislator. A rural Republican would hardly credit labor with much skill in presentation. When the question was phrased to include the word "powerful" different responses were obtained. In this case, legislators who disagreed with the policies of the group were more likely to name that group as powerful. The evidence of occupational sympathies in Indiana demonstrates again the amateur status of state legislators. Since serving in the state legislature is in many cases a part-time job, legislators retain active ties with their businesses or professions. The possibility of "built-in" access exists because state legislatures are likely to contain more people without the perspective of a career politician and more people engaged in private business on an active basis than the national legislature.

CHOICES OF STRATEGIES.   When establishing a contact with a friendly legislator in order to transmit the position of his organization, the lobbyist has a choice of strategies. In most cases he will choose to operate through the official channels of the legislature by giving testimony at committee hearings, because most legislators rely heavily upon them. Over three-quarters of the legislators in Massachusetts, North Carolina, and Oregon indicated that committee hearings were their primary source of information. In Utah the figure was 48 per cent.[82]

Lobbyists believe that testimony in committees is most effective when it is supplemented by other communication contacts that will lend credibility to the hearing and familiarize the legislator with different points of view. This belief, of course, is not at all surprising since lobbying is to a considerable extent a process of bringing about opinion change, or getting someone to see things in a slightly different light. When the changes are of major proportions because of the attitudes of many legislators, the lobbyist may run into trouble. Thus, it is to his advantage and to the advantage of those seeking to bring about a change in existing legislative priorities to prepare legislators for what is to take place in the committee hearing — thereby reducing the chances that ambiguity and hostility will obstruct a fair consideration of the issues.

When faced with strong opposition, the experienced lobbyist is likely to rely upon indirect methods, most notably working through another legislator who is more favorable toward the legislation championed by the lobbyist and has access to those he seeks to influence. In this manner the lobbyist attempts to reduce gradually the discrepancy between attitudes. Although he prefers an intermediary who is another legislator, "lobbyists will frequently try to buttress the work of other legislators with contacts by influential constituents. When the lobbyist is unable to persuade a legislator to lobby for him, constituents become the major agent of mediation." [83]

This kind of activity is especially conducive to change and to involving articulate segments of the community in decision making. Lobbyists "frequently interpret opposition as a difficulty in communications rather than as a problem of ideology,[84] which indicates that those seeking representation through the mediation of interest groups are inclined to work within the system and to have faith in its ability to fulfill their demands.

To supplement testimony, lobbyists seek informal meetings with committee members. This alternative was used frequently by Utah lobbyists who must face formal hearings conducted rapidly. Meetings by appointment with individual legislators are also used. Chance meetings and social gatherings are generally not relied upon to any great degree.[85]

Contrary to popular belief, a very effective strategy for the lobbyist is building a reputation for knowledgeability and honesty. Since perceptions of pressure are most likely to arise from those who imagine that the lobbyist is out to push a particular viewpoint, credibility and expertise are important lobbying resources. One lobbyist, frequently called upon by legislators to provide information, indicated that he would discuss the bad as well as the good points of bills even though he supported them. As he put it:

> I am not going to try to fool you. I'm not going to be as persuasive
> with the other arguments as I am going to be with my own, but I will
> tell them to the limit of my ability the other side.[86]

Lobbying techniques depend to some extent upon the political system in which the lobbying takes place. Interest groups have been able to establish a more permanent web of interaction with administrative agencies than with the legislature because of the inherently monopolistic tendencies of administrative politics. At the state level, each agency is responsible for a narrowly defined set of operations and comes into almost daily contact with a clientele whose interests are affected by the agency's operations. Constantly associated with a specific clientele, administrators see very little of a more general public and gradually tend to identify their values with those of their clientele. The establishment of a set of mutually shared values between agency and clientele can be useful not only in turning legislative defeat into administrative victory but also in the pursuit of group goals through legislation. A combination of private interest group and administrative agency is valuable in the event that a group without access to the agency tries to change the structure of power through the legislature.[87]

Because of the unstructured nature of state legislatures, lobbyists devote much time to cultivating valuable personal relationships. Consequently, the full-time, experienced lobbyists prefer to operate as what Patterson calls "contact men." In his article on Oklahoma, Patterson describes the contact man as one who

> conceives of his job as primarily that of making contacts, personal acquaintanceships and friendships with various legislators, and of maintaining these contacts. The Contact Man provides a direct communications link between the interest group and the individual members of the legislature. When faced with a legislative problem for his group, the lobbyist with a Contact Man orientation is likely to propose as the solution the personal contacting of as many members of the legislative body as possible, directly presenting the interest group's case to them.[88]

Patterson found that more than half the Oklahoma lobbyists were contact men but, more important, a substantially greater portion of the contact men were on the job more than half the time. Similar findings appear in De-Vries's study of Michigan.[89] The lobbyists in the top of the effectiveness scale were more likely to rely on personal presentation of arguments than those at the bottom of the scale, and less likely to rely on formal presentation at committee hearings than those at the bottom of the scale.

In Massachusetts, North Carolina, Oregon, and Utah, lobbyists who were high job investors — individuals who devoted most of their time to the lobbying profession — were more likely to be contact men than administrators who spend most of their time preparing testimony, writing speeches and letters, or observing the legislative calendar for bills affecting their client organization [90] (see Figure 4).

Lobbyists spending a lot of time on the job are also more likely to consider themselves professionals and to be experienced; the chances of legislators interacting with them increase accordingly.[91] Thus, no significant differences for the high investment category appear between the states, although North Carolina, a weak-lobby state, has fewer high investigators who are able to take the contact man approach. When the sample is viewed as a whole without regard to experience or job investment, however, we see that lobbyists in the weak-lobby states are more likely to be administrators than their counterparts in strong-lobby states (Figure 5). Where access is difficult, as in Massachusetts, where strong party cohesion and many legislators confound the problems of achieving success by contacting a few key members of important committees, the less direct administrative technique is preferred. In Oregon, the reverse is the case.[92]

FIGURE 4

Comparative Percentages of Lobbyists in the High Job Investment Category Who Are Classified as Administrators or Contact Men

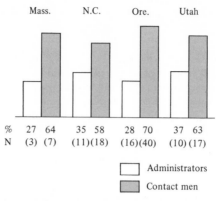

	Mass.		N.C.		Ore.		Utah	
%	27	64	35	58	28	70	37	63
N	(3)	(7)	(11)	(18)	(16)	(40)	(10)	(17)

☐ Administrators
▨ Contact men

Source: Zeigler and Baer, *Lobbying,* 80. Percentages do not equal 100 in all cases because the category "both administrator and contact man" is omitted here.

THE FLOW OF COMMUNICATION. The question of whom to contact is answered to some extent by the structure of the legislature and the role of the political party in determining legislative policy. Needless to say, lobbyists do not spend much time talking to legislators they regard as unimportant. They want to communicate with party leaders in states with strong party discipline and cohesion, and with the chairmen of standing committees in states with a tradition of committee dominance like that of Congress. In states where the parties and their satellite interest groups exist in a well-defined system of interaction, the problem of access does not exist. Business groups can talk with Republicans and labor unions can talk with Democrats with confidence that their views will be taken seriously. Only in legislatures without the control of a party organization does the job of locating and impressing the key decision makers become acute. Jewell has noted that standing committees in state legislatures rarely exercise the independence of Congressional committees. Most important bills are guided to a few committees dominated by a few legislators, usually party or faction leaders.[93] To establish and maintain access to these committees becomes a major goal of the state lobbyist. It is here that competition is keenest. In the frantic atmosphere of a legislature that meets only for a few months every other year, the rush of legislation makes the task of the lobbyist difficult. Time becomes quite important. Consequently, the patient cultivation of goodwill can make the difference between talking to a legislator or waiting

FIGURE 5
Comparative Percentages of Lobbyists Classified as Administrators or Contact Men

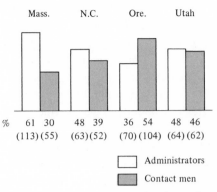

Mass.   N.C.   Ore.   Utah

%   61   30   48   39   36   54   48   46
    (113) (55)   (63) (52)   (70) (104)   (64) (62)

☐ Administrators
▨ Contact men

Source: Zeigler and Baer, *Lobbying,* 79. Percentages do not equal 100 because the category "both administrator and contact man" is omitted here.

all day without so much as a glimpse: "The harassed member will give his ear to those advocates he knows and likes in preference to persons he knows only distantly." [94]

The lobbyist concentrates his energies on those who are neutral and can swing a vote, or those who are already inclined to favor his viewpoint. As indicated earlier, he will use indirect rather than direct means if he thinks he must reach a legislator strongly opposed to his position. Thus

> the overwhelming majority of lobbyists who spend most of their time talking to supporters do so because they want these supporting legis- lators to line up further support. . . . When a persuasion-oriented lobbyist is talking to a supportive legislator, much of the conversation is related not to the merits of a bill, but to the role the legislator can play or is willing to play in contributing to the defeat or passage of the bill.[95]

LIMITS ON THE EFFECTIVENESS OF TECHNIQUES.   This discussion of the techniques of the lobbyist should not obscure one fundamental point. The techniques of lobbying as practiced by a representative of an interest group are less important than the group itself in contributing to any given legislative outcome. In the words of the authors of *The Legislative System,* "reasons connected with a group's claim to be represented or with its gen- eral political power appear . . . to be more significant than reasons asso- ciated with its lobbying activities in the legislative arena itself." [96] General political power, of course, is difficult to define and is probably best under- stood as a subjective definition on the part of the individual legislator.

Groups represented by experienced lobbyists rarely will threaten a legislator with electoral defeat and they will rarely flaunt economic power openly. On the other hand, wealth or potential electoral strength are credited by legislators as being critical factors in the effectiveness of groups. One plausible explanation is that frequently legislators perceive political power and representative quality in an organization as synonymous. For example, the Florida Dairy Products Association, an organization representing practically all the milk distributors in Florida, had a virtual monopoly on access to the house Public Health Committee, which would never report out a bill opposed by the organization. Those who sought alterations in the laws governing the sale of milk in Florida did not go to the legislature or to one of its committees. They went first to the Florida Dairy Products Association. Why was this true? The large milk distributors in the association such as Sealtest, Borden's, and Foremost are economically powerful, but it is difficult to believe that control of the legislative committee was due exclusively to wealth. Nor was the strength of the association due to its voting strength. It is more likely that its representative quality made the legislative committee willing to accord it the role of legitimate spokesman for an economic interest.[97]

CONCLUSIONS

Just as the strength of political parties varies from state to state, the significance of interest groups varies depending upon circumstances outlined in this chapter. A major variable is the political and social structure of the state. The long-assumed notion that pressure groups do not thrive in states with cohesive political parties has some validity, but in many cases peaceful coexistence and mutually beneficial cooperation are possible. Political parties as cohesive agencies direct pressure away from the individual legislator and perhaps reduce the salience of pressure politics for the rank and file. Within a politico-economic structure, the importance of pressure groups varies with the peculiarities of the situation. Groups powerful in some situations are powerless in others. Even states characterized by a few strong and active groups are likely to have a pluralistic rather than a monolithic structure of power. This conclusion is supported both by the decline in the number of states in the single dominant interest category and the fact that high pressure lobbying by powerful interests is not a satisfactory technique of persuasion. In addition, the power of public opinion and conscience influences the legislative process more than it has in the past, further circumscribing the area of action available to one or two powerful interests. Interest groups may be conceptualized as one of several actors in the political process with influence that increases or diminishes in relation to other actors.

The importance of lobbying as a technique of persuading and communicating information has increased with the decline in de facto control of the legislative process by single or amalgamated group interests. Faced with increasing industrialization and urbanization, interest groups have changed their tactics. The techniques used to exert influence have become less flamboyant and more closely attuned to the political dynamics of individual state legislatures. Overt pressure has been replaced by the subtleties of the legislator-lobbyist interchange.

The inverse relation between party strength and interest group dominance need not imply that the importance of the interest group in the political process of the American states has declined greatly or that interest groups can be expected to fade from the scene in a short time. Rather, the resulting changes have shifted the analysis from an emphasis upon the specific, presumably invariant attributes of interest group power to the more complex and often contingent relationships that determine the outcome of interaction between the legislator and the lobbyist.

SELECTED BIBLIOGRAPHY

Buchanan, William. *Legislative Partisanship: The Deviant Case of California.* University of California Publications in Political Science, Vol. 13. Berkeley and Los Angeles: University of California Press, 1963. A careful evaluation of the changing nature of interest groups in California with particular emphasis upon the relationship between interest groups and political parties.

Francis, Wayne L. *Legislative Issues in the Fifty States: A Comparative Analysis.* Chicago: Rand McNally, 1967. A study of legislative issues and conflict in the states.

Hacker, Andrew. "Pressure Politics in Pennsylvania: The Trucker vs. the Railroads," in Alan F. Westin (ed.), *The Uses of Power.* New York: Harcourt, Brace & World, 1962, 324–376. An analysis of the role of public relations firms in the development of group strategy.

Wahlke, John C., Heinz Eulau, William Buchanan, and Leroy C. Ferguson. *The Legislative System.* New York: John Wiley & Sons, 1962. Chapter 14 contains an analysis of legislators' role orientations toward interest groups in California, New Jersey, Ohio, and Tennessee.

Zeigler, L. Harmon, and Michael A. Baer. *Lobbying: Interaction and Influence in American State Legislatures.* Belmont, Calif.: Wadsworth Publishing, 1969. A study of lobbying based on questionnaires administered to legislators and lobbyists in four states.

Zeigler, L. Harmon, and Michael A. Baer. "The Recruitment of Lobbyists and Legislators," *Midwest Journal of Political Science,* 12 (1968): 493–513. An examination of the backgrounds and political socialization of legislators and lobbyists in relation to their respective rates of interaction and influence.

Zeigler, L. Harmon. "The Effects of Lobbying: A Comparative Assessment," *Western Political Quarterly,* 22 (1969): 122–140. A discussion of the effects of lobbying and the elements that significantly act to determine these effects.

PART THREE

THE POLICY-MAKING ARENAS

CHAPTER FIVE

State Legislative Politics

Thomas R. Dye

Generalizing about American state legislatures is difficult. Some legislatures are highly professional lawmaking bodies with well-paid members who devote a significant portion of their lives to the problems of their states. Other legislatures are very amateur bodies composed of part-time lawmakers who meet a few weeks each year and then hurry home to their businesses and law practices. Some are important political bodies that make the crucial decisions about public policy in their states. Others simply rubber stamp the decisions of a strong governor, influential party leaders, or powerful interest groups. Some legislatures are completely dominated by a single party and there is little likelihood that the minority party will ever capture control. In other states a more competitive situation exists and control of the state legislature frequently shifts from one party to the other. In some state legislatures voting is frequently along party lines, whereas in other states voting is more affected by factional rivalries or constituency pressures than by party loyalties. In some the conflict between rural and urban interests dominates legislative politics, whereas in others conflict between regions, between legislature and governor, between liberal and conservative, or between labor and industry may take precedence. In short, state legislatures can be quite different from one another. The problem facing anyone who wants to talk about legislative politics in fifty states is not only in describing these differences from state to state but in explaining these differences.

THE FUNCTION OF LEGISLATURES

From a legal view point, the function of state legislatures is the enactment of statutory law. If the volume of statutory writing and revision were the criterion upon which state legislatures were judged, it could rightly be said that legislatures have never functioned so well as they have in recent years. In the 1950–51 biennium, American state legislatures considered over 47,000 bills; by the 1966–67 biennium this figure had grown to over 136,000.[1] * The total number of state legislative enactments grew from approximately 15,000 to over 41,000 in that same period. As a society grows more complex and becomes increasingly urban, the need for formal statutory control seems to grow. Table 1 indicates that in general the states that enacted over 1,000 statutes in the 1960–61 and 1966–67 legislative sessions were more urban than the states that enacted fewer than 1,000.

TABLE 1
Urbanization and Numbers of Laws Enacted by State
Legislatures

		1966-67
Number of enactments	No. of states	Mean urban percentage
Over 1,000	11	71.0%
500-1,000	18	58.8
Less than 500	21	59.8

The range of subject matter of the bills considered even in a single session is enormous. A legislature may consider the authorization of a billion dollars of state spending, the extension of the hunting season on raccoons, participation in the national defense highway system, the designation of an official state flower, an increase in teachers' salaries, and whether or not license plates bearing the inscription, "The Poultry State," would cause the state to be called "chicken." Obviously, these considerations range from the trivial to the vital; yet every bill that comes into a legislature is important to someone. In addition to the enactment of statutory law, legislatures share in the process of state constitutional revision, approve many executive appointments, establish congressional districts, and consider amendments to the United States Constitution. But perhaps their single most important legal function is the passage of the appropriations and tax measures in the

* [See pp. 576–580 for notes to this chapter. — Eds.]

state budget. No state monies may be spent without a legislative appropriation, and it is difficult to think of any governmental action that does not involve a financial expenditure. Potentially, a legislature can control any activity of the state government through its power over appropriations, but as a practical matter this legal power over fiscal affairs does not amount to political control.

From a political viewpoint, the function of state legislatures is to assist in the formulation of public policy. It is misleading to say merely that "the legislature makes policy," for obviously the legislature is not the only group that shares in this task. The governor, the courts, executive agencies, organized interests, the press, political parties, and many individuals — the interested as well as the apathetic — share in making public policy. How, then, do we distinguish the role of the legislature from that of other groups? For example, do legislatures merely ratify and thereby lend legitimacy to the decisions that are actually made by the governor, or the bureaucrats, or the organized interests? Or are legislatures an important part of the process of proposing, deliberating about, and deciding public policy? If they are an important part of the decision process, what function do they perform? Does the legislature merely referee the struggles between political interests in the state, recording the terms of surrender, compromise, or conquest in the form of statutes? Or does the legislature exercise independent influence over policy? If the latter is the case, on whose behalf does it exercise this influence — the parties, the constituencies, or particular interests in the state? Are legislatures initiators of public policy or do they merely articulate expressions of public sentiment in favor of, or in opposition to, policies initiated by others? These are the critical questions about the function of legislatures in state policy making. This chapter attempts to consider these questions.

THE PARTISAN SETTING
OF LEGISLATIVE POLITICS

There are ninety-six partisan legislative chambers in the United States; Nebraska and Minnesota legislatures are elected on a nonpartisan ballot. Over the years the Democratic party has tended to dominate American state legislative politics; only recently have Republican party fortunes improved. The high-water mark of Democratic success in controlling state legislatures came in 1964, when Democrats controlled thirty-four upper houses, thirty-nine lower houses, and thirty-three governorships. Since then the GOP has been growing in strength in legislative chambers and governors' chairs. The ups and downs of Democratic party fortunes in controlling state legislative chambers and governorships are graphically displayed in Figure 1.

Divided government, when the governor's chair is held by one party and one or both chambers by the opposition, occurs frequently in the states. Governors who have succeeded in winning by only a small margin are more likely to face opposition legislatures than those elected by wide margins. When Democratic governors are elected in the normally Republican midwestern and upper New England states, they usually face a Republican legislature. On the other hand, Republican governors elected in the traditionally Democratic border and southern states are generally faced with Democratic legislatures.

What types of states are most likely to experience Democratic or Republican legislative control? State legislatures can be classified according to the proportion of total seats in both houses of the legislature held by

FIGURE 1
Democratic Party Control of Upper and Lower Chambers of State Legislatures and Governorships, 1954-1968

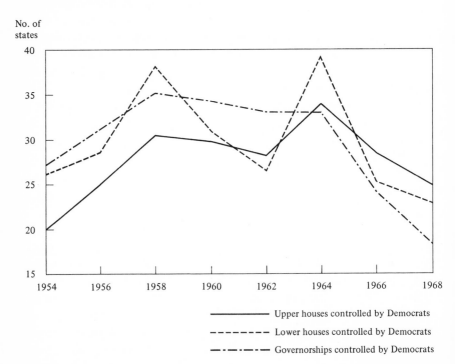

each party from 1964 through 1968. Table 2 divides the states into five categories: one-party Democratic (70 per cent or more of the legislators elected to both houses from 1964 through 1968 were Democrats); Democratic dominant (over 50 per cent of the legislators elected to both houses were Democrats); divided (over 50 per cent of the legislators elected to one house were Democratic but over 50 per cent elected to the other house were Republican); Republican dominant (over 50 per cent of the legislators elected to both houses were Republican); and one-party Republican (over 70 per cent of the legislators elected to both houses from 1964 through 1968 were Republican). It is clear from Table 2 that socioeconomic development does not consistently favor one party or the other.[2] Rather, high levels of urbanization, industrialization, income, and education foster party competition for legislative control. Both one-party Republican and one-party Democratic legislatures occur in rural, agricultural states with populations possessing lower income and educational attributes. This pattern is

TABLE 2
Socioeconomic Development and Party Control of State Legislatures, 1964-68

| | Indices of socioeconomic development[a] (mean scores) | | |
	Urbanization	Income	Education
One-party Democratic: Over 70 per cent of both houses Democratic (14 states)[b]	57.1%	$4,437	9.5 yrs.
Democratic dominant: Over 50 per cent of both houses Democratic (13 states)[c]	67.1	5,922	10.8
Divided: One house over 50 per cent Democratic; one house over 50 per cent Republican (7 states)[d]	69.0	5,975	11.2
Republican dominant: Over 50 per cent of both houses Republican (10 states)[e]	64.0	5,705	11.3
One-party Republican: Over 70 per cent of both houses Republican (4 states)[f]	43.5	4,741	10.5

[a]Indices are as follows: urbanization is the percentage of population in urban areas in 1960; income is median family income in 1959; education is median school year completed by population over 25 in 1960.
[b]Alabama, Arkansas, Florida, Georgia, Louisiana, Wyoming, Mississippi, North Carolina, Oklahoma, Rhode Island, South Carolina, Texas, Virginia, West Virginia.
[c]Alaska, California, Connecticut, Delaware, Hawaii, Kentucky, Massachusetts, Michigan, Missouri, Nevada, New Mexico, Pennsylvania, Tennessee.
[d]Arizona, Illinois, Indiana, Montana, New York, Oregon, Washington.
[e]Colorado, Idaho, Iowa, Maine, New Hampshire, New Jersey, Ohio, Utah, Wisconsin, Wyoming.
[f]Kansas, North Dakota, South Dakota, Vermont.

likely to prevail through the 1970s, despite the growing party competition in southern and midwestern states in gubernatorial, congressional, and presidential elections. Interestingly, the growth in party competition in these elections has *not* been accompanied in these states by any comparable growth in party competition for state legislative seats. Despite the election of Republican governors, United States Senators, and presidential electors in many southern states, southern state legislatures have remained firmly Democratic. Likewise, the midwestern and New England legislatures have remained firmly in Republican hands.

What difference does it make whether a state has competitive or non-competitive legislative politics? First, one-party states do not have cohesive party organization with power to hold legislators in line on crucial legislative decisions. In one-party legislatures, divisions over public policy follow constituency, factional, or interest group lines rather than party lines. Parties exercise more influence in legislative decision making in competitive than in noncompetitive states.

It is often argued that competitiveness results in increased benefits for citizens because the parties are forced to bid for votes, implying that policy choices of competitive legislatures are different from those of noncompetitive legislatures. It is true that levels of public spending for education, welfare, and many other benefits and services tend to be higher in the states with more party competition, but the problem in trying to determine the effect of party competition on specific policies is that it is always possible that party competition does not itself produce liberal welfare policies or high educational expenditures. Party competition and these policies may occur together because some third intervening variable produces both of them. Since it is known that competitive and noncompetitive states differ in their degree of socioeconomic development, most policy differences between competitive states may be due to differences in socioeconomic development rather than party competition itself. In general, recent research literature supports the view that *most* of the variation among the states in levels of public taxing, spending, benefits, and service can be accounted for by differences among the states in levels of wealth, although party competition does have effects on certain welfare benefits.[3]

The visibility of parties in a competitive system may produce the most important differences between competitive and noncompetitive systems. A party label in a competitive system is a very conspicuous attribute of a candidate for the legislature. One-party states may have important factions of varying durability. Yet in two-party states a party label must be worn on election day and can be seen by every voter. It is not so obscure as a vague alignment with a faction. Most of the students of state party systems think that it is more difficult to hold factions responsible for policies than it is to hold competitive parties responsible, even though the latter is difficult to accomplish. Factions are fluid and change their personnel and policies much more frequently than parties. Even in Louisiana, which has one of the more durable bifactional systems among the one-party states, observers have found factionalism to be "considerably inferior to two-party politics." [4] V. O. Key argues that southern factional systems obscure politics for most voters and permit conservative interests to manipulate factional groups.[5] Many people who have little knowledge about policies and membership in various factions are easily misled by factional systems. This is not to say that many voters are not confused about the policies of parties in a competitive state, or that competitive parties can always hold their legislators responsible, but party competition is more likely than factional politics to clarify issues for the voter. Even if policy differences between parties are vague, voters at least can identify an "in-party" and an "out-party" at election time. Finally, in one-party states and even in states with limited competition, the minority party very often fails to run candidates in many legislative districts, giving a voter in such a district no opportunity to exercise a choice in the general election.

THE COMPOSITION OF LEGISLATURES

Legislative Districts

Elements of the politics of representation are the size and composition of legislative districts and the question of who gains and who loses from the variations. Inequality of representation, or malapportionment, is claimed when there are differing numbers of people in districts that receive the same number of representatives in the legislature. For example, if one legislator represents a district of 10,000 inhabitants and another a district of 40,000, the right to vote in the smaller district is worth four times what it is in the larger district.

Prior to 1962 malapportionment was widespread in American state legislatures. Small minorities of the population could elect a majority of the house or senate or both in most of the states (see Table 3). Generally the rural voters in a state controlled a majority of legislative seats, and the urban voters were discriminated against in the value of their vote. In order to determine the degree of discrimination against urban areas in American

TABLE 3

Changes in Representation Resulting From Reapportionment of Legislatures, 1962, 1968

	Minimum percentage of population that could elect a majority			
	Senate		House	
	1962	1968	1962	1968
Alabama	25	48	26	48
Alaska	35	51	49	48
Arizona	13	52	NA	51
Arkansas	44	49	33	48
California	11	49	45	49
Colorado	30	50	32	54
Connecticut	33	48	12	44
Delaware	22	53	19	49
Florida	12	51	12	50
Georgia	23	48	22	43
Hawaii	23	50	48	43
Idaho	17	47	33	47
Illinois	29	50	40	49
Indiana	40	49	35	49
Iowa	35	45	27	45
Kansas	27	49	19	49
Kentucky	42	47	34	45
Louisiana	33	48	34	47
Maine	47	51	40	43
Maryland	14	47	25	48
Massachusetts	45	50	45	46
Michigan	29	53	44	51
Minnesota	40	48	35	47
Mississippi	35	49	29	48
Missouri	48	52	20	49
Montana	16	47	37	48
Nebraska	37	49	–	–
Nevada	8	50	35	48
New Hampshire	45	52	44	46
New Jersey	19	50	47	50
New Mexico	14	46	27	46
New York	41	49	33	49
North Carolina	37	49	27	48
North Dakota	32	47	40	47
Ohio	41	50	30	47
Oklahoma	25	49	30	49
Oregon	48	47	48	48
Pennsylvania	33	50	38	47
Rhode Island	18	50	47	49
South Carolina	23	48	46	46
South Dakota	38	47	39	47
Tennessee	27	49	29	47
Texas	30	49	39	47
Utah	21	48	33	48
Vermont	47	49	12	49
Virginia	38	48	37	47
Washington	34	48	35	47
West Virginia	47	47	40	46
Wisconsin	45	48	40	45
Wyoming	27	47	36	46

Source: Council of State Governments, *Book of the States, 1968-69,* 66-67.

state legislatures, David and Eisenberg compared the "value" of a vote cast for a state legislator in rural and urban areas in every state.[6] Table 4 shows the national averages of the value of a vote in four categories of counties by population. Clearly, the more populous counties in the nation were underrepresented in American state legislatures. Prior to 1962 it did not seem that the situation was improving with time.

For many years the federal courts avoided the distasteful task of compelling legislative reapportionment by asserting that this was a legislative rather than a judicial function. Underrepresented populations were told by the courts that their remedy was to elect a legislature that would do its duty.[7] This was a worthless prescription, of course, since electing a legislature was the very thing underrepresented populations could not do. The position of the courts changed radically, however, after the United States Supreme Court's decision in *Baker* v. *Carr*.[8] This case involved the complaint of urban residents in Tennessee, where the largest district in the lower house was twenty-three times larger than the smallest district. Petitioners argued that such inequalities in state apportionment laws denied them "equal protection of the laws" guaranteed by the Fourteenth Amendment and that the federal courts should grant relief from these inequalities. The Supreme Court decided: (1) that even though apportionment is a legislative function, the federal courts can accept jurisdiction where a constitutional question is involved; (2) that voters in underrepresented areas are entitled to judicial relief from apportionment laws that violate constitutional mandates; and (3) that discriminatory and arbitrary state apportionment laws can violate the Fourteenth Amendment's prohibition against laws that deny citizens equal protection. The Supreme Court returned the Tennessee case to a lower federal court, which ordered reapportionment.

TABLE 4

Relative Values of a Vote for State Legislators, National Averages for Counties by Size, 1910-1960

Categories of counties by population size	1910	1930	1950	1960
Under 25,000	1.13	1.31	1.41	1.71
25,000 to 99,999	1.03	1.09	1.14	1.23
100,000 to 499,999	.91	.84	.83	.81
500,000 and over	.81	.74	.78	.76

Source: David and Eisenberg, *Devaluation of the Urban and Suburban Vote,* 8. David and Eisenberg first computed the average size of the constituency of a single member in each state. Actual constituencies were then compared to this average constituency; the "value" of a vote was the ratio of a real constituency to the average constituency in the state. For example, in a constituency twice the size of the state average, the value of a vote is .50; in a constituency half the size of the state average, the value of a vote is 2.0. The average value of a vote in rural and urban areas can be compared in this manner both within a single state and between states. See *ibid.,* 2.

Reaction to the decision was immediate and widespread. Underrepresented voters throughout the nation petitioned federal courts to order state legislative reapportionment on the basis of the equal protection clause of the Fourteenth Amendment. Federal courts found themselves struggling with the mathematics of apportionment. The courts did not decide on any firm mathematical standard of correct apportionment, holding only that "as nearly as practicable, one man's vote should be equal to another's." [9] State after state was induced to reapportion its legislature under the threat of judicial intervention. Federal courts generally allowed legislatures time to reapportion themselves but found token reapportionment unacceptable. The courts even threatened to bar legislative elections by districts in states that failed to meet constitutional standards of apportionment. In addition to requiring legislative apportionment on a population basis, the Supreme Court also required population equality in congressional districting by state legislatures [10] and threw out the county unit system of voting in statewide elections.[11] The philosophy underlying all of these decisions was expressed by the Court: "The conception of political equality from the Declaration of Independence to Lincoln's Gettysburg Address, to the Fourteenth, Fifteenth, Seventeenth, and Nineteenth Amendments can mean only one thing — one person, one vote." [12] The Court made no distinction between malapportionment that was a product of state law and malapportionment that was embodied in state constitutions; both forms of malapportionment were declared to be in violation of the Fourteenth Amendment.

Two years after *Baker* v. *Carr* the Supreme Court decided that representation in the second house of a state legislature also had to be based on population. Most state constitutions based representation in the upper chamber upon some unit of local government rather than population. The justifications for such an arrangement are rooted deep in American democratic theory. The idea of bicameralism was based in part upon the advantages of having two separate systems of representation in a legislature. The *Federalist Papers* vigorously defended a second chamber capable of checking the popular majority represented in the lower chamber and protecting interests that might be threatened by that majority. However, in 1964 in *Reynolds* v. *Sims,*[13] a case involving Alabama's attempt to base representation in its senate on counties, the Court decided that *both* houses of a state legislature must be fairly apportioned according to population. In the words of Chief Justice Earl Warren, writing for the Court:

> Legislators represent people, not trees or acres. Legislators are elected by voters, not farms or cities or economic interests. . . . The complexions of societies and civilizations change, often with amazing

rapidity. A nation once primarily rural in character becomes predominantly urban. Representation schemes once fair and equitable
became archaic and outdated.[14]

The Court dismissed the federal analogy as "irrelevant" because "political
subdivisions of states . . . never have been considered as sovereign entities." [15] The court argued that requiring both houses to have the same basis
of representation did not make bicameralism meaningless, because differences between the houses in numbers, terms of office, and size of constituencies would still remain.

By 1968 every state had reapportioned one or both houses of its legislature, generally in response to a federal court order. The results have been
startling: today there is very little malapportionment in any state and "one
man, one vote" is the prevailing style of representation (see Table 3).

What has reapportionment done to state legislative politics? Reapportionment has significantly increased the representation afforded urban interests. Of course, this is what reapportionment was expected to do, but it
is still interesting to observe the results of reapportionment in increasing
urban representation and decreasing rural representation. Table 5 illustrates
what happened in many states. The percentage of Georgia's population living in various types of urban communities is shown in the left column.
These figures are compared with the percentage of house and senate seats
afforded these communities "before" and "after" reapportionment. Georgia's
urban counties, which contain 53.3 per cent of the state's population, increased their representation in the senate from 28.7 to 52 per cent and in
the house from 24.9 to 48.8 per cent. Rural counties, which contain 46.7
per cent of the state's population, decreased their representation from 71.3
to 47.9 per cent in the senate and from 75.1 per cent to 51.2 per cent in
the house.

Finally, there is evidence that reapportionment has a significant impact
on the kinds of people who win seats in state legislatures. Reapportionment
appears to bring younger, better-educated, more prestigiously employed men
into the legislature. It also brings many new people into legislative politics
who have had little or no previous experience in public office. However,
this may be a temporary effect that will disappear after reapportionment
legislatures have met for several years.

How has reapportionment influenced the policy choices of state legislatures? There is no doubt that significant political differences exist between
big-city and small-town or rural legislators and that malapportionment
granted a real political advantage to the latter. If the perceptions of state
legislators themselves about legislative conflict are to be considered, then

TABLE 5
*The Effects of Reapportionment on the Representation Afforded
Urban Communities in Georgia*

| | | Percentage representation | | | |
| | *Percentage of state popula- tion* | Senate | | House | |
		Before	*After*	*Before*	*After*
Atlanta metropolitan area	20.0	6.0	24.3	6.3	12.2
All metro areas	39.0	14.3	44.3	15.1	29.1
All nonmetro areas	61.0	85.7	55.7	84.9	70.9
Urban counties (Over 50 per cent urban pop.)	53.3	28.7	52.0	24.9	48.8
Rural counties (Less than 50 per cent urban pop.)	46.7	71.3	47.9	75.1	51.2
Counties with cities over 50,000	28.2	11.2	37.0	10.2	28.1
Counties with cities 10,000 to 50,000	21.2	21.4	22.1	19.5	22.1
Counties with cities 10,000 or less	49.4	67.4	40.8	70.3	49.8

rural-urban conflict is not only discernible but is the most important conflict in American state legislatures. Rural-urban conflict was the only type
of conflict rated "important" by over half of the legislators interviewed in
four separate states.[16] It seems safe to say that legislators from large central
cities and those from rural areas and small towns differ over the following:
housing and welfare measures, aid for urban renewal and mass transit, the
division of the state's tax dollar, state aid to schools, the location of highways, and the regulating authority granted cities.[17] In some southern states,
urban legislators represent a "moderate" approach to race relations, and
rural legislators are more often segregationists. According to the Advisory
Commission on Intergovernmental Relations, the unrepresentativeness of
state legislatures forced big cities to take their cause to the federal government where they thought they could obtain a fairer hearing.[18] The commission claimed that the rural character of state legislatures meant that cities
bypassed the states in requesting direct federal-to-local grants-in-aid, such
as the federal public housing and urban renewal programs.

However, we must be cautious in estimating the policy consequences
of reapportionment. In the past, proponents of reapportionment were overly
enthusiastic about its expected consequences. Having attributed the lack of
party competition, unfair distribution of state funds, conservative tax
schemes, unprogressive education policies, and penny-pinching welfare programs to rural overrepresentation, they naturally expected to see these poli-

cies change significantly with reapportionment. Empirical evidence gives little support to such hopes.

In the first place, even before *Baker* v. *Carr* there was no evidence that the policy choices of well-apportioned states differed significantly from the policy choices of malapportioned states. There were no significant differences between well-apportioned and malapportioned states in levels of expenditures for welfare and education, the quality of public education, the tax burden, the revenue structure, the liberality of welfare benefits, or the extent of state participation in education, health, and welfare.[19] Most differences among the states in these policies were accounted for by differences in socioeconomic environment; apportionment practices seem to have little direct impact on these policies. Of course, it is possible that the policy impact of reapportionment will be subtle and diverse, and that reapportionment will have a greater influence on the rural-urban division of *marginal increases* in public expenditures, in contrast to *overall levels* of public expenditures, sources, or benefits. But there is little evidence that the "one man, one vote" movement will dramatically change the nature or extent of state involvement in urban problems, and reapportionment is not likely to solve any of the pressing problems of the nation's cities such as poverty, racial tension, slum housing, or congestion.

Certainly we need more "before" and "after" studies of the effect of reapportionment on the policy choices of legislatures in order to identify the actual policy changes that have been brought about by reapportionment. The problem with such "before" and "after" comparisons is that so many other things were changing in the states during the reapportionment movement of the 1960s that it is difficult to sort out the policy changes that resulted from reapportionment from the policy changes that resulted from other factors — for example, increased black voting, increased party competition in the South, or riots in big cities.

If reapportionment does increase urban representation, why would it not lead to major policy changes? Within urban areas, city and suburbs have many real conflicts of interest based upon the different attributes of persons living in each area. Crowded slum dwellers living in the central city have different opinions about public policy than inhabitants of suburban split-levels on half-acre lots. Blacks in ghettos have different policy positions than whites in suburbs. Often residents of medium-sized cities differ with residents of a large central city in a metropolitan area. In contrast, rural legislators are much more likely to agree on policy issues and to vote in a bloc. On some issues we even find a conservative coalition of suburban and rural legislators. Several studies of legislative voting have indicated that urban legislators have difficulty in agreeing on policy positions and in voting as a bloc.[20]

Prior to reapportionment, Florida was one of the most malapportioned states in the nation, and many observers expected dramatic changes with reapportionment. There were many policy changes in Florida in the 1960s, perhaps even some that could be attributed to reapportionment. But as one Florida solon explained:

> The fellows from the upstate counties control the state's politics, no matter what happens with the one-man one-vote law. Those fellows work together and vote together whenever there's something really important coming up. They can stop the big cities cold whenever they want to.
>
> Here's why: Take Dade County [Miami] for example. They've got 22 representatives in Tallahassee and you'd think that would give them a lot of power, but they're always fighting among themselves. When they split down the middle, they end up with a majority of one. That gives Dade County one vote while the Porkchoppers [rural legislators] are putting up a couple of dozen solid votes all one way.[21]

Social Characteristics of Legislators

The assumption that a representative's social background is directly associated with his behavior in office is questionable. Although it is true that in the general population class position correlates with opinion on a variety of public issues, many people deviate from the majority opinion on every class level. And, as Peter Rossi explained, these deviators among persons of high status may attract the popular support of lower-status groups.[22] Class position, then, may affect decisions of voters, but it is a poor predictor of the decisions of elected representatives. Each representative is involved in a whole series of well-defined relationships with other individuals and groups, and these relationships may establish criteria for his behavior.

Perhaps the real value of studying the social background of legislators is to reveal the nature of the influences to which they will be subjected during their tenure. Mosca has observed that decision makers will usually possess "some attribute real or apparent which is highly esteemed and very influential in the society in which they live." [23] Both the local party and the constituency tend to select representatives who reflect the dominant social values in the district. Of course, a representative need not himself be typical of his constituency in order to fully represent their goals and aspirations. Background data on legislators should tell something of the criteria recruiters have in mind when they search for candidates.

Evidence indicates the "birthright" characteristics — race, religion, ethnic, and national background — tend to be essential in the recruitment formulas to which candidates must conform. In a thorough study of state legislative representation in Pennsylvania, Frank Sorauf found that the religious composition of constituencies had a distinct influence on both Democratic and Republican candidates for the state legislature.[24] Protestant candidates came from Protestant districts and Catholics came from Catholic districts. These religious differences paralleled ethnic differences. The Democratic party in that state, although heavily Catholic, did not run Catholic candidates in the Protestant "bible-belt" counties. Nor did the predominantly Protestant Republican party run Lutherans or Presbyterians in the Irish and Italian wards of Philadelphia.

Another social characteristic to which constituents demand conformity is race. Of the nearly 8,000 state legislators in the nation, no more than 200 are black. Blacks are reasonably well represented in the legislatures of northern urban, industrial states (see Table 6) where the black population is concentrated in core areas of large cities. Blacks are seriously underrepresented, however, in the legislatures of rural southern and border states. This underrepresentation occurs not only because of the segregationist history of these states, but also because blacks are spread out in rural areas rather than concentrated in urban constituencies. The vast majority of the nation's black state legislators are Democrats elected from ghetto areas of large cities.[25] At present this is true in the South as well as in the North. For example, all Georgia's black legislators are from Atlanta's ghetto area, although some predominantly black rural constituencies in the Deep South states, particularly Mississippi, soon may elect some black legislators. For the foreseeable future, it is very likely that all, or nearly all, of the nation's black state legislators will come from majority black constituencies. From the viewpoint of representation, the ghettos, with their concentration of black voters, grant blacks an advantage in capturing legislative seats. That advantage is lost when the black vote is spread out and diluted. For the same reason single-member legislative districts grant blacks an advantage in capturing legislative seats over multi-member districts, which dilute the black vote to less than a majority.

Another important criterion that constituencies establish for their representatives is place of residence. Legislators are far less mobile than the population as a whole; they tend to have deep roots in their constituencies. Sorauf reports that in Pennsylvania, a state with considerable population mobility, the odds against a "newcomer" with only twenty or twenty-five years' residence in a district are prohibitively high.[26] In 1957, 83 per cent

TABLE 6

Social Background of State Legislators, Selected States

	College graduates	Professional, managerial, or sales	Farmers and farm laborers	Catholics	Blacks (1967)
California					
Population	10%	48%	2%	22%	5.6%
Legislators (1957)	54	86	13	17	5.8
New Jersey					
Population	8	45	1	37	7.5
Legislators (1957)	63	92	2	36	4.4
Ohio					
Population	7	40	3	18	8.1
Legislators (1957)	58	88	10	23	8.8
Tennessee					
Population	5	35	10	1	16.5
Legislators (1957)	46	84	13	2	6.0
Pennsylvania					
Population	6	39	2	27	7.5
Legislators (1958)	32	76	5	34	4.4
Georgia					
Population	6	35	8	0.9	28.5
Legislators (1961)	57	78	22	0.4	4.2
Wisconsin					
Population	7	37	11	29	1.9
Legislators (1953)	40	68	22	33	1.0

Sources: Figures are derived from the following: John C. Wahlke, *et al., The Legislative System,* 486-491; Frank J. Sorauf, *Party and Representation,* 69-71; *The Wisconsin Blue Book 1954* (Madison, 1954); *Georgia Official and Statistical Register 1961* (Atlanta, 1961); National Council of Churches of Christ, *Churches and Church Membership in the U.S.* (New York: National Council of Churches of Christ, 1956); U.S. Bureau of Census, *U.S. Census of Population 1960,* "United States Summary" PCI (1)-IC (Washington,. D.C.: United States Government Printing Office, 1962); Congressional Quarterly Service, *Revolution in Civil Rights,* 4th ed. (Washington, D.C.: Congressional Quarterly Services, 1968), 114.

of the state legislators of New Jersey had been born in the district they represented or had lived there over thirty years; in Tennessee this figure was 76 per cent and in Ohio it was 88 per cent. Even in California, one of the states with the highest population mobility, 56 per cent of the legislators had been born in their district or had lived there thirty years, and only 10 per cent had lived in their districts less than ten years.[27]

Certain social characteristics, however, escape the constituents' demand for conformity. More than three-quarters of the nation's state legislators have been exposed to a college education, a striking contrast to the educational level of the total population. Legislators are also concentrated in prestigious occupations. A great majority of legislators are either engaged in the professions, or are proprietors, managers, or officials of businesses. Farmers constitute a sizable minority of legislators in all but the most urban states, and lawyers are the largest single occupational group. The feminine half of our population is seldom represented by more than 5 per cent of the members of any state legislature. Sorauf reports that the legislative chambers bear signs of a male club such as highly burnished cuspidors. The female legislator "may be viewed as an intruder in the smoking-room company." [28] Women are somewhat better represented (up to 18 per cent) in the less populous New England and western states with less professional legislatures; the large urban industrial states with more professional legislatures have few female representatives.[29]

Since the populations of the fifty states vary in ethnic and religious composition, we can expect state chambers to reflect these variations. Table 6 indicates that legislators in every state have higher educational and occupational levels than the general population. Legislatures do reflect their states in certain characteristics, however. The Catholic percentage of the population in New Jersey, Pennsylvania, and Wisconsin is higher than the other states, and there are more Catholics in their legislatures. Tennessee and Georgia have very few Catholics in their populations or their legislatures. The farm populations of Tennessee, Georgia, and Wisconsin are larger than those of the other states; correspondingly more farmers hold legislative office.

Social background information on state legislators also indicates that legislators usually come from the upwardly mobile sectors of the population.[30] Many of them are among the second rung elites in the status system rather than from established wealth. Although the sons and grandsons of distinguished old families of great wealth are increasingly entering presidential and gubernatorial politics in the states, they seldom run for state legislature. In contrast, state legislators have tended to take up occupations with more prestige than their fathers. Legislators are frequently among the middle or upper-middle status groups for whom politics is an avenue of upward mobility. Constituencies accept higher educated, more "prestigiously" employed candidates because of success, status, and the popular conceptions of qualifications for the legislative job. In general, constituencies seek gregarious, socially rising men from the prevailing racial, religious, and nationality groups of the district. Candidates should be respectable in whatever ways the local mores define that term. The voters seem to want candidates typical of themselves in religion, race, and ethnic background, but with education, occupation, and social status above the average. In short, constituents seem to prefer that their legislators be "local boys made good." [31]

Occupational data also clearly reflect the fact that the state legislator's job is part-time and lacks a self-supporting salary. Legislators must come from occupational groups with flexible work responsibility. The lawyer, the farmer, and the business owner can adjust his work to the legislative schedule, but the office manager cannot. The overrepresented occupations are those involving extensive public contact. The lawyer, insurance agent, farm implement dealer, tavern owner, and undertaker establish in their business the wide circle of friends necessary for political success. In short, the legislator's occupation should provide free time, public contacts, and a sense of social respectability.

In the urban industrial states, Democratic and Republican legislators differ in their social attributes. For example, Catholic legislators are more likely to be Democrats than Republicans in these states. Legislators with strong ethnic ties are also likely to be Democrats, as are Negro legislators. Sorauf found marked differences in educational levels of Democratic and Republican legislators in Pennsylvania.[32] He discovered that Republican legislators in Pennsylvania on the whole held higher status occupations than Democratic legislators. These differences between the legislators of the two parties in the urban states do not grow out of the parties' expressed preference for specific types. The differences are imposed by the separate constituencies represented by each party in most of the urban states. Urban, low-income, and ethnic constituencies are usually represented by Democrats, and rural, high-income urban, and suburban districts are usually represented by Republicans. In the more rural states the constituencies of the parties more closely resemble each other in their social composition, and hence Republican and Democratic legislators cannot be clearly differentiated according to their social attributes.

Constituents demand certain social characteristics from their legislators but what is the social status of the office of state legislator? Sorauf reports, "If there is an order of accessibility to public office, the state legislature in Pennsylvania apparently stands just above small city borough and township office, below county and large city office, and greatly inferior to statewide or national office." [33] Certainly the record of turnover of state legislators indicates that returning to office is not particularly high on their scale of values. Over half of the nation's state legislators are new at each session, and the lower chambers have a greater percentage of new members than the upper chambers. This turnover is clearly not a product of competition for the job; only a very small proportion of legislators are turned out of office at the polls.

Recruitment of Legislators

The constituencies fix broad standards of social acceptability for candidates within which specialized recruiting agencies must operate. Party or nonparty recruiters must set more specific criteria and go through the mechanics of recruitment within the broad outlines of constituency expectations.

Why does a legislator decide to run for office? It is next to impossible to determine the real motivations of office seekers — they seldom know themselves. It is even difficult to establish the real circumstances surrounding their recruitment. We can ask legislators why they ran for office, who asked or encouraged them to run, and how the party influenced their decision. Yet the story we are likely to get usually magnifies the legislator's political initiative and independence, describes his motivations in socially acceptable terms, and understates his debt to the party or other nominating groups. The chief rationalization for seeking office seems to be an interest in or a sense of obligation to public affairs:[34] "The reason I was interested was that I felt I could do the community a service"; "I felt it a civic duty to run." Only seldom are the reasons for candidacy expressed in personal terms: "Oh, I just think it's lots of fun." Seldom will a legislator say that he ran to feed his ego, but occasionally a frank answer relating candidacy to professional or career aspirations is encountered: "It was an opportunity to expand my knowledge of the law and also good during the lean years of practice." Running for office is the classic form of "ethical advertising" for lawyers. Politics has a special lure all of its own: "It gets into your blood and you like it." However, despite some frank reasons for seeking to enter the state legislature, most decisions to run are cloaked in impersonal rationalizations: "I would like to serve the public as guaranteed by the principles as set forth by the constitution." Attempts to quantify these rationalizations seem fruitless, and the reasons for seeking legislative office are not very different from state to state.

The circumstances of a legislator's recruitment are almost as obscure as his motives. Many legislators declare that they were prevailed upon by friends, constituents, backers, or party leaders to seek office, fulfilling the old tradition that the office should seek the man. Few legislators seem willing to perceive their careers as party-sponsored. We should expect that in the more competitive party states, legislators would be more likely to see the party as the necessary vehicle for a political career. Sorauf found that "party is obviously the chief stimulus to candidacy in Pennsylvania."[35] *The*

Legislative System studies also found that more legislators in the competitive states were willing to view their career as party-sponsored than legislators from the noncompetitive state of Tennessee.

It also appears that the more competitive the state's party system, the more likely it is for legislators to have had some prior governmental experience, particularly service at the local level. The most common prelegislative service is on city councils, county boards, and school boards. *The Legislative System* studies show the following percentage of legislators having some prior local government experience: New Jersey, 58; Ohio, 43; California, 33; Tennessee, 29.[36] These percentages seem related to the degree of party competition in each state. Separate studies confirm this relationship between local government experience and party competition by reporting the following percentages of state legislators with experience in locally elected bodies: Wisconsin, 71; Massachusetts, 54; Oregon, 43; Utah, 37; Nebraska, 33; West Virginia, 15; South Carolina, 8.[37] In competitive party systems the party is more likely to participate in the nominating process, and state legislative offices are likely to be regarded as a reward for faithful party service at the local level.

How much competition exists for legislative seats? Not as much as we might expect. First, let us consider competition in primary elections. Studies in Pennsylvania and Wisconsin reveal that more than half of the legislators ran unopposed in primary elections.[38] In the noncompetitive states, primary competition may occur more frequently in the majority party primaries, but competition in the minority party primaries is very unlikely. Competition is also measured by the closeness of the races. Many legislators engaged in primary contests face only token opposition. Available evidence suggests that primary competition is greater where the likelihood of victory in the general election is greater. V. O. Key has shown that most primary competition occurs in a party's "sure" districts, some contests occur in "close" districts, and few contests occur in districts where the party's chances are poor.[39]

The recruitment process culminates in the general election. Yet one party or the other is so entrenched in many legislative constituencies that the voters have little real choice in the general election. A sampling of legislatures by Malcolm Jewell shows that the proportion of contested seats to total seats in general elections can range from a low of 41 per cent (North Carolina senate, 1956–1960; New Hampshire house, 1950; Kentucky house, 1947–1957) to 100 per cent (Rhode Island senate and house, 1952–1956; Michigan senate, 1958–1960; New York house and senate, 1958–1962).[40] In most of the legislatures sampled about 80 per cent of the seats were contested in the general election. More seats are contested in states with close, two-party competition. In the southern and border states, where the legislatures are heavily Democratic, there is little competition in the general election for legislative seats, although primary competition in the majority party is frequent in these states. In contrast, party competition in New York is so intense that both parties are given maximum incentive to run full legislative slates throughout the state. Statewide competition is only one of the factors explaining contested elections. Party organization and cohesion is another factor; even a party that obtains frequent statewide victories may experience local problems in organization strength resulting from a failure to run candidates. It takes time and work to build up local party organizations to produce a complete legislative slate.

Competition means more than a name filed under the opposition party label. Generally, a competitive election is one that the winning candidate wins by something less than a 2 to 1 margin. Under this realistic definition of competition, the absence of truly competitive politics in legislative elections is striking. In Pennsylvania, one of the more competitive states, over half of the legislators are elected by margins in excess of 2 to 1.[41] Similar findings are reported for competitive Massachusetts and Michigan.[42] Usually legislators from noncompetitive districts face a legislative session with little danger of defeat in the next election, and their behavior in the legislature differs from the behavior of legislators from competitive districts (see page 167).

THE STRUCTURE OF LEGISLATURES

Public Support

Public support of state legislative institutions is reasonably high, despite many criticisms from reformers. There is some evidence that Americans have considerable confidence in state governments in general. A national survey in 1967 asking Americans "Which do you think spends the taxpayer's dollar more wisely — the state government or the federal government?" received the following responses: state government, 49 per cent; federal government, 18 per cent; neither, 17 per cent; no opinion, 16 per cent.[43] A more detailed study of public support for the state legislature in Iowa revealed considerable commitment among the general population to the legislature as an institution: 88 per cent would not consider abolishing the state legislature; 78 per cent would not consider abolishing it even if it persistently passed disagreeable laws; and 67 per cent opposed a reduction in its power.[44] Consistent with many studies showing that support for American political institutions varies with the social, economic, and educational backgrounds of individuals, the Iowa investigators found that the greatest support for the state legislature came from the college-educated, professional, managerial, and high-income groups. Moreover, support was strongest among those citizens who had higher levels of political knowledge and who had higher political participation rates.

Professionalism

Some state legislatures are highly "professional," others are not. Professional legislatures are those with well-paid members who think of their jobs as full-time positions; well-staffed members and committees with good informational services available; and a variety of legislative services, such as bill drafting and statutory revision, that are well supported and maintained. In unprofessional legislatures, members are poorly paid and regard their legislative work as part-time, legislators or committees have little staff; legislative assistance and services are nonexistent.

In the 1960s John Grumm constructed a "professionalism index" based upon (1) the compensation of legislators, (2) the total length of the legislative sessions in a biennium, (3) the expenditures for legislative services, and (4) a legislative services score awarded each state by the Citizens Conference on State Legislatures.[45] The results in rank order were:

Highly Professional	*Professional*	*Less Professional*	*Nonprofessional*
California	Wisconsin	Rhode Island	South Dakota
Massachusetts	Texas	North Carolina	New Mexico
New York	Ohio	Arizona	Tennessee
Pennsylvania	Oregon	Oklahoma	Vermont
Michigan	South Carolina	Nebraska	New Hampshire
New Jersey	Delaware	Maine	North Dakota
Illinois	Florida	Mississippi	Utah
Hawaii	Louisiana	Indiana	Idaho
	Georgia	Colorado	Montana
	Connecticut	Alaska	Wyoming
	Maryland	Kentucky	
	Minnesota	Kansas	
	Missouri	West Virginia	
	Washington	Iowa	
	Alabama	Virginia	
		Nevada	
		Arkansas	

Environment

The pay, prerequisites, and working conditions of legislators vary a great deal from state to state. In general, the more populous, urban, industrial states provide more comfortable environments for their legislators than the smaller rural states. California legislators, for example, receive an annual salary of $16,000, and legislators in Massachusetts, Michigan, and New York receive compensation in excess of $10,000 per year. In contrast, New Hampshire pays its legislators only $200 for the biennium. It is not surprising that turnover is higher among legislators from rural than from the urban states. However, the larger urban states tend to consider more legislation, remain in session longer, and demand more time from their legislators, who probably devote a small proportion of their time to private business and become more dependent on their legislative salary than legislators from rural states.

Rules and Procedures

The formal rules and procedures by which a legislature operates are designed primarily to make the legislative process fair and orderly. Without established customs, rules, and procedures, it would be impossible for 50, 100, or 200 men to arrive at collective decisions about the thousands of items submitted to them during a legislative session. Yet the formal rules and procedures of legislatures also lend themselves easily to use by those who seek to delay or obstruct legislative action. It is a difficult process for a bill to become a law; legislative procedures offer many opportunities to defeat legislation. Since the legislature is a political institution that functions as an arbiter, rather than an initiator, of public policy, it was designed to minimize deliberation even at the expense of granting advantage to those who would oppose change.

Legislatures follow a fairly standard pattern in the formal process of making laws. Table 7 provides a brief description of some of the more salient procedural characteristics of legislatures. It illustrates the deliberative function of legislatures and the consequent advantage given to those who do not want action to be taken.

Rules of the Game

Partly to counteract the formal rules and procedures, legislatures develop informal rules of the game. These unwritten rules are not merely

TABLE 7
Summary of Legislative Procedure for Bill Passage

1. *Introduction of bill* (house or senate)	One or more members file bill with clerk or presiding officer, who gives it a number and refers it to a committee. This constitutes the first reading.
2. *Committee hearings*	Important bills may be given public hearings at which all interested persons or groups may testify. Committee may speed or delay hearings.
3. *Committee report*	Committee meets in executive (closed) session. Bills may be amended or pigeonholed or reported favorably or unfavorably.
4. *Bill placed on calendar*	Bills reported by committee are placed on calendar for floor consideration. Urgent or favorite bills may get priority by unanimous consent or informal maneuvering; other bills may be delayed, sometimes indefinitely.
5. *Floor debate, amendment, vote*	The second reading of the bill before the entire chamber is usually accompanied by debate and perhaps amendments from the floor. Often the crucial vote is on an amendment or on second reading.
6. *Third reading and passage*	Usually a bill is delayed one calendar day before it is brought to the floor for third reading. On third reading debate is not customary and amendments usually require unanimous consent. After final vote, bill is certified by presiding officer and sent to second house.
7. *Referral to second chamber*	Bill is sent to second chamber where steps 1 through 6 must be repeated. Bills must pass both chambers in identical form before going to governor.
8. *Conference committee*	If there are differences in wording in the bills passed by each house, one or the other house must accept the wording of the other house or request a conference committee. This committee is made up of members of both houses and it agrees to a single wording for the bill.
9. *Vote on conference committee report*	Both houses must vote to approve conference committee wording of bill. Bills may be shuttled back and forth and eventually die from lack of agreement between both houses.
10. *Governor's signature or veto*	An identical bill passed by both houses becomes law with the governor's signature. It may also become law without his signature after a certain lapse of time (e.g., 10 days) if the legislature is still in session. If the legislature had adjourned during this time, the governor's failure to sign is the same as a veto. A governor may formally veto a bill and return it to the house of origin for reconsideration. An unusual majority is generally required to override a veto.

quaint and curious folkways. They support the purposes and functions of the legislature by helping to maintain the working consensus among legislators essential to legislative output. Legislators are aware of these rules, which carry clearly recognized sanctions that can be imposed upon errant members. A great majority of legislators appear to accept the functional utility of informal rules, some by stating clearly that observance of the rules contributes to legislative efficiency, others by giving reasons why certain rules are necessary.

Some rules contribute to the legislative function by *promoting group cohesion and solidarity*.[46] In the words of legislators themselves, "Support another member's local bill if it doesn't affect you or your district"; "Don't steal another member's bill"; "Accept the author's amendments to a bill"; "Don't make personal attacks on other members"; "Oppose the bill, not the man": "Don't be a prima donna, an individualist, an extremist or a publicity hound"; "Don't be overambitious"; "Don't divulge confidential information"; "Defend the legislature and its members against outsiders." Another category of rules *promote predictability of behavior within the system:* "Keep your word"; "Abide by commitments"; "Don't conceal the real purpose of bills or amendments"; "Don't engage in parliamentary chicanery"; "Notify in advance if you can't keep a commitment." Some rules *channel and limit conflict:* "Be willing to compromise"; "Accept half a loaf"; "Go along with the majority of the party"; "Respect the seniority system"; "Respect older members"; "Don't try to accomplish too much too soon"; "Respect committee jurisdiction"; "Don't vote to discharge a committee." Other rules are designed to *expedite legislative business:* "Don't talk too much"; "Don't fight unnecessarily"; "Don't introduce too many bills and amendments"; "Be punctual and regular"; "Take the job seriously"; "Don't be too political"; "Don't call attention to the absence of a quorum."

A most important informal device is the granting of unanimous consent for the suspension of the formal rules; this permits a legislature to consider bills not on the calendar, to pass bills immediately without the necessary three readings, to dispense with time-consuming formalities, to permit nonmembers to speak, and to otherwise alter the formal procedures. Another informal rule is the practice in many states of passing local bills without debate or opposition when the local delegation unanimously supports the measure.

Committee Systems

While it is most convenient to study legislative decision making by observing floor actions, particularly the division of ayes and nays, the floor is not the only locus of important legislative decisions. Many observers and legislators think that committee work is essential to the legislative process. In committees public hearings are held, policies pleaded and debated, legislation amended and compromised, bills rushed to the floor or pigeonholed. Harmon Zeigler and Michael Baer write: "The committee hearing is generally the most important source of information for legislators, and lobbyists tend to flock to the committee rooms as the focal point of their contact with legislators." [47] The committee system reduces legislative work to manageable proportions by providing for a division of labor among legislators. But by so doing the committees themselves often come to exercise considerable influence over the outcome of legislation, and provide another opportunity for delay and obstruction by less than the majority of legislators, sometimes by a single committee chairman. Duane Lockard reports that "what a new legislator soon finds is that there is no choice but to depend upon his colleagues to inform him about issues assigned to their committees, and, like it or not, he is reduced to following their advice unless he knows the subject well enough to have an opinion. It is a source of surprise to many new members how many issues they are too ignorant to have an opinion about." [48]

A typical legislative chamber will have between twenty and thirty standing committees which consider all bills in a particular field, such as revenue, appropriations, highways, welfare, education, labor, judiciary, or local government. Many houses operate with a rules committee that governs house proceedings and determines the priority given the bills on the legislative calendar. Committees may prevent the bill from coming to the floor for vote by inaction ("pigeonholing") although twenty states require every committee to report on every bill either favorably or unfavorably.

The importance of committee systems seems to vary from state to state. Malcolm Jewell argues effectively that state legislative committees do not exercise the independent influence over legislation that Congressional committees enjoy. He offers several reasons "why legislative standing committees are but pale shadows of their Congressional counterparts." [49] Most state legislatures meet only a few months every other year, giving committees very little time for any careful review of bills. Committees seldom have any staff assistance, legislative turnover is high, the seniority system is not as prevalent as it is in Congress, and committee members seldom acquire the experience and expertise of their Congressional counterparts. In most state legislatures the rules committee does not have the power to determine what bills will reach the floor as does the rules committee of the United States House of Representatives. The committee system, in short, does not offer the state legislator an independent source of power separate from party or factional basis of power. Of course, the fact that legislative committees are not independent sources of power does not mean that they are never used as important instruments of party or factional control. [50]

We can suggest four variations among the states and their committee systems: (1) Committees exercise less independent influence over legislation in two-party states where party discipline is high; (2) Committees exercise less influence in two-party states when the governor and the legislature are of the same party and more influence under divided government; (3) Committees are not likely to play an independent role in states where the governor, the party, or a faction exercises strong influence over the legislature; (4) Committees are more likely to be influential in one-party states where the governor does not exert strong leadership.

Legislative Roles

Roles are expectations about the kind of behavior people ought to exhibit. Expectations are placed upon a legislator by fellow legislators, the party, the opposition party, legislative leadership, constituents and interest groups, friends, and himself. A legislator may change roles to fulfill different expectations. Some expectations loom so large in the eyes of certain legislators that these men can easily be categorized according to the roles that seem to dominate their behavior.

Perhaps the most important and distinctive set of roles in the legislative process is that of the leadership.[51] The typical legislative chamber has a presiding officer, majority and minority floor leaders, committee chairmen, and a steering committee. The expectations with regard to these officers are rather consistent, and their behavior is subject to the restraints and demands of the membership. The functions of leaders are similar to the functions of rules. First, leaders are expected to help make the legislative system stable and predictable. They are expected to maintain order, to know the rules and procedures, to follow the rules, and to show fairness and impartiality. This, of course, is more true of presiding officers and committee chairmen than of party leaders. Leaders are also expected to help focus the issues and resolve conflict by presenting issues clearly, narrowing the alternatives, organizing hearings, and promoting the party or administration point of view on bills. The majority leader is supposed to "get the administrative program through" while the minority leader tries to develop criticism, "find party issues," and "develop a constructive opposition." Leaders are also expected to administer the legislature and expedite business. This includes "promoting team work," "helping individuals," "being accessible," "cracking the whip in the interest of time and smooth operation," starting the sessions on time, keeping them on schedule, and distributing the work load. It also involves communication, coordination, and liaison with the governor, administrative departments, and the other chamber. Finally leaders are expected to know what is going on, including the subject matter of bills. Role conflict can occur when different expectations are placed upon leaders. This problem is particularly important for presiding officers, who are both referees and partisan leaders. As one legislator explained: "He should be fair to both sides — except in a real pinch."

Another set of legislative roles that are commonly encountered and that make important contributions to the legislative process are the "subject matter experts." Unlike the role of the leader, the role of subject matter experts is not embodied in formal offices. However, the existence of subject matter experts is closely associated with the committee system and the practice of recognizing seniority within the committee. The committee system introduces specialization into the legislative process; the seniority system places at the head of each committee the majority member longest exposed to information about the subject matter of the committee. Subject matter experts are widely recognized among legislators; they occur in the fields of law, finance, education, agriculture, conservation, local government, labor, and transportation. Legislators often acquire a reputation for expertise through their occupations. Others become expert through contact with the dominant interest in their constituency. Still others see the acquisition of expertise as a source of influence and personal advancement.

Legislators might also be classified according to the way they perceive the legislative function — in other words, according to the expectations they place upon their own behavior as legislators. *The Legislative System* found four discernible types of self-conceptions among legislators: the ritualist, the tribune, the inventor, and the broker.[52] The ritualist sees his job through the mechanics of legislative operations. He is preoccupied with parliamentary rules and routine, and their mastery appears as his principal task. Legislative maneuvering becomes an end in itself. He views passing a budget as a necessary routine rather than as an important policy-making act. Committee work is important to the ritualist. The technical perfection of laws seems almost as important to him as their policy implication. Some ritualist orientations were expressed as follows: "Primarily I should acquaint myself with parliamentary procedures and rules and regulations, in finding out where I may avail myself with the necessary information to enable myself to represent my constituency to the highest degree"; "The most important thing which isn't done enough is to watch the type of bills that pass and to watch the language of bills."

The tribune perceives himself "as the discoverer or connoisseur of popular needs, as the defender of popular interests, or as the advocate of popular demand." He sees his principal task as one of understanding local problems, making himself available to the people back home, and keeping track of public opinion: "Well, most important is to keep in close touch with your constituents and find out what they want"; "A legislator has an obligation to protect people's rights — every time you pass a law, you take away from them"; "With me the only reason is to improve things for the ordinary man and the underdog — big business and rich people have attorneys, accountants, and loopholes in the laws but damn few people are interested in the underdog and minorities."

The inventor, a type chosen by few legislators, sees himself as the initiator and creator of public policy. He wants the legislature to lead in solving the current major problems in his state. He believes the legislature "should be in front of things." That few of the legislators interviewed even claimed to approach their task in a creative manner is evidence that legislators themselves recognize that the function of policy initiation has shifted from the legislatures to the governor, executive agencies, and interest groups. The true inventors in the legislature are probably frustrated men, since the legislature seldom does anything but respond to the inventiveness of the governor, civil servants, or active pressure groups. Only in those two-party states where legislature and executive are controlled by two different parties is it likely that the legislature will attempt to compete with the governor in making public policy. Still, many legislators persist in seeing their task in grand proportions: "Like a doctor, this job is to cure ills. This state has many economic and social problems, and a legislator with lots of background can grasp these problems and introduce legislation to better them. He can cure just like a doctor can."

The broker sees himself as a referee in the struggle between interest groups, constituencies, and executive agencies. His task is to balance, to compromise, and to arbitrate between conflicting interests. Although the role of broker is probably a realistic appraisal of the functions of legislatures as a whole, only a minority of legislators will state that this is their personal role. However, those that do may be the more discerning and efficacious legislators. As one legislator expressed the brokerage role: "It's important to see the other man's point of view. Even if you feel that what you want is the absolute best, give a bit and get the next best thing."

Still another way of describing characteristic behaviors is to discover the legislator's orientations toward the expectations of constituents and party. Legislators have been classified as either trustees (those who are guided in legislative affairs solely by their personal conscience and judgment), delegates (those who are guided by the instructions or wishes of their constituents), or partisans (those who look to the party leadership for guidance). Despite the concern of political scientists since the time of Burke with the classic question of whether legislators should represent their party, their constituency, or their conscience, few legislators actually exhibit in their behavior a firm commitment to any of these. The fact that most legislators claim in interview situations to be guided solely by their own conscience is not relevant in behavioral terms since legislators when facing specific issues do not perceive any conflict among the wishes of their constituents, their party, or their own judgment. Even when they do perceive conflict, most legislators attempt to balance conflicting demands rather than opt exclusively for one role or the other. One legislator whisked the whole problem away with a little semantic trickery: "A representative's judgment should arise from knowing the needs and wants of his district and state." [53] For most legislators the formal attribution of the role of trustee is little more than a verbalism. It reflects the heroic image of the independent and courageous defender of the public interests who acts out of personal virtue and conviction regardless of the consequences. A few legislators in every chamber approach the pure type of trustee, delegate, or partisan.

The more politically experienced legislator is more likely to assume the posture of a trustee. There is some evidence that legislators who come to the office with little prior experience as public officials, and those with less service in the legislature, are more likely to respond in the fashion of a delegate or politico, while their more experienced colleagues prefer the trustee role.[54]

The future political ambitions of legislators also influence their legislative roles and behavior. Legislators who express the desire to remain in the legislature for several terms and those who express a desire to run for higher public office are more likely to see themselves as trustees using their own judgment in reaching legislative decisions.[55] In contrast, legislators who express little desire to remain in public office are more likely to see themselves as delegates representing their constituents' opinions. Furthermore, the more ambitious legislators are more likely to express a "state orientation" to legislative issues in contrast to a "district orientation." Apparently the politically ambitious legislator seeks to broaden his constituency in legislative affairs and to assume a more state-oriented role.

DECISION MAKING IN LEGISLATURES

Legislative Conflict

Many of the decisions made by state legislatures do not involve conflict. Most bills are enacted into law without a single negative vote. Several studies suggest that 70 to 80 per cent of total roll calls in state legislatures are unanimous.[56] Yet this does not mean that legislative chambers are free from conflict; unanimous bills are generally local or minor bills involving decisions that are not deeply devisive.

What are the principal types of conflicts that affect legislative decision making? If we can rely on the perceptions of legislators about the conflicts that consume their energies, then Table 8 is a valuable indicator of the types of conflicts prevailing in four different states. In California, regional conflicts rank as most important, although such conflicts were not perceived as particularly intense in New Jersey, Ohio, or Tennessee. Conflicts between the legislature and governor appeared important in New Jersey and Tennessee but not in California. Only rural-urban conflicts were rated as important by over half of the legislators in all four states.[57] What kinds of issues generate conflict in legislatures? Wayne L. Francis reports the kinds of issues that are generally important and those that generate party, factional, regional, and interest group conflicts according to a national sample of 838 state legislators from all fifty states.[58] As Table 9 shows, legislators rate taxation as the most important issue but it does not generate the most conflict. Elections generate the most partisan conflict but little factional, regional, or interest group conflict. Thus the issues over which disputes occur vary according to the context in which the conflict is considered.

Party Influence

The influence of parties in legislative decision making in the fifty states is by no means uniform. It is obvious that parties in one-party states do not exercise tight party discipline over the voting of legislators. In terms of legislative behavior, in fact, one-party states are really no-party states. As a Tennessee legislator expressed it: "You never thought about the Demo-

TABLE 8

Conflicts Perceived as Important by State Legislators in Four States

	Percentage declared "important," house and senate							
	California		New Jersey		Ohio		Tennessee	
Conflict	H	S	H	S	H	S	H	S
Rural-urban	65	74	53	50	79	65	91	63
Party	26	26	96	85	49	59	23	17
Governor-legislature	18	24	76	70	36	38	89	96
Liberal-conservative	58	74	22	25	52	59	29	37
Labor-management	65	62	18	15	61	55	54	67
Regional	69	44	18	40	17	10	13	20

Source: Wahlke, *et al., The Legislative System,* 425.

TABLE 9

Legislative Issues Arranged by Conflict

		Conflict			
Ranking	Party	Factional	Regional	Interest group	Issue "importance"
1	Elections	Liquor	Apportionment	Labor	Taxation
2	Labor	Constitutional revision	Local government	Liquor	Apportionment
3	Land	Agriculture	Constitution revision	Business	Education
4	Finance	Civil rights	Social welfare	Civil rights	Finance
5	Administration	Business	Civil rights	Gambling	Labor
6	Apportionment	Apportionment	Gambling	Water resources	Health
7	Taxation	Gambling		Agriculture	Business
8	Social welfare	Taxation		Taxation	Civil rights

Source: Derived from Francis, *Legislative Issues in the Fifty States.*

cratic party unless the Republicans were trying something — for example reapportionment." [59]

The extent of partisanship in legislative decision making varies even among the more or less competitive states. One common measure of party influence on voting is the percentage of nonunanimous roll call votes on which a majority of Democrats voted against a majority of Republicans. Compilations by the *Congressional Quarterly* show that the proportion of Congressional roll calls in which the two parties have been in opposition has ranged from 35 to 50 per cent. Table 10 suggests that party voting may be higher in the legislatures of New York, Pennsylvania, Ohio, Delaware, Rhode Island, Massachusetts, New Hampshire, and Michigan than it is in Congress. Party voting is also common in Indiana, New Hampshire, New Jersey, Washington, and West Virginia. Parties appear less influential in Idaho, Illinois, Missouri, Oregon, Kansas, Nevada, Utah, and California. Notice Table 10 excludes unanimous or nearly unanimous votes in determining the influence of parties. Since most legislative decisions are unanimous, party votes would represent only a very small proportion of *all* roll call votes. Yet this does not justify the conclusion that parties are insignificant in legislative decision making. The function of political parties is to offer alternatives where significant conflict exists, and a unanimous vote is evidence that no real demand existed for an alternative decision. Thus, the importance of parties is best observed on nonunanimous votes.

Table 10 also shows party cohesion, which may be defined as the tendency of legislators to vote with their own party majority on roll calls in which a majority of one party votes in opposition to a majority of the other. The party cohesion of individual legislators is measured by the percentage of roll calls in which parties were in opposition and in which the legislator sided with his own party; the average party cohesion of Democratic or Republican legislators is simply their mean party cohesion scores. Party cohesion is high in Connecticut, Delaware, Ohio, New Jersey, New York, Massachusetts, Michigan, Pennsylvania, Rhode Island and West Virginia. It is low in Idaho, Kansas, Kentucky, Missouri, Utah, Nevada, New Hampshire, Vermont and California.

On what types of issues do the parties exercise great influence? Minor bills involving the licensing of water well drillers, beauticians, or barbers do

TABLE 10
Party Voting in State Senates

State	Party votes: Percentage of nonunanimous roll calls with party majorities in opposition[a]	Mean index of cohesion on party votes	
		Democrats	Republicans
California	17	48	57
Connecticut	50	90	67
Delaware	62	84	87
Idaho	30	58	62
Illinois	27	75	63
Indiana	51	65	68
Iowa	39	69	60
Kansas	35	49	82
Kentucky	39	51	59
Massachusetts	74	78	77
Michigan	58	81	75
Missouri	35	49	63
Montana	37	54	56
Nevada	28	70	43
New Hampshire	62	63	38
New Jersey	46	85	90
New York	70	76	88
Ohio	69	83	71
Oregon	29	55	64
Pennsylvania	82	82	90
Rhode Island	100	99	96
South Dakota	44	67	67
Utah	26	41	53
Vermont	40	63	41
Washington	50	60	78
West Virginia	54	85	73

[a]All roll calls in which at least 10 per cent of those voting dissented from the majority position.

Source: Derived from Hugh L. LeBlanc, "Voting in State Senates: Party and Constituency Influences," *Midwest Journal of Political Science,* 13 (February, 1969): 36.

not usually become the subject matter of party votes, and only infrequently will the parties divide over such matters as the designation of an official state bird. Rather, as Table 11 shows, two kinds of issues attract cohesive party votes.

The first involves organizational matters in government agencies, the legislature, and elections. Parties often exhibit an interest in bills proposing to transfer powers from an office controlled by one party to an office controlled by the other, or bills proposing to create or abolish non-civil service jobs. Parties display considerable interest in bills affecting the organization of local government, state administration, the civil service, registration and election laws, and legislative procedure. On issues that directly affect their organization and prestige, the parties react as interest groups.

The second category of issues on which the parties vote with cohesion concerns the most important issues of the day — taxation, appropriations, education, health and welfare, regulation of business and labor, and problems involving natural resources. Party influence in budgetary matters is particularly apparent since the budget often involves basic issues of social welfare and class interest on which parties are split. In addition, the budget is clearly identified as the product of the governor and carries the label of the governor's party. Legislators are urged to support the budget of the governor of their party, while opposition legislators are stimulated to force changes in the budget in order to create issues for coming elections. Party cohesion is not related to the majority or minority status of parties in the legislature. On the basis of his twenty-six-state study, LeBlanc concluded that party cohesion was no greater among minority party legislators than among those of the majority party. Nor was the level of cohesion obtained by a party affected by whether or not it controlled the office of the governor.

Constituency Influence

What factors distinguish those states in which the party substantially influences legislative decision making from those states in which it does not? Party cohesion is found in the competitive states rather than the noncompetitive states. Since the noncompetitive states are the rural nonindustrial states, party voting appears related to urbanism and economic development and occurs more frequently in the legislatures of urban industrial states. California is an exception to this observation. Party cohesion is really strongest in those urban industrial states in which the parties represent separate socioeconomic constituencies, and in which Democratic legislators represent central-city, low-income, ethnic and racial constituencies,

TABLE 11

Party Cohesion on Roll Call Votes by Issue Category in State Senates

	Mean index of cohesion	
	Democrats	Republicans
Election administration	78	66
Legislative organization	73	70
State administration	68	63
Local subdivisions	64	58
Judicial and legal	61	58
Appropriations	70	69
Labor	67	79
Education	65	57
Taxation and revenue	63	68
Regulation of business	58	57
Transportation	57	62
Health and welfare	55	66
Natural resources	55	59

Source: Derived from LeBlanc, "Voting in State Senates: Party and Constituency Influences," 43.

and Republican legislators represent middle-class, suburban, small town and rural constituencies.[60]

What then is the basis of party cohesion in the states where it exists? Is party cohesion a product of effective party organization and discipline? Or is it really a result of similarities in the constituencies represented by each party? For example, is Democratic party cohesion in industrial states a result of party organization pressures? Or is it a result of the fact that Democrats typically are elected from metropolitan centers with strong labor groups, many Catholic voters, racial and ethnic minorities, and persons with few skills and poor education? Do constituency similarities really hold Democratic legislators together? Do Republicans cohere in these states because they typically represent middle-class suburbs, small towns, and rural areas, and these types of constituencies have similar ideas about public policy?

It is unlikely that party organization and discipline alone cause party voting, for organization and discipline can only be effective under certain conditions. Evidence seems to support the hypothesis that party influence is only effective where the parties represent separate and distinct socio-economic coalitions. Where the constituencies of a state are divided along social and economic lines and where the party division coincides with these constituency divisions, party program and discipline will be effective in shaping policy in legislative chambers.

After investigating the correlations between party cohesion and constituency characteristics in twenty-six state senates, LeBlanc found that:

(1) senators were more loyal to their party when their constituents voted heavily for their party in gubernatorial and presidential elections; (2) senators were more loyal to their party in partisan states where the Democratic party was heavily supported by racial and ethnic minorities, low-income groups, and the poorly educated; (3) senators were less loyal to their party in states where a more ambiguous relationship existed between the Democratic party and socioeconomic constituencies. He observed:

> It is understood, of course, that constituency influences on legislative voting are sometimes difficult to disentangle from party influences and the dictates of the legislator's own conscience or convictions. Often the several influences reinforce one another. Thus an individual of liberal convictions is politically involved in the Democratic party for that reason and, as the Democratic party's candidate for senator, is victorious at the polls in a constituency conventionally associated with Democratic party success — perhaps a racially mixed, low-income, urban constituency, heavily populated with industrial workers. In voting to increase workmen's compensation payments, the senator could be said to vote his convictions, his party's program, and his constituency.[61]

Pennsylvania is an excellent example of a state in which Republican and Democratic legislative districts are clearly differentiated by socioeconomic variables. The parties are first divided along rural-urban lines; within urban areas they are further divided along indices of socioeconomic status. Republicans dominate in rural areas and in the wealthier urban areas (upper middle-class suburbs and several "silk stocking" districts in Philadelphia and Pittsburgh). Democratic districts are found predominantly in the less wealthy, urban areas of the state. A similar pattern emerges when we consider occupational, religious, or racial characteristics. Republican districts within urban areas have greater concentrations of professional, managerial, sales, and clerical people, and Republican candidates fare badly among Negro voters. The Democrats dominate southern and eastern European, Irish, and Catholic districts, which are frequently the big-city, mining, or mill districts. The Republicans draw heavily in the Anglo-Saxon, northern and western European, Protestant districts of the state. This same sort of party division of legislative districts has been documented in Massachusetts and Michigan.[62]

This division of constituencies is the basis of party cohesion and influence in the legislature. Further support for this view is provided by examining the voting behavior of legislators elected from *atypical* districts. Since rural and high-income urban districts in Pennsylvania generally elect Republicans, and low-income urban districts generally elect Democrats, atypical districts are rural or wealthy urban districts that elect Democrats and low-income urban districts that elect Republicans. Studies in Pennsylvania, Massachusetts, and Michigan of the voting behavior of representatives from these atypical districts show that they tend to cross party lines much more frequently than representatives elected from districts typical of their party.[63] The threat to Democratic party cohesion in these states comes from small bands of rural Democrats; insurgency within the Republican party originates from the urban Republican legislators. Since party cohesion breaks down among representatives elected by districts atypical of their party, cohesion may really be a function of constituency similarities rather than party organization and discipline.

One of the more rigorous investigations into the causes of party voting in a state legislature is Thomas A. Flinn's study of party voting in Ohio.[64] Flinn expresses the constituency basis of party cohesion in the following hypothesis: "Legislators from similar constituencies will vote together and in opposition to legislators from constituencies with contrasting characteristics. To the extent that parties find their support in contrasting constituencies, party responsibility is the consequence." Flinn argues that constituency factors alone do not fully explain party cohesion, since members of the same party representing dissimilar districts show greater cohesion than members of the rural and urban blocs. On the other hand, the experience in Ohio does indicate a relation between constituency and party loyalty. Within each party, members from districts typical of their party in socioeconomic attributes support the party position more often than members from districts atypical of the party. Flinn concludes:

> Party responsibility is a consequence of party competition. . . . Various factors may intervene to inhibit or promote party responsibility, but the only important one located with substantial confidence . . . is constituency. Prospects for increased party responsibility depend, therefore, on the spread of party competition and upon a sorting out of legislative constituencies so that the districts represented by the respective parties are more homogeneous.[65]

The effect of constituency on voting behavior can be observed in still another fashion. In the urban states, "close" legislative districts, where the margin of victory is less than two-to-one, are those in which typically Republican socioeconomic characteristics balance typically Democratic socioeconomic differences. In contrast, "safe" districts, where the margin of victory is greater than two-to-one, are those with a socioeconomic imbalance favoring one or the other party. Legislators elected from safe districts generally show greater party loyalty on roll call votes than legislators elected from close districts.[66] Legislators with relatively thin margins of victory reflect the socioeconomic balance of their districts in their voting and exhibit less party loyalty.

Constituency characteristics, then, help to explain not only the outcome of elections but the behavior of the elected. The constituency basis of party cohesion has been studied in Pennsylvania, Michigan, Massachusetts, Ohio, and Kansas and appears to be operative in New York, Illinois, and many other states as well.[67] In contrast, Washington presents an example of a state where party lines do not follow constituency differences and, as a consequence, party unity is lower despite a high degree of organization in the legislature.[68] The constituency of each party in Washington includes both rural and urban legislative districts in reasonable, balanced proportions. Democratic party cohesion is broken down by the existence of liberal and conservative wings that roughly follow a rural-urban division. In California, too, the parties do not clearly follow rural-urban divisions within the state, and the result is a lack of party cohesion and influence in the legislature. The California system of apportionment, which grants one senate seat to each county regardless of population, strengthens the rural wing of the Democratic party in the senate and contributes to a lower level of party voting in the senate than in the assembly. The tradition of nonpartisanship in California has also tended to reduce the influence of party in the legislature. Phrases such as "playing at parties" and "captive of your party" from interviewed legislators attest to the persistence of antiparty bias in California.[69] Party voting is also low in Missouri, and there, too, we do not find a clear rural-urban or metropolitan out-state alignment of the parties.[70] Both parties draw their votes from rural and urban constituencies in approximately equal proportions. Salisbury reports that economic and social conflicts are not developed along party lines and that, as a result, Missouri is a "politically bland" state.[71]

To say that constituencies make themselves felt in legislative decision making is not to swallow whole the image of a legislator as an errand boy, a delegate, or a "lackey." In fact, most legislators seem to side with Burke's classic argument that the representative should be guided not by "local purposes" or "local prejudices," but by "his unbiased opinion, his mature judgment, his enlightened conscience." Sixty-three per cent of the legislators in four states identified themselves with the Burkean position, rather than subscribed to the role of district delegate or even admitted to balancing personal views with those of constituents.[72] It is not surprising that most legislators perceive themselves as unfettered decision makers drawing their wisdom chiefly, if not completely, from their own virtue, knowledge, and experience. Yet formal protestations of independence in an interview obscure more than they reveal the real influence of constituencies. Aside from the social incentive to assert their independence, legislators themselves are seldom conscious of the many ways in which their constituency impinges upon their behavior. The classic choice posed by Burke between district demands and personal judgment is an artificial issue to most legislators. They are products of their constituency and they share its goals and values. Conflicts between their district's views and their own are rare. We have seen that legislators have roots deep in their constituencies — many organizational memberships, life-time residency, shared religious and ethnic affiliations, for example. The party with which the legislator identifies is also a creature of the constituency; it accedes to local interests, local political mores, local political style. The legislator is so much "of" his constituency that he needs little direct prompting or supervision. As one discerning legislator commented:

> Basically you represent the thinking of the people who have gone through what you have gone through and who are what you are. You vote according to that. In other words, if you come from a suburb you reflect the thinking of people in the suburbs; if you are of depressed people, you reflect that. You represent the sum total of your background.[73]

Organized Group Influence

The character and influence of organized groups in legislative decision making varies from state to state. Elsewhere in this volume the reader will find a discussion of interest groups in state politics and an analysis of their relative influence in the fifty states. One way to approach interest group activity in the legislative process is to ask legislators what groups, if any, they perceive as being powerful. This was the approach of the authors of *The Legislative System.* In the course of their interviews, California legislators referred to fifty-six specifically named organizations; New Jersey legislators named thirty-eight formal organizations; Ohio legislators mentioned sixty-eight organizations; and Tennessee lawmakers mentioned forty organizations.[74] Thus, there seems to be little doubt that most legislators are aware of considerable organized interest group activity. There is also considerable agreement among legislators about which types of interest groups were the most powerful. Business interests were named as "most powerful groups" more often than any other interests in all four states. Educational interests ranked second in three states and tied for third in the other, and labor interests ranked third in all four states. Agricultural interests, government interests (associations of city, township, and county governments, and government employee associations), ethnic and demographic interests, and religious, charitable, and civic interests also were mentioned as powerful interests.

It is difficult to measure the effects of lobbying in the legislative process, although we can ask legislators what they perceive to be the impact of lobbying activity. This was the approach of Harmon Zeigler and Michael Baer in their study of lobbying in four states.[75] They asked legislators to evaluate the worth of the information they received from lobbyists, the degree to which they depended upon this information, and how much they believed they had been influenced by lobbyists. Their results are shown in Table 12. Legislators in different states differ considerably in their estimate of the effects of lobbyists. Only about one-fifth of the legislators in Massachusetts and North Carolina admitted that lobbying activity "frequently" or "occasionally" changed their position on an issue, while closer to one-half of the legislators in Oregon and Utah made such an admission. Legislators in Massachusetts and North Carolina had less confidence in the information supplied by lobbyists than legislators in Oregon and Utah. Zeigler and Baer reported that, generally, the greater the number of contacts between legislator and lobbyist, the greater the degree of influence enjoyed by the lobbyists. Also lobbyists and legislators tend to share similar socioeconomic backgrounds; many lobbyists, like legislators, are lawyers and have held previous governmental positions.

Legislators disagree about the usefulness of interest groups in the

TABLE 12
Perceived Effect of Lobbying by Legislators in Four States

	Massachusetts	North Carolina	Oregon	Utah
Persuasion				
Percentage of legislators believing that they have been influenced to the extent of:				
Changing from one position to another	20	18	51	42
Leaning more to the views of lobbyist	31	20	42	38
Questioning a previously held opinion	34	22	45	32
Information				
Percentage of legislators indicating they:				
Depend upon information from lobbyists	50	41	83	80
Have confidence in information from lobbyists	55	56	88	70
Find information from lobbyists helpful	41	28	61	43

Source: Derived from data supplied in Zeigler and Baer, *Lobbying.*

legislative process. *The Legislative System* classified 36 per cent of the legislators interviewed in four states as "facilitators" (those having knowledge of group activity and a friendly attitude toward it); 37 per cent as "resisters" (those having knowledge of group activity but a hostile attitude toward it); and 27 per cent as "neutrals" (those having either little knowledge about group activity or no strong favorable or unfavorable attitudes towards it). Facilitators were more ready than neutrals or resisters to attribute importance to the views of interest groups and were more ready to use the aid of lobbyists in drafting bills and lining up support for their own bills. Resisters and neutrals were less likely to feel that the views of interest groups were important in shaping the opinions of legislators. Facilitators and resisters could not be differentiated with regard to income or occupational status or rural-urban residence or age. However, better-educated legislators tended to be facilitators more than other legislators. This finding suggests that increased knowledge of the complexity of society is associated with greater realization and acceptance of group activity.

On what kinds of decisions are interest groups most likely to exercise influence? Party and constituency interests are most apparent on broad social and economic issues. On narrower issues parties are likely to have neither an interest nor an opinion. The legislator is, therefore, freer to respond to the pleas of organized groups on highly specialized topics than he is on major issues of public interest. The absence of both party and constituency influences on certain types of issues contributes to the effectiveness of organized interests. Economic interests seeking to use the law to improve their competitive position are a major source of group pressure on these specialized topics. Particularly active in lobbying are the businesses subject to extensive government regulation. Truckers, railroads, and liquor interests are consistently among the most highly organized and active lobbyists in state capitals. Organized pressure also comes from associations of governments and of government employees. State chapters of the National Education Association are persistent in presenting the demands of educational administrators and occasionally the demands of the dues-paying teachers as well. Lobbying is largely unregulated except for registration requirements established by about half of the states. Duane Lockard summarized interest group activity from the perspective of the legislator:

> Their pleas are not stated in terms of relative competitive position, yet that is exactly what is involved when large garages attempt to exclude small ones from making major automobile repairs; when liquor stores seek to prevent the sale of liquor in drug stores; when druggists seek to sell liquor at later hours than are permitted the liquor stores;

when farmers, dentists, engineers, and countless others get into squabbles over their internal affairs. The arguments are put in terms of public safety, health standards, free enterprise, or fair trade, and the legislator is subjected to a drum fire of telegrams, letters, telephone calls, personal pleading, and propaganda on such bills. Should automobile dealers be allowed to sell insurance on the cars they sell? For some reason — all connected with the highest motive of public welfare naturally — insurance men doubt the ability of auto dealers to advise wisely on insurance and they therefore propose to prohibit the sale of automobile insurance by car dealers. Not only does this bring forth vigorous pleas from the auto dealers and insurance men in the legislator's district, but a legislator who has no particular connection with business soon notices that his colleagues who do have connections frequently become unashamed lobbyists within the legislature. While the incidence of outright bribery and corruption in most American legislatures is nowadays slight, the practice of acting in behalf of one's economic interests — in the most flagrant disregard of the moral obligation to avoid conflict of interest — is all too common; indeed it is unusual to see a legislator refrain from taking advantage of his inside position.[76]

The Governor in the Legislature

The responsibility for the initiation of major statewide legislative programs falls upon the governor, who relies heavily upon his staff and executive personnel to fulfill his responsibility. There is not much incentive for a governor to shirk his responsibility. In the eyes of a large segment of the public the governor is responsible for everything that happens in the state during his term of office, whether he has the authority or capacity to do anything about it or not. There is a general public expectation that every governor will put forward some sort of legislative program, even a governor committed to a caretaker role. The governor's programs are presented to the legislature in various governor's messages and in his budget. Through his power of policy initiation alone, the governor's influence on the legislature is considerable. The governor sets the agenda for public decision making, and he largely determines what the business of the legislature will be in any session. Few major state undertakings ever get off the ground without gubernatorial initiation. In setting the agenda of legislative business he frames the issues, determines their context, and decides their timing. Few would argue that these functions have little to do with the outcome of issues. However, as influential as a governor can be through policy initiation alone, few seem content with the role of initiator; most interject themselves into the role of arbiter as well.

A variety of formal and informal powers accrue to governors that enable them to directly involve themselves in legislative decisions.[77] Among the formal powers is the governor's right to call special sessions. By utilizing this power a governor can bring attention to an issue and intensify pressure on the legislature. Another formal power is the veto that every governor has, except in North Carolina. Thirty-five states require a two-thirds vote rather than a simple majority to override a veto. The governor has an item veto on appropriations measures in forty-one states. The closing days of any legislative session generally see a flurry of bills passed. A governor can exercise his veto on these measures after the legislature has adjourned and for all practical purposes foreclose the opportunity of being overridden. Overriding vetoes is a difficult process, since a governor is seldom so weak that he cannot count on at least one-third of the legislature to sustain his veto. The mere threat of a veto also can change the course of legislative action. The state constitution may limit or strengthen the governor's influence in the legislature by determining his frequency of election and ability to succeed himself. All other things being equal, a governor with a four-year term and an opportunity to succeed himself should be in a stronger position than a governor who faces election every other year or one who cannot serve more than four years.

The governor's informal powers over legislatures derive from his role in the state political system. The governor's office carries prestige in any state; no man becomes governor without considerable political resources. It is natural that a governor will attempt to use his prestige and resourcefulness to influence legislatures. The governor is the most visible state official. His comments are more newsworthy than those of legislators, and he is much more sought after for television, radio, and public appearances. As a consequence, he is able to direct public attention to issues that he deems important. Perhaps he will not always be able to influence opinion, but he has ample opportunity to be heard. Skillfully used, the power of publicity can be more influential than any formal power. Legislators must respect the governor's greater access to the communication media and hence to the minds of their constituents.

In addition to the influence inherent in his office, a governor will also be an important figure in his party, perhaps even its dominant figure. In states with competitive two-party systems, the program of the governor is likely to be identified in the public's mind as the program of his party. Legislators know that they will carry that same party label into the next election. In some measure they will share with the governor the responsibility for the success or failure of his program because of their common party label. It may be sufficient for a governor to tell his party leaders in the legislature that he thinks that his prestige is at stake on a particular measure and that he expects the support of the party faithful. The governor thus can be instrumental in bringing to bear upon the legislature all of the cohesive forces described earlier that are associated with party. In the urban industrial states, where party lines reflect socioeconomic, religious, and ethnic affiliation, the governor can exercise great power over legislators in his party by making any issue a party issue and thereby activating these underlying affiliations.

Given the absence of divided government, gubernatorial influence in lawmaking appears strong in a competitive two-party state. When a governor in a competitive two-party state faces a legislature controlled by the opposition party, the linkage of the governor's program with the fortunes of his party reduces his influence over the legislature rather than strengthens it. The more his program bears a party label, the more likely it is to activate the cohesive forces of the opposition party. In contrast to the situation in competitive two-party states, the governor of a one-party state cannot inspire either intense loyalty or intense opposition by party identification alone. Legislators run independently of the governor and have no political stake in the success of the governor's program.

In the one-party states where party appeals are insufficient, the astute use of patronage and pork is indispensable in securing support for the governor's program. Pork can include construction contracts, roads, parks, hospitals and other institutions, state insurance contracts, and innumerable other items. State jobs look most attractive and local pork is most important in one-party states, with their rural economies, lower family incomes, and poorly educated work forces. Frank Sorauf reports that patronage jobs in urban industrial economies are insecure and unattractive, at best "short-term desperation job alternatives." [78] But in economically depressed states including large parts of the South, state jobs are more highly valued.[79]

It is apparent that the legislative influence of governors varies from state to state and over time within states. Ira Sharkansky has attempted to isolate the factors that influence the success of state executive agencies and governors in getting legislatures to approve their budgetary requests.[80] A more detailed report of this research is found in Chapter 7 but it is interesting to note here some of the key findings about interaction between governors and legislatures. (1) More acquisitive agencies get their requests cut down more by governors and legislatures than less acquisitive agencies. However, the more acquisitive agencies end up with generally higher appropriations than the less acquisitive agencies. (2) The governor's support appears to be a critical ingredient in the success enjoyed by executive agencies in their budgetary requests to the legislature. Legislatures respond more to governors' recommendations than to agency requests. Agencies with the largest budget expansions were those that enjoyed the greatest gubernatorial support. (3) The governors who enjoyed the greatest budgetary success in the legislature tended to be governors who could be reelected. Governors with high tenure potential were better able to elicit legislative cooperation in funding requests than those who could not expect to remain in office because of constitutional limitations on their terms.

Another study of the success of governors in passing their legislative programs in a number of states produced the following interesting conclusions: [81] (1) Governors appear more successful in competitive two-party states where their party holds a small majority in the legislature than in one-party states where their party holds an overwhelming majority in the legislature. We might think that the more seats the governor had to spare, the more successful he would be, but this is not the case. Apparently the governor is better able to rally support within his own party when he has only a modest majority; when his party has a large majority, he has a more difficult time holding the support of various factions within his party. (2) A governor is more successful when he wins a large popular vote in a general election. Moreover, his success in the legislature is also closely related to his showing in the primary election. Apparently strong opposition in the party's primary indicates factionalism within the party, resulting in the inability of the governor to secure the support of party members in the legislature.

CONCLUSIONS

At least three general propositions about state legislatures emerge from the discussions in this chapter. First, state legislatures reflect the socioeconomic environment of their states. Levels of urbanization, income, and education, the level of legislative activity, the degree of interparty competition, the extent of party cohesion, the professionalism of the legislature, the nature of legislative conflict, the level of interest group activity and influence, and the nature of legislative relations with the executive in the fifty states help explain many of the differences encountered in state legislative politics. Of course, there are some unique features of legislative politics in each of the fifty states based upon particular events, individuals, or historical experiences. But generally, the characteristics of a state's legislative system are closely linked to a state's environment.

Second, it seems safe to say that most state legislatures function as arbiters of public policy rather than as initiators. Policy initiation is the function of the governor, the bureaucrat, and the interest group. These elements develop policy proposals in the first instance; legislatures are placed in the role of responding to the stimulus provided by these groups. The structure of legislatures clearly reflects their deliberative function. Their rules and procedures and their leadership and committee systems do not lend themselves to policy initiation so much as they lend themselves to deliberation, discussion, and delay. The size and complexity of state government has reached a scale where expert knowledge rather than lay enlightenment is the critical ingredient in policy formation. For example, the state budget, perhaps the single most important policy-making document, is drawn up by bureaucrats subordinate to the governor, who modifies it before submitting it to the legislature. Legislatures make further modifications but they seldom undertake to rewrite an executive budget. Legislatures are still critical obstacles through which appropriation and revenue measures must pass; they are still the scenes of fierce battles over the ends for which public money is to be spent. Yet prior to legislative deliberation, the agenda for decision making has already been drawn up, the framework for conflict has already been established, and the issues have already been placed in particular bills. Sophisticated lawmakers are aware of their function as arbiters rather than initiators of public policy. As one of them said: "We're the policy-making body of the state government, and basically we should give leadership necessary to meet the problems the state faces. But in practice it comes from the executive branch." [82]

A third general proposition about legislatures is that they inject a parochial influence into public decision making. Legislatures represent locally organized interests that are manifested in local rather than statewide constituencies. Legislators have deep roots in their local constituencies. They have the religious and ethnic affiliations of their constituents, they have lived among them for most of their lives, and they meet them frequently in their businesses and clubs. The process of recruiting legislators is carried on at the local level. State legislators clearly represent local interests in state politics. This local bias has been often attributed to malapportionment and rural overrepresentation in state legislatures but actually it derives from the decentralized character of legislative and party systems in the American states. Precisely because the constituency of the legislature is territorially defined as many small segments of the state, the legislature will exhibit a parochial bias in decision making. Any representative body whose members are chosen by partial interests throughout a society represents that society in a manner different from a representative body chosen by the society at large. By representing small segments of a state, each legislator represents a more homogeneous constituency than the governor, who is chosen by the state at large. The legislator's constituents share a local environment, whether it be rich or poor, rural or urban, mining or manufacturing. As a result they are more likely to have roughly similar opinions on policy matters. The constituency influences on legislators are relatively clear, unmixed, and unambiguous. A governor, on the other hand, must please a wider, more heterogeneous constituency. No single local interest can dominate his judgment; he can balance one interest against another; he is free to represent widely shared interests throughout the state; and he is free to direct himself to statewide problems.

SELECTED BIBLIOGRAPHY

Dye, Thomas R. *Politics, Economics, and the Public: Policy Outcomes in the American States.* Chicago: Rand McNally, 1965. A comprehensive analysis of the linkages between socioeconomic environment, the character of state political systems, and public policies in education, health and welfare, highways, taxation, and public regulation.

Flinn, Thomas A. "Party Responsibility in the States: Some Causal Factors," *American Political Science Review,* 58 (1964): 60–71. A summary and critique of studies of party voting in state legislatures in the light of data derived from an analysis of roll call votes in Ohio.

Francis, Wayne. *Legislative Issues in the Fifty States: A Comparative Analysis.* Chicago: Rand McNally, 1967. An analysis of the results of a mail survey of legislators in fifty states describing key policy issues and the involvement of parties, factions, interest groups, and regions in these issues.

Jewell, Malcolm. *The State Legislature.* New York: Random House, 1962. Dealing exclusively with state legislative politics, this volume provides an excellent summary of material on the fifty states while extolling the virtues of party competition.

LeBlanc, Hugh L. "Voting in State Senates: Party and Constituency Influence," *Midwest Journal of Political Science,* 13 (February, 1969): 33–57. An excellent comparative analysis of the role of party and constituency influences on voting behavior in selected state senates.

Sorauf, Frank J. *Party and Representation.* New York: Atherton Press, 1963. On the basis of extensive interviewing, this study examines the many ties legislators in Pennsylvania have with their local constituents and describes the parochialism of legislative politics in that state.

Wahlke, John C., Heinz Eulau, William Buchanan, and Leroy C. Ferguson. *The Legislative System.* New York: John Wiley & Sons, 1962. This volume reports the results of comprehensive interviews with legislators in four states focusing on the perceptions legislators have of their jobs.

CHAPTER SIX

The Politics of the Executive

Joseph A. Schlesinger

The politics of administration relates political decisions to the business of the state. How do political objectives affect the manner in which laws are carried out? Does the arrangement of state agencies and personnel have anything to do with the fate of political goals? The American states are excellent laboratories in which to study such questions since they are unencumbered by well-ordered bureaucracies. Students of bureaucracy often can only sense the conflicting goals that are obscured by an orderly hierarchy of authority. But the American states, for the most part, consist of a variety of agencies whose relations are either so ill defined that they are uncertain of their jurisdictions or so well defined that they can act independently of each other. The observer, therefore, does not need to probe too deeply to discover how politics impinges upon administration.

States failed to develop neat administrative hierarchies in large part because state governments were not created at once but are the products of the gradual accretion of new functions and agencies.[1]* When a new problem arises, the pressures for action often force the state to use the simplest administrative solution, the creation of a new agency. A water pollution control board may be set up outside the bureau of conservation partly because its existence is a symbol that the state is doing something about the problem, but also because of a suspicion that the old bureau would not be interested enough in forcefully executing new policy. Then too, functions that at first appeared unrelated, such as recreation and conservation, came into conflict when the growth of population created a need for coordination that had not existed originally. Even states that have sought to develop neat

For assistance in gathering data for the revision of this chapter I wish to thank Harold Old.
*[See pp. 580–582 for notes to this chapter. — Eds.]

administrative hierarchies by establishing functional departments must face new problems. Thus, since New York State has constitutionally limited the number of its departments to twenty-one, it has had to use the executive department as a catchall to include such unrelated agencies as those for liquor control and atomic development.[2]

Of primary importance in the study of the politics of state administration is the intermediary and ambiguous role of the state in the American political system. The intermediate position of state government leads to uncertainty about policies and responsibilities and to laxity about standards of performance. This does not mean that state government is unimportant, or that it does not deal with matters having a direct impact on the daily lives of its citizens. A state may have an excellent department of public health on which the localities, in fact, do depend for the prevention of disasters. The state police may be the principal instrument for crime prevention or for preserving traffic flow in metropolitan areas. A state's tax policy may influence the economic health of its industries. But no one can ever really pinpoint the state's role. The capacity of a state to develop programs rests upon its revenues, which depend on the general condition of the economy. If people in California and New York are not buying automobiles, Michigan's revenues suffer and so does its ability to govern effectively.

A state may avoid solving its problems as long as people can turn either to the cities or the national government. Indeed, the general failure of states to handle adequately the problems of expanding metropolitan areas has led increasingly to direct relations between cities and the federal government, for the cities cannot tolerate a breakdown in transportation and health, and neither can the federal government, which is politically more receptive to urban problems than many states. Consequently, the intermediate character of state government means that a great variety of administrative arrangements never face hard tests. They may or may not be successful; but the costs of failure are not always clear. Thus, as Anton argues, many of the activities of state governmental leaders are best explained dramaturgically. They act out symbolic power roles without really accepting responsibility for the consequences.[3]

ORGANIZATIONAL CONSEQUENCES
OF INDETERMINATE GOVERNMENT

Political Parties

The unclear function of state administration, its varied character, and its relative freedom from public reckoning affect the ways in which men organize to achieve political goals at the state level. In most states organization has generally been weak. Although some American states are reasonably competitive, most states are dominated by one or the other major party.[4] But as a party tends to dominate a state its organization often becomes more fragmented, although it may contain persistent factions. Even when the states are more or less competitive for the top executive position of governor, lesser executive offices are often much less competitive, reflecting the willingness of the voter to dilute as well as to divide party control of the state executive (see Table 1).[5] More often than not, governors must govern either with executives of the opposite party or with executives of their own party who are freed of the constraint of having their reelection dependent upon the head of state.

Whether a state is competitive or not, the turnover in the office of governor is generally high, placing further limits on the governor as party leader. In close to three-fourths of the states a governor can expect to hold office for less than five years, and in eighteen states for less than four years. Such high turnover is not simply a product of constitutional restraints on reelection since it occurs even where there are no restraints.

The willingness of the voter to tolerate and even to impose weak party organization at the state level is partly a consequence of the national two-party mold, and partly a result of the nature of state government. National politics can stifle strong state party efforts. Yet state parties often stand in sharp contrast to strong one-party control at the local level. Lincoln Steffens long ago pointed out that the party "machine" imposed critical functions upon local government.[6] The failure of state party machines to

TABLE 1

Competition for Elective Offices, 1914-1958 (Southern states excluded)

	Number of states[a]	Type of competition (Percentage)		
		Competitive[b]	Cyclical[b]	One-party[b]
Governor	36	50	6	44
Lieutenant governor	24	21	25	54
Treasurer	26	15	35	50
Auditor	21	14	34	52
Secretary of state	30	13	30	57
Attorney general	26	11	31	58

[a]The number of states varies since minor officers are not elected independently in each of them.

[b]An office is rated as competitive if no party held it for more than 70 per cent of the time during the period 1914 to 1958, and if there was a change of party control in 30 per cent or more of the elections. If the rate of turnover was less than 30 per cent, it is a cyclical office. The office is considered as one-party if one party won over 70 per cent of the elections.

Source: Table is based on Joseph A. Schlesinger,"The Structure of Competition for Office in the American States," *Behavioral Science,* 5 (1960): 200.

develop is one indication of the uncertain political expectations that we have of the states. The brief tenure of the typical governor limits his opportunities for developing a personal political machine that could coordinate state government. Brief tenure tends to release from the governor's influence all the nonparty officials who know they can outlast him, such as civil servants, lobbyists, and others with long terms of office.

The fact that state government is something of a halfway house for men with political ambitions also reinforces its indeterminacy. This can be seen most clearly in the careers of governors, for few have been able to sustain a career in state government or politics. The typical governor arrives in office somewhere in his mid-forties at the peak of his political vigor. Twenty or more active years lie ahead of him. Yet, typically a governor can hope to spend at most four years in office. Where can governors go? The answer most clearly is not into some other state position but rather into the federal service. In Table 2, we see the postgubernatorial office careers of men who served in the decade from 1900 to 1909 and who served in the 1950s. Many of the latter are still active at this writing, although only Nelson Rockefeller of New York is still a governor.

The political careers followed by the governors of these two decades shows little significant difference. In each instance about 40 per cent did something else in politics after being governor. The greater proportion either became United States senators or obtained some administrative post in the federal government. About 12 per cent of the governors became senators, and, in fact, about one-fourth of all senators have been governors. Un-

TABLE 2
Public Office Careers of Former Governors

Postgubernatorial office experience	Percentage of governors serving during	
	1900-1909	*1950-1959*
United States Senate	13.6	12.5
United States House of Representatives	2.6	1.6
State legislature ·	1.9	1.6
Judicial office at all levels	2.6	5.5
Federal administrative office	14.3	18.7
State administrative office	8.9	1.6
Elected executive (governor again, mayor, or major party presidential or vice presidential nomination)	1.9	4.7
No evidence of postgubernatorial office	61.7	56.2
N	(154)	(128)

like the office of governor, however, the Senate with its six-year term and high frequency of reelection offers a man a long-term career.

A few governors, of course, can aspire to the presidency or vice-presidency. Many more gain top administrative positions in the federal government. Seven governors who served in the 1950s held cabinet level posts in either the Eisenhower, Kennedy, or Johnson administrations (Douglas McKay, Luther Hodges, Orville Freeman, Christian Herter, Abraham Ribicoff, Sherman Adams, and Adlai Stevenson). Many other filled subcabinet posts, took jobs on federal commissions, or obtained diplomatic assignments. A few such as Earl Warren became federal judges.

The typical route for politically ambitious men is upward, and for governors up means only the federal government. Of course, some remain in their states. Among the governors of the 1950s, Bracken Lee of Utah became mayor of Salt Lake City and Theodore McKeldin of Maryland became mayor of Baltimore. Two even returned to their respective state legislatures. But these are the conspicuous exceptions. The eyes of governors usually turn away from state politics, for their political futures, if any, lie elsewhere.

The flow of personnel from the state to federal government runs below the gubernatorial level as well. Nearly 40 per cent of all second-level federal political executives from the Roosevelt through the Kennedy administrations had some form of state or local office experience, the most common being as head of a state agency.[7] To the extent, then, that a man's outlook on his present job is altered by his ambitions, we must conclude that many of the most important officials in state government have their thoughts directed at the federal government. This does not mean that they do good or bad jobs for their state masters. It does mean that the state, in whatever sense one chooses to perceive that entity, is not really their master at all. State officials are ruled by those individuals and groups inside and outside the state who influence their destiny at the federal level. Thus the indeterminacy of the states as political units within the federal system is reinforced by the intermediate position of state administration within the careers of the governor and lesser administrative state leaders.

The advantages that may accrue to a governor from his position of influence within the national structure vary considerably from state to state. All states are not equal in the federal system. For example, career outlets in some states certainly provide better advantages for gaining a federal position than others. Although this is obvious for the office of the presidency, it is also true regarding lesser positions in the presidential complex such as Cabinet appointments and positions in the Supreme Court. Twelve states between 1900 and 1958 received no presidential appointment to the Cabinet or Supreme Court. On the other hand, a few states such as New York and Massachusetts received more than two and three times the number of such positions as their population size warranted.[8]

Such differences in the relative positions of the states in the federal system have a great effect on the states' administrative politics. The more closely the state and federal career ladders are joined, the more influence persons outside the state have over the state administration. Also within the state those who have some say about promotions have more influence over the behavior of administrators. In other words, if we try to assess the relative influence of governors of two states over their administrations, it is not enough simply to know the formal controls available to them, or even all about the internal politics of the state. The fact that one governor is in an excellent position to gain the presidency whereas the other has no prospects is equally important, if not more so, in describing what they can do or what prospects they have for attaining their goals within their own state. V. O. Key has pointed out that the party systems of states vary in their degree of interdependence with the national system; some states are closely bound to national trends and others are effectively divorced from them.[9] The same is true of administrative politics. Some states are more closely bound to the nation by ties of personnel and their careers.

In effect, the governor has great freedom to define his relation to his administration. His leadership is essentially political. He must be concerned whenever conflict arises, as well as whenever scandals emerge. But his relations with day-to-day administration can be very tenuous. Governors find it more important to maintain their political standing than to influence administration directly through daily supervision. In surveying the distribution of the governors' time each week Ransone found that only 10 per cent was devoted to talking with department heads, even though governors typically hold two press conferences a day.[10]

Being head of a state administration does not hold a man close to his desk. He can make extensive out-of-state political forays, and he is only restrained by fears of what political conflicts might break out at home while he is away. Writing in 1948 Warren Moscow, the political reporter of *The New York Times,* said that, compared with the task of being mayor of New York City or president of the United States, the job of being governor of New York was a

> soft snap. Save in rare emergencies, the press of work is not so much greater than that of any big-business executive. The physical strain is light enough so that any man of sound mind and sound politics with

the ability to pick trustworthy subordinates can function adequately
as governor.

The reason for this is simply that the important part of the job
of governor lies in the fields of policy-making rather than in the
handling of administrative detail. The Governor is not awakened late
at night or early in the morning by recurrent crises in international
affairs, nor is his executive domain so vast that the number of
minutes in the calendar week is insufficient to permit even ab-
breviated conversations with each of his lieutenants, a difficulty
which plagues a modern president.[11]

The governor does not even have to assert policy leadership, for rarely
does he face such hard tests of success as a mayor or the president. In the
severe governmental crises caused by the race issue, for example, the governor, among all elective executives, has had the greatest choice for involvement. Many governors have involved themselves deeply on one side or the
other, while others have chosen to avoid the issue. None has had involvement thrust upon him in the way local race riots and aggressive demonstrations for school desegregation have involved mayors and four presidents of
the United States. Even such a prominent governor as Nelson Rockefeller
was able to continue his convalescence after the political battles for the Republican presidential nomination, while the New York City race riot of
July, 1964, brought Mayor Robert Wagner home from vacation in Switzerland and caused President Johnson to assure the public in a press conference that the FBI was supplying him with daily reports on the New York
situation. In the recurrent crises in New York City during the 1960s involving strikes of subway workers, garbagemen, and school teachers, the governor's decision whether or not to intervene was as much a product of his
political conflict with Mayor Lindsay as of any generally accepted sense of
state responsibility.

Interest Groups and the Executive

Interest groups form the second principal way of influencing state government and its administration.[12] Although we have no reliable tests of the
influence of interest groups at various levels of government, it does appear
that they are exceptionally important in determining what the states do.
Here again the intermediate character of the state is the underlying factor.
As party organization weakens, it is reasonable to expect other methods of
gaining influence to become stronger. Also, when there are no clear expectations about the functions of a unit of government, the way is open for
interested organizations to use that unit for their own purposes. Thus, we

conclude that the many state boards regulating a great range of professions and trades including doctors, lawyers, barbers, morticians, architects, cosmetologists, and psychologists were created to regulate competition among the practitioners as much as to protect the public. This is most evident when members of a regulatory agency are drawn primarily from the practitioners themselves. Similarly, state government often becomes an extension of local industries empowering tourist councils and economic development agencies to give preferential tax treatment to new industries and even to build factories. Since the late 1930s Mississippi has had a program to "Balance Agriculture with Industry" (BAWI). It has been estimated that at least a fourth of the state's industrial payroll comes from plants built by the program through bonds backed by tax revenues.[13] State administration has long been closely entwined with farm organizations through the agricultural extension services and the county agents. Much of the latter relationship has been fostered through the grant programs of the federal government.

Indeed both the federal and local governments act as pressure groups upon the states and may even register as lobbyists. In providing inducements to the states through matching grants, the federal government has not only strongly influenced state policies, but it has also sought to define effectively the manner in which the programs are administered. For example, merit systems, although far from being all-inclusive in state employment, do exist in those agencies dealing directly with federal grant programs. In the day-to-day administration of programs the responsible federal agency must be considered. Local governments exert some of the most persistent pressures on state administration because all of their powers and much of their revenue come from the state.

As with political parties, the activities of pressure groups vary from state to state. Powerful economic groups often alter the governments of the states in which their principal resources are based. Thus the Anaconda Copper Company was almost synonymous with state government in Montana until the federal government became a formidable competitor [14] during the New Deal. Similarly, Ford, General Motors, and the United Auto Workers have had their most direct impact upon state government in Michigan. At the same time, certain states, principally New York and California, are often singled out for special attention by groups with nationwide concerns. In 1966 the California highway budget was larger than the entire budgets of thirty-five other states, and New York spent more on education than forty-three states did on all of their functions.[15] A pressure group, by getting one of these states to adopt an innovation such as the requirement that seat belts be installed in every new car, can force changes that will be felt in all states.

DOCTRINAL CONSEQUENCES
OF INDETERMINATE GOVERNMENT

People respond differently to the uncertainty that surrounds the states' functions and their varied organizational consequences. Some may simply withdraw. Most people pay little attention to state government. In a survey of one Michigan city, only 2 per cent of the respondents considered the problems of state government to be of great interest or importance, while 59 per cent thought national problems were highly significant.[16] Uncertainty about the future or about the consequences of choices may, on the other hand, lead to the development of a doctrine, or a set of prescriptions, about the "good" state. In other words, those who do take an interest in state government will tend to react less pragmatically than logically or rhetorically.[17] If a person does not know the consequences of administrative structure — of giving more or less power to the governor, for example — yet thinks that the structure is important, he is forced into making ideological responses.

As they have developed historically all levels of government have been affected by arguments about administrative reform. But it is a measure of the great indeterminacy of state government that the arguments have had extraordinary influence. Most of them have served the establishment and maintenance of a nonhierarchical state administration, keeping the governor from having much formal influence over the rest of the state government. The first argument, which emerged from the colonial experience, was "fear of the executive." It remains today and can be heard at every attempt to give more power to the governor. Characteristics of state government such as short terms of office, restrictions on reelection, the election of lesser executives, restraints on the governor's appointive and removal power, and overlapping terms all express the desire to prevent a governor from gathering too many of the instruments of control.[18]

A second argument, which emerged during the Jacksonian era, was that of "popular democracy." This argument followed logically from the fear of the executive, and asserted that the way to assure popular control of state government was to elect most of the important administrators. It dominated throughout the nineteenth century when the constitutions of most states were being framed. One of its major results was the establishment of many popularly elected executive officials. Their numbers are given in Table 3. This argument, however, has run its course. Elective officials tend to head agencies that were important during the last century, but are much less so today. The major new agencies that provide for health, welfare, and highways and carry the great share of state effort are usually not headed by elective officials. Education, one of the earliest functions of state government, is the only major function that is headed by an elected executive in many states.[19]

The representative character of state government is also reflected in the construction of boards and commissions to head agencies. Collective executives derive their rationale from the assumption that each member may represent a divergent interest. Thus, various groups may be permitted to control the naming of personnel, assuring a breadth of access and influence.

In the politics of state administration, "antipolitics" has been one of the most pervasive themes. Many Americans undeniably have distrusted political parties, politicians, and any activity that might be called political. In the late nineteenth and early twentieth centuries this feeling dominated the American states. In electoral politics it had its expression in the movement for the direct primary and for nonpartisan offices. The idea of removing politics from administration arose from the same sentiment. No one yet has found a way of achieving that feat, but some have suggested a state manager as a counterpart to the city manager. The antipolitics theme has been most successful in establishing the civil service systems in place of patronage appointments.

A variation of the same theme is the goal of separating state politics and administration from national politics and administration. As an approach to state politics, this goal rejects the national parties as having any proper relevance to state affairs. This separation is most commonly sought

TABLE 3
Number of States with Popularly Elected Officials, 1969

Governor	50	University regents	5
Attorney general	42	Mining commission	5
State treasurer	41	Tax commission	3
Secretary of state	39	Printer	2
Lieutenant governor	38	Board of equalization	1
State auditor	29	Railroad commission	1
Superintendent of education	23	Corporation commission	1
Public utilities commission	14	Commissioner of charities	1
Agriculture commission	12	Adjutant	1
Board of education	11	Examiner and inspector	1
Controller	10	Highway commission	1
Insurance commission	9	Fish and game commission	1
Land commission	7	Custodian of voting machines	1
Labor commission	6		

Source: The Book of the States, 1968-69, (Lexington, Ky: The Council of State Governments, 1969), 134-137.

by timing the elections of state officials so that they occur in non-presidential years. Recent changes regarding the office of governor give him a four-year term when elected in that manner. New Jersey, Virginia, and Louisiana elect their governors in odd-numbered years, avoiding any coincidence of federal and state elections.

A fourth theme, "administrative efficiency," emerged in part as the positive side of the antipolitics notion. It was also essential to the development of a merit system for hiring and promoting personnel. Administrative efficiency, however, has developed its own momentum since 1900, producing organizations such as the National Municipal League dedicated to the creation of administrative structures more efficient than the nonhierarchic state. In the reform rhetoric, efficiency has become equated with coordinated government, with central responsibility placed on the governor. The many "little Hoover commission" reports framed after World War II were dominated by this trend and usually advocated a reduction in the number of departments, more functional integration, and more power in the governor's office. As an argument about the proprieties of administration this theme counters the earlier positions. The argument for strengthening the governor has surely not swept all other arguments before it, but whenever major changes are made today by conventions or legislatures they usually work in that direction.[20]

The indeterminate character of state government suffuses every aspect of its administrative organization. For the citizen, the federal and local governments are the most conspicuous governmental units, and those he can most easily approach. Having only the dimmest notion of what he can or should expect from state government, he accepts a variety of arrangements. For politicians, too, the state is very often a halfway house. Many governors and other state executives consider state government only an intermediate point in a career leading to federal office. Those who have the clearest and most direct involvement in state government are organized interests or pressure groups; they leave their mark everywhere. But, because political expectations have been vague, the most frequent doctrinal responses to the problems of state administration have also been vague.

A COMPARISON OF THE RELATIVE
POSITIONS OF GOVERNORS

Since the governor's role is central to administrative-political relations, an assessment of the relative position of the governors in the several states is very illuminating. We have mentioned strong and weak governors. Now we will examine some major organizational devices that observers often think define the strength of the governor. We will rate the governors according to each, and then combine the various ratings to obtain an overall measure of the relative political strength of the governors in state administration.

One element that defines the influence of an administrator over others is status. The factor is difficult to quantify, however. The organizational chart of a state is largely a definition of the relative status of individuals, departments, and agencies. In part, status may be defined as who appoints whom, but it also derives from the placement of agencies within larger entities. An agency head beneath the governor is expected to consult with him. If an agency is a unit within a larger department, then it is to be expected that its head will consult with others in the same department and will report to the head of the overall department. An organizational chart, therefore, is a statement of formal communication channels and the influence that derives from control of information.

While the organizational chart is overtly a statement of who has the power to tell others what to do, it is also a chart of the incentive system of the state. We have argued earlier that an official is as much driven by his ambitions as by those forces or individuals that have put him into his present place. The organization of the state is the means whereby those ambitions are defined. A finely graded bureaucracy that constantly holds out the hope of promotion is the most capable of controlling the behavior of its members. The more extensively an organization seeks to control the behavior of its members, the more refined must be the status system.

In most states the organizational status system is not very clearly defined, which affects the behavior of administrators. An agency head whose unit is one of many in a large department may temper his devotion to his own agency because he hopes to be promoted to department head. The more independent the agency, the more he is likely to devote himself to internal goals exclusively. No doubt agencies and their clientele resist integration of their departments with others because they know their independence will be diminished.

Status is also defined by salary. The governor outranks all other political executives, and the discrepancy between the governor's salary and that of other executives does vary greatly. One exception to the salary-status system does exist. In many states the members of administrative boards may be unpaid or may be reimbursed simply for expenses. In Delaware most administrative agencies are headed by such unpaid boards.[21] It is difficult not to conclude that when the state does not provide the salary incentive for these men charged with executing its policies, nongovernmental employers of such officials will find their influence increased. The existence of this method of employment is another sign of the extent to which the state governments are not neatly closed systems but are bound up with the group structure of their states. The boundary between the government office structure and society is never so clean that officials are free of external influence. But what is characteristic of the states is the extent to which a customary device for defining the boundaries of an organization from its environment — the use of salaries and wages to define to whom an official is responsible — can also be extended to the larger society and economy.

Let us turn now to some aspects of the governor's administrative position that can be measured.

Tenure Potential

We have already stated that governors typically have short terms of office that may reduce their influence. When the governor's tenure is compared in Table 4 with the tenure of the other elected executives we can see that he is at a further disadvantage. In the period from 1914 to 1958 no governor could expect to be in office more than eight years, but over half of the secretaries of state could; in twelve states the typical secretary's term ran to over ten years. A similar relationship exists for the other minor executive posts, with the exception of lieutenant governor and attorney general, which are also positions of high turnover. Since ambition is probably related to opportunity, the possibility of long tenure for lesser elected officials helps determine the extent to which they can be controlled through their career expectations by a governor or anyone else.

TABLE 4

The Governor's Tenure in Office Compared with That of the Secretary of State

	Distribution of states			
Average tenure in	Governor		Secretary of state[a]	
years (1914-1958)	N	%	N	%
Under 3	3	7	0	0
3.0-3.9	15	31	4	10
4.0	12	25	4	10
4.1-4.9	5	10	3	8
5.0-7.9	13	27	8	20
8.0-9.9	0	0	8	20
10.0 plus	0	0	12	32
	48	100	39	100

[a]States with an elective secretary of state.

Source: Turnover figures for governors and secretaries of state derived from state manuals and blue books.

The term of office for governors ranges today from two to four years, although it has been as short as one year. Both the length of term and the stipulations on reelection state the improbability of long tenure for governors. In Table 5 the states are ranked according to the governor's tenure potential. All four-year-term states have a higher rating than any two-year-term state, regardless of restraint on reelection, in accord with experience. The longest tenure is found in those four-year-term states that permit reelection. In these states we would expect a governor to last long enough in office to put his mark on the state administration.

The shortness of the governors' tenure is due to various factors. Most important is the American attitude rejecting long tenure for chief executives. The attitudes that led to the Twenty-Second Amendment of the federal Constitution restricting a president to two terms have produced similar restraints on the terms of governors. Elective state treasurers and auditors also frequently have limited terms, reflecting the constitution writers' distrust of those put in charge of the state's monies. Yet lesser officials often overcome the constitutional restraint by the practice of rotation, as in Colo-

TABLE 5
Governors' Tenure Potential, 1969

Four-year term, no restraint on reelection (5 points)[a]			
California	Illinois	Montana	Utah
Colorado	Massachusetts	Nevada	Washington
Connecticut	Michigan	New York	Wisconsin
Hawaii	Minnesota	North Dakota	Wyoming
Idaho			
Four-year term, one reelection permitted (4 points)[a]			
Alaska	Maine	Nebraska	Oklahoma
Delaware	Maryland	New Jersey	Oregon
Louisiana	Missouri	Ohio	Pennsylvania
Four-year term, no consecutive reelection permitted (3 points)[a]			
Alabama	Indiana	North Carolina	Virginia
Florida	Kentucky	South Carolina	West Virginia
Georgia	Mississippi	Tennessee	
Two-year term, no restraint on reelection (2 points)[a]			
Arizona	Iowa	New Hampshire	Texas
Arkansas	Kansas	Rhode Island	Vermont
Two-year term, one reelection permitted (1 point)[a]			
New Mexico	South Dakota		

[a]The points are used for the construction of the General Power Index, Table 10.
Source: The Book of the States, 1968-69, 133.

rado where the state treasurer and auditor frequently alternate positions over a series of elections. No governor has circumvented the constitutional intent, which indicates that the formal restraint upon the chief executive has popular support. The closest to an actual circumvention of a constitutional limitation was the election of George Wallace's wife, Lurleen, to succeed him as Alabama's governor in 1967.

Despite popular support, the consequences of formal restraints upon the governor's tenure are by no means clear. The governor who cannot run for reelection undoubtedly has limited control over the personnel who hope to outlast him. On the other hand, the governor himself is freed from the control of the gubernatorial electorate and can carry on his administration with greater flexibility. The unexpected behavior of some southern governors is probably related to restraints on gubernatorial tenure that are characteristically a southern rule. Therefore, it is not always easy to predict from his campaign how a southern governor will react to the civil rights crisis. In 1958 S. E. Vandiver, Jr., was elected governor of Georgia on a strong segregationist platform that pledged that no school would be integrated while he was governor.[22] Nevertheless, in 1961 he lent the power of his office to further peaceful integration of the University of Georgia.

Vandiver's subsequent behavior in aiding integration may be the result of his need to change his constituency in order to continue his political career. Unable to succeed himself as governor he had no place else to go in Georgia politics. The road to the Senate was effectively blocked. Both of the state's senators, Russell and Talmadge, were powerful figures and, in any event, Vandiver was related by marriage to the former and had been a campaign manager for the latter. With the election of John Kennedy as president, Vandiver was pushed strongly for under secretary of the army, an appointment civil rights groups managed to block because of his campaign stands. But the experience pointed the way to future national office.[23]

Vandiver's behavior contrasts with that of Orval Faubus of Arkansas, a state that allows its governors reelection. Considered a moderate, Faubus nevertheless in 1956 sparked the first major crisis over school integration. He was reelected five times, breaking a long-standing two-term tradition for Arkansas governors.

It is true that in most states where a governor may not succeed himself he may run for reelection after an interval. But the politics of such reelections are more complex than reelecting an incumbent governor, and they are not a common occurrence. The most prominent examples of governors who were reelected after an interval are George Wallace of Alabama, A. B. "Happy" Chandler of Kentucky, Theodore G. "The Man" Bilbo of

THE POLITICS OF THE EXECUTIVE 225

Mississippi, Earl K. Long of Louisiana, and Gifford Pinchot of Pennsylvania. In seeking reelection to the governorship after an enforced interval, a strong personality is undoubtedly an essential asset.

The decade of the 1960s has seen a considerable improvement in the tenure potential of governors. Between 1960 and 1969 the number of states allowing governors four-year terms jumped from 19 to 29. According to our point score for tenure potential, the average for all states increased from 3.26 in 1960 to 3.68 in 1969. The increase in potential does appear to be reflected in an actual trend toward increased tenure. Looking at a sequence of decades since the beginning of the republic in Table 6 we can see that the number of years spent in office for governors serving in the 1950s begins to approach the experience of a typical governor in the first decade of the nineteenth century. Yet we must conclude that the greater proportion of these recent governors (69.5 per cent) serve four years at most. It is indeed a significant departure that governors such as Mennen Williams in Michigan or Nelson Rockefeller in New York can serve twelve or more years. The increase in tenure for most governors, however, appears marginal.

The Power of Appointment

The most widely appreciated means of controlling officials is the power to name them. Presumably, if a person can name an official, not only is the official beholden to him, but that person can also name someone whose values are close to those he wishes to implement. A sign of the diffusion of administrative control in the American state is the diversity of ways in which men are named to office. As we have seen, many are popularly elected. The governor, with varying degrees of freedom, may name others. Boards or commissions may name even more.

TABLE 6
Tenure in Office of Governors (Figure is percentage of all governors who served during the decade)

Number of years spent in office of governor	1800-1809	1820-1829	1850-1859	1870-1879	1900-1909	1920-1929	1950-1959
10 plus	14.3	3.5	0.8	0.0	1.3	1.0	4.0
5-9	16.1	14.0	5.6	11.8	8.5	15.1	26.5
3-4	30.3	40.2	40.4	49.1	54.4	53.5	50.3
1-2	39.3	42.3	53.2	39.1	35.7	30.4	19.2
N	56	92	124	154	154	185	151

Source: Joseph A. Schlesinger, "The Governor's Place in American Politics," *Public Administration Review,* 30 (1970): 4.

We can measure a governor's appointive power by defining the extent to which he is free to name the heads of the major agencies. Taking sixteen principal functions and offices we can score each according to the relative formal influence that the governor has over the appointment of the head of the function. The range of values is a statement of the likelihood that the governor can influence the administrator on the basis of formal appointive powers alone.

For each of the sixteen major functions the governors have been rated and the scores for each function have been totalled in Table 7. Since not all states have each of the sixteen functions, the index has been converted into a percentage of the possible maximum rating in a state. Thus, if a governor rated a 5 for all of the functions in his state, he would get a 100. If, on the average, he rated a 4, i.e., he appointed everyone with the approval of one house of the legislature, then he would rate an 80. If he usually appoints with the approval of both houses, he would rate a 60.

The ranking of the governors shows a great range, from 73 in Tennessee to 17 in Arizona. States such as New Jersey and New York that, along with Tennessee, have had major state constitutional revisions in the last thirty years also rate highly. States such as Illinois and Virginia, which pioneered in administrative reforms in the first part of the century, also rank highly.[24] Thus, the rating reflects the extent of the impact of the dominant trend in management reform on the several states.

A better idea of what the rankings mean can be derived from looking at selected states. Tennessee ranks as high as it does because the governor, with the exception of three public utilities commissioners, is the only elective officer, and most of the other positions are filled by him without the need of legislative approval. Even in Tennessee, however, some major officers — the secretary of state, the treasurer, and the controller — are chosen not by the governor but by the legislature. At the other extreme, Arizona's governor has weak appointive powers not only because such positions as secretary of state, attorney general, treasurer, and auditor are popularly elected, but also because the major functional departments such as agriculture, labor, and health are headed by men appointed by boards and commissions. North Dakota's governor has weak appointive powers because, in addition to the usual elective offices, such positions as tax, agriculture, labor, insurance commissioners are also elective.

The ratings given here of the governors' appointive powers are necessarily indicative only of gross differences. Not all offices and functions are equal in importance, nor do the values of our point scale have any inherent validity. As we said earlier, there is a historical difference between the older elective offices and the newer functions of great importance that are more

TABLE 7

The Appointive Powers of the Governor

		State rankings (index scores)[a]		
5 points	4 points	3 points	2 points	1 point
73 Tennessee	50 Arkansas	44 Alabama	37 Maine	29 Texas
72 Pennsylvania	50 California	44 Missouri	37 Oregon	27 Colorado
69 Hawaii	50 Connecticut	44 Washington	35 Nevada	26 Georgia
68 New Jersey	49 Idaho	43 West	35 Wisconsin	26 Mississippi
64 Indiana	49 Kentucky	Virginia	34 Louisiana	25 North
59 Massachusetts	48 Michigan	42 Alaska	33 New	Dakota
58 New York	48 Minnesota	42 Nebraska	Hampshire	24 New
56 Maryland	47 Ohio	42 Rhode	33 North	Mexico
56 Virginia	46 South Dakota	Island	Carolina	21 South
55 Illinois	46 Vermont	41 Utah	32 Kansas	Carolina
		40 Iowa	31 Wyoming	20 Oklahoma
		39 Montana	30 Florida	17 Arizona

The figure for each state is based on the governor's powers of appointment in sixteen major functions[b] and offices. It indicates the degree to which the governor can be assumed to have sole power over the sixteen functions or offices.

For each function, the index is scaled according to the governor's powers of appointment according to the following formula:

$$\text{Index} = \frac{\text{Values of } P_1 + P_2 + P_3 \ldots (100)}{\text{Maximum values of } P_1 + P_2 + P_3 + \ldots P_n}$$

where $P = $ 5 if governor appoints;

4 if governor and one house of legislature approves;

3 if governor and both houses of legislature approve;

2 if appointed by director with governor's approval or by governor and council;

1 if appointed by department director, board, by legislature, by civil service;

0 if elected by popular vote;

and where subscript indicates the chief administrator for each of the sixteen major functions and offices.

[a]The points are used for the construction of the General Power Index, Table 10.
[b]Functions are: administration and finance, agriculture, attorney general, auditor, budget officer, conservation, controller, education, health, highways, insurance, labor, secretary of state, tax commissioner, treasurer and welfare.
Source: The Book of the States, 1968-69, 136-137.

often appointive positions. It is probably more important for a governor to appoint a welfare director than a state auditor, or even a secretary of state. Of all the older elective offices the attorney general's is probably the most important because the judgments and legal advice he is called upon to give may have great political importance. Attorneys general and lieutenant governors are the minor elected executives who have most effectively been able to use their posts to advance to the governorship or the United States Senate. In this connection it is interesting that the earliest state official resistance to the 1954 desegregation decision of the Supreme Court came from southern attorneys general, a fact that Krislov has attributed to their aspirations for local office.[25]

State executives are quite sensitive to the influence of the appointing power. Deil Wright questioned department heads in all fifty states and found a strikingly positive relation between those who were appointed by the governor, their perception that they were controlled by the governor, and their preference for such control.[26] Popularly elected department heads, in contrast, were least likely to see or prefer a governor with much influence over their agencies.

Again, it is well to look at the governor's appointive powers within the total context. While the power to appoint is an obvious means of controlling subordinates, once the appointment is made the influence fades rapidly unless it is backed either by the use of power to remove or more preferably by control over future appointments. Since a governor with the power to remove an official is constrained by the resulting wrangle, he uses this power only as a last resort. Control through the hope for reappointment or for advancement is far more effective. Here lies the significance of political parties in state administration. Although governors may come and go, a party organization has a memory that enables future governors to reward administrators for past services.

That governors indeed may expect to influence ambitious administrators is indicated in Swinerton's study of the agency heads of six states.[27] He found that the more ambitious agency heads tended to view their function as aiding the governor in carrying out his program. Agency heads whose career goal was primarily to remain in that particular office had a less governor-oriented view of their function.

Party organization may modify our ratings in another respect. In our scale we have rated elective positions as those over which the governor is likely to have the least influence. This is true only to the extent that an individual does not owe his nomination and election to the governor. In a competitive state it is likely that a governor or candidate for governor will be closely involved in the selection of his party's candidates for lesser state offices, and to the extent that they can ride his coattails they are as dependent on him as any formal appointee. As we have already pointed out, if the lesser official develops independent electoral support, the governor's influence is lessened. However, it is also likely that men who run for elective offices are sensitive to political protocol and will conflict with a governor only if they feel it will aid their political ambitions.

Control over the Budget

One important control over administrative agencies is the power of the purse, which may transcend weaknesses in the appointive power. In general, this power is shared by the governor and the legislature, most states having placed the authority to prepare the budget in the hands of the governor. We can define the governor's strength again on a five-point scale according to the extent to which the budgetary authority originates with him:

5 if the governor has the responsibility for preparing the budget and shares it only with persons appointed directly by him;
4 if the governor has the responsibility for preparing the budget but shares it either with a civil service appointee or an appointee of someone other than himself;
3 if the governor shares responsibility with the legislature;
2 if the governor shares responsibility with another major elected official (no contemporary examples);
1 if the governor prepares the budget only as a member of a group, usually consisting of other elected state officials or members of the legislature.

As may be seen from Table 8, most states today give the main authority for budgetary preparation to the governor, although diffuse control exists in many states. For example, it is common practice to earmark funds for particular purposes, such as gasoline taxes for highways. Then, too, many states finance special projects such as highways, bridges, and power resources through tolls and fees. Such devices reduce the governor's control by providing the agencies concerned with an independent income.

The Veto Power

Finally, the governor's formal strength may be defined by his power to veto bills passed by the legislature. Although not, strictly speaking, a control over administration, the veto is a means by which a governor can prevent administrators from going over his head and obtaining support from the legislature. This is particularly true when the governor has the item veto, i.e., the power to veto a particular item of an appropriation without being forced to accept or reject the entire bill.

As with budgetary powers, the governors are typically strong with respect to the veto. Most enjoy an item veto, which requires an extraordinary majority of the legislature to be overridden. Some, however, lack such a power; in other states either a majority of the total membership of legislature or even a simple majority of those present can override the veto. These differences provide us with a five-point scale of veto powers, shown in Table 9.[28]

The veto, too, must be considered within the total political context. For

TABLE 8
The Governors' Budget Powers

	Full responsibility (5 points)[a]		
Alabama	Iowa	Nevada	Pennsylvania
Alaska	Kentucky	New Hampshire	South Dakota
Arizona	Maine	New Jersey	Tennessee
California	Maryland	New Mexico	Utah
Delaware	Massachusetts	New York	Vermont
Georgia	Michigan	North Dakota	Virginia
Hawaii	Minnesota	Ohio	Washington
Idaho	Missouri	Oklahoma	Wisconsin
Illinois	Montana	Oregon	Wyoming

Shares responsibility with a civil service appointee or with
person appointed by someone else (4 points)[a]

Colorado	Kansas	Nebraska	Rhode Island
Connecticut	Louisiana	North Carolina	

Shares responsibility with legislature (3 points)[a]

Arkansas

Shares responsibility with another popularly elected official (2 points)[a]
No example

Shares responsibility with several others with independent
sources of strength (1 point)[a]

Florida	Mississippi	Texas	West Virginia
Indiana	South Carolina		

[a]The points are used for the construction of the General Power Index, Table 10.
Source: The Book of the States, 1968-69, 144-152.

instance, even though he has no veto, the governor of North Carolina does not appear weaker in relation to the legislature than other southern governors. Even weak governors can dominate their legislatures on matters of policy because if the governor is weak in formal powers, the state legislatures are still weaker as instruments of policy leadership. Legislatures have only the barest capacity to provide any kind of oversight of the state administration.

A General Index of the Governors' Formal Powers

To arrive at a general rating of the governors' formal powers we combined in Table 10 the four measures of each governor's strength already presented: his tenure potential, his appointive, budgetary, and veto powers. The maximum possible rating is 20, found only in New York, Illinois, and Hawaii. The lowest rating is 7, found in Texas. The median score is 15. Although each measure is independent of the others, they appear to go together. Formal powers for the governor are cumulative and

TABLE 9
The Governors' Veto Powers

Very strong (5 points)[a]
Item veto plus at least 3/5 of legislature to override

Alaska	Illinois	Mississippi	Ohio
Arizona	Kansas	Missouri	Oklahoma
California	Loúisiana	Nebraska	Pennsylvania
Colorado	Maryland	New Jersey	Utah
Delaware	Michigan	New York	Washington
Georgia	Minnesota	North Dakota	Wyoming
Hawaii			

Strong (4 points)[a]
Item veto plus majority of legislature to override

Alabama	Arkansas	Kentucky	Tennessee

Medium (3 points)[a]
Item veto plus more than majority of members of legislature present to override

Connecticut	Massachusetts	Oregon	Texas
Florida	Montana	South Carolina	Virginia
Idaho	New Mexico	South Dakota	Wisconsin

Weak (2 points)[a]
No item veto, but speical legislative majority required to override

Iowa	Nevada	Rhode Island	Vermont
Maine	New Hampshire		

Weakest (1 point)[a]
No item veto and simple legislative majority required to override, or no veto at all

Indiana	North Carolina	West Virginia

[a]The points are used for the construction of the General Power Index, Table 10.
Source: The Book of the States, 1968-69, 62-63.

their adoption undoubtedly reflects similar, overall views of the governor's role.

A cursory examination of the general ratings shows that there is a relation between the size of the states and the formal strength of their governors. Texas is the only populous state where the governor's formal strength is low. All of the urban giants — New York, Illinois, California, Pennsylvania, and New Jersey — have high ratings. Indeed, the nine states with a formal power index of 19 and 20 contain almost 42 per cent of the total population of the United States.

Undoubtedly, the many factors that account for the variations in population among the states account for the variations in their formal power index. Factors related to the size of the states also relate to the power index, as shown in Table 11. Therefore, the higher the proportion of urban population in a state, the higher the formal power index.

Since the formal strength of the governor is positively associated with the size of the state, we may generalize that as the complexity of a state

TABLE 10

A Combined Index of the Formal Powers of the Governors

	Tenure potential	Appointive powers	Budget powers	Veto powers	Total index
New York	5	5	5	5	20
Illinois	5	5	5	5	20
Hawaii	5	5	5	5	20
California	5	4	5	5	19
Michigan	5	4	5	5	19
Minnesota	5	4	5	5	19
New Jersey	4	5	5	5	19
Pennsylvania	4	5	5	5	19
Maryland	4	5	5	5	19
Utah	5	3	5	5	18
Washington	5	3	5	5	18
Ohio	4	4	5	5	18
Massachusetts	5	5	5	3	18
Wyoming	5	2	5	5	17
Missouri	4	3	5	5	17
Alaska	4	3	5	5	17
Tennessee	3	5	5	5	17
Idaho	5	4	5	3	17
North Dakota	5	1	5	5	16
Kentucky	3	4	5	4	16
Virginia	3	5	5	3	16
Montana	5	3	5	3	16
Nebraska	4	3	4	5	16
Connecticut	5	4	4	3	16
Delaware	4	1	5	5	15
Oklahoma	4	1	5	5	15
Alabama	3	3	5	4	15
Wisconsin	5	2	5	3	15
Colorado	5	1	4	5	15
Louisiana	4	2	4	5	15
Georgia	3	1	5	5	14
Oregon	4	2	5	3	14
Nevada	5	2	5	2	14
Arizona	2	1	5	5	13
South Dakota	1	4	5	3	13
Maine	4	2	5	2	13
Vermont	2	4	5	2	13
Kansas	2	2	4	5	13
Arkansas	2	4	3	4	13
Iowa	2	3	5	2	12
New Hampshire	2	2	5	2	11
Rhode Island	2	3	4	2	11
New Mexico	1	1	5	3	10
North Carolina	3	2	4	1	10
Mississippi	3	1	1	5	10
Indiana	3	5	1	1	10
Florida	3	2	1	3	9
South Carolina	3	1	1	3	8
West Virginia	3	3	1	1	8
Texas	2	1	1	3	7

TABLE 11

Governors' Power Index Related to Selected Social and Political Characteristics of the States

	Distribution of total population in United States, 1960	
Power index	*No. of states*	*Percentage of total population*
18-20	13	52.3
16-17	11	12.0
13-15	15	15.9
7-12	11	19.8

	Distribution of states according to percentage urban, 1960			
Power index	*Over 75%*	*60-74%*	*45-59%*	*Under 45%*
18-20	6	7	0	0
16-17	1	1	6	3
13-15	0	9	3	3
7-12	2	3	2	4

	Distribution of states according to degree of party competition[a]			
Power index	*1st quartile (most competitive)*	*2d quartile*	*3d quartile*	*4th quartile*
18-20	6	6	0	0
16-17	3	2	3	2
13-15	2	2	6	5
7-12	1	2	3	5

	Distribution of states according to percentage of national leaders coming from them (1900-1958)[b]			
Power index	*2.5% plus*	*1.0-2.1%*	*0.42-0.84%*	*0.0*
18-20	8	3	1	0
16-17	2	3	2	3
13-15	0	2	7	6
7-12	3	3	2	3

[a]The measure of party competition is that in Richard I. Hofferbert, "Classification of American State Party Systems," *The Journal of Politics,* 26 (1964): 550-567. Does not include Alaska and Hawaii.
[b]Distribution of sources of national leadership, Schlesinger, *Ambition and Politics,* 24.

increases, the governor's need for explicit means of control over his administration also increases. We have already pointed out that the formal devices for administrative control are not necessarily related to the governor's influence. Within their states the governors of Mississippi and North Dakota may have as much, if not more, influence as the governors of New York and Illinois. A governor trying to oversee the spending of a $6 billion budget has a much harder task than one dealing with a budget of $150 million. The terms "state" and "governor" mask differences in administrative problems not unlike those separating the small neighborhood dress shop from the larger department store.

Regardless of differences in the size of the operation, the government of the small, rural state has more economic responsibility than that of the industrial state. An industrial, urbanized state has separate and sizable aggregates of wealth and population. The president of a major manufacturing concern, the head of a labor union, and the mayor of a metropolitan center can compete with a governor. On the other hand, in a state with no large cities and only minor industries no figure is as important as the governor. Thus, if a governor of New York had to work with the administrative apparatus of Mississippi he would be helpless in competition with its varied interests. Yet it would be a mistake to infer that the governor of Mississippi is helpless. The minor jobs, the contracts, and the patronage that a Mississippi governor dispenses provide him with the influence over legislators, administrators, and interest groups that his formal powers appear to deny him.[29] For a New York governor such patronage in a vast domain would be a crushing burden; he needs the order that formal, hierarchical controls provide.[30] Should the rural state governor obtain these controls he might have an excess of power. Perhaps this explains the resistance of rural, particularly one-party rural, states to the arguments for administrative reform.

But political factors must also be considered. Political indices as well as the factors of size relate to the power index. The more highly competitive states tend to concentrate power in the hands of the governor. Also there is a direct relation between the extent to which a state contributes to the national leadership corps (defined as presidential candidates and appointees to the Cabinet and the Supreme Court) and the formal power index. These political characteristics, of course, also are related to the size of the state and its degree of urbanization. Yet party competition, the need for parties to make their mark in a competitive political situation, may be the critical factor. The principal aberrations from the gradation of power according to size are those states out of line in terms of competition as well. Thus, one-party Texas has a weak governor, while the highly competitive but thinly populated mountain states of Utah, Montana, and Wyoming have strong governors.

THE POLITICAL EFFECT OF THE STATES' ADMINISTRATIVE ARRANGEMENTS

The measures we have presented of the governors' powers are based on constitutional and statutory provisions. Most observers have considered these basic in giving governors influence in their states but they have done little actual testing of this thesis. We have already noted that agency heads think they do. What do governors think? In 1965, a questionnaire was sent to all governors asking "What powers, both formal and informal, do you lack that could aid you significantly in effecting your programs?" Thirty-nine usable responses were received. Beyle reports a close relation between a limitation in a governor's power according to our index and his perception of that limitation as a weakness.[31] Thus, the budget power, which we have seen is mostly in the hands of governors, is far less frequently mentioned as a problem than the power of appointment, which many see as a principal weakness.

Some additional concerns of governors emerged from Beyle's survey. The second most important weakness mentioned was the related power of administrative reorganization. This power is not widely found in the states. The New York legislature in 1969 followed the federal precedent of permitting the chief executive to submit reorganization proposals that would become effective in sixty days unless vetoed by the legislature. Were such a system to become widespread governors would undoubtedly be less constrained by administrative organization.

The other major problem for governors was their relationship with the legislature. Any true evaluation of gubernatorial powers over legislators must examine all the subtleties of influence between two independently elected bodies. A governor facing a legislature composed of a majority of his own party clearly has different problems from a governor who must deal with a majority of the opposition. One of the more interesting recent findings is that of McCally, who tested the influence of governors over their legislative parties by observing their success with vetoes.[32] The best relationship she found had nothing to do with past events, such as the size of the governor's vote, or the size of his party's legislative majority. The best "predictor" of a governor's success with his own party members was how well he did in a subsequent primary election. We can interpret such a finding in several ways, but the interpretation that fits well with our underlying thesis is that politicians are most responsive to their expectations, and a governor who has a good chance of returning gains a great deal of influence. This interpretation suggests also that of the elements in our power index, tenure potential is perhaps the most important.

Although men think that administrative arrangements have much influence on policy outcomes, the actual effect is not easily determined. One problem is that of defining what we should expect from one arrangement or another. Should we expect a state to spend more or less money on education, highways, and the like in relation to the number of independently elected executives? Will we find that states that give their governors more formal power also spend more on redistributive policies such as welfare? The only answer that seems obvious is that the greater a governor's formal powers, the more he ought to be able to implement his program, whatever that may be. If, however, we assume that loose administrative arrangements work to the advantage of conservative interests, then lack of power in the hands of the governor ought to mean less money spent on education, health, and welfare. Thomas Dye [33] has tested these propositions and has found them to be true. As Dye is quick to point out, however, larger, more industrialized, and wealthier states both spend more money on redistributive policies and give their governors greater powers. When the economic factors are controlled, the effects of the political structure tend to be eliminated, indicating that the economic base of the state is the significant factor in determining policies (see Table 12).

However important the economic base of a state is in defining how much it spends on services, its politics still largely determines which groups pay and which receive. Fry and Winters have developed measures of the extent to which the taxing and spending policies of the states redistribute goods from the rich to the poor.[34] Their findings showed that political factors such as political participation, apportionment, and civil service coverage, as well as the governor's power and tenure potential affect the net redistribution more than the socioeconomic indicators, even when controlled for the latter. These findings help to clarify and restore the importance of politics. Of greatest interest in the present context is that the governors' tenure potential proved relatively significant, even more so than the total power index.

Again, the most significant improvement in the governor's power in the last ten years, according to our index, has been in tenure potential. His budget and veto powers were already strong in most states. His appointive powers have not increased much, and in some instances they have declined. Thus, the principal structural response to the ever increasing demands on

TABLE 12

Coefficients of Simple Correlation Between Governors' Formal Power and Public Policy Outcomes

	Number of elected state agency heads	Governors' formal power index
Per pupil expenditures for education	−.43	.49
Unemployment benefits	−.34	.52
Per capita tax revenue	−.22	.42

Source: Adapted from Dye, "Executive Power and Public Policy in the States," 931, 937.

state government has been to strengthen the governor in what our theory and evidence indicate to be the most effective way. If tenure potential is turned into the reality of governors with long terms, the gubernatorial office could become a true position of political leadership in the states.

SELECTED BIBLIOGRAPHY

Kallenbach, Joseph E. *The American Chief Executive: The Presidency and the Governorship*. New York: Harper & Row, 1966. A general text.

Lipson, Leslie. *The American Governor, from Figurehead to Leader*. Chicago: University of Chicago Press, 1939. History of the early reform movement.

Institute of Government and Public Affairs. *The Office of Governor*. Urbana: University of Illinois, 1963. A good collection of papers dealing primarily with the office of governor in Illinois.

Ransone, Coleman B., Jr. *The Office of Governor in the United States*. University, Ala.: University of Alabama Press, 1956. Useful surveys of the operations of the governor's office from the orthodox administrative reform point of view.

Schlesinger, Joseph A. *How They Became Governor*. East Lansing: Governmental Research Bureau, Michigan State University, 1957. Analysis of career backgrounds of governors from 1870 to 1950.

———. *Ambition and Politics: Political Careers in the United States*. Chicago: Rand McNally, 1966. Study of the political system as a response to the structure of political opportunities.

CHAPTER SEVEN

State Administrators in the Political Process

Ira Sharkansky

INTRODUCTION

Administrators do most of the work that we think of as "state government." They run universities and hospitals, design highways, and collect taxes. To be sure, the legislature must approve the statutes that empower the administrators, and the governor's program is usually the primary legislative debate. Yet we find administrators active in the formulation of basic policies. When the governor or a member of the legislature has an idea for a new program, he typically checks it out with the department that would be responsible for its administration. Depending on what the experts say, the elected official is likely to modify or to drop his own proposals. Much of the time the governor's proposals originate in the administrative departments. Program officers have lots of ideas for adding to their activities. What is announced as the program of the governor may be only his choice from many proposals that begin in the administration.

Who are state administrators? Many of them carry out routine tasks that have been detailed by actions of the legislature. In this category is the state tax auditor, who makes the first decision about a merchant's sales tax return and charges for additional taxes that have not been paid. Other administrators manage routine operations. The auditor's superior allocates work loads, processes vacation schedules, sees to the maintenance of his office, and may deal with clients who are not satisfied with the decisions of his subordinates. Still other administrators involve themselves in the most innovative work of government. They help push forward the frontiers of social progress by drafting proposals for new programs and by lobbying

238

in behalf of these proposals with the governor and members of the legislature. Administrators must also implement controversial programs. The way in which an administrator uses his discretion can mean success or failure for a project involving the intense feelings of many citizens. An official of the state department of education who negotiates as an intermediary between local school systems and the United States Office of Education about racial desegregation is vital to his program's success. Schools do not desegregate by themselves or simply in response to court or administrative orders. State administrators must have great sensitivity to the political constraints operating on a local school board. A state administrator may help balance sharply conflicting interests in order to help local officials accede to the wishes of the government in Washington without losing their local support. Increasingly, the services of state governments require the employment of highly trained professionals, who represent another kind of administrator. Most of them do not run extensive programs as department heads, nor do they perform routine tasks under a superior's direction. Professors at state universities and physicians at state hospitals, for example, use their skills and discretion under conditions of loose supervision in order to accomplish agency tasks.

The label "public administrator" is used in different ways. In some contexts, it denotes all the employees of a government except those in the legislative and judicial branches and the elected chief executive. Such a designation includes the file clerks and sweepers, as well as persons in high- and middle-range positions in state departments. In other contexts, the term is reserved for high-level employees of departments or agencies, i.e., the personnel who make the nonroutine decisions or set the standards to be carried out by their subordinates. For the most part, we shall concern ourselves with middle- and upper-level employees who employ substantial discretion in their activities within administrative units, or who speak for their units in dealings with other branches of government.

There is much variety in the state institutions that employ public administrators. They are called "departments," "bureaus," "agencies," "offices," "commissions," "services," "divisions," "units," or any name that the designers of a service may select. From one state to another the same kind of programs may be administered by units with different names. The names of the state libraries, for example, include Public Library *Service* (Alabama), *Department* of Library and Archives (Arkansas), *Bureau* of Library Services (Connecticut), Free Library *Commission* (Wisconsin), and *Division* of State Library, Archives and History, State Department of Education (New Jersey).

We actually know very little about the activities of state administrators. The major advances in the research techniques of political science and systematic efforts to build theories that describe and explain political behavior have passed by the agencies of state governments. Part of the problem, perhaps, lies in the intellectual background of public administration. Political scientists who specialize in the study of public administration often find themselves on the defensive. They suffer from a legacy that subordinates their field to other aspects of political science, or makes it appear wholly different from political science. Part of the legacy is an alleged dichotomy that contrasts "administration" with "politics." This contrast reached its height in the reform movements of the late nineteenth and early twentieth centuries. Administration was said to be different from politics, and was properly isolated from political control. Another intellectual legacy that threatens public administration is the division of government into three parts: legislative, judicial, and executive. Where is the administrator? Typically he is submerged within the executive branch. Each of these legacies tempts the political scientist to ignore the workings of administration. Either it is different from politics and thus not the natural domain of a political scientist, or it is subordinate to the executive branch, and less important than the chief executive himself.

Not all the literature discourages a study of administration. Perhaps the best-known defense of the field is Pope's couplet:

> For forms of government let fools contest —
> That which is best administered is best, —

Alexander Hamilton quoted this passage in the *Federalist Papers,* but could "not acquiesce in the political heresy of the poet." [1] * Hamilton helped shape our intellectual heritage by concentrating on the chief executive as the principal figure in politics.

There are several reasons for insisting on the distinction between the executive and administrative branches of state governments. These reasons stand as the crucial differences between executives and administrators and as features of the political process that will be ignored if we continue to think about administrators merely as the governor's subordinates. Administrators provide permanence and professionalism to the states. They typically acquire their positions by virtue of training and specialization rather than electoral success of alliance. They usually survive the periodic transfer in the control of the state capitol by one or another party or faction. Administrators design and implement public policies. As the per-

* [See pp. 582–584 for notes to this chapter. — Eds.]

manent professional employees of state governments, they are often the best informed about current programs. They are sensitive to the range of popular demands that are not being satisfied by current programs. More than other officials, administrators in each state are in touch with their counterparts in other states, in federal agencies, and in related specialities in universities and private enterprise. Professional administrators often enjoy the respect of elected officials for their expertise. Legislators and executives generally refer new ideas to administrators for their comments. Administrators typically draft the bills that legislators approve and the governor signs.

A common designation of administrative units that distinguishes them from the executive branch is the term "line." The administrative branch of state governments includes the line units that provide services directly to the people. Line units differ from the "staff" units that serve the governor and help him supervise and control the administrators. The governor's staff usually includes a budget unit, personal aides of the governor, and perhaps — depending on the state — a personnel unit to supervise the selection, promotion, and dismissal of employees in the administrative branch.

Admittedly, porous borders surround the administrative branches of most state governments. We know that administrators in all states do not simply carry out decisions that are made in the legislative, judicial, and executive units of government. Administrators do much of the work that is ascribed to other branches. They suggest policies and write bills that are enacted by the legislative and executive branches. Certain agencies have adjudicative functions and operate like the courts. Some organizations serve part-time as units of public administration and part-time as members of the private sector (e.g., government contractors). It is especially difficult to separate cleanly the administrative branch from the executive branch of state governments. The heads of many state departments are directly elected and have the potential for acting as independent executives. Over half of the states fill by direct election the offices of attorney general, treasurer, secretary of state, auditor, and superintendent of education. The voters of several states elect the chief administrators of agriculture, insurance regulation, public utilities regulation, higher education, highways, tax collection, railroad regulation, conservation, the national guard, and the printing of public documents. Many department heads are not only directly elected; they are also elected independently of the governor. The candidates for each office run their own campaigns, and the candidates of different parties may win positions in the same election. The result may be departments loosely held together by respect for the governor's program or by whatever control the governor can exert over departmental budgets. Or, the result may be a plural executive whose members carry on sharp disputes in public and sometimes keep each other from realizing their goals (see Chapter 6). Although the administrative branch deserves our concern as a distinctive institution that is important in state politics, we cannot define this branch in any way that fits the realities in all states.

This chapter explores the distinctiveness of administration in the political process of American states and its importance in the design and implementation of state policies. The sections that follow describe four traditions that figure in the design of administrative branches; show how these traditions are mixed in the structures of most administrative branches and their ties with executive and legislative branches; outline important differences in the administrative features of the states and show how these differences correspond with other peculiarities of each state, and show how certain administrative features correspond with the policies provided in each state.

ORGANIZATIONAL TRADITIONS
AND ADMINISTRATIVE DIVERSITY

The administrative branches of the state differ. Some of the differences reflect the choices made in each state from beliefs about the structures of administrative units and their relationships to the executive and legislative branches. Many organizational theories motivate those who design government programs and organizations in the abstract. In each state practical considerations also have led officials to modify their abstract plans as they build new structures or alter existing ones. The choices of organizational modes have varied from one state to another, and within each state from one era of administrative design to another. Four separate bodies of organizational tradition are prominent in the administrative structures of state governments and in the control devices that tie them to the executive and legislative branches.[2] It is stretching the meaning of theory to use the term for the thoughts involved in the development of administrative structures. They tend to be loosely related ideas, lacking specific assumptions, precisely derived propositions, or accepted bodies of fact. It is more appropriate to think about four "intellectual roots" or "traditions" that are evident in the arguments that address questions of administrative organization. Each tradition is associated with certain political goals that are inconsistent with the goals of other traditions. The administrative branches of each state government show some features of each tradition. In most cases the mixture is so thorough it is difficult to say which tradition prevails. If nothing else inserts controversy into the construction of administrative institutions, the attempt to adhere to certain features of each tradition guarantees that conflict. The four traditions are: (1) the desire to maintain political accountability in public administration; (2) the desire to maintain an equilibrium among the three constitutional branches of government by preserving the system of separation of powers and checks and balances; (3) the desire to ensure that professional and technical skills are brought to bear on relevant matters of policy formulation and implementation, and (4) the desire to maximize the efficient use of resources by means of a hierarchical form of organization.[3]

Political Accountability

The general principle of political accountability of public administration is pursued in radically different ways. There are such sharp controversies between the proponents of different forms of accountability that they could be termed distinctly antagonistic approaches to administrative organization. One approach, which can be termed classical by virtue of its historical lineage, maintains that elected officials should have the final say over the activities of administrative agencies. This means that agency programs are defined by laws subject to the approval of the legislature and the chief executive. Moreover, annual or, in the case of many state governments, biennial budget requests are subject to similar lawmaking procedures and require the approval of the legislature and the chief executive. An element that sometimes accompanies this form of political accountability is gubernatorial and legislative control over agency personnel. At the extreme, this means both control over individual appointments and the insistence that all administrators be contributing members of the party in power. The excesses of Jacksonian patronage are decreasingly apparent in state governments. Yet for many years, public bureaucracies experienced mass turnover with a change in party control of the state house. Patronage still flourishes in important departments of Massachusetts, Illinois, Indiana, and many other states. Other features also testify to the strength of political accountability in state agencies. Governors often fill senior positions with an outsider brought in from private life, rather than with a person who has devoted his career to a department. In this way, administration is thought to remain responsive to the wishes of the people, either because the governor makes the top appointment or because the appointee himself is a citizen rather than a professional bureaucrat. We have seen that another approach to political accountability — the direct election of department heads — hinders the governor's control over his administration.

A third approach to political accountability is direct client-participation in agency decisions. This feature has attracted considerable public attention recently when implemented through local community action programs. As these efforts began, there were direct clashes between two approaches to political accountability. Governors thought their own control of administrative activities would be undercut by citizen selection of policy-making councils and citizen control over the selection of agency personnel. There was intense political conflict over the design of administrative structures. Governors charged that citizen participation would put untrained and irresponsible persons in charge of public resources. They predicted that huge sums would be siphoned off for the support of new political organizations, that untrained supervisors would waste resources in poorly conceived and poorly managed programs, and that cadres of new revolutionaries would gain control of state programs and use them to challenge established norms. From the other side, the spokesmen for citizen participation alleged that existing programs for welfare, health, and education were poorly conceived to assist those people who were most in need and that recipients were the best qualified to formulate policies for their own benefit.

The recent political uproar over citizen participation in administration suggests that it is a radically new structure; but this is not the case. Several old and respected government programs include provisions for client control. State programs to license and regulate the professions and trades typically include members of the regulated group on the policy-making boards. A board of physicians oversees the regulation of the medical profession, and boards of barbers, plumbers, and electricians supervise the regulation of their trades.

Separation of Powers — Checks and Balances

A second tradition of administrative structure supports the separation of powers and checks and balances. The framers of the United States Constitution implemented this mode of organization and established it as a tradition to be followed by the builders of state governments. In the federal government, the separation of powers takes the form of a bicameral legislature, a separately elected chief executive, and an independent judiciary. Each of the state governments adopted the separation of powers and the checks and balances, although with slight variations in individual branches. Only Nebraska does not have a bicameral legislature, and only North

Carolina does not permit the governor to veto acts of the legislature. If any general statement can be made about the structures of state governments, it is that they are even more divided and beset with internal checks than the national government. In contrast to the opportunities of the president to appoint all the major officers in his administration, each governor must work with high-ranking department heads who are separately elected or are appointed by quasi-independent boards or commissions. In contrast to the freedom with which the United States Congress can determine its own prerogatives on matters of legislation, most of the state legislatures are limited to short sessions, are prohibited from borrowing sizable funds in a convenient manner, and have numerous other constraints against the types of legislation they may approve.

The pervasive attachment of state constitution makers to the separation of powers and to checks and balances has several implications for administrative organizations. First, control of administrative units is not given entirely to any one of the other branches. Second, this concern to divide the leadership of administration precludes the use of a simple administrative hierarchy in which control of the hierarchy is given to the governor. He must share his prerogatives over administration with the legislature and the judiciary. The judiciary hears cases that aggrieved citizens bring against administrators and may void or restrict certain powers that the administrator had exercised. The legislature has many opportunities to affect the structure, procedures, and programs of administration: review of new program proposals, periodic review of agency budgets, the approval of key personnel appointments, special legislative investigations into the operation of certain programs, the legislature's ability to initiate (and to pass over the governor's veto) new programs or to make changes in existing programs, and informal arrangements in which administrators seek the approval of key legislators for certain kinds of decisions. Third, each administrative unit may be subject to demands from competing superiors. A committee in the upper or lower house of the legislature and the governor may send conflicting directives to the administrator. While at times this may benefit the administrator — by providing him with the excuse of conflicting instructions to explain his lack of compliance with any one of them — the conflict between superiors also presents problems for administrators. Each potential superior may have his spokesman within an agency; the unit may be affected by internal conflict over the choice of superiors. Multiple loyalties among subordinates can upset the department head's control over his own agency at the same time that they inhibit clear control by either the governor or the legislature.

Professional Expertise

Another tradition of administrative structure seeks to elevate professional and technical competence to secure positions in each agency. This has several manifestations, some of which have generated severe conflicts with spokesmen for contrasting forms of organization. One prominent manifestation is the civil service movement. Several reform organizations have sought to protect state employees from patronage, the spoils system, or political control. Their goal is a merit system.

Employment on the basis of merit is only part of the more inclusive concern with technical competence. The merit programs remove the criteria of partisanship from personal decisions; until quite recently they have not been concerned with the development of recruitment, selection, and training programs to increase the level of technical competence in administrative agencies. The later movements reflect the increased preoccupation of state agencies with natural and social scientific programs that require highly trained specialists. Yet this concern with professionalism has its political opponents. The motivation for citizen participation in welfare and education administration comes partly from those who think that established professions are insensitive to the needs of certain clients. In another kind of conflict the spokesmen of hierarchical organization battle with those who want professionals in charge of their own administrative structures. In a university, this conflict is called administration versus faculty. That part of a professional's training that leads him to make his own judgments about a client's needs clashes with the principles of hierarchical management that lead a superior to assert agency policies against the decisions of his subordinates. Where the manager and the professional employees do not share similar professional training and norms of service, the intraagency clash may find professional workers on one side and management on the other.

Hierarchical Management

Although the administrative hierarchy is often violated due to other traditions or to the exigencies of special demands, it does have its own intellectual justification. It enjoys the support of a management theory that corresponds closely with some principles of managing large private firms. This body of dogma is responsible for the hierarchical outline evident in the organizational charts of most governments and private business firms in the United States. Its principles are: [4]

1. Activities should be grouped by purpose, process, clientele, place, or time and made the responsibilities of small units under the direct control of a supervisor.
2. Work units should be organized vertically so that several units are controlled by a single supervising unit, or supervisor, that is subsequently grouped with other units or supervisors under the control of a yet higher supervisor.
3. There should be a narrow span of control, with a limited number of subordinates under each supervisor. In this way, supervisory personnel can give sufficient attention to each subordinate unit or person.
4. There should be a clear chain of command and communications through channels so that superiors will have full information about the activities of subordinates and be assured that their directives will control their subordinates.
5. Executives should have sufficient authority to appoint and remove their subordinates.
6. Personnel appointments and promotions should be made on the basis of competence with no interference from politicians seeking to reward fellow partisans.
7. Executives should control the expenditures of administrative units.
8. Staff services should provide the executive with the sufficient information to understand and control the activities of subordinates.

These management principles have enjoyed strong support in the reports of prestigious groups charged with proposing administrative reforms in state governments. Several presidential commissions have stimulated spin-off groups in the states (e.g., "Little Hoover Commissions") that have supported administrative reforms to increase the governor's control of the administrative hierarchy. However, recent investigations have challenged several of their basic assumptions.

Among the major shortcomings of hierarchy in both a private and a public organization are: its failure to account for complex motivations of employees; conflict within administrative units, and the executive's inability to master all the information necessary to control his subordinates. For a hierarchy to operate according to design, subordinates must accept their superior's definition of organizational goals. However, state employees come to their task with a variety of personal and professional interests.[5] It is no easy task for a governor to win their loyalties for any common goal. Indeed, it is often difficult even to define the common goal. Department heads may not agree with the governor on the proper tasks of their organizations. Conflict within a hierarchy may reflect the imperfect knowledge that the governor has about a department head when he appoints him to office; the department head's need to compromise his own desires with those of his subordinates; or the diverse nature of the department head's own interests and his willingness to accept some, but not all, of the governor's goals for the department. Although the theory of managerial hierarchy prescribes strict adherence to the decisions of a superior, that standard is difficult to obtain. The result of different goals, different levels of motivation, and different loyalties is often the inability of an organization to articulate its goals clearly. It may be easier for a governor and his team to muddle through on the strength of agreements about specific programs without raising the spectre of long-range goals. A result, of course, is the lack of clear normative standards against which an executive can screen his prospective subordinates or can test their loyalty once they are employed.[6]

The intrusion of other organizational traditions into state governments also presents severe qualifications to the hierarchical nature of superior-subordinate relationships. The direct election of department heads weakens the governor's control over a hierarchy in the name of political accountability. The legislature's right to confirm — or deny — major appointments and to modify the governor's budget qualifies the hierarchy in the name of separation of powers and checks and balances. The prerogative of a state university to make its own decisions about the selection of students and faculty qualifies the hierarchy in the name of professional expertise.

Another feature that qualifies the hierarchical nature of state administration is the disinclination of many governors to use their available powers in a manner that will bolster their hierarchical control. When a governor wants to get a job done in a hurry he is tempted to cut through red tape. This means that he will circumvent the normal chain of command and involve himself directly in the operation of a department's program. This is fine from the perspective of those who want speedy action, but it also may weaken the control of the department head over his own subordinates and pose yet another threat to the tradition of hierarchical administration.

In order to see how the interaction among the four traditions of administrative organization have influenced the state governments, we will describe the major features of state administrative branches and important structures in the executive and legislative branches that operate as mechanisms of administrative control.

AN OUTLINE OF STATE ADMINISTRATIVE
BRANCHES AND CONTROL MECHANISMS

Many features of the administrative branches of state governments and their executive and legislative controls resemble those of the national government. Each state has departments that administer the major programs of the state. Their structures resemble a hierarchy that culminates in the governor's office. Also, as in the case of the federal government, there are numerous compromises with hierarchical principles. The compromises reflect the traditions of political accountability, the separation of powers and checks and balances, and professional competence, as well as particular concerns relevant to each program. What distinguishes the administrative structure of state from federal governments is the extent of these compromises. The architects of state governments have been hypersensitive to the notion of political accountability and to the principle of separation of powers and checks and balances. The results show themselves in the top levels of administrative departments and in governors and legislators whose controls over administrative units are weaker than their counterparts in the federal government.

The separation of powers and checks and balances and political accountability are highlighted in most state governments by severe limitations on the authority of the governor to control his administration. Direct elections choose the heads of major departments; other department heads are selected by boards or commissions over which the governor has only partial control. The governor is obligated to share budget controls with individuals who are not directly responsible to him, and the governor's tenure is more severely restricted than the president's. Because governors have little direct control over several important department heads, internal tension and discord are highly probable in the formulation of state policy. At times the tensions break out dramatically. During a period of party division between Republicans and Democrats in Wisconsin's legislative and executive branches, the Republican treasurer refused to honor the salary voucher of a man appointed to a state commission by the Democratic governor. Because the Republican attorney general also opposed the governor on this appointment, the chief executive had to obtain private legal counsel in order to press his case for control over his administration.

The budget powers of most governors are woefully inferior to those of the president. Whereas the president formulates his administration's budget with the assistance of an expert budget bureau headed by his personal appointee, several governors must share budget formulation with persons who are politically independent. In Florida and West Virginia the governor is chairman of a budgeting board that includes the separately elected secretary of state, comptroller, treasurer, attorney general, superintendent of public instruction, and commissioner of agriculture. In Mississippi, North Dakota, and South Carolina the governor is chairman of a group containing separately elected administrative heads, plus the chairmen of the legis-

lature's finance committees and members of the legislature named by the
presiding officers. The governor of Indiana has only indirect access to the
formulation of the budget; his appointee sits on a board with legislators
appointed by the presiding officers of the house and senate. In thirteen
other states the governor works with a chief budget officer who is either
separately elected or chosen by the legislature or Civil Service Commission.[7] A study of state budgeting in Illinois summed up the financial powers
of the governor with a crisp analogy:

> The budget document may be compared to a huge mountain, which
> is constantly being pushed higher and higher by underground geo-
> logic convulsions. On top of the mountain is a single man, blind-
> folded, seeking to reduce the height of the mountain by dislodging
> pebbles with a teaspoon. That man is the Governor.[8]

The governor's control over the administration is diminished not only
by structural features of the state government, but also by the temptations
to dissipate his energies across many different fields. The governor must
attend to all fields of the state's public services. As a politician with personal
ambitions that may range beyond the state house, he must attend to numerous matters that have regional, national, or international extensions. Although the governor may have a skilled and loyal executive staff, he cannot
match the specialization and expertise of administrative units.

If the governor's proposals threaten the established activities of administrative agencies, he may be drawn into a squabble that diminishes his public standing. Administrators can openly dispute the executive's position or
can supply information to interest groups or legislators who oppose the executive. At times like this, the governor's best weapon may be his informal
power to persuade the policy makers within the administrative organization.
Aiding his power of persuasion is his prominent public position, his claim
to represent all of the people, and the technical arguments that his aides
provide. The weaknesses of persuasive power are the time that it con-
sumes and the publicity it may give to the governor's problems. Governors
win some of their confrontations with administrators, but the time and political costs involved may lead them to concede all but the most vital concerns to the administration.[9]

The lofty position of the chief executive helps isolate him from many
administrative arenas where important decisions are made. The chief executive may have direct access to his department heads, but the operating
bureaus are submerged within the departments. Unless the chief executive
is willing to break through the hierarchical lines on his organization chart,
he is separated from most policy makers in the administration. One study
of presidential relations with bureau chiefs may be relevant for many state

governors. It found that the heads of twenty bureaus had served a total of 170 years as bureau heads, but had met a total of only seventy-nine times with the president. This averages to one meeting every two years for each bureau head. These meetings include ceremonial and social functions as well as policy sessions. Seven of the twenty bureau heads had no contacts with the chief executive except for social or ceremonial occasions; and two had no contacts with him at all.[10]

The features that restrict the governor's control over the state administration are mirrored in restrictions on the legislature's controls. State legislatures lack several of the features that enable the federal Congress to supervise and regulate administrative provisions. Among the states there is a dearth of strong committees bolstered with seniority provisions or staff units that can spend all their time on the tasks of administrative oversight (see Chapter 5). Without seniority provisions, state legislatures are unlikely to develop any expertise among their members. Where committees do not provide tenure and an opportunity for members to learn their jobs, they are likely to become highly dependent upon the recommendations of administrative agencies.

State legislatures are restricted further by the nature of decisions they are allowed to make about administrators' programs. In dealing with budget policy, many state legislatures face difficult requirements that do not present themselves to Congress. While Congress can decide about expenditures separately from revenues (with the federal government's borrowing power making up for the deficit), the constitutions of several states require that expenditures not exceed projected revenues. This means that legislators cannot develop new public services without going through the obnoxious task of raising sufficient taxes. Additional restrictions occur in some states. The legislatures of Maryland and West Virginia may reduce the funds that the governor recommends for any agency but may increase only those recommended for the legislature or, in West Virginia, the judiciary. In Nebraska, a simple majority may reduce the governor's recommendations, but a three-fifths vote is necessary to increase them.

Another feature that weakens the legislature as a policy-making body is the tendency of its members to fragment their energies. This is not out of keeping with the numerous responsibilities of state legislators and is not unexpected in view of their diverse educational and occupational backgrounds. Their problems resemble those of the governor. Besides formulating policy or supervising ongoing programs, legislators must also accommodate constituents who want assistance in dealing with administrative agencies. This typically requires individual legislators to tend a much broader field than any of them can master. Constituents seek government jobs and contracts, assistance in qualifying for routine services, or help in appealing cases after being denied their first application. State legislators deal with constituents who are denied admission to the state university or mental hospital or who are denied release from the same mental hospital or a parole from the penitentiary. Legislators also service local governments. They introduce local bills to the legislature, testify in behalf of their community's needs, and steer the bills through committee. Where the state government controls many functions in the local community, legislators are kept busy as delegates from city hall and the county courthouse. Legislators must also attend to their own political careers. Many legislators feel a continuing need for an opportunity to express their views or to solicit funds for their next campaign.

Whereas members of the legislature, and the governor, often dissipate their resources in many distinct activities, administrators concentrate their resources by specializing in the affairs of a single agency, or more likely, a single program. For many administrators, specialization begins in college or in graduate school and continues through their career. Few elected officials have the knowledge or the inclination to match the expertise available to administrative agencies.

Legislators and executives do not accept administrative primacy as a matter of principle. The separation of powers and all its bulwarks of structure and tradition make the elected branches the natural antagonists of the bureaucracy. Yet the embarrassing realities of the policy-making process often limit the politicians to incremental adjustments on the administrators' budgets.

STATE-TO-STATE DIFFERENCES IN ADMINISTRATIVE FEATURES

Two features of state administrative branches are prominent in this discussion: the magnitude of fiscal resources allocated to administrators in each state; and the extent to which each state's administrators show the marks of professionalism.[11]

Fiscal Resources

The fiscal resources of state administrators are appropriated by the actions of the legislative and executive branches. As a matter of practice, however, both the governor and the legislators depend heavily on the budget recommendations that come to them from administrators. By noting the resources allocated to the administrators of each state, we can gauge the magnitude of service responsibilities that are given to them, as opposed to those left to the administrators of local governments or to the free enterprise operations of the marketplace. We can also use state expenditure figures to measure the success of state administrators in producing desirable levels of public service. We use total state government expenditures as our standard of the fiscal resources allocated to state administrators. Only a tiny fraction of this total is used to support the governor, the legislature, or the judicial branch. Figures compiled by the United States Bureau of the Census for 1968 show these branches were allocated an average of only 0.7 per cent of state government expenditures. Connecticut spent the highest portion of total funds on the executive, legislative, and judicial branches; it allocated them only 2.1 per cent of its total.

In studying state-to-state differences in expenditures, we must correct raw figures for the state-to-state differences in population. We also must eliminate state expenditures for liquor stores and insurance trust funds. The resulting figure, the general expenditures per capita, is the measure that is used most frequently to judge the fiscal resources made available in each state to support its public services. Table 1 ranks the states in total general spending, per capita, as of 1968. Table 2 shows how state spending corresponds with various social, economic, and political traits. Alaska and Hawaii outspend the other states, due partly to the high cost of goods and services outside of the older states. The lowest spender is New Jersey. This may come as a surprise to those who automatically look for Mississippi at the bottom of the state rankings. Other wealthy states scoring near the bottom of this list are Illinois, Missouri, and Ohio. These state governments have been lethargic in supporting programs that are popular elsewhere, and they have left massive spending responsibilities to their local governments. (When state and local spending is combined for each state, Mississippi settles to its customary place close to the bottom — just above North Carolina and Arkansas for 1968.)

We noted above that state expenditures indicate the magnitude of resources employed by state administrators instead of local authorities or the private sector of the economy. Table 2 shows expenditures are highest in those states where local governments are relatively weak, as shown by a low percentage of state and local expenditures made by local governments; and where private resources are relatively meager, as shown by low scores on population and industrialization. State administrators seem to compensate for weaknesses that exist elsewhere in their jurisdiction. Where citizens and

TABLE 1

Total General Expenditures Per Capita of State Governments,
1968, by Rank

	Rank	Expenditures per capita[a]
Alaska	1	$999.00
Hawaii	2	555.89
Wyoming	3	526.00
Vermont	4	491.81
Delaware	5	466.27
New Mexico	6	429.76
Nevada	7	412.06
North Dakota	8	406.66
Washington	9	392.78
California	10	392.62
New York	11	387.02
Utah	12	374.71
Rhode Island	13	373.26
Louisiana	14	372.15
Wisconsin	15	371.10
Oklahoma	16	365.99
Minnesota	17	357.12
Oregon	18	350.60
Montana	19	336.34
West Virginia	20	335.72
Arizona	21	333.81
Iowa	22	328.92
Kentucky	23	324.56
Colorado	24	323.94
South Dakota	25	322.54
Michigan	26	317.22
Maryland	27	306.47
Massachusetts	28	296.97
Idaho	29	298.67
Connecticut	30	290.95
Alabama	31	286.20
Georgia	32	273.77
Pennsylvania	33	273.42
Indiana	34	272.02
Maine	35	271.26
Mississippi	36	270.91
North Carolina	37	269.15
Arkansas	38	264.21
Virginia	39	259.65
Kansas	40	254.45
South Carolina	41	248.97
New Hampshire	42	248.77
Tennessee	43	238.66
Illinois	44	235.92
Florida	45	232.36
Texas	46	229.99
Missouri	47	228.96
Nebraska	48	226.38
Ohio	49	219.76
New Jersey	50	197.94

[a]General expenditures are for those functions pursued in common by almost all the states. They exclude expenditures of state liquor stores and insurance trust funds.

Source: United States Bureau of the Census, *State Government Finances in 1968* (Washington, D.C.: United States Government Printing Office, 1969).

TABLE 2
*Coefficients of Simple Correlation Between Total State General
Expenditures Per Capita, 1962, and Selected Independent
Variables[a]*

Total population	−.32
Percentage of labor force in manufacturing	−.51
Value added by manufacturing per capita	−.38
Population density	−.30
Percentage of state and local expenditures spent by local govts.	−.54
Previous state spending per capita, 1957	.85

[a]Selected from a list of social, economic, political, and governmental variables to
represent those strong enough to pass a test for statistical significance.
Source: Data from Ira Sharkansky, *Spending in the American States* (Chicago: Rand
McNally, 1968), 40, 60, 61.

local governments are poor, state authorities tend to have sizable revenues
and, presumably, offer a disproportionate share of the services received by
the population.

Several features help explain the high levels of state expenditures
where the private economy and local governments are not able to meet
service demands. Low-income citizens cannot provide for themselves the
levels of education, health, or recreation that are obtained through the market mechanisms in affluent settings. Moreover, many local governments in
poor states, especially in rural counties, are hard pressed to meet service
demands with their own resources. Part of the problem faced by local governments rests on their enforced reliance on a tax base that is dependent
upon the local economy. State constitutions generally restrict localities to
the tax on real property located within their borders, imposing a severe burden on poor localities.

State governments have the resources to make up for the needs of local authorities under low-resource conditions: the states have legal access
to the economic resources within their larger jurisdiction; they benefit from
a more generous selection of federal aids; and they have a more productive
tax system to extract revenue from available resources. The state levies on
personal income and general sales and state excises have remained more
productive in the face of depressed economic conditions than has the local
property tax.

INCREMENTAL BUDGET MAKING.   A prominent finding about the resources of state administrative branches is that each state tends to remain
in the same position relative to other states for many years at a time. This
is evident in the strong relationship between a state's spending in a current
year and in the recent past. The routine practice of incremental budgeting

is crucial in the allocation of resources among the administrative departments of a state. Incremental budgeting places severe constraints against sharp increases in spending and inhibits most states from moving sharply ahead of the pack in the process of annual or biennial budgeting. Incrementalism shows itself in other features of policy besides the budget. A study of state adoptions of economic opportunity and community action programs during the 1960s shows the operation of incrementalism in the development of programs that are thought to be new. The states with well-developed programs in the fields of education, health, and welfare made the greatest use of the new federal grants. Policy norms held by state administrators and other decision makers — with many of these norms going back to the New Deal or earlier — seemed crucial for the innovations made in the 1960s.[12] The pervasive importance of incrementalism in state budget making leads us to probe into its procedures and the elements that support it.

The common ingredient of incrementalism in state governments is a fixation upon previously made decisions. When administrators plan their budget requests, their paperwork requires them to list current and previous expenditures and to compare these figures with their estimates for the coming year. Moreover, agency personnel must justify their increment of increase with respect to the guidelines announced by supervisors. These guidelines estimate the increases in revenue that are expected, or they indicate the priorities to be given individual programs. Last year's budget has the greatest legitimacy in the eyes of governors, central budget officers, and members of legislative appropriations committees. It represents the funds considered necessary to operate established programs, and these funds tend to escape current review. Budget examiners are most likely to question the funds that would increase appropriations, and they are most likely to cut from these requests in order to minimize budget growth. By looking at relationships between the nature of agency requests, the governor's recommendations to the legislature, and the subsequent actions of the legislature, we can see how the governor and the legislature actually make their budget decisions in an incremental fashion.

Administrative agencies and the governor play the most consistent roles in the state budget process. In each of nineteen states reported in Table 3 for budget periods from 1963 to 1969, the agencies requested a sizable annual increase (4 to 53 per cent) over their current appropriations and the governor pared the increase in his recommendations (by 4 to 31 per cent). Agencies requested an average 24 per cent increase over their current budgets, and the governor's recommendation trimmed an average

TABLE 3

Average Annual Percentage Changes at Major Stages in the Budget Process, by State

State, showing year of budget analyzed	Agency request as percentage of current expenditure	Governor's recommendation as percentage of agency request	Legislature's appropriation as percentage of governor's request	Legislature's appropriation as percentage of agency's current expenditure	Legislature's appropriation as percentage of agency request
Florida, 1965-67	120	90	93	109	84
Georgia, 1965-67	153	86	100	139	87
Idaho, 1967-69	119	93	92	109	86
Illinois, 1963-65a	118	83	102	108	85
Indiana, 1965-67	123	83	103	112	86
Kentucky, 1966-68	120	90	93	109	84
Louisiana, 1966-67	121	90	101	110	91
Maine, 1965-67	114	85	108	109	92
Nebraska, 1965-67	122	87	119	124	104
North Carolina, 1965-67	120	84	105	112	87
North Dakota, 1965-67	124	74	111	111	82
South Carolina, 1966-67	117	96	104	116	99
South Dakota, 1967-68	136	82	98	109	80
Texas, 1965-67	128	82	104	117	86
Vermont, 1965-67	121	87	106	115	91
Virginia, 1966-68	120	92	100	114	91
West Virginia, 1966-67	125	88	92	101	81
Wisconsin, 1965-67	115	96	98	111	94
Wyoming, 1967-69	133	69	109	112	75

aThe Illinois data come from the Appendix of Thomas J. Anton's *The Politics of State Expenditure in Illinois* (Urbana: University of Illinois Press, 1966). All other data come from the official budgets and financial reports of the states.

Source: Ira Sharkansky, "Agency Requests, Gubernatorial Support and Budget Success in State Legislatures," *American Political Science Review*, 63 (December, 1968), Table 1. Reprinted with the permission of the *American Political Science Review*.

14 per cent from their requests. The legislature's final appropriation typically remained close to the governor's recommendation, but varied from a cut of 8 per cent below his recommendation to an increase of 19 per cent above his recommendation. Six of the legislatures cut agency budgets below the governor's figure, and eleven appropriated more than the governor asked. In only one case, however, did a legislature, in Nebraska, give more money to the agencies than they had requested themselves. The average legislative grant for the coming period was 13 per cent below the agencies' request, but 13 per cent above the agencies' current budget.[13]

When we examine the response of governors and legislatures to the budgets of individual agencies, we find some evidence for the administrators' domination of the expenditure process. This is consistent with our discussion above about the resources, including the opportunities for specialization, that each branch can bring to policy making. The acquisitiveness of the agency requests plays a crucial role in the decision of the governor and the legislature. The absolute size of agency budget requests does not appear to influence the decisions made by the governor or legislature. Budget reviewers in the governor's office and the legislature are more likely to respond to the percentage increment of change that is requested (i.e., agency acquisitiveness) than to the sheer size of the request. In most of the states examined, the governor and legislature direct the greatest percentage cuts at the agencies that request the greatest percentage increases (see Table 4). However, only the acquisitive agencies come out of the legislature with substantial increases over their previous budgets. There are strong positive relationships between the percentage increase requested by the agency and the percentage growth in agency expenditures. Both the governor and the legislature are using similar decision rules: *cut the budget of the agencies that ask for a large increase; do not recommend a budget expansion for those agencies that ask for no increase.*

The failure of either the governor or the legislature to impose additional funds on those agencies that do not ask for them illustrates how much the incremental budget makers depend on someone else to initiate policy innovation. Budget reviewers in the governor's office and the legislature have let this initiative pass over to the agencies. This is part of the often-observed shift in the locus of innovation from elected officials to professionals. It is said to reflect the increasing technological sophistication of public services and the need for professional training in order to comprehend the public's needs or to design alterations in current programs. It is consistent with their other traits that incremental budget makers expect recommendations for policy change to come from the agencies. The incre-

TABLE 4

Coefficients of Simple Correlation Among Budget Requests of State Agencies and the Actions of the Governor and Legislature

	Correlation between			
	Agency budget request and percentage of agency request approved by:		Percentage increase requested by agency and percentage of agency request approved by:	
	Governor	Legislature	Governor	Legislature
Florida, 1965-67	.04	.03	−.80	−.63
Georgia, 1965-67	.08	.02	−.86	−.82
Idaho, 1967-69	.45	.04	−.70	−.80
Illinois, 1963-65	.07	.03	−.52	−.51
Indiana, 1965-67	.10	.04	.13	−.27
Kentucky, 1966-68	.18	.06	−.94	−.77
Louisiana, 1966-67	.12	.00	−.82	−.48
Maine, 1965-67	.08	.24	.22	.18
Nebraska, 1965-67	−.23	−.09	−.59	.51
North Carolina, 1965-67	−.05	−.04	−.20	−.20
North Dakota, 1965-67	−.01	.17	−.84	−.80
South Carolina, 1966-67	.06	.00	−.30	−.17
South Dakota, 1967-68	.02	.00	−.75	−.70
Texas, 1965-67	−.10	−.25	−.63	−.06
Vermont, 1965-67	−.16	−.12	−.67	−.61
Virginia, 1966-68	.12	.07	−.56	−.27
West Virginia, 1966-67	.16	.01	−.57	−.65
Wisconsin, 1965-67	−.03	−.08	−.61	−.28
Wyoming, 1967-69	−.15	−.18	−.82	−.70

Source: See Table 3.

mental routine is hostile to innovation. It signals a reluctance on the part of governors and legislators to control policy in a comprehensive fashion through the medium of the budget.

Incremental decision making is popular among budgeteers for several reasons. One reason lies in the appeal of routines in comparison with the rational assessment of the whole budget document. Rather than attempting the impossible task of considering all the issues relevant to a budget, officials in administrative units as well as in the executive and legislative branches have grown used to conceding the propriety of expenditures used to finance existing programs; they focus attention on the increment that represents a growth in expenditure, and presumably a change in the agency's program. To do otherwise would continually reopen past accommodations between the parties interested in each item of an agency's program. This would make each item always controversial, would preclude administrators or clients from counting on the continuation of current programs, and would require an extraordinary magnitude of investigatory resources just to supervise each part of every agency's program and to prepare the information necessary for an annual decision.[14]

Another reason for incremental decision making lies in the commitments built into each budget. In some cases, relatively little can be changed in an agency's expenditure from one budget period to the next. Some parts of an agency's budget may represent earmarked funds, monies that cannot legally be spent for any other than certain purposes and, thus, are not likely to be challenged by either the executive or legislative branches. Also, commitments to government employees and to the clients of public services limit a serious inquiry into an agency's established level of expenditure. Large numbers of employees cannot be threatened with dismissal or transfer during each year's budget review, and large numbers of citizens cannot be threatened with a curtailment or shifting of major components of their public services. These inflexibilities, reflecting common agreements as to what is practical, impose real limits on the thorough review of an agency's budget.

VARIATIONS IN INCREMENTAL BUDGETING.   The routines of incremental budgeting lead reviewers to reduce the estimates of growth-oriented bureaus, and to withhold increases from the bureaus that have not sought more funds. Nevertheless, these decision rules are not uniform. Some governors and legislatures are more or less likely than their counterparts in other states, or in their states during other years, to grant or withhold funds to agencies that request increments. By examining the nature of budget relationships between agencies, the governor, and the legislature in conjunction with several other characteristics of each state, we can gain some insight into the elements that influence budget decisions. Actually, the findings are not crystal clear. Although some relationships prevail between the nature of budget decisions and several traits of the state's politics and economy, many instances of budget decisions do not correspond to the general patterns. Variations from incremental budget routines are not governed by objective forces of economics or politics. They often develop in the individual context of each state despite the presence of economic or political conditions that make the variations unexpected.

Two characteristics associated with strong gubernatorial restraint against agency budget development are the governor's possession of strong formal veto powers and high state government expenditures. The already high expenditures may incline the governor against further large increases in state spending, and the power of a veto may strengthen the governor's resolve to impose a severe review on the agencies when they submit requests to him.

The governor is unusually generous toward agency requests for budget expansion when there is relatively intense party competition. A competitive party situation may lead him to advance his own career, and his party, by supporting innovation agencies. Where the legislature is particularly restrictive against agency budget development there tends to be relatively high state government expenditure and debt and a low incidence of state officials who are separately elected. Like the governor, the legislature appears to resist an acquisitive agency in the face of already committed state resources, i.e., high expenditures and debt. With a scarcity of separately elected executives, agency heads may lack politically independent allies who can promote their budget through the legislature.[15]

The role of incrementalism in state budgeting sets outside limits to the percentage of change that is feasible, instead of defining precisely the direction and magnitude of the change that will occur. An examination of budget changes during eleven periods between 1903 and 1965 found only weak patterns between the change in each state's spending and its expenditures in an earlier year. It is not possible to predict the level of expenditures in a forthcoming year simply by knowing the current level of expenditure. Although most states' expenditures in a year $a + i$ are close to the same relative positions as they were in year a, the direction and magnitude of change is inconsistent. Several states go up slightly in their spending, others may drop, a few demonstrate sizable changes in position, and many maintain their same position during the period. A major exception to these findings occurred from 1929 to 1939 when clear patterns of correspondence appeared between spending in the first year of each period and the direction and magnitude of change. The low spending states showed consistently greater increases in spending than the high spending states, and the gap between high and low spenders lessened considerably. This may have been the product of several new federal aid programs that were started during the depression. Indeed, one justification for these programs was their capacity to redistribute resources between have and have-not states.[16]

Professionalism in State Administration

Professionalism is the second feature of administrative branches that we shall measure and analyze on a state-to-state basis. When we say that a state administration is highly professional, we have in mind several attributes: personnel have advanced training in their fields of specialization; they have an active concern to stay abreast of the latest developments; and they have a desire to implement the most advanced level of service available. A state that wanted creditable professionals would, presumably, offer high salaries and fringe benefits to recruit the best possible candidates and would support their activities with generous budgets.

Deil Wright reports an opinion survey of 933 state administrators from across the country that shows one dimension of their professionalism.[17] The large majority of his respondents (76 per cent) wanted to expand their own agencies' services and expenditures. The administrators had a choice of expansion at the levels of 0 to 5 per cent, 5 to 10 per cent, 10 to 15 per cent, and 15 per cent plus. Almost one-third of the respondents chose the uppermost range of expansion. If Professor Wright's alternatives had reached higher, we might have been able to gauge the upper limits of administrators' desires. As it is, many administrators seem to want a greater magnitude of expansion than Professor Wright expected (see also Chapter 6).

Different features of administrative professionalism have varied in the ways they have been adopted in the states. By subjecting several measures of professional characteristics to a factor analysis, we can see how the various characteristics cluster together in their adoption, and we can see how each state scores on each cluster of professional attributes.[18] For this factor analysis, we considered measures for the salary of top figures in the administrative branches of state governments plus average salaries and fringe benefits for all state employees. At the present time there are no adequate state-by-state measures of administrators' training or attitudes about their work. We have to make do with measures of the economic resources that states invest in the pay and perquisites of the bureaucracy and assume that these correspond with other aspects of professionalism.

A factor analysis reveals two separate dimensions in these measures of administrative professionalism. They are identified in Table 5 and are named according to the variables that load highest on each factor: salary and fringe benefits. The first factor reflects the salaries paid to state employees and heads of major departments.[19] The second factor reflects the coverage of state-financed health and life insurance. Table 6 ranks the states on each of these factors.

It is illustrative of the multidimensional nature of administrative professionalism [20] that a high, or low, score on one factor is generally not reflective of high, or low, scores on the other factors. Only seven states score consistently *low* on both factors: Arizona, Delaware, Montana, Nebraska, South Dakota, West Virginia, and Wyoming.[21] Connecticut, Georgia, New Jersey, and Wisconsin score high on both factors. Several of the states with

TABLE 5

Measures of Professionalism in State Administration, by Their Loading on Two Principal Factors

	Factor loadings	
	Salary	Fringe benefits
Average salary, state employees	.824	−.146
Salary of chief budget officer	.801	−.024
Salary of chief education officer	.869	.050
Salary of chief welfare officer	.799	.147
Salary of chief health officer	.713	.291
Percentage of state employees with state-financed health and hospital insurance	.274	.859
Percentage of state employees with state-financed life insurance	−.158	.913

Sources of data are given in note 18.

national reputations for the quality of their civil service score high on only one of the factors: California, Michigan, Minnesota and New York. California and New York pay high salaries, but are far behind most of the states in their support for the fringe benefits we have measured. The salary factor seems responsive to the level of economic resources in a state; Table 7 shows that it corresponds in particular to the level of industrialization.[22] A high level of industrialization may provide the resources necessary to support high levels of spending on the civil service, and it may also provide the models of salary levels that are adopted in the public sector.

These factors do not reflect several attributes of administrative professionalism that may have crucial importance in the policy-making process: professional training, employees' attitudes toward their work, the distribution of resources among professional-technical and other employees, and the culture of state departments with respect to the pursuit of public improvements or private gain. State rankings on these features of professionalism may, or may not, correspond with rankings on salary and fringe benefits. Moreover, these as yet unmeasured features of professionalism may prove to be far more important determinants of state policies.

Another dimension of administrative professionalism that is not subject to factor analysis concerns the distribution of professional employees among the local jurisdictions of a state. If there is not an equivalent level of professionalism at both state and local levels within a state, then the state administrators may be frustrated in their attempts to upgrade public services. Much of the work of state agencies consists of working with localities. State funds, program standards, and informal suggestions are important in

TABLE 6

Rankings of States[a] on Two Principal Factors of Administrative Professionalism

	Salary	Fringe benefits
New York	1	28
California	2	38
Ohio	3	32
Michigan	4	15
Pennsylvania	5	31
Illinois	6	27
Washington	7	23
Texas	8	45
Georgia	9	7
Connecticut	10	2
New Jersey	11	4
Wisconsin	12	9
Florida	13	41
Maryland	14	30
Colorado	15	18
Massachusetts	16	24
Minnesota	17	5
Oregon	18	39
Oklahoma	19	16
South Carolina	20	42
North Carolina	21	33
Indiana	22	22
Missouri	23	35
Iowa	24	21
Rhode Island	25	3
Nevada	26	17
Kansas	27.5	26
Virginia	27.5	21
Kentucky	29	36
Vermont	30	14
Utah	31	8
Alabama	32	25
Arkansas	33	34
Tennessee	34	10
Maine	35	29
New Mexico	36	12
Arizona	37	40
New Hampshire	38	13
West Virginia	39	44
North Dakota	40	19
South Dakota	41	46
Nebraska	42	43
Montana	43	37
Louisiana	44	6
Delaware	45	47
Idaho	46	1
Mississippi	47	11
Wyoming	48	48

[a]Alaska and Hawaii are omitted.

TABLE 7
Coefficients of Simple Correlation Between Two Factors Measuring Social and Economic Traits and the Two Factors of Administrative Professionalism

Social and economic factors	Administration factors	
	Salary	Fringe benefits
Industrialization	.68	.15
Affluence	.20	−.04

the policy processes of many localities. Liaison with local governments occupies vast energies in the state departments of education, transportation, health, and welfare. As we see below, the distribution of professionalism among the local governments of a state has more to do with the nature of state and local policies than with traits of state administrators alone. Table 8 shows how one measure of professionalism, average salaries, occurs in thirty-six states.[23] One statistic, the coefficient of variability, measures the equality of administrative salaries among the counties of a state; other measures show how salaries are combined in the counties of each state with the economic traits of industrialization and income.[24] Table 9 shows how these distributions of administrative professionalism correspond with statewide economic traits.

There appear to be statewide standards for the salaries of local government officials. When we compare within-state distributions of administrative salaries with the distributions of other economic and political traits, we find that salaries are the most likely to be distributed equally among the counties of each state.[25] Perhaps the salary standards are enforced in each jurisdiction by the workers' unions or associations. Several state legislatures have enacted statutes to set a minimum salary for certain local employees. Yet salaries are not perfectly equal throughout each state, and salaries are most equal in the poorest states.[26] The differences in salaries that exist tend to correspond with local economic resources: the wealthier counties in most states pay the highest government salaries. The economic-professionalism juxtapositions are most apparent in wealthier states, as Table 9 shows. Examples include California, Illinois, Massachusetts, Michigan, New Jersey, New York, and Ohio. Perhaps a generally high level of wealth throughout a state permits the relatively wealthy jurisdictions to use their resources for a professional cadre of administrators. In the less wealthy states, several of the most wealthy counties may spend their resources for items that contribute more visibly to citizen benefits.

TABLE 8

Measures of Within-State Distributions of Administrators' Salaries,
County Coefficients of Correlation

	Coefficients of variability	Industrialization and salaries	Income and salaries
Alabama	.087	−.26	.38
Arizona	.074	.16	.03
Arkansas	.085	−.11	.34
California	.134	.29	.68
Colorado	.129	.50	.63
Florida	.088	−.14	.47
Georgia	.136	−.11	.01
Illinois	.134	.66	.85
Iowa	.098	.60	.79
Kansas	.089	.32	.60
Kentucky	.117	.05	.19
Louisiana	.088	.10	−.21
Maryland	.116	−.18	.62
Massachusetts	.087	.40	.73
Michigan	.139	.50	.76
Minnesota	.029	.57	.81
Mississippi	.092	−.19	.22
Missouri	.093	.34	.57
Montana	.101	.36	.48
New Jersey	.104	.52	.84
New Mexico	.092	.23	.55
New York	.104	.23	.78
North Carolina	.079	−.19	−.41
North Dakota	.095	.39	.46
Ohio	.119	.59	.81
Oklahoma	.070	.29	.29
Oregon	.074	.01	.49
Pennsylvania	.091	.24	.62
South Carolina	.094	.03	.31
South Dakota	.074	.50	.55
Utah	.075	.47	.35
Virginia	.143	−.03	.18
Washington	.088	.41	.51
West Virginia	.115	.23	.59
Wisconsin	.104	.68	.76
Wyoming	.059	.13	.33

THE IMPORTANCE OF ADMINISTRATIVE
FEATURES FOR PUBLIC POLICY

In earlier sections we described certain features of the administrative, executive, and legislative branches that affect their roles in state policy making. We also saw how the procedures of incremental budgeting focus executive and legislative deliberations on the requests of administrators. In this section we take another look at the fiscal resources and the profession-

TABLE 9

*Coefficients of Simple Correlation Between Two Factors Measuring
Statewide Economic Traits and the Measures of Within-State
Distribution of Administrators' Salaries*

	Measures of within-state distribution[a]		
Statewide traits	*Coefficients of variability*	*Industrialization-salaries correlation*	*Income-salaries correlation*
Industrialization	.40	.24	.48
Affluence	−.09	.51	.55

[a]From Table 8.

alism of state administrators and test their importance for the public services offered in the states. We want to know if there is any evidence that the resources or the professionalism of administrators has had the expected effects on the quality or quantity of public services.

Administrative Resources, Professionalism, and Policy Scores

By themselves, the features of administrative resources that we have measured provide little insight into the policy-making processes of the states. For the most part, there are only weak statistical relationships between government expenditures and the public services provided in the states. Yet these findings are not entirely disappointing. They lead to a richer conception of the administrative-policy linkages, and hopefully will guide research to specify those linkages. Two studies in different contexts have shown that relationships between government spending and levels of public service are neither strong nor pervasive. A study of 163 Georgia school districts shows only weak relationships between measures of educational spending and service outputs.[27] Another study of state and local government spending and services across the country found that only 16 of 27 service measures (59 per cent) showed sizable relationships with government spending.[28] Some of the spending-service relationships are negative, meaning that high scores on spending correspond with low scores on the measure of service. In the highway field, low-spending states develop the most extensive system of rural roads and also experience the most enviable records of highway safety.

The evidence is also discouraging for the expectation that an increase in spending will produce a clear improvement in services. Only ten out of twenty-seven measures of changes in services from 1957 to 1962 showed sizable positive relationships with changes in the spending of state and local governments in the same years. Perhaps the lag between an increase in spending and a change in service levels is greater than five years. Or perhaps an increase in spending is not powerful enough to cope with all of the nonfinancial elements in bringing about a change in the nature of services.

To explain the weak statistical relationships between measures of public service and our measures of administrative resources, we can cite the range of other features that seem likely to affect levels of service. Aggregate government spending is only one influence. After some reflection, that in itself seems far less important than the sensitivity and skills involved in allocating funds among the different items that may be purchased. These and other attributes of state administrators have not yet been subject to comparative, quantitative measurement. Until such research is attempted, it would be foolhardy to conclude that characteristics of state administrators do not show an important correspondence with the nature of services provided. Sufficient funds may be a sine qua non for public services. However, several other determinants of service outcomes may be provided in generous or stingy proportions by different jurisdictions whose total budgets are nearly equal. By varying the allocation of funds among different elements, policy makers may make a budget of a certain total more or less productive of service outcomes. Some of the policies that have important effects on outcomes may be independent of spending levels.

When dealing with our limited indicators of professionalism among state administrators — salaries and fringe benefits — we also fail to uncover any strong or pervasive correspondence with two summary measures of public service. Table 10 shows simple and partial relationships between factor scores for welfare-education and highway-natural resources and factor scores for salary and fringe benefits.[29] The weakness of these findings may reflect the different arenas examined. The salary and fringe benefit factors reflect conditions in state governments alone. The policy factors reflect the activities of state and local units within each state. Some greater importance for administrative professionalism appears when we compare the policy factors with the distributions of professional traits among local jurisdictions. Welfare-education and highway-natural resource services are most generous in those states where high administrative salaries occur in the most industrialized counties. Where the competence and service motivations of professional administrators are found in conjunction with high levels of economic resources, there may be the greatest opportunity for their service-oriented training and motivation to affect program development. Also, the even distribution of professionalism within a state seems to provide hospitable conditions for highway-natural resources programs.

TABLE 10
*Coefficients of Simple and Partial Correlation Between Measures
of Administrative Professionalism and Two Factors Measuring
Welfare-Education and Highway-Natural Resources Services*

	Measures of public service	
	---	---
Measures of administrative professionalism	*Welfare-education*	*Highway-natural resources*
Simple correlation		
Salary factor	.41	−.52
Fringe benefit factor	.18	−.06
Within-state coefficient of variability	−.03	−.44
Within-state industrialization-salary correlation	.69	.12
Within-state income-salary correlation	.65	−.07
Partial correlations		
Salary factor[a]	.23	.11
Fringe benefit factor[a]	.23	.08
Within-state coefficient of variability[b]	.03	−.40
Within-state industrialization-salary correlation[b]	.66	.41
Within-state income-salary correlation[b]	.25	.11

[a]Controlling for measures of industrialization and affluence.
[b]Controlling for counterpart statewide measures for industrialization, income, and salary.

A suggestion for further research is contained in this finding of stronger policy relationships for our measures of the distribution of professionalism than for our measures of professionalism in state governments alone. Perhaps it is not the gross levels of administrative attributes that exist in a jurisdiction but how they are distributed and combined with other traits that has the greatest importance for public services. More detailed comparative studies of discrete programs in different states may uncover persuasive findings about the policy importance of administrative resources and professionalism. Such features as administrators' training, attitudes, and opportunities for program research and experimentation may show close relationships with program outcomes. Also, more refined measures of service should have greater sensitivity to administrative influences than the measures considered here. Surveys of client satisfaction, changing rates of service-use over time, changes in the tangible outputs of certain state agencies, and changes in measures of client well-being should be considered for their correspondence with administrator's traits.

SUMMARY AND CONCLUSIONS

This chapter combines a verbal analysis of the distinctiveness and the importance of the administrative branch in the policy-making processes of state governments with a series of quantitative analyses that show only occasional evidence for the administrators' importance. We described four traditions that are evident in the design of administrative branches: political accountability; separation of powers and checks and balances; professional expertise, and hierarchy. We produced state-by-state indicators for only one of these traditions, however, and our indicators for professionalism measure only a few of the traits that ought to be considered. The quantitative revolution in political science has passed by many features of public administration. At the present time, it remains an undeveloped field in the systematic and comparative study of state politics.

It is too soon to admit the weakness of administrators in state policy making. In the discussion of state expenditures, we found that executive and legislative branches respond to the budget increments that are requested by the agencies. If an agency does not request an increase, it is rare that the other branches will impose additional funds (and program responsibilities) upon the administrators. The agencies that request the largest increases end up with the largest increases, even after executive and legislative cuts. When we examined the distribution of administrative professionalism among the counties of several states, we saw their importance in welfare-education and highways-natural resources policies. The lack of policy findings for our measures of state salaries and fringe benefits may only reflect the comparison between administrative traits of the state government alone and policies that are defined by the state and local governments together.

It is often pretentious to end a discussion with the claim that we need more information. In this case, however, the need is sufficiently great to warrant attention. Although we have found some indications of four separate traditions in the design of state administrations, we have produced measurements for only one of these traditions. In our measures for professionalism, we have been unable to provide state-by-state measures for employees' training or for their attitudes toward their jobs. These traits are essential to any discussion of professionalism. Likewise, a concern for political accountability, separation of powers and checks and balances, and hierarchy should figure in any discussion of the ways that features of state administrations may influence state policy. This field begs for additional research with indicators that show state-by-state differences in administrative characteristics. Until we have more information, we can claim only superficial knowledge about the functions of administration in the state policy-making process.

SELECTED BIBLIOGRAPHY

Anton, Thomas. *The Politics of State Expenditure in Illinois.* Urbana: University of Illinois Press, 1966. A perceptive analysis of expenditure politics in Illinois.

Crecine, John P. *Government Problem-Solving: A Computer Simulation of Municipal Budgeting.* Chicago: Rand McNally, 1968. An example of the application of computer simulation to the theory and practice of municipal budgeting.

Morse, Eliott R., *et al.* "Fluctuations in State Expenditures," *Southern Economic Journal,* 33 (April, 1967): 496–515. A systematic analysis of the variations in state expenditures over time.

Redford, Emmette R. *Democracy in the Administrative State.* New York: Oxford University Press, 1969. An analysis of administrative practices and principles from the viewpoint of democratic theory.

Sharkansky, Ira. *Public Administration: Policy-Making in Government Agencies.* Chicago: Markham Publishing Co., 1970. An analysis of the policy-making aspects of public administration.

Wright, Deil S. "Executive Leadership in State Administration," *Midwest Journal of Political Science,* 11 (February, 1967). A report of survey data on the attitudes and perceptions of over 900 state administrators.

CHAPTER EIGHT

State Courts

Kenneth N. Vines and Herbert Jacob

From a perspective of politics concerned with the allocation of values, the political functions of state courts are difficult to observe. Courts seldom engage in activities that are as visibly distributive as are legislative appropriations, gubernatorial presentation of budgets, or establishment of utility rates by public service commissions. Demands made of the courts lack the salience of such activities as lobbying in the legislatures or executives and decision making in the courts is neither as open to public inspection nor as widely publicized as in legislatures and some other state agencies. In addition judicial processes are formalized by the constraints of litigation, insulated from the public by legal traditions and codes of ethics, and conducted in the language and symbols of the law. As a result judicial activities are not often associated with the rough and tumble aspects of state politics that determine "who gets, what, when, how": Courts seldom appear involved in power conflicts or the resolution of major issues in the states." [1] *

Nevertheless, state courts, no less than legislatures and executives, are omnipresent features of state government. All states — the rich and the poor, the large and the small — conduct aspects of state politics by means of judicial institutions. Yet courts, possibly because they are less visible than other state agencies, have been less systematically investigated than have other aspects of state government. All too often their conception according to formal, legalistic terms has not emphasized the value allocation functions they share with other state agencies.

Justice William J. Brennan, Jr., one of the three justices who served on a state court prior to elevation to the Supreme Court, has provided useful insights on the political functions of state courts. State courts con-

---

* [See pp. 584–585 for notes to this chapter. — Eds.]

tribute to the allocation of values, he observed, by "measuring how well America attains the ideal of equal justice for all. The fifty states . . . determine vital issues of life, liberty and property of human beings of this nation." More specifically, he explained, this means that courts probe deeply into the important values of life in the American states by dealing with such matters as labor relations, issues of family life, property rights, criminal prosecution, and consumers' rights.[2] Although these issues handled by the courts seldom make headlines, they involve many of the basic values of day-to-day existence and deal with vital issues of personal and social life. Moreover, Brennan, who had the experience to make such a comparison, thought the composite work of state courts was more significant in measuring how well the ideal of equal justice for all is attained than the work of the more widely publicized Supreme Court.

State courts are well suited for the comparative analysis that we shall conduct. With the exception of Louisiana, in which only traces of civil law heritage remain, state courts all have a common institutional culture springing from the common law, and they are all set in a common context of national constitutionalism. On the other hand, wide disparities occur among the states both in the character of their inputs, such as court organizations and judicial selection, and in the nature of their judicial processes. There are also major differences in the political and social environments of the courts.

For our analytical framework in this chapter we will use systems theory and consider the courts, as a whole, as subsystems of the larger American political system. It is advantageous to keep the concept of judicial subsystems in mind, for it demonstrates how the various aspects of judicial politics relate to each other. A specific political model is especially important for judicial analysis because the legal forms and terminology tend to obscure the political character of the courts. Like other political subsystems such as legislatures and executive offices, courts receive inputs in the form of pressures and demands and convert these inputs through institutional decisional processes into outputs or decisions. First we examine the inputs into state courts, next look at conversion or decision-making processes, and finally examine outputs of the state judiciaries.

INPUTS INTO STATE COURTS

Demands for court action and support for the legal system are channeled in many different ways to the courts. However, courts differ from legislatures and executive agencies in the ways they handle inputs. Often courts are quite aloof from interest group and political party activities. In general, political groups are kept at arm's length in the processes of litigation and in relationships with judges although they participate more actively in questions involving the organization and structure of courts and the selection of judges. These groups operate only in very limited ways inside the courts by sponsoring test cases, filing amicus curiae briefs, or stimulating litigation. Far from being central to the life of the courts, they are peripheral, occasional participants.

Indeed, lobbying in the usual sense of the word is not possible in state courts. Although judicial codes rarely mention interest groups explicitly, judges clearly are expected to avoid contacts and associations with groups. Effective representation of group interests requires a variety of informal contacts and communications by groups with political officials. This is prevented in the courts by the insulated position of the judges and the lack of opportunities for contact as in other political institutions.

The strongest instance of group influence has been their sponsorship and encouragement of litigation. An excellent example of such group activity has been the role of the NAACP in encouraging civil rights litigation in southern state courts. In an important case growing out of NAACP activity in the South, the Supreme Court held that group activities to foster litigation were protected by constitutional guarantees of free political expression:

> Groups which find themselves unable to achieve their objectives through the ballot frequently turn to the courts. Just as it was true of the opponents of New Deal legislation during the 1930's for example, no less is it true of the Negro minority today. And under the conditions of modern government, litigation may well be the sole practicable avenue open to a minority to petition for redress of grievances. . . . For such a group, association for litigation may be the most effective form of political expression.[3]

Political parties are also restricted in the judiciary. Although political parties are often deeply concerned about judicial recruitment and organization, they are not visible in litigation or in interactions with judges. Parties provide an important basis for the organization and control of legislatures and are actively involved in the conflict over control of executive agencies, but they remain in the wings of the judiciary. Judges may have partisan affiliations and past associations but no American court is organized along party lines nor are any judicial procedures conducted in partisan terms. Whereas partisan influences are accepted as legitimate and necessary in legislative halls and executive offices, legal ethics prohibit their use in the courtroom. Formal statements of such prohibitions against partisan influence have been adopted as rules of the court in many states. For example, the American Bar Association's canons of judicial ethics have been adopted by thirty state supreme courts and by thirteen bar associations or judicial conferences. Only the states of Alabama, Maine, Massachusetts, New Hampshire, North Carolina, Rhode Island, and South Carolina are without codes of ethics.[4]

Studies have demonstrated the relations between partisan affiliations of judges and their decisions, reminding us that partisan inputs do affect state judges.[5] Such partisan influences are primarily psychological and indicate internalized values and perceptions of judges. It is not difficult to hypothesize the source of judges' partisan values. Since many judgeships are desirable state governmental positions, party activists have an advantage in obtaining them, and it is no surprise to learn that many state judges are former active participants in party affairs. Although judges cease partisan activities once on the bench the effects of their political past are still important. The imprints of party identification, the association with party ideologies, and habits of partisan thought remain as part of their personal, intellectual and evaluative equipment. Moreover, many questions handled in the courts are similar to those that stimulate partisan reactions outside the courts. The issues of liberty, authority, criminal rights and justice, and social and economic problems reappear with modified legal symbols and in new forms.

Demands for court actions and support for the legal system flow through several channels into the courts. They come to the courts in the form of complaints by policemen about the criminal behavior of defendants and pleas by private citizens for redress of grievances caused by marital conflict, automobile accidents, breaches of contract, and dozens of other circumstances. Other significant inputs are channeled to the courts through conflicts over who shall be judge and what views of society, political equality, and legal activism shall be represented on the bench. Still other inputs enter the courts in the struggle to determine their organization, for instance whether special interests such as tenants or landlords shall have their own forum in a housing court or whether they must take their cases to the general court and wait their turn there. Many other demands are expressed in conflicts over the location, jurisdiction, and forms of courts. These struggles provide occasions for important inputs of support.

Criminal and Civil Litigation as Inputs

Reliable data about the cases filed in court are not available in the United States because few courts have professional administrators who know how to keep track of the case load. Most courts still use the ledger book filing systems developed at the beginning of the nineteenth century, with ballpoint pens rather than quill-and-ink as the only innovation. Consequently, our evidence on the volume of cases the courts handle is fragmentary.

Table 1 presents data about the two circumstances that contribute most to the business of the state courts. Crimes known to the police represent the pool of potential criminal cases. These crime data are not very reliable indicators of the amount of crime because some people do not report crimes against them to the police, and police departments vary considerably in the accuracy of the records they keep about complaints made to them. But crimes that are unreported or that the police do not even record certainly do not lead to arrests or criminal prosecution. Therefore, the crime rate is a fairly accurate indicator of variations in the potential case load for the state criminal courts.

California and New York lead in the number of crimes known to the police, even if we hold population constant. There is great variation among the states, however, and the rate varies from 320.75 crimes per thousand population in California to 57.49 per thousand population in Mississippi.

The most frequent source of civil litigation is automobile accidents. Not all accidents lead to litigation, but many claimants have their lawyer file a suit in court to expedite settlements with insurance companies. Most suits are settled before coming to trial. Column 2 of Table 1 shows the potential cases arising from traffic accidents. Again, substantial variation appears, ranging from 38.96 accidents per thousand in Wyoming to 13.53 accidents per thousand in Mississippi and 4.51 accidents in Tennessee.

These two sources of court business are not closely related. Wyoming, the state with the most accidents per thousand inhabitants, ranked thirty-six in its crime rate, and California, the state with the highest crime rate, ranked twenty-seven in its accident rate. Whereas crimes are known to be especially high in urban areas, accidents seem to occur most frequently in those states with relatively small and scattered populations. For instance, among the top ten states with automobile accidents, only two, Indiana and Michigan, have highly urbanized populations. On the other hand, all ten states with the highest crime rate are highly urbanized, including Nevada and Arizona, most of whose populations live in cities.

Other major sources of demands contribute to the millions of cases filed in state courts each year. All divorces are granted by state courts; all wills must be probated in them. All actions seeking the eviction of tenants, the garnishment of wages, the settlement of most disputes about contracts

TABLE 1

Indicators of Litigation Inputs to the State Courts

State	Crimes known to the police per 1,000 population	Rank	Automobile accidents per 1,000 population[a]	Rank
California	32.075	1	25.39	27
New York	29.080	2	22.59	38
Nevada	27.631	3	33.48	9
Maryland	26.612	4	25.16	30
Arizona	26.576	5	26.69	25
Florida	25.850	6	33.28	11
Michigan	25.300	7	34.94	7
Hawaii	22.181	8	17.98	47
Rhode Island	21.141	9	24.39	32
Oregon	19.810	10	38.17	2
New Jersey	19.796	11	19.21	45
Alaska	19.706	12	28.90	20
Washington	19.457	13	28.52	22
New Mexico	19.311	14	27.78	24
Colorado	19.150	15	37.26	3
Missouri	19.040	16	32.39	14
Massachusetts	18.629	17	25.32	29
Illinois	18.531	18	31.99	15
Texas	17.848	19	33.26	12
Delaware	17.082	20	30.20	16
Louisiana	16.844	21	35.03	6
Utah	16.218	22	33.40	10
Connecticut	15.881	23	29.13	18
Minnesota	15.581	24	29.13	18
Indiana	15.575	25	36.00	5
Tennessee	15.313	26	4.51	50
Ohio	15.059	27	21.13	44
Virginia	14.236	28	26.20	26
Georgia	13.659	29	18.13	46
Oklahoma	13.642	30	23.54	36
Kansas	13.316	31	22.49	39
Alabama	13.139	32	28.96	19
Montana	13.044	33	24.05	34
Kentucky	13.021	34	22.69	37
South Carolina	12.915	35	21.62	40
Wyoming	12.686	36	38.96	1
North Carolina	12.488	37	21.30	42
Wisconsin	11.211	38	24.64	31
Pennsylvania	10.922	39	23.88	35
Nebraska	10.820	40	28.15	23
Arkansas	10.086	41	15.00	48
Iowa	10.071	42	28.58	21
Idaho	9.854	43	37.23	4
Vermont	8.345	44	33.84	8
South Dakota	8.131	45	21.40	41
Maine	7.989	46	24.17	33
New Hampshire	7.067	47	29.89	17
West Virginia	6.587	48	21.22	43
North Dakota	5.961	49	35.27	13
Mississippi	5.749	50	13.53	49

[a]National Safety Council, private correspondence. Total accidents for Alabama, Alaska, California, Louisiana, Minnesota, Missouri, New Jersey, Vermont, and Washington are estimated by the author on the bases of the ratio of deaths: accidents for the entire United States and the deaths reported for those states by the National Safety Council.

Source: Federal Bureau of Investigation, *Uniform Crime Reports for the United States for 1968* (Washington, D.C.: United States Government Printing Office, 1970), 60-64.

as well as appeals against decisions made by zoning boards, state regulatory agencies, and school systems come to the state courts. Collectively, these and other demand sources account for an enormous amount of litigation, most of it individualized inputs.

INPUTS FROM JUDICIAL SELECTION
IN THE STATES

The selection of state judges offers one major input channel for influencing state courts. In contrast to the choice of state legislators and executives, who are selected according to some variant of popular election, recruitment of the state judiciary reflects more complex political factors. State selection systems have been responsive to innovations in democratic practice, but they have also reflected the pressures of legal traditionalism and professionalism since judicial recruitment is linked not only to the political systems of the states but also to their legal systems. Political parties and party officials, as well as legal professional groups such as bar associations and judicial conferences, have been interested in influencing the selection of judges.

Legal groups are professionally interested in judicial selection. The judges who are selected, their qualifications, and the manner in which they conduct the judicial process determine to a large extent the conditions under which legal practice is carried on. Prominent legal groups favor judges who adhere to important legal ethics and values and who identify closely with legal groups. Hence, these groups want to be consulted on judicial appointment, and they want to participate in the selection process. They are especially pleased when legally qualified judges are chosen.

Political parties, on the other hand, find the large number of state judgeships an attractive source of patronage. Major judicial posts are not only well paid and relatively secure, but they combine these occupational amenities with intellectual challenge and opportunities for the exercise of power and influence. Moreover, judgeships are particularly desirable posts for certain groups. For ethnic and racial minorities, for example, judgeships with their high social and professional prestige are especially desirable goals towards which the upwardly mobile may aspire.[6] Lawyers active in state politics look upon high judicial positions as the supreme attainment of a successful legal career. Also, the number of judgeships available in state politics remains large in the states and has not been drastically reduced by either civil service or administrative reorganization as have been some administrative positions.

Judicial Selection Systems

Presently, the states use five different selection systems, each of which favors somewhat different kinds of inputs. They are:

PARTISAN ELECTION. In this plan judges are chosen in elections where parties participate freely. This system maximizes the influence of electoral parties and popular participation.

ELECTION BY LEGISLATURE. The influence of the legislative party is predominant although sometimes the governor has great influence over legislative choices.

APPOINTMENT BY GOVERNOR. In appointing judges the governor may function as leader of his party but a variety of groups often influence the courts through the governor.

MISSOURI PLAN. Under this plan the governor makes the appointment from a list of nominees submitted by a nominating commission. Because the commission usually includes legal representatives, law groups are influential but so also are party groups and others who have access to the governor.

NONPARTISAN ELECTION. Partisan groups are formally excluded but free opportunities are afforded inputs from legal and other groups.

The states seldom agree on ways of selecting their judiciary, as shown in Table 2. Recruitment by election is the most popular method but seventeen utilize partisan elections, whereas fifteen hold nonpartisan elections. Ten states have adopted Missouri plan methods, seven retain appointment by the governor, and five use election by the legislature. The states, then, reflect both traditional ideas and modern orientations toward judicial recruitment, retaining plans that emerged from reform movements of the past and recently adopting methods growing out of contemporary model selection plans.[7]

Two major developments have dominated the character of inputs into state courts. The first culminated in the widespread adoption of partisan election plans for choosing judges during the middle of the nineteenth century. The second de-emphasized partisan inputs by inaugurating nonpartisan reforms in the latter part of the nineteenth century; the contemporary Missouri plans strengthened bar influence and revived the appointive powers of the governor. Table 3 portrays these developments.

TABLE 2

Methods of Judicial Selection in the States (Appellate and Major Trial Courts)

Much party influence and little bar influence			Little party influence and much bar influence	
Partisan election	Election by legislature	Appointment	Nonpartisan election	Missouri plan
Alabama	Connecticut[b]	Delaware	Arizona	Alaska
Arkansas	Rhode Island	Hawaii	California[a]	California
Florida	South Carolina	Maine	Idaho	Colorado
Georgia	Vermont	Maryland	Michigan	Illinois
Indiana	Virginia	Massachusetts	Minnesota	Iowa
Kansas[a]		New Hampshire	Montana	Kansas
Kentucky		New Jersey	Nevada	Missouri
Louisiana			North Dakota	Nebraska
Mississippi			Ohio	Oklahoma
Missouri[a]			Oregon	Utah
New Mexico			South Dakota	
New York			Tennessee	
North Carolina			Washington	
Oklahoma[a]			Wisconsin	
Pennsylvania			Wyoming	
Texas				
West Virginia				

[a]States listed under more than one heading select judges for different courts by different methods.

[b]Formally legislature, actually by nomination of governor.

Source: State Court Systems (Lexington, Ky.: Council of State Governments, 1970); *The Extent of Adoption of the Non-Partisan Appointive Elective Plan for the Selection of Judges* (Chicago: American Judiciary Society, 1969).

TABLE 3

Initial Adoption and Change of Judicial Selection Systems in the American States by Historical Periods

	Period			
Method of selection	1776-1831	1832-1885[a]	1885-1933	1934-1968[b]
By legislature	48.5%	6.7%	0.0%	0.0%
Gubernatorial appointment	42.4	20.0	10.7	5.6
Partisan election	9.1	73.3	25.0	11.1
Nonpartisan election	0.0	0.0	64.3	11.1
Missouri plan	0.0	0.0	0.0	72.2
	100.0%	100.0%	100.0%	100.0%

[a]Toward less governmental and more partisan influence.

[b]Toward less partisan and more bar influence.

Source: Charles Haynes, *The Selection and Tenure of Judges,* National Conference of Judicial Councils, 1944; *Journal of the American Judicature Society,* various volumes.

Colonial American judges were appointed by the executive but many post-Revolutionary state governments reacted against use of the executive power by changing to legislative election. The five states that utilize legislative election are states from among the original thirteen colonies that have retained the post-Revolutionary system. Of those states that utilize gubernatorial appointment, five are from the original thirteen colonies. One state, Maine, was admitted shortly after the Revolution, and only Hawaii has adopted the system in recent times, simply retaining the practice of appointment used before statehood.

Two major political movements, both concerned with reform in political institutions in their time, account for the adoption of electoral methods. The first of these movements, that of Jacksonian popular democracy, swept through the states during the 1830s and 1840s, changing courts and other institutions to bring officials under popular control by partisan elections. The nonpartisan movement, which reached its peak in the latter part of the nineteenth century, reacted against political parties as corrupt and oligarchical and sought to return control of state institutions to the people through the recruitment of political officials by nonpartisan elections. Thus nonpartisan selection of the judiciary is used in those western and midwestern states where the nonpartisan and Progressive movements were strong. Popular election, on the other hand, is retained in the states that initially provided for judicial elections during the Jacksonian period or else changed to partisan election under the influence of Jacksonianism.

As in other matters affecting the judiciary, professional legal groups sponsor contemporary reform selection plans for the judiciary. The model plan endorsed by the American Bar Association and the American Judicature Society recommended that judges be chosen in the states by a Missouri-like plan.[8] This plan, a variant of appointment, would increase the influence of professional lawyers by having the governor choose from among candidates nominated by a panel that included legal members along with other lay or political members. The Missouri plan also appears to minimize the role of political parties and the influence of the popular electorate. Popular control, while entirely excluded in the initial selection process, is admitted subsequently through the provision that after selection judges must submit to a referendum vote on their record. If the vote is negative the judge is replaced. Not only has the Missouri plan dominated recent changes but during the past twenty-five years no state has changed to any method other than the Missouri plan. (Hawaii did not change at statehood but continued territorial practices.)

Processes of Judicial Selection

As Table 3 shows, political parties have tended to be de-emphasized in the recent adoption of recruitment plans. In actual practice, however, informal behaviors not present in the formal rules and assumptions of the plans have provided channels for partisan inputs into the courts. Indeed, the actual processes of selection sometimes contradict the plans' formal expectations. In the resulting modifications, the most important outcome has been the growth of the power of the governor to make choices, both as leader of the state's party and as the head of its political system. In the process the role of electoral participation has been minimized while the influence of bar groups remains high.

PARTISAN AND NONPARTISAN ELECTIONS. A prominent characteristic of judicial recruitment in states that elect their judges is that most judges are not initially elected; they are appointed. In an analysis of the period from 1948 to 1957 Herndon found that in elective states 192 Supreme Court justices first attained office by election but that 242 entered office by appointment.[9]

This rather discrepant method of selection in an elective system is made possible by the governor's power of interim appointment. It works in this manner: Apparently acting in conformity with a general understanding, many judges will resign or retire a short time before the end of their terms. The governor then exercises his power to appoint someone to the unexpired term of the judgeship. These interim appointments often become permanent selections because of the great success that judicial incumbents have in elections. In one study of subsequent elections involving such appointees in Wisconsin, more than one third were not contested and in those contested less than 10 per cent of the appointed judges were defeated.[10]

Where nonpartisan elections are used partisan influences are nonetheless often present in the process of selection. For example, about half of the judges in nonpartisan states list some form of party affiliation in official biographies. Party organizations, under secretive disguises, often play an active part in the campaigns.[11] This is the case in Minnesota where judges have run as a bloc and where political parties have endorsed judges, making the partisan affiliations of judicial candidates easily visible. In Michigan, a nonpartisan state, judges are openly nominated at party conventions and then supported without pretense by party organizations in ensuing campaigns.[12]

In partisan elections of the judiciary we might expect more competition, more vigorous activity, and more intense partisanship. But partisan elections seldom live up to their name. Although judicial offices are generally contested at the same elections and appear on the same ballots as other offices, judicial contests are generally characterized by low turnouts, lackadaisical campaigns, and voter acquiescense. In general there is a more pronounced tendency than in other elections not to contest incumbent office holders and, if contests occur, for the incumbents to win. For example, in Louisiana between 1945 and 1960 there were 7 defeats out of 304 elections for district and appellate courts involving 169 different judges. In the same state 26 judges had served a period of time covering three elections. Of these, 1 had never faced opposition, 16 had faced opposition in only one election, and 5 had been opposed in two elections. Only 2 had been opposed in all three elections.[13]

Most judicial elections are inactive and the rare active elections are apt to occur under partisan systems. Experience indicates that it is all but impossible to arouse voters in judicial contests occurring in nonpartisan elections, even when contenders bring into the campaign the seemingly explosive questions of judges' handling of sex and Communism issues.[14] On the other hand, two states, Louisiana and Pennsylvania, furnish examples of heated contests for judicial office, including a number of elections for the state supreme court. Among the many instances of highly partisan campaigns for judgeships in these states, Chief Justice Fournet's career furnishes the most colorful example. Justice Fournet secured his office originally in 1934 through a manipulative stratagem of Huey Long. Judge Pony, an opponent of Long, referred to the court decision that validated Long's stratagem: "[The judges who ordered a new primary] are stool pigeons of that lying scoundrel, Huey P. Long, who has forfeited his right to live" and have "disgraced the court. In my opinion they have put themselves in the class of hog thieves." [15] Two terms and twenty-eight years later Chief Justice Fournet faced formidable opposition in the Democratic primary. James Nelson Lee, his chief opponent, attacked Fournet's honesty and business dealings while on the court; Fournet accused Lee of circulating a "lie-laden sheet" and acting "below the dignity of any man who seeks the important office of supreme court justice." [16] The vote was extremely close in both primaries, and bitterly fought to the end. The vote was:

First primary		*Second primary*	
Fournet	47.6%	Fournet	51.5%
Lee	46.3	Lee	48.5
Thompson	6.1		

Fournet's partisan career is typical of partisan politics for judicial selection in Louisiana and Pennsylvania, and these two states have frequent instances of partisan factionalism in judicial elections.

GUBERNATORIAL APPOINTMENT. Most state appointive systems are much like the presidential system of appointment of federal judges except that there is no equivalent of senatorial courtesy on the state level. More important are the background of the judge, the political needs and strategies of the governor, and the actions of such groups as the state bar association and political party factions. Many of the governor's appointees to judicial office have previously served in the legislature, where they have established a reputation for service that was beneficial to the party and to the state. At other times the governor may appoint a candidate from a particular section of a state in order to bolster his influence where his strength or his party's prospects are weak.[17]

One careful study of a gubernatorial appointment in a western state has analyzed the campaign undertaken by a candidate for the appointment.[18] The campaign was as carefully planned and energetically carried out as campaigns for elective office. Attention was concentrated on the mobilization of important political groups of several kinds. Private groups such as labor and public utility firms were enlisted, ethnic and minority groups normally found in the governor's party were mobilized, and local party organizations were brought into service. Finally, an effort was made to secure the support of a variety of law firms and sitting judges in order to project the image of a legally qualified nonpartisan aspirant. Despite his energetic campaign the candidate failed to get the appointment, for the governor made the appointment to serve his own needs.

A governor can make an appointment in order to serve a variety of purposes. He can make the appointment to gain immediate political advantage or to reward specifically for past services, or he can appoint someone who stands out primarily because of his legal reputation and the endorsement of legal groups. A governor makes his appointments according to political needs and his conception of his role as recruiter. One governor was described as making appointments that "invariably . . . have had a . . . readily apparent connection to a gubernatorial strategy for election and re-election." [19]

MISSOURI-LIKE PLANS. Legal reformers pressing for the adoption of this method of recruitment frequently say that it will take judicial selection "out of politics." Few could be so naive as to believe that the selection of judges could possibly be nonpolitical in nature. What they mean, presumably, is that a Missouri plan would remove selection from partisan politics. A thorough study of the operation of the Missouri plan in Missouri indicates that not only has judicial selection there evolved a political pattern of its own, but also that recruitment of judges has been linked in important ways to Missouri politics in general.[20]

One of the most interesting features of the plan is the great influence of the judiciary in selecting their own colleagues. Each of the three commissions in Missouri that nominates judges for different courts consists of a combination of laymen, lawyers, and a sitting judge who presides over the commission. The lawyers are elected by all attorneys in the court's district, the lay members are appointed by the governor, and the judge on the commission is the presiding judge of the court of appeals of that area. Because he has a greater stake than do the other members of the commission in the nomination of judicial colleagues, the presiding judge ordinarily works more devotedly and with more energy. His influence with the other commission members is great because he has common professional ties with the lawyers and receives deference and respect from the laymen because he is a chief justice. In addition, the judge has an appreciation of the political perspective of the governor because his own appointment was an outcome of that perspective. For these reasons the judge is the most effective member of the commission in forming politically influential combinations.

The lawyer members of the commission are less influential than is generally assumed under this plan. They not only defer to the presiding judge but their influence is weakened by divisive interests. A common mistake is the assumption that all lawyers agree on such questions as judicial appointments and do not have divergent perspectives. In fact, lawyers tend to be polarized around two general orientations, that of the plaintiff lawyers who represent and identify with injured persons in personal injury cases and that of the defendant lawyers who have as clients the parties being sued such as insurance companies and business concerns. Plaintiffs' lawyers and defendants' lawyers usually have separate bar associations and in Missouri each association fields a slate of candidates for membership on the commission and conducts vigorous campaigns. Lawyer members of the nominating commissions rarely were able to form a united front.

The influence of lay commission members is weakest of all, despite the implicit assumption in the Missouri plan that they would represent the public interest. Because of their lack of familiarity with and general awe of the technicalities of the law, the lay members turn both to the lawyers on the commission and to the judge for direction. Their most positive contribution is the representation of the governor's perspective. On occasion, lay members convey direct statements from a governor but more generally they convey the governor's point of view by their general awareness and experience with personalities and problems in his political life and with how judicial appointments might affect them.

Somewhat unexpectedly, the influence of the governor is exceptionally strong in Missouri plan operations. His influence is not only channeled through lay members but is represented by the judge, himself a product of gubernatorial appointive politics. Indeed, the most realistic assessment of the Missouri operation is that it embodies a process of gubernatorial selection in which the perspective of the bar, the judiciary, and the public, expressed through the commission, simply set the outer limits of the governor's influence. Indeed, this study of the Missouri plan operation in Missouri concludes that governors "have used their appointments to reward friends or past political supporters" and have implemented the plan very largely from a personal and political standpoint.[21]

A most important effect of the plan has been the institution of life tenure for judges in Missouri under its auspices. The plan formally provides for electoral review of judges after one year's service on the bench. The judge runs unopposed on his record. In practice the reviews have been virtually without effect since in only 1 of 179 elections held under the plan has a judge been turned down — and that under highly extraordinary circumstances. Because of general public timidity and unawareness of judicial issues, judicial elections provide no protection for the public. The safe tenures of Missouri plan appointees are in marked contrast to preplan conditions when both circuit and appellate judges met with frequent defeats, particularly in general elections.

Impact of Different Selection Systems

Efforts directed toward judicial recruitment have led to a moderately large amount of activity in state politics. Although most of the effort has probably been inspired by thoughts of reward, profit, and patronage in judicial positions, concern has been shown about the character of judges likely to be produced by certain selection systems. Most often, these aims have been expressed by Missouri plan advocates who were sure their plan would recruit judges with superior qualifications. But does it? Are there any differences between judges selected according to the Missouri plan and those selected according to other methods?

Herbert Jacob has systematically investigated and compared the characteristics of judges chosen under the five different selection systems.[22] He finds that judges chosen under the different methods do differ but sometimes not as we might expect. For example, judges chosen by the Missouri plan do not have notably better legal educations than judges chosen under other plans, and Missouri plan judges are more localistic — educated and born in the vicinity of their court — than other judges. This is contrary to the picture of the Missouri plan judge as highly educated and cosmopolitan. In an investigation of judges from the state of Missouri, Watson and Downing also find that Missouri plan judges have rather minimal legal educations and tend to be associated with local factors rather than out-of-state or national experiences.[23] But they have had somewhat more previous experiences as judges than other groups. On the other hand, both those judges chosen by the state legislature and those elected under partisan systems more frequently have had political experiences such as legislative and law enforcement positions than other groups of judges. This is precisely what we would expect from the closer involvement of these selection plans with the institutions of state government and with political parties. Jacob also finds that governors appoint an unusually large proportion of former legislators to judicial positions, and we would expect that the governor's involvement with legislators in effectuating his state programs would lead to obligations payable via judicial appointments.

Although seldom fully articulated, selection plans imply some pattern of behavior for those the system chooses. For example, legal advocates of the Missouri plan generally claim greater objectivity and legal expertise of those selected while partisan advocates claim that those elected will be more sensitive to democratic impulses. Critics of the Missouri plan claim, on the other hand, that judges so selected will be conservatively biased and act in terms of conformity:

> The point is that the Missouri plan will not produce a maverick. On the other hand, if you select your judges under the elective system, you may get all kinds of wacky characters going on the bench, who will frequently dissent from the views of their colleagues, and who will air different viewpoints and thus let a little ventilation into the process of justice.[24]

Investigation of the Missouri plan reveals that attorneys believe that Missouri plan judges are about as objective as those who were previously selected under a different method. Moreover, the investigators were able to find no significant differences in the judicial behavior of judges chosen under the plan. Also, plan judges actually dissented more.

Conflict over Court Organization as an Input

In contrast to the individualized inputs in the litigation process, conflict over court organization, like controversies over judicial recruitment, provides an occasion for interest group activity and partisan influence. While state courts have been no more disposed to change their institutional forms than have other political institutions, quite a few modifications have been made in the structure of the state judiciaries. Different kinds of group demands have been responsible for changing court organization in different periods. Figure 1 portrays the evolution of court organization in the states from the colonial period to the present time.

One period of great change in state court structures began around the middle of the nineteenth century when the United States had started the transformation from a rural agricultural society into an urban industrial one with an increasingly heterogeneous population and a large number of foreign born. In consequence, courts were soon called upon to resolve issues having to do with automobile accidents and traffic problems, employee injury suits, labor cases, and consumers' suits. Demands were made for special courts to handle the litigation and for judges to staff them. Traffic, municipal, small claims, and domestic relations courts originated in response to these demands.[25] Interest groups sometimes seek specialized courts that will handle only one kind of cases and deal more expeditiously with them than the general courts. However, such prominent interest groups as unions and trade associations are not involved in court organization demands, for their concern is not intense enough to justify their involvement.

Concern for court organization also provides occasions for political parties to make demands on the judiciary. Parties are especially interested in the geographical distribution of courts, for it is important to them that courts are available in all major subdivisions of the state, particularly in cities and counties so that municipal and county party organizations can participate in the patronage that courts distribute. Patronage in the forms of appointments to the bench, assignment of lawyers to administer estates where there is no will, selection of persons to estimate the value of estates, and other judicial business is the source of many campaign contributions and a strong attraction for some young lawyers and others to work under a party banner.

Demands for change in court organization often come from bar associations. Lawyers are concerned about the identity and location of courts since they want courts that are convenient for their practice and that will deal efficiently with the cases they bring. Oddly enough, the American Bar

FIGURE 1
The Evolution of State Courts

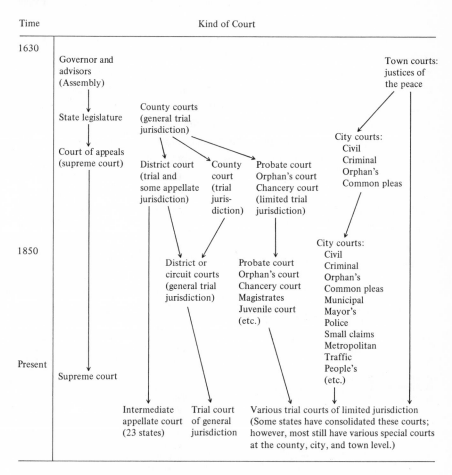

Source: Henry Robert Glick and Kenneth N. Vines, *State Courts* (Englewood Cliffs, N.J.: Prentice-Hall, forthcoming), ch. 2.

Association has taken a stand against specialized courts, quite contrary to the tendency of specialization in other occupations.[26] Undoubtedly, this stand is related to the general identification of lawyers as "attorneys-at-law" and nothing more.

Reform in judicial organization has been urged by professional legal organizations, particularly the American Bar Association and the American Judicature Society, who make demands in the form of advocating model organizational plans. The model plan sponsored by the ABA calls for four courts in a state judiciary: a supreme court, one intermediate appellate court, one trial court of general jurisdiction, and one set of magistrates courts. This relatively centralized court system entirely lacks special courts and thus simplifies and conveniently concentrates the facilities for the practice of law. The inclusion of an intermediate court of appeals, on the other hand, broadens and enhances the possibilities for appeal of cases, thus maximizing the appellate litigation that can be carried on. By 1971, however, only North Carolina had adopted the model plan, and only Arizona, California, and Washington had approximated closely the ABA's model. Table 4 compares court organizations in the different states.

Only six states have court organizations that place them in a category close to the ABA model plan. Although every state has one court of last resort only 23 have intermediate appellate courts. Others fail to meet ABA specifications for a modern court system by having multiple courts of general jurisdiction and many still retain a multitude of trial courts of limited

TABLE 4
Differences in State Court Organizations[a]

Simple and modern			Complex and traditional
Group 1 N = 6	Group 2 N = 20	Group 3 N = 20	Group 4 N = 4
Arizona	Alabama	Connecticut	Arkansas
California	Alaska	Idaho	Delaware
Illinois	Colorado	Iowa	Mississippi
North Carolina	Florida	Kansas	Virginia
Oklahoma	Georgia	Kentucky	
Washington	Hawaii	Maine	
	Indiana	Massachusetts	
	Louisiana	Minnesota	
	Maryland	Montana	
	Michigan	Nebraska	
	Missouri	New Hampshire	
	Nevada	North Dakota	
	New Jersey	Rhode Island	
	New Mexico	South Carolina	
	New York	South Dakota	
	Ohio	Tennessee	
	Oregon	Utah	
	Pennsylvania	Vermont	
	Texas	West Virginia	
	Wyoming	Wisconsin	

[a]States were placed in categories according to their approximation to the ABA model plan for state court organization. Points were allocated to states according to possession of a court of last resort, one intermediate appellate court, one trial court of original jurisdiction and one special court. Each aspect of court organization was measured on a 4 point scale using the ABA plan as the measuring rod.
Source: State Court Systems, (Lexington, Ky.: Council of State Governments, 1970) and Henry Robert Glick and Kenneth N. Vines, *State Courts,* (Englewood Cliffs, N.J.: Prentice-Hall, forthcoming) ch. 2.

jurisdiction. The correlates of court organization are not clear but western states appear to lead in the achievement of modern organizations while southern states retain traditional forms of court organization.

LEGAL PROFESSIONALISM AS AN INPUT

Legal groups, as we have seen, are quite active in sponsoring inputs for state courts. On questions of judicial selection, court organization, judicial administration, tenure, and salary, legal groups advocate reforms, propose model plans and pursue interested activity. Although many of these plans are presented as reforms or achievement of model plans, they generally would increase the influence of legal groups in the court system and create conditions perceived as favorable for legal professionalism. The increased intervention of legal groups in questions concerning state judiciaries correlates with the growth of professional training and organization in the law. In turn legal organizations have increased in scope and numbers and evidenced interest in bringing legal orientations into state courts. While there is a diversity of legal groups and not all groups agree on all questions, there appears to be substantial agreement on major aspects of court politics. On the other hand legal groups are often opposed on such matters as judicial selection and court organization by partisan organizations and other special interests.

We have measured the extent of legal professionalism in the states by means of a composite index. This index consists of major features of state court systems and includes judicial selection, court organization, judicial administration, tenure systems and salary levels. The extent of legal professionalism is measured by the approximation of states to the model plan or statement on each feature advocated by the American Bar Association and the American Judicature Society, chief spokesmen for legal reform in the states. State scores are evidence of the relative success of legal groups in modifying judicial institutions. Table 5 presents scores and rankings for the states.

Although the states as a whole are distributed along a continuum, there are pronounced differences among states at the ends. In general, states that ranked highest appear to be urban and industrial, whereas southern states have the lowest rankings. Inspections of the correlates of legal professionalism in Table 6 confirm this observation.

Legal groups have been most successful in bringing modern legal orientations into judiciaries in the wealthier, urban states with social and

TABLE 5

Legal Professionalism in the American States

Rank of States	Composite Score
1. California	21.7
2. New Jersey	18.0
3. Illinois	17.7
4. Massachusetts, New York	16.7
6. Alaska, Michigan	16.3
8. Maryland	15.3
9. Hawaii	15.3
10. Pennsylvania	15.0
11. Colorado, Washington, Wisconsin	14.3
14. Ohio	14.0
15. North Carolina	13.7
16. New Hampshire	13.4
17. Arizona, Oregon, Rhode Island	13.3
20. Nevada	13.0
21. Connecticut	12.6
22. Idaho, Minnesota, Oklahoma	12.0
25. North Dakota	11.3
26. Kentucky	11.0
27. Iowa	10.9
28. Maine, Wyoming	10.7
30. Vermont	10.3
31. Florida, Montana, Virginia	10.0
34. Delaware, Louisiana, Missouri	9.6
37. New Mexico, Utah	9.3
39. Nebraska, South Dakota	9.0
41. South Carolina	8.7
42. Georgia, Kansas, Tennessee, Texas	8.0
46. Indiana	7.6
47. West Virginia	7.3
48. Alabama	6.0
49. Arkansas	5.3
50. Mississippi	3.4

Source: Data is from *The Book of the States 1970-71, State Court Systems,* and various issues of *Journal of the American Judicature Society.*

TABLE 6

Simple Correlations of Legal Professionalism with Selected Social and Political Indicators

Indicator	Correlation
Percentage urban	.65
Per capita income	.75
Social and economic heterogeneity	.76
Interparty competition	.56
Political innovation	.77
Legislative professionalism	.56

Source: Kenneth N. Vines and Judson B. Fisher, "Legal Professionalism in the American States," mimeo., State University of New York at Buffalo, 1971.

economic heterogeneity. Greater legal professionalism is also present in those states with more partisan competition and political innovation. In addition we find that legal and legislative professionalism tend to occur together in the states and represent aspects of modernization and political development. Quite likely modernization is correlated with the growth of an urban industrial society and the development of professional orientations toward political institutions.

Support for the State Courts

Like all political institutions, state courts also require support from the general population and from other institutions of government. Courts are provided some support through the respect accorded judges. But material support is meager. All the states together spent $205 million during the fiscal year 1967–68 for judicial activities. This figure represents 3 per cent of their total expenditures! On a per capita basis, the mean expenditure for judicial activities in the 1967–68 fiscal year was $1.53. Only six states spent more than $3 per capita, and they were mostly small states: Connecticut, Alaska, Delaware, Idaho, Rhode Island, and Vermont. Twenty-six states spent less than $1 per person per year on their courts. Moreover, our primitive data suggest that legislatures and governors are not very responsive to the needs of the courts because those states with potentially heavy court loads do not give the largest funds to their courts. Table 7 shows the simple correlations between several indicators of potential court work load and per capita expenditures for the courts. None show a high relationship. Rather, we are left with the impression that the amount of money given the courts is an accidental outcome of tradition, personality, and sporadic attention to the needs of the judiciary. Unlike other agencies,

TABLE 7

Simple Correlation Between Indicators of Potential Work Load of Courts and Per Capita Expenditure on State Judiciary

Crime rate[a] and expenditures[a]	.13
Accidents[c] per 1,000 pop. and expenditures	.04
Divorce[d] rate and expenditures	−.05

[a]See Table 1.
[b]United States Bureau of the Census, *Criminal Justice,* State and Local Government Special Studies No. 55 (Washington, D.C.: United States Government Printing Office, 1970), 11.
[c]See Table 1.
[d]United States Bureau of the Census, *Statistical Abstract of the U.S., 1969* (Washington, D.C.: United States Government Printing Office, 1969), 61.

the courts do not have a strong lobby of clients who continually urge a higher expenditure rate on legislatures and governors.

MAKING JUDICIAL DECISIONS

Organizational Structure of Decisions

Decisions in state courts are made within an organizational framework established to accommodate the different phases of the legal process. In the American state legal process three different kinds of activities take place, each requiring a distinctive kind of court organization. The three types of organizations are: (1) courts of general jurisdiction that handle broad categories of trial cases; (2) special courts that handle litigation in specialized areas and on particular subjects; and (3) appellate courts that review cases already heard. With these types of courts states can fulfill the rudiments of the legal process that include a first hearing in courts of general jurisdiction or special courts depending on the nature of the case and at least one review of the decision in an appellate court. However complex and detailed the judicial organization in a state, each court fulfills one of these functions.[27]

Although the general classifications of courts are broad and general, state variations of the three types of courts offer a bewildering variety of names and court forms. As the result the outward appearances of state court systems often bear little resemblance to each other.

Cases of general significance are handled in trial courts of general jurisdiction, which occur in the states under many names. The most common are district, circuit, or county courts but they are also called common pleas courts, courts of general sessions, and superior courts. In New York the courts of general jurisdiction are called supreme courts. Thirty-eight of the states utilize only one type of trial court of general jurisdiction, but nine states have two types, two states have three types, and one state has four kinds of trial courts of general jurisdiction.

Special cases that arise out of limited jurisdiction are handled in trial courts of limited jurisdiction. The richest variety of names and special types is found in the states among these courts. A few examples to illustrate the variety are recorder's courts, courts of domestic relations, police courts, orphans courts and corporation and hustings courts. Only eight states have as few as two types of these courts, ten states have three different kinds, twenty states have four or five, and twelve states have six or more different kinds.

There are two types of appellate courts in the states: supreme courts and intermediate appellate courts. Supreme courts are uniform throughout the states. Every state has one and they all serve as the final court of appeal. In most states this court is called simply, the supreme court. In a minority of states, however, other names are given to the court. These include: court of appeals, supreme judicial court, and supreme court of errors.

Only twenty-three states have intermediate appellate courts. However, Oklahoma, Tennessee, and Texas have two intermediate appellate courts, one for civil cases and one for criminal cases. Intermediate appellate courts also have a variety of names such as superior court, court of appeals, and appellate division of the supreme court or superior court.

As the previous description suggests, state judiciaries differ widely in both the pattern and the substance of their organizational forms. Some, such as New York and Florida, are complex and highly specialized, consisting of a multitude of courts. Other states such as Wyoming and Hawaii have few courts, fulfilling only the basic functions of the legal process. The court systems of Hawaii and New York illustrate two extreme instances of complexity and simplicity:

Hawaii courts	*New York courts*
Supreme court	Court of appeals
Circuit courts	Appellate division of supreme court
District courts	Appellate terms of supreme court
	Supreme court
	Court of claims
	Surrogates' courts
	Family courts
	County courts
	City courts
	Civil courts
	Municipal courts
	Criminal courts
	District courts
	Justice courts
	Police justice courts
	Traffic courts
	Recorders' courts
	Police courts
	Courts of special sessions

Both state organizations have certain elements of the ABA plan. Hawaii has no special courts but also has no ABA recommended intermediate court of appeals. New York has an intermediate appellate court, the appellate division of the supreme court, but also has many special courts.

Judicial decision making resembles decision making in other state institutions in some basic ways. Like other agencies the judiciary must render decisions by considering demands and interacting with those who make them. Like the legislature, for example, it must be aware of problems of power and conflicts of interest. It must resolve internal differences and finally reach a decision by voting. However, judicial decision processes have distinctive features. These include the use of quite formal legal procedures, customary utilization of adversary conflicts for litigations, and the limitation that courts cannot initiate cases but hear only those that are brought before them.

Resolution before Trial

Although we generally associate judicial decision making in lower courts with trials, many cases are settled before ever reaching the trial stage.[28] A trial is a formal procedure that takes place in a courtroom before a presiding judge and involves the participation of attorneys. It proceeds according to formal methods and follows legal rules. In the final stages a decision is made by the judge or often by a jury.

Before the trial begins in criminal cases, many important steps must be taken. An arrest must have been made, a charge filed, the possibility of bail considered, prosecution decided upon, and a plea made. In civil cases equally important steps are necessary before trial is begun. The suit must be filed, the defendant must answer, and both parties must be determined to go to trial rather than give in or compromise. Thus, in both criminal and civil cases the decisional process is complex.

An important feature of these pretrial decisions is the active participation of the decision makers, whether they be policemen, prosecutors, attorneys, or litigants. Because of their usual lack of visibility and public reputation, pretrial decisions are sometimes assumed to involve no active participation but to be subsumed under automatic and routinized methods of the law. In reality nothing could be further from the truth.

The discretion of the prosecutor in deciding both whether to press charges after the arrest has been made and in negotiating the settlement of cases without trial has long been accepted as necessary and proper. The enormous authority of the prosecutor in pretrial decisions has led some to speak of him as a de-facto judge. Much of the political sensitivity of the prosecutor's role is linked to the character of his office and especially to the necessity for the prosecutor to maintain a good record. A good record is ordinarily defined as a good score of case convictions, but it may also include sensitivity to the social and personal problems involved in criminal prosecution. The prosecutor is usually elected, often in partisan elections, and uses his public reputation and the public record of his activities not only to retain his position but as a stepping stone to higher political office.

The negotiated guilty plea is a particularly useful device by which the prosecutor can build up his record of convictions. At the same time guilty pleas help clear crowded dockets and are a simple way of speeding up judicial decision making while retaining a high percentage of convictions. Table 8 shows the prevalence of negotiated guilty pleas in the trials of some states.

Trial by Single Judge

Most cases are settled out of court by procedures such as those just described. The decisions in cases that come to trial are made by a jury or by a single judge. There is very little analysis of trial decision making and we are unable to draw any state comparisons. In addition to the problem of a very large amount of data (millions of cases are involved), trial decisions

TABLE 8
*Prevalence of Guilty Pleas in Trial Courts of General
Jurisdiction of Selected States*

State (1964 unless otherwise noted)	Total convictions	Percentage of guilty pleas
California (1965)	30,840	74.0
Connecticut	1,596	93.9
Hawaii	393	91.5
Illinois	5,591	85.2
Kansas	3,025	90.2
Massachusetts (1963)	7,790	85.2
Minnesota (1965)	1,567	91.7
New York	17,249	95.5
Pennsylvania (1960)	25,632	66.8

Source: Task Force Report on Administration of Justice, *The Courts* (Washington, D.C.: United States Government Printing Office, 1957), 9.

are usually not published by the states and can only be gathered on occasion from court files. Without convenient, reliable records, therefore, it has been difficult to examine trial decisions.

Kenneth Dolbeare made a careful case study of trial court decisions in a New York urban county.[29] He found that there were consistent differences in the ways judges decided cases such as those dealing with zoning and taxation. Although Dolbeare's study does not permit us to make generalizations concerning trial court behaviors in the states, other judicial studies raise expectations about trial court decision making.

We could anticipate, for example, that a trial judge does not make decisions *tabula rasa* but reflects his social background traits and the character of his prejudicial experiences. We would expect the judge to be sensitive to the pattern of political power in his constituency. Indeed, if a single party or faction dominated a community we might believe that trial judges would reflect that fact and, if a single figure dominated an area, judges would likely be beholden to him.

Such expectations are plausible if trial judges make decisions in a manner similar to appellate judges, but Dolbeare's study casts some doubt on these assumptions. However, both the findings of studies of appellate decision making and the close fashion by which judicial recruitment is linked to state politics would logically lead us to look for a link between trial decisions and judges' former environment.

Appellate Decision Making

In contrast to trial court decisions, appellate court decisions are the most frequently studied phase of the judicial decisional process. Whereas state trial court decisions often are not systematically recorded and published, appellate decisions are reasonably well reported and regularly published in state and regional reports. Also, whereas trial decisions often do not provide an adequate body of cases for study since particular judges often decide few cases in important policy categories, all judges on collegial appellate courts usually sit for all cases and thus generate enough cases for comparison. Since appeals courts always have more than one member, these courts have special problems in making decisions, concerning how the members of the court interact in case voting; whether they tend to agree or disagree establishes the environment of the court, making it an atmosphere either of conflict or harmony.

The simplest and most direct way to describe conflict and agreement on appeals courts is to note the extent, the frequency, and the patterns of dissent. Because conflict can be expressed in other ways (e.g., arguments, conference, or personal statements to other justices), expression by means of a vote of dissent has special importance. Votes of dissent are formal actions that appear in the record and emphasize the split vote on a decision. A decision delivered with dissents has political implications that are lacking in a unanimous decision that appears to convey total agreement. Moreover, courts that have a great deal of dissent in their decisions operate in a different atmosphere than do courts that are relatively free of dissent. Rivalries and disagreement sometimes become public and tensions hamper interpersonal cooperation and agreement in arriving at decisions. Also, conflicts expressed in dissents may reinforce personal animosities. A court that produces few split vote decisions, on the other hand, operates in an environment of apparent harmony and agreement. Such an atmosphere must surely help in reaching agreements and compromising differences.

The supreme court in Pennsylvania regularly produces many divided decisions and vigorous dissents.[30] The Pennsylvania court often leads state supreme courts in its rate of dissent, and it is also well known for personal animosities, some of them public, among its members. Many supreme courts present public facades of harmony with few dissents. Among them is the supreme court of Wisconsin, where personal animosity is rare.[31] The Wisconsin court has an atmosphere of nonpartisanship and confidence in its ability to resolve differences and effect compromises.

Are state supreme courts generally like the Pennsylvania court or more like the Wisconsin court? To provide materials for comparison we have collected data on dissenting opinions for the supreme courts of forty-eight states. (Hawaii and Alaska are omitted.) Presented in Table 9, the data include figures for three years for each state. The years chosen are 1966, 1941, and 1916 so that we may investigate the development and decline of dissent over a fifty-year span.

Dissent rates in state supreme courts varied widely in each period. In 1966, the most recent year examined, dissent in Michigan, New York, and Pennsylvania courts approached the level of the national Supreme Court (over 50 per cent) whereas in Massachusetts, Rhode Island, and Alabama dissents were barely more than 1 per cent of all decisions made. In 1941 and in 1916 levels of dissent in most states were lower than they were in 1966. A good example is Pennsylvania whose 41% dissent rate in 1966 was not equaled in 1941 or 1916 when the rates were 5 per cent and 1.5 per cent respectively. On the other hand, some states had rather high

TABLE 9

Percentage of Dissenting Opinions in State Courts for the Years 1966, 1941, and 1916[a]

Rank in 1966	State	1966	1941	1916
High dissent courts — Pennsylvania model *(Dissent rate > 20%)*				
1	Michigan	46.5	19.0	9.6
2	Pennsylvania	41.0	5.0	1.5
3	New York	41.0	15.8	34.1
4	Ohio	34.9	14.1	14.8
5	California	32.3	16.7	5.3
6	Florida	28.2	17.7	4.1
7	Oklahoma	26.5	19.7	.1
8	South Dakota	24.3	12.0	18.6
Low dissent courts — Wisconsin model *(Dissent rate < 20%)*				
48	Massachusetts	1.2	.6	0.0
47	Alabama	1.7	4.1	6.1
46	Rhode Island	1.4	5.4	6.5
45	North Carolina	2.4	17.8	13.2
44	Tennessee	3.0	2.3	1.6
43	South Carolina	3.4	8.3	17.0
42	Delaware	3.4	15.4	15.0
41	Connecticut	3.6	3.9	11.9
40	Mississippi	3.9	8.0	.1
39	Missouri	4.1	.7	17.4
38	Maine	4.2	7.0	2.5
37	Vermont	5.9	1.7	5.4
36	Maryland	5.4	8.6	5.6
35	New Mexico	6.0	10.3	6.2
34	Arizona	6.1	1.8	8.3
33	Minnesota	6.8	10.8	5.9
32	New Jersey	7.1	30.2	14.0
31	Illinois	7.2	15.7	15.0
30	New Hampshire	7.3	1.4	3.3
29	Virginia	7.4	19.6	.1
28	Wisconsin	8.0	3.9	8.6
27	Kentucky	8.1	3.0	.1
26	Georgia	8.3	7.2	5.8
25	North Dakota	8.4	15.1	10.0
24	Idaho	9.0	35.6	12.2
23	Oregon	9.1	12.2	9.1
22	Wyoming	9.7	4.3	2.6
21	Nevada	9.8	6.8	11.4
20	Colorado	9.8	26.3	18.5
19	West Virginia	10.7	14.3	4.8
18	Nebraska	11.2	7.1	36.5
17	Washington	11.5	28.7	10.0
16	Indiana	11.5	5.7	7.1
15	Utah	11.7	33.0	7.7
14	Montana	11.9	16.1	.1
13	Kansas	12.1	13.4	8.5
12	Louisiana	12.7	.9	12.8
11	Arkansas	13.6	14.3	9.6
10	Texas	19.1	3.4	5.7
9	Iowa	19.7	14.4	5.2

[a]Includes *per* curiam but not memorandum opinions.
Source: State and regional reports for 1966, 1941, and 1916.

percentages of dissent in earlier years that did not persist into 1966. Nebraska's courts made 36.5 per cent of its decisions with dissent in 1916 but only 7.1 per cent in 1941 and 11.2 per cent in 1966.

Comparing the distribution among the states for the three years systematically by means of simple correlations we find that state dissents for 1916 correlated .22 with those for 1941 and .15 with those for 1966. The correlation between the years 1941 and 1966 was .22. Thus, our sample years show little relationship between the states from one generation to the next. The low correlations indicate neither an orderly increase nor a diminution among the states for the years examined. In general the average level of dissent in state supreme courts has remained much the same. Since 1916 dissent rates have increased only 2 per cent. Unlike the national Supreme Court, where dissent has become quite frequent, state courts today dissent about as seldom as they did in 1916. The picture of the average court in 1966 as well as in 1916 and 1941 is closer to the Wisconsin model than to the Pennsylvania model. Exceptions occur, but most cases in the states are decided without an expression of overt conflict in voting and with a facade of nonpartisan, harmonious decision making.

Reasons for Conflict

One explanation for variations in political conflict emphasizes social and political conditions within states that lead to varying degrees of conflict. Among the conditions associated with conflict are urbanization, industrial development, and the character of the state's population. Perhaps some social and economic conditions also lead to conflict in judicial decision making. Possibly judges, who often have practical political experiences before recruitment, bring with them attitudes and predispositions to interpret judicial policies in ways that reflect these basic social and political conflicts. Judges might interpret cases involving urban-rural problems, civil rights difficulties, or economic conflicts in ways that reflect social and political orientations.

We can investigate this hypothesis by observing whether judicial conflict embodied in dissents is associated with major social and political variables. If it is, then dissents should occur more often in states where these variables are strongest and less frequently where the variables are weaker. Table 10 presents the results of such an investigation.

According to the table, several factors are associated with dissent rates among the states. Party competition, urbanization, Negro population, and foreign-born population all show positive associations with rates of dissent.

TABLE 10
*Relationships Between Rates of Dissent in State Supreme Courts
and Certain Social and Political Variables, 1966 Dissent Rates*

	Correlation with rate of dissent	
Variable	*All states*	*States with intermediate appellate courts*
Background variables		
Percentage of urban population, 1960	.28	.40
Percentage of foreign born, 1960	.16	.49
Percentage of Negro population, 1960	.12	.30
Multiple R of three variables above	.29	.51
Interparty competition (Ranney index)	.16	.33
Legal professionalism index	.33	.48
Court organization variables		
Number of judges on court	.35	.43
Total number of cases heard	.08	.23
Percentage of court dominated by one party	.31	.38
Percentage of total cases affirmed	.27	.34
Other variables		
Per capita state taxes. 1964	.02	.14
Crime rate, 1965	.23	.15
Number of state government employees, 1964	.28	.16
Public assistance expenditure, 1964	.12	.09

Also, some suggestive relationships are present with the number of judges on the courts and the presence of an intermediate appellate judiciary in the states. There is some confirmation that a tendency to dissent is associated with the number of judges on a court. The relevance of intermediate courts of appeal to higher dissent rates is that they increase the number of difficult cases that supreme courts handle. Intermediate courts were created to siphon off the purely routine appeals, with the assumption that the more contentious and politically controversial cases would be appealed further to the supreme court. An increase in controversial and difficult cases, then, would also increase the amount of conflict in decisions made by those courts.

Quite a few of the variables investigated in Table 10 overlap with each other, for example, urbanization, Negro population, and foreign-born populations. Factor analysis of the variables in Table 10 reveals two basic dimensions that are related to judicial conflict in the state supreme courts. One, which we call the urban dimension, includes urbanization, crime, legal professionalism, and tax rate variables; the second, which we call the complex population factor, includes party competition rates, Negro population, and foreign-born population.

Although the overall correlation of dissent rates with legal professionalism is modest, the link is stronger when the highest ranked groups from both variables are considered. For example, the five states with highest dissent rates in 1966 also have high legal professionalism scores. This relationship suggests that the propensity to state dissents is an outgrowth of modernization of state courts. As the states develop modern and socially complex societies, their court systems, as we have shown, become more legally professionalized. Judges on such courts become more aware of social conflict and less insulated by traditional legal orientations. When traditional legal methods fail to resolve conflicts on the courts, state judges express disagreement more frequently by dissenting votes.

Methods of Achieving Conflict and Agreement

Many of the supreme courts with low dissent rates exist in states with major social and political divisions, which are expressed in litigation and in the selection of judges. The political and social differences expressed in some states with low dissent rates are as sharp and visible as those in states with high dissent rates. Wisconsin, for example, has a low dissent rate and a nonpartisan facade in decision making. Yet, Wisconsin has as much party competition, as many diverse interests, and as many sharp political disagreements as do the more divided and dissentious states of Michigan and Pennsylvania. Moreover, judges on the Wisconsin court reflect as many political and social differences in their background as do the Michigan and Pennsylvania judges.

This apparent inconsistency between voting differences on the court and potential dissent among the judges and in the states suggests differing processes of decision making. In Michigan and Pennsylvania courts, potential differences are translated into votes in decision making and political differences may be expressed in the majority and dissenting votes. In Wisconsin courts, state political divisions that come into the court are resolved in the decision-making process before the final vote. The large number of unanimous votes indicates that the members of the courts have usually resolved their differences.

The minimal differences expressed in low dissent rates emphasize the importance of the decision-making process in state courts. The process of decision making provides several alternative means of handling differences of opinion on supreme courts. Voting these differences, which results in both majority and dissenting opinions, is one way the differences are handled. Voting unanimity means that differences have been settled by other means, prior to the vote. Although unanimous voting may express a facade of unanimity this does not mean that differences have not been present earlier.

Including the expression of differences through the vote, differences in the court can be settled by four means.[32] These are: (1) persuasion; (2) compromise; (3) logrolling; and (4) voting. The first three enable the court to present a facade of legalistic, bipartisan unanimity to the outside world. The fourth, settling the differences only by vote, pictures a court that appears dissentious and divided.

Persuasion is utilized after differences become evident, when judges try to bring other judges to accept their views by arguing with vigor and eloquence or skillfully analyzing a case. The chief justice or other judges who have special status through seniority or other means may persuade members of the court to abandon their own position and adopt the views of others.

Compromise is used to settle differences through the process of mutual give-and-take rather than through conversion by argument or victory by persuasion. When a judge agrees to include or remove a section of his opinion to gain the support of other judges, each is compromising part of his own point of view to achieve consensus. Judges may also support a majority opinion in the hope of obtaining equal consideration in exchange when they write an opinion for the court.

Because of its similarity to the exchange of support in the legislature the third method of decision making has been called logrolling. This way of securing unanimity has been described at work in the Maryland Court of Appeals.[33] Because the writing of opinions is rotated among members of the court, the practice has developed in certain cases of allowing the opinion writer to determine the direction of the decision. Other members of the court go along with him, and he in turn goes along with others when they write opinions. In this way some internal contradictions occur in certain policy areas decided by the court because of differences among various members. Logrolling preserves a facade of unanimity and largely avoids written dissents.

When persuasion and compromise fail to resolve conflicts or when logrolling is not used, differences of opinion concerning decisions are settled by means of voting. A vote can be recorded simply as disagreement with the majority opinion, or it can be expressed in a written dissenting opinion. Differences expressed in conference and in head-counting do not appear as votes on the record and do not settle differences. Only when the opposition to the majority opinion records its position are differences voted and the validity of the majority opinion formally questioned.

The most divisive kind of decision making is voting accompanied by disagreements embodied in dissenting opinions. Not only do the dissenters question the validity of the majority vote for the record but they also put forward their differences in explanations and suggest at some length that the differences are worth attention. They also imply that the differences are worthy of public notice and deserve equal billing with the majority opinion. Dissenting views sometimes supplant the majority opinion at a later date when differences recur.

Pennsylvania-like courts, with their frequent dissents, represent more than simple disagreements, for disagreements can always be settled by discussion or argument (persuasion), by interpersonal negotiation (compromise), or by exchange of supports (logrolling). Frequent dissents indicate major areas of disagreements that cannot be settled by means other than formal voting. Disagreements that are voted are public displays of an institutional schism and suggest that the court is incapable of reconciliation, compromise or solving problems through nonpartisan and legal methods.

Confronted by these implications, some judges of dissenting courts have defended state court dissents by recourse to both legal and democratic theory.[34] They argue that differences ought to be argued and debated openly. Moreover, they argue that such expression of differences assists the development of law by establishing a decisional dialectic. Judges on Wisconsin-like courts, on the other hand, argue for reconciliation of differences before voting. They stress the importance of nonpartisan, legal decision making in which differences are subordinated to more important legal and institutional values.

OUTPUTS OF THE STATE JUDICIARY

The decisions of state courts are responses to the complaints and suits filed before them. Since most litigation is filed by individuals or consists of complaints against individual defendants, no extragovernmental agency has taken the trouble to compile the results, nor do the courts. Therefore, we have only fragmentary information about who benefits the most from the decisions of state courts and who is most disadvantaged. For instance, we have information about divorce rates, but we have none about how often mothers get custody of their children or what the mean alimony and child support rates are. We have no systematic data about the costs of probating wills through the courts. We even have no exhaustive data about the average sentence meted to thieves, robbers, or rapists.

Outputs of Trial Courts

Table 11 presents limited data about two forms of output on which we have reliable information for almost all the states. On both indicators, substantial differences among the states reflect both state law and local practice. The divorce rate is affected principally by the rigidity of state laws. New York's divorce rate, for instance, is so low because in 1966 New York had a very stringent law that permitted divorce only where adultery was proved. Consequently, those New Yorkers seeking a divorce who could afford it went to Mexico or Nevada; others lived apart from their spouses without a divorce. Since 1966 New York's law has been liberalized and its divorce rate has increased substantially.

The number of prisoners sent to state penitentiaries is also an important output of the state courts. The data indicate that the courts sent an average of 3.5 prisoners per 10,000 population to state institutions. Maryland had the highest rate (11.3), whereas Hawaii had the lowest (.7). This output of the courts is not strongly related to the crime rate in the states ($r = .22$) for several reasons. Many crimes reported to the police go unsolved, and many persons convicted of crime are released on probation, suspended sentence, or sent to city and county jails and are not included in our data. The low correlation coefficient indicates as yet unexplained variation from state to state, with some states sentencing a much higher proportion of their convicts to state institutions than others.

Outputs of Appellate Courts

The outputs of appellate courts are easy to examine because many appellate cases are reported in legal journals and semiofficial publications. By reading the cases and observing which parties are favored, it is possible to construct indices that show which segments of society are most favored by the appellate decisions and how these decisions are related to the inputs we have already described.

Nagel has conducted a leading study of appellate outputs.[35] He was interested in seeing whether such input factors as judges' party affiliation and social background characteristics of religion and ethnicity were related

TABLE 11
Selected Outputs of State Trial Courts

State	Convicts sent to state prisons per 10,000 population 1967	Rank	Divorces per 10,000 population 1966	Rank
Maryland	11.3	1	2.0	32.5
Oklahoma	6.6	2	4.9	4
Colorado	5.7	3	3.7	12.5
Florida	4.9	4.5	4.3	7.5
South Carolina	4.9	4.5	1.2	45
Georgia	4.7	6	4.3	7.5
Arkansas	4.6	7.5	5.7	2.5
Texas	4.6	7.5	4.0	10
Nevada	4.5	9	21.4	1
Michigan	4.3	10.5	2.6	25.5
Oregon	4.3	10.5	3.5	15
Alabama	4.2	12	3.2	16
South Dakota	4.0	13.5	1.4	41.5
Vermont	4.0	13.5	1.5	38.5
Kentucky	3.9	15	2.1	30.5
Louisiana	3.9	15	NA	–
North Carolina	3.9	15	2.3	28
Maine	3.8	19.5	2.7	22.5
Montana	3.8	19.5	3.0	19.5
Nebraska	3.8	19.5	1.8	35
Wyoming	3.8	19.5	4.6	5
Arizona	3.7	22	5.7	2.5
New Mexico	3.6	23	NA	–
Missouri	3.5	24	3.1	17.5
Delaware	3.4	25	1.6	36
Kansas	3.3	26.5	2.7	22.5
Tennessee	3.3	26.5	3.0	19.5
New Jersey	3.2	29	1.0	47
Ohio	3.2	29	2.7	22.5
Virginia	3.2	29	2.1	30.5
Connecticut	3.0	31.5	1.5	38.5
Washington	3.0	31.5	3.8	11
Wisconsin	2.8	33	1.3	43
California	2.7	35	3.7	12.5
Idaho	2.7	35	4.4	6
Indiana	2.7	35	3.6	14
New York	2.6	37	.4	48
Iowa	2.5	38	2.0	32.5
Mississippi	2.4	39	2.7	22.5
West Virginia	2.1	40	2.2	29
Illinois	2.0	41.5	2.6	25.5
Utah	2.0	41.5	3.1	17.5
New Hampshire	1.6	43	2.5	27
Massachusetts	1.4	45	1.9	34
North Dakota	1.4	45	1.2	45
Pennsylvania	1.4	45	1.5	38.5
Minnesota	1.2	47.5	1.5	38.5
Rhode Island	1.2	47.5	1.4	41.5
Hawaii	.7	49	1.2	45
Alaska	NA	–	4.1	9

to the partisan direction of decisional outputs. He predicted that the following relationships would occur:

1. In civil rights cases Democrats would support the claimant.
2. In taxation cases Democrats would support the claims of government or taxing authority.
3. In workmen's compensation cases Democrats would support the claims of workingmen claimants.
4. In business regulation cases Democrats would support the claims of the government as regulator.
5. In insurance cases Democrats would support the claimants against insurance companies.
6. In criminal cases Democrats would vote for the defense.
7. In labor-management cases Democrats would vote for the labor unions.
8. In debtor-credit cases Democrats would vote for the debtor.
9. In landlord-tenant cases Democrats would vote for the tenant.
10. In employee injury cases Democrats would vote for the employee.

He predicted that Republicans would support the opposing sides.

In the first comparative analysis of the problem Nagel gathered data on the votes of all appellate judges in forty-eight states for cases decided in 1955. The results were then compared to the political party affiliations of judges and to their ethnic and religious background. All three were found to be related to votes on the cases. Moreover, both Democratic and Republican judges decided cases in the ways predicted above. However, some relationships were stronger than others.[36]

Nagel's study raised so many questions that a number of persons have replicated it or portions of it. One replication that followed Nagel closely was Bowen's study of appellate judges' decision making.[37] Using somewhat more careful statistical methods but also departing from some of Nagel's research methods, Bowen confirmed the observation that groups of judges with similar background characteristics did tend to vote differently from judges with other characteristics. After his careful analysis Bowen concluded that "a number of these associations hold up with astonishing consistency over a large number of different types of cases."

The intriguing aspects of judicial behavior, particularly the impact of party affiliations upon judges' decisions, also have been investigated for several individual states. In Michigan, party affiliations have been shown to be quite strongly related to patterns of decision making on the supreme court.[38] Michigan judges, although nominally elected by a nonpartisan system, are previously nominated to run in the election by party conventions. Consequently, their partisan identity is not only not hidden but is strongly emphasized in Michigan politics. During his lengthy tenure as governor of Michigan, G. Mennen Williams undertook to pack the supreme court by securing the election of a majority of members who were "Williams Democrats." When he took office Williams governed with a supreme court dominated by a Republican majority of 6 to 2. During subsequent years, through special and regular elections, Williams was able to place five Democrats of his choice on the court. The result was a major change in the character of decisions made on the court, for a majority of justices began to vote in favor of liberal Williams positions on important social and economic questions. The new liberal majority was composed of Williams Democrats and they were opposed by Republican justices and one non-Williams Democrat.

Another investigation examined four state supreme courts with high dissent rates: New York, Pennsylvania, California, and Michigan.[39] Differences in decision making were related to different background characteristics by detailed analysis in the three states of Pennsylvania, New York, and California. Partisan identifications of judges were found to be associated with different decisional tendencies. In New York little relationship was discovered. In Pennsylvania and Michigan the partisan association was strong; in California it was only moderate.

A cogent demonstration that divisions in case votes are sometimes not due to partisan affiliations may be found in Adamany's investigation of the Wisconsin court.[40] The division of members in the court's dissenting behavior was related very little to the party divisions of justices. The unimportance of party considerations was explained by the genuine nonpartisan environment in which the Wisconsin court operated. Unlike Michigan where nonpartisanship is only nominal, the entire election process of Wisconsin judges from nomination through balloting lacks division and activities along party lines. Indeed, if anything, judicial elections in Wisconsin are bipartisan in character. Judges are nominated in nonpartisan primaries and in campaigns the fortunate ones, usually the incumbents, receive support from party, legal, and communications elites who join in a bipartisan effort. Moreover, even the electorate votes along bipartisan lines and voting in judicial elections is not strongly associated with partisan patterns in other elections.

As we have indicated, two models of decision making seem to exist in state supreme courts. One, exemplified by the Michigan and Pennsylvania courts, occurs in a milieu of factionalism expressed in dissenting opinions. Often the character of differences in voting behavior is associated with significant background factors such as ethnic-religious affiliations, age, state, region, and political party affiliation. The strongest involvement is with political parties. Partisan division may actually help produce dissenting factions on the courts. The decisional differences often continue outside of court and are expressed in judges' rivalry in party affairs and in other political contests.

The second type of court, exemplified by the Wisconsin court, usually has a low dissent rate in decisions. The consistent divisions and opinions that can be found are only weakly associated with social and political features of the justices. The court presents an effective facade of nonpartisan, legal consensus in which differences are resolved by informal procedures and implicit legal agreements. Disagreements are not openly expressed either in decisions emanating from the court or in activities outside the court. At present the typical state supreme court appears to be more like the Wisconsin than the Michigan-Pennsylvania model.

CONCLUSIONS

We have investigated state courts systematically by examining their functions in the political system. We have also called attention to the variations among state judiciaries with respect to inputs into the courts, decision-making processes and judicial outputs. In seeking explanations for these differences we found that judicial practices are related, as are other aspects of state politics, to a variety of political and social conditions in the states.

However, judicial politics does have distinctive qualities. Courts are shaped by a variety of legal orientations that permeate every phase of the states' judicial process. Legal influences impose on the courts an environment of insulation, the inhibitions of codes of ethics, the constraints of the litigation process, and the practices of legal traditionalism. As a result, most aspects of judicial politics are less visibly political than other aspects of state politics. But with careful investigation the influences of political parties and interest groups and the effects of the political and socioeconomic environment can be discerned at every level of judicial activity.

Although adequate data for many aspects of state courts is lacking, comparative analysis has revealed contrasting patterns of judicial activity. These varieties of judicial activity have documented how — recalling the introduction to this chapter — state judiciaries participate in the allocation of values. Although practiced with many features of legal orientations, judicial politics in the states evidenced no less conflict and variability than other aspects of state politics.

SELECTED BIBLIOGRAPHY

Glick, Henry Robert and Kenneth N. Vines. *State Courts.* Englewood Cliffs, N.J.: Prentice-Hall, forthcoming. A systematic analysis of courts in the fifty states.

Jacob, Herbert. *Debtors in Court: The Consumption of Government Services.* Chicago: Rand McNally, 1969. A useful case study of the Wisconsin judiciary that looks at judicial activities as consumption of government services.

————. "The Effect of Institutional Differences in the Recruitment Process: The Case of State Judges," *Journal of Public Law,* 13 (1964): 104–119. A comparative study of the differences in judicial recruitment among twelve states representing different systems of selection.

————. *Justice in America.* Boston: Little, Brown, 1965. A systematic and politically aware treatment of the whole judicial process in the United States, bringing together the diverse elements into an integrated description.

Nagel, Stuart. "Political Party Affiliation and Judges' Decisions," *American Political Science Review,* 55 (1961): 843–851. An inquiry into the influence of political party preferences on judicial decision making.

Council of State Governments. *Trial Courts of General Jurisdiction in the Forty-Eight States.* Chicago, 1951. A useful tabulation and description of the structure and function of trial courts in the states.

Ulmer, Sidney. "The Political Party Variable on the Michigan Supreme Court," *Journal of Public Law,* 11 (1962): 352–362. An analysis of the dynamics of party influences on decision making in the Michigan Supreme Court.

Vines, Kenneth N. "Southern State Supreme Courts and Race Relations," *Western Political Quarterly,* 18 (March 1965). An analysis of decision making in the southern supreme courts in the area of race relations.

———— and Herbert Jacob. *Studies in Judicial Politics.* Tulane Studies in Political Science. New Orleans, 1962. Exploratory studies into several aspects of local judicial politics including politics and criminal prosecution, judicial selection, and political functions of courts.

PART FOUR

POLICIES
AND PROGRAMS

CHAPTER NINE

Dimensions of State Policy

Ira Sharkansky and Richard I. Hofferbert

Policy is what politics is all about. Many of the classical arguments in politics are about policy. Officials in all branches of government as well as politicians and politically aware citizens propose, investigate, debate, or administer public policy. Political scientists recognize that scholars and commentators disagree over the meaning of "public policy." Some restrict the term to the basic set of goals or targets that government activities are designed to serve. Others question whether there are specifiable goals or targets for many government programs.[1] * Policy, then, may cover all actions of government, whether or not they are part of a basic set of goals. Some people would broaden the definition of policy to include effects that government actions have upon the populations they are designed to serve. These effects go under various names: outputs, outcomes, or impacts of government action.[2] Others use policy to describe the style of government actions. Officials are thus described as taking active, passive, innovative, or lethargic policies, with these terms suggesting a mode of approach to a wide variety of governmental activities. Despite these differences in meaning, one ingredient is common to the various conceptions: public policies are government actions important enough to merit notice. Their importance may refer to economic resources or people affected by the actions, or they

Separate grants to each of the authors by the Social Science Research Council's Committee on Governmental and Legal Processes made possible portions of the research reported in this chapter.

* [See pp. 585–591 for notes to this chapter. — Eds.]

315

may be important because understanding certain policies clarifies our view of how the political system works.

POLITICAL SCIENCE AND STATE POLICIES

The public policies of state governments include the provision of public services (e.g., education, welfare, hospitals), the regulation of personal and corporate activities (e.g., by the police, market inspectors, and tax auditors), the celebration of holidays and other symbolic events (e.g., Columbus Day, Confederate Memorial Day, Evacuation Day [3]), and the control of policy-making processes (e.g., changing the apportionment in the legislature, requiring officials to register Negro voters, combating graft in a state agency). Some policies are solely the responsibility of state officials. For the most part, however, state officials work in conjunction with officials of federal or local governments. Most public activities involve the cooperation of different governments in setting program standards, providing funds, or administering activities.[4] Although our primary interest is state politics and policy, it is impossible to deal with this topic without referring to other governments. We will study policies in each state, and concede that they reflect the work of many hands.

Policy is not a new subject of political science. Classical political philosophies examined the actions of public officials, the conditions that fostered policy, and the implications of policy for a society. The current interest in policy departs from past interests even while it shares the same basic concerns. The chapters in this volume illustrate several new dimensions of political scientists' concern with policy: a primary interest in explanation rather than prescription; sophisticated comparisons between the policies of different jurisdictions; the investigation of economic, social, historical, political and governmental features for their influences upon policies, and an effort to cumulate the research of different scholars in order to build theories about policy. These attributes are related to one another. The shift to explanation from prescription allows political scientists with different policy preferences to cooperate on common projects. The eclectic search for the determinants of policy also profits because it is relatively unhampered by an overt attachment to one political philosophy or another. The concern for additive theory building stimulates various scholars to make their own analyses relevant to the findings of their colleagues, which helps integrate studies of different kinds of policy.

Explanation and Causation

One of the most exciting developments in political science is the comparison of policies found in different states. The question is not simply "How do policies differ from one state to another?" More complicated questions concern the most salient or distinctive differences in state policies and the elements in each state that are related to its distinctive policies. Scholars who want to explain policy differences use policies as dependent variables and try to identify the economic, social, or political characteristics of each state that shape those policies. Those who want to explain the effects of different policies use policies as independent variables and try to identify the economic, social, and political results of differences in policies.

Strictly speaking, it is inaccurate to say that current research identifies the *influence* that certain elements exercise over policies, or the changes that policies *cause* in their economic, social, or political surroundings. The closest we come to causation is the discovery of relationships that are consistent with causal patterns. If we hypothesize that element *A* brings about policy *B* we can infer support for that hypothesis if we find element *A* and policy *B* typically associated in the same time and place. Of course, we also must determine if the coexistence of *A* and *B* are due to some common trait *C* that might cause *A* and *B* to occur together. In other words, we must control the relationship between *A* and *B* to see if it might not simply be a product of *C*.

One hypothesis, for example, contends that high levels of political participation bring about generous levels of public service. If we find that states showing high citizen participation also show generous levels of public service we have superficial support for the hypothesis. But we must check other explanations for the findings as well. A high level of economic well-being might influence both political participation and generosity of public services. We know that people who are wealthy and well educated show more than average interest in politics, and we know that wealth has something to do with the resources needed to support public services. So economic wealth in a state may lead it to have high (or low) levels of both political participation and generosity in public services. On the other hand, it is possible that the political cultures in certain states lead their citizens to participate more (or less) actively than expected on the basis of their wealth, or to lead their government officials to greater (or lesser) levels of commitment in offering public services. In the absence of research, it is not clear whether participation has a relationship with public services that is independent of a state's economic character. In a later section of this chapter, we show that some aspects of participation seem to affect levels of policy in ways that do not merely reflect economic influences.

Analysis and Improvement of Policy

The current approach to policy analysis is not devoid of interest in the proper forms of policy. Indeed, an interest in the features of states that influence policy and in the influence that policy exerts on other features represents the attempt of social science to produce better information about the policy-making process. Sophisticated techniques of analysis can define which features of politics or the economy help to shape policies and which features of policy may influence other dimensions of state politics, economics, or society. This research is of interest to the government official who must understand the policy-making process, as well as to the student of political science who cares about changing policy. Some policies have more latitude for change than others. Even where policies generally depend on the level of economic conditions in a state, some states show higher (or lower) scores on policies than are expected on the basis of their economic conditions. No policies are so much influenced by intractable environmental conditions that a concerted campaign cannot alter them. Some officials try hard to produce policies that meet high standards of generosity. Citizens' groups pressure administrators and legislators to force greater governmental effort. The political culture of some states is more public-minded than it is elsewhere and facilitates higher rates of taxation and more generous levels of service than expected on the basis of economic conditions.[5]

CONSTRAINTS ON STATE POLICY: ECONOMIC DEVELOPMENT AND POLITICAL ROUTINES

Even though it provides no objective way to identify superior or inferior policies, sophisticated analysis of state politics can help officials and citizens identify the areas of likely constraint and the areas of flexibility in the policy process. Two factors have been identified in recent studies as constraints on policy making. The first is the level of economic development within a jurisdiction, which presumably limits the magnitude and quality of the policy outputs that the jurisdiction may produce. The second comes from the routine decision processes that government officials find useful.

These threaten to screen out messages that might demand a basic change in policies. Both economic constraints and those of routine decision processes can limit an official's capacity for innovation. It is important to understand which limitations may come to the policy maker from economics and which from his own decision routines, and under what conditions these limitations are likely to inhibit innovation.

Constraints on the Policy Maker from the Level of Economic Development

Thomas R. Dye provides the clearest statement of the argument that the level of economic development within a state imposes severe limits on the nature of policy outputs.[6] High levels of economic development — measured by such variables as per cent urban, per capita personal income, median education level, and industrial employment — are generally associated with high levels of expenditure and service outputs in the fields of education, welfare, and health. Service outputs in these fields are measured by teacher salaries, the rates of pupil attendance in schools and student success on a national examination, average welfare benefits, and the incidence of medical facilities. Economic development may provide the wherewithal to purchase these services or increase the service demands of clientele. In contrast to these findings, however, are results in the fields of highways and natural resources. In these fields, economic development is inversely associated with levels of spending and services (as measured by highway mileage and the magnitude of state hunting, fishing, and park activities). Explanations are tentative and in some cases conflicting. Highway and natural resources programs may draw their impetus from wide-open spaces and long distances between population centers. The politics of rural states may facilitate the use of pork barrel or logrolling techniques to authorize a dense network of roads between scattered settlements. In contrast, the population congestion produced by industrialization and urbanization may render highway construction prohibitively expensive and politically controversial. Or because urban highways transport many vehicles more efficiently than rural highways, industrialization and urbanization may actually reduce the per capita cost of the roads needed.

Dye emphasizes the importance of economic development for the policy maker by comparing the economic impact on policy with the impact from characteristics of the "state political system." He finds that measures of political characteristics long thought to affect policy (voter participation, the strength of each major party, the degree of inter-party competition, and the equity of legislative apportionments) have only weak relationships with measures of policy that are independent of economic development. A well-developed economy seems to affect both a high participatory, high competition political system and a pattern of policy outputs. Dye warns his reader to be cautious in expecting policy changes to result from alterations in the political system. He does not encourage the policy maker who must work in the face of economic constraints.

Analysis of Economic Development as a Constraint on Policy

Several problems of the economy-policy research caution against a simple acceptance of its findings. These problems should not lead us to discount the importance of economic development in policy outputs, however. Looking closely at the data, we can acquire a more refined understanding of where — and how much — the level of economic development is likely to restrain the policy maker.

The first problem in the economy-policy linkage lies in the temptation to exaggerate its strength. It is true that economic development and policies generally stand in relation to one another as outlined above. Yet the relations are not so strong as to preclude noneconomic factors from being crucial to public policy. Dye reports 456 coefficients of simple correlations between policy measures and his four economic measures of income, urbanism, industrialization, and education, but only 16 of them (4 per cent) are strong enough to indicate that an economic measure explains at least one-half the interstate variation in policy. He also reports 54 coefficients of determination that show the combined strength of his four economic measures with policy measures. Only 19 of these (35 per cent) indicate that all economic measures together explain one-half of the interstate variation in policy. Governments in many states either surpass or fail to reach the policy norms that generally are associated with their levels of economic development.

A second problem with the economy-policy proposition is that its proponents have not presented a fair opportunity for noneconomic factors to show their influence on policy outputs. In Dye's book and in other publications, measures of party strength and competition, voter turnout, and the equity of legislative apportionment have had to carry the entire burden of representing "political factors that might influence policy independent of economic conditions." [7]

A third limitation in the economy-policy argument is its tendency to overlook the likelihood that the economy varies in its influence over policy makers. Variation can occur between different levels of government, different periods of time, different kinds of public service, or at different levels of affluence. Economic influences on policy processes appear to be strongest in local governments and weakest in state governments. Data for 1962 show that the coefficient of simple correlation for per capita personal income with the per capita expenditures of state governments is .14. It is .82 with the total spending of local governments within each state, and .62 with the total of state and local government spending within each state. A variety of research techniques show similar findings. The officials of localities, not state agencies, feel the greatest pressure from their economic surroundings.[8]

　　　Differences in economic resources and fiscal opportunities help to explain the greater dependence of local governments — as opposed to state governments — on the economic resources within their jurisdiction. Most local governments must draw upon a limited geographical area for resources, and they are confined to only one major revenue source, the property tax, which generates a great deal of political controversy.[9] State governments draw upon their larger judisdiction and can transfer resources from have to have-not communities. State officials also have wider revenue options that include taxes on income and retail sales. The state income and sales taxes appear to be less upsetting politically than the local property tax, and state taxes appear to be less vulnerable to an economic downturn.[10] As a result, state officials can escape many of the economic constraints that limit the policy discretion of local government officials. Federal officials can also escape economic constraints, partly because of their ability to tax resources of wealthy areas throughout the country, and partly because of their power to borrow when deficits occur in the taxing-spending balance. The federal government operates numerous programs to control levels of employment, interest, and wages, and may be as much the master as the subordinate of the economy. Moreover, not all local governments are equally influenced by the nature of the local economy. Where the locality has adopted reformed government structures there is less of an economy-policy linkage than where local government has an unreformed structure. The principal features of a reformed local government structure are a professional city manager, nonpartisan elections for local offices, and a council selected at-large rather than by wards. These features seem to depoliticize the social and economic cleavages within a community, permitting local officials to make their policy decisions with less concern for economics.[11]

The influence of economic conditions on state and local government policies appears to be diminishing. Table 1 shows a continuing decline in the economy-policy relationship since 1902. Policy makers now have more opportunities to spend at levels above the norm of their economic conditions. Some of this increased flexibility may reflect increases in federal aid. By transferring resources from have to have-not jurisdictions, grants-in-aid make up for some of the differentials between states. Also, state and local governments have been developing more flexible tax structures. With state taxes on personal incomes and/or retail sales now used by over forty states (no state used either tax at the beginning of the century), and numerous local governments now turning to these forms of taxation, policy makers can tap an increasing proportion of the resources within their own jurisdictions. Even the poorest states — Mississippi, South Carolina, Arkansas, Vermont — have some pockets of wealth that can help support services in their poorest counties.

It is also apparent that economic conditions exercise less constraint on some kinds of policy than upon others. The political salience of a policy is one factor that can lessen the influence of economics. If programs are made the subject of prominent disputes among individual candidates and political parties, they can provoke the use of substantially more resources than normally associated with the jurisdiction's level of wealth. Officials try harder under the impetus of public demand. When public demand runs counter to a program, there is less performance than expected on the basis of economic conditions.[12] Another line of research has examined different conceptions of economic resources (total economic resources, and the distribution of those resources among income groups) as they affect different conceptions of public policy (the total service output of a jurisdiction, and the distribution of benefits among income groups). The magnitude of

TABLE 1

Relationships Between Per Capita State and Local Government Expenditures and Per Capita Personal Income: Coefficients of Simple Correlation[a]

1903	.920
1932	.839
1942	.821
1957	.658
1962	.645
1964-1965	.558

[a]Alaska and Hawaii are omitted in state analyses here and elsewhere because of inadequate data.

Source: Alan K. Campbell and Seymour Sacks, *Metropolitan America: Fiscal Patterns and Governmental Systems* (New York: The Free Press, 1967), 57.

resources in a jurisdiction may exercise greater influence over services than does the nature of income distribution in a jurisdiction.[13] Also, the magnitude of resources may affect the total volume of benefits produced more than it affects the distribution of benefits to different kinds of residents.[14]

Constraints on the Policy Maker from His Own Routines

Political routines are another kind of restriction that, like economic resources, can limit the policy discretion of certain officials. Political routines are decision processes that win the favor of policy makers because they simplify complex considerations. A routine either prescribes the decision that will be made with respect to certain types of problems, or it identifies those criteria that should receive priority consideration in decision making. Several routines are used by policy makers in state governments.[15] They include incremental budgeting, legislators' acceptance of the executive's budget recommendations, regional patterns of consultation among the policy makers of different states, and the assumption that improvements in public services will result from increases in governmental expenditures. The archetype of the policy routine is incremental budgeting. Because it is so characteristic, and because it has received the greatest attention in the literature, it serves as the focus for this consideration of routines.

Charles Lindblom provides the clearest explanation for the attractiveness of political routines among policy makers. In several publications he documents the limitations inherent in the often prescribed "rational-comprehensive" method of decision making.[16] A rational-comprehensive technique requires that an official recognize the whole range of alternatives that face him, identify his goals, rank his preferences for each alternative, define the resources necessary for each alternative, and make the final selection on the basis of all relevant information. Lindblom writes that this approach to decision making fails to take into account the limitations of intelligence, time, organization, and policy discretion available to public officials. Limitations of time and intelligence restrict the capacity to identify the full range of alternatives and resources available at the moment of decision. Limitations of organization and politics restrict the clear announcement of long-range goals and the preference-ranking of alternatives. The announcement of basic goals may generate conflict among participants with different goal-expectations who might have agreed on specific proposals. Other problems for rational-comprehensive decision making come from the strong legal and political traditions that rest upon the constitutional separation of powers and checks and balances. Our governments were designed to hinder swift agreements on centrally designed policies. Conflict and accommodation are more characteristic of policy making in the United States than are rational efforts to identify and serve the public interest.

Analysis of the Incremental Routine

Incremental budgeting, and other routines, are popular among officials who find themselves incapable of practicing rational-comprehensive decision making. Routines limit the number and type of criteria that policy makers feel obliged to consider before they reach a decision. Incrementalists do not consider the full range of an agency's budget. Rather than risk opening old controversies, they accept the legitimacy of established programs and continue the previous level of expenditure that has provided for these programs. They limit their task to examining the increments of change proposed for the new budget and considering the narrow range of goals represented in these departures from established activities.

The power of incremental budgeting is apparent in the statistical relationship between current and previous levels of government expenditures. Table 2 shows coefficients of simple correlation between total per capita state expenditures in 1965 and those in eleven previous periods back to 1903. When past and present spending are considered only three years apart, the correspondence is virtually perfect. Although state governments increased their spending from 1963 to 1965, they remained in essentially their same positions relative to one another. The power of previous expenditures inhibits policy makers in most states from embarking on programs that call for markedly greater increases in spending than are possible in other states.

As the span between current and previous expenditures increases, the correspondence between spending positions lessens. Factors that are remote from the situations have increasing opportunity to enter the budget process. Yet the expenditures of the past continue to be the standard for later expenditures. Despite several major wars, population shifts, transformations in the economy, and increases of many times in the expenditures of each state, some resemblance remains in the spending positions of most state governments now and in the past.

Under a system of incremental budgeting, reviewers are reluctant to permit major increases in the expenditures of individual agencies. As we note elsewhere (pp. 256–257), governors and legislatures react negatively to acquisitive agency requests. Both the governor and the legislature im-

TABLE 2
*Coefficients of Simple Correlation (Product-Moment) Between
Total State Government Expenditures Per Capita in 1965 and
Those in Previous Years*

1962	.94
1957	.85
1952	.85
1947	.63
1942	.72
1939	.61
1929	.61
1924	.53
1918	.49
1913	.52
1903	.44

Source: Ira Sharkansky, *Spending in the American States* (Chicago: Rand McNally, 1968), 40.

pose the largest budget cuts on the agencies that request the greatest increase in funds. The size of the agency request appears to be unimportant in the decisions of the governor and the legislature. Budget reviewers respond primarily — and negatively — to the size of increments.

Incremental budgeting seems to be most confining in those arenas that feel the greatest pinch from their level of economic development, that is, in state and local, rather than federal governments. At the federal level, incrementalists seem willing to examine the changes in expenditure and service outputs that are requested for each agency.[17] The state and local governments that have been examined closely, however, concentrate more narrowly on the increments of dollars that are requested. In his study of budgeting in Illinois, Thomas J. Anton finds decision makers relying on a simplistic set of rules that reveal little concern for program-related values.[18] Decisions rely almost entirely on the dollar value of agency requests as they compare with previous budgets and on the reviewers' estimates of the tax revenue that will be available in the coming biennium. Because reviewers tend to cut new requests without regard to their effects on programs, administrators in Illinois often expand services by shifting funds within budgets that reveal minimal changes. Thus, the state budgetary process stands as a deterrent to innovation that policy makers must circumvent, rather than as a device for the executive or the legislature to inspect and adjust to proposed innovations.

Several factors may explain the federal-state differences in budget makers' consideration of increments in programs as well as dollars. Federal budgeting proceeds with more and better trained staff assistance within both the executive and legislative branches. Moreover, the federal government has more productive revenue devices, particularly its ability to borrow easily in the face of an expected budget deficit. In contrast, many state authorities must balance expenditures with revenues, or can borrow only by using the revenue bond for limited services, typically those that pay their own way, such as toll roads or college dormitories. Better staff and more resources at the federal level may produce a greater awareness of program opportunities on the part of budget analysts, and a greater likelihood that program values will be built into their considerations of budget increments.

Implications for the Policy Maker in Economic Determinism and Political Routines

Both the economic dependence of public policy and the routinization of decision making may inhibit the innovative potential of government agencies. The level of economic development in a jurisdiction may restrict innovation, especially among local officials. Because routines lead officials to rely on fixed criteria, they make it difficult for new or unusual circumstances to provoke a major deviation from the normal pattern of decisions. Officials are reluctant to break with their routines. Although routines are flexible in the face of environmental upsets, it may take something approaching a national trauma to provoke nonroutine decisions. One study found that events of the depression, World War II, the Korean conflict, and postwar economic reconversions produced only limited and temporary departures from incremental budgeting.[19]

DIMENSIONS OF STATE POLICY AND THEIR DETERMINANTS

From the discussion in the introduction, it should be clear that dozens of different products of state political systems could be labeled policy. We shall study but a few of these alternatives. Even with a limited list of indicators of policy, one should not assume that one factor or direction can characterize the differences between the states. Some states may be leaders in one field and followers in another. Oklahoma and Louisiana make relatively heavy welfare expenditures. New York is a pacesetter in educational innovation in the elementary and secondary grades. Kansas is a laboratory for some kinds of mental health policies. Mississippi invented the sales tax. No state is outstanding or completely out of date in all policy areas.

But the fact that states vary in their areas of policy emphasis should not lead to the conclusion that policies themselves are unrelated. It may well be that the states that lead the way in welfare also tend to lead in other areas. There may be some associations between the systems of policies. In technical language, there may be identifiable dimensions of policy performance. Policies that are seemingly different (e.g., welfare and education or parks and highways) may in fact be a part of a common dimension.

In the remaining pages of this chapter, we make some effort at defining certain dimensions of policy that distinguish the public services of each state and identify several features of the economics and politics of each state that help to explain each state's policy scores. We also show that general patterns of relationship between economics, politics, and policy do not hold for certain states. We identify the states that provide more generous — and less generous — levels of policy than their environmental conditions suggest, and we propose some explanations for these "deviant cases."

The Definition of Policy Dimensions

In seeking to identify distinctive dimensions of state policy, we are limiting our conception of policy to government expenditures for, and the outputs of, major public services. However, we still have to face the questions of: (1) how to measure government expenditures and source outputs and (2) how to arrange our measurements to clarify the differences among states. To decide the features of policy to be measured, we follow the guidelines implicit in the existing literature. That is, we use the measures that have proved most useful to political scientists. These are measures of total per capita government expenditures, and the separate expenditures for education, highways, public welfare, health, and natural resources. For each state the figures show the combined expenditures of state and local governments.[20] Other measures show various features of the services provided by government agencies in each state under the categories of education, highways, welfare, health, and natural resources. They combine features of what are labeled elsewhere as outputs and outcomes. Our analysis shows a correspondence within certain fields of policy of both output and outcome measures. First we will consider statewide levels of policy for each state; later we will measure how policies are distributed within each state.

Data arrangement and presentation are crucial to any analysis of state policies. If one seeks to attach numbers to a concept, mutiple measures are likely to be more accurate than any single measure.[21] Multiple measurement, however, cannot determine the common element of the many variables used. Averaging scores or ranks and constructing composite indices of unweighted items runs the risk of making several unwarranted and unnecessary assumptions. It allows for no indication of the relative importance of the items included. Thus, while a strong case can be made for a lengthy list of indicators, one also needs a mechanism for sorting out their commonality and diversity. If used with some sensitivity, factor analysis serves this need. Factor analysis will tell which common traits exist in the phenomena being measured by several individual variables. These will be the principal dimensions of state policy, the features that most clearly distinguish the policies of one state from those of other states. Factor analysis will also provide state scores for each of the policy dimensions. These scores will permit the use of additional statistical techniques to determine what social, economic, and political features of the states explain their levels of policy.[22]

State Policy Factors

Our list of policy measures is not designed to measure everything government does. Some measures of government activity seem better conceived as measures of the state political system than as measures of policy. In a later section, we justify including measures pertaining to government personnel, government structure, and revenue among our political variables. In brief, they represent features of government structure and tax demands that may affect officials' responses to citizens' needs and demands. Our policy measures are more narrow in representing the expenditures and services that governments actually direct at their citizens within the prominent categories of service.[23] Appendix 1 lists the variables in the factor analysis of policy.* Those items asterisked remained after weakly loaded and ambiguous variables were screened out on the preliminary factor analysis. Our measures reflect conditions from 1960 to 1962.[24]

The measures of educational policy show the capacity of secondary schools to convince students they should remain until graduation and the success of each state's residents on a nationwide examination. The rate of high school graduations assesses the schools' ability to serve the needs of the students, whether they are inclined toward college preparation or immediate placement in business or the trades. The incidence of examination passes reflects the quality of information and the intellectual skills that state residents possess by the time they finish secondary school.

The measures of highway policy record the mileage of various types of state roads in relation to population. Population seems to be the best

* [See Appendix 1 to Chapter Nine. — Eds.]

measure of traffic needs that is readily available.[25] Therefore, the measures show the incidence of various roads in relation to the demands of traffic. Admittedly, road location is not considered. Some states may build many miles of roads but place them unwisely with respect to centers of population and commerce. The completion rate of the interstate system provides some indication of state highway department administrative skills and capacity to respond quickly to a major opportunity. The inverted death rate provides a measure of road safety. A high state score on the latter measure should indicate high standards of road design and maintenance and/or an adequate system of highway patrol.

Policy measures of public welfare reflect both the generosity of payments and the coverage of public assistance programs. These programs represent much of the work carried out by state departments of public welfare. The indicators do not assess quality or quantity of counseling services or activities under the programs sponsored by the United States Office of Economic Opportunity.

Measures of health policies assess the likelihood of white and non-white children surviving their first year. These variables cover only a small portion of health relevant services within each state and they show the influence of many social and economic processes. Nevertheless, we assume that high scores on these scales reflect the presence of health and hospital facilities that are adequate to cultural and medical needs.

Natural resources variables measure how frequently state residents use the programs and facilities offered by state departments of parks and wildlife. High scores on these variables should signal attractive programs. The basic assumption is that an adequate program will stimulate usage by state residents.[26]

Two principal policy dimensions were identified by one factor analysis. Their variables are shown in Table 3. Welfare-education emphasizes generous welfare payments, the tendency of high school pupils to remain until graduation, and the success of state residents on the national examination. Highway-natural resources measures rural highway mileage and highway expenditures, plus measures of fish and wildlife services and expenditures for natural resources. A variable that is loaded highly on this factor is the incidence of recipients of old age assistance. At first glance it seems out of its proper place in the welfare-education factor. Aid to the aged, however, is the product of a policy process distinct from that of other welfare and education programs. A number of rural states that have paid little attention to the average level of welfare benefits have made their program for the aged available to many beneficiaries. Some of this concern may be related to the political strategy of state governmental decision makers.

TABLE 3
*Policy Variables in the Order of Their Loadings on Two
Principal Factors*

Variables on welfare-education[a]
  AFDC payments (10)
  OAA payments (11)
  High school graduates (1)
  AB payments (12)
  Examination success (2)
  APTD payments (13)
Variables on highways-natural resources[a]
  Rural road mileage (5)
  Hunting licenses (24)
  Highway expenditures (9)
  Fishing licenses (23)
  Natural resource expenditures (25)
  OAA recipients (15)

---

[a]The parenthesized numbers correspond to the variable numbers in Appendix 1.
Source: Sharkansky and Hofferbert, "Dimensions," 876-879.

Along with welfare mothers, who are tainted with a stigma of illegitimacy, the aged are the largest group of potential welfare recipients eligible to vote.[27]

As a result of this factor analysis of policy measures, we know the dimensions that most clearly differentiate the policies of the states. Because the computation seeks the policy dimensions that are most distinct from one another, the scores of most states on one dimension do not correspond with their scores on the other dimension. However, Minnesota, Oregon, and North Dakota score relatively high both on welfare-education and on highways-natural resources; while Florida, Georgia, North Carolina, South Carolina, and Virginia score relatively low on both factors. Massachusetts, New Jersey, and New York score high on welfare-education but low on highways-natural resources. We shall postpone an explanation of these findings until we explore other dimensions of state policy and the socioeconomic and political characteristics of the states that seem likely to account for their policies.

Political and Socioeconomic Determinants
of State Policies

To explain state-to-state differences in policies, we rely on a three-part conception of the state policy making system, grouping the elements into policy, political determinants, and socioeconomic determinants. The measures of policy are those already defined. We use similar techniques of factor analysis, as defined above, to identify salient dimensions of each state's political and socioeconomic characteristics. Then we compare each state's scores on the political, socioeconomic, and policy factors to identify the relative weight of socioeconomic and political determinants on state policies.

Political Factors

In choosing items for computing state political factors, we tried to include all the characteristics that political scientists have considered: measures of participation and party competition; the character of the legislative, judicial, and executive branches of state government; and the individual and mutual aspects of state, local, and intergovernmental fiscal structures. Appendix 2 lists the specific variables.*

The measures of participation and competition assess prominent aspects of the electoral process, including contests for both governor and United States representative, the spread of the vote received in recent elections in each state, and the distribution of legislative control between parties and over time.

The variables of government structures, personnel, and revenues examine some aspects of state and local government that may affect officials' perception of and responsiveness to citizen interests. The legislative variables include three separate indices of apportionment equity, the number of legislators, the length of the legislature's session, the number of committees, the salary of members and total expenditures for legislative services, plus the number of bills introduced and passed at a recent session. Other scholars have used these variables to assess the representativeness of state legislatures, their professionalism, and their activism.[28] Several of the variables for the executive branch assess the magnitude and professionalism of the civil service and the formal nature of leadership in the executive branch. They show the relative number of employees and their conditions of work. Two measures of executive leadership are the score of each state's governor on an index of formal authority[29] and the number of administrative officials who are directly elected. The age and length of the state constitution and the number of its amendments have been used by one scholar to assess the activism of state interest groups and their orientation toward constitution-building.[30] Also examined are terms, official qualifications, compensation, and pension opportunities of the state judiciaries. Insofar as professionalism in the judiciary is related to other features of state politics, these measures should denote some central aspects of that professionalism.

* [See Appendix 2 to Chapter Nine. — Eds.]

We measure state and local tax systems by the proportion of revenues raised from the major taxes. Each tax has a different effect upon various segments of the population.[31] Thus, the composition of state and local revenue systems may have an important bearing on the demands and supports of different groups and on the services that governments are likely to render in response to these demands and supports.

Several measures of intergovernmental relationships assess the mutual dependence of state and local governments and the role of federal agencies in financing public services. These variables answer the question: Which government pays the bills? Federal, state, and local taxes vary in their progressivity-regressivity. A state that relies heavily on locally financed services may generate a different response among taxpayers than a state that relies on state or federal revenues. It is also likely that each level of government differs in its responsiveness to demands. Thus, a state that emphasizes services financed by federal or state agencies may present different demand gratifications than a state that is localist in orientation. Finally, the supervision of aided programs is likely to differ from that of locally financed programs. A heavy reliance on federal and state revenues, therefore, may have administrative implications that influence other dimensions of state politics.

No two political variables measure the same phenomena in exactly the same manner. It is possible, however, that our penchant for a comprehensive list of indicators will overload the factor analysis in favor of phenomena (e.g., party competition) that have been the subject of several earlier measurements. To guard against this overloading, we computed a matrix of simple correlation coefficients between all of our political variables. Where variables measuring similar phenomena showed high coefficients of correlation ($r > .7$), we eliminated one of the highly correlated pair from the factor analysis. Those variables that survived this first screening process are indicated in Table 5 (see p. 335).

Once we had limited our political variables in this manner, we ran a factor analysis with the remaining forty-one variables. On the basis of the results of that analysis, the second screening process was employed, eliminating irrelevancies and ambiguities, to purify the factors. The factor analysis of political variables described above produced two principal factors. The eleven variables retained for this analysis and their loadings are portrayed in Table 4.

The first principal factor that we isolated is labeled "Professionalism-Local Reliance." It draws its name from the positively loaded measures of reliance upon state government expenditures and federal aids. States scor-

TABLE 4

Political Variables in the Order of Their Loadings on Two
Principal Factors

Variables on professionalism-local reliance[a]
Compensation of judges (25)
Compensation of legislators (15)
Legislative service expenditures (16)
Number of bills introduced (18)
State and local revenues from own sources (46)
State and local revenues spent by localities (48)
Variables on competition-turnout[a]
Competition in lower house seats (6)
Gubernatorial election turnout (1)
Competition in gubernatorial votes (4)
Liberal suffrage laws (3)
Competition in lower house in terms of tenure (9)

[a]The parenthesized numbers correspond to the variables listed in Appendix 2.
For the sake of simplicity in presentation, the labels of the variables are changed in the case of those having negative loadings. For the loadings of each variable, see Sharkansky and Hofferbert, "Dimensions," 867-879.

ing high on this factor show high salaries for judges and legislators, well-financed legislative staffs, and primary reliance on locally raised and spent revenues. The inverse juxtaposition of professionalism in government and the use of state and federal aids makes sense in terms of functions that intergovernmental payments are reputed to serve. They are often defended as devices used most by governments to redistribute resources from have to have-not jurisdictions. In addition, states making heavy use of intergovernmental assistance have judicial and legislative institutions that are less developed than average.

The second factor, "Competition-Turnout," has as its highest loaded variables the measures of turnout in a gubernatorial election, an index of suffrage liberality, and (negatively) one-party dominance in the state legislature and in recent elections for governor. The competition-turnout dimension provides some post hoc justification for the many studies of state politics that have almost exclusively examined electoral processes and interparty struggles. Books and articles by V. O. Key, Duane Lockard, and John Fenton, among others, view party competition and electoral behavior as the primary stuff of politics.[32] Our factor analysis shows that an electoral-party dimension is important as a distinct component of state politics.

Socioeconomic Factors

The socioeconomic features of the states, like their political and policy features, may have several dimensions. Yet much of the literature from economics assumes that socioeconomic differentiation is linear and uni-dimensional — that one central form of development or growth is most salient within changing societies.[33] The argument we are presenting, however, is that the social structure of the states differ in more than one way and that each kind of differentiation has its own consequences for state politics and policy.[34]

As we noted above in our discussion of state politics and policies, identifying and labeling significant social and economic dimensions present technical and theoretical problems. The terms employed include economic development, social structure, social environment, and ecological systems. Little consideration has been given to the likely multidimensionality of the various lists employed to represent these concepts. That is, development may proceed in more than one direction within and between the states. Differences in the social systems of Mississippi and Connecticut may have measurable consequences for the politics and policies of these states. Other attributes separating New Jersey and Wyoming may also be politically relevant — but in ways different from the Mississippi/Connecticut syndrome. Thomas R. Dye measures the effect of urbanization, nonagricultural employment, income, and education upon various public policies in the states. He labels these environmental characteristics, collectively, "economic development." Yet, even though these all correlate highly with one another, there is no prima facie reason why we should assume they are measuring one thing in the social systems of the states. Dye found, for example, that urbanization and industrialization often related to policies differently than did income and adult education.[35]

Socioeconomic Index Construction

The first step in the construction of indices is to find and select data that are likely to produce valid and useful pictures of the characteristics being represented. We will devise socioeconomic indices by the same procedure by which we used factor analysis to construct indices of state policy and politics.

The socioeconomic variables employed and their loadings on two major factors are presented in Table 5. Table 6 ranks forty-eight states on the factors developed for state policy, politics, and economics.

The first socioeconomic factor is industrialization. The states scoring high on this dimension have large industrial production, a heavy emphasis on manufacturing employment, and a congested population. Conversely, those states that score low have many large farms.

TABLE 5
*Socioeconomic Variables in the Order of Their Loadings on Two
Principal Factors*

Variables on industrialization[a]
  Value added by manufacture per capita
  Percentage employed in manufacturing
  Value per acre of farm land and buildings
  Population per square mile
  Percentage foreign
  Total population
  Percentage urban
  Telephones per 1,000 population
  Average number of employees per manufacturing establishment
Variables on affluence[a]
  Median school years completed
  Estimated value of real property per capita
  Percentage non-Negro
  Personal income per capita
  Motor vehicle registration per 1,000 population
  Telephones per 1,000 population

---

[a]Only variables with a loading of at least ± . 600 are listed. For simplicity of presentation, the names of negatively loaded variables have been altered. For the loadings of each variable, see Hofferbert, "Socioeconomic Dimensions of the American States, 1890-1960."

We use affluence as the label of Factor II. This dimension is heavily regional, along North-South lines. The eleven states of the Confederacy scored relatively low not only in the industrialization dimension, but also in affluence. The mean rank of these eleven states is 27 on the industrialization factor, whereas it is 40 on the affluence index.

Aside from this distinct clustering of southern states at the bottom of the affluence factor, we see that the features of affluence include the characteristics of modern, secular, wealthy cultures. The strong negative loading of percentage Negro is indicative of the general economic and cultural deprivation of nonwhite Americans, and is consistent with the correspondingly heavy loading of property values at the positive end of the spectrum. Affluence reflects high educational attainment and entry into a less parochial culture, measured either negatively in terms of illiteracy or positively by median school years completed. Some may find it strange that "percentage foreign born" is positively associated with affluence. But it should be noted that the major portion of the white immigrants to the United States settled in the states that already were affluent as defined by wealth, educational attainment, and economic opportunity.[36]

Reflection on the economic history of the states will further underscore the value of these separate indices of socioeconomic characteristics. Economically, large sections of the South are now and always have been

TABLE 6
Rankings of the States on Policy, Political, and Socioeconomic Factors

State	Welfare-education	Highways-natural resources	Profession-alism-local reliance	Competition-turnout	Industrial-ization	Affluence
Alabama	46	29	32	45	31	45
Arizona	30	16	19	29	41	16
Arkansas	41	19	40	43	40	44
California	1	26	2	17	10	2
Colorado	17	11	29	13	35	4
Connecticut	10	42	13	15	2	11
Delaware	32	39	15	23	8	12
Florida	37	35	12	37	32	14
Georgia	43	33	16	46	22	41
Idaho	26	4	44	4	43	13
Illinois	5	44	46	7	5	21
Indiana	23	28	17	6	13	28
Iowa	11	20	24	19	25	15
Kansas	9	21	21	18	34	9
Kentucky	38	30	35	33	33	39
Louisiana	36	27	18	42	24	43
Maine	33	12	34	27	26	37
Maryland	29	40	9	34	12	29
Massachusetts	2	48	3	26	4	20
Michigan	15	34	5	14	11	23
Minnesota	4	10	10	3	21	17
Mississippi	47	23	26	44	39	48
Missouri	31	25	14	20	15	34
Montana	27	3	45	5	44	7
Nebraska	18	13	30	2	37	8
Nevada	34	2	27	30	42	1
New Hampshire	7	15	38	24	16	30
New Jersey	7	46	6	10	1	19
New Mexico	22	14	36	39	45	24
New York	6	45	1	40	3	18
North Carolina	40	43	23	31	18	46
North Dakota	8	9	41	11	48	31
Ohio	20	37	7	22	9	22
Oklahoma	14	24	39	32	38	26
Oregon	16	8	25	9	28	5
Pennsylvania	25	38	4	23	6	33
Rhode Island	19	47	31	25	7	36
South Carolina	44	41	20	47	23	47
South Dakota	28	5	42	28	46	25
Tennessee	45	22	33	36	20	42
Texas	12	32	11	38	29	27
Utah	24	7	43	1	36	10
Vermont	35	6	48	35	30	35
Virginia	39	36	28	41	19	38
Washington	13	18	22	12	17	6
West Virginia	42	31	37	21	27	40
Wisconsin	3	17	8	8	14	32
Wyoming	21	1	47	16	47	3

poor relative to the rest of the country. In this respect, the South has some similarities to plantation economies in some of the less developed countries of the contemporary world. To the extent that the South has industrialized, it has done so late. But the analyses presented here would suggest that the absence of industrialization alone does not explain the relative poverty of the region. Several southern states that scored very low on industrialization in 1890 have moved into the ranks of the more industrialized in recent years. North Carolina, which was thirty-fourth in industrialization in 1890 was eighteenth in 1960. During the same period, however, North Carolina moved downward from forty-second to forty-sixth in affluence. Conversely, Montana dropped from twenty-sixth to forty-fourth in industrialization while remaining as one of the most affluent states.[37] Relative to New Jersey, Michigan, and Illinois, the states of the plains and Rocky Mountains are not industrialized. Yet Nevada has one of the highest levels of per capita income and education in the country. We cannot describe Wyoming as economically underdeveloped, despite the absence of factories. The nonindustrialized, agrarian regions of the plains and the West are not poor in the way that so many areas of the South are poor — often in spite of considerable industrialization. To lump Idaho with Arkansas merely because both have few factories is to cause many problems of analysis and to conceal some politically critical differences.

If we reflect upon the style and economic role of southern agriculture and compare it to the agriculture either of the Midwest or the Plains, the differences become obvious. When we try to relate socioeconomic differences to political behavior or policy, indiscriminate categorization could cause severe problems. Arkansas has one of the lowest competition-turnout scores in the country. Idaho has one of the highest. This difference is not unrelated to differences in their social structures, but to detect this, we must have reliable indices of social structure that are sensitive to these differences. The two indices of industrialization and affluence tap some of the multiple social and economic differences among the states. In the next section, we show how they relate to the political and policy dimensions that we describe above.

Socioeconomic and Political Relationship with the Policy Factors

Citizens are more likely to participate in politics, and parties are most likely to compete with one another where people are wealthy and well educated. Table 7 shows a strong positive association between competition-

TABLE 7
*Coefficients of Simple Correlation Between Political and
Socioeconomic Factors*

	Industrialization	Affluence
Professionalism-local reliance	.73	.14
Competition-turnout	.11	.66

turnout and the affluence dimension of state economics. This finding is not new, but it is an important relationship in the political and economic systems of American states that is highlighted by the use of factor analysis. The greater involvement in the national, secular milieu that increased affluence implies has its political counterpart in the involvement of voters in political systems beyond the confines of their own local community.

Another strong relationship is that between the professionalism-local reliance dimension of state politics and the industrialization dimension of state economics. Apparently the value of industrial output and the incidence of industrial employment — instead of education, wealth, or ethnicity — have the most to do with the development of legislative and judicial professionalization and the tendency of local authorities to rely on their own economic resources. It may be that a large industrial tax base and an urbanized population permit governments to rely on locally raised revenues. An industrial economy may encourage states to develop professional, active policy-making institutions in response to comparable models and organizational complexity in the private sector.

Some regional patterns appear in the political factors. States in the middle Atlantic and Great Lakes regions score highest on professionalism-local reliance, while mountain states score lowest on that dimension. Mountain and Great Lakes states score highest on competition-turnout, while southeastern states score predictably lowest on that dimension.[38]

The welfare-education dimension of state policy responds most to competition-turnout and affluence, with neither being significantly more important than the other. This is evident from the coefficients of partial correlation in Table 8. The elements of popular interest, competition, and economic resources may provide the stimuli and the wherewithal for public officials to provide generous welfare payments and successful educational services. This finding of importance for the competition-turnout factor with respect to welfare and education services provides some latter-day support for hypotheses derived from V. O. Key and others that electoral and party characteristics of state politics have something to do with the nature of services that are provided.[39] The nature of state politics do make a difference for state policy. Our findings do not, however, fit the linear, single determinant structure of causality suggested by some of Key's followers. Rather, the data suggest that not any one element of state politics, but an underlying factor only partly measured by individual variables independently influences public services. The prominence of this finding is increased by the importance of the policy factor involved. Welfare and education services consume much of state and local government resources: 49 per cent of general expenditures and 51 per cent of government employment in 1965–1966. Policy making in welfare and education have been troubled by sharp controversy and affected by electoral and partisan processes in a manner quite different from other areas of public policy.

The highway-natural resources dimension of public policy shows its primary dependence on economic factors. It is inversely and strongly related to industrialization and directly related to affluence. Perhaps low levels of population density and urbanization together with high levels of personal wealth and education incline a state toward heavy investments in roads (especially in rural areas) and active fish and wildlife programs. Wide-open spaces present an abundance of recreational opportunities, a need for highway facilities, and rural interests that have concentrated their political efforts in behalf of these services.

Why the lack of dependence on political factors for highway and natural resources policies? The programmatic activities of these policies do not use the symbolic continua that are most commonly the objects of parti-

TABLE 8
Coefficients of Simple, Partial, and Multiple Correlation, and Multiple Determination Between Socioeconomic, Political, and Policy Factors

	Welfare-education	Highways-natural resources	Welfare-education	Highways-natural resources
	Simple Correlation		Partial Correlation[a]	
Professionalism-local reliance	.39	−.54	.26	−.24
Competition-turnout	.68	.25	.47	−.02
Industrialization	.37	−.69	.17	−.55
Affluence	.69	.43	.43	.53
	Multiple Correlation		Multiple Determination	
Socioeconomic factors	.77	.82	.59	.68
Political factors	.78	.60	.61	.36
Socioeconomic and political factors	.83	.84	.69	.70

[a]Controlling for the other factors.

san controversy. Highway and natural resource policies produce conflict, but few of these issues seem to array taxpayers and the economic haves against recipients of services and the have nots in contrast to education and welfare policies. Highways, parks, and conservation programs are financed by earmarked taxes, licenses, and user fees; thus, recipients pay for most of the benefits received.

What Remains after Statistical Analysis: Deviant Cases of High and Low Scores

We have provided general explanations for interstate variations in several features of public policy. We know that high scores on the welfare-education dimension of policy usually correspond with high levels of competition and turnout in state politics and high levels of affluence in the economy. High scores on the highways-natural resources dimension of policy depend upon high levels of affluence and low levels of industrialization. Although these relationships characterize conditions in most of the states, they do not explain all states' policies. A number of states show higher (and lower) levels of each policy than expected on the basis of social, economic, or political characteristics. We should not overlook these deviations. They indicate that economic or political forces do not always have their expected effect on a state's policies. Plenty of room remains for extraneous elements to influence state policies. State traditions that favor, or discourage, effort on behalf of certain programs, or the assertiveness of contemporary officials or interest groups may affect decisions about individual programs in the legislative or executive branches. Politics is a dynamic process not wholly explained by statistical analyses that seek out and highlight the general trends.

We can identify policy scores that do not fit state traits on the socioeconomic and political factors by means of regression equations that show the usual relationships between socioeconomic, political, and policy factors. We compare each state's actual policy scores with those predicted for the state on the basis of its socioeconomic and political scores. Table 9 shows the states that stand appreciably above, or below, the scores expected for them on the welfare-education and highways-natural resources dimensions.[40]

We must be careful in suggesting explanations for the deviant states. These findings represent our errors in trying to explain policy by reference to socioeconomic and political characteristics. However, we can make some limited inferences. First, if a state shows high positive or negative deviation for both measures of policy, we can infer the presence of tendencies sup-

TABLE 9

*States Showing Higher and Lower Scores on Policy than Expected
on the Basis of Socioeconomic and Political Factors*

Welfare-education	Highways-natural resources
States scoring higher than expected, by rank[a]	
Oklahoma	Wyoming
New Hampshire	Nevada
North Dakota	Vermont
Wisconsin	New York
New Mexico	Wisconsin
Massachusetts	South Dakota
Iowa	Idaho
Rhode Island	Montana
Minnesota	Minnesota
Kansas	
California	
South Carolina	
States scoring lower than expected, by rank[b]	
Nevada	Florida
Delaware	Oklahoma
Florida	Kansas
Tennessee	New Mexico
West Virginia	Arizona
Mississippi	Texas
Texas	Nebraska
Missouri	Colorado
Utah	Iowa
Montana	Washington
Indiana	

[a]Highest deviations shown first.
[b]Lowest deviations shown first.

portive or unsupportive of public services in the state political cultures. Such tendencies may lead state officials to consistently more or less generous provisions of service than seems warranted by our measures of environmental traits. In both policy areas, the states of Minnesota and Wisconsin stand out as being generally supportive of public services, while Florida and Texas stand out as being generally unsupportive.

Second, if a state shows a high positive deviation on one policy factor but a high negative deviation on the other, we can infer policy-making peculiarities that favor one kind of service over others. Kansas, New Mexico, Iowa, and Oklahoma seem to favor the welfare-education dimension over the highway-natural resource dimension, and Nevada and Montana seem to favor highway-natural resources over welfare-education.

The identification of deviant cases in this manner allows for two further steps in analysis. First, it suggests which instances are idiosyncratic.

For example, Oklahoma's supportive orientation to welfare-education reflects its extraordinary contribution to various forms of public assistance.
This is due to a decision many years ago to write into the state constitution
a provision earmarking certain funds for welfare. An exact counterpart
of this situation is found in few states. This provision explains Oklahoma's
situation, although it is not very interesting in building general theory. Second, deviant case analysis contributes suggestions for further inquiry. Our
identification, in light of political and social structures, of the states most supportive and most unsupportive of a policy may identify attributes that these
states share. The individual political and economic histories of the states
may provide unique explanations for these and other residuals.

At the present time we cannot explain high scores on welfare-education in New Hampshire and North Dakota or the high scores for highway-
natural resources in Vermont and Wyoming. Rather than wrestle with our
own speculations, it seems appropriate to admit the weaknesses of our general findings. Politics is, after all, carried on in different ways from one state to
another. Some states may just be different, period.

Before we admit total defeat in the effort to build general propositions, an additional aspect of interstate variations in state policy deserves
careful attention. We are mindful of the fact that many differences between
states are not tapped by measures of central tendency. In 1960, both Ohio
and Michigan were 73.4 per cent urban. Knowing this tells us something
interesting about Michigan and Ohio compared to, for example, Idaho or
Mississippi. But the distribution of Ohio's urban population contrasts
sharply with the Detroit-outstate split in Michigan. Ohio has no single
dominant city with which the rest of the state competes, either for political
offices or for the benefits of policy. The reverse is true in Michigan. Geographic distributions of social, economic, and political traits, and policies,
can be just as important to political systems as levels of those features.

THE DISTRIBUTION OF STATE POLICIES

In the realm of public policy, it may be as interesting to examine the style
of administration of a particular policy in various areas of the state as it is
to examine the comparative, average level of policy activity. Statewide
averages do not measure the sensitivity of officials to clients' needs, the
receptivity of officials to innovative procedures within their programs, or
the distribution of benefits among different kinds of clients and into different communities. We cannot examine all these questions with available

data, but we can examine some aspects of the problem of intrastate distribution.

We have computed several measures that show how welfare payments are distributed among the counties of thirty-six states.[41] These measures of distribution are compared to state averages for welfare payments and the welfare-education factor. We are concerned with two questions: (1) How equally are welfare payments distributed among the counties of each state? and (2) Within each state, do social or economic traits affect the distributions of payments in any patterned way? State policy makers do not make their decisions only with an eye toward macro-levels of state performance. Not "how much?" but "who should get how much?" is the subject of many policy debates. We cannot say which question is faced most often by policy makers. However, we can see if the answers to the two questions — statewide macro-levels of policy or the distribution of policies — are made in similar ways in each state.

Depending on the policy involved, distributions among the counties of a state can be influenced by local officials alone or by the combined efforts of officials from several governments. When policies reflect the combined efforts of local, state, and/or federal authorities, their distribution may depend on the actions that local authorities take within the standards established by state or federal agencies, or upon the actions of local authorities outside established standards. When formulated outside established standards, the distribution of policy may depend upon the tolerance of state or federal officials for local deviations, or the weakness of state and federal controls vis-à-vis local actions.

This section explains the distribution of policies that depend on the combined actions of state and federal, as well as local officials. Sometimes we see the effects of local authorities working out the policy discretion that is legally theirs; at other times, it appears that local officials deviate from state and federal standards. In the latter instances officials of the superior governments are either unwilling or unable to control the deviations. Our subjects are payments given to individuals under the five major public assistance programs. These are aid to the aged, aid to the blind, aid to the permanently and totally disabled, aid to families of dependent children, and general assistance. We focus on the average monthly grants per recipient that are made for each of these programs in each county of thirty-six states.

Each of the welfare programs except general assistance receives federal aid and is regulated by federal and state standards. Supposedly, county or municipal welfare boards in each state must accept statewide standards in making payments. These standards denote the qualifications that a recipient must meet and the amounts that can be allowed, under each program, for each major item on a household budget (food, clothing, shelter, personal items). Federal as well as state auditors check disbursements in each county to determine if state standards are followed. Yet these procedures permit county-by-county variations in the generosity of welfare payments. The state standards emphasize maximum or minimum payments that can be made for each item in a recipient's budget. Officials can hold down expenditures within each item that are considered excessive for the circumstances of each recipient. If an aged family of two members is living in a four-room dwelling, for example, they may be given a shelter allowance sufficient only to cover their needs, determined as a two-room dwelling. Similar economies can be affected in the portion of welfare payments allowed for other expenses. However, welfare officials may be slow in requiring a recipient to move into a smaller dwelling after the death of a family member and thus continue higher monthly payments than the standards indicate. Some authorities are "client oriented" while others are "rule oriented." [42] Also, the state standards permit local variations according to the price and availability of goods, services, and accommodations.

Some of the county-to-county variations that we find may be due to conditions of price, family size, or other features not subject to the control of county welfare officials. However, much of the variation is consistent with county differences in economic and political traits that suggest the workings of different policies toward welfare clients, i.e., differences in average size of payments that officials are willing to give. In many states the general assistance program is completely in the hands of county or municipal welfare officials. They decide what kinds of people to aid and how much to give to each recipient.

Measuring Intrastate Policy Distribution

To answer our questions about the distributions of welfare payments, we first calculated state-wide means and coefficients of variability (V's) for each state. The coefficients of variability show the equality of policies among the counties in each state. A low coefficient signifies a more equal distribution of policies; a high coefficient signifies a distribution that is highly skewed from the mean.[43] By comparing coefficients of variability with means in each state, we can see if the states with a generally high level of welfare payments also show equal distributions of payments in different counties. Our concept of equality is arithmetic identity. We make no claim that it approximates more elaborate concepts of equity. A concern with equity would lead to a complex and controversial discussion of the criteria that officials ought to consider when making their decisions. By looking merely at the differences in payments from one county to another within each state, we have an empirical goal: determining where county-to-county differences exist and what features of counties and states account for the differences.

Second, we computed for the counties of each state separately, and for the counties of all states together, coefficients of correlation between each county's policy and the median family income of county residents. These correlations describe if and how average welfare payments are distributed in linear relationships with income, i.e., the counties that show the largest, and the smallest, monthly welfare payments.

Within-State Distributions of Welfare Payments

Counties differ substantially in the ways they make their welfare payments. Table 10 shows coefficients of variability. Recall that low scores on coefficients of variability indicate equal average payments among the counties of a state; high coefficients of variability indicate unequal payments. The equality of county payments in each state often varies from one welfare program to another: in Colorado, for example, average county grants for the aged and the families of dependent children are more equal than the nationwide average, and average county grants for the blind and disabled are less equal than the national average. The states that show relatively equal county payments under several welfare programs include Alabama, Arizona, Louisiana, Missouri, and Oklahoma. In contrast, states showing marked inequalities in several programs include Michigan, Montana, and North Carolina.

Average payments for the aged and dependent children show the most equal distributions within the states; payments for general assistance show the most skewed distributions. The equal distributions for the aged and dependent children may reflect the political visibility of these programs and the severity of state controls exercised over county welfare authorities. The program for the aged provides grants to the largest group of welfare recipients who are eligible to vote. It is often seen as the most legitimate of the welfare programs, insofar as it provides funds to citizens who have made their own contributions to society in the past. In a number of states where welfare programs generally receive little support, the aged received the most generous treatment. In contrast, the program to aid the families of dependent children receives more than its share of political attacks. In

TABLE 10
Per Recipient Monthly Payments: County Coefficients of Variability, by State

	Payments for:				
	Aged	Blind	Disabled	Children	General assistance
Alabama	.063	.092	.080	.080	.072
Arizona	.052	.050	.043	.037	.083
Arkansas	.072	.238	.131	.125	.274
California	.061	.077	.090	.102	.473
Colorado	.108	.460	.245	.109	.792
Florida	.076	.182	.086	.086	.639
Georgia	.188	.184	.106	.086	.806
Illinois	.187	.355	.217	.120	.423
Iowa	.297	.259	.283	.198	.444
Kansas	.198	.562	.299	.280	.415
Kentucky	.087	.398	.115	.160	.778
Louisiana	.125	.098	.091	.045	.067
Maryland	.115	.191	.096	.068	.205
Massachusetts	.124	.109	.124	.075	.274
Michigan	.197	.552	.279	.095	3.870
Minnesota	.114	.381	.154	.135	.346
Mississippi	.100	.169	.025	.059	.663
Missouri	.141	.092	.076	.071	.120
Montana	.209	.383	.167	.227	.703
New Jersey	.092	.159	.178	.082	.326
New Mexico	.051	.247	.083	.092	.580
New York	.169	.271	.206	.230	.272
North Carolina	.628	.665	.190	.646	.735
North Dakota	.180	.444	.189	.132	.479
Ohio	.153	.311	.198	.189	.528
Oklahoma	.062	.194	.075	.056	.192
Oregon	.137	.332	.286	.130	.280
Pennsylvania	.171	.061	.171	.173	.120
South Carolina	.153	.186	.168	.187	.051
South Dakota	.212	.422	.330	.338	1.092
Utah	.152	.450	.269	.169	.472
Virginia	.236	.540	.295	.244	.487
Washington	.142	.380	.276	.165	.217
West Virginia	.111	.132	.122	.054	.195
Wisconsin	.149	.461	.241	.121	.627
Wyoming	.241	.277	.202	.160	.504
State means	.154	.288	.172	.148	.517

those states where it is most vulnerable to antiwelfare sentiments, the equality of county payments reflects uniformly low payments. State and federal administrators may audit this program closely in order to protect themselves against interest groups that would oppose marked inequalities in county policies. The unequal distribution of general assistance payments reflects the opportunities for local discretion built into that program. Of the five major welfare programs, general assistance is the one that receives no federal aid and is subject to no federal regulation. In many states, the state government does not participate in general assistance; each county or municipal welfare board makes its own policy. Many counties offer no aid at all, and others provide only enough so that an indigent person can move on to the next county.

By comparing these coefficients of variability with each state's average welfare payments, we see the justification for this separate analysis of within-state distributions of policy. For the most part, the equality of welfare payments within a state does not correspond with the state's average welfare payments. Different influences obviously work in within-state distributions.

Sharp state-by-state variations occur in the kinds of counties that give more and less generous welfare payments. Table 11 shows correlation coefficients between county measures of policy and income. By looking at the counties of all states together, we see a pattern that is consistent with aggregate state data: high state averages in welfare payments occur with high income. Yet prominent exceptions appear in the counties of individual states. For various programs, low-income counties in Louisiana, Massachusetts, New Mexico, and Oklahoma give the highest welfare payments. In many instances, income and average county welfare grants have no particular linear association.

Socioeconomic and Political Relationships with Distributions of Welfare Payments

We can look for some patterns in the distributions of welfare payments by examining state-by-state means, coefficients of variability, and county coefficients of correlation, and by comparing them with socioeconomic and political factors that seem likely to influence the distributions. This is not easily done. Few sizable relationships exist between state socioeconomic and political characteristics and our measures for the distribution of county welfare payments. We saw above in connection with the welfare-education factor that strong forces having to do with economic resources, population traits, participation, and partisanship may work at the state level to influence overall commitments to certain welfare programs. Statewide policy is set, by and large, by legislatures that operate relatively in the open, and are subject to public pressures from the governor, the mass media, prominent individuals, and organizations. Monthly payments tend to be high in states with high scores on industrialization, affluence, and competition-turnout. Of these factors, affluence and compe-

TABLE 11

Within-State Coefficients of Simple Correlation Between Each
County's Median Family Income and Average Welfare Payments,
by Program

	Payments for:				
	Aged	*Blind*	*Disabled*	*Children*	*General assistance*
Alabama	.29	.03	.34	.22	.36
Arizona	−.18	.23	−.05	.30	−.02
Arkansas	.03	−.11	.16	.03	−.06
California	.22	−.06	.32	.29	.69
Colorado	−.26	.17	.36	.01	.04
Florida	.19	.02	.09	.07	.22
Georgia	.07	.11	.18	.03	.32
Illinois	.13	−.01	−.03	.34	.21
Iowa	.13	−.04	.21	.04	−.20
Kansas	.20	.11	.24	.04	.28
Kentucky	−.11	−.05	−.03	−.08	.36
Louisiana	−.44	.00	−.28	−.25	−.24
Maryland	.60	.21	.13	.60	.14
Massachusetts	−.62	.65	−.10	−.14	.61
Michigan	.16	.09	.17	.24	−.10
Minnesota	.30	.26	.17	.35	.16
Mississippi	.04	−.04	−.06	−.05	.07
Missouri	−.07	−.01	.13	−.19	−.22
Montana	.05	.14	.17	.14	.28
New Jersey	.18	.11	.06	.59	.36
New Mexico	−.42	−.14	−.58	−.08	−.20
New York	.37	.35	.35	.66	.46
North Carolina	.00	.02	.32	.13	.29
North Dakota	−.26	.04	−.04	.11	.15
Ohio	−.15	.11	.32	.53	.53
Oklahoma	−.70	−.20	−.63	.13	−.18
Oregon	−.18	.10	.06	.15	.28
Pennsylvania	.15	.00	.19	.16	.36
South Carolina	.29	.26	.26	−.09	.35
South Dakota	.27	.00	.37	.15	.05
Utah	−.21	.13	−.28	−.05	.09
Virginia	.52	.00	.43	.52	.37
Washington	−.03	.17	.07	.03	.28
West Virginia	.37	−.17	.44	.56	.31
Wisconsin	.44	.00	.45	.48	.41
Wyoming	−.27	.30	.07	−.05	.30
Correlations for the counties of thirty-six states considered together	.27	.22	.28	.49	.07

tition-turnout are most important for the level of benefits offered under
most programs. None of these environmental factors relate in a strong or
consistent way with the equality of welfare payments among a state's coun-

ties. Affluence, for example, shows sizable relationships with statewide averages for welfare payments, but bears no strong relation with the county equality of welfare payments. In only one program (disabled) is there a slight relationship between affluence and the equality of grants (.38). Thus, more affluent states tend to have less equal county grants. The equality of welfare payments throughout a state is a measure of policy that may not reflect economic or political conditions widespread throughout a state. The equality of payments can be skewed by the peculiar actions of a few county welfare boards, whose work is less public than that of state officials. It may be easy for personal norms, political bargains, or numerous other factors to enter the decision process in individual counties and lead to welfare payments that vary greatly from the statewide norms. There is a slight tendency for payments to the blind and disabled to be most unequal from one county to another in those states with high scores on competition-turnout (r's = .38 and .45), suggesting that prominent and competitive politics result in frequent disputes about welfare programs and that the results of those disputes differ markedly from one county to another.

The particular way in which we conceive the distribution of welfare benefits within states affects the findings we obtain. When we think of within-state distributions strictly in terms of equality of welfare payments among the counties of a state, we do not find clear patterns with state social, economic, or political characteristics. There are substantial state-to-state differences in the equality of county payments. However, the reasons for these differences in within-state distributions eludes this analysis. Measures of equal or unequal distribution show only weak relationships with measures of state resources, population, and political traits. When we conceive of within-state distributions in terms of the kinds of counties that give high or low welfare payments, we find stronger patterns with respect to state resources, population, and political traits. By examining the correlations between county welfare benefits and median family income, by state, we can identify the kinds of states where high welfare grants seem dependent on an abundance of local resources, and the kinds of states where high grants are made available in poor counties.

The states where poor counties give high welfare payments [44] (where resources seem to be redistributed from wealthy to poor economies) have a low industrial base and low levels of professionalism in government. Louisiana and New Mexico are the best examples. The low level of economic resources may provide both the need and the justification for a redistribution welfare policy. In Louisiana a patronage tradition in the civil service accompanies redistributive welfare policies and may reflect a more general tendency to use the powers of the state government to affect the allocation of economic resources.[45]

SUMMARY AND CONCLUSIONS

In recent years, the systematic, comparative analysis of state politics has come into its own as an area of sophisticated social scientific inquiry. No longer is the field characterized exclusively by bald exhortation and polemical criticism. Nor is it tied exclusively to bland description of formal, legal institutions or to individual case studies in a theoretical vacuum. A model of rigorous inquiry has emerged and demonstrated its utility. That model has been employed in this chapter to demonstrate both its shortcomings and its potential for guiding students of state politics into a set of questions which are both substantively interesting and capable of empirical test.

The model with which we have worked, and the one that underlies most of the studies in this volume, posits state policies as a function of socioeconomic and political systems. That is to say, the differences in the patterns of public policies between states are conceived to reflect, in some measurable degree, corresponding differences in their socioeconomic and political characteristics. Foremost in our inquiry has been the idea of dimensionality. In any area of inquiry into human affairs, attaching unwarranted importance to a single measure or variable is risky. Policy as a concept is very difficult to define, let alone measure. In constructing measures, we have employed rigorous statistical devices for relating several indicators in order to extract the portion of each that most closely approximates the common phenomena in each sector of our model. We wished to avoid the assumption, however, that policy or political system or social structure is necessarily a simple phenomenon. Each sector of the model has several parts. We demonstrated the problems, for example, in assuming that social and economic differences among the states follow a single line of development.

It would be naive to assume that all state policies are pursued with equal vigor. Yet it would also be unwarranted to assume no clustering or common threads in the programs pursued by various states. The policy factors we discovered — welfare-education and highways-natural resources — fit with a reasonable expectation of what programs might be related to one another in the policy mechanisms of the states. It seems reasonable to group programs in this manner for purposes of exploring both the constraints and the resources that influence the formulation of policies.

As with social structure and patterns of policy, various attributes of state political systems group themselves into distinct clusters. Professionalism-local reliance taps an attribute of the sophistication and distribution of authority within the states; it may explain more of the variation in policy choices than shown in this chapter.[46] Competition-turnout reflects concepts used extensively in studies of state politics since the 1940s. As we have seen, this new formulation revives some of the confidence formerly held in the importance of state politics for public policy.

The three components of our policy model show some interesting relationships. We find that welfare-education policies and highways-natural resources policies serve different clients and are shaped by different economic and political features.

Highway and natural resource policies find support in the vigor of local governments, the professionalization of the public service, and the absence of industry and population concentrations. Attributes of the electoral arena, however, as measured by competition and turnout, as well as the levels of personal income and education have little to do with policies in this area.

Welfare-education policies, in contrast, are related closely to levels of competition, turnout, and affluence. The most politically vigorous and well-off states are the most prone to support programs for uplifting the population through schools and assistance to the poor. Although less important than competition-turnout and affluence, the vigor of local governments and the professionalism of the civil service supports welfare and education policies.

The attributes of the socioeconomic and political systems we have measured account for about two-thirds of the interstate variation in statewide policies for welfare-education and highways-natural resources. The range of choice for the policy maker, then, independent of socioeconomic and political constraints, is about 30 per cent. Decision makers in each field must take account of different constraints and resources, but the balance of limitations on their options is comparable from one field of policy to another. On the basis of our findings, we expect that conflicts in the highway-natural resources area are less likely to spill over into partisan disputes than those in welfare or educational issues. Regardless of social or economic conditions, it seems unlikely that significant changes can occur in welfare or education policies without substantial political conflict.

All of the conflicts over policy and all the differences between the states, however, do not concern statewide levels of support. Many important questions of policy making and the analysis of policies have to do with the distribution of policies within states. Here the patterns are not so clear. When we examined all of the counties in thirty-six states their social and political systems were found to relate generally to policy in the same manner as when state averages were used in the analysis. But the extent to which socioeconomic features related to policy within individual states varied considerably. To some extent, the responsiveness of states to unevenly distributed economic and social claims is a function of the overall level of development of the state's economy. The generalizations we have to offer in this regard, however, are less firmly grounded than the explanations offered above for the variation in state level performance.

Despite the confidence with which we may have explained two-thirds of the variation in certain statewide policies or some smaller fraction of the patterns of intrastate distribution, we have by no means closed the door on alternative explanations. It is clear that there is room for considerable departure from the general patterns. It is the deviant cases that we must examine for still more attributes of the policy systems. And we have enough respect for the leadership ability and cantankerousness of individual state political figures to know that they can always smudge up any neat model we might propose. Each state has, simply by virtue of its relative autonomy in politics and policy making, experienced a unique history. Each has presented unique opportunities for the impact of leadership.

Leadership, we would argue in conclusion, may be that of the hero or that of the bum. One's heroes may be liberals and his bums conservatives or vice versa. But either way, the leader is the political figure who takes his state down a policy path at variance with the normal route for its economic and political characteristics. We have discovered what some of these economic and political characteristics are. The leader is the politician — be it a governor, a legislator, or an influential bureaucrat — who restricts his policy involvement in the face of pressures for expansion, or the figure who promotes a policy despite short economic resources. Someone who simply rides the tide of social and political forces should not be called a leader. The governor of a rich, competitive state who advocates a dollar increase in welfare programs is perhaps exercising less leadership than his counterpart in a one-party, poor state who may be seeking less money but more structures of constraints in his state. To discern the effects of leadership a state must be compared not to an abstract national average standard, but to the constraints and resources operative in the state policy systems. By means of comparative analysis, we have tried in this chapter to identify some of the principal constraints and resources in state policy systems.

SELECTED BIBLIOGRAPHY

Davis, James, Jr., and Kenneth Dolbeare. *Little Groups of Neighbors: The Selective Service System.* Chicago: Markham Publishing Co., 1968. A policy case study of the draft and its administration through the selective service system.

Hofferbert, Richard I. "State and Community Policy Studies: A Review of Comparative Input-Output Analyses," forthcoming in James A. Robinson (ed.), *Political Science Annual, 4.* Indianapolis: Bobbs-Merrill. A critical review of the literature of input-output analysis.

―――― and Ira Sharkansky (eds.). *State and Urban Politics: Readings in Comparative Public Policy.* Boston: Little, Brown and Co., 1970. Readings and commentary on policy problems in state and urban politics.

Keech, William A. *The Impact of Negro Voting: The Role of the Vote in the Quest for Equality.* Chicago: Rand McNally, 1968. An investigation of the effects that attainment of the vote had upon policies affecting the voters.

Sharkansky, Ira (ed.). *Policy Analysis in Political Science.* Chicago: Markham Publishing Co., 1970. Selections dealing systematically and critically with aspects of policy analysis.

Wilson, James Q. (ed.). *City Politics and Public Policy.* New York: John Wiley & Sons, 1968. Selections dealing with public policy in an urban setting.

CHAPTER TEN

Innovation in State Politics

Jack L. Walker

One sure way to compliment a state official is to call him a pacesetter in his field. The federal system encourages comparison and competition among the states, and, according to its advocates, places a premium on the pioneering development of governmental programs. In the words of justice Louis D. Brandeis: "It is one of the happy incidents of the federal system that a single courageous state may, if its citizens choose, serve as a laboratory and try novel social and economic experiments without risk to the rest of the country." [1] * The belief that the federal system encourages experimentation is widely held. In fact, the performance of state governments traditionally has been judged by the relative speed with which they have accepted new ideas or programs. Wisconsin, for example, because of its leadership during the Progressive period and its early adoption of the direct primary, the legislative reference bureau, and workmen's compensation, gained a reputation as a pioneering state that it has never lost.

State political leaders are quick to remind us of those instances where pioneering states have created programs later adopted by most other states or the federal government.[2] In Governor Nelson D. Rockefeller's words:

> Time and again, states like Massachusetts, Wisconsin, or New York acted on their own initiative to protect the health, safety, and welfare of the individual. . . . This was true of factory inspection or the limitation of hours of labor. It was true of child labor or women's labor. It was true of unemployment compensation and social security. In all such cases, the ferment of ideas and innovations worked its way up through the federal system — often from private initiative.[3]

* [See pp. 591–597 for notes to this chapter. — Eds.]

354

Many accept and frequently repeat in discussion these impressions about the operation of the federal system, but political scientists have made almost no systematic effort to test their accuracy. If it is true that some states consistently adopt new programs more rapidly than others, it should be possible to measure the phenomenon and to roughly identify the pioneers and the laggards. If information and policy cues regularly follow the same channels, the passage of these messages should be evident and the communications network should be identifiable and describable. Pioneering states ought to have identifiable characteristics that facilitate the rapid adoption of innovations. In short, if it is true that some states change more readily than others, a study of the way states adopt new ideas might lead to some important insights into political change and development.

We are not trying to decide whether state governments are doing enough in protecting civil rights, in providing housing for the poor or the elderly, or in reducing air pollution. We are not asking if the states are innovative enough, according to some standard of social need. I believe Press and Adrian are correct when they charge that "our state governments are sick" because they have lost touch with the most progressive and adaptive elements in the society.[4] Most state governments are simply ignoring many of society's serious social problems, especially those arising in the cities. In this chapter, however, we are only trying to explain why some states act more rapidly than others, and once they have acted, how new forms of service or regulation spread among the American states.

DEFINITIONS AND DISTINCTIONS

Several terms have already been used here with ambiguous meanings. Let us define them. Most important, and potentially misleading, is the term innovation. An innovation is simply a program or policy that is new to the states adopting it, no matter how old the program may be or how many other states may have adopted it. Although bureaucratic innovations or new departures by regulatory commissions or courts are mentioned in the course of the discussion, the data used to measure the relative speed of adoption of innovations consists exclusively of legislative actions, simply because the data was readily available only in that form.

We are studying the relative speed and the spatial patterns of the adoption of new programs, not their invention or creation. Inventing workable, relevant solutions to pressing problems is an important activity and has been the subject of fascinating research.[5] We will concentrate on the way organizations select from proposed solutions the one that seems most suited to their needs, and how the organizations come to hear about these new ideas in the first place.[6] We are not trying to specify the circumstances under which new ideas or programs will be conceived or developed; we are studying instead the conditions under which state decision makers are most likely to adopt a new program.

Sometimes states enact legislation that is virtually copied word for word from other states. The California fair trade law, adopted in 1931, "was followed either verbatim or with minor variations by twenty states; in fact, ten states copied two serious typographical errors in the original California law."[7] Another piece of agricultural legislation drafted as a model bill by officials of the federal Department of Agriculture was adopted eventually by all states, usually with only minor amendments. "At least one state was apparently so anxious to qualify its farmers for federal aid that the state legislature even enacted the footnotes in the model act, footnotes intended simply to give advice to state officials with respect to alterations in the model that would be necessary to 'fit' it to the situation of particular states."[8]

New legislation on the same subject is not written in exactly the same language by every legislature. It is unlikely that the highway department established in Wyoming in 1917 had the same organizational format as the one adopted by Wisconsin in 1907, or that the council on the performing arts created in Kentucky in 1966 bears an exact resemblance to the one created by New York in 1960. In each case, however, a commitment was made to offer a new service, establish a new principle of regulation, or create an agency that had never existed before. Our concern is the origin and spread of an idea, not the detailed characteristics of institutions created in each state to implement a policy.

No ideological bias was employed in selecting issues for study. The patterns of diffusion for each issue have been treated equally, and no effort was made to develop any method of determining the relative importance or desirability of the programs.[9] Programs are sometimes enacted only to provide symbolic rewards to groups within the population and once created are left with inadequate funds or otherwise disabled.[10] Oklahoma's legislature, for example, emulated other states by creating a state civil rights commission, but once the commission was established only $2,500 was appropriated for its operation.[11] For the purposes of this study, however, all adoptions are equal. My goal is to provide an explanation of the relative speed of adoption and the patterns of diffusion of innovations; I am not interested in the effectiveness of Oklahoma's civil rights commission, but in where the legislature got the idea to create such a commission and why it acted when it did.

The Innovation Score

My first aim is to explain why some states adopt innovations more readily than others. I assume that the pioneering states gain their reputations because of the speed with which they accept new programs. The study must begin, therefore, with an attempt to devise an innovation score that will represent the relative speed with which states adopt innovations.

The innovation score is based on analysis of the eighty-eight different programs listed in the appendix * that were enacted by at least twenty state legislatures prior to 1965, and for which reliable information was available on the dates of adoption. In order to make the collection of programs as comprehensive and representative as possible, I adopted a list of issues similar to the one employed by the Council of State Governments in its bi-annual reports in the *Book of the States*. I tried to study six to eight pieces of legislation in each of these areas: welfare, health, education, conservation, planning, administrative organization, highways, civil rights, corrections and police, labor, taxes, and professional regulation. I studied issues ranging from the establishment of highway departments and the enactment of civil rights bills to the creation of state councils on the performing arts and the passage of sexual psychopath laws. Most of the programs were adopted during the twentieth century, but sixteen of them diffused primarily during the latter half of the nineteenth century.

The eighty-eight lists of dates of adoption were used to create an innovation score for each state. The first step was to count the total number of years that elapsed between the first and last recorded legislative enactment of a program. Each state then received a number corresponding to the percentage of time that elapsed between the first adoption and its own acceptance of the program. If the time between the first and last adoption of a program was twenty years, and Massachusetts enacted the program ten years after the first adoption, then Massachusetts received a score of .500 on that issue. The first state to adopt the program received a score of .000, and the last state received 1.000. If all states have not yet adopted a program, the states without the program were placed last and given a score of 1.000.[12] The innovation score for each state is 1.000 minus the average of the sum of the state's scores on all issues. The state that has been faster, on

* [See Appendix to Chapter Ten. — Eds.]

the average, in responding to new ideas or policies receives the higher innovation score. The issues may be divided into groups according to subject
matter or time periods, and separate scores can be created for these smaller
groups by following the same procedure. The results of this scoring procedure, using all eighty-eight issues, are presented in Table 1.

A note of caution should be sounded before the results of this exercise are analyzed. We are endeavoring to measure a highly complex process with an enormous number of idiosyncratic influences. An official with
an unusually keen interest in a program, a chance reading of an article or
book by a governor's aid, or any number of other circumstances peculiar
to any one issue might lead to the rapid adoption of a piece of legislation
by a state usually reluctant to accept new programs. Mississippi, which has
the lowest average score and ranks last among the states in relative speed
of adoption, was nonetheless the first state to adopt a general sales tax and
in 1936 was the first to pass legislation permitting cities and counties to
incur indebtedness for industrial plants leased to private firms.[13]

If this reservation is kept in mind, the data in Table 1 provide a crude
outline of the typical pattern of diffusion of new programs or policies

TABLE 1
Composite Innovation Scores for the American States[a]

New York	.656	Kansas	.426
Massachusetts	.629	Nebraska	.425
California	.604	Kentucky	.419
New Jersey	.585	Vermont	.414
Michigan	.578	Iowa	.413
Connecticut	.568	Alabama	.406
Pennsylvania	.560	Florida	.397
Oregon	.544	Arkansas	.394
Colorado	.538	Idaho	.394
Wisconsin	.532	Tennessee	.389
Ohio	.528	West Virginia	.386
Minnesota	.525	Arizona	.384
Illinois	.521	Georgia	.381
Washington	.510	Montana	.378
Rhode Island	.503	Missouri	.377
Maryland	.482	Delaware	.376
New Hampshire	.482	New Mexico	.375
Indiana	.464	Oklahoma	.368
Louisiana	.459	South Dakota	.363
Maine	.455	Texas	.362
Virginia	.451	South Carolina	.347
Utah	.447	Wyoming	.346
North Dakota	.444	Nevada	.323
North Carolina	.430	Mississippi	.298

[a]Alaska and Hawaii were omitted from the analysis because data for their years of
adoption were often missing.

among the American states. The states at the top of the list tend to adopt
new programs much more rapidly than those at the bottom. Why should
New York, California, and Michigan adopt innovations more rapidly than
Mississippi, Wyoming, and South Dakota?

The Correlates of Innovation

DEMOGRAPHIC FACTORS.   After studying the acceptance of technological innovations by both individuals and organizations, several writers
have concluded that the decision maker's relative wealth, or the degree to
which "free floating" resources are available, are important determinants
of the willingness to adopt new techniques or policies.[14] If "slack" resources
are available, either in the form of money or a highly skilled, professional
staff, the decision maker can afford the luxury of experiment and can more
easily risk the possibility of failure.[15] Other studies, especially in the areas
of agriculture and medicine, have shown organizational size to be a strong
correlate of innovation.[16] These results from prior studies in other fields
might prepare us to find that the larger, wealthier states — those with the
most developed industrial economies and the largest cities — would have
the highest innovation scores. The great cosmopolitan centers in the country, the places where most of the society's creative resources are concentrated, would likely be the most adaptive and sympathetic to change and,
thus, the first to adopt new programs.

In order to test these assumptions, several measures of social and economic development were correlated with the innovation score. We can see
in Table 2 that the larger, wealthier, more industrialized states adopt new
programs somewhat more rapidly than their smaller, less developed neighbors. Fairly strong relationships exist between the innovation score and the
value added by manufacturing, the average per acre value of farms, the
size of the urban population, and the average per capita income. These relationships remain virtually unchanged in all time periods. In fact, the
only relationship that changes substantially over time is that between innovation and the percentage of illiterates in the population, which declines
steadily across the three time periods. This declining relationship and the
low correlation between innovation and the median school year completed
is caused primarily by the states in the Rocky Mountain region that have
the highest rankings on median school years completed and yet are among
the slowest to adopt new programs.[17] The median of educational attainment in the states with the highest innovation scores is pulled down by the
presence of a large, poorly educated lower class, living primarily in the

TABLE 2

*Correlations Between Innovation Scores and Five Social and
Economic Variables, by Time Periods*

Social and economic variables	Innovation scores[a]			Com-posite score
	1870-1899	*1900-1929*	*1930-1966*	
Percentage of population urban	.62[b]	.69	.62	.63
Total population	.52	.40	.50	.59
Average income, per capita	c	.62	.50	.55
Value added per capita by manufacturing	.46	.55	.57	.66
Average value, per acre, of farms	.70	.52	.52	.54
Percentage of population illiterate	−.58	−.44	−.12	−.23
Median school years completed	c	c	.24	.26

[a]In order to insure that the innovation score and the social and economic variables came from comparable periods, separate innovation scores were calculated for three time periods: 1870-1899, 1900-1929, and 1930-1966. In constructing this table each innovation was placed in the time period during which the first ten states adopted it. Thus, if a program was adopted by only four states during the 1890s, and completed its diffusion during the 1900s, the program is placed in the second time period, 1900-1929, even though its first adoptions took place during the nineteenth century. Social and economic data are taken from the years 1900, 1930, and 1960. The composite score is correlated with social and economic data from 1960.
[b]The table entries are Pearson product-moment correlations.
[c]Measures of these phenomena corresponding with these time periods do not exist.

inner cities. The highly industrialized states with large urban concentrations are characterized by great inequality of social status and attainment. It would seem, however, that the elements necessary to foster innovation are present in these states even though they do not have highest average level of educational achievement.

POLITICAL FACTORS. Although students of policy making have begun to doubt the importance of the political system as an independent determinant of the behavior of decision makers, it seems likely that both the degree of party competition and a state's system of legislative apportionment would affect its readiness to accept change. It would seem that parties that often faced closely contested elections would try to outdo each other by embracing the newest, most progressive programs, naturally encouraging rapid adoption of innovations. Lowi argues that departures in policy are more likely at the beginning of an administration, especially when a former minority party gains control of the government.[18] If this tendency exists it would also seem likely that state political systems allowing frequent turnover and offering the most opportunities to capture high office would more often develop the circumstances in which new programs might be adopted.[19]

Another prerequisite for the rapid adoption of new programs might be a system of legislative apportionment that fully represented the state's urban areas and that did not grant veto power to groups opposed to change. Such a system might be expected to allow consideration and debate of new policies and programs in all areas. Some recent findings, such as Barber's study of legislators in Connecticut,[20] lead us to speculate that representatives from newly developing urban and suburban areas are more cosmopolitan, better informed, and more tolerant of change. If nothing else, urban legislators are probably more willing to deal with problems of sanitation, planning, transportation, and housing peculiar to large metropolitan areas.

No matter what the composition of the legislator's constituency, however, the presence of competent staff, superior clerical facilities, and supporting services should allow him to give serious consideration to a larger number of new proposals. Several studies of the diffusion of technological innovations have demonstrated that the best informed individuals are most likely to pioneer in the use of new techniques or tools.[21] Therefore, the states that provide the most extensive staff and research facilities in their legislatures ought to pioneer in the adoption of new programs.[22]

Table 3 displays efforts to test some of these hypotheses in different time periods. Measures of political variables are usually based on evidence only from contemporary periods because data are seldom available on state and local elections or the operation of legislatures in earlier decades. Measures are available, however, for the degree of party competition and the extent of legislative malapportionment.[23] Party competitiveness is not con-

TABLE 3

Correlations Between Innovation Scores and Measures of Political Variables, by Time Periods

	Innovation scores			Com-posite score
Political variables[a]	1870-1899	1900-1929	1930-1966	
Party competition for governorship	.36	.02	.14	.24
David-Eisenberg index of malapportionment	b	.07	.55	.65

[a]The index of party competition used in this table is the percentage of the total vote going to the gubernatorial candidate coming in second, times 2. This yields a scale from 0 to 100. It was created by Richard Hofferbert. The apportionment index appears in Paul T. David and Ralph Eisenberg, *Devaluation of the Urban and Suburban Vote* (Charlottesville: Bureau of Public Administration, University of Virginia, 1961).

[b]Measures of this phenomenon corresponding with this time period do not exist.

sistently related to the innovation score, at least as it is measured in Table 3.[24] Legislative apportionment is not correlated with the innovation score in the 1900 to 1929 period, but is related in the 1930 to 1966 period. Since legislatures steadily became less representative of urban populations after 1930, we may have here some empirical evidence of the effect of malapportionment on policy making in the states.

Recent studies of state expenditures have shown that the explanatory effects of political variables could be eliminated if statistical controls for social and economic variables were applied. Table 4 presents both the zero-order correlations of the composite innovation score and measures of legislative apportionment, party competition, turnover in office, and legislative professionalism,[25] and also partial correlations with four social and economic variables controlled. The control variables are value added by manufacturing, percentage of urban population, total population size, and per capita personal income, all of which earlier proved to be independently related to the innovation score. In Table 4 each control variable is displayed separately along with the combined impact of all four. The results tend to corroborate earlier analyses that minimize the independent effects of these political variables on policy outcomes. The Schlesinger index of opportunity, which measures the difference among the states in the average number of times major offices have changed hands, and the Hofferbert index of interparty competition seem to have some independent influence on innovation, although it is greatly weakened when all four control variables are combined. This finding lends some credence to Lowi's argument that turnover in office fosters change.

Certainly, the most important result depicted in this table is the consistent strength of the correlation between innovation and the David Eisenberg index of urban representation. Earlier studies, using expenditures as a measure of policy outcomes, have consistently found that apportionment has little importance as an explanatory variable.[26] Our findings indicate the opposite. Although the other political factors do not have great independent impact on innovation, the clear implication arising from Tables 3 and 4 is that those states that grant their urban areas full representation in the legislature adopt new ideas more rapidly, on the average, than states that discriminate against their cities.

The results of this correlational analysis might lead us to conclude that New York, California, and Michigan adopt new programs more rapidly than Mississippi, Wyoming, and South Dakota primarily because they are bigger, richer, more urban, more industrial, have more fluidity and turnover in their political systems, and have legislatures that more adequately

TABLE 4

Relationships Between the Composite Innovation Score and Measures of Legislative Apportionment and Party Competition

	Zero-order	Partials				
		Value added manu-facturing	Per-centage urban	Total population	Per capita income	Four factors combined
Apportionment:						
David-Eisenberg index	.65	.47	.64	.67	.60	.58
Party competition:						
Hofferbert index	.54	.35	.34	.50	.26	.12
Turnover in office:						
Schlesinger index of opportunity	.53	.40	.39	.32	.34	.24
Legislative services:						
Grumm's index of legislative professionalism	.63	.38	.33	.41	.51	.11

represent their cities. Although these findings are important, they do not answer many important questions. The political system does not react automatically to the growth of manufacturing industries or to the increase in the percentage of the population living in cities. Developments of this kind obviously cause problems that public officials might try to solve, but the mere presence of such a stimulant does not cause public officials to act, nor does it determine the form the solution will take, or which state might act first to meet the problem. Our analysis has provided us with evidence that change and experimentation are more readily accepted in the industrialized, urban, cosmopolitan centers of the country, but we have not improved our understanding of the institutions and decision-making processes that cause strong statistical relationships between industrial output and innovation. Also, we have not explained the way innovations spread from the pioneering states to those with lower innovation scores. To explain these processes we must go beyond the search for demographic correlates of innovation and develop generalizations that refer to the behavior of the men who choose new programs.

EMULATION AND DECISION MAKING
IN THE STATES

We are searching for answers to three major questions: Why do certain states consistently adopt new programs more rapidly than other states. Are there more or less stable patterns of diffusion of innovations among the American states? If so, what are they? I want to develop an approach to governmental policy making that will lead to a better understanding of decisions made by bureaucrats, political executives and other governmental officials. Rather than focus upon conflict among factions within the legislature or the administrative agencies, I will search for the criteria employed by legislators and administrators in deciding whether a proposal is worthy of consideration. This search rests on the belief that whoever the decision maker may be — administrator, lobbyist, party leader, governor, or legislator — and however controversial a particular issue may become, a set of general criteria exists in every state that establishes broad guidelines for policy making. Regardless of the interests supporting an innovation, no matter whether the decision system is primarily monolithic or pluralistic, if a proposal for change does not fall within those guidelines its chances for acceptance are slim.

We are drawing here, in part, on insights from the theories of organizational decision making developed in recent years by writers such as Simon, March, Cyert, and Lindblom.[27] At the heart of these theories is the concept of the decision maker struggling to choose among complex alternatives and constantly receiving much more information about his environment than he is able to digest and evaluate. An ordinary decision maker, required to make frequent choices and faced with an inconclusive flood of reports, programs, suggestions, and memos, must somehow simplify his task. According to Simon, he does not — cannot — always search for the best possible solution to the problems he faces; he has neither the time nor the energy. Instead, he finds an alternative that he believes is good enough to preserve whatever values are important to him. The limits of human rationality prevent him from maximizing his benefits in every situation; rather, he "satisfices," or chooses a course of action that seems satisfactory under the circumstances.

The individual in a complex organization, therefore, does not deal directly with all sources of information potentially available to him, nor does he evaluate every conceivable policy option. In place of the debilitating confusion of reality he creates his own abstract, highly simplified world containing only a few major variables. In order to achieve this manageable simplicity he adopts a set of decision rules or standard criteria for judgment that remain fairly stable over time and that guide him in choosing among sources of information and advice. With these rules, he decides both where to look for cues and information and how to choose among alternatives. The rules also embody the current goals and aspirations of his organization, or the values the organization is designed to advance and protect. Hence, if we wish to predict the decision maker's behavior, we should try to discover these rules of thumb, or "heuristics" as they are sometimes called. We could then explain his choices by the alternatives he considers, his knowledge of each alternative, the sources of his knowledge, and the standard decision rules he applies in cases of this kind.[28]

Taking cues from these theories of human choice and organizational decision making, our explanation of the adoption of innovations by the states is based on the assertion that state officials make most of their decisions by analogy. The rule of thumb they employ might be formally stated as follows: *look for an analogy between the situation you are dealing with and some other situation, perhaps in some other state, where the problem has been successfully resolved.*[29]

We are looking to what has been called the "inter-organizational context," [30] or the *horizontal* relationships among the states within the federal system, for the principal influences that regulate the speed of adoption and the patterns of diffusion of innovations. Most work on intergovernmental relations and federalism concentrates on the question of centralization within the American system of government. In line with the general interest of most political scientists in the factors that affect the access of organized groups and the lines of authority within a political system, many writers study the virtues of centralization or decentralization and try to determine how much of either exists in the system. They have studied primarily the vertical relationships among national, state, and local governments, and have usually identified the party system and its demands as the institutional influence most responsible for maintaining the present, decentralized, federal relationships.[31] I want to focus attention on the mutual perceptions and relationships among state governments and to show how these relationships affect the behavior of state decision makers.[32]

One of the most common arguments used in state legislatures against raising taxes or regulating business is the fear that such measures might retard industrial development or force marginal plants to leave the state. Lawmakers often must handle problems that arise when one or two states establish extremely permissive standards for the granting of licenses, such as the corporation laws in New Jersey and Delaware, or the divorce laws in Nevada. However, interstate competition does not always drive standards down; it has a positive side as well. State decision makers are constantly looking to each other for guidance in many areas of policy, such as the organization and management of higher education, or the provision of hospitals and public health facilities. In fact, this process of competition and emulation, or cue taking, determines in large part the pace and direction of social and political change in the American states.[33]

Uncertainty and the fear of unanticipated consequences have always been formidable barriers to reform. Proponents of new programs have always had to combat the arguments of those who predict dire consequences if some innovation is adopted. Even though American history is full of cases where the opponents of change have later had to admit that the dangers they feared never materialized, inertia and the unwillingness to take risks have prevented a more rapid rate of change.

Inertia can more easily be overcome if the proponent of change can point to the successful implementation of his program in a similar setting. If a legislator introduces a bill that would require the licensing of probation officers, for example, and can point to its successful operation in a neighboring state, his chances of gaining acceptance are markedly increased. As Harsanyi has asserted:

> It is not an overstatement to say that a very considerable part of the social values of most societies is based on sheer ignorance. . . .
> One of the reasons why other persons' example is so important in

encouraging changes in people's value and behavior lies in the fact that it tends to dispel some groundless fears about the dismal consequences that such changes might entail. Another reason is of course that people can more easily face the possible hostility of the supporters of the old values if they are not alone in making the change.[34]

In fact, once a program has been adopted by a large number of states it may become recognized as a legitimate responsibility for all states. When this happens it becomes extremely difficult for state decision makers to resist even the weakest kinds of demands to institute the program for fear of arousing public suspicions about their good intentions. When a program gains the stamp of legitimacy it has a momentum of its own. As Lockard found in studying the passage of fair employment practices laws, the actions of other states are sometimes key factors in prompting reluctant politicians to accept controversial programs.

> Pressure mounted in New Jersey during 1944 and 1945 for some stronger policy, and when New York passed its FEP law certain key politicians in New Jersey decided to act. Governor Walter E. Edge concluded, apparently reluctantly, that he had to commit himself to such a law. "As the session drew to a close," Edge wrote in his autobiography, "minority racial and religious groups pressed for adoption of an antidiscrimination program. While it was a subject which I would have preferred to give greater study, politically it could not be postponed because New York had passed a similar measure and delay would be construed as a mere political expedient." [35]

For similar reasons there have been numerous efforts to enact a program of homesteading in Hawaii as a way of disposing of its arable public lands even though the circumstances there are quite different from other states where homesteading was successfully introduced.[36] In Connecticut one of the most powerful arguments in favor of introducing the direct primary system during the 1950s was simply that all the other states had adopted one.[37]

The Connecticut case illustrates some generalizations we are developing. Lockard points out that the leaders of both political parties privately opposed the introduction of a primary system but thought that an endorsement of the idea had to be put into their platforms to avoid having their opponents charge them with bossism. Demands for the primary came for the most part from small groups in the state's suburban areas that were interested in the issue as "a consequence of the influx of migrants from states with primaries." [38] Speaking as a professional political scientist as well as a legislator, Lockard was well suited to counter the fears expressed by the party leaders who predicted that party organizations would be completely destroyed if primaries were introduced. Reasoning by analogy to the experience in other states, Lockard both countered the opponents of change and shaped his own moderate position:

> I expressed my considerable doubts about the effect of party primaries on party organization. From observations of politics in some of the most thoroughgoing party primary states, [however] it seemed that the party organizations had been shattered with many undesirable consequences. In my campaign I expressed support only for a limited form of a primary and not one calculated to wreck the party system.[39]

Events like these illustrate that the agenda of controversy in a state is determined, at least in part, by developments in other states. They also show how experiences and examples from outside the system help to overcome the natural reluctance of any institutional structure to risk the consequences of change. The constituent units of any federal system are under pressure to conform with national and regional standards or accepted administrative procedures. These norms result primarily from the processes of emulation and competition we have described and also from the efforts of nationally organized interest groups. They are affected also by the growth and development of professional organizations and other forms of communication among state administrators, and by the natural circulation of active, politically involved citizens among the states, such as the Connecticut suburbanites who began agitating for a primary system in their adopted political home.

Regional Reference Groups and Standards of Evaluation

Nationally accepted standards or norms provide a convenient measure that can be used by interested citizens or political leaders to judge the adequacy of services offered in their own states. But these norms have an ambiguous influence on the performance of state governments. On the one hand, the existence of national standards probably encourages higher performance among the poorer members of the federation than we could expect if functions and service levels were established independently within each unit of government, solely as a result of internal demands. An example of this tendency was discovered by May in his study of Canadian federalism:

> Newfoundland chose for a long time to remain outside the Canadian federation, thus not subjecting itself to the forces of national reorientation, and when, after joining the Dominion, a royal commis-

sion reported on its financial position, the commission observed that Newfoundland's public services were very backward in relation to those of the other provinces, including even the maritimes.[40]

In the United States, Mississippi, Vermont, and North Dakota are good examples of relatively poor states that make unusual efforts to bring their public services into closer approximation of national standards.

On the other hand, national standards and norms can have a conservative impact, especially in the richer, industrial states that are able to provide services somewhat above the national averages with relatively little effort.[41] Hansen complains of this tendency when he points out that:

> Some northern states fall considerably below their northern neighboring states in public service standards. . . . Their fiscal problems arise not because they are poor but because their tax levels are low by northern standards. This is notably true for example of a tier of large industrial states — Illinois, Indiana, Ohio and Pennsylvania. . . . These states are not excessively hard pressed by tax burdens relative to the country as a whole.[42]

This statement is drawn from an essay in which Hansen expresses disapproval of what he considers the inadequate public services of large industrial states with relatively low tax burdens. But the statement contains several ambiguities. For example, Hansen charges that "some northern states fall considerably below their northern neighboring states in public service standards," but then he specifically points as examples to Illinois, Indiana, Ohio, and Pennsylvania, states that border each other. It is not clear whether we are being asked to compare these states to their neighbors, to other northern states with higher tax burdens, or to "the country as a whole." In Illinois, however, decision makers are probably comparing their own performance with their counterparts in Indiana, Ohio, Pennsylvania, or New Jersey. Officials in Illinois may know of the procedures and performance levels in New York or California, but they are unlikely to think of events in these states as legitimate guides to action.[43]

When examining the public policy of any state, therefore, it is important to discover in which "league" it has chosen to play. In New York, for example, decision makers seem to take great pride in being first to adopt new programs or in providing better public services than offered by any other state. In 1968, for example, Governor Rockefeller proposed a huge new health program containing several unprecedented elements. In defense of his proposal the governor argued:

> This state leads the nation in the actions it has taken to expand the availability and the equality of health facilities. More remains to be done and the legislation I am urging will go far in that direction. This

program would give New York State the opportunity to pioneer in the field of heart disease, as it has done so notably in the field of cancer.[44]

New York's political leaders conceive of themselves as national leaders [45] and this belief determines their relative tolerance for innovation. Missouri's leaders, on the other hand, seem to find more virtue in caution and conservatism. Salisbury, in a statement much like Hansen's, reasons by analogy in arguing that Missouri does not provide as much aid for its schools as its potential resources might warrant. He points out that in 1959 the "state ranked 18th in per capita income but 38th in per capita expenditure for local schools." [46] This relatively low level of support seems to result from the correspondingly low aspirations of the officials of the Missouri State Teachers Association who, according to Salisbury, "have chosen to get what they can with a minimum of agitation or conflict rather than attempt broader public campaigns in behalf of larger objectives." [47] The officials of MSTA "are fully conscious of the gap between the Missouri school aid level and that of, say, neighboring Illinois," but they are quick to point out "that by comparison with other neighboring states — Arkansas, Oklahoma, or Nebraska, for example — Missouri's record is much more impressive." [48] It would seem from this example that Missouri's leaders, at least those concerned with public education, are emulating and competing primarily with the states to their south and west, rather than with the Great Lakes states to their north and east, or the Rocky Mountain states, the Deep South, or the Far West. The choice of relatively poor states such as Arkansas and Oklahoma as the principal, legitimate reference groups establishes an upper limit of aspirations considerably below what might exist if Missouri's accepted basis for comparison were the public services of Illinois, Wisconsin, or Michigan.[49]

Regional Groupings among the States

We have come far enough in our analysis to see that our original presentation of the innovation scores in Table 1 as a linear distribution masked some pertinent information. A more useful representation of the data, which would conform more closely to the actual patterns of diffusion, would have to be in the form of a tree. At the top of the tree would be a set of pioneering states linked together in a national system of emulation and competition. The rest of the states would be sorted out along branches of the tree according to the pioneer, or set of pioneers, from which they take their principal cues. States such as New York, Massachusetts, California, and Michigan should be seen as regional pacesetters, each with a group of followers, usually within their own region of the country, that tend to adopt programs only after the pioneers have led the way. For example, Colorado, which ranks ninth in Table 1, might be seen as the regional leader of the Rocky Mountain states. The rest of the states in that region are much farther down the list: Utah is twenty-second, Idaho is thirty-third, Arizona is thirty-sixth, Montana is thirty-eighth, New Mexico is forty-first, Wyoming is forty-sixth, and Nevada is forty-seventh. All of these states, with the possible exception of Utah, which may share in the leadership of the region, might be seen as Colorado's followers, usually picking up new ideas only after the regional pioneer has put them into practice.

Retirement systems for state employees were first instituted by Massachusetts in 1911 and by most other states in the years directly after World War II. The pattern of diffusion of this innovation illustrates the process of regional comparison and cue taking. In Table 5 the country is divided into eight regional clusters.[50] Each state is categorized according to the year in which it adopted a retirement program for its employees. The pattern that emerges when the data are arranged by region and time of adoption closely approximates a tree. Several regional pioneers appear, such as California, Colorado, Minnesota, Ohio, New York, and Massachusetts, who adopted and tested the program. After a time lag (twenty-five years in the New England states), the rest of the members of the region began falling into line and most adopted the program within a short period.

In Table 5 the states are arbitrarily clustered, but if we are right about these general patterns of competition and emulation, it should be possible to discover in these data some evidence of regional clustering among the states. In an effort to test for the existence of such groupings, a factor analysis was performed (varimax rotation) on a matrix of pair-wise comparisons of all state innovation scores on all eighty-eight issues.[51] If regional groupings of states respond to new programs as a unit, adopting some new ideas with relative haste and lagging behind on others, the factor analysis should be able to identify most members of the regional units.

Our factor analysis of these data produced five groupings of states. The states identified by this method — all those with factor scores above .500 — are shaded on the map in Figure 1. Several ambiguities in these results are difficult to explain, such as the presence of Nebraska in a group that otherwise includes southern states, New York's appearance in two groupings, California's appearance with border and Great Lake states, and Louisiana's appearance with northwest and lower plains states. These unexpected findings may reflect only the ambiguities of our data and the

TABLE 5
Dates of Legislative Adoption of Retirement Systems for State Employees

Year of adoption	Far West	Mountains	Southwest	Plains	Great Lakes	Southeast	Mid-Atlantic	New England
1910								Mass. 1911
1920							N.Y. 1921 N.J. 1922 Pa. 1923	
				Minn. 1929				
1930	Calif. 1932	Colo. 1931			Ohio 1935			R. I. 1936
1940								Conn. 1939

Regional Grouping

TABLE 5 (Continued)

Year of adoption	Far West	Mountains	Southwest	Plains	Great Lakes	Southeast	Mid-Atlantic	New England
1940						N. Car. 1941	Md. 1941	
					Ill. 1943	Va. 1942		Me. 1942
					Mich. 1943	Ala. 1945		
	Ore. 1945	Mont. 1945		Iowa 1945	Ind. 1945	Fla. 1945		Vt. 1944
						S. Car. 1945		N. Hamp. 1945
						La. 1946	Del. 1946	
	Wash. 1947	Utah 1947	N. Mex. 1947	N. Dak. 1947	Wisc. 1947	Tenn. 1947		
	Nev. 1947	Wyo. 1949	Tex. 1947			Ga. 1949		
1950			Ariz. 1953	Mo. 1954		Miss. 1952		
		Idaho 1954	Okla. 1954	Neb. 1954		Ark. 1954		
				S. Dak. 1954		Kent. 1956		
1960				Kan. 1961		W. Va. 1961		
1970								

Source: *The Book of the States, 1952-53*, 194-254, and the files of the Council of State Governments.

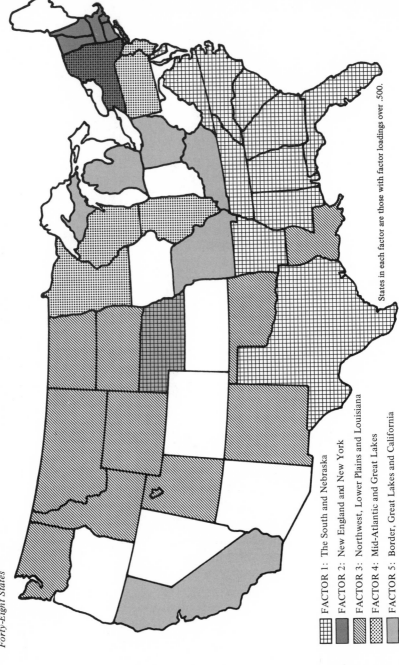

FIGURE 1
Graphic Presentation of Varimax Factor Analysis of Innovation Scores for Forty-Eight States

States in each factor are those with factor loadings over .500.

FACTOR 1: The South and Nebraska
FACTOR 2: New England and New York
FACTOR 3: Northwest, Lower Plains and Louisiana
FACTOR 4: Mid-Atlantic and Great Lakes
FACTOR 5: Border, Great Lakes and California

limitations of our methods. New York and California, for example, consistently lead the country in the adoption of new programs, so they may not appear to be members of a cohesive regional group or league of states, a fact that may prevent their categorization through factor analysis. Although these five clusters are not as clear as we might have hoped, they are generally recognizable as contiguous, regional groupings of states.

Specialized Communications among the States

Our analysis has provided evidence for the existence of a continuum that ranges from those states usually quick to accept innovations to those typically reluctant to do so. We also know something about the correlates of innovation and have evidence of regional groupings among the states, but it is not always easy to identify a regional pioneer or to know exactly which states make up each league or subsystem of cue-taking and information exchange. Some states have connections with more than one region and may regularly receive cues from states in both groupings. As the American political system develops an increasing number of specialized communication systems cut across traditional regional lines and bring officials from many different regions into contact with each other and with federal and local officials, journalists, academic experts, and administrative consultants.

Several organizations now exist, such as the Council of State Governments, the Federal Commission on Intergovernmental Relations, and the recently established Citizen's Conference on State Legislatures, whose primary function is to improve communications among the states. Most important of these specialized communications networks are the professional associations of state officials, such as the National Association of State Budget Officers, or the National Association of State Conservation Officers. Associations of this kind were first created late in the nineteenth century and more are forming each year. Only five existed prior to 1900, but by 1930 there were approximately thirty-one; by 1966, at least eighty-six.[52] Memberships in these groups often include federal and local, as well as state officials working in the policy area. All the associations regularly hold national, and sometimes regional, meetings and conventions. Approximately 40 per cent of the associations have full-time executive directors, and about 70 per cent regularly publish journals, newsletters, or the proceedings of their annual meetings.[53]

These groups serve two general purposes. First, they are sources of information and policy cues. By organizing conferences or publishing newsletters they bring together officials from all over the country and facilitate the exchange of ideas and knowledge among them, thus increasing the officials' awareness of the latest developments in their field. Second, these associations serve as "occupational contact networks" that expedite the interstate movement or transfer of personnel. Through the efforts of these groups, officials become aware of desirable job openings in other states and are able to create professional reputations that extend beyond the borders of their own states.[54]

By rapidly spreading knowledge of new programs among state officials and by facilitating the movement of individuals to jobs in other states, professional associations encourage the development of national standards for the proper administration and control of the services of state government. The executive secretaries of professional societies and the staff members of agencies such as the Commission on Intergovernmental Relations have contacts with officials from almost all the states. From their central positions they are able to evaluate the relative merits of state programs and can communicate these judgments to others, thus reinforcing the reputations, both good and bad, of individual administrators or state agencies. By circulating information, these national agencies help to shape the professional consensus in their policy areas concerning ideal or desirable programs and indirectly set policy agendas in many states. Just as in other sectors of American life such as the business, the military, and the academic worlds, as individuals increase their mobility, their role perceptions are likely to change; they are likely to adopt a more cosmopolitan perspective and to cultivate their reputations within a national professional community rather than merely within their own state or agency.[55]

Since general awareness of new developments is achieved much more quickly now than ever before, we would expect that the time that elapses from the first adoption of an innovation by a pioneering state to its complete diffusion throughout all the states would be greatly reduced. Certainly, several recent innovations, such as educational television or state councils on the performing arts, have diffused rapidly. Table 6 measures the average speed of diffusion in years for three periods of time: 1870 to 1899, 1900 to 1929, and 1930 to 1966. The results in the first column of this table show that the speed of diffusion has been constantly increasing as time passed. This measurement, however, is somewhat misleading. The second column of the table indicates the average number of years it took the first twenty states to adopt the programs in each time period. The same trend toward increased speed of diffusion is evident here, but the differences among the three time periods are much smaller.[56] This evidence

TABLE 6
Average Time of Diffusion in Years for Innovations in Three Time Periods

Time periods	Time for all adoptions	Time for first twenty adoptions
1870-1899	52.3	22.9
1900-1929	39.6	20.0
1930-1966	25.6	18.4

suggests that the pioneering states, those with high innovation scores, adopted new programs about as quickly in the early part of this century, prior to the development of many specialized communication links, as they did in the 1960s. The total time of diffusion has decreased, however, primarily because the laggard states, those with low innovation scores, are now reacting more quickly. This development results partly from the efforts of the federal government to stimulate state action through grants-in-aid, and partly from the increasing professional development in state government. Both tendencies seem to have affected the behavior of the parochial states more than the cosmopolitan, pioneering states.

Officials in the more parochial states are made aware of developments in the pioneering states through contacts with federal officials, conversations with their counterparts in other states during professional meetings and conventions, reports and articles in newsletters or journals, or in model bills patterned after legislation already enacted in the pioneering states. The suggested state legislative programs issued annually by the Advisory Commission on Intergovernmental Relations (ACIR) are one source of model legislation. The program includes the text of the suggested legislation ready for enactment merely by inserting the appropriate state names and official titles. In some cases the legislation has been drafted by the commission staff, but usually the bills are either copied from legislation already enacted in some states, or are model bills currently being advocated by professional associations of state or local officials.

In the 1970 ACIR legislative program model, bills from several organizations were presented, including the Council of State Governments, the United States Council of Mayors, the National League of Cities, the National Municipal League, the American Society of Planning Officials, the National Association of Counties, and the Conference of State Sanitary Engineers. Draft legislation is often prefaced by information about the operation of similar programs already enacted in other states. One such example of ACIR's efforts to facilitate diffusion is the following preface to suggested state legislation on municipal charters:

> Information regarding the New Jersey law upon which the draft is based and experience under it over a period of 15 years is available in a report entitled *New Jersey's Optional Municipal Charter Law* published by the National Municipal League. While the specific form of the options presented in the New Jersey act is somewhat different and while there are other differences, the general discussion and descriptive material, the review of experience under the act, and the citation to judicial rulings provide useful annotation.[57]

The majority of the suggested pieces of legislation in the ACIR proposals have already been enacted in at least one state. The 1970 ACIR legislative proposals were used to make Table 7. Each time a state was cited as the source of the proposed legislation, the state was given a point. The total points awarded to each state create an index upon which the ranking in Table 7 is based. Even though the ACIR concerns itself with a limited range of legislation dealing primarily with taxation, planning, and intergovernmental relations, and the ranking is based on only a single year's program, the results strikingly resemble the innovation scores presented in Table 1. New York leads both lists. The top ten states on the innovation table all receive multiple mentions in the ACIR ranking while only one of the bottom ten on the innovation table (Missouri, 39th) is mentioned by the ACIR as a source of legislative cues. From documents such as these state officials are kept informed of the latest pioneering developments in states all over the country. Merely by passing the word, and providing the stamp of professional endorsement, groups such as the ACIR are speeding up the diffusion of innovations among the states.

The Persistence of Regionalism

Improved communications and greatly increased contacts of all kinds among state officials seem to be accelerating the process of diffusion, but this does not necessarily mean that the regional clusters or leagues of states to which we have referred have been destroyed. Evidence from several sources indicates that regional differences are persisting in America, even though strong nationalizing currents have been flowing for several decades.[58] During the last thirty years in state government many new professional associations have been formed and more interstate and federal agencies have begun facilitating communications and encouraging national

TABLE 7

*Index of Citations of States from the 1970 State Legislative
Program of the Advisory Commission on Intergovernmental
Relations*

State[a]	Index number	State	Index number
New York	11	West Virginia	1
New Jersey	8	Vermont	1
Michigan	7	Florida	1
Wisconsin	7	Nebraska	1
California	6	Maine	1
Oregon	6	Montana	1
Maryland	6	Illinois	0
North Carolina	6	New Hampshire	0
Missouri	6	Louisiana	0
Connecticut	4	Utah	0
Colorado	4	North Dakota	0
Minnesota	4	Iowa	0
Pennsylvania	4	Alabama	0
Virginia	4	Arkansas	0
Alaska	4	Idaho	0
Hawaii	4	Arizona	0
Massachusetts	3	Delaware	0
Ohio	3	New Mexico	0
Tennessee	3	Oklahoma	0
Georgia	3	South Dakota	0
Kentucky	3	Texas	0
Kansas	2	South Carolina	0
Washington	1	Wyoming	0
Rhode Island	1	Nevada	0
Indiana	1	Mississippi	0

[a]When ties occur, the states are arranged in the order in which they occur in Table 1.
Source: United States Advisory Commission in Intergovernmental Relations, *1970 State
Legislative Program.*

uniformity, but there is still a pronounced regional bias in the specialized
networks through which state officials communicate.

Evidence of regionalism appeared in answers given by administrators
in a survey of ten states conducted during 1968 and 1969.[59] These answers
were ranked in Table 8A so that the communication patterns of each state
emerge. The respondents were top administrators in the departments of
education, labor, mental health, welfare, the budget bureau, legislative
reference service, and the governor's chief assistant for program development.[60] In an effort to identify the channels of communication employed by
these administrators, two questions were asked about interstate contacts.
First, respondents were asked if they, or the members of their staffs, ever
contacted officials in other states to get advice or information. The answer
to that question was yes in 93 per cent of the cases. Those who said yes

were then asked: "In your field which states would you say are the best sources of information and new ideas?" Each time a respondent mentioned a state it received one point. States receiving more than two points were recorded in the table.

States are arranged roughly according to geography in Table 8 with Oregon, the most western state, on the left of the table and Rhode Island, the most eastern state, on the right. An inspection of the rankings reveals that all states seem to seek information and new ideas from some pioneering states. California, for example, was mentioned as a contact by every state, and New York was mentioned by all but Arizona. Four other Great Lake states — Wisconsin, Michigan, Illinois, and Minnesota — were mentioned in at least six of the ten cases. Besides these "national league" states, however, each state reported making contact with other states in its immediate region. Rhode Island reported extensive contacts with its New England neighbors, North Carolina with other southeastern states, Kentucky with other border states and some southern states, and Michigan with other Great Lake states. In all cases there is a mixture of regional and national communication, although Oregon, Colorado, and Michigan, the more innovative states, exhibit weaker ties to their regions than states with lower innovation scores such as Arizona or Rhode Island.

The evidence in Table 8A suggests that state administrators look to both the pioneering states and to their immediate neighbors when searching for policy guidance. The respondents were also asked if *they* were ever contacted for advice or information by officials from other states. Those who said yes to this question, 98 per cent of the total, were then asked to name the states that "usually" contacted them. Answers to this question were arranged in rankings for each state and are presented in Table 8B. This question about incoming messages reveals strong regional patterns of communication. North Carolina, for example, reported extensive contact with its neighboring states of Georgia, Tennessee, South Carolina, and Virginia; Oregon with Washington, California, and Idaho; Colorado with Utah, Wyoming, Kansas, and Nebraska; and Iowa with all six of its neighbors. The national league states, however, which are the objects of numerous inquiries, also seem to initiate contacts with states all over the country. California, Michigan, Wisconsin, and Minnesota appear in several rankings (California is mentioned six times), and Michigan reports extensive contacts from other national league states, but most of the reported inquiries for most states come from other administrators in their immediate region.

The earlier question about the "best sources" of information and new ideas may have prompted respondents to name states whose programs they admire and would like to emulate, even though they may have had infrequent direct contact with the administrators from these states. Our Michigan respondents did not report an unusually large number of inquiries from other states even though they were identified as good sources of information in six of the other nine states in our study. We are dependent on the memories of our respondents, of course, and have no empirical measure of these communication flows that could be used to check the validity of the answers. Nevertheless, the findings in Table 8B suggest that the communications system among state officials is even more affected by regional bias than indicated by the data in Table 8A. Interviews of the kind being relied on here cannot provide us with an exact picture of the flows of information among our respondents, but these data provide ample evidence that a strong sense of regionalism persists among the American states.

Our interviews reveal that state administrators communicate most readily with their counterparts in states that they believe have similar resources, social problems, and administrative styles. Usually this means states in their immediate region. We also found, however, that California, New York, Wisconsin, Michigan, Minnesota, and Illinois were mentioned by many respondents from far outside their regions as good sources of information and new ideas. This national league appeared again when we tried to identify the states our respondents used as models worthy of emulation.

An index of approval, presented in Table 9, is based upon the results of three questions asked on our survey concerning the evaluation of programs in other states.[61] The scores for each state in Table 9 represent simply the total number of times a state was mentioned favorably by one of our respondents when he was asked to identify either the sources of an innovation he had recently instituted in his own department, the state program in his area that came closest to his ideal, or states that could be generally characterized as pioneers in government and public affairs. This index reveals that our respondents in all parts of the country are substantially agreed on which states have the most desirable programs. Both New York and California are mentioned in every state; they received more than half the favorable mentions in Michigan, Oregon, and Colorado, the states with the highest innovation scores. Wisconsin, Michigan, and Illinois also are prominently mentioned in most states. In fact, Wisconsin received more favorable mentions from our Iowa respondents than either New York or California.[62] There is a small regional bias in these data reminiscent of the patterns in Table 8. New York predominates east of the Mississippi River,

TABLE 8

Communication Patterns Among Administrators in Ten States

A. Best Sources of Information and New Ideas

Oregon (N=27)[a]	Arizona (N=22)	Utah (N=23)	Colorado (N=24)	Missouri (N=23)	Iowa (N=25)	Michigan (N=24)	Kentucky (N=24)	North Carolina (N=21)	Rhode Island (N=23)
Cal. 18	Cal. 11	Cal. 12	N.Y. 14	Cal. 6	Mich. 8	N.Y. 19	Ohio 7	Cal. 8	Mass. 11
Wash. 14	Region[b] 3	N.Y. 5	Cal. 12	Minn. 6	Wisc. 8	Cal. 15	N.Y. 5	N.Y. 5	Conn. 9
N.Y. 7		Colo. 4	Wisc. 7	N.Y. 5	Minn. 7	Wisc. 12	Cal. 5	Fla. 5	N.Y. 8
Wisc. 6		Wisc. 4	Ill. 6	Wisc. 5	Cal. 6	Ill. 5	Penn. 5	Minn. 4	Cal. 3
Minn. 5		Ill. 4	Ohio 4	Ill. 5	Ill. 6	Minn. 4	Ga. 5	Va. 4	N.H. 3
Colo. 4		Fla. 3	Mich. 3	Mich. 4	Mo. 6	Ohio 4	Mich. 4	Region[b] 3	Vt. 3
Mich. 4		Ore. 3	Minn. 3	Region[b] 4	Region[b] 5		Wisc. 4		Me. 3
Ill. 4		Tex. 3	Utah 3	Penn. 3	Indiana 3		Colo. 4		Region[b] 3
Utah 3			Fla. 3	Kan. 3	Neb. 3		N.C. 4		
Tex. 3			Region[b] 3		Kan. 3		Tenn. 4		
Ohio 3							Fla. 3		
							Md. 3		
							Va. 3		
							Region[b] 3		
Total Mentions[c] 83	28	65	59	66	80	76	74	42	57

B. States That Usually Ask for Advice and Information

Oregon (N = 27)	Arizona (N = 22)	Utah (N = 23)	Colorado (N = 24)	Missouri (N = 23)	Iowa (N = 25)	Michigan (N = 24)	Kentucky (N = 24)	North Carolina (N = 21)	Rhode Island (N = 23)
Wash. 17	Nev. 9	Idaho 12	Utah 10	Iowa 8	Neb. 10	N.Y. 10	Tenn. 11	Va. 11	Mass. 15
Cal. 10	Region[b] 7	Colo. 11	Wyo. 9	Ill. 5	Ill. 8	Cal. 6	Ohio 10	S.C. 8	Conn. 11
Idaho 10	Cal. 4	Nev. 7	Kan. 8	Cal. 4	Wisc. 7	Ill. 5	W. Va. 6	Ga. 7	N.H. 6
Mont. 5	Ore. 4	Wyo. 7	Neb. 6	Minn. 4	Minn. 6	Ind. 5	Ind. 6	Fla. 5	Me. 5
Minn. 4	Utah 4	Mont. 7	Cal. 3	Wisc. 3	Mo. 6	Wisc. 4	Ga. 6	Cal. 4	Vt. 4
Utah 4		Ariz. 6	Mich. 3	Kan. 3	Kan. 6	Minn. 4	Ill. 5	Tenn. 4	
Ariz. 4		Ore. 5	Ore. 3	Tex. 3	S.D. 5	Ohio 4	Va. 5	N.Y. 3	
Conn. 3		N. Mex. 4	Mont. 3		Ohio 4		N.J. 3	Mich. 3	
Md. 3		Wash. 4	Ga. 3		Region[b] 4		N.C. 3	Md. 3	
Neb. 3							Fla. 3		
Fla. 3							Region[b] 3		
Tex. 3									
Alaska 3									
Total Mentions[c] 92	29	75	77	50	77	60	83	62	52

[a]N is number of administrators questioned.
[b]These entries represent general references to surrounding states.
[c]This figure is the total number of mentions by all respondents, including states that do not appear in the table because they received less than three mentions. It is not the total of the column above.

TABLE 9
Index of Approval Scores From Administrators in Ten States[a]

	Oregon (N=27)[b]	Arizona (N=22)	Utah (N=23)	Colorado (N=24)	Missouri (N=23)	Iowa (N=25)	Michigan (N=24)	Kentucky (N=24)	North Carolina (N=21)	Rhode Island (N=23)
	Cal. 26	Cal. 12	Cal. 20	Cal. 16	Cal. 15	Wisc. 16	N.Y. 36	Cal. 21	N.Y. 15	N.Y. 16
	N.Y. 26	Region[c] 7	N.Y. 15	N.Y. 13	Wisc. 12	Cal. 15	Cal. 26	N.Y. 19	Cal. 14	Mass. 11
	Wisc. 13	N.Y. 6	Colo. 8	Wisc. 6	N.Y. 10	N.Y. 15	Wisc. 13	Wisc. 13	Wisc. 8	Cal. 10
	Wash. 7		Mich. 6	Mich. 5	Ill. 9	Mich. 9	Ohio 10	Ga. 6	Fla. 7	Conn. 10
	Colo. 6		Wisc. 5	Ill. 3	Mich. 8	N.J. 6	Penn. 9	Ohio 5	Mass. 4	Wisc. 6
	Minn. 6		Minn. 5		Minn. 8	Fla. 6	Ill. 8	Fla. 5	Ill. 4	N.J. 4
	Mich. 4		Fla. 5		Conn. 4	Penn. 4	N.J. 5	Ill. 4	Mich. 3	Mich. 3
	Haw. 4		Ill. 4		Penn. 4	Minn. 4	Colo. 3	Colo. 3	Ga. 3	
	Ill. 3		N.C. 3		Md. 4	Neb. 4		N.C. 3		
					Fla. 4	Mo. 4				
					Kan. 3	Ohio 3				
					Iowa 3	Ill. 3				
Total Mentions[d]	135	44	109	60	109	106	141	92	82	86

[a]This index is based on the answers to three questions: (1) Respondents were asked to identify "the most important single new program or policy change" introduced in their departments during "the recent past, the last five years or so." Once this was done they were asked follow-up questions including: "Would you happen to know if such a program had already been adopted in other states before it was adopted here in (state name)?" (2) Respondents were asked to describe "the best possible program" for their departments. Once this was done they were asked follow-up questions including: "Do you know of any other states that have developed programs of this kind?" (3) Respondents were asked: "Speaking generally, do you feel that any state governments are outstanding enough to be called 'pioneers' or taken as models by other states, or are the differences so small that no states deserve to be singled out?" If pioneers exist, "Which states are these?" Each time a state was mentioned by a respondent it received one point. All those states receiving more than two points were recorded in the table.

[b]N is number of administrators questioned.

[c]This entry represents general references to "the western states," and "some of the southwestern states."

[d]This figure is the total number of mentions by all respondents, including states that do not appear in the table because they received less than three mentions. It is not the total of the scores in the column above.

with the exception of Kentucky; California is the leading state in the West. Wisconsin's popularity is greatest in Michigan, Iowa, and Missouri, the states in our sample in closest proximity to it. Once again it should be remembered that we are using open, unstructured questions and relying on the ability or willingness of respondents to recall past incidents or volunteer opinions, but even with these reservations, the data in Table 9 indicate a high level of national consensus among state administrators about which states have the most desirable programs.[63]

Interviews with state officials confirm that established modes of communication and evaluation based on traditional ties of region and common culture are persisting, but some of these data indicate that the system may be slowly changing.[64] The widespread consensus we discovered on the quality of state programs suggests that state administrators are developing a broader, national focus based on new lines of communication that extend beyond regional boundaries. The diffusion process is operating much faster today than ever before, especially among those states that have traditionally lagged behind in adopting new ideas. As communication and transportation systems improve and the professionalization of state government increases, the desires of administrators to obtain, maintain, or increase their prestige within a national professional community also grows. Pressures are increasing on even the most isolated and backward states to fall into line with national standards or adopt programs that have gained popularity within developing national professional communities.[65]

SUMMARY AND CONCLUSIONS

Many influences shape decisions by state officials; no two innovations diffuse in exactly the same way. There is resistance to change in every state, even the most innovative, usually stemming from fear of unanticipated consequences that a new policy or procedure might produce. A natural and understandable reluctance to take risks is the principal source of inertia in state governments. Such a formidable obstacle to change can sometimes be overcome if the proponents of a new idea can point to examples of its successful implementation in a comparable setting. As a result, when state policy makers become aware of a problem, usually they look for a similar situation in states where solutions to the problem have been found and emulate these solutions.

The search for policy cues has traditionally been limited to states that the decision makers believe to be appropriate sources of comparison, usually those in the immediate region. This process of emulation and competition has led to the development of regional groupings or leagues of states within which roughly similar levels of public service are offered. The likelihood of a state adopting a new program increases if any other state has already adopted the idea, but it becomes higher still if the innovation has been adopted by a state viewed as a point of legitimate comparison. Decision makers are likely to adopt new programs, therefore, when they become convinced that their state is relatively deprived, or that some need exists to which other states in their league have already responded.

Before states may respond to new programs adopted in other states their leaders must be aware of these developments, so interstate communications are important to diffusion. All states, even those with the highest scores on our innovation index, seem to have substantial ties to their immediate regions, but a small group looks beyond its neighbors and strives to compete with regional leaders from all parts of the country. Policy makers in these national league states are often key members in the professional communities in their policy areas. Their own programs are usually as closely in accord with professional standards as possible, and they are taken as models by administrators in other states who are anxious to receive recognition within professional circles. The professional communities that have grown up during the last thirty years play an important part in defining social needs, proposing solutions for social problems, and generally establishing both the agenda for change and the standards of evaluation for existing programs in their policy areas. New ideas and information are circulated within these nationwide professional communities and from these interchanges policy norms or national standards of administration are established.[66]

The limitations of our data allow us only to sketch the outlines of this national system of policy formulation, emulation, and competition. The system we have described links together the centers of research and generation of new ideas, national associations of professional administrators, interest groups, and voluntary associations of all kinds into an increasingly complex network connecting the pioneering states with the more parochial ones. Much more investigation will be necessary before we can gain a full understanding of this system and its function as a device for controlling the pace and direction of policy development in the American states. Once we know more, it might be possible to prescribe with confidence some changes in the decision-making system, or the creation of some new governmental institutions that might accelerate or redirect the adoption of innovations.

SELECTED BIBLIOGRAPHY

Grodzins, Morton. *The American System.* Chicago: Rand McNally, 1966. The book provides an insightful review of the development of several important policies and underlines the importance of professional associations of state officials as influences on decision making.

Rogers, Everett M. *Diffusion of Innovations.* New York: The Free Press, 1962. A good introduction to diffusion research in other disciplines.

Scott, Thomas M. "The Diffusion of Urban Governmental Forms as a Case of Social Learning." *The Journal of Politics,* 30 (November, 1968): 1091–1108. A good case study of diffusion of innovations in an urban setting.

Sharkansky, Ira. *Regionalism in American Politics.* Indianapolis: Bobbs-Merrill, 1970. A good review of research on regionalism.

Taylor, Donald, W. "Decision Making and Problem Solving," in James G. March (ed.). *The Handbook of Organizations.* Chicago: Rand McNally, 1965. An exceptionally clear review of the literature on decision making that has obvious implications for students of politics and public administration.

Walker, Jack L. "The Diffusion of Innovations Among the American States." *The American Political Science Review,* 63 (September, 1969): 880–899. A somewhat more technical discussion of the argument made in this chapter.

CHAPTER ELEVEN

State Politics and Education

Robert H. Salisbury

In 1961 state and local governments spent 5 per cent of the personal income of their citizens on education. Thirty-six and six-tenths per cent of the total expenditures of state and local governments was devoted to public education. The sum of $112.40 was spent on schools for each person in the nation, and $432.00 was spent for each pupil in average daily attendance in public school.[1] * These figures suggest the magnitude of the education function performed by state and local governments. Only 3.2 per cent of the revenue (1962–63) for elementary and secondary schools comes from the federal government. Education not only involves vast expenditures of money but it also involves many of the major social and political controversies of the mid-twentieth century. Whether the issue is the international competition between the U.S.S.R. and the United States, racial segregation, church-state relations, or "why Johnny can't read," the school system is at the center of the discussion.

We cannot hope to deal with all the important issues that impinge on education or are affected by the school system in a single chapter. We will concentrate on an examination of which states spend more and which states spend less on their schools, and we shall try to explain why. To do so re-

[The author of this chapter did not have the opportunity to revise it for this edition. For that reason the chapter from the first edition is reprinted, supplemented by a Postscript from the author on recent developments in the politics of education in the states. Although the relationships revealed by the original analysis remain, the data on which they are based comes from the early 1960s. The reader may wish to examine more recent expenditure data published by the National Education Association in its annual Rankings of the States. Other current data may be found in the Council of State Government's *Book of the States* which appears biennially. — Eds.]
* [See pp. 597–599 for notes to this chapter. — Eds.]

quires looking at the historical background of today's school systems, the group interests and pressures that operate, as well as interstate variations in expenditure. We must remember that education is a function of both state and local authority, and one question of continuing importance concerns the balance between state and local authority and the conditions under which it changes.

We will examine public higher education and identify interstate variations in this field, which, in terms of interests and political processes, is largely separate from the elementary and secondary school issues. Finally, we will look briefly at some of the major social issues that, though in a sense tangential, are intertwined with the politics of public education.

THE RISE OF THE PUBLIC SCHOOL

The educational system has been the object of important political controversy almost since the first settlers landed on the shores of North America.[2] The extent to which governmental authority should be invoked to require education, make public money available for it, or indoctrinate through the schools is among the oldest American political questions. In 1642, for example, the Massachusetts General Court directed parents to see to it that their children received a basic education, and in 1647 Massachusetts towns were required to establish schools. These initial steps were, in time, taken by the other colonies — with important differences among them — until, by the early days of the Republic, every state constitution included some recognition that education was a responsibility of the state.

The notion that education was a public matter was founded on the conception that among the state's primary duties was the maintenance of religious orthodoxy. Each colony tended to be religiously homogenous, and it was not difficult to accept the view that compulsory public education, under suitable auspices, could reinforce the training received in the church. The result would be a literate population better able to develop the opportunities of colonial life and also more articulate and learned in their faith.

This view had much to do with the initial structures established for school systems. In much of the South the Church of England was dominant and was regarded as the institution primarily responsible for both secular and religious education. School systems were organized for the whole of a colony relying on the episcopal structure of the church for the units of organization, rather than on secular entities like the county. Southern civil authorities were regarded as responsible only for educating orphans or apprentices or other young people unable to utilize the private schools run by the Church of England. In New England, on the other hand, the congregational structure of the dominant religious group lacked any centralized authority through which to establish schools, and so governmental authority was invoked to implement the educational goals of the Puritan ideal.

Despite the early recognition of the principle of state responsibility, however, during the seventeenth and eighteenth centuries local bodies came more and more into effective control of their own educational destinies. In the eighteenth century, especially during the Great Awakening of the 1740s, the growth of religious heterodoxy throughout the colonies undercut the original reason for having publicly supported schools, the propagation of the true faith. If several denominations competed in a colony, then the only acceptable form of public education was local control of schools according to locally predominant sentiment. The result was that colonial or state authority was extensively delegated to county (in the South), town, or district agencies to establish and maintain schools as they chose. Where state monies were provided for local schools they were turned over to local bodies, often even to religious groups, to run the schools according to whatever the prevailing local conditions might require.

Needless to say, the result of such extreme decentralization was that school systems varied enormously in quality. Southern public schools were generally less well supported than those in New England since they were primarily designed as charity institutions. By no means everyone outside the South was agreed on the desirability of public education, however. As a rudimentary class structure began to differentiate those with greater wealth from those with less, the potential impact of public education upon the social structure became a matter of controversy. Groups argued that general public education would destroy the structure of privilege and open opportunity to all or, alternatively, that it would undercut the roots of wisdom that higher status provided and thereby threaten the stability of the social order. Thus, where the school system had been an object of religious controversy, during the first half of the nineteenth century it also became embroiled in the socioeconomic conflicts of the day.

Implicit in both types of controversy was the assumption that education was not a neutral force but one that would benefit some groups at the expense of others. A dominant religious denomination could reinforce its position through public education. A dominant social class might protect its position by resisting public education. In a state with diverse interests — religious and social — public education might languish as each minority feared that schools would threaten their position. It required the growth of new ideas: that a broadly democratic society could allow all groups to pursue their interests; that education could provide skills essential for this pursuit; that schools could be instruments of secular instruction that need not affect directly the articles of religious or group faith; in short, that general public education was possible and desirable in a society of diverse and conflicting interests — for public schools to become a fully accepted part of the American scene.

These articles of public belief were, of course, part of the Jacksonian creed that came to prominence, indeed dominance, in the decades prior to the Civil War. Jacksonian democracy took root more easily, in regard to schools as well as other issues, in the trans-Appalachian West. The growth of genuinely public schools, supported by public money, controlled by public officials, and open to everyone, found relatively easy acceptance in the West. Especially was this true in the Northwest Territory where the Northwest Ordinance of 1787 provided that one-sixteenth of one section of each township be set aside for support of public schools. Similar provisions were included in other federal grants of land in the new states. But frontier life also frequently bred an "anti-book-larnin" spirit. Furthermore, the social and political complexion of the various parts of the new West reflected in many ways the origins of the settlers. Identification with a political party, attitudes toward slavery, inclinations toward religious denomination and constitutional theory, and, not least, attitudes toward schools reflected the divergent conceptions and institutions of New England and the southern states.

Considerable variety had already developed among the older states, as we have seen. Public education was more firmly and widely established in New England than in the South. Moreover, the local school district had been widely adopted to provide for and control New England schools, while the county remained the southern unit of administration. Generally, until the Civil War, publicly financed education in the South — with North Carolina a partial exception — was primarily charity for the poor.

In the North we find Massachusetts enunciating the principle of general tax support for schools in 1789; Connecticut establishing a school money fund from the proceeds of the sales of public land in 1795; New York providing state funds to match local money in 1812. These early efforts, however, fell far short of achieving completely free common schools, and another half-century of effort was required before schools entirely supported by public money were available even to the children of New York.

The Emergence of State Control

The task was not simply to establish the principle of free public education but also to create mechanisms to make the principle effective. The problem of quality in education began to rear its head along with the related problem of equality among districts within a state. Extreme decentralization of the educational function had led to a bewildering variety of pattern and achievement. This was partly a result of the great variations among religious, national, and private academy groups that controlled the schools in particular localities. Partly it was a result of inequalities of resources and commitments to education among various sections of each state. Partly, too, it was a result of the lack of centralized leadership and focus. The key developments of the pre-Civil War era in public education in one way or another all attacked these problems.

The assertion of public control by placing the schools in the hands of public agencies supported by public money was one side of the development. This, in turn, led to a neutralizing of the curriculum by removing its theological elements and underplaying controversial political and social themes. If the schools were to be a public function they had to function on the common ground of social consensus. Further, public control sooner or later meant establishing minimum standards of competence in educational offering. Otherwise, public money would be spent without any standards of achievement to guide the decisions. The effort to raise and equalize standards led to the establishment of state agencies to provide leadership and stimulation. None of these changes occurred easily or without opposition, but by about 1850 all northern and western states had accomplished them, and a few of the states in the Old South had moved part way along the path.

New York led the way in the formal creation of state agencies for educational leadership. The Board of Regents of the University of the State of New York was established in 1784, and in 1812 New York established the first state superintendent of schools. In terms of effective, standard-setting state leadership, Massachusetts under Horace Mann and Connecticut under Henry Barnard were in the vanguard. The Massachusetts Board of Education was established in 1837 and Mann was named as the first secretary. Barnard accepted a similar assignment in Connecticut in 1839. For twelve years Mann used all the devices available to him to raise standards throughout the state. He organized teacher institutes, held public meetings to stimulate lay support, argued his case in annual reports to the legislature, and published the bi-weekly *Common School Journal*. Although there was much opposition to Mann's work — often labeled "Prussianization" of the schools at the expense of local control — Mann and Barnard did succeed in establishing and legitimizing an active role in education for state authority.

In the post-Civil War era the vital decisions affecting both quality and quantity of public education were made increasingly by the states. Although the extent of financial support, the hiring and firing of teachers, and details of the curriculum continued to be decided largely at the local level, more and more educational standards were set by state authorities.

In the postbellum South it was difficult to legislate at all in order to raise educational quality. The southern states had a much weaker tradition of public education and they were now confronted by two further inhibiting factors, dire poverty and the race problem. Not until nearly the end of the century was segregation firmly established, deferring indefinitely the fears of southerners who equated public schools with integration. By 1900 various philanthropic agencies, particularly the Rockefeller-sponsored General Education Board, began their efforts to upgrade southern education, but by this time an enormous gap had been opened between most southern school systems and those elsewhere in the country.

Outside the South, rapid strides were being made. Compulsory school attendance laws were passed as early as 1852 in Massachusetts and thirty-two states had them by 1900. Compulsory attendance presaged many other changes, of course, one of which was the enlargement of the public school systems to include high schools and universities. The high school grew rapidly in the 1870s and 1880s, displacing the older private academies but also serving the ever growing school population of all social levels, instead of only the college preparatory students. This same period, roughly 1865 to 1900, is also the period of rapid growth of parochial schools.

The great growth in school attendance of the post-Civil War era required further development of the mechanisms of leadership and control. By 1880 all thirty-eight states had established a position of chief state educational officer, and all these officers found that their functions were increasing. School consolidation as a means of increasing the quality of education was specifically permitted by Massachusetts in 1869, and by 1910 a majority of the states had permissive consolidation statutes. In some, indeed, substantial consolidation of districts had been achieved. By 1911, a majority of the states had laws relating to teacher certification, and in many states *only* the state could certify a teacher.

An important assist in providing for overall state control of standards was given by the state universities. Beginning with the University of Michigan in 1870 and spreading rapidly to other states, students graduating from public schools accredited by the state university were automatically admitted to the university. Thus, the state school officials and the state universities could work together to establish and enforce minimum standards of teacher training and curriculum that local school authorities were bound to accept.

The ultimate lever for setting standards, of course, was money. In 1890, as now, state patterns of school support varied widely. Generally, in the South the states provided a larger portion and the local units a smaller proportion of the total expenditures than in other parts of the country. The overall level of expenditures, however, was much higher in those states with longer and stronger public school traditions: New England, New York, and the upper Middle West. In addition, the states where Progressivism was strong expressed that ethos through generous support for schools. But the growth of large urban centers within many of these states led to new sources of variation and complexity in educational systems and new sources of conflict over the kind of program and the means of support to be used.

We will examine the present patterns of state support for schools later in the chapter. Suffice it to say for the moment that the imprint of the historical development we have described is still clearly visible today.

THE STRUCTURE OF STATE SCHOOL DECISIONS

From 1787 to the present the federal government has played a role in public education. Periodically, direct support from federal money or land has been given to the state for schools. In the twentieth century a series of programs has been adopted providing support for specialized educational functions, such as vocational education or foreign language training. Though no legislation providing broad grants to public schools has to date become law, such legislation has been seriously proposed more or less regularly since the Civil War.[3] No federal program or authority, moreover, has provided American education with common administrative structures, standardized curricula, or uniform systems of financial support. Each state has made these decisions on its own authority. Yet it is remarkable that out of the welter of state and local experiences a high degree of consistency has developed in these matters.

The State Board

All states except Michigan, Illinois, and Wisconsin have state boards of education with general supervisory authority over the administration of the states' educational program.[4] In some states a variety of boards may deal with specialized fragments of the program, but by far the most common arrangement is one board with broad responsibility. Until recently, almost all boards were appointed, usually by the governor. During the 1950s, however, the number of popularly elected boards has tripled, from three to nine. As of 1961, in twenty-three states the board appointed the chief state school officer, more than twice as many as in 1947. The tendency seems to be, therefore, to vest increasing responsibility for overall direction of state educational affairs in a board directly responsive to the electorate.

Some boards are important in the decision-making process. The New York Board of Regents, for example, the oldest state board of education, is probably the most powerful, and certainly has the most prestige. Its members are chosen by the legislature for thirteen-year terms! The result is substantial autonomy and substantial power over school administration in New York.

Yet it is unusual for the state board to "run" the schools of a state. As Bailey, *et al.,* point out, state boards

> are less independent forces in their own right than sympathetic responders to the executive and administrative officials they oversee. . . . Strong commissioners of education, exercising forceful professional leadership, have a ready sounding-board and supporting officialdom in their state boards.[5]

The board may serve as an ultimate court of appeals for contending groups or as a device for recruiting lay spokesmen for education interests. But it rarely exercises power to match its authority.

The State School Officer

The operating head of the state system is the chief state school officer, who may be called commissioner or superintendent or something similar. The authority of this officer varies, of course, from state to state, but generally he and his department perform two types of functions: first, they provide specialized technical service, advice, and information to local school officials; and second, they establish and enforce minimum local school standards for curriculum, teacher certification, school construction, and other aspects of school administration. The former category of service is difficult for all but the largest and wealthiest local districts to provide for themselves, and gradually through the years local districts have come to rely on the state department for help in accounting methods, building plans, personnel programs, and a variety of other matters ancillary to the primary concern of education. Of course, the department also provides guidance on curriculum, teaching aids, testing methods, and a host of other matters. In many state departments research of various kinds is carried on to assist the development of educational techniques. The districts most in need of this kind of help and least able to provide for it themselves are the rural or outstate districts, and these generally develop the closest working relationships with the state departments.

The standard-setting functions of the state department involve substantially greater exercise of power and hence more conflict. Much of the authority of the state department derives from the fact that it disburses money to the local districts. Programs of both federal and state aid, whether categorical such as vocational education of NDEA, or general assistance such as the state foundation programs, are administered by the state departments. They set many of the standards by which the money is to be given out, and to get the money the local district must meet the standards. As a result, disputes over how many hours of education courses a prospective teacher must take in order to receive a certificate usually revolve around the state department and chief state school officer. They are rarely legislative issues.

The state departments of education are thus arenas of significant or potential conflict. There are strong tendencies, however, to repress much of this conflict and preserve the appearance of nonpolitical administration, devoted only to elevating the professional standards of education. With state money as the lever, state educational administrators have come to dominate the local districts with respect to standards of recruitment and promotion of personnel and, in the process, have exercised great influence over the training programs for teachers. Recent critics of American education have charged that the result has been to create an "interlocking directorate of educationists" who eliminate intellectual substance from teacher training in favor of trivial courses in teaching methods.[6] Yet the rationale behind standard-setting is the desire to raise minimum preparation, to eliminate the untrained teacher, to assure the technical competence to organize courses and control classes, etc. Moreover, by requiring technical teacher training for certification (and certified teachers for a school to receive state money), more uniformity of experience and identification can be achieved among teachers and this, in turn, can lead to greater professionalism among them.[7] The institutional heart of the system is the state department of education.

The educational administrators in the state departments do not work in a vacuum, of course. They act on behalf of or with reference to "the educational establishment" — the teachers, the teachers of teachers, the school administrators, the school boards, and other groups more or less deeply involved in the issues of public education. State departments and chief school officers are invariably recruited from the ranks of the professional educators. Generally, they come from professional backgrounds that make them sensitive to the needs of the less developed parts of the state school system — the rural areas rather than the metropolitan centers, for example. Insofar as public school educators are in substantial agreement among themselves, the state department may act vigorously and with confidence that its clientele supports its action. Where the clientele is split, the state department may often reflect the split by its own inaction. To understand the administrative politics of education, therefore, it is necessary to look at its clientele.

In concluding this brief discussion of the structure of the decision making, we should discuss the role of the legislature and the governor. They are ultimately the authoritative decision makers on all matters, of course, but, in effect and often explicitly they have delegated considerable authority to the state boards and/or departments. The ultimate issue, however, in education as in so many matters, is finance — how much money will be available, how it is to be raised, and, broadly, who will get it. These are questions that governors and legislators cannot delegate. Accordingly, these agencies are the sites of regular conflicts among educational groups and between them and other interests over money.

MONEY AND SCHOOLS,
THE FOUNDATION PROGRAM

The overriding issue in public education is money. Other questions and conflicts may often be present, too, but nearly all of them are shaped by the consideration of finance. Is there a rural-urban split? This takes the form of disputing how much state aid should go to the cities as against the rural areas. Is there opposition to school district consolidation? This is likely to be expressed as sentiment pro or con some state aid formula. Does the religious question intrude? This is manifested mainly in arguments over aid to parochial schools, parents, or students. Money provides the leverage for upgrading teacher preparation, for improving curricula, and for reorganizing the structure of education.

As we have seen, the historical growth of state responsibility for public education was accomplished largely by the use of money — state money dispensed to local schools. By 1900 every state provided significant aid to local schools, but most did so with bewildering varieties of techniques and programs. Through the years each state had tended to work out ways of either giving special assistance to poor districts or providing incentives to greater local effort, or both. Not until 1905, however, with the publication of Ellwood Cubberley's study, *School Funds and Their Apportionment*,[8] were these common denominators brought into focus. Cubberley conveyed intellectual order to the diverse practices then in existence, and during the next two decades professional educators labored hard to explore further the possibility of articulating general principles to govern state aid to schools. Many of these efforts centered around the faculty of Columbia University's Teachers College as its members assisted state after state in studying present practices and recommending future direction. Men such as George Strayer, Robert Haig, and Paul Mort were especially influential, and their efforts developed the conception of the *foundation program* that continues to dominate the discussion of state aid today.[9]

Essentially, a foundation program is a formula that sets forth the particular pattern of support the state proposes to give its local schools. The formula of one state may vary greatly from that in a neighboring state, but when adopted into law the foundation formula provides a continuing basis for allocating state money. It sets a minimum total amount and prescribes the bases for dividing the total among local districts.

All the formulae in a foundation program stress equalization. Clearly expressed by Strayer and Haig, the equalization principle calls upon the state to assure a satisfactory minimum program in every district. The local district would raise as much of the cost as its resources permit; a wealthy district might finance its entire program. State aid would go to all the districts that were below the minimum in resources. Equalization does not encourage districts to make more than the minimum effort, and many foundation programs include a good deal more than equalization. Nevertheless, the concept of equalization leading toward a minimum educational program throughout the state has been central in developing foundation systems.

The advantages of having a foundation formula are substantial. First, it brings system and order, though often of a very complex kind, to the business of state aid to local schools. The rationale underlying the state programs is made explicit, the relationship of state to local programs is clearly set forth, and, in the process, a very large part of the discussion of educational policy is converted, by formula, into dollar values. With a foundation program, it is possible to set a figure of, say, $300 per pupil in average daily attendance as the desired minimum, compare this with other states, assess the revenue requirements necessary to meet the figure, evaluate local district support, and, in short, make concrete and tangible a host of thorny policy questions.

The second great advantage of the foundation concept is that once a formula is written into state law, further discussion can be centered on the simpler issue of more or less aid, rather than ranging over all the possible combinations of support programs that might be possible. The foundation program concept has greatly simplified the agenda of state policy making for the public schools. It has also simplified and made more manageable the political struggles over state aid to schools. To those groups with the greatest active interest in the issue, the professional educators, this is a great advantage indeed.

Having said this, however, it is necessary to repeat that states vary considerably in the particulars of the programs they have adopted. Mort, *et al.,* concluded that eleven states rely almost wholly on flat grants with virtually no equalization included.[10] Nine states provide little except equalization. The other states range between these two extremes. These two elements, equalization and flat grants, are the basic ingredients of state aid regardless of the formula used, and the rest of the formula will then be devoted to indicating how much there will be of each and how the dollar amounts are to be computed.

The flat grant may be one of several kinds. It may take the form of a minimum payment made by the state to every district regardless of other considerations. Many states adopted such provisions when their foundation programs went into operation in order to avoid a net loss to any district as compared with earlier patterns of state aid. In other cases, the flat grant may be provided in order to assure that wealthy districts receive some state money, thereby persuading their legislative representatives to support equalization money for the poorer parts of the state. A third aspect of flat grant payments, or at least of payments not based on equalization needs, is the payment for incentive or as reward. A variety of such payments exist to encourage the local district to undertake more than a minimum program by adding state money to the additional local money raised. Generally speaking, the poorer parts of a state desire that the foundation program emphasize equalization while the wealthier sections, which usually include the metropolitan areas, seek larger flat grants and incentive payments. Once a balance is struck, however, and a program is passed, strong pressures maintain the basic formula.

GROUPS AND INTERESTS

It has been fashionable for critics of contemporary American education to blame the shortcomings of the system on an interlocking directorate of professional educational groups and interests, often labeled the "educationists." [11] The educationists are said to dominate the colleges of education where teachers are trained. Their ideas command the allegiance of practicing teachers and administrators and shape public policy decisions. The educationists determine who shall teach and what shall be taught. The critics often go on to allege that this tightly knit group is incompetent to wield this massive power in the public interest. These assertions make it clear that we must look at the question of power and its distribution among education interests.

The amount and concentration of power over public policy possessed by professional educators varies considerably from state to state. As with most conspiracy theories of politics, that employed by the critics of education fails to do justice to the complexity and variety of educational interests. At the same time, there are kernels of truth in the arguments also. Considerable uniformity of policy demands among the fifty states grows out of widely shared values that were shaped by a few intellectual pioneers and that are sustained, at least in part, through an organizational framework encompassing the whole country.

The Innovators

In the northeastern states it is widely acknowledged that George Strayer, Paul Mort, others from Columbia University's Teachers College, and Alfred Simpson from Harvard were responsible for much of the content of state actions affecting education.[12] Over the past half-century these men directed research on what was happening in education to establish empirical bases for alternatives. They articulated formulae for new policy proposals, including the whole idea of the foundation program. Not the least contribution, they trained scores of professional educators who moved into academic posts in other universities and into state administrative posts, and from both kinds of positions the disciples spread the doctrines. In many states, of course, the Columbia or Harvard men were not directly involved, though the number of states in which they did serve in an official advisory capacity is remarkable. But it is fair to say that the intellectual shape of educational policy throughout the country was given in outline by these innovators. From them came the ideas of equalization aid and the guaranteed minimum program that are the bases of the foundation approach. These same forceful leaders were among the principal spokesmen for the movement to upgrade teacher preparation, and, again, the people they trained carried this gospel throughout the land. Nor can one forget the enormous impact of John Dewey upon the curriculum.

A recognition of the influence of these innovators, however, does not commit us to the position that today Columbia Teachers College dominates the American educational scene. In most states we hear neither direct nor indirect reference to the intellectual roots of the policy disputes. Indeed, the innovators of the 1960s — those who advocated significant changes of direction in educational policy — were largely from outside the "educational establishment." Interestingly, in the published studies dealing directly with state politics and education we find few references to James Conant, Arthur Bestor, Hyman Rickover, or the other intellectual gadflies of American education. The ferment that they and other innovators in the teaching of mathematics and science have helped create conditions the atmosphere within which state governments make their decisions about schools. The decisions themselves rarely have to do with curriculum, and on the matter of finance or reorganization the "lay" critics have been much less vocal. Conant's work on teacher education does go to the heart of an important state-determined policy area — certification. It may therefore find its way into the hands of legislators, but if so it will be exceptional.

The Teachers Associations

Most of the continuing efforts to gain and exercise influence over state educational policy are made by organized groups. Foremost among these groups and active in nearly every state is the state affiliate of the National Education Association. State affiliates go by various names but invariably they are the largest and most active group dealing specifically with questions of public school policy. Nearly two-thirds of the people professionally employed in elementary and secondary school work belong to one or another of the state teachers associations. Membership is much greater proportionately in outstate areas than in cities, however. In seven of the largest cities, for example, only 13 percent of the school people belong to the state association.[13]

The state associations usually speak for both classroom teachers and school administrators, though in some states the latter have their own organization. Many teachers hope to become administrators eventually and refuse to see a sharp distinction between the two roles. Generally the state teachers associations have reflected this view, as does the NEA. Rather than conceiving of teachers as workers and superintendents or school boards as bosses, the NEA position is that the educator is a professional person with a special commitment to his function in society — educating the young.[14] This conception has policy consequences. Many state teachers' associations have been relatively inactive in seeking teacher welfare legislation, such as tenure protection or fringe benefits. Partly for this reason the state associations have lost members in many large cities to local chapters of the American Federation of Teachers (AFL-CIO). The latter tend to take a trade union view of the teacher, bargain hard for economic benefits and job security, and use the traditional weapons of the union including the strike.

In the state political arena the AFT groups have so far demonstrated little except an ability to needle the NEA group into going farther on teacher welfare than it might otherwise have done. If the union continues to grow, however, it will represent a real threat to the "spokesman-for-education" role presently held by the state teachers groups.

The Other "Schoolmen"

In many states a continuing effort is made by "the schoolmen" to achieve a united front. Much of their ability to shape the content of public policy rests on their status as experts in the field. For a group representative to be able to claim expert status, he must not be challenged by opponents with equally professional credentials. Later on we will examine some of the mechanisms for securing agreement among school interests, but we should note here that this partly accounts for the tendency of school interests and groups to pool their resources, often under teachers association leadership. We have mentioned the tendency of administrators to merge with teachers in a single group. Where administrators have operated separately, as in Michigan, for example, the teachers association has moved sharply in the direction of making greater demands for teacher welfare. Indeed, in Michigan the broad conflict over education issues is both intensified by and stimulating to the divisions among educators.

In most states the school boards have separate organizations, and often these organizations have distinct interests to pursue in the state legislature. The boards are likely to be concerned with matters involving the structure of school government, for example, which are of little interest to the teachers. Potentially, the boards and the teachers are opponents in what amounts to a labor-management controversy. Again, Michigan offers an example of considerable direct conflict between the two groups. In many states, however, the school boards and the teachers join forces in behalf of one policy objective that both desire, increasing state aid to schools. In states where more or less formal machinery has been developed to help unify the schoolmen, the school boards are included. Illinois, New York, and New Jersey provide examples. In Missouri the coordination is more informal, with the Missouri State Teachers Association taking the leading role as spokesman and the school board interest playing a supporting role.

Still further removed from the center of activity are the PTAs or their equivalents. They are sometimes given formal representation on coordinating committees, as in New York and New Jersey, but their role seems generally confined to providing the appearance of lay support in large numbers for the professionals' recommendations.

Other school groups are visible in some states but participate on a more specialized basis. For example, in Michigan the county superintendents constitute a separately organized group devoted primarily to defending the functions of, or finding new duties for, the county superintendents. In many other states these officials are active in matters of reorganization, and frequently they are significant members of county political groups. Thus, they are often influential with legislators on the specific questions related to their self-interest.

Another specialized education interest, though often with little influence in the state arena, is the big-city school system. Many of these systems are largely autonomous in their governmental structure, separate both from other school systems in the state and from the political system in the city. Therefore the city's legislators are often relatively indifferent to the desires of the city's schoolmen. The problems of the latter are often special, unlike those of nonmetropolitan schools. The spokesmen for education at the state level are leaders of groups with little strength in the large city. The result is that the big city schools get a less sympathetic hearing in many states than do the outstate schools. Again, coordinating mechanisms in New York and Illinois include the city schools as a separate interest entitled to separate representation. Generally, however, the big-city school interests, to the extent that they are dependent on increased state aid for meeting their problems, are in a weaker bargaining position than other schoolmen.

Associated Interests

The politics of education encompasses a broad range of specific questions frequently involving the direct interests of groups not primarily associated with education itself. For example, a bill to provide special counseling for delinquent children in the schools may draw its principal support from social workers. A bill to loosen the requirements for auditing school accounts may be opposed by the association of certified public accountants. And a bill to provide state aid to bring symphony concerts to the public schools may be introduced at the instigation of a metropolitan symphony society seeking a way out of its perpetual financial crisis. While all these groups may participate in disputes over particular bills, they are not part of the continuing process of decision making whereby the major shares of state resources are assigned.

We should not conclude, however, that no noneducational groups are directly involved in school issues. Business, labor, and farm associations are relevant in most states to a wide range of the major issues. Certainly they are a part of the process of making public school decisions. Their involvement varies from state to state, both in the extent of impact and the mode of participation. For the most part, these groups become active because the issue of the state's role in education is so largely a question of finance. How much tax money is to be made available to schools and how is it to be raised? Schoolmen are generally inclined to say, "We'll take any live program." Any tax proposal with a reasonable chance of passage is likely to get their support. But labor groups may oppose increased sales taxes or cigarette taxes, while business groups oppose programs that depend on the income tax for financial support. Farm associations are often major spokesmen for nonmetropolitan interests of various kinds. They are likely to oppose any program that may increase the tax burden on real property. They may also take an interest in school consolidation, working to slow down the rate at which small rural schools are abandoned in favor of a larger unit.

None of these groups would allow itself to be put in the position of seeming to oppose schools per se. Schoolmen would always insist that these groups were all friends of the schools, and that any disagreements were minor squabbles over the means to achieve ends that all desired. Nevertheless, decisions to be made are always about means, and the disagreements are often significant barriers to what the schoolmen want. The rhetoric with which the schoolmen advance their cause stresses the consensus among all the interests about the value of education, but they cannot escape the necessity of striking a specific bargain in each state with the interests active in that state's political system.

In cataloging interests we must note, finally, groups that have so far played only a small role in most states but whose presence is often noted and frequently reacted to by persons with authority to decide school questions. One such group is the Catholics. Bailey and his colleagues concluded that "there is no evidence whatsoever to suggest that the Roman Catholic Church has been a depressant upon state aid to public education," [15] although the church might have had some such impact at the federal and the local levels. There have been efforts by Catholics, the Citizens for Educational Freedom being one organized group involved, to secure state aid for transportation, books, and the like for children attending parochial schools. These efforts have been sporadic and have had varying degrees of success. What must be recognized, however, is that schoolmen in many states believe that the religious schools and the families whose children attend them pose a *potential* problem of great seriousness. In Illinois, for example, it was found that "the real controversial questions — those dealing with religion, race, federal aid, etc. — are just never brought up. . . . They are too controversial and would divide us." [16]

The sense that these questions are too hot to handle can be translated into some specific strategies for dealing with educational issues. The major one is the strategy of letting the big city schools work out their own problems apart from the rest of the state. Most blacks and a large proportion of Catholics are inside the big cities, and by granting local autonomy the state schoolmen may also avoid the divisive issues of race and religion. In turn, by avoiding divisive issues schoolmen improve their chances of maintaining the united front they need to support their claim of disinterested expertise.

A further aspect of this issue is that in many states schoolmen are strengthened in their commitment to the nonmetropolitan part of the state by this fear of the divisive potential of the social composition of the big cities. The fear may be reinforced by a suspicion of organized labor and occasional conflict with the unions over, for example, a proposed increase in the sales tax. When the teachers' union is strong there is a further basis for schoolmen, meaning usually the NEA affiliate, to regard the cities with suspicion.

Bailey and his colleagues are probably correct, not only for the Northeast but for states in general, in saying that the parochial school issue has not held down state spending for public schools. Neither has the race issue, as such, had a direct impact in nonsouthern areas.* But in a variety of subtle and often unspoken ways these issues are an integral part of the process by which state decisions about schools are made. Most observers would agree that they are coming closer and closer to the surface.[17]

---

* It must be remembered that we are discussing *state* action, not local. In the latter arena, of course, the race issue is at the forefront of school affairs.

Bases of Power and the Quest for Unity

The groups we have identified in the preceding discussion all have some degree of influence over the decisions made by the state officials concerning the public schools. On the basis of the studies made of some states it is possible to specify a number of factors that help to account for this influence. Particularly we are interested in the bases of power of the most influential groups, the schoolmen themselves.

The state education associations derive a very substantial portion of their effectiveness from the classic source of influence in a democratic society, strategically placed numbers. There are thousands of teachers and other school people in each state, located in every town in every county in every legislative district. The school people are relatively well educated; they have considerable prestige, especially when the school board members are included; they are part of an organizational structure that alerts them to legislative prospects and does so more effectively than most interest groups because the teachers are easily located in the school itself and, being teachers, are responsive to the written communication of a newsletter. All of these elements combine to produce a group that is alert to its interests and well situated to contact legislators. We must recognize, however, that the access is only potential until skillful leadership transforms strategically placed numbers into genuine power. Leadership is notoriously difficult to identify, much less to measure. Thus, it is difficult to speak confidently about the school leaders, comparing them with other group spokesmen or contrasting leaders in one state with those in another. What is clear, however, is that in some states the school leaders are regarded as extremely skillful. This perception is held by legislators whose positive estimate may partly be based on the tendency of school spokesmen to adapt their demands to what they think the legislators will accept.[18] In other states the school leaders might be less adaptive and more inclined to insist upon the virtue of their claims regardless of the larger political context in which the claims are pressed. When schoolmen are adaptive they and the legislators believe that they achieve all that is possible. Their adaptation is partly a matter of tailoring their demands to fit the larger political context of the moment and partly a matter of personal style. A rural-dominated legislature is more readily influenced by a schoolman whose background and accent are similar to those of the legislators.

Legislators are likely to respond favorably to groups whose claims on state resources are made in tangible terms. That is, a claim made in behalf of excellence is all very well but has no specific content applicable to a legislator's frame of reference. A claim for an additional allotment of dollars for school districts in a legislative constituency or a demand for more money to be used to raise the salaries of teacher-constituents is concrete. Moreover, it has the ring of respectable self-interest. Partly for that reason, schoolmen may get a more sympathetic hearing than, say, social workers or mental health advocates.[19]

Finally, we may note interlocked variables that vary significantly from state to state. The central factor is that of cohesion among the schoolmen — the extent to which they speak with one voice. This factor is often cited in connection with interest group strength. With education interests, however, there is a complicating factor rooted in the drive among educators for professional standing. If schoolmen are to gain recognition as professionals they must behave with the restraint and unity of purpose that characterizes a professional group. To achieve unity among the disparate elements that make up the schoolmen — classroom teachers, administrators, board members, etc. — may often require sacrifice or compromise on goals. As we have noted in discussing the teachers union movement, compromise on teacher interests may reduce the enthusiasm of teachers for their organizational spokesmen, and the whole structure of consensus among the schoolmen may break apart as a result.

Maintaining maximum agreement among schoolmen is a central objective of both the political and professional activity of school leaders. If many competing "experts" are advising the legislature, the legislators are likely to trust none of them. The desire for professional standing leads logically to the quest for unity. So does the notion so widely articulated among educators that education issues are or should be nonpolitical, i.e., beyond conflict. Moreover, schoolmen believe that in unity there is strength, and that the public schools will receive more state aid when schoolmen are unified.

Not least among the factors facilitating unity among schoolmen is the view frequently expressed by legislators that little political advantage can be gained from school issues. In the past decade or so legislative wariness regarding school matters has been a matter not just of indifference but of "avoiding the heat." Many, perhaps most, legislators represent areas where changes in the population and in its expectations have produced pressures on the local schools. Some of these pressures are felt in the state house, and as individuals the legislators can do little to satisfy the demands. If a legislator can turn to a united and presumptively expert group, he may channel the pressure away from himself in a constructive way. Several states have created machinery to try to achieve greater agreement among those with a real stake in state decisions affecting the schools.

Missouri provides an example of the simplest kind of integrative mechanism. The Missouri State Teachers Association has very successfully preempted the field as spokesman for the public schools and has managed to keep the various elements of its constituency — teachers, administrators, etc. — reasonably harmonious. MSTA representatives work closely with legislative leaders, and although they are thoroughly in tune with the norms and folkways of Missouri state politics, MSTA leaders feel that they succeed in getting all the state aid that the Missouri political system is likely to provide. To get very much more would require a striking change in the whole state's scheme of things.

Illinois also achieves substantial unity among the various school interests but employs a highly institutionalized mechanism for doing it. The School Problems Commission, formally established in 1949, serves as the principal agency to screen and evaluate major school proposals before they are sent to the legislature. The SPC includes in its membership state legislators who usually bring a special interest in education to the commission and take a highly developed expertise back to the legislature. Members appointed by the governor have regularly included representatives of the Illinois Education Association, the Illinois Agriculture Association, the State Association of School Boards, the Chicago Board of Education, and often the Illinois Chamber of Commerce. The SPC members have developed a deep commitment to achieving unity among themselves. They tend to avoid the most controversial questions when they can, and try hard to go to the governor and the legislature with unanimous recommendations. For the most part the SPC has been successful in achieving unity, and almost invariably the legislature accepts the commission's recommendations.

Neither Missouri nor Illinois, however, ranks high in the proportion of personal income devoted to public education. Certainly part of the reason is that the whole political system in these states makes it difficult to pass high spending programs. In part, however, it may be that unity among schoolmen carries a price in terms of the level of state aid attainable.

Michigan is an example of a state where the school interests are divided both organizationally and ideologically. Efforts to achieve a consensus program by creating a broadly inclusive education council have broken down completely. Yet Michigan spends a higher share of its income per capita on schools than do Illinois or Missouri. Obviously the factors affecting the level of state support for the schools are more numerous and complicated than the simple issue of unity vs. disunity among the schoolmen, and we shall need to examine these factors further.

Nevertheless, the drive of school groups to achieve not only unity but some predictability in the process of making school decisions — a quest for regularity and normalization — does seem characteristic, even though it may not pay off immediately in getting more state money for the schools. In part, this desire may be linked to the myth that education and politics have nothing in common. To the extent that school groups are unified they may be able to perpetuate this myth, since little overt conflict will arise over state educational policy. The vigor of the myth will, in turn, reinforce the position of professional educators as prime movers on matters of public school policy.

Bailey and his colleagues found that in all the states of the northeast there was at least some evidence of "the urge to coalesce." In Massachusetts there was only a short-lived, *ad hoc* group. In Rhode Island and New Hampshire the state department of education sparked the formation of a broader group. In New York and New Jersey more durable and effective organizations have been established. The "Princeton Group" in New Jersey brings together in relatively informal coordinating or clearing-house meetings representatives of the State Department of Education, the teachers association, the PTA, the school boards, and the superintendents. In New York the New York State Educational Conference Board was created in 1937, modeled after a comparable conference board of farm organizations. Though some nine school groups are formally members, the dominant elements seem to come from the state department, the teachers association, and the school boards association.

How the Public Decisions Are Made

Education policy finally must be determined by the state legislature, often acting on recommendations of the governor, and is therefore caught up in much the same policy-making processes as other major areas of state concern. The generic state decision-making processes are discussed elsewhere in this volume, so we shall note here only distinctive aspects of legislative and executive behavior regarding education.

It is often impossible to separate the governor's impact on public school policy from his general leadership. Much of his control in this area comes as a by-product of his fiscal and budgetary leadership. Thus governors have been known to set a flat ceiling figure for state aid and force schoolmen to work out a formula for allocating that size of pie. When the governor seeks to increase taxes he may try to gain broad public support for the increase by promising a part of it to the schools. Generally, however, the governors are not likely to become involved in the details of state school policy. Except as school issues are entwined in finance, the state executive is likely to pay them only sporadic attention.

The legislature is a far more significant arena for determining the specifics of education policy. The myriad of local school decisions are made here, and usually the governor plays no role whatever on these items. Bills affecting reorganization or even state aid may be hotly controversial in the legislature without invoking the governor's participation. The result is that education is a major item on the legislative agenda with important consequences for the ultimate policy product.

Educational interests, we have seen, attempt to maintain the maximum unity in order to sustain their reputation as experts. Within the legislature also, education questions tend to become the domain of experts. Wahlke *et al.*, found education to be the third most frequently named area of specialization among the legislators of four states.[20] They also found that legislative experts authored more successful bills than nonexperts.[21] Masters *et al.*, found that in Missouri the sponsorship of the *crucial* education bills — those most desired by the schoolmen — was usually placed in the hands of one or two legislators who combined experience and sympathy for school interests with status and prestige among fellow legislators. Moreover, the relationship tended to be quite durable over time. In Illinois the most advanced stage of specialization could be observed as the legislative members of the School Problems Commission tended to dominate the legislature's consideration of school issues almost completely. The greater the controversy, the more difficult it is for the legislative experts to dominate the discussion; as a consequence, education groups and their specialized legislative friends are agreed that intense controversy on school questions is undesirable. Therefore, they attempt to minimize controversy even though it may cost something in short-run achievements.

MONEY AND SCHOOLS: WHO SPENDS WHAT

We discussed the growth of public school systems and pointed out the early origins of regional differences among them. In organizational structure and in strength of public financial support the southern states were quite different from New England, while Middle Atlantic and trans-Appalachian states also developed along distinctive lines. Today, a surprisingly large residue of these early differences can still be observed. Reinforced by economic and social factors of more recent growth, the states tend to support public education in patterns that exhibit interregional variations and intraregional similarities.

Analysis of state support of the public schools is complicated by reporting and measurement problems. The criteria for determining how much a state spends on education are fuzzier than we might expect. Many reports show the amount of dollars spent in the state per pupil in average daily attendance (ADA) in public school. This calculation is well understood and highly standardized since it is used as a main basis for calculating state aid under a foundation program. Also, it is a highly relevant figure in terms of the quality of support given public education in the states.[22] Money spent per pupil is more indicative than money spent per adult when talking about education. Money spent per pupil in ADA leaves out the parochial school children, and this results in striking differences in the relative ranking of many states. New Jersey, for example, ranks second in expenditures per pupil in ADA but twenty-second in school expenditures on a per capita basis.

Expenditures per pupil can only be used for some of the comparisons we want to make, however, since the recent available reports do not distinguish between the support per pupil in ADA that the state government provides and the support given by local governments in the state. Clearly, if we are to assess the role of the state, we must differentiate between state and local effort, but to do this we must employ data on per capita expenditures rather than per pupil expenditures.*

A possible further complication might be introduced if, in comparing states in expenditures for schools, we accidentally hit on a year that displayed particularly eccentric patterns. Any given year might show this effect, and we have no way of knowing which year, if any, is "normal." The level of school expenditures in all states has risen rapidly, nearly 300 per cent between 1952–53 and 1960–61, with states and local governments increasing their spending at about the same rate. These increases not only accommodated the growing population but permitted the average expenditure per pupil to rise from $228 to $390. These increases have come unevenly, however; one state moving ahead strongly one year, another state catching up two years later. To examine any single year, therefore, might lead to misinterpretation based on short-run fluctuations. This analysis rests primarily on 1960 to 1962 data. The above-mentioned strictures apply to these years as to others, but state and local expenditures per pupil in ADA during 1961–62 were discovered to be highly related to expenditures in 1937–38.† At least between those two academic years the variation in rela-

---

* Per capita state and local expenditures for local schools (1961) and per pupil expenditures (1962–63) show a rank-order correlation of .74. Although this is quite high, there are some striking variations in rank for particular states. These will be noted in the discussion below.

† The rank-order correlation coefficient is .91.

tive position of the states was slight, reflecting a tendency for short-run fluctuations in school spending to be cancelled out in the long run. States retain their relative rankings because the rankings are consequences of certain durable long-run characteristics of the states.

The most striking finding with respect to support of public education is its dependence upon wealth.[23] The richer the state the more its spends on schools,* and this is particularly the case in the less urbanized states.† If we control for income, on the other hand, neither urbanization nor party competition seems to affect the level of expenditure,‡ confirming the findings of Dawson and Robinson.[24] The only point we may add to their analysis is that in the highly urbanized states even income does not seem to predict expenditure. This may mean that the highly urban states, which are also the wealthiest states, reach a high plateau in school spending. The plateau is a goal to be striven for in less well-to-do states, but once affluence permits its realization, efforts to climb still higher depend on factors such as educational leadership or group activity rather than broad socioeconomic conditions.

Table 1 shows the twenty-seven states that spend money on schools in some rough proportion to their income. Eleven states spend more than might be expected from their income and ten states spend less.

Nine of the eleven high spending states are upper midwestern and western with a tradition of Progressivism that is associated with a strong commitment to education. We shall also take note of this tradition in connection with the rise of the state university since several of these states were also prominently among the leaders in developing public higher education. The low spenders have no such geographic bonds, and we must look elsewhere for whatever characteristics may account for their relative reluctance to support public education.

One possibility would be that the low-spending states are generally conservative in public expenditures and that low school spending is simply one aspect of this conservative ethos. The rank-order correlation of school

---

* The rank-order correlation coefficient is .89. The relationship between wealth and per capita expenditure yields a rank-order correlation coefficient of .65.

† On the basis of per capita expenditures in the sixteen most urban states, the correlation of income and expenditures is .19. In the middle sixteen and lowest sixteen, the correlations are .71 and .77, respectively.

‡ Party competition (using Dawson and Robinson's average ranking, "Inter-Party Competition," 275–276 n. 24) shows a correlation with per capita expenditures of .52. Controlling for income by breaking the state into high income, middle income, and low income categories, the correlations are −.16, .26, and .32, respectively. Following the same procedure for urbanization, the correlations are −.34, .01, and .04.

TABLE 1

Per Pupil Expenditures for Schools in Relation to Per Capita Income, 1961

Expenditures high in relation to income (11 states)	Expenditures proportionate to income (27 states)	Expenditures low in relation to income (10 states)
Minnesota*	California*	Colorado
Oregon*	Connecticut*	Massachusetts
Rhode Island*	Delaware*	Nevada
Wisconsin*	Illinois*	Ohio
Wyoming*	Maryland*	Indiana
Arizona	New Jersey*	Missouri
New Mexico	New York*	Nebraska
Iowa	Washington*	New Hampshire
Montana	Kansas	Maine†
Louisiana	Michigan	Virginia†
North Dakota	Pennsylvania	
	Florida	
	Oklahoma	
	South Dakota	
	Texas	
	Utah	
	Vermont	
	Alabama†	
	Arkansas†	
	Georgia†	
	Idaho†	
	Kentucky†	
	West Virginia†	
	Mississippi†	
	North Carolina†	
	South Carolina†	
	Tennessee†	

*Denotes highest school spenders.
†Denotes lowest school spenders.
Source: National Education Association, *Rankings of the States,* Washington, D.C.: Research Division, National Education Association, 1963. Alaska and Hawaii are omitted.

expenditure and total expenditure is .67, so there is a fairly strong connection between the two. As Table 2 shows, twenty-seven states spend on schools about what we might expect, judging from total state-local expenditure. Eleven states spent more than might be expected; ten spent less. If we combine the material summarized in Tables 1 and 2, several types of relationships emerge, and we can group them in the following way:

1. *School spending highly related to income:* Alabama, Arkansas, California, Georgia, Iowa, Kansas, Kentucky, Maine, Michigan, New Hampshire, New York, South Carolina, Tennessee, Washington, and West Virginia (fifteen). This group includes most of the southern and low-income states plus several of the most wealthy.

TABLE 2
Per Pupil School Expenditure in Relation to Total State and Local Government Expenditure, 1962

School expenditure high in relation to total government expenditure (11 states)	School expenditure proportionate to total government expenditure (27 states)	School expenditure low in relation to total government expenditure (10 states)
Connecticut*	California*	Colorado
Illinois*	Delaware*	Montana
Wisconsin*	Minnesota*	Nevada
Maryland*	New York*	North Dakota
New Jersey*	Oregon*	Vermont
Rhode Island*	Washington*	Louisiana
Indiana	Wyoming*	South Dakota
Ohio	Arizona	Utah
Pennsylvania	Iowa	Idaho†
Missouri	Kansas	Maine†
Texas	Massachusetts	
	Michigan	
	New Mexico	
	Florida	
	Nebraska	
	New Hampshire	
	Oklahoma	
	Alabama†	
	Arkansas†	
	Georgia†	
	Kentucky†	
	Mississippi†	
	North Carolina†	
	South Carolina†	
	Tennessee†	
	Virginia†	
	West Virginia†	

*Denotes highest school spenders.
†Denotes lowest school spenders.
Source: National Education Association, *Rankings of the States, 1963,* and Council of State Governments, *The Book of the States, 1962-63.* Alaska and Hawaii are omitted.

Perhaps it may be said that in these states a normal proportion of the state wealth is spent on schools.

2. *School spending high in association with generally high expenditures:* Arizona, Minnesota, Oregon, Rhode Island, Wisconsin (five). These states all provide a generally high level of public services, ranking higher in spending than in income. Education fully participates in the results.

3. *School spending high in relation to income, low in relation to expenditures:* Louisiana, Montana, New Mexico, North Dakota, South Dakota, Wyoming (six). In these states most public services are generously provided for. Some of this generosity spills over to benefit the schools, but schools trail other functions in money received. The Great Plains concentration in this category is patent.

4. *School spending low in relation to income, high in relation to expenditures:* Massachusetts, Missouri, Ohio, Virginia (four). These states are generally rather conservative in fiscal affairs, significantly less so with regard to their schools than in other areas, but low spenders for schools, nevertheless.

5. *School spending a function of income, high in relation to expenditures:* Illinois, Indiana, Maryland, New Jersey, North Carolina, Pennsylvania, Texas (seven). These states are conservative in non-education functions but support public schools in rough proportion to their respective incomes.

6. *School spending a function of income, low in relation to expenditures:* Connecticut, Idaho, Mississippi, Oklahoma, Vermont (five). These states are high spenders in some areas but neither high nor low in education.

7. *School spending low in relation to income, consistent with expenditures:* Delaware (one). Although Delaware falls in the highest quartile of the states in expenditures, it ranks several places lower in spending than it does in income.

8. *School spending low in relation to both income and expenditures:* Colorado, Florida, Nebraska, Nevada, Utah (five). These states seem to single out education for particularly penurious treatment. Utah, however, has a very high proportion of school-age residents and on a per capita basis its school expenditures rank third rather than thirty-fourth! Nevada jumps from nineteenth to fourth when looking at per capita expenditure, and Colorado's position also improves. Florida and Nebraska are low spenders by either measure.

These eight categories continue to display certain regional patterns. In the South, the upper Midwest and Plains, and the Far West considerable homogeneity is apparent. Yet the differences are striking within, as well as between, regions. The groupings are too numerous and each is too small to permit useful statistical tests to determine what common factors, if any, may bind each group together.

We must make still another breakdown of states in order to determine in which states the local governments provide the bulk of the school money and where the state authority bears the larger share. To a considerable extent, state expenditure and local expenditure are inversely related.* We would expect to find this since expanded state aid has been predicated on foundation assumptions and has sought to equalize educational opportunities in the state at an acceptable minimum level. The less the local units spend, the more the state must help.

---

* The rank-order correlation is —.47, using per capita expenditures rather than expenditures per pupil.

Generally speaking, in the wealthier and more urbanized states, the local governments provide much the larger share of the school money. Income correlates with per capita local expenditures for local schools at .5, with state expenditures for local schools at −.02. Moreover, in the sixteen least urban states, income correlates with local expenditures at .86, with state expenditures at −.73. This is broadly true within each state as well, and we may recall the point made earlier that schoolmen tend to speak primarily in behalf of the outstate parts of the state. In part, however, these relationships may be the result of another kind of regional-historical factor. The strength and longevity of local school support in New England is great. We noted its early origins and connections with the growth of religious diversity. This tradition grew hardly at all in the antebellum South, and after "The War" extreme poverty delayed the expansion of local school systems still more. Public education did not really come to maturity there until substantial state-aid programs had begun to supplement local efforts in other parts of the country. Naturally, the state's role was proportionately larger. In states such as those in the upper Midwest, the New England pattern of strong schools, locally supported, was given early and continuing support by successive generations of settlers.

Table 3 shows the contemporary pattern of state-local relations. This pattern, moreover, is remarkably durable over time. Mort et al., found that between 1890 and 1956 the proportion of local school money coming from the state increased in most states; eighteen states provided 30 per cent or more of the money in 1890, while thirty-one states provided that proportion in 1956. Only a few states changed their support relative to other states, however, and Mort concluded that "the posture of the several states in regard to state support had already become fairly well fixed by 1890." [25]

The factors associated with relative changes in state aid as against local school support are not entirely clear, but some tendencies can be identified. The historical picture shows state aid increasing in relative contribution most strikingly during economic recession. Thus, total state and local expenditures for schools increased about 10 per cent between 1930 and 1940, but local support decreased. We observed earlier that state aid is proportionately high in the poor southern states. Conversely, in periods of prosperity, past and present, state aid increases but local support for local schools increases faster. Thus the state's role with respect to education tends to be that of supplementer; it is strongest in poor states or in general economic recession. Again, this is true not only between states but within each one, as the state program tends, albeit imperfectly, to give primary attention to raising up the poorest districts.

There are individual state exceptions to this broad pattern, of course. Delaware, for example, has provided almost all of its school money from the state, virtually treating the entire state as a single district. Nebraska, on the other hand, has a strong tradition against state expenditure and provides well over 90 per cent of its school money locally.

In summary, we may say that the most important factor in determining state spending for local schools is income, but historical tradition, manifested in regional groupings of states, also plays an important role in conditioning the perspective with which state decision makers view the school needs of their state. Finally, the special circumstances of each state's political system affect education issues as they affect all the decisions made in the political arena.

TABLE 3

Per Capita School Expenditures by State Governments in Relation to School Expenditures by Local Governments, 1961

State expenditures high in relation to local expenditures (22 states)	State expenditures proportionate to local expenditures (6 states)	State expenditures low in relation to local expenditures (20 states)
Minnesota	California*	Arizona*
Nevada	Michigan	Oregon
New York	Connecticut	Colorado*
Utah	Idaho	Montana*
Wyoming	Rhode Island	North Dakota*
New Mexico	Virginia	Indiana
Washington		Maryland
Alabama†		Utah†
Delaware†		Iowa*
Georgia†		Wisconsin*
Louisiana†		Nebraska*
Oklahoma		New Jersey*
Pennsylvania		South Dakota*
Texas		Kansas*
Florida†		Illinois
West Virginia†		Massachusetts
North Carolina†		Ohio
Mississippi†		Maine
South Carolina†		Missouri
Tennessee†		New Hampshire
Arkansas†		
Kentucky†		

*Denotes highest local school expenditures.
† Denotes lowest local school expenditures.
Source: National Education Association, *Rankings of the States, 1963.* Alaska and Hawaii are omitted.

PUBLIC HIGHER EDUCATION

The role of the state in higher education followed a cycle similar to that regarding the common schools.[26] In colonial times it was common for the government to appropriate funds for privately established colleges. Harvard, for example, received public money on more than one hundred occasions before 1789. Williams College received as much from the state between 1793 and 1823 as from private sources. Indeed, in many eastern states, the legislatures continued to support private colleges well into the twentieth century. A convenient date to divide this intermixture of public and private money and authority from the later growth of exclusively public institutions is 1819. In that year the U.S. Supreme Court held that the state of New Hampshire could not alter the terms of the charter of Dartmouth College.[27] The state, therefore, could not take over private institutions and convert them to public facilities.

> The Dartmouth College decision, by encouraging college-founding and by discouraging public support for higher education, probably helped to check the development of state universities for half a century.[28]

Following the Dartmouth decision there was a great wave of private college founding, particularly under the auspices of the various religious denominations. Sectarian colleges could not be given state aid without inviting conflicts among all the rival denominations. The more secular institutions, such as Harvard, lost their claim to state support as they sought to broaden their geographical coverage by attracting students from other parts of the country. As a result, public higher education languished. In 1834, for example, the Missouri legislature petitioned Congress to be allowed to use money earmarked for universities in the common schools. By the Civil War era the concept of public support of higher education, especially of private universities, was regarded as an insidious threat to the American way. Opposing the creation of a tax-supported national university, President Charles Eliot of Harvard said, in 1873, that "our ancestors well understand the principle that to make a people free and self-reliant, it is necessary to let them take care of themselves, even if they do not take quite as good care of themselves as a superior power might." [29]

In pre-Civil War America, therefore, the college had become a private, often sectarian institution and, moreover, by maintaining a relatively rigid classical curriculum, had become largely alienated from the Jacksonian temper of public opinion. It was primarily in the South that the state university achieved a firm footing in the antebellum years. There the colleges served as centers of cultural adornment, buttressing the social status quo. Accordingly, state-supported universities could exist as minor luxuries of a distinctive socioeconomic system. But, while they existed, they did not grow or serve a broad audience. And in the post-war era the universal poverty of the South afflicted its colleges as it did the rest of southern educational institutions.

In the West conflicting forces were at work. Land grants had long been used to support higher education, the culmination being the Morrill Act of 1862. In the East most states were slow to respond to the stimulus to create or expand public higher educational facilities. West of the Alleghenies, however, the Jacksonian spirit was stronger, and many dirt farmers looked askance at universities. The prospect of college-trained or "fancy" farmers and mechanics produced by state universities supported by Morrill Act funds was by no means regarded as an unmixed blessing. Middle-class reformers sponsored technical institutes both for farmers and for urban dwellers but met with an indifferent response. It was not until "practical science" research began to pay off in the immediate post-Civil War period that broad popular approval was achieved. The heirs of the Jeffersonian ideal of public higher education for large numbers of people, men such as James B. Angell of Michigan, were successful in articulating and selling the notion of state-supported higher education. Under their leadership

> the growth of a body of applied agricultural science, the experiment stations, farmer approval, and federal and state assistance all fed upon one another, helping to develop the land-grant colleges into a significant educational movement.[30]

As we have noted, the state universities led the way in creating public secondary schools. For a time most of the universities relied on college preparatory programs that they themselves operated to bridge the gap between the common school and college. Beginning with Michigan in 1870 the university's accreditation of state public schools so stimulated the expansion of public high schools that the preparatory school became largely unnecessary.

The state university also led the way toward introducing modern subjects into the college curriculum and broadening the curriculum of the high school as well. By 1910, for example, the University of California accepted thirty different subjects for admission credit while Yale and Princeton accepted only thirteen.

In the twentieth century, of course, the state university systems expanded enormously, especially in recent years. Even in this burgeoning, however, we can still observe the regional differences that emerged nearly a century ago. The midwestern states were in the vanguard of the state university movement. In Michigan, Wisconsin, and generally throughout the Great Plains service-oriented higher education came to be one facet of the Progressive spirit. The state of the West likewise reflected this ethos. The South lagged behind for its own special historical reasons, poverty and the race problem combining to slow down the growth of all public educational institutions. In the eastern states the numerous strong private universities perhaps made state institutions less necessary than in the West. Many eastern universities received mixed public and private support — some like Cornell and Pennsylvania still do. The result was that the concept of strictly public institutions of higher learning grew much more slowly in the seaboard states, and state support was consequently modest. Only in the last decade has New York, for example, begun to operate a full set of state universities. The regional differences may gradually disappear but they and their historical roots remain visible today.

Higher Education Expenditures

In this field the historical patterns that have emerged run parallel to the patterns of support for local schools, i.e., the states have tended to develop a kind of state perspective regarding education that conditions the level of support given to both higher education and the public schools. Table 4 relates state expenditures per capita for higher education to those for public schools. The result is that on a per capita basis there is a .68 correlation in rank orders among the states on the two types of expenditures. But expenditures for higher education bear a much lower relation to local support for local schools (.39) or state support for local schools (.28). Moreover, higher education spending is unrelated to income (.03), although in the least urbanized states there is a greater association (.49). Higher education expenditure is unaffected by party competition (.03) though again in the less urban states there is some relationship (.54). Urbanization bears a somewhat negative relation to spending for higher education (−.34). Yet all of these relationships seem to be largely the result of the strong regional variations in the traditional strength of public

TABLE 4

*Per Capita Expenditures for Higher Education in Relation to Per
Pupil Expenditure for Public Schools, 1961-62*

Expenditures for colleges high in relation to public school expenditures (20 states)	Expenditures for colleges proportionate to public school expenditures (14 states)	Expenditures for colleges low in relation to public school expenditures (14 states)
Colorado	California*	Delaware
Kansas*	Washington*	Minnesota
Michigan*	Wyoming*	Wisconsin
New Mexico*	Oregon*	Illinois
Montana*	Nevada	Maryland
Utah*	Arizona	Ohio
Vermont*	Iowa	Connecticut†
North Dakota*	Nebraska	New Jersey†
Indiana	New Hampshire	New York†
Oklahoma	Texas	Rhode Island†
South Dakota	Maine†	Massachusetts†
Louisiana	South Carolina†	Pennsylvania†
West Virginia	Tennessee†	Missouri†
Virginia†	Georgia†	Florida†
Alabama		
Arkansas		
Idaho		
Kentucky		
North Carolina		
Mississippi		

*Denotes highest college expenditures.
†Denotes lowest college expenditures.
Source: National Education Association, *Rankings of the States, 1963.* Alaska and
Hawaii are omitted.

higher education that we noted in tracing the growth of publicly supported
colleges and universities.

The foregoing discussion of state expenditures for higher education
may tend to imply that state appropriations constitute the sole source of
income for state colleges and universities and that, consequently, the comparative quality of the states' schools may be measured rather directly by
examining the spending figures. Actually, only about one-half of the money
for publicly controlled institutions comes from the state governments, the
rest being derived from student fees, research contracts, endowments, football tickets, and other sources. Various federal programs are of growing
importance, providing nearly one-fourth of the income of publicly controlled institutions. In recent years several states have departed from the
traditional paths of direct appropriation, finding other means to give aid
to public higher education. Many states have chosen to issue bonds for
capital improvements in colleges and universities rather than paying for

them as they were built. The results of these efforts, of course, are to channel more state resources into higher education than the short-run expenditures would seem to report.

The Politics of Higher Education

Public higher education bears little political relationship to elementary
and secondary schools. In organizational structure, in methods of financing,
and in the pressures and politics of decision making, state colleges and
universities are part of a different system from the schools. We noted the
impact of the state universities on the high schools with regard first to
establishment and then to development. Publicly supported colleges have
both trained the teachers and provided the critics who denounce teacher
training. Much of the intellectual innovation in education comes from the
universities' scholars, and the public and private universities are intellec-
tually indistinguishable from one another. Thus, functionally the two kinds
of educational enterprise are closely linked. But politically the differences
are major, indeed.

The governing structures of public colleges and universities vary
widely from state to state, but in virtually every case these structures are
separate from the state departments of education and the chief state school
officers.[31] In some states the governing authority of the universities is
vested in trustees who are popularly elected, but the more common pattern
is to have appointed boards. In the past there were separate boards for
each institution in the state, but in one state after another the enormous
expansion of public higher education has made it necessary to establish
coordinating boards or councils. California has proceeded the farthest in
developing a complex but highly integrated system of colleges and universities in which each institution fits into a broad pattern. As the costs of
education rise, however, other states are moving in this direction in order
to achieve the greatly expanded services required of higher education in
the face of rising enrollments at manageable cost levels.[32]

In many states, however, a unified system on the California model is
far from realization, and the task of getting appropriations from the legislature is pursued through the traditional processes of political negotiation
and bargaining. Although board members have prestige and influence, the
chief spokesmen of the universities and colleges are their presidents.
Whereas the public schoolmen work largely through associations, pressing
their claims through a mass membership, the demands of higher education

are more often expressed by prominent individuals occupying the highly political roles of public university presidents.

The ability of a university, through its president, to command public funds often depended in the past on the specific services rendered by the university to the state and its legislative representatives. A state teachers college, for example, might get money primarily on the ground that it trained teachers for a specific region of the state. Representatives from the several regions could trade off in logrolling fashion, either by having the college representatives get together beforehand to develop a package to present to the governor and the legislature, or by negotiating in the legislature itself. The university served through its service-oriented research, analyzing the mineral resources of the state, developing crop strains suitable for the state's climate, or advising local governments of the state on their personnel practices. Other university functions were appreciated too: admission or special treatment of marginal student-constituents might be of service to a legislator; a winning football team or a fancy marching band stimulated legislative enthusiasm that, in turn, would support research on medieval poetry.

All these considerations are still part of the political foundation of public education. Unquestionably, too, the traditional posture in the state toward education — the value placed on good schools — provides a context within which legislators operate and that context has much to do with the level of appropriations. California, Kansas, and Michigan are simply more generous toward public higher education than Missouri or Connecticut, and variations in the quality of their football teams will not explain the difference.

Support for higher education has changed in recent years, however. First-rate universities have come to be regarded as a positive asset of a state. Their research facilities and their intellectual resources may attract new industry and professional people to locate there. Government contracts for space research may be forthcoming. Moreover, the sharp increase in broad public demands for higher education for everyone requires greatly enlarged facilities. The cultural norms have shifted to require both excellence and universality of public higher education, and legislators have had to respond with vastly increased appropriations.

The politics have changed, too. The tendency toward coordinating boards has already been noted. In many states, however, the inter-university competition is greater rather than less. Many erstwhile teachers colleges have become universities, for example, and have begun to compete for funds directly with the older land-grant institutions. In this competition educational quality is not only a goal but also a persuasive argument for more money. Alumni may be organized, pride in a section of the state appealed to, and both Rose Bowl and College Bowl victories celebrated — all in an effort to get a larger slice of the rapidly growing appropriations pie. Such open competition may be short-lived, however, for the pie cannot always grow, and coordinating mechanisms are emerging to help bring order to each state's system of public institutions of higher education.*

The Junior College

We may conclude our discussion of public higher education by noting the dramatic increase in the number of junior colleges. Publicly supported two-year institutions of higher education have existed since the turn of the century. Only in the last decade or so, however, have they come to perform such an important role in the educational system. Most of the nearly four hundred such colleges derive much of their support from the local communities that are their primary service areas. The state then supplements this support with state money. The result is that for a growing portion of the system of public higher education the state-local relations are similar to those regarding elementary and secondary schools. Junior colleges, of course, are designed to help meet the great increase in college enrollments. As college training becomes more and more universal it may be that a still greater similarity will develop between public school politics and the politics of higher education.

CONCLUSION

We conclude this chapter with a brief mention of some important questions regarding the politics of education that have hardly been mentioned in the foregoing pages. Some of these are major social issues that involve the schools because they are basically social institutions. Foremost among these issues is race.

It is not possible to separate the controversies over race relations from those over education. The historic *Brown* v. *Board of Education* [33] decision involved the public schools as have a large portion of the related cases

---

* In 1957 seventeen states created formal agencies to coordinate higher education. Others have done so since then, bringing the total to about twenty-five.

providing basic interpretations of individual rights to equal protection of the laws. More recently the militant protests of blacks seeking to implement their *de jure* rights with more thorough *de facto* integration, have focused much attention on the schools. Indeed, almost every question of education, in the metropolitan centers at least, has become partially a race question too. That this intertwining will become increasingly relevant to the state politics of education is obvious. We have not examined it here because in the northern states its impact on state decisions is still primarily in the future. In the South, of course, race and education have been intimately bound up for a century, and that fact helps account for the distinctive patterns of southern behavior we have observed earlier.

A second area we have neglected includes more strictly educational issues of intense controversy. Debates over the proper function of the public schools have been carried on seriously for generations and never more vigorously than today. Questions of what a curriculum should include, what facilities a school should have, and how its teachers should be prepared are constantly argued in local communities across the nation. Teacher certification is primarily under state control and thus is involved in the state political system. We alluded earlier to the administrative politics involved in certification and related matters and noted that it was relatively rare for these questions to descend on the legislature for resolution. Money for schools must be provided in competition with all other public functions. Certification and curriculum questions do not involve conflict with non-educational groups, and their resolution largely follows the relative strength of contending interests within the professional education world.* The issues are important, but they are only marginal to the central processes of state politics.

We said little about reorganization of school districts. The justification for omitting this question is that it is so largely accomplished. During the past thirty years the number of school districts has been reduced from 127,422 to 36,880. Consolidation is continuing but in most states without very much controversy. The defense of "the little red school house" once aroused deeply felt emotions, but seldom does it do so now.[34]

Last in our list of omissions is the matter of federal aid to education. The federal government already provides a noticeable portion of the total public school budget. Vocational education has long been supported with

---

* We should not entirely overlook the attacks of strongly conservative groups on school administrators in various communities. For the most part, these controversies have been confined to particular school systems, but in California the issue became statewide in the 1962 election campaign for state superintendent of public instruction.

federal funds. The school lunch program is unchallengeable. The National Defense Education Act of 1958 provided federal help for science, language, and mathematics programs. Substantial sums of money are provided to assist the schools in areas where large federal installations have swollen the public school population. The Impacted Area program, as it is called, provides a sizable portion of the federal money, which in Alaska, Arizona, and Georgia amounts to more than 10 per cent of the total expenditure on public schools.

Existing federal aid programs are significant. Prospective programs expanding federal aid would be even more important. Yet it is most unlikely that any federal programs will relieve the states of the need to provide increasing sums of money for schools. This being so, the connections between state politics and education will continue to be important subjects of public concern.

POSTSCRIPT

No other American institution has been subjected to the tension, the pressures, and the demands for change that the public schools have experienced during the last decade. From nursery school through doctoral programs education has become a battleground for a large share of the contending groups, ideas, and forces in our society.

There are many reasons for the dramatic position of schools in the crises of contemporary life. One of them is size. The expanded birth rates of the 1940s and 1950s brought more children to school. Parochial school systems, hit by rising costs, have closed many of their schools. In the cities especially, the rapidly growing black population sent children to public schools in much larger proportions than European ghetto residents had done in previous generations. Economic affluence underwrote a rapid increase in the college population. The cultural emphasis on academic training as a prerequisite for work led others to demand the opportunity for higher education.

The pressure of numbers had several consequences. One, of course, was that the physical facilities for education had to be enlarged substantially. New campuses have sprung up and old ones have been massively expanded. New schools have been built and old buildings enlarged and renovated. The capital invested in American educational facilities during the 1960s amounted to many billions of dollars.

As education became a growth industry the status of the teacher changed. At every level, but especially in higher education, qualified teachers and academic administrators were scarce in relation to rising demand and, accordingly, their salaries went up. Among public school teachers, self-conscious and often militant organization to press for still further increases has made great headway. Unthinkable a few years ago, strikes by public school teachers are by now not only thinkable. They happen. A slightly delayed result of the growth of education was to increase markedly the "production" of doctorates to staff the new or expanded colleges and universities. Since graduate training is also academically prestigious for a university, each new institution hoped to establish its respectability by instituting graduate programs. Graduate teaching and research add disproportionately to the costs of educational institutions, however valuable they may be on other grounds.

The force of numbers has thus generated pressures for massive additions to the amount of money available for education. Some of these pressures have been directed toward the federal government, and, through the Elementary and Secondary Education Act of 1965 and other measures the federal share of the costs of education has increased. Universities, public and private, have come to depend especially heavily on federal money to support scientific research and graduate training.

Some of the pressures have weighed most heavily on the local school districts. Increases in local school taxes have been dramatic in most parts of the nation. In states that require public approval of the school tax levy the campaigns to boost the levy have recurred nearly every year and have met increasingly stiff resistance. Teachers have not been alone in bringing the schools to a halt. In a number of communities the voters have refused to approve school taxes and schools have closed down for months at a time.

The main demands for school money come from the local districts but much of the money itself comes from state revenue raised through taxes imposed by the state legislature. As local pressures and conflicts have intensified, community activists and professional schoolmen alike have acquired a more sophisticated appreciation of the complex interplay among national, state and local authority in education. The issue is not always money. The local district gets its power from the state. The state prescribes how tax money can be raised and establishes a large share of the rules and procedures by which local school boards, administrators, and teachers must operate. The state mandates the organizational pattern of the schools, sets the district boundaries, fixes teacher qualifications, and prescribes much of the educational program itself. If any of these features is altered it can ease, or worsen, the local fiscal burden. A state requirement that every school have a library, for instance, will cost the local district extra money. A state-funded capital improvements bond issue, on the other hand, may allow some schools to be built without much direct cost to the local district. Under fiscal pressure local school and community interests in many states have increased both the scale of their efforts and the variety of their proposals to get the state legislature to help them. But money is still the heart of the matter and the battle over state funding of education has become increasingly intense as the sums involved go up and the counter-demands for economy grow more insistent.

How have the states responded to this intensification of political conflict over the financing of public education? Most noticeable, perhaps, has been the enormous increase in state spending. But there have been other responses as well. There has been a resurgence in political popularity for public officials who advocate a stronger voice for nonprofessionals in education. Politicians treat schoolmen with less admiration and deference. In recent years they have come to be looked upon less as experts and more as expansion-minded claimants to public money.

This view is associated with another question: How far ought elected public officials direct the course of public education? If educators are truly experts then it is surely foolish for laymen to intrude into the schools and specify how they should be run. But if there are no experts, then public officials can properly take part, as they have done, especially if they seem to represent a substantial section of public opinion. Ample evidence shows that educators have not succeeded in wiping out the educational deficiencies of blacks, Chicanos, or Puerto Ricans. In the schools of slums and suburbs alike there is precious little academic achievement or even elemental peace and good order. Hardly anyone is content; neither parents nor students; neither teachers nor the community. Scores of prescriptions for change have been written, but the cacophony reveals that professional educators can no longer muster sufficient agreement among themselves to persuade others to treat them as experts.

This greater assertiveness regarding education on the part of nonprofessionals has been expressed by several types of public figures. In some states governors have run on a platform of restoring order in the schools. Legislators have jockeyed for power by exploiting public discontent over school costs, teacher militancy, and student demonstrations. There have been other levels of nonprofessional assertiveness, too, however. In the ghettos of some cities black parents and community leaders have demanded a larger share of control over the schools in their part of town. Classroom teachers in several parts of the country have demanded greater control over school policy at the expense of school administration and school boards. Students, learning quickly from the examples of others, have added their insistence on the right to participate in setting school policy.

Nearly all these demands find their way into the state political arena. Sometimes this is because state legislative permission is required to satisfy the demands. Often the demands for change have taken the form of reorganizing the schools, and this invariably requires state action. Efforts to decentralize New York City schools, or alter the authority of the Chicago School Superintendent, or change from citywide to ward election of a school board must be pursued, in part, in the state capital. And always there is the question of money. Many state officials have felt that they had none to spare, but the legal possibility of raising state taxes for the schools has always been present even when it seemed politically suicidal to do it.

Thus, again, state political arenas have been severely fractured by the militant conflicts over public education. But this is only one side of the picture. Another response to escalating costs and political pressures of school policy has entailed efforts to develop comprehensive, statewide plans for educational finance and organization and to build semiautonomous institutions that will coordinate and hopefully control the diverse interests and pressures. The object is to achieve some form of rational long-range planning of school programs throughout the state so as to gain greater efficiency in the allocation of resources. The form of these institutional mechanisms varies and not all states have yet established any. Where they exist, they buffer some of the pressures and shield the legislature by allowing the latter to pass the buck of school finance decision to the special commission. The latter, typically composed of some senior legislators and some notable laymen, is likely to feel less constrained by public demands.

These contradictory tendencies — using education as a focus for political dispute and building semiautonomous mechanisms to work out school policies in a less turbulent atmosphere — underscore an important facet of contemporary educational politics. They are in an extraordinary state of flux. Very little can be taken for granted or projected with confidence into the future. As we noted earlier, there are important, long-term continuities in the patterns of financial support and organizational arrangements in particular states and regions. Present day discontents over school policy are connected to these historic patterns, too, as ghetto protests, teacher militancy, and student demonstrations occur within a context of the unique personalities and circumstances of a specific community.

But there are powerful national, indeed international, forces at work, too. A demand made in one city is quickly known and often imitated in others. An idea propounded on one coast is soon argued about on the other. Much commonality results throughout the nation in the issues that each state and community must face, the proposals made for change, and the rhetoric with which the disputes are expressed.

The balance of political forces at the state level remains very different from that of most local communities. In education the difference shows itself most strikingly in regard to the school-related interests of two groups, Catholics and Negroes. In many states Catholics have sought state aid for their parochial school system and have received some success. In general, however, the degree of subsidy has fallen far short of what has been needed to maintain the parochial system in full operation. Analogous efforts are being made by private institutions of higher education, seeking state funds to avoid financial collapse. Some states have responded, but many have not. Nevertheless, under the pressure of rising costs, the demarcation between private and public education is gradually being reduced in importance.

Black Americans have gained a substantial political voice in most of the nation's large cities, and this has meant considerable influence over local educational policy. Gradually, this influence is being felt also in "close-in" suburbs where blacks have begun to move in significant numbers. But often the school issues most vital to blacks cannot be effectively resolved at the local level, no matter how much control they have. Redistricting to achieve integration must cut across municipal boundaries. Recruiting the best teachers for the toughest ghetto jobs requires salary differentials that cannot be gained without state authority, state money, and statewide political support. In most state legislatures the impact of the blacks, though growing, is still much slighter than is required to achieve ambitious proposals for changes in state public policy.

In these comments we have not generally tried to distinguish the politics of public schools from the politics of higher education. Partly this is for want of space, but partly it is because in recent years the two policy areas, once clearly separate and distinct, have come together. There are differences still, of course. Higher education continues to involve scientific research and therefore industry supports its appropriations. Medical training and football both have constituency support that is meaningful in the legislatures and is quite absent from state public school politics. The balance of imports and exports, native and out-of-state students, is not faced in elementary and secondary education. And protests, riots and demonstrations, while not entirely absent from high schools, have not had the dramatic impact university student behavior has had on state officials.

Yet the features in common are perhaps more important. The changing status of teachers and of students can be observed on every school level. The unsettled character of curriculum and teaching methods characterizes education from kindergarten through graduate school. The growth of junior colleges on a statewide basis provides an institutional unit between the public school and the university, and the design, control, and funding of a state system of these units has built further political links among the historically separate educational levels. The building of new state colleges, universities, and branches has given nearly every section of every state an institution of higher education. In turn, however, these institutions are increasingly administered as a state system rather than simply a collection of regional favorites trading off with one another for state money. The latter pattern is not wholly absent, to be sure, but the trend — and it is a political trend reflected in the attitudes and behavior of state officials — is toward seeing higher education as a comprehensive problem, integrally related to elementary and secondary schools, embracing a broad complex of issues and institutions and requiring planning and action on a statewide, or on a few problems even interstate and regional, basis.

SELECTED BIBLIOGRAPHY

Bailey, Stephen K., Richard T. Frost, Paul E. Marsh, and Robert C. Wood. *Schoolmen and Politics: A Study of State Aid to Education in the Northeast.* Syracuse: Syracuse University Press, 1962. One of two major studies of the politics of state decisions affecting education.

Benson, Charles S. *The Economics of Public Education.* Boston: Houghton Mifflin, 1961. A broad examination of economic relationships in this field.

Butts, R. Freeman, and Lawrence A. Cremin. *A History of Education in the United States.* New York: Henry Holt, 1953. A thorough general survey by two leading scholars in the history of American education.

Glenny, Lyman A. *Autonomy of Public Colleges.* New York: McGraw-Hill, 1959. One of a series of studies of American higher education centered at the University of California.

Masters, Nicholas A., Robert H. Salisbury, and Thomas H. Eliot. *State Politics and the Public Schools.* New York: Alfred A. Knopf, 1964. Provides detailed material on a subject that has received little attention from political scientists — covers Missouri, Illinois, and Michigan.

Moos, Malcolm, and Francis Rourke. *The Campus and the State.* Baltimore:

The Johns Hopkins Press, 1959. Survey of the governing arrangements for public higher education.

Mort, Paul, Walter Reusser, and John Polby. *Public School Finance*. 3rd ed. New York: McGraw-Hill, 1960. Useful survey and guide to more detailed literature. The senior author was a leading innovator in state aid issues a generation ago.

Munger, Frank J., and Richard F. Fenno. *National Politics and Federal Aid to Education*. Syracuse: Syracuse University Press, 1962. An excellent short review of the history and the contemporary struggle over this thorny question.

Rudolph, Frederick. *The American College and University*. New York: Alfred A. Knopf, 1962. An excellent study of the growth and development of the American system of higher education.

The Economics and Politics of Public Education Series, published by the Syracuse University Press, contains ten other titles in addition to the works by Bailey, *et al.*, and by Munger and Fenno listed above. Any or all of these may be of interest to the reader, even though they are not specifically noted in the present discussion.

CHAPTER TWELVE

State Welfare Policies

Richard E. Dawson and Virginia Gray

INTRODUCTION

Public welfare programs are one of the most significant areas of policy making in the American states. Along with education and highways public welfare is a leading object of state expenditures. Within the federal structure welfare policy remains one of the arenas in which state politics substantially determines the issue of "who gets what, when, how." During the year 1968 American state governments spent $8.7 billion for programs of public welfare and social welfare.[1] * This constituted 14 per cent of the money spent by the fifty states during that year.

As have other types of governmental activities, the number and scope of welfare programs and the amounts of public funds expended in the area of social welfare have increased greatly over the past few decades. In 1929 total state and local governmental expenditures for public aid and other social welfare (excluding social insurance programs) totaled only $134 million. Federal expenditures for the same program areas came to $1.4 million.[2] Prior to the 1930s states and their local subdivisions participated in only a few types of welfare activities. There was little uniformity in programs from state to state, and efforts even varied among local units within the same state. Today federal, state, and local governmental units maintain, jointly or singularly, several dozen types of welfare programs. The form and operation of programs is similar from state to state.

Prior to the 1930s active responsibility for and participation in public welfare activities was concentrated in local governments. State governments

---

* [See pp. 599–601 for notes to this chapter. — Eds.]

were only beginning to develop and operate extensive and uniform programs for social welfare. Over the past four decades responsibility for initiating, operating, and financing welfare programs has shifted simultaneously to the states and to the federal government. The federal government, through programs of grants-in-aid, has taken on an increasing amount of the financing of most state welfare programs.

Despite the movement toward uniformity in types of programs and the growing role of the federal government in establishing central guidelines and in financing key welfare programs, the states still vary considerably in the extent and generosity of welfare efforts. State political processes still determine to some extent the amount of payments given to various categories of recipients, the criteria for eligibility, and some administrative arrangements. The great variations in payments per recipient, in the number of persons receiving aid, and in the proportion of need met under various programs reflect the wide discretion held by the states.

In this chapter we will describe and compare the welfare efforts of the American states and identify some of the state conditions and processes that influence state welfare policies. In the first section we present a brief historical overview of the development of welfare policies in the United States, stressing the lingering influence of early Anglo-American tradition formulated in the seventeenth-century Elizabethan Poor Law, as well as more recent developments of state-federal cooperation. In the second section we outline the present scope, structure, and content of state welfare policies. Then, we turn to a comparative description of state welfare efforts, pointing out several different dimensions of state welfare efforts and the considerable variations among the states. Finally, we analyze what characteristics of the American states tend to be related to varying types and amounts of welfare effort. What types of states tend to spend the most money for welfare? Are welfare expenditures and the number of recipients more closely related to the needs of the population, the state's economic capabilities, or political characteristics?

Two points of qualification concerning the content and focus of our discussion should be made. First, we attempt here to portray and compare welfare efforts in all of the American states. This means developing comparable and often gross measures applicable to each of the states. It also means that our analysis does not include detailed or individualized discussion about political, economic, or program conditions of particular states. Nor do we discuss the particular patterns of interest groups, local traditions, and leadership efforts that are a part of each state's welfare activities. Second, in developing measures of comparative state welfare efforts and in the statistical analysis of state conditions, we concentrate on the several public assistance programs in operation in nearly all of the states. Space and data management necessitate this limitation. We stress, however, that public assistance programs are the core of state welfare efforts. They involve the bulk of state welfare expenditures, and most of the interests and controversies pertaining to state public welfare are applicable to these programs.

THE DEVELOPMENT OF WELFARE POLICY

In very simple terms public welfare policies involve the acceptance by the society at large of the responsibility to provide for the basic needs of persons who are unable, for one reason or another, to provide for themselves. The principle that the public treasury should help provide life's necessities for the destitute has long been part of the social law or custom of most societies. This concept has been part of Anglo-American common law for several centuries. In *Commentaries on the Laws of England,* written in the late eighteenth century, William Blackstone stated this principle:

> The law not only regards life and member and protects every man in the enjoyment of them, but also furnishes him with everything necessary for their support. For there is no man so indigent or wretched, but he may demand a supply sufficient for all the necessaries of life from the more opulent part of the community, by means of the several statutes enacted for the relief of the poor.[3]

In the development of Anglo-American public welfare, the early secular concern with public care for the destitute evolved out of the disintegration of the feudal and religious institutions of the Middle Ages. Early concern focused on the regulation of beggars and the control of the movement of laboring classes.[4] By 1572 the English Parliament had recognized the principle of public provision for the destitute and had put responsibility for raising funds for poor relief upon local governments. However, the Poor Relief Act of 1601, the Elizabethan Poor Law, formally and firmly established the nature and techniques of governmental responsibility for the care of the poor. This act codified earlier legislation and practice. It has influenced the subsequent policies for relief of the poor and public welfare in both England and the United States for more than three and a half centuries.

In acknowledging governmental responsibility for the care of the destitute, the Poor Relief Act delegated the provision of aid to the smallest unit of local government, the parish. It allowed for tax funds to support poor relief and to establish workhouses and almshouses. It recognized the principle that relatives have legal responsibility to support impoverished members of their families. It also established residence or settlement requirements to discourage indigent travelers. Through the centuries these basic provisions have generally been written into welfare and relief legislation. Some continue as provisions in current state welfare programs. Only in 1969, for example, did the federal courts declare residence requirements for welfare eligibility unconstitutional.[5] Until that time some form of residence requirement was part of most state welfare provisions.

The early laws reflected the sentiment that poverty is a personal disgrace caused by individual laziness, moral weaknesses, or other individual or personal shortcomings. This underlying notion still influences some welfare provisions and the outlook of many toward public welfare.

The English colonists who settled the North American continent during the seventeenth and eighteenth centuries brought with them the basic principles formulated in the Elizabethan Poor Law. The general public obligation, the reliance upon local government, and the residence requirements are all found in the poor relief provision of Plymouth Colony, which stipulated in 1642 that

> every township shall make competent provisions for the maintenance of their poor according as they shall find most convenient and suitable for themselves by an order and general agreement in public town meeting. And notwithstanding the permission that all such person and persons as are now resident and inhabitant and within the said towns shall be maintained and provided for by them.[6]

By the time the American states attained independence a vague public policy for poor relief was generally in effect. Its most important political feature was that local governments were relied upon to establish, support, and administer welfare programs. The New England colonies had designated the town as the appropriate unit for carrying out this function. Southern colonies delegated relief first to the local parish and later to the counties. Middle Atlantic states assigned responsibility either to township or county governments.

These central features of welfare policy were carried westward as new territories and states were settled. The 1790 statutes of the Northwest Territory and the 1815 statutes of the Missouri Territory contained the principle of local responsibility for poor relief. The states formed from these territories adhered to this principle in establishing their own poor laws.[7]

State legislation dealing with the care of the poor was enacted from time to time, but such legislation merely delegated responsibility to local governmental units or granted them permission to act if they wanted to. This pattern of reliance upon local government existed throughout the nation until the mid-1930s. Table 1 outlines the frequencies with which various local units were responsible for public welfare as of 1934.

By the latter part of the nineteenth century states had begun to develop programs for specialized cases. The earliest form of direct state responsibility had to do with relief for the "unsettled poor" or for those poor or needy persons not classified as residents of any local community. State laws and court decisions, some going as far back as the colonial period, assumed or designated state responsibility for such persons. State governments, especially after the Civil War, also began to adopt programs for disaster relief and for assistance to military veterans. By 1910 all but six states provided for relief of Civil War veterans, and some states also provided for veterans of other wars and military conflicts.[8]

Others who early received direct aid from state governments were dependent persons such as children without parental support, the deaf, the dumb, the blind, the feebleminded, and the insane. Aid for these persons first came in the form of special state institutions, asylums, and homes. Virginia had established a colonial institution for the insane as far back as 1769. Kentucky founded an asylum for the insane in 1822 and an institution for the deaf and dumb the same year. New York opened a House of Refuge for Delinquents in 1826; Massachusetts set up a school for feeble-minded and idiotic youth in 1848. The number of state institutions for the care of various special categories of needy persons grew steadily throughout the nineteenth century. Their establishment was the first major assumption of direct state responsibility for welfare, as distinguished from the delegation of such responsibility to local governments.[9]

TABLE 1
Political Unit Responsible for Poor Relief, 1934

Number of states	Units
24	Counties
7	Counties, townships, and cities
6	Counties and cities
5	Towns (all 5 in New England)
3	Counties, townships, cities, and villages
2	Counties and townships
1	Towns and cities (Rhode Island)

Source: Lucy W. Brown. "Poor Relief Laws: A Digest," American Public Welfare Association, 1934; taken from Brown, *Public Relief: 1929-1939.*

Next, the states established state boards of charity to supervise and inspect the operation of such institutions and programs. The first such agency was set up in Massachusetts in 1863. New York followed in 1866, and within a decade nine other states had done likewise: Ohio (1867); Illinois, North Carolina, Rhode Island, Pennsylvania (1869); Kansas and Michigan (1871); Connecticut and Wisconsin (1873). A few other states set up similar boards during the last few decades of the nineteenth century, but in 1904 only fifteen states had boards of charities. During the early twentieth century most other states moved in this direction. In 1931 the White House Conference on Child Health and Protection reported that only five states did not have a department concerned with general public welfare problems. For the most part these boards merely inspected and supervised the administration of state and local institutions. Only in a few instances did their jurisdiction extend to noninstitutional welfare activities.[10]

With the exceptions of special cases of persons mentioned above, state programs of welfare assistance to the needy outside of institutions, "home relief," were not instigated by the states until the early twentieth century. During this period some states began to formulate programs entailing direct aid to categories of needy individuals such as the blind, the aged, and dependent children. Under these programs needy individuals were granted money or other payments while continuing to reside at home. Wisconsin passed the first such state law involving aid to the blind in 1907. Illinois adopted the first program of aid for dependent children in 1911. Montana and Nevada enacted the first programs of aid for the aged in 1923. Because these programs granted aid to specified groups, they became known as categorical assistance programs. This form of assistance program, later established under the structure of the 1935 Social Security Act, has emerged as the core of state welfare programs.[11]

The adoption of such programs by the states, however, proceeded slowly. By 1934, just prior to the enactment of the national Social Security Act, only twenty-four states aided the blind, twenty-eight states helped the elderly, and forty-two states assisted mothers of dependent children (Alabama, Arkansas, Georgia, Mississippi, New Mexico, and South Carolina had no operative programs of aid to dependent children).[12] Some of the programs enacted were not applicable or available in all counties of the states. Even in states in which these categorical assistance programs had been adopted, they were only partially operative and, on the whole, not very effective.[13]

Despite the severe limitations on their scope and effectiveness, these state programs significantly developed the nation's basic structure of welfare policies. The categorical relief program radically altered concepts and methods of public assistance that had prevailed since the passage of the Elizabethan Poor Law. Basic changes emerged in the criteria by which aid was awarded, the form in which it was given to the recipients, the administrative procedures, and the kind and extent of state government participation.

While direct activity of state governments in the area of public welfare was slow to develop during the first hundred and fifty years of the United States, federal participation was almost nonexistent. No consistent comprehensive welfare policy was formulated by the federal government until the 1930s. The federal government did from time to time grant aid for specific relief in the case of large-scale catastrophies such as floods, large municipal fires, and earthquakes. Such emergency relief, however, was sporadic and did not result in the establishment of any overall policy.[14]

Largely as a result of the efforts of the pioneer reformer, Dorothea Dix, Congress did pass a bill authorizing federal aid in the form of land grants to the states for the benefit of the insane in 1854.[15] This bill was vetoed by President Franklin Pierce in a message that is representative of the prevailing attitude of the federal government toward welfare involvement until the Federal Emergency Relief Act became law in 1933. Pierce maintained that the welfare clause in the Constitution did not give Congress the power to provide for indigent persons. Aid to the insane, he pointed out, could lead to aid to the indigent in general and transfer to the federal government the charge of the poor in all the states. Pointing out that this would lead to the dependence of states upon the federal government, he argued

> that if Congress is to make provision for such objects, the fountains of charity will be dried up at home, and the several states instead of bestowing their own means on the social wants of their own people, may themselves, through the strong temptation, which appeals to states as to individuals, become humble supplicants for the bounty of the Federal Government, reversing their true relation to this Union.[16]

Despite the aid given to states for education by the land-grant act of 1862 and for agriculture by the 1887 Hatch Act authorizing agricultural experiment stations, the reluctance of the federal government to involve itself in welfare aid continued until the fourth decade of the twentieth century.

As it did in other areas of public policy and in intergovernmental relationships, the Great Depression of the 1930s marked a major watershed in the development of public welfare policies. There was a major increase in the amount of money expended for public welfare, a proliferation in the types and scope of welfare programs, including major changes in the basis and form of aid granted, and a shift from local to both state and federal participation in the financing and operation of programs. Though the establishment of the old-age, survivors', and disability insurance program by the federal government was the most dramatic innovation of the 1930s, very important developments also occurred in other forms of welfare assistance. Table 2 vividly points out the radical alterations in the amount of money expended for assistance and work programs from 1930 to 1941 and the shift from local to state and federal governmental units in financing such programs. In this twelve-year span the local proportion decreased from 91.3 per cent to 10.9 per cent. The federal percentage rose from 0 to 66.5; state contributions rose from 8.7 per cent to 22.6 per cent.

The magnitude of change in such a short period of time stemmed from two factors. First, governments in the United States had been very slow in responding to the changing social needs and economic alterations that had accompanied industrialization. In areas such as social security and unemployment relief the United States was behind developments in other industrialized nations. Second, the severity of the economic crisis and the magnitude of unemployment brought home the need for greater governmental welfare activity. The economic and social needs created by the depression rapidly overtaxed the meager and haphazard system of private and local

TABLE 2
Sources of Public Expenditures for Assistance and Work Programs,
1930-1941.

Year	Total amount (in thousands of dollars)	Percentage federal	Percentage state	Percentage local
1930	98,024	0.0	8.7	91.3
1931	217,043	0.0	18.0	82.0
1932	421,370	17.5	21.9	60.6
1933	1,059,675	63.9	11.7	24.4
1934	1,779,313	75.8	10.0	14.2
1935	1,871,315	73.3	13.1	13.6
1936	2,505,580	77.4	13.4	9.2
1937	2,173,580	71.0	18.2	10.8
1938	2,827,300	72.9	17.5	9.6
1939	2,638,869	69.4	20.1	10.5
1940	2,309,068	68.6	20.7	10.7
1941	1,950,269	66.5	22.6	10.9

Source: "Trends in Financing Public Aid, 1930-1941," in *Public Assistance 1941,* The Federal Security Agency, Social Security Board, Bureau of Public Assistance, No. 4.

relief, charities, and other programs. The widespread economic disruption also assaulted traditional outlooks concerning social welfare, economic insecurity, and the role of government in the society in general.

At the beginning of the depression many states supplemented their local welfare activities through greater state aid and state participation. In 1931 New York, the first state to adopt a relatively long-term program of financial aid for the unemployed, created a Temporary Emergency Relief Administration to distribute money to local relief agencies. Many states followed with programs of their own.[17] Even in the midst of the economic crisis, however, states clung to the tradition that welfare or public aid was basically a local responsibility. The programs generally consisted merely of emergency state aid to assist local operations.

Active participation in relief by the federal government began in mid-1932 with the enactment of the Emergency Relief and Reconstruction Act. Although this was a small measure, it represented the first major departure from the traditional nonparticipation of the federal government in welfare. The act authorized loans at 3 per cent interest to states as advances on future federal grants for highway construction.

The movement toward active participation of the federal government in public welfare during the 1930s took place in two stages. First, emergency and temporary programs were designed to meet the immediate crisis. One of these was the Emergency Relief and Reconstruction Act of the Hoover administration. In 1933, under the new Roosevelt administration, a more extensive emergency relief bill was passed, the Federal Emergency Relief Act. This legislation appropriated money for unemployment relief to the states in the form of grants rather than loans. It created a Federal Emergency Relief Administration to supervise the disbursement of the funds to the states. Other emergency relief and public works programs were enacted during the first year of the Roosevelt administration — the Civilian Conservation Corps, the Federal Emergency Administration of Public Works, the Public Works Administration. All these programs involved the federal government in the field of welfare and relief, but all were designed as temporary measures to prop up or supplement the existing welfare system in a particularly bad economic situation.[18]

The second stage of the development of federal activity in welfare came in the mid-1930s. By that time a permanent federal-state social insurance and public assistance program had aroused considerable interest. In 1934, President Roosevelt created the Committee on Economic Security to study the problems of economic insecurity and want and to propose more permanent solutions for these problems. The committee submitted its report to the president in January, 1935. On the basis of its findings the president made recommendations to Congress. With congressional modifications these proposals became the Social Security Act in August.[19]

This legislation has served as the basic framework for public welfare programs of nearly all types and has affected welfare activities at all levels of government. The act set up both programs administered and financed entirely by the federal government and programs administered and financed jointly by the federal government and the several states. Although the act authorized extensive federal participation, especially through financial assistance and minimum standards, it retained the basic responsibility of the state governments for most programs. Congress has amended this act several times, but its essential features have remained the same. The provisions of the act combined a variety of approaches to the problems of economic insecurity and public welfare. It included programs of social insurance in which persons paid money during their productive years and received benefits during periods when they were not working — old-age, survivors', and disability insurance and unemployment compensation — provisions for federal grants-in-aid for state categorical assistance programs, and a wide variety of child welfare services. The old-age, survivors', and disability insurance program was largely run by the federal government. Under the provisions for unemployment compensation, the categorical assistance programs, and the child welfare services, the states were induced by federal grants-in-aid to set up and operate programs that met minimum federal standards.

We have stressed the great innovations that took place in public welfare policy during the 1930s and especially the new role played by the federal government. These developments were, indeed, very important and did much to alter the provisions and character of public welfare. However, it would be misleading to stress only the changes that took place. As with many policy changes that occurred during the depression the innovations were mixed in with and modified by persistent adherence to traditional principles and modes of operation. Even as the federal government set up a social insurance program and began to finance a major portion of public assistance programs, the principle that basic responsibility for public welfare rested upon the states was maintained and reaffirmed. The states retained basic responsibility for setting up and operating programs, and they continued to have a great deal of discretion in how such programs operated. Though the principles and operating procedures of the Social Security Act altered traditional forms of welfare programs, the act fell short of a total attack on the traditional poor law system, especially as it was reluctant to interfere with state operations. In some regards the act involved a retreat from innovations in federal participation that had occurred under the earlier Federal Emergency Relief Act. Under that act federal participation in policy making and administration had been much more direct. States and local units had much less discretion in the administration of emergency relief funds than they were to have under the programs set up under the Social Security Act. Congress made provisions giving more say to state and local governments and watering down federal standards. These provisions modified the proposals of the Committee on Economic Security. Congress was deliberately reacting against the provisions of and experience under the Federal Emergency Relief Act and was seeking to return control to the states.[20]

As we suggested above, the provisions of the 1935 Social Security Act outlined the major provisions and principles of subsequent public welfare policy. The basic structure of public welfare policy, containing a mixture of traditional concepts and the innovations of the 1930s, remains the core of public welfare policy today. Only during the past few years have attempts been made to alter significantly these provisions. The Supreme Court recently disallowed residence requirements. The Nixon administration in 1969 proposed standardizing welfare payments from state to state. There is considerable interest in some form of family allowance plan or guaranteed income arrangement.

CONTEMPORARY WELFARE POLICY

Contemporary public welfare policy includes a complex of programs, representing a variety of governmental units, servicing different clientele, and financed through a variety of formulas. As we suggested above, this hodgepodge of programs has developed over a long period of time and has been influenced by a variety of conditions and philosophies. Prior to the depression programs and their administration and organization from state to state were not uniform. Since the enactment of the Social Security Act in 1935, which set up some federal programs and provided strong financial incentives for the states to formulate programs of their own, more uniformity in the types and structures of state programs has been established. Public welfare activity has developed over the past few decades as a cooperative venture, participated in by state, local, and federal governments. In a very broad sense welfare could include health care, prisons and reformatories, and labor and employment affairs. We will mainly study income maintenance programs, especially those such as public assistance that today constitute the core of state welfare efforts.

Some programs are handled exclusively by the federal government; we will not examine them here. The old-age, survivors' and health insurance program, railroad workers' insurance, and services to veterans are examples of such programs. Other programs are joint federal-state programs. These include old-age assistance, aid to the blind, aid to dependent children, aid to the permanently and totally disabled, unemployment compensation, child welfare services, and crippled children's services. Other programs — general assistance, workmen's compensation, and disability insurance — have remained wholly state or state and local.

The public assistance programs are currently the keystone of nonsocial insurance welfare programs. These programs include the various categorical assistance programs operating under the provisions of the Social Security Act and state general assistance programs that are maintained entirely by state and local governments and that have the most direct link to the traditional poor law provisions. As suggested above, many states already had semblances of categorical assistance programs in operation prior to 1935. The original Social Security Act provided a system of matching grants to the states if they would set up and operate certain categorical assistance programs that met certain standards. The original act provided for three such programs; old-age assistance, aid to the blind, and aid to dependent children. In 1950 the act was amended to provide a program for aid to the permanently and totally disabled. In 1960 a program of medical assistance for the aged was added, followed by a more general program of medical assistance in 1965. The latter program replaced the 1960 program and contained provisions for meeting the cost of medical services for persons receiving aid under the various categorical assistance programs. All states currently operate each of the four categorical assistance programs, with the exception of Nevada, which has no program of aid to the permanently and totally disabled.[21]

In order to participate in the federal matching programs a state must develop and administer its own programs within the framework of limitations and requirements established by the federal government. Under the federal requirements the state must design a program and submit it to the federal government. The plan must be operative in the entire state, and the state itself must participate in financing it. The program must be administered by a single state agency whose employees operate under civil service provisions. Eligibility may be determined by the state, but the federal law provides that the recipient of aid must be in "need"; that the state must consider a person's available income and resources in determining the amount of assistance; and that the state may not establish age and citizenship requirements beyond those permitted by federal law. The state must also provide for a fair hearing for any person whose application for aid is denied.[22] These provisions have been important in spurring the states to adopt and participate in common statewide programs. Prior to the 1930s, many states merely provided that local governments might enact programs and did not participate themselves, or maintained programs that were applicable only in some parts of the state.

The federal provisions do give the states latitude in determining eligibility, defining need, and determining the amount of payments to be made. This gives the states great leeway over the extent, scope, and generosity of their welfare efforts. In 1969 the Supreme Court ruled out residence requirements on the grounds that such requirements violated the equal protection of the law provided by the Fourteenth Amendment and interfered with the citizen's freedom to move.[23] As late as 1970, on the other hand, a federal court upheld the right of the states to set their own ceilings on the amount of payments to recipients.

The financing of these categorical assistance programs is shared jointly by federal, state, and local governments. The provisions in the original act called for federal grants to match équally state payments per recipient up to a certain maximum above which all of the money came from the state. These formulas have been altered from time to time with the federal government coming to provide an increasingly larger proportion of the funds. Currently, the provisions allow for the federal government to pay higher shares of the lesser proportions of payments per recipient. For example, the formula for computing the federal share of old-age assistance payments is 31/37th of the first $37 of the average maximum monthly payment and a share varying between 50 per cent and 65 per cent of the next $38 of the average maximum payment.[24] Thus, if a state had an average maximum monthly payment of $37, the federal government would pay $31. For each extra dollar over the first $37 up to $75, the federal government would pay between $.50 and $.65, depending upon the state's per capita income. The federal government would not pay for any of the money entailed in an average per recipient payments of over $75. Since the federal government pays a higher proportion of the funds for lower average payments, a state that wants to maximize aid from the federal government might pay small amounts of money to large numbers of people. The proportion of welfare aid that comes from the federal government, then, is highly related to per recipient payments. In recent years the federal formulas have provided for the federal government to pay higher proportions of the money expended in states with lower annual per capita incomes than in states with higher per capita incomes. This provision has been designed to help the poorer states increase their welfare provisions. Federal contributions to state public assistance payments have been about 60 per cent for the entire nation. However, on a state-by-state basis the federal proportion in 1968 varied from 39.1 per cent in New Jersey to 82.0 per cent in Mississippi.[25]

In addition to the several categorical assistance programs in which the federal government plays a part, each state has some form of general assistance program financed entirely by state and local funds. These programs furnish aid to individuals or families who do not qualify for aid under the federally aided programs. Operated outside the context of any federal standards, these programs vary widely from state to state in eligibility requirements, in amount and duration of payments, and in administration procedures. In some states the state public assistance agency administers the general assistance program. In others local authorities administer the program with the supervision of the state. In still others it is administered at the local level without any form of state supervision. As more categorical assistance programs have come into operation the number of persons aided by general assistance programs has decreased. The number of recipients of general assistance payments, more than for the categorical assistance programs, varies according to general economic conditions. When economic conditions are bad, and many are unemployed, the number of persons aided under general assistance tends to rise.

The basic pattern of federal-state public assistance programs and two social insurance programs — old age, survivors', and disability insurance and unemployment insurance — were put into operation during the extreme economic conditions of the Great Depression. It was expected that as economic conditions improved and as the social insurance programs went into effect the various public assistance programs would diminish in importance and cost. However, neither the abatement of the economic crisis nor the operation of the social insurance programs have put the various public assistance programs out of operation. Since 1935 there have been increases in the number of assistance programs in operation, the number and rate of recipients, and the amount of money expended under these programs. The graphs in Figures 1 and 2 show the changes in the numbers and rates of recipients and in total payments to public assistance recipients that occurred between 1936 and 1965. Payments to recipients and recipient rates went down or leveled off during World War II but in most instances began to rise after the war. Only general assistance has

FIGURE 1
Public Assistance: Total Payments to Recipients

Public assistance payments were nearly $5.3 billion in 1965. Of this amount, 39 per cent was paid to recipients of old-age assistance; 33 per cent, for aid of families with dependent children; 10 per cent, for aid to the permanently and totally disabled; 6 per cent, for general assistance; 10 per cent, for medical assistance for the aged; 2 per cent, for aid to the blind.

Billions
of dollars

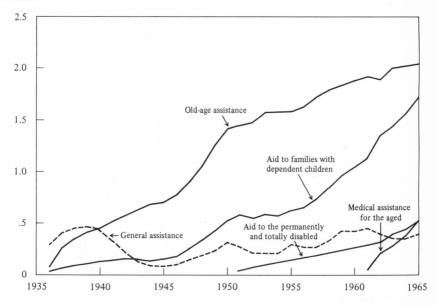

Source: United States Department of Health, Education and Welfare. *Health, Education and Welfare Trends, 1966-67,* Part I, S-116.

shown a dramatic decrease in the numbers of cases and recipients. Old-age assistance rates have decreased somewhat since the late 1940s. AFDC rates, on the other hand, have more than doubled since 1940.

We have presented an outline of the basic state welfare programs, concentrating upon the various public assistance programs or nonsocial insurance income maintenance programs, which, we have argued, constitute the core of state welfare policies today. All states currently participate in the three categorical assistance programs covered under the original Social Security Act. All but Nevada have a program of aid to the permanently and totally disabled. All have some form of general assistance program, and most states participate in one of the two medical assistance grant-in-aid programs. All states have a central state welfare agency that oversees the administration of the public assistance programs.

FIGURE 2
Public Assistance Recipients

Substantial increases in aid to families with dependent children and general assistance brought the total number of people on public assistance rolls to 8.2 million in December, 1965. Compared with December, 1964, there were increases of 164,700 in aid to families with dependent children, 54,500 in medical assistance for the aged, and 47,700 in aid to the permanently and totally disabled; and decreases of 102,000 in general assistance, 31,800 in old-age assistance, and 10,400 in aid to the blind.

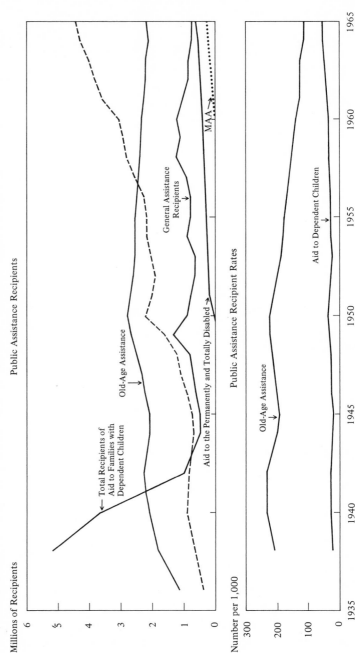

Federal-State Public Assistance Program b Recipients in Thousands

Year (as of December)a	Old-age assistance		Medical assistance for the aged h	AFDC d				APTD e		Aid to the blind	General Assistance c	
	Total f	Rate g		Total i	Total	Children Rate j		Total	Rate k		Recipients	Cases
1936	1,106	—	—	—	404	—		—	—	45	—	1,510
1940	2,066	228	—	—	891	22		—	—	73	3,618	1,239
1945	2,056	195	—	—	701	17		—	—	71	507	257
1946	2,196	202	—	—	885	21		—	—	77	673	315
1947	2,332	208	—	—	1,060	24		—	—	81	739	356
1948	2,498	216	—	—	1,214	27		—	—	86	842	398
1949	2,736	227	—	—	1,521	32		—	—	93	1,337	562
1950	2,789	224	—	2,234	1,662	34		69	—	98	866	413
1952	2,646	200	—	1,992	1,495	30		164	—	99	587	280
1953	2,591	190	—	1,942	1,464	28		195	—	100	618	270
1954	2,565	181	—	2,174	1,640	29		224	—	102	880	351
1955	2,553	173	—	2,193	1,661	30		244	—	105	743	314
1956	2,514	167	—	2,271	1,732	29		269	—	107	731	305
1957	2,487	161	—	2,498	1,913	30		291	—	108	907	344
1958	2,455	154	—	2,851	2,185	34		328	—	110	1,246	434
1959	2,394	148	—	2,953	2,273	35		350	—	109	1,107	399
1960	2,332	141	15	3,080	2,377	35		374	4	108	1,244	431
1961	2,269	134	72	3,582	2,770	39		396	4	103	1,069	411
1962	2,226	128	110	3,828	2,873	42		437	5	100	900	358
1963	2,194	123	150	3,981	2,987	42		479	5	98	872	352
1964	2,159	119	225	4,292	3,218	45		528	—	96	779	346
1965	2,127	115	280	4,457	3,358	47		575	6	86	677	310

a. Alaska and Hawaii are included throughout the period. b. Programs administered by the federal government under the Social Security Act of 1935 (P.L. 271, Title I, IV, X, and XIV, as amended, 42 U.S.C. Beginning with December, 1950, data include cases having payments made directly to the suppliers of medical or remedial care in behalf of recipients. c. Supported entirely by state and local funds; recipient data partly estimated. d. Aid to families with dependent children. e. The program of aid to the permanently and totally disabled (APTD) was initiated in October, 1950. f. Includes a small number of recipients aged 60-64 to whom or in whose behalf payments are made without federal participation. g. Per 1,000 population aged 65 and over, based on data excluding recipients aged 60-64. h. Program initiated in October, 1960 under Public Law 778. i. Includes children and, beginning October, 1950, one parent or other adult relative in families in which the requirements of at least one adult were considered in determining the amount of assistance; beginning October, 1962, may include both parents. j. Per 1,000 population under 18 years of age. k. Per 1,000 population aged 18-64.

Source: United States Department of Health, Education and Welfare. Health, Education and Welfare Trends, 1966-67, Part 1, S-115.

COMPARISON OF STATE WELFARE EFFORTS

Despite the operation of similar programs and the financial incentives and standards of the federal government great variations persist among the states in the extent and generosity of their welfare efforts. In making comparisons among the states we included a time dimension, asking how state welfare efforts have changed over the past few decades. We developed measures of state welfare efforts at three consecutive time points: 1940 through 1942, 1951 through 1953, 1966 through 1968. Most states did not participate in the several categorical assistance programs before 1940. Important alterations were made in the formulas and proportions of federal contributions in 1950, along with the introduction of the aid to the totally and permanently disabled program. The 1966 through 1968 period is the latest for which data are available. By using three years instead of a single year to measure most aspects of welfare efforts and by averaging the figures of each year, we hoped to avoid the influence of very short-range deviations in a state's expenditures or assistance. For example, a change in federal formulas may cause states to spend more money after alterations are made in their own provisions by the legislature and welfare administration agencies. Since all states may not make alterations at the same speed, a state's expenditures for one single year are more likely to misrepresent its general effort than are averages for a three-year period.

In assessing the public welfare policies of the states six dimensions of state activity or effort can be identified, each of which indicates some aspect of state welfare effort.[26] The first dimension, how much a state spends for the various welfare programs, must be measured on a per capita basis, since the populations of the states vary greatly. *Total welfare expenditures per capita* include all expenditures, regardless of whether the funds come from state, federal, or local sources.

A good proportion of the money a state gives for public welfare comes from the federal government. The remainder comes from state and local sources. In order to assess better both the effort of the state and its dependence upon the federal government, two additional per capita indices were used: a measure of state-local contributions, *state welfare expenditures per capita,* and an indicator of the federal contribution, *federal welfare grants per capita.*

Another aspect of a state's welfare effort is the proportion of its money that goes for public welfare programs — *welfare expenditures as a per cent of general expenditures.* For the 1960 period Oklahoma ranks highest, with 24.8 per cent of its total expenditures going for welfare. Wyoming ranks lowest with only 4.0 per cent.

In addition to the amounts spent by the states we should measure how many receive aid and how much they receive. How many people or what proportion of the population of the state receives benefits under the various public assistance programs? For an indicator of this dimension we added the number of recipients of aid under the various programs for the middle year of each of the three periods and divided that by the total population of the state. We then converted that figure into *the number of recipients per 1,000 population receiving aid under one or more of the various programs.* On this measure for the late 1960s Oklahoma again ranks highest with 79.7 per thousand persons receiving public assistance. Indiana ranks lowest with 14.6 per thousand.

Most of the public assistance programs provide monthly payments to persons who are in need and qualify for aid. Federal guidelines allow the states great discretion in setting the amount of payment per recipient. State conditions such as amount of need, resources available, and state political pressures can thus influence the amounts of money awarded to each recipient. In order to measure the liberality of state payments we took average payments per recipient and computed an average of these monthly payment figures for each of the programs for the three years making up each time period. This created an *average monthly payment per recipient* for each of four programs in the early 1940s and the early 1950s and for five programs in the late 1960s. Average payments per family are used for the aid to dependent children program. For the third period the average monthly payments under the old-age assistance programs ranged from a high of $99.45 in California to a low of $38.31 in Mississippi. Under the programs of general assistance the range for the same time period runs from a high of $71.36 in Maryland to a low of $4.02 in Arkansas.

Data were compiled giving the states' scores on each of these six measures for each of the three time periods. These scores and the comparative rankings of the states for the six indices in the third time period are presented in Table 3. In all instances the smaller the rank number of the state, the more the state spends or gives in comparison to other states. Table 4 shows the rankings of the states for three of the indices for each of the three periods — total per capita expenditures; number of recipients per 1,000; and average monthly payment per family, AFDC. By presenting the data in this way we can readily see the stability and change in the relative efforts of the states.

The data in Table 3 indicate several interesting comparative features

TABLE 3
State Scores and Ranks for Six Indicators of State Welfare Efforts, 1966-1968

	Total per capita expenditure		State per capita expenditure		Federal per capita welfare grants		Welfare exp. as percentage of gen. expenditure		Number of recipients per 1,000		Average monthly payment per family, AFDC	
	Score	Rank	Score	Rank	Score	Rank	Score	Rank	Score	Rank	Score	Rank
Alabama	$37.19	13	$ 9.30	36	$27.89	7	14.1%	12.5	56.7	7	$ 56.00	47
Arizona	22.62	40	8.10	40	14.52	39	7.0	43	41.0	17	121.00	34
Arkansas	41.01	10	9.86	32	31.15	4	16.7	8	58.4	6	73.00	44
California	70.49	2	28.86	2	41.63	3	20.1	3	63.9	5	181.00	10
Colorado	48.68	7	20.97	7	27.71	8	16.0	10	53.7	9	148.00	22
Connecticut	33.92	19	15.74	14	18.18	27	14.5	11	27.4	36	214.00	3
Delaware	32.47	22	18.85	8	13.62	41	7.4	42	38.4	19	133.00	28
Florida	20.87	40	4.93	44	15.94	35	9.7	33.5	42.0	15	69.00	45
Georgia	23.50	26	7.68	41	23.50	15	12.9	17	50.3	12	95.00	42
Idaho	28.52	32	10.11	29	18.43	25	9.9	31	25.8	38	173.00	12
Illinois	35.35	16	16.18	12	19.17	23	17.1	6.5	24.3	23	200.00	5
Indiana	11.48	47	4.03	45	7.45	47	4.8	46	14.6	48	122.00	33
Iowa	29.97	28	13.73	16	16.24	33	10.7	27	29.0	33	172.00	13
Kansas	27.54	33	11.24	23	16.30	32	11.4	24.5	28.6	34	182.00	9
Kentucky	38.26	12	10.02	30	28.24	5	13.5	14.5	54.2	8	110.00	37
Louisiana	59.61	3	16.72	10	42.89	2	17.1	6.5	74.0	3	104.00	41
Maine	33.48	20	13.62	18	19.86	21	13.5	14.5	41.1	16	111.00	36
Maryland	30.73	27	14.83	15	15.90	36	11.6	23	34.5	24	153.00	18
Massachusetts	52.03	6	23.84	5	28.19	6	20.3	2	37.6	20	213.00	4
Michigan	32.91	21	15.78	13	17.13	30	11.4	24.5	32.4	29	177.00	11
Minnesota	31.46	25	8.79	38	22.67	18	10.4	28	30.2	32	184.00	7.5
Mississippi	34.18	18	9.41	35	24.77	13	14.1	12.5	82.6	1	37.00	48
Missouri	36.38	14	11.22	25	25.16	12	17.2	5	49.2	14	106.00	38
Montana	24.41	39	10.26	27	14.15	40	7.9	40.5	25.7	39	143.00	24
Nebraska	26.43	35	9.04	37	17.39	28	12.7	18	23.7	42	128.00	29
Nevada	25.35	36	10.13	28	15.22	37	6.7	44	22.5	44	123.00	32

New Hampshire	20.06	41	9.97	31	10.09	45.5	9.0	37	19.0	46	171.00	14
New Jersey	19.57	45	9.48	34	10.09	45.5	11.7	22	27.3	37	221.00	2
New Mexico	41.45	9	13.72	17	27.43	9.5	10.0	30	50.8	11	124.00	30.5
New York	52.79	5	25.36	4	27.43	9.5	16.3	9	52.5	10	233.00	1
North Carolina	19.82	44	3.48	47	16.34	31	8.1	39	35.8	21	105.00	39.5
North Dakota	34.19	17	11.18	26	23.01	17	9.7	33.5	25.0	41	184.00	7.5
Ohio	25.27	37	12.23	24	13.04	42	7.9	40.5	35.0	22	144.00	23
Oklahoma	81.23	1	26.51	3	54.72	1	24.8	1	79.7	2	134.00	26.5
Oregon	31.63	24	16.65	11	14.98	38	9.6	35	28.0	35	152.00	19.5
Pennsylvania	29.01	31	13.00	20	16.01	34	12.3	19.5	32.8	28	158.00	17
Rhode Island	56.53	4	30.91	1	25.62	11	17.8	4	50.0	13	166.00	16
South Carolina	14.71	46	3.85	46	10.86	44	6.6	45	22.7	43	67.00	46
South Dakota	29.20	30	9.70	33	19.50	22	10.1	29	31.2	31	152.00	19.5
Tennessee	24.98	38	6.64	42	18.34	26	10.9	26	40.6	18	105.00	39.5
Texas	27.19	34	6.50	43	20.69	20	13.2	16	33.8	26	92.00	43
Utah	31.74	23	13.16	19	18.58	24	8.9	38	32.2	30	149.00	21
Vermont	40.38	11	16.94	9	23.44	16	9.8	32	33.7	27	134.00	26.5
Virginia	10.76	48	3.41	48	7.35	48	4.6	47	17.9	47	124.00	30.5
Washington	44.29	8	23.26	6	21.03	19	12.3	19.5	34.3	25	168.00	15
West Virginia	36.12	15	11.53	22	24.59	14	11.9	21	66.0	4	115.00	35
Wisconsin	29.61	29	12.35	21	17.26	29	9.1	36	21.0	45	190.00	6
Wyoming	19.92	43	8.49	39	11.49	43	4.0	48	25.4	40	139.00	25

Data on state welfare expenditures, payments, and recipients are published monthly by the Department of Health, Education and Welfare, as are more comprehensive summary reports on state and national welfare programs. These data and reports can be found in the following sources: Council of State Governments, *Book of the States* (Chicago: Council of State Governments), a biennial publication beginning with Vol. I in 1935; United States Department of Commerce, Bureau of the Census, *Compendium of State Government Finances* (Washington, D.C.; United States Government Printing Office); United States Department of Health, Education and Welfare, Social Security Administration, *Social Security Bulletin* (Washington, D.C.: United States Government Printing Office), a monthly publication beginning with Vol. I in 1937; United States Department of Health, Education and Welfare, Welfare Administration, *Welfare in Review* (Washington, D.C.: United States Government Printing Office), a monthly publication beginning with Vol. I in 1963; United States Department of Commerce, Bureau of the Census, *Statistical Abstract* (Washington, D.C.: United States Government Printing Office).

In compiling our measures of welfare efforts we have drawn data from each of these sources. Because of the large number of individual data sources and the fact that many of them are used only indirectly in our discussion and data presentation we do not provide exact sources for our data.

TABLE 4

*Comparative Rankings of States at Different Time Periods for
Three Measures of Welfare Effort*

State	Total per capita expenditure			Number of recipients per 1,000			Average monthly payment per family, ADC		
	40s	*50s*	*60s*	*40s*	*50s*	*60s*	*40s*	*50s*	*60s*
Alabama	48	40	13	47	8	7	48	46	47
Arizona	7	11	40	8.5	26	17	21	25	34
Arkansas	44	20	10	a	7	6	47	44	44
California	2	5	2	18	15	5	3	3	10
Colorado	1	1	7	1	4	9	17	16	22
Connecticut	29	19	19	45	45.5	36	1	8	3
Delaware	39	42	22	42	43	19	6	26	28
Florida	36	15	40	21.5	12.5	15	37	42	45
Georgia	42	22	26	36	14	12	39	35	42
Idaho	16	16	32	13.5	31	38	24	31	12
Illinois	8	18	16	11	36	23	10	9	5
Indiana	20	43	47	8.5	41	48	30	31	33
Iowa	24	21	28	21.5	31	33	34	12	13
Kansas	25.5	17	33	21.5	28.5	34	18	22	9
Kentucky	41	37	12	37.5	9	8	38	43	37
Louisiana	31	4	3	11	2	3	32	39	41
Maine	15	14	20	24.5	16	16	13	29	36
Maryland	35	45	27	37.5	47	24	25	24	18
Massachusetts	5	7	6	13.5	21.5	20	2	2	4
Michigan	21.5	24	21	18	36	29	11	18	11
Minnesota	17	34	25	7	27	32	19	17	7.5
Mississippi	47	41	18	44	6	1	44	47	48
Missouri	25.5	6	14	5	3	14	31	37	38
Montana	11	8	39	6	19.5	39	29	20	24
Nebraska	21.5	27	35	11	39	42	28	23	29
Nevada	18	31.5	36	28	44	44	35	a	32
New Hampshire	19	29	41	31	31	46	7	10	14
New Jersey	37	46	45	42	48	37	22	15	2
New Mexico	38	13	9	35	11	11	26	33	30.5
New York	6	26	5	31	38	10	4	4	1
North Carolina	43	44	44	40	24	21	46	41	39.5
North Dakota	30	25	17	26.5	33.5	41	23	14	7.5
Ohio	13	33	37	24.5	33.5	22	15	28	23
Oklahoma	9	3	1	2	1	2	41	27	26.5
Oregon	23	9	24	26.5	28.5	35	8	7	19.5
Pennsylvania	12	39	31	18	42	28	12	21	17
Rhode Island	27	10	4	39	24	13	5	19	16
South Carolina	45	40	46	42	19.5	43	45	45	46
South Dakota	14	23	30	15.5	21.5	31	33	30	19.5
Tennessee	40	36	38	31	12.5	18	42	38	39.5
Texas	33	31.5	34	31	17	26	43	40	43
Utah	4	12	23	3	24	30	9	11	21
Vermont	32	30	11	34	18	27	27	34	26.5
Virginia	46	47	48	46	45.5	47	40	36	30.5
Washington	3	2	8	4	10	25	6	1	15
West Virginia	34	28	15	15.5	5	4	36	32	35
Wisconsin	10	38	29	21.5	36	45	14	5	6
Wyoming	28	35	43	31	36	40	20	13	25

aInsufficient data available to determine state score and rank.

of state welfare efforts. Not only do scores among the states differ, but state rankings along different dimensions often vary greatly. For example, Alabama ranks in the upper third of the states in total per capita expenditures for welfare (13th), in the percentage of total state expenditures allocated to welfare (12.5th), and in the number of recipients per 1,000 population who receive aid (7th). At the same time, Alabama ranks in the lower third of the states in average monthly payments (47th) and in the per capita expenditures for welfare coming from state and local sources (36th). These figures suggest that Alabama spends a good deal of money for welfare, and welfare spending constitutes a relatively high proportion of its total expenditures. It gives a small payment to a large number of recipients. A relatively small proportion of that money comes from internal state and local sources. It ranks relatively high in federal grants per capita. Arkansas shows a similar pattern in its ratings on the several dimensions of welfare effort.

By way of contrast, Iowa and Kansas give relatively large amounts of money to relatively few recipients. The total per capita expenditures are lower than those of Alabama and Arkansas, but the per capita expenditures from state and local sources are higher. The percentage of state expenditures allocated to welfare is lower than that of Alabama and Arkansas. California represents yet another pattern. California ranks in the top ten along all dimensions. It gives high payments to many people, spends a large amount of money per capita (including large amounts of internal money) and allocates a relatively high percentage of its total expenditures to welfare. The welfare efforts of the state of Washington form a pattern similar to that of California. At the opposite end of the continuum is Indiana, which ranks near the bottom on all five measures, spending small amounts of money and a relatively small proportion of its expenditures to make small payments to few people. Virginia's welfare efforts look much like those of Indiana.

Overall, states exhibiting high effort along one dimension do not necessarily exhibit similarly high effort along another. For the late 1960s a particularly wide discrepancy appears in state welfare efforts as indicated by the number of recipients aided and the amount of payments made per recipient. Those states that give money to many people are not necessarily the same states that give out high average payments. The tendency, in fact, runs in the opposite direction. Taking the rankings of a state along these two indicators, it is possible to develop a two-dimensional typology that shows a clearer pattern of comparative welfare efforts by the various states. A six-category typology was constructed by dividing the states into two

groups (high and low) according to their ranks on average monthly payment per family, AFDC, and dividing the states into three categories according to the number of recipients per 1,000 population. For the second
dimension the upper third of the states constitutes a category of "payments
to many," the middle third a "medium" number category and the lower
third a "payments to few" category. By taking the rankings of states along
both of these indicators we come up with six categories ranging from high
payments to many to low payments to few. The states falling into these
categories are shown in Table 5.

These listings clarify the pattern suggested above. Those states that
give aid to many tend to give relatively small payments per recipient. Those
states that give payments to few persons tend to give higher payments. The
states at the two extremes — high effort along both dimensions and low
efforts along both dimensions — are very easily identifiable. California,
Colorado, New York, and Rhode Island give high payments to many.
Indiana, Nebraska, Nevada, South Carolina, Virginia, and Wyoming give

TABLE 5
Classification of States for Late 1960s According to Combined
Measures of Number of Recipients and Average Family Payments, AFDC

High payments to many recipients (4)	High payments to medium recipients (10)	High payments to few recipients (10)
California	Illinois	Connecticut
Colorado	Maryland	Idaho
New York	Massachusetts	Iowa
Rhode Island	Michigan	Kansas
	Minnesota	Montana
	Ohio	New Hampshire
	Pennsylvania	New Jersey
	South Dakota	North Dakota
	Utah	Oregon
	Washington	Wisconsin

Low payments to many recipients (12)	Low payments to medium recipients (6)	Low payments to few recipients (6)
Alabama	Arizona	Indiana
Arkansas	Delaware	Nebraska
Florida	North Carolina	Nevada
Georgia	Tennessee	South Carolina
Kentucky	Texas	Virginia
Louisiana	Vermont	Wyoming
Maine		
Mississippi		
Missouri		
New Mexico		
Oklahoma		
West Virginia		

low payments to few people. As Table 3 indicates, the "high to many" states rank high in both total and state per capita expenditures, whereas the states making low payments to few rank low on both measures of per capita expenditures.

This pattern has not remained constant over the time span. Using the same typology for the 1940s data, we see that the same states do not always occupy the same positions for the earlier period that they do later. These states are listed in Table 6. The relationship between the two dimensions also is different than in the later years. In the 1940s states making low payments tended to give them to few people and states making high payments tended to give them to many people. For this period it is easier to identify many high effort and low effort states. Nineteen of the forty-eight states fall in the extreme categories in the early 1940s, in contrast to only ten in the late 1960s.

Most of the changes that have taken place in the categories in which the various states fall have occurred along the number of recipients dimen-

TABLE 6

Classification of States for Early 1940s According to Combined Measures of Number of Recipients and Average Family Payments, AFDC

High payments to many recipients (8)	*High payments to medium recipients (11)*	*High payments to few recipients (5)*
Arizona	California	Connecticut
Colorado	Kansas	Delaware
Idaho	Maine	New Jersey
Illinois	Michigan	New York
Massachusetts	New Hampshire	Rhode Island
Minnesota	North Dakota	
Utah	Ohio	
Washington	Oregon	
	Pennsylvania	
	Wisconsin	
	Wyoming	

Low payments to many recipients (8)	*Low payments to medium recipients (5)*	*Low payments to few recipients (11)*
Indiana	Iowa	Arkansas
Louisiana	Nevada	Alabama
Missouri	Florida	Georgia
Montana	Tennessee	Kentucky
Nebraska	Texas	Maryland
Oklahoma		Mississippi
South Dakota		New Mexico
West Virginia		North Carolina
		South Carolina
		Vermont
		Virginia

sion rather than the payment per recipient dimension. The state rankings given in Table 4 substantiate this point also. Many relative rankings change over the years in the number of recipients columns, but relatively few change in the average payment per recipient columns.

Another indicator of significant changes in relative welfare efforts among the states is shown by changes in ranks by many states in the per capita expenditures for welfare and the percentage of state expenditures going for welfare. States moving significantly upward and downward in ranks along each of these two indices are shown in Table 7. Eight states have moved up more than ten positions from the 1940s to the 1960s in relative rank along both of the indices. Nine states have moved down in rank more than ten positions along the two indices. With the exception of Rhode Island all of the states showing substantial relative increases in these two aspects of welfare efforts are southern or border states. With the exceptions of Indiana and Ohio all of those moving downward substantially are mountain or prairie states. Looking back to the data presented in Tables 4, 5, and 6, we see that all of the states showing substantial increases in per capita and proportional expenditures for welfare moved from payments to only a few to payments to many. Conversely, most of the nine states dropping substantially in rank (except for Ohio and Wyoming) moved from payments to many in the 1940s to payments to few or medium in the latter period.

Another change in state efforts in welfare is the relationship between total per capita expenditures and per capita welfare expenditure from state and local funds. For the early 1940s in most states the state per capita expenditure is slightly more than half of the total per capita expenditures. This proportion rises considerably higher in a few states such as New York

TABLE 7
States Showing Substantial Change in Relative Rankings Along Two Measures of State Welfare Effort Between 1940-42 and 1966-68

Increased Ranking	Decreased Ranking
1. Alabama	1. Arizona
2. Arkansas	2. Idaho
3. Georgia	3. Indiana
4. Kentucky	4. Ohio
5. Louisiana	5. Montana
6. Mississippi	6. Nebraska
7. New Mexico	7. South Dakota
8. Rhode Island	8. Utah
	9. Wyoming

and New Jersey. The ranks of the states along these two indices are very close. By the 1950s there is a considerably wider variation in the proportion of total welfare expenditures per capita coming from internal sources. There is still a fairly high correspondence in state ranks along both indices.

By the 1960s the relationship between total per capita expenditures and state per capita expenditures was different. State rankings on the two measures were much less likely to correspond. For example, Arkansas ranks in 10th place in total per capita expenditures for welfare, but only 32nd in per capita expenditures from state and local sources. Delaware, on the other hand, ranks only 22nd in total expenditures but 8th in per capita expenditures from state and local sources.

These changes reflect the alterations in the participation of the federal government and in its formulas for determining its grants to the states for welfare programs. In the early days of the matching programs, reflected in the figures for the early 1940s, the federal government matched equally the money states spent in payments under the categorical assistance programs. States tended to contribute around 50 per cent of the per capita expenditures, accounting for the very close correspondence in state ranks for these two measures. By the 1950s the federal government was paying a higher proportion of the money spent under the state-federal programs and was making up a higher proportion of lower per recipient payments than of large per recipient payments. In the late 1960s these trends continued to accelerate. The federal government was paying a more disproportionate share of low per recipient payments, and at the same time, it was seeking deliberately to equalize welfare efforts by paying a higher proportion of payments to states with low annual per capita incomes. What this means is that in order to maximize the amount of federal contribution and minimize state-local contribution the state could give small payments to large numbers of people. Thus, Arkansas received 76 per cent of its expenditures from the federal government and gave small payments (it ranks 44th for AFDC) to many persons (it ranks 6th in number of recipients per 1,000).

This brief survey of comparative state welfare efforts has suggested that patterns of welfare expenditures and payments are complex and have changed substantially over the several decades during which the federal-state public assistance programs have been in operation. One factor that has contributed much to the complexity of and changes in welfare efforts is the increasing and changing role played by the federal government. The federal government has come to pay an increasingly higher proportion of the bill for public assistance, and its formulas for making grants to the states have been altered so that poorer states and those states that pay out relatively small per recipient payments get a proportionately higher amount of their welfare expenditures federally funded. Among other things, the increased role of the federal government and its formulas for determining the proportion of its expenditures have contributed to the increased number of recipients receiving aid in states such as Arkansas, Alabama, Mississippi, and Kentucky. It has also meant that between the early 1940s and the late 1960s a state such as Arkansas was able to increase its total per capita expenditures for welfare by twenty-two times while increasing its state per capita expenditures by only nine and a half times.

One goal of federal welfare policy has been to equalize welfare efforts among the several states. This has been one reason for the development of the special formulas determining federal contributions discussed above. In order to examine whether the gap between the welfare efforts of the states has increased or decreased over time we computed coefficients of variation for nine welfare indices for each of the three time periods. This coefficient measures the amount of dispersion in the welfare scores for the forty-eight states for each period. The higher the coefficient the greater the discrepancy in scores for that particular measure. The coefficients of variation for the nine welfare measures for each of the time periods are presented in Table 8.

The figures in Table 8 suggest that over the three time periods the states have become less discrepant in welfare effort. The differences among the states in size of payments per recipient have decreased for all programs except for general assistance. Since general assistance is an entirely state program, it is not directly affected by federal contributions and formulas.

TABLE 8
Coefficients of Variation for Nine Measures of State Welfare Effort

	Time period		
	1940-1942	*1951-1953*	*1966-1968*
Measure	*Coefficients of variation*		
Total per capita welfare expenditures	55.2	50.3	43.7
State per capita welfare expenditures	57.7	63.4	12.2
Federal per capita welfare grants	60.3	47.0	51.8
Welfare expenditures as percentage of general expenditures	46.2	39.9	52.8
Number of recipients per 1,000 population	33.9	41.6	40.1
Average payment per recipient, AFDC	37.6	34.8	31.5
Average payment per recipient, AB	39.9	31.1	21.4
Average payment per recipient, OAA	35.2	27.6	20.2
Average payment per recipient, GA	38.8	37.5	53.9

The discrepancy among the states in the number of recipients has increased since the early 1940s, reflecting the radical increase in the number of persons receiving welfare aid in the southern and border states. The states have been becoming more alike in the share of their budget going for welfare and in the amount of contributions coming from state and local sources. The discrepancy between states in total per capita welfare expenditures and per capita federal grants decreased between the 1940s and 1950s, but then increased between the 1950s and late 1960s.

STATE CHARACTERISTICS
AND WELFARE EFFORTS

Which kinds of states tend to spend more money on public welfare? To what extent is a state's welfare effort influenced by the welfare needs of its populace, its socioeconomic characteristics and resources, or by some aspects of its politics? How are need, socioeconomic characteristics, and politics related, and how has the role of the federal government affected the influence of these various factors on state welfare efforts?

One theory in the literature on state politics and policy holds that party competitiveness may contribute to greater welfare effort. This theory maintains that in a politically competitive situation the threat that those out of power might win control and the possibility that the incumbents might be ousted cause the political leaders to appeal to lower socioeconomic groups (the persons least likely to vote without specific efforts at mobilization) for electoral support by offering public policies beneficial to them. Welfare programs, of course, are likely to be of great interest to the have nots. Duane Lockard articulated the theory as follows: "In the two-party states the anxiety over the next election pushes political leaders into serving the interests of the have-less elements of society, thereby putting the party into the countervailing power operation." [27]

An early statement of this thesis can be found in V. O. Key's *Southern Politics in State and Nation.* Key observed that the southern states with loose multifactional party systems, in which the coherence and continuity of competition is low, pursue more conservative policies — i.e., policies more favorable to the interests of upper socioeconomic groups. States with regular competition between two cohesive and enduring factions adopted more liberal policies — i.e., policies more responsive to the interests and needs of the have nots.[28]

Later studies, such as those by Dawson and Robinson, Dye, and

Dawson,[29] conclude that the amount of money states spend for various policies is more a function of socioeconomic factors than of political conditions. Consequently, a contrary thesis may be entertained: some states devote more resources to public policies benefitting the have nots because they have more economic resources or because their citizens have more objective need for welfare benefits.

Various authors, employing different definitions of politics and economics, have come to different conclusions about which explanation is more accurate.[30] Our purpose here is not to enter into this debate, but rather to try to ascertain which political and socioeconomic factors are associated with different patterns of welfare effort. In order to investigate these questions we used the measures of welfare for each of the three time periods and developed indicators of welfare need, socioeconomic conditions, and political characteristics.

One possible influence upon a state's welfare activity is the objective need of its citizens, the extent to which there are persons in the state who are generally without basic sustenance. Because of the goals of welfare programs, we might expect that *the greater the need, the greater the welfare effort.* We used two general indicators of need: (1) the percentage of the state's population under a poverty line ($3,000 in 1960; $1,000 in 1950; comparable data not available in 1940); and, (2) the number of infant deaths per 1,000 live births in 1964, 1950, and 1940. High infant mortality is a good indicator of generally low living standards and, hence, should indicate a need for welfare benefits. Measures of need were selected for the years immediately prior to the beginning of the three welfare time periods.

Another factor presumed to have an impact upon state welfare activity is the state's socioeconomic conditions. We hypothesized that *the higher the level of wealth and urbanization, the greater the welfare effort.* A state may pay out more money for welfare simply because it has more money available. Urban residents are usually more supportive of welfare programs than rural residents. As indicators of socioeconomic conditions we used: (1) per capita personal income (1965, 1950, and 1940); (2) median family income (1959, 1950, and 1940); and (3) percentage urban based on the census definition of urbanization (1960, 1950, and 1940). As with the need measures, these readings were made for points nearest to the three welfare periods.

A third factor we hypothesized to be related to welfare effort is certain political conditions. We looked at two political variables: interparty competition and voter turnout. We anticipated that *the greater the party com-*

petition, the more extensive a state's welfare effort. The indicators of party competition include: (1) the average percentage of seats held by the major party in the upper house of the state legislature during the designated time period; (2) the average percentage of seats the major party held in the lower house; and (3) the average percentage of total vote received by the major party candidate for governor.[31] One minus the average percentage yields an average competition score; a small number represents little competition, and a large number signifies vigorous competition.

The other political variable used, voter turnout, is closely related to party competition, and the expectation is that *the higher the level of voter turnout, the greater a state's welfare effort.* Since high turnout indicates participation by people from lower socioeconomic classes, and since these people are likely to benefit from welfare policies, it follows that their presence at the polls might influence the policy enactments of political leaders in the direction of more extensive welfare effort. Turnout in gubernatorial elections was used; the score was the average percentage turnout for the two elections prior to 1941, prior to 1951, and prior to 1966 in the gubernatorial primary or general election, whichever had the larger number of votes cast. By allowing the interest of voters, as expressed in turnout, to determine whether the primary or general election is the real election, the turnout scores for many southern states are substantially higher than usually reported.

In order to see if needy states respond with proportionately greater welfare effort, if states of high socioeconomic development spend proportionately more, and if competitive states spend proportionately more, we computed simple correlation coefficients (Pearson product moment) for the 1940, 1950, and 1960 periods. The difference in the correlation for two variables in the 1940s and for the same two variables in the 1950s can be used to trace important changes in their relationship over time. Finally, to ascertain the relative importance of need, socioeconomic development, and politics in explaining the level of state welfare activity, we perform regression analysis. The R^2 expresses the proportion of the dependent variable (welfare effort) explained by a particular set of independent variables (need, socioeconomic development, political characteristics).

This statistical analysis is feasible because the states vary widely on measures of welfare effort, need, socioeconomic development, and political competition. In the earlier sections we saw which states rank high in welfare effort and which rank low, and we got an idea of the magnitude of differences among states (see Table 8). On this section we use log bar graphs along with the coefficient of variation to display the relative magnitude of

FIGURE 3
Coefficients of Variation and Ranges Among the States for Infant Mortality

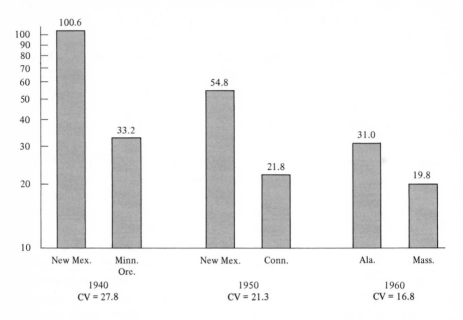

Source: The indicators of need and socioeconomic characteristics were computed from data found in United States Department of Commerce, Bureau of the Census. *Statistical Abstract* (Washington, D.C.: United States Government Printing Office); United States Department of Commerce, Bureau of the Census; *Census of Population, 1940, 1950, 1960* (Washington, D.C.: United States Government Printing Office).

differences among the states on a select number of independent variables; one measure is chosen from each factor (need, socioeconomic development, political competition, and turnout).

On measures of need, the states exhibit wide variations. Figure 3 shows how the magnitude of these variations has changed over time for infant mortality and which states ranked highest and lowest in each period. The log bars show that the differences among states in infant mortality have lessened. The states also vary widely on measures of socioeconomic development. The variance in median family income has decreased, as the bar graph in Figure 4 suggests. Finally, the states vary widely in political competition and voter turnout, but as Figures 5 and 6 show, the states have moved closer together in the level of gubernatorial competition and voter turnout.

Some states are at the same time needy, poor, and noncompetitive, for example, Mississippi; other states are low in need, high in economic resources, and competitive, as is Connecticut. The relation of these variables is a common finding of studies of state politics. Table 9 shows the

FIGURE 4

Coefficients of Variation and Ranges Among the States for Median Family Income

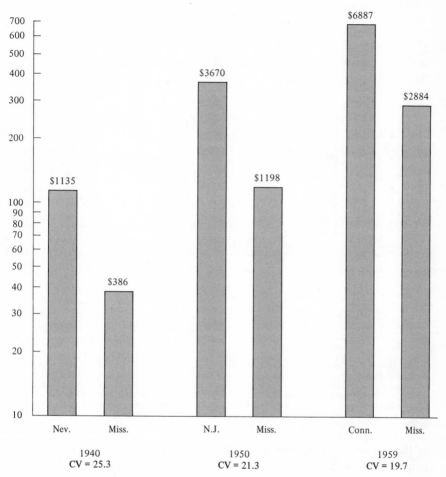

Source: The measures of political competition and voter turnout were computed from data found in George Gallup, *The Political Almanac, 1952* (New York: Forbes, 1952); Alexander Heard and Donald S. Strong, *Southern Primaries and Elections, 1920-1949* (University, Ala.: University of Alabama Press, 1950); United States Department of Commerce, Bureau of the Census, *Statistical Abstract* (Washington, D.C.: United States Government Printing Office); *Book of the States* (Chicago: Council of State Governments); United States Department of Commerce, Bureau of the Census, *Current Population Reports;* Richard M. Scammon, *America Votes,* Vols. 2-7 (New York: Macmillan Co.).

patterns and extent of these relationships. The relationships between socio-economic conditions and party competition are always positive; the higher a state's median family income, the more competitive is the state. In general, a positive relationship prevails between socioeconomic development and turnout; in wealthier states, more people tend to participate in gubernatorial elections. The wealthier states generally have fewer needy persons

FIGURE 5
Coefficients of Variation and Ranges Among the States for Average Percentage of Vote for Winning Gubernatorial Candidate

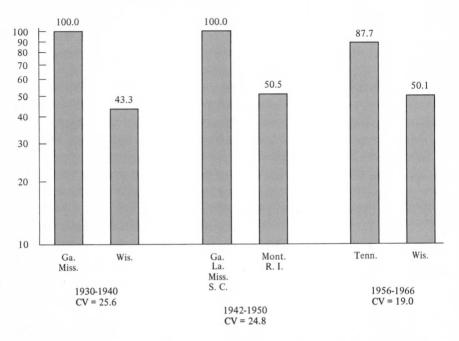

Source: The measures of political competition and voter turnout were computed from data found in George Gallup, *The Political Almanac, 1952* (New York: Forbes, 1952); Alexander Heard and Donald S. Strong, *Southern Primaries and Elections, 1920-1949* (University, Ala.: University of Alabama Press, 1950); United States Department of Commerce, Bureau of the Census, *Statistical Abstract* (Washington, D.C.: United States Government Printing Office); *Book of the States* (Chicago: Council of State Governments); United States Department of Commerce, Bureau of the Census, *Current Population Reports;* Richard M. Scammon, *America Votes*, Vols. 2-7 (New York: Macmillan Co.).

as the negative correlations demonstrate. The needy states tend to be less competitive, and they tend to have lower rates of voter turnout.

Recognizing how states differ in competition, socioeconomic development, and need, we looked to see if the welfare efforts of rich and poor states, competitive and noncompetitive states, needy and less needy states differ. In short, what are the socioeconomic and political characteristics of high effort states and of low effort states? In an earlier section we pointed out which states exerted more and less effort along several dimensions of welfare activity. Now we try to see what kind of state spends more than others. Again we display only one indicator from each of the several independent variables.[32]

Needy states are characterized by low average per recipient payments for AFDC, and after the 1940s, by a large number of recipients. By the

FIGURE 6

Coefficients of Variation and Ranges Among the States for Average Percentage of Gubernatorial Turnout

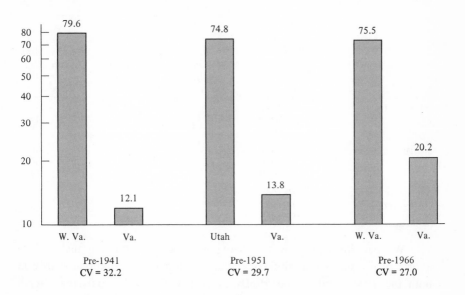

Source: The measures of political competition and voter turnout were computed from data found in George Gallup, *The Political Almanac, 1952* (New York: Forbes, 1952); Alexander Heard and Donald S. Strong, *Southern Primaries and Elections, 1920-1949* (University, Ala.: University of Alabama Press, 1950); United States Department of Commerce, Bureau of the Census, *Statistical Abstract* (Washington, D.C.: United States Government Printing Office); *Book of the States* (Chicago: Council of State Governments); United States Department of Commerce, Bureau of the Census, *Current Population Reports;* Richard M. Scammon, *America Votes,* Vols. 2-7 (New York: Macmillan Co.).

1960s they began to devote a comparatively higher proportion of their budget to welfare, with comparatively more money coming from federal grants than had been the case in the 1940s. The needy states themselves contribute proportionately less to per capita welfare expenditures, and their total welfare expenditures tend to be less than those of well-off states. In Table 10 are the correlations of the six welfare measures with infant mortality, median family income, average competition for governor and percentage of turnout for governor.

Since we know that needy states are often low in socioeconomic development, we can surmise that financially they are less able to support extensive welfare benefits themselves. Since they are often less competitive and have lower voter turnout levels, there may be less organized political pressure on behalf of the have nots. Over the last thirty years the federal government increasingly has become the provider; the federal aid formulas give more money to the needy states, thereby helping to equalize public assistance expenditures among the states.

TABLE 9

Relationship of Need, Socioeconomic Development, and Politics
(Simple correlation coefficients)

		Median family income	Average competition for governor (1930-1940, 1942-1950, 1956-1966)	Percent turnout for governor (pre-1941, pre-1951, pre-1966)
Infant mortality	1940	−.47	−.48	−.42
	1950	−.47	−.29	−.41
	1964	−.32	−.47	−.65
Median family income	1940		.74	.60
	1950		.75	.64
	1959		.62	.17
Average competition	1930-1940			.82
for governor	1942-1950			.72
	1956-1966			.58

We can illustrate this equalizing influence by studying the welfare efforts of six states that ranked among the top ten in infant mortality in both the 1940s and in the 1960s. Alabama, Georgia, Louisiana, North Carolina, South Carolina, and New Mexico received 40.0 to 46.9 per cent of their welfare expenditures from the federal government in 1940; in the 1960s these six needy states could rely on the federal government for 66.7 to 82.4 per cent of their welfare expenditures, a percentage substantially higher than for less needy states. Four of the six states made dramatic shifts upward in their rankings on total per capita expenditures between the 1940s and the 1960s. In the earlier period they extended benefits from 14.0 to 37.0 recipients per 1,000; in the 1960s from 22.7 to 74.0 per 1,000 received aid in the same states. In this way, the change in federal formulas has resulted in more welfare money divided among more people.

States with higher median family income are characterized by high average payments for AFDC (see Table 10). In the early period rich states showed a slight tendency toward aiding many recipients, but since 1950 this trend has reversed itself so that wealthy states tend to have fewer recipients than poorer states — though some like California, New York, and Rhode Island do aid many persons.

The wealthier states in some years devote a higher percentage of the budget to welfare. In 1940 these states tended to have higher total welfare expenditures per capita than other states, but in the 1950s this association is greatly attenuated, and in the 1960s it is reversed for the income measure. Likewise, in 1940 wealthy states tended to get more federal grants per capita; in the 1950s the correlation is in the opposite direction; in the

TABLE 10

Relationship of State Welfare Efforts and Need, Socioeconomic Development, Politics (Simple correlation coefficients)

		Total per capita welfare expenditure	State per capita welfare expenditure	Federal per capita welfare grants	Welfare expenditure as percentage of general expenditure	Total number recipients	Average payment AFDC
Infant mortality	1940	-.32	-.39	-.16	-.25	-.14	-.50
	1950	-.01	-.15	.16	-.12	.33	-.60
	1964	-.20	-.56	.30	.28	.38	-.69
Median family income	1940	.64	.69	.47	.30	.30	.72
	1950	.08	.34	-.27	-.07	-.58	.70
	1959	-.07	-.13	-.07	.28	-.33	.69
Average competition for governor	1930-1940	.53	.57	.38	.39	.32	.58
	1942-1950	.08	.26	-.17	.01	-.37	.58
	1956-1966	.05	.08	-.04	.04	-.32	.65
Percentage turnout for governor	pre-1941	.53	.55	.43	.48	.44	.49
	pre-1951	.21	.36	-.02	.17	-.19	.56
	pre-1966	.33	.61	-.31	-.34	-.20	.51

1960s the pattern is indeterminate. State welfare spending per capita tended to be higher for rich states in 1940 and 1950, although the positive association no longer prevails in the 1960s for the income measure. Once again, the federal formulas seem to have been instrumental in equalizing public assistance spending by reducing the advantage possessed by states of high socioeconomic development.

States that are competitive for governor over a ten-year span share certain common patterns of welfare effort; Table 10 displays the correlations of welfare effort and competition. The more competitive states grant higher average payments for AFDC than do the noncompetitive states, and the strength of this correlation increases in the 1960s.[33] A decline occurs in the relationship with the percentage of the budget devoted to welfare: in 1940 competitive states gave welfare a higher priority, whereas in 1950 and 1960 the relationship is nonexistent. Likewise, competitive states in 1940 had higher total welfare expenditures; in 1950 and 1960 competition had little association with total welfare spending. In the 1940s competitive states gave money to larger numbers of recipients, but in 1950 and 1960 the association disappears.

The reversals or attenuations seem to be due to the change in patterns of state-local and federal support for welfare. In 1940 the federal government gave more to competitive states than to others, because these states paid out more of their own money and at that point the federal government matched state payments. In 1950 and 1960 competitive states sometimes received less federal money. In 1940 high competition was associated with a high level of state-local support for welfare; by the 1950s the correlation was greatly reduced, and by the 1960s it dropped nearly to zero.

Thus far, when discussing measures of competition we have relied on the ten-year periods (long-term system competition) because the short-term (two election) measures coincided almost exactly. The only period of competition that seems to have changed in the short-run is gubernatorial competition in the 1960s. The forty-eight states apparently became more competitive in the two elections prior to 1966, and the differences among the states on this measure, as described by the coefficient of variation, decreased from 26.0 in the 1940s to 10.1 in the 1960s, which is the narrowest range of any variable.

Short-range gubernatorial competition in the 1960s had a stronger and appreciably different relationship with several welfare indicators than did the long-term gubernatorial competition just discussed. For instance, the states that were competitive in the short run devoted a smaller share of their budgets to welfare $(-.78)$, got less federal money $(-.64)$, and spent more of their own money on welfare (.89) than did other states. Here, political competition is strongly related to welfare spending.

As Table 10 shows, states with high voter turnout characteristically have higher average payments for AFDC, higher total welfare expenditures, and higher state-local expenditures. In the 1940s these states had more recipients and received more federal money; however, in the 1950s and 1960s these trends reversed so that high turnout states now have fewer recipients and receive smaller amounts from the federal government. In 1940 and 1950 states with high turnout gave higher budgetary priority to welfare than did other states, but the correlation is just the opposite in the 1960s.

Since we know that need, socioeconomic development, and political competition are related to welfare effort and are themselves related, we need a way to separate the influences in order to see whether political or socioeconomic factors (need, income, urbanization) are the most important determinants of the state's welfare efforts. Regression analysis is one method we can use to achieve this purpose; in Table 11 the R^2 tells how well several independent variables (need, wealth, urbanization, and politics) predict the dependent variables (five of the most important welfare measures)

TABLE 11

Percentage of Variance in Five Welfare Measures Explained by Need, Socioeconomic Development, and Political Measures

		Need, socio-economic R^{2a}	Political R^{2b}
Total per capita welfare expenditures	1940-1942	.49	.33
	1951-1953	.32	.07
	1966-1968	.30	.17
State per capita welfare expenditures	1940-1942	.56	.38
	1951-1953	.39	.13
	1966-1968	.82	.50
Welfare expenditure as percentage of general expenditure	1940-1942	.29	.24
	1951-1953	.28	.10
	1966-1968	.79	.20
Total number of recipients	1940-1942	.35	.20
	1951-1953	.48	.20
	1966-1968	.47	.16
Average payment AFDC	1940-1942	.65	.35
	1951-1953	.66	.38
	1966-1968	.74	.50

[a]Need, socioeconomic R^2 includes median family income, personal income per capita, per cent urban, infant mortality, and percentage poor (except in 1940).
[b]Political R^2 includes average per cent of winning party in governorship, lower house, upper house, and percentage turnout in gubernatorial elections.

in each of three time periods. A comparison of the relative magnitude of the socioeconomic R^2s and the political R^2s reveals which of the two is more important.

Generally, we see that socioeconomic factors explain more of the variance in the welfare measures than do political factors. Six of the fifteen welfare measurements have 50 per cent or more of their variance explained by need, income, and urbanization, whereas for only two variables does politics explain as much as 50 per cent. Need-wealth-urbanization seems to predict better than do political characteristics for every dependent variable in each period. Total welfare spending and number of recipients are the only welfare variables for which need-wealth-urbanization does not explain at least half the variance in at least one period. In contrast, AFDC average payment and state-local spending are the only variables for which politics explains as much as half the variance in a time period.

Another way we can evaluate the relative importance of socioeconomic factors and political factors is to combine the most powerful predictors of each independent variable into a single regression. The partial correlation coefficient indicates the relative strength of the independent variables, and thus we can find out if politics predicts welfare effort independent of need, wealth, and urbanization.

Regressing a combination of the most powerful political and socioeconomic variables on the five welfare measures in the three time periods does not increase the number of welfare variables for which half the variance is explained. Nor does the predominant status of need-wealth-urbanization change much. Politics is a less important predictor than need-wealth-urbanization in all but five of fifteen cases. The exceptions are total welfare expenditures in 1950, state-local welfare expenditures in 1960, and percentage of the budget devoted to welfare in all three periods. The short-term gubernatorial competition variable was the strong variable accounting for the predominance of politics in 1960 on the latter two measures. The relatively greater importance of politics in explaining proportion of the budget than in explaining level of the budget was predicted by other scholars.[34] The strongest socioeconomic predictors are median family income, percentage urban, and percentage poor.

CONCLUSION

In this chapter we have traced the development of public welfare policy in the American states, outlined the major welfare programs in which the states play a major role, developed a series of measurements of various dimensions of state welfare effort, used these indices to compare state welfare activities, and examined how different patterns of welfare activity are related to selected social, economic, and political conditions. Our study has been narrow in regard to the scope of welfare activities, but broad and general in regard to the variables we have dealt with and the indicators we have employed in our analysis. We have concentrated on gross conditions for which comparable data were readily available for nearly all the states. Consequently, we said nothing about the factors that might influence welfare decisions in any particular state. Nor did we say much about the configurations of interest groups, leaders, public opinion, and values that influence state welfare commitments and actions.

The widespread commitments to public welfare by the states, and the expenditures of large sums of money for public welfare programs have been phenomena of the past four decades. During this period three trends have developed simultaneously: greater governmental welfare involvement, an increase in the responsibilities of the state governments in setting up and administering public welfare programs, and increasingly active participation by the federal government in defining and financing public welfare. These patterns are likely to continue in the future. Public responsibility for providing and guaranteeing minimum sustenance is likely to increase. The federal government most likely will assume more importance in nearly all aspects of public welfare activities.

We stressed the variety of dimensions to look at in considering the amount of effort a state gives to public welfare, even when concentrating on the amounts of money spent and the numbers of persons aided. During the early 1940s comparative rankings of states along the several dimensions or aspects of welfare effort tended to be somewhat similar. States that ranked high in effort along one dimension tended to rank high along the others. States that gave money to many persons tended to give out high per recipient payments and to make high per capita welfare payments. By the late 1960s state rankings diverged along the several dimensions. States ranking high in one aspect of welfare effort did not necessarily rank similarly high in others. This was particularly true of the measures of persons per 1,000 receiving welfare assistance and the amount of payments per recipient. Relative state rankings for the amount of average payments per recipient have remained fairly constant, but many states have changed in relative ranking in the number of recipients aided. The most significant change in state efforts over the years has been the movement of many poor states with high levels of welfare need — states that tend to be concentrated in southern and border areas — to change from making small payments to comparatively few individuals to making small payments to relatively many individuals. These same states have tended to rise considerably higher in comparative rankings for total per capita welfare expenditures. These changes, it seems fairly clear, have been strongly influenced by the increased level of and altered patterns of federal financing of public assistance programs.

Great variations continue in all indicators of the level of state effort, although the discrepancies lessened over time. One important area in which the opposite trend — greater variation in state effort — has occurred is in the measure of numbers of public assistance recipients per 1,000 population. The overall trend suggests that federal policy directed in part toward equalization of welfare benefits has been partially successful.

Following the lead of other studies of state policies, we investigated several hypotheses regarding the relationship between the objective need for welfare assistance, economic conditions, and some selected political factors and state welfare efforts. For the contemporary period, as one would expect from the divergence of state positions along the several indices of welfare effort, the pattern of these relationships is complex. In regard to the level of average payments per recipient, the needier states, the poorer states, and the states ranking lower in party competition and voter participation consistently make smaller payments than other states. Between these three conditions and number of recipients per 1,000 population, the relationship is the same for the early time period (needier, poorer, less competitive, and lower turnout states do less in the field of welfare), but by the 1960s the relationship is reversed, with the poorer states and the states with lower levels of party competition and voter turnout tending to give aid to a comparatively larger proportion of people. Though the pattern of reversal is not as great as for the number of recipients aided, some change has occurred over time in the relationship between these several conditions and total per capita welfare expenditures. Whereas the relationships between median family income, party competition, and per capita expenditures was fairly strong and positive in the 1940s, by the late 1960s it is negligible.

In the argument current in the literature of state politics and policy as to whether socioeconomic conditions or political factors such as party competition and political participation are most strongly associated with the level of policy output, our analysis tends to support the relative importance of the socioeconomic conditions. In most instances the correlation coefficients computed between socioeconomic conditions and level of effort are higher than those relating the political factors. The regression analysis similarly suggests that socioeconomic conditions predict a larger portion of the variance than political factors.

The present system is a patchwork of programs developed over a long time, incorporating a variety of ideas and compromises. The past decade has witnessed growing discontent over the structure and operation of the public welfare system. During the past few years major assaults have been launched against the system or against individual programs from a wide variety of standpoints and perspectives. Both conservatives and liberals have argued that the system has not worked nor been very effective. Conservatives, on the one hand, argue that we have a very costly series of programs that have not helped much in solving the problems of poverty and insecurity. More money is constantly being paid out to more people in a manner that tends to foster social and economic irresponsibility, they allege. Many liberals and pro-welfare partisans, on the other hand, while agreeing that the present system has not worked very successfully, argue that welfare provisions have not been liberal enough either in amounts of payments or ease of access to benefits. They still find aspects of the program degrading for the individuals receiving aid. Groups of welfare recipients and strong supporters of better benefits and more sophisticated treatment of welfare recipients have become better organized and more militant in pressing their demands for more liberal welfare provisions. This has been particularly true in regard to AFDC recipients — AFDC has been one of the fastest growing and most controversial of the categorical assistance programs. Other segments of the population with different values may be organizing and becoming more militantly opposed to public assistance programs and any attempts to liberalize them. Because a substantial proportion of welfare beneficiaries are black — this is particularly true of AFDC recipients — opposition or support of public assistance often takes on racial significance.

Another current issue of controversy surrounding the public assistance programs is the unequal payments to recipients made by different states. As we have shown in our program and data analysis, states retain the authority to determine the level of payments to beneficiaries, and payments for the same program vary widely from state to state. We pointed out that a recent federal court decision involving the state of Maryland upheld the right of the state to determine the maximum amount of payments provided under the categorical assistance programs. The welfare reform proposals of the Nixon administration include provisions calling for the standardization of welfare payments from state to state. Among complaints lodged against the diversity of payment levels from state to state is the contention that it encourages migration from states, such as southern and border states, in which welfare payments are low to states, such as New York and California and other northern and western states, where per recipient payments are much higher.

In addition to proposing changes in the current welfare structure, some advocate more drastic alterations in welfare policy. One of the most prominent of these proposals is some variation of a guaranteed annual income, a family maintenance allowance, or a negative income tax. All of these are variations of programs that would attempt to provide every family with a minimum income. Such a program would be a major departure from the current system of categorical assistance programs. The idea has widespread support among economists and public welfare officials and has become a part — though one of the most controversial — of the Nixon administration's proposal for broad revision of the current welfare system.

SELECTED BIBLIOGRAPHY

Brown, Josephine. *Public Relief: 1929–1939*. New York: Henry Holt, 1958. This is a good source book for material on the historical background and development of public welfare policies in the United States, especially the developments leading up to and including the 1935 Social Security Act.

Council of State Governments. *Book of the States*. Chicago: The Council of State Governments. This biennial publication is a good source of political, policy, and expenditure data for the states.

Dawson, Richard E., and James A. Robinson, "Inter-Party Competition, Economic Variables, and Welfare Policies in the American States." *Journal of Politics*, 25 (May, 1963): 265–289; and Charles Cnudde and Donald J. McCrone, "Party Competition and Welfare Policies in the American States," *American Political Science Review*, 58 (September, 1969): 858–866. These two articles deal with the impact of party competition upon state welfare policies.

United States Department of Health, Education and Welfare, Social Security Administration. *Social Security Bulletin*. Washington, D.C.: U.S. Government Printing Office. This monthly publication contains a great deal of data concerning most aspects of federal and state welfare programs and activities, as well as articles dealing with social security and public welfare.

CHAPTER THIRTEEN

State Politics and Highways

Robert S. Friedman

Highways are among the most costly, pervasive, and politicized areas of state policy making. More is spent by state and local government in the United States for highways than for any other activity except education. This fact alone is enough to make a careful examination of highway decision making important in studying American state politics. Two additional factors make it critical. First, highway decisions are relevant to most other areas of activity. The consolidation of rural schools, the development of state parks, the redevelopment and restoration of urban central business districts, and the development of land-use patterns in suburbia are all dependent on highway decisions. Second, despite the extensive expertise and advanced technology in highway engineering, professionals and technicians in the field recognize the political nature of highway decision making.

Until quite recently state politics witnessed consistent victories for supporters of expanded freeways and expressways at the expense of advocates of other modes of transportation. Slowly but perceptibly this trend has begun to turn toward those opposed to a system of transportation dominated exclusively by the superhighway and the private automobile. Although some uniformity in the pattern of decision making has permeated the highway politics of most states, there are noticeable differences both in decision style and outcomes among the states. In this chapter I will describe and attempt to explain these similarities and differences.

To accomplish this goal, it is necessary to describe the setting for highway decision making. This description will include the historical growth and development of American highways, the components of a highway system, and the relationships among levels of government in highway activities. We must also examine the structure in which decisions are made, some of the issues about which controversies develop, and the participants in conflicts that occur. Finally, we will test some of the factors that have resulted in variations among states in highway outputs.

THE SETTING

Growth and Development of Highways

Any discussion of state highway politics must begin with the extraordinary expansion of the highway system in the twentieth century. In 1900 the entire United States had only 128,500 miles of surfaced roads. By 1968 Texas alone had over 170,000 miles of surfaced roads and the national total exceeded 2,800,000 miles. In 1900 only 8,000 motor vehicles were registered; by 1967 almost 97 million registered vehicles were being driven by over 103 million drivers.[1] * Consequently, governmental expenditures in 1900 for highway construction and maintenance were minuscule except at the municipal level. Presently all levels of government are significantly involved. In fact, in approximately twenty states the total state and local expenditures for highway purposes range from one-fifth to one-third of all governmental expenditures, and in no state is the figure under one-tenth. These proportions represent a small decline in the past few years in comparison with other services. Nevertheless, when we consider the magnitude of political activity undertaken on behalf of governmental participation in education, health, welfare, public safety, or recreation, the successes scored by the supporters of an ever expanding highway system are all the more impressive.

The general growth in highways and highway use in all fifty states has been fairly uniform and is closely associated with a steady increase in motor vehicles of all kinds. The same categories of highway demands are found throughout the states. Construction specifications, with allowances for peculiarities in terrain and climate within each category, are similar. The financing of highways varies, but here again similarities outweigh differences. The political game of highway building and maintenance has similar categories of players; the arenas, the structure of the arenas, and the rules of the game have only modest variation from state to state.

Nevertheless, these uniformities must not obscure numerous differences. When one highway official was asked about the comparative quality of highway systems among the states, he had little difficulty in distinguish-

* [See pp. 601–604 for notes to this chapter. — Eds.]

ing what he regarded to be the very best highway systems from the very worst.[2] When we compare expenditures, we must judge that some states earmark a substantially larger segment of the budget for highways than others.*

Highway Needs

Highway engineers often describe the need for new highways in terms of optimum traffic flow, based on safe speeds in urban and rural areas. Underlying these needs are differences in demands from various classes of highway users. Users compete in the political market place for scarce dollars to construct and maintain the kinds of roads socially and economically necessary to them. Retail merchants in the core city demand expressways in the heart of the city to compete with growing suburban shopping centers. Rural school administrators urge improvement of rural roads to enable school buses to complete their daily rounds. The interstate trucking industry supports improved, primary intercity roads. Operators of highway motels, restaurants, and gas stations press for more access roads to interstate highways. Farmers demand paved roads from farm to market. Residents of suburbs insist upon paved neighborhood streets.

Until World War II, the major question about these demands was which would be met.[3] From the advent of the automobile until World War II, emphasis was on construction of rural roads, both primary and secondary. Cities had created street networks that were able to service motor vehicle needs reasonably well, especially with the continued vitality of street railway systems. Road conditions in rural America were so poor that even the railroads joined in support of improved farm-to-market roads in order to guarantee access to railroad terminals.[4] As a result, state after state created highway departments charged with constructing primary rural highways, and schemes were devised whereby state aid was granted to local units of government, other than cities, to relieve the problem of inadequate farm-to-market roads.

Highway Classification

Since World War II, the dominance of motor vehicles in the field of surface transportation has engendered great demand for highway construction activity in both urban and rural areas. In general, the response to the

---

* Because of the difficulty in distinguishing local from state expenditure, for comparative purposes our discussion of expenditures includes both state and local expenditure.

demands for all categories has been extremely favorable. Exceptions to this have begun to develop within urban areas where some resentment to construction of interstate highways has occurred. However, the most common sources of conflict continue to be allocation of cost, location, and construction specifications.

The burden of cost is a knotty problem since it encompasses not only the tax system but also the distribution of state aid to local government units and the scheme of highway classification.[5] A system of highway classification has been devised in many states to provide orderly development and a scheme of responsibility for state and local roads. Categories vary, but a typical classification scheme divides the system into rural and urban roads. Rural roads are then subdivided into primary, secondary, and land service systems and urban into primary, secondary, and local.[6] Designation of roads in these categories influences policy decisions, for it determines the level of government — state, county, or city — charged with construction and/or maintenance. It also settles the source of funds for construction or maintenance — state taxes, local taxes, or special assessments on property adjoining highways.[7]

The most frequently adopted criterion for inclusion in the state system is the stipulation that "the primary system shall connect all counties or county seats." In the view of one observer this system "strongly favors rural interests in that it allocates equal weight to each area of the state regardless of the sparsity or density of its population." [8] Another frequently used criterion to define the state primary system is "roads which connect population and market centers." Although this kind of provision permits discretion, it is undoubtedly more favorable to the more concentrated population centers. Other stipulations include development of natural resources, development of business, industry, agriculture, traffic needs, public welfare, provision for an integrated system, and the financial capacity of the state. All permit wide leeway and political flexibility.

A leading student of highway financial policy has argued that although in theory highway classification is designed to differentiate arteries of statewide from local importance for purposes of establishing revenue and expenditure policy, in practice it serves as an additional form of state aid. His argument is based on the fact that in many states pressure is exerted successfully by local interests to transfer roads from classification as locally maintained roads to state highways. The purpose of this pressure is to relieve the burden upon local revenue sources and also to obtain higher quality road service.[9]

Control and administration of rural roads by state agencies varies among the states. In eighteen states rural, secondary, or country roads are under state jurisdiction. In three of these, Delaware, North Carolina, and West Virginia, all county roads are state administered.[10] These states do not fit regional patterns nor are they in like categories of urbanization, industrialization, or political party competition. Furthermore, the practice of including secondary and county roads under state jurisdiction does not seem to be related to the independence of the highway department from the governor.[11] Similarly, this pattern seems to be as common in states with strong governors as in states with weak governors (using the Schlesinger index of gubernatorial power).[12] Whatever distribution of responsibility and control is agreed upon within the state political system, the categories of highways outlined earlier are found to some extent in all states.

Cost Variations

Differences in costs of highways result not only from differences in population but also from several other conditions.[13] Variations in soil and terrain account for differences in highway cost. It is relatively cheap to construct highways on desert sands, but expensive in rocky terrain. Similarly, the prairie lands of the Midwest present few obstacles in comparison with mountainous regions of the Rockies or even West Virginia. Climatic conditions also add to the cost of highways in some regions. The need for snow removal and for repairs due to damage by deep winter frost both represent expenses not found in the South. On the other hand, excessive rainfall adds to highway costs in some areas. In short, within the general uniformities in highway needs are variations resulting from natural factors that are not a product of the vicissitudes of the political system.

Federal Aid Programs

Perhaps the most important factor in highway politics and one that encourages uniformity in state highway systems has been the program of federal aid. Since 1916 the federal government, through the Bureau of Public Roads, has provided funds for highway construction under standards of organization and procedure established at the national level. In order for a state to participate in the program initiated by the Federal Aid Road Act of 1916, it was required to have a highway department.[14] Plans for highway construction under the program were to be drawn up by individual highway departments but submitted to federal highway authorities for approval. Plans were required to show locations of roads to be constructed, specifications, and cost estimates. Money was only available for construction purposes and was limited to the intercity road system. An amendment enacted in 1921 stated that aid was to be limited to a maximum of 7 per cent of the total road mileage of the state. Federal appropriations were made from the general fund and allocated on the basis of one-third according to area, one-third according to population, and one-third on the basis of total mileage of rural delivery and star routes* in the state. States were required to match federal grants dollar for dollar.[15]

Two changes of lasting significance were instituted during the depression. The National Industrial Recovery Act provided that at least one-fourth of the federal aid funds allocated to the states be used on extensions of federal aid highways into or through incorporated municipalities. In addition, up to one-fourth of the funds could be used for secondary or feeder roads. These changes were predicated upon work-relief policies rather than highway policies, but their adoption gave added support to the advocates of highway aid for purely urban and rural needs in later years.[16] The highway act of 1944 specifically incorporated these policies into the permanent highway program. Under the act, appropriations were made specifically for primary roads, urban extensions of primary roads, and secondary roads. A mileage limitation was continued on aid to the primary system, but none was placed on either of the other two programs. Three separate allocation formulae were used. The primary system continued to receive aid on the formula of one-third area, one-third population, and one-third mail route mileage. The secondary system allocation was similar, except that only rural population was used. Urban area funds were apportioned on the basis of population in urban areas, with 5,000 being used as the minimum population for urban classification.[17]

Later Innovations

The Federal Highway Acts of 1944 and 1956 had an impact on state highway politics because they created for the first time a single network of primary highways with uniform minimum standards. The result of these enactments has been to increase the role of the United States Bureau of Public Roads in decision making in matters previously left entirely to state and local authorities.

---

* The post office department is authorized to contract for the transportation of mail over a post road other than a railroad, and such contract may include collection and delivery service to patrons of the postal service. Such roads are designated star routes. 39 USCA 6401.

The 1944 act created for the first time a system of interstate highways designed to connect the principal metropolitan areas, cities, and industrial centers by as direct a route as possible. The system, when completed, will total 42,500 miles of road. State highway departments were required to cooperate with departments in adjoining states to determine routes, subject to federal approval. No specially designated funds, however, were earmarked for these roads until 1952.[18] The net effect of the act was to shift federal highway activity from rural to urban areas. It also provided the Bureau of Public Roads with meaningful supervisory tools that guaranteed it major decision-making powers in the construction of primary roads. Specifically, the bureau was granted an important part in highway classification and route selection. Each state was awarded a portion of interstate highway mileage. If a state did not designate the artery desired by the Bureau of Public Roads, the mileage and money could be given to another state. The bureau has occasionally recommended major modifications of route alignment or recommended the selection of entirely different routes.[19]

Other features of the act have enhanced the position of the Bureau of Public Roads and have assured uniformity among the states. One is the requirement that all interstate highways be controlled access roads. Another provision discouraged signs and billboards along highway rights-of-way. Any state regulating such signs on rights-of-way acquired after 1956 was granted a .5 per cent reduction in its share of the cost of the program. Finally, the act froze maximum size and weight limits at their 1956 level.[20] The Bureau of Public Roads has permitted flexibility in these provisions. However, the shift from a 50–50 matching of funds to an arrangement under which the federal government paid 90 per cent of the program cost assured continued control by the Bureau of Public Roads.

One other aspect of the federal program is important to an understanding of state highway politics. The distribution of funds for the first several years of the interstate program was based one-half on population and one-half on the primary road system formula developed in 1916. Since then, distribution has been based on the need for completion of the program. Determination of need has been left largely to the states with only minimum specifications set by the Bureau of Public Roads. This has benefited states that had ignored their interstate roads during the period before 1956 in favor of construction of other roads. States, particularly in the congested northeast and the Pacific coast, that had used federal and state money earlier for their interstate highways were simply "out of luck." [21]

The actual completion rate of segments of the interstate system has lagged somewhat behind the expected completion date of 1972 for the entire system. The median percentage of designated interstate highways among the fifty states open to traffic on June 30, 1969, was 66 and only in six states was more than 80 per cent of the designated mileage open to traffic. However, well in excess of 90 per cent of the designated mileage was under construction if not open. In only eight states, Colorado, Connecticut, Florida, Hawaii, New Jersey, North Dakota, Rhode Island, and Wisconsin, was the figure less than 90 per cent.[22]

As the interstate program nears completion, a national controversy has developed regarding the disposition of the Highway Trust Fund, the money collected by the federal government from gasoline taxes. Two issues are at stake. First, should the tax be continued? Second, if it is continued should the money be used for maintenance and reconstruction of interstate highways, should it be used for primary and secondary road systems that may have been neglected during the period in which state highway department energy has built the interstate system, or should some or all of it be diverted for use in innovating other modes of public transportation?

The following evaluation of the controversy by a leading business magazine suggests one possible outcome of the controversy:

> The highway lobby has behind it some of the most powerful state political machines in the U.S. . . . In many states, the highway department produces the grease that keeps the machines running. Since the gasoline pump is one of the most efficient tax collection agencies ever devised by man, in many states it takes in more money than any other state department. It has more contracts to give; it has more favors to offer. . . .
> Finally, like the gun lobby, the highway lobby has the strength of a great mystique. There are millions of Americans who just plain love cars. They will make any sacrifice to own and drive a car.[23]

Although it is improbable that highway interests will be severely set back, some small inroads have been made in favor of other modes of public transportation. The impetus for this has come from the passage in 1964 of the Urban Mass Transportation Act and from the creation of a federal Department of Transportation in 1966. The 1964 act encouraged research and planning and authorized some finances for facilities, equipment, and the relocation of individuals displaced by the development of mass transportation projects. The 1966 act created a cabinet level department in which the Federal Highway Administration is formally subordinated to the secretary in the same way as the Federal Railroad Administration, Urban Mass Transportation Administration, U.S. Coast Guard, and Federal

Aviation Administration. Realistically, neither of these developments is likely to reduce the support for highways, but they do provide the machinery for a countervailing force that, together with pressures from inner-city dwellers and their supporters, may ultimately change the balance in the system of public transportation.

State-Local Relations

Although the focus of our attention is on state highway politics, the political and administrative relation between state and local highway systems is so close that we should mention the impact of the state highway department on local road affairs. Customarily, highway construction and the maintenance of local roads, urban and rural, have been local responsibilities. Local road systems were in operation long before state highway networks were on the drawing board. In recent years, local governments have had to rely more on state funds for their local road programs, leading to increased supervision by state highway departments and greater state control of local roads. We have already referred to the great variation among states in the percentage of local roads under state control. Equally varied is the amount of influence accruing to the state from control of the purse strings. Influence in some instances appears potentially great, but is only minimal in practice. In instances in which local road organizations are popularly elected or chosen politically, freedom to defy state edicts is maximized. Nevertheless, dependence upon state revenue determines how much local officials will flex their muscles.

City highway organizations are far freer from state supervision than their rural counterparts. They have participated in state aid programs in relatively few states. Where no money is dispensed, little control is exercised. With the advent of the federal program for urban roads, however, the pattern changed. In some states, however, even after the legislation, the inability of city forces to marshal legislative strength meant little state aid. In Louisiana, for example, in the late 1940s and early 1950s the cities of New Orleans and Baton Rouge, which had city-county consolidations, did well because of their eligibility for parish (county) road funds. So did towns having under 5,000 population in which urban extensions of primary state roads represented the main street of the city. Cities of intermediate size were receiving nothing. State legislation in 1955 and the interstate program have altered this situation.[24] In general, however, except for coordination and general street planning, city highway departments remain independent of the state system.

INSTITUTIONAL STRUCTURE

One of the ironies of highway politics is that, despite the highly charged conflicts that prevail, strong endorsement is found in many states for a highway organization that is superficially removed from partisan political decision making. For example, during the 1961–62 Michigan constitutional convention, highway groups such as the Michigan Road Builders Association, the Associated Petroleum Industries of Michigan, the Oil and Gas Association of Michigan, and the Good Roads Federation all argued for the retention of an independently elected highway commissioner. They argued that highway building needed to be removed from regular political channels, using the following rationale:

> Michigan's economy depends on highways, and highway construction and maintenance are something apart from other functions. The governor's views might control elsewhere but not with respect to highways. Michigan has an outstanding system and this is due to two factors, a highway commissioner separately elected and a system of earmarking revenues for highway needs.[25]

Relationship to the Governor

What are the consequences for highway politics of differences in organization and relationships of the highway department with the governor? We propose that the control the governor exercises over highway policy partially determines the competitive position of highway building and maintenance vis-à-vis other programs. If the highway department is under the wing of the governor, it will have to compete with other programs for support. Where the department is independent its supporters and staff are freer to plead their own cause. Because highways are visible and tangible, only vigorous action by a governor is likely to restrain legislatures from pouring money into highways, rather than mental health and similar programs. Even a strong governor operates with a handicap in states with independent highway departments.

A highway department that is organizationally independent differs from one that is dependent upon the governor or the executive branch. As with other complex organizations, formal structures do not entirely describe the decision-making patterns. In Louisiana, for example, the governing body of the highway department is a multimembered board appointed by the governor for staggered terms whose length exceed his own. The board appoints and removes the highway director. In actuality, however, recent governors have "arranged" upon taking office to have the legislature remove "undesirable" commissioners by a device known as "addressing out of office." [26] Through this technique any governor so desiring may name his own highway director and exercise strong gubernatorial control over the department. In some states, formal structures probably do reflect actual practice.

We may use several criteria to measure the independence of highway departments from governors or their dependence upon them. These include plural- versus single-headed governing authority, independent election or prescriptive gubernatorial confirmation versus unrestricted gubernatorial selection, legislative confirmation versus no confirmation, term of office exceeding that of the governor versus coincidence of term of office, and removal only for cause versus service at the pleasure of the governor. A dependent highway department would be one in which a governor was free to name his own department head without restrictions on partisanship or professional background and without legislative veto power. The highway director would serve at the pleasure of the governor. An independent department would be governed by a multimembered board chosen by the governor, but with prescriptions neutralizing partisanship and perhaps guaranteeing occupational and regional representation. Legislative confirmation would be required and the term of office would exceed that of the governor. Removal would be for cause only. In addition, control over the appointment of the highway director would be entirely within the purview of the board, and usually professional qualifications would be written into the system.

Very few states use either of the models.[27] However, using these, we have classified formal structure of state highway departments under three heads: independent, partially dependent, and dependent. Table 1 lists the distribution of these structures among American states. This classification was used to test the hypothesis above and the evidence casts doubt on its validity. This doubt is based on examination of the five year averages of state and local expenditures based on per capita, per $1000 income, and percentage of all expenditures. The means for partially dependent states were higher on all three measures of expenditures than in independent or dependent states. In addition the per capita expenditures in dependent states averaged more than in independent states — $88.84 to $82.56.

TABLE 1
Relationship of Highway Department to Governor

	Independent	Partially dependent	Dependent
	Arizona	California	Alabama
	Arkansas	Kansas	Alaska
	Colorado	Louisiana	Connecticut
	Delaware	Maryland	Hawaii
	Florida	Minnesota	Illinois
	Georgia	Nevada	Kentucky
	Idaho	Nebraska	New Jersey
	Indiana	Oklahoma	New York
	Iowa	Oregon	North Dakota
	Maine	South Dakota	Ohio
	Massachusetts	Vermont	Pennsylvania
	Michigan	Virginia	Rhode Island
	Mississippi	West Virginia	Tennessee
	Missouri	Wisconsin	
	Montana		
	New Hampshire		
	New Mexico		
	North Carolina		
	South Carolina		
	Texas		
	Utah		
	Washington		
	Wyoming		

Source: See note 27.

Board Representation

Several states employing highway commissions stipulate that commissioners represent geographical districts rather than the state at large. The usual rationale for such provisions is that problems vary from place to place and the district highway commissioner is able to convey this to the highway department. Variations of this device are used in approximately half the states. Commission members in these states are usually appointed from geographical districts, such as counties, highway districts, supreme court districts, judicial districts, congressional districts, and in some instances from cities.[28] Proponents of coordinated highway planning for the state highway network frown on this device as a deterrent to the accomplishment of their ends and charge that localism results from it.[29] It would be difficult to measure the validity of the charges. However, the interstate highway program most likely has diminished the probability of localism in state highway affairs, regardless of the presence or absence of a district system for appointing highway commissioners.

In organizing some governmental functions, commissions have been created with occupational or professional requirements designed to represent either affected economic interests or professional standards. No legislation requires highway commissions to represent specific occupations. However, some occupations may be informally recognized. One state in which the highway director is required by law to appoint an advisory committee makes a conscious effort to represent "affected" industries. The highway director in question was very prompt to point out that the committee does not make policy and serves at most as a sounding board. Professional qualifications are seldom required of commissioners. West Virginia sets technical requirements for the executive who heads its highway department.[30] This standard is also frequent for highway directors in commission states.

State Departments of Transportation

A new development that may ultimately have far-reaching implications for state highway politics is the creation of state departments of transportation in which highway agencies are subordinate units. An informal survey made in 1969 revealed that five states — Florida, Hawaii, New Jersey, New York, and Wisconsin — had taken this step. The threat of this new and broader organization mechanism to highway independence is illustrated in proposals enacted by the Pennsylvania and Maryland legislatures in 1970. The Pennsylvania act provided for a transportation department that included highways, motor vehicle licensing, traffic safety, aeronautics, and mass transportation. It left untouched the earmarking of highway user revenues. The Maryland act made it the first state to establish a comprehensive transportation trust fund. Under the act the new trust fund is to be supported by revenues from highway user charges, motor vehicle fees, port authority revenues, fuel taxes, etc. Expenditures are no longer limited to highways but include other forms of transportation as well.[31] Since highways will lose their organizational and financial independence, they will also lose their preeminence over other forms of transportation.

Organizational issues such as departmental autonomy, multiple versus single executive, and the method of selecting the agency head have apparently made little difference in highway policy among states. On the other hand, subsuming highways under departments of transportation, especially if highway user revenues are not confined to highway expenditures, could vary policy.

ISSUES IN HIGHWAY LOCATION,
CONSTRUCTION, AND FINANCE

Highway engineers and economists have developed technical standards for highway location, rights-of-way, construction practices, use of highways, and finance.* Nevertheless, each of these has been a source of political conflict in some states, as statements from policy makers in a state highway department in a large industrial state exemplify. These officials were asked to list individuals and interest groups most directly affected by the services performed by the department. They were also asked which groups they thought felt benefited and which felt they were harmed by these services. To a large degree, when administrators mentioned groups harmed they mentioned only those affected by "technical aspects" of highway building. The head of the department, for example, identified owners of roadside services on highways that had been relocated and persons whose property had been purchased for highway rights-of-way. Only after further questioning did he mention the competitive facets of highways and the railroad and airline industries. The department's director of administration in response to the same question identified local communities by-passed by primary trucklines, people whose homesteads are in the path of highways, railroads that are required to resolve the grade crossing problem, and the road building industry, which is compelled to meet high specification standards. A similar answer was given by the department's public information officer.

Highway Location

Controversy surrounding highway location is well documented in Alan Altshuler's description of the location of an intercity freeway in the Minneapolis-St. Paul area.[32] The decision to build was never in doubt. The route through the city of St. Paul, however, was the source of continuing conflict for several years. State highway engineers proposed a route that represented the least dollar expenditure and the best route from the standpoint of travel time. Their choice was based on easily quantifiable data that were readily available to them. The St. Paul city planner balked at this route because of what he considered to be its aesthetic and social cost. He thought it would detract from the appearance of the city and would tear up

---

* The Highway Research Board of the National Academy of Sciences-National Research Council is perhaps the leader in this field. The highway construction industry has itself been active in research and development.

a homogeneous Negro neighborhood. Because his planning skills were not based on techniques that were regarded to be as sophisticated as those of the highway engineer, his alternate route never was given serious consideration. The Negro community did obtain some concessions in the form of highway depression to maintain the integrity of their neighborhood. Apart from this, other sources of opposition, including central business district merchants fearful of the development of competing commercial establishments outside the central business district adjacent to the freeway, were unsuccessful in altering the route. As Altshuler put it, "It was a crucial advantage of the highway engineers in freeway disputes that they possessed and believed in a set of clear normative propositions, applicable to the most important of their problems and convincing to the vast majority of the people with whom they had to deal." [33]

Therefore, emphasis on technical aspects of highway policy making may tend to obscure controversy, but controversy, nevertheless, occurs frequently, on many issues. Decisions on highway location enhance property values for some and diminish values for others. Highways encourage commercial and industrial development nearby and discourage activity along abandoned or downgraded routes.[34] In some instances, conflicts occur between the builders of highways and those displaced from their homes, or those opposed to tampering with historical sites or areas of scenic beauty. Some dislocation conflicts have been alleviated by the Federal Highway Act of 1962, which authorizes states to enact legislation to reimburse property owners dislocated by highway building. Those who wish to retain the aesthetic character of urban areas, defeated in earlier controversies, began to see hope for future victory when, in the summer of 1969, United States Secretary of Transportation Volpe ordered the abandonment of an interstate highway route in the French Quarter of New Orleans because it would ruin the appearance of the area.*

Rights-of-Way

The disposition of rights-of-way for highway purposes is a delicate process in which public officials must participate in real estate transactions. Despite fairly elaborate rules of conduct, discretion permits manipulation that can be used to the economic advantage of some and the political advantage of others. The flexibility essential in this kind of activity sometimes allows officials to be charged with impropriety. Congressional hearings conducted by a House of Representatives subcommittee, chaired by Representative Blatnik of Minnesota, disclosed conduct the committee considered

* For a further discussion of this decision, see p. 507.

questionable in several states, but especially in Massachusetts and Florida.[35] In its report on land purchase and disposition in Florida the committee pointed to the sharp differences in costs between the land-boom states of Florida and California. It found that despite similar land value increases, California highway officials were purchasing land at a far lower cost than their counterparts in Florida.[36]

Construction Policies

Uniformities prevail in highway construction partly as a result of federal program specifications and partly because of developments in highway engineering practices. Nevertheless, the range of discretion occasionally has encouraged activities that have raised the specter of scandal. In Massachusetts allegations were made that grateful highway contrators held a testimonial dinner for a highway official who was rewarded the net proceeds of the dinner in return for services rendered. In the same state the Public Works Department, which builds the highways, was charged with dividing contracts into pieces of less than $1000 so that competitive bidding could be waived and "deserving" contractors rewarded.[37]

More commonly, highway politics leads to disputes like the one in Minnesota that began in the late 1930s and was not settled for a decade. A local manufacturer of natural cement requested that the highway department be required to use a blend of Portland and natural cements, which, he argued, would prevent scaling caused by winter weather and would also aid local industry. Highway department officials rejected the request on the ground that the claims made for the blend were not substantiated by research. As a result the blend had to compete in bidding with Portland cement. Since the latter was less expensive, the effect was to remove the blend from competition. The struggle that ultimately led to this decision involved not only the highway department and the affected industries, but also the legislature, the governor, and the United States Bureau of Public Roads.[38]

Weight Limits

Undoubtedly the most controversial technical problem is that of the use, or "wear and tear," on highways. Highway use by different classes of motor vehicles has varying physical effects on the highway.* Because of

---

* One element of the problem concerns differences in benefit derived from highway use and, therefore, questions inequities in the incidence of the financial burden. This is discussed in connection with highway revenue sources on pp. 493–495.

the generally accepted notion that heavy trucks have a deleterious effect on highways, many states have placed limitations upon truck weight. Some states have been more zealous than others with politically stronger trucking groups and competing transportation facilities.

A classic example of this occurred in Pennsylvania. Pennsylvania is a key state for the transportation industry not only because it is populous and industrial, but also because it bridges the eastern seaboard and the Midwest, and the North Atlantic and South Atlantic regions. In addition, the home office of one of the nation's largest railroads, one of the predecessors of the Penn Central, is located in the state.

In 1943 the overall weight limit for trucks in Pennsylvania was fixed at 45,000 pounds, the strictest limit of any state in the United States, except Kentucky.[39] Neighboring states had load limits of 60,000 to 70,000 pounds. The railroads hoped that trucks would have to unload before entering Pennsylvania and that some shippers might be frustrated enough to turn to the railroads. In addition, the heavily taxed railroads thought that a relaxation in the weight limit would give truckers an unfair competitive advantage. The trucking industry launched a counteroffensive in the 1950s that led to the passage of a law supported by Democratic Governor Leader that increased the weight limit to 60,000 pounds. Although Republican Governor Fine, Leader's predecessor, had vetoed a similar measure, the conflict was not primarily partisan. In fact, party lines were sharply broken. The division involved an intense campaign between the two directly affected interests, each of which created coalitions with numerous other groups that either had indirect interest or owned some allegiance to one of the protagonists. The struggle may have been more heated in Pennsylvania than elsewhere, but similar issues have arisen in numerous states.

In summary, the politics of highway construction and maintenance handles many conflicts over mundane technical issues. The state highway department must resolve these controversies, although in exceptional circumstances the governor, legislature, courts, and other agencies of federal, state, or local government may enter the picture before a settlement is reached.

Highway Finance — Revenue

Although issues of location and construction are important, the questions at the heart of the highway political game are who will benefit from highway construction, what money will be spent for, and who will pay.[40] Before the automobile became a major means of transportation, highway expenditures were derived from the general fund and revenue came mostly from property taxes. Automobile travel has changed highway finance substantially and has led to an increased reliance upon highway-user revenue sources. The earliest of these devices was the motor vehicle registration fee, initiated for purposes of identification but used increasingly for revenue purposes. Shortly after World War I, sales levies were begun on gasoline. Again, the theory behind the tax was that those who benefit from highways ought to pay for them. This point of view was supported most vigorously by railroad men, who argued that since use of the highway is free of charge, failure to charge the user more directly creates unfair competition for the railroads.

At present, over 50 per cent of all highway receipts are derived from the gasoline tax. Prior to the vast state highway building programs begun in the 1950s, much variation existed in the size of the gasoline levy. Southern states often had levies ranging up to seven cents per gallon even during depression years, in contrast to two or three cents in the northeast. Gasoline taxes began inching up around 1950 and now all states levy gasoline taxes from five to nine cents. In most states vehicles not using highways are exempt from the tax, which proves extremely beneficial to farmers.

Another major state revenue source for highways is the motor vehicle registration fee. In some states, particularly in the South, this source continues to be used almost exclusively as a regulatory device, and fees are very low. More than half the states increase the fee for heavier weight automobiles. Trucks and buses usually pay even higher fees on the grounds that they damage highways more than cars do. Again, many states reduce fees for farm vehicles that it is argued, do not use highways as extensively as other vehicles of the same size.

Several states recently have levied the so-called third structure taxes. These taxes combine heavy vehicle weight and high level travel. In other words, heavy trucks and buses carrying greater weight and traveling more miles are taxed at a higher rate. The technique is strongly supported by railroad interests and equally strongly opposed by truckers and bus companies. Thus far, it has been a very small revenue producer.

Because of the backlog of highway needs that had accrued by the end of World War II, many states resorted to bond issues to finance highway construction. This approach to the problem spreads out the time in which payment must be made and in some cases transfers the burden from the highway user exclusively to the population in general.

The use of toll roads has gained support in a number of states, particularly in the Northeast. The burden, of course, is placed directly on the highway user. Railroads have frequently endorsed this approach, but automobile clubs, truckers, and bus companies complain that they are facing double taxation on the grounds that they have already been compelled to pay motor vehicle and motor fuel taxes. In practice, the toll road is a most useful device for states that handle a great deal of through traffic. Over half of all toll receipts are collected in the states of New York, New Jersey, and Pennsylvania.

Earmarking of Funds

In a few states general revenues are used for highway purposes, but the huge revenue derived from highway levies has reduced these totals to negligible proportions. Funds raised from highway sources are heavily earmarked for highway expenditure. Pressed by highway groups, more than half of the states have adopted constitutional provisions forbidding or restricting diversion of highway revenues from highway purposes to other expenditures. Other states have adopted similar provisions by state or administrative practice. Such provisions specifically designate that revenues from highway sources may be used only for highway construction, maintenance, and related purposes. In states employing anti-diversion provisions, it is forbidden to appropriate highway user revenues for nonhighway purposes. The device guarantees road building funds even in circumstances in which legislative politics might otherwise favor a reduction in activity. Highways are given preferential treatment. In Michigan's notorious cash crisis of 1959 when the general fund was depleted, no financial problem existed for the highway building agency.

In the anti-diversion concept, permissability and actual diversion are related to the amount of highway spending in the states in relation to other governmental activities. As Table 2 demonstrates, in 1967 nine states diverted in excess of 10 per cent of highway revenues from highway purposes; another nine states diverted from 2 to 10 per cent. Only two of these ranked in the top quartile of states in terms of the percentage of highway expenditures to all other expenditures in the period 1963 to 1967, and six were in the last quartile.* Quite a number of the states were highly urbanized; yet even when urbanization is held constant diversion and highway expenditures seem related. Of the twenty-five most rural states in the

---

* In this analysis the dependent variable used is the percentage of highway expenditure to all state and local expenditures. Its use is based on the notion that anti-diversion provisions are a direct part of the struggle for scarce resources between highways and other agencies of government.

TABLE 2

Highway User Revenue Diversion and Highway Expenditures

State	Percentage diverted, 1967	Rank order according to percentage of highway expenditure to all state and local expenditure, 1963-1967
New Jersey	43.7	44.5
Florida	33.6	37
Texas	23.6	22.5
Washington	21.5	33
Oklahoma	17.4	30.5
California	17.0	48
Rhode Island	13.9	39
Tennessee	11.1	18
Alaska	10.6	2
New Mexico	6.9	22.5
Hawaii	5.7	49
Oregon	5.6	24.5
Wisconsin	5.2	34
New York	3.3	50
South Carolina	3.2	35.5
Arkansas	3.1	20
North Dakota	2.9	8
Illinois	2.1	43
Alabama	1.2	21
Colorado	1.0	42
Kansas	0.9	19
Minnesota	0.6	27
Georgia	0.3	41
Utah	0.3	24.5
Missouri	0.1	32
Maryland	0.1	44.5
Arizona	0	30.5
Connecticut	0	35.5
Delaware	0	11
Idaho	0	10
Indiana	0	19
Iowa	0	16.5
Kentucky	0	14
Louisiana	0	26
Maine	0	9
Massachusetts	0	46
Michigan	0	47
Mississippi	0	16.5
Montana	0	5
Nebraska	0	13
Nevada	0	12
New Hampshire	0	7
North Carolina	0	39
Ohio	0	28
Pennsylvania	0	39
South Dakota	0	3
Vermont	0	4
Virginia	0	15
West Virginia	0	6
Wyoming	0	1

Sources: United States Department of Transportation, Bureau of Public Roads, *Highway Statistics 1967,* 89; and United States Bureau of the Census, *Governmental Finances in the United States,* Volumes for 1966-1970 (Washington, D.C.: United States Government Printing Office, issued annually).

United States,* seventeen had no (or negligible) diversion. Only four did not rank in the top half of the states in the ratio of highway to other expenditures; nine were ranked in the top quartile. Of the eight rural states with some or substantial diversion, only two ranked in the top quartile in expenditures and three ranked in the lower half. Earmarking and anti-diversion provisions are symptomatic, therefore, of the success scored by supporters of highway expenditures.

Federal and Local Revenue

Federal and local revenues are also vital to state highway finance because of their relation to state taxes. Historically, local highway work was paid for by taxes on property and by special assessments on abutting property owners. These still remain the major locally raised revenue sources. Because of traffic congestion and the financial burden upon central cities, in recent years parking meters and "wheel taxes" on vehicles using city streets have provided an increasing amount of funds in many places.

During World War I the federal government entered the field of highway taxation by levying a tax on motor vehicles and parts that expired at the end of the war. In 1932 the federal government instituted a one cent per gallon tax on gasoline and taxed new automobiles and auto accessories. With the expansion of federal expenditures, the gasoline tax has been increased to four cents and the tax on new vehicles to 10 per cent. In the first twenty years of the vehicle tax, trucks and buses were taxed at a somewhat lower rate than autos, and some observers have concluded that this gave truckers and bus companies an advantage that they have never relinquished. In addition to these revenue sources, diesel fuel has been taxed since 1951 and a tonnage weight levy has been put on trucks since 1956. The petroleum industry and other groups have opposed the expansion of the federal government in the area of highway taxation, but the very extensive revenue derived directly from these taxes has neutralized this opposition. This is especially true in states that have benefited most, particularly the rural South and West.

Highway Finance — Expenditures

In addition to looking at total highway expenditures, it is also important to examine the distribution of expenditures within states and differ-

---

* For purposes of analysis, percentage of population in standard metropolitan statistical areas has been used to measure state urbanization. The choice of this measure is based on the assumption that for highway purposes urban concentrations largely distinguish urban and rural needs.

ences in level of expenditures between states. One of the most difficult aspects of highway systems to measure is overall quality and its relation to political strength. Nevertheless, overall highway expenditures do provide a rough measure of the extent to which the supporters and users of the highway system have achieved their ends.[41] Therefore, the state expending the greatest ratio of its budget for highways need not be the state with the best system, but it may be the state in which supporters of the system are strongest politically.

Highway engineers might expect the division of funds for various categories to be determined primarily by highway use. In practice this has not been the case. In most states, until the presence of the interstate system began to be felt, rural secondary roads used by farmers and small-town dwellers were favored above rural primary and urban roads. Burch found that in each of sixteen selected states the percentage of the total state expenditure devoted to secondary rural highways exceeded the estimated percentage of secondary to total rural travel on state highways. In Alabama, Florida, South Carolina, and Virginia the percentage was more than double. By 1959, in all instances the percentage expenditure on these roads had declined and in some instances it had declined to a point beneath the figure for percentage traveled.[42]

Expenditures in urban areas are even more out of line. In only a few states do cities receive state highway expenditures commensurate with use. Add to this that cities receive relatively little financial help from state aid to localities and the picture is complete. One of the most frequent explanations made for this is the underrepresentation of urban areas in the legislature.[43] In order to examine the validity of this explanation, the percentage of "fair share" that urban areas were receiving from state expenditures as developed by Burch was compared with the David-Eisenberg index of representativeness.[44] In using the technique of rank-order correlations, no relation was found, either positive or negative. In short, the answer must be sought elsewhere. We found a modest, positive relation between states responding most favorably to urban needs and the degree of urbanization of the state. States such as Rhode Island, Illinois, New Jersey, Connecticut, California, Massachusetts, and Ohio ranked in the top ten in terms of "best" ratio of actual to "proper" expenditures for urban areas. Similarly, the bottom ten states in terms of "poorest" effort in providing aid to urban areas were predominantly rural. It seems apparent, therefore, that malapportionment has not been a factor of consequence in determining state aid to cities. In states with large metropolitan concentrations aid has been forthcoming. Where urban dwellers are a relatively small force, even when adequately represented, they have not had the influence to obtain state highway expenditures.

The most important change in recent years, of course, has been the increased activity in urban areas resulting from the interstate highway program. The visibility of this activity has not been lost on rural officials. A series of interviews was conducted in 1960 with parish (county) officials in Louisiana asking them to comment on whether state aid to local government gave adequate consideration to urban needs. The response from rural respondents was invariably that the larger cities were doing extremely well under the interstate program and that this more than compensated for lack of state aid to these cities.[45]

State Aid to Localities

State financial aid to local highway systems bulks large in the local highway operation in most states. Justification for such aid has been based on arguments that a state needs at least minimum highways, that resources and technical skills are inadequate at the local level, and that the state wants to guarantee to less wealthy areas at least a minimum highway program. Within the range of possibilities for determining a distribution of funds, a need formula would be at one end and at the other would be the ability of local political leaders to negotiate for funds. The difficulties associated with each of these approaches has led to some fairly fixed formulae that most states use either singly or in combination. Some of the yardsticks used are road mileage, vehicle miles traveled, gasoline consumption, population, motor vehicle registration, area, and equal amounts for each subdivision. Formulae such as vehicle miles traveled, gasoline consumption, population, and registration are more favorable to urban areas; road mileage, area, and equal dollar distribution and devices are conducive to more favorable treatment for rural areas.

Increasing influence of urban centers among legislative bodies in recent years has brought about a more equitable distribution of funds from an urban point of view. An interesting example of this was the revision of the highway aid formula in Louisiana in 1955. Louisiana by the time of the 1950 census had approximately half of its population situated in metropolitan areas. A need study had been done by the Automotive Safety Foundation in the early 1950s that found substantial road deficiencies in the state. A larger proportion of these deficiencies was found in counties with high urbanization than in rural counties. The 1955 legislation granted counties highway aid on the basis of a need formula with a minimum built in to guarantee some aid to all areas. In addition, older programs were continued under a gasoline consumption formula and a flat sum grant. A sop was thrown to municipalities with assurances of state assumption of the main cost of urban extensions of state highways. Finally, a classification system in state highways was written into law that included a primary, secondary, and farm-to-market system. The net result was to remove highway deficiencies, particularly in urban counties, without alienating rural constituencies.[46] However, since county highway departments were forbidden to work within city limits, the needs of central cities, in some cases, remained unfulfilled.

In general, aid formulae have been geared to counties and sometimes town or township needs but seldom to the needs of municipalities. Approximately sixteen states, mostly in the Northeast and the South, provide little or no direct assistance for local highway needs in municipalities. Assistance is limited in most of the rest. In fact, in only ten states does state aid represent one-third or more of the municipal street revenues. Furthermore, in some states county road agencies do not provide either construction or maintenance services within city limits. In Louisiana, for example, where a gasoline consumption formula has provided a substantial sum of money at the county level and has included gasoline consumed in municipalities, none of the money may be used within city limits except in New Orleans and Baton Rouge, which have consolidated city-county governments. Interviews with local highway officials in Louisiana brought out many more feelings of discrimination against cities because of this restriction than feelings of discrimination because of inadequate aid to urban areas under the general state formulae.[47]

Recent figures published by the United States Bureau of Public Roads, however, show that large sums of money are being spent in counties in metropolitan areas. While little of this expenditure of funds benefits municipalities, much of it does benefit urban highway users in surrounding areas. In summary, it is possible that patterns of aid distribution are changing to the advantage of urban counties, but limitations on the activity of county highway units within municipalities in some states has continued the lag.

Expenditure Variations

Finally, which states spend more on highways and which spend less? The explanation of these differences is reserved for the concluding section, and at this point we shall simply attempt to describe some of the differences. Yet, even a simple description is fraught with hazards. If our purpose is to be comparative, figures on total expenditures are meaningless because they do not control for size and population. We have used three measures for comparison: expenditures per capita, expenditures per $1,000 income, and highway expenditure as a percentage of all state and local expenditure. In each instance we have used a five-year average for the period 1963 through 1967. The expenditure measures used combine state and local spending because of the lack of uniformity across state lines in definition of state and local roads. We have used three measures because each has some drawbacks. Area differences among states, problems of terrain leading to cost variations, population concentration and sparsity factors, differences in right-of-way costs between urban and rural areas limit dollars spent per capita. Expenditure levels per $1,000 income look superficially like an excellent measure, but the heavy input of federal funds based on formulae that take no account of the ability of states to pay for highways distorts the meaning of any relation found using this measure. Highway expenditure as a percentage of all state and local expenditure is limited since it labels as "high effort" those states that spend proportionately little on other programs, making them appear to be big highway spenders, while making those that put a great deal of money into schools, health, welfare, etc. appear to be niggardly on highways. The principal advantage of this measure is that it provides an excellent guideline for discovering how important highway activities are in the affairs of the fifty states. Peculiarities of cost, terrain, and the like tend to be neutralized.

Table 3 lists the states in rank order for the period 1963 through 1967, based on the percentage of highway expenditures to total state and local spending. It lists per capita and per $1,000 income average expenditure and rank for the same five-year period. The three measures correlate highly.[48] The most striking feature about the highest ranked states using all three measures is that they are rural. Wyoming, Alaska, South Dakota, Vermont, and Montana are among the most rural states in the United States. Similarly New York, Hawaii, California, Michigan, Massachusetts, New Jersey, Maryland, and Illinois are all among the twelve states in which more than 70 per cent of the population lived in standard metropolitan statistical areas in 1960. Each ranks low using all three measures.

In the concluding section of this chapter we shall examine expenditure variation using each of the three measures included in Table 3 and relate them to some socioeconomic and other environmental variables, including urbanization, as well as several political variables.

TABLE 3
Comparative State and Local Highway Expenditures

State	Percentage of highway expenditures of all state and local expenditures, 1963-1967 average	Rank	Per capita highway expenditures, 1963-1967 average	Rank	Expenditures per $1,000 personal income, 1963-1967 average	Rank
Wyoming	32.5	1	$217.51	2	$ 82.53	2
Alaska	30.5	2	326.98	1	101.65	1
South Dakota	29.4	3	132.44	6	60.14	4
Vermont	29.3	4	141.97	4	60.62	3
Montana	27.9	5	135.54	5	55.72	5
West Virginia	23.9	6	86.77	16	41.45	10
New Hampshire	23.8	7	89.72	13	35.70	18
North Dakota	23.3	8	118.01	8	52.21	6
Maine	23.1	9	84.08	19	36.62	16
Idaho	23.1	10	93.13	11	41.30	11
Delaware	22.9	11	124.49	7	36.78	15
Nevada	22.5	12	147.23	3	45.95	7
Nebraska	22.2	13	86.20	17	34.40	22
Kentucky	22.0	14	78.72	22	38.32	14
Virginia	21.9	15	76.22	26	32.15	27
Iowa	21.8	16.5	97.37	9	36.09	17
Mississippi	21.8	16.5	69.63	30	43.65	8
Tennessee	21.2	18	69.20	31	34.63	21
Kansas	20.2	19	80.74	20	31.23	28
Arkansas	20.1	20	61.76	37.5	34.16	23
Alabama	19.9	21	65.88	32	35.26	20
New Mexico	18.9	22.5	92.59	12	42.52	9

Texas	18.9	22.5	65.57	34	28.05	31
Oregon	18.6	24.5	93.44	10	35.58	19
Utah	18.6	24.5	88.73	14	38.41	13
Louisiana	18.2	26	78.43	24	38.42	12
Minnesota	18.1	27	87.78	15	33.12	25
Ohio	17.8	28	64.75	35	22.99	39
Rhode Island	17.6	29	77.92	25	27.40	32
Arizona	17.2	30.5	80.35	21	33.92	24
Oklahoma	17.2	30.5	73.78	27	32.65	26
Missouri	17.0	32	61.67	39	23.04	38
Washington	16.8	33	85.09	18	29.18	29
Wisconsin	16.7	34	78.44	23	28.82	30
Connecticut	16.5	35.5	71.95	28	21.10	42
South Carolina	16.5	35.5	50.67	49	24.33	36
Florida	16.1	37	61.76	37.5	25.93	33.5
Indiana	15.7	39	59.07	40	21.18	41
North Carolina	15.7	39	47.81	50	23.06	37
Pennsylvania	15.7	39	58.36	41	20.88	43
Georgia	15.5	41	52.71	47	24.80	35
Colorado	14.0	42	70.43	29	25.93	33.5
Illinois	13.8	43	53.66	46	16.52	49
Maryland	13.5	44.5	56.52	42	19.06	45
New Jersey	13.5	44.5	52.21	48	16.22	50
Massachusetts	12.9	46	56.26	43	18.21	47
Michigan	11.9	47	53.96	45	18.31	46
California	11.2	48	65.87	33	20.42	44
Hawaii	10.5	49	62.18	36	22.16	40
New York	10.0	50	55.05	44	16.78	48

Source: United States Bureau of the Census, *Governmental Finances in the United States, 1963-1967.*

POLITICAL CONFLICTS

Earlier discussion provided numerous examples of conflict in highway policy making. These areas of conflict must be brought into focus. Primarily, conflict in highway affairs can be classified under four major headings: (1) conflicts among transportation media for a share of the transportation market; (2) conflicts among economic interests that are dependent in varying degrees upon highways; (3) conflicts among producers of highway materials and building contractors; and (4) conflicts over partisan and constituency service needs in which contestants are only incidentally concerned with highways. Each of these conflict areas illustrates the kinds of contestants, the kinds of struggles about which conflict occurs, and the universality of these struggles throughout the United States.

Transportation Industry

Conflicts within the transportation industry are directly related to economic competition. This includes competition for freight between truckers and railroads, competition for long distance passengers between buses and, indirectly, automobile users and manufacturers on the one hand, and railroads and (to a lesser extent) airlines on the other, and competition for urban transport between the automobile and transit facilities. Each of these competitors has allies but, for purposes of simplicity, only the primary protagonists are listed. Issues about which conflicts occur include level of highway expenditure, classification of highways for which expenditures are made, impact and incidence of the revenue systems, and limitations on weight carried by motor vehicles traversing highways.

Railroads have been in the forefront of all of these conflicts for many years. In the late nineteenth century, curiously enough, the railroad industry participated prominently in the good roads movement.[49] At the time, this movement was mainly in support of highways from farm to town. This, of course, was encouraged by railroads because it expedited transportation from farm to train depot. When the good roads movement extended its interest to primary roads and eventually to urban streets, the posture of the railroad industry changed, sensing a threat to its own survival. Now, railroads are avoiding endorsement or opposition to the construction of various classes of highways. Instead they attack the incidence of taxation and truck weight limits.[50] In general, they have supported the principle that highway users should pay for highways in proportion to the use and damage done to the highways. Specifically, this has led to support for the use of revenue bonds rather than general obligation bonds for long term indebtedness in order to avoid transfer of the incidence of the cost from highway users to the general taxpayers. They have argued for fuel taxes, including those on diesel fuel, that reflect the added use given to roads by heavy vehicles. Railroad people also have urged the maintenance of a toll structure under which commercial vehicles would pay according to weight. They have also recommended weight limitations on heavy motor vehicles and penalties for violations that are stringent enough to discourage further violations.

The point of view of the railroads is challenged strongly by truckers and, to a lesser extent, by other highway users. In general, all components of the automotive transportation industry have joined in this effort. In Michigan, for example, the Good Roads Federation has included officers from such diverse organizations as the Associated Petroleum Industries of Michigan, Chrysler Corporation, Corregated Metal Pipe Association, County Road Association of Michigan, Ford Motor Company, General Motors Corporation, Michigan Asphalt Paving Association, Michigan Bell Telephone Company, Michigan Construction Equipment Dealers Association, Michigan Farm Bureau, Michigan Municipal League, Michigan Road Builders Association, Michigan Sand and Gravel Producers, Michigan State Highway Department, Michigan State Grange, Michigan State Police, Michigan Trucking Association, Oil and Gas Association of Michigan, Portland Cement Association, and Allied Chemical Corporation. Auto transport groups have urged maximal highway spending. With respect to financing highway programs, they have opposed toll roads and encouraged anti-diversion provisions in connection with the use of funds derived from highway user taxes. They have also supported general purpose bonds as opposed to revenue bonds, and the truckers have opposed third structure taxes, taxes on motor vehicle accessories, diesel fuel, etc. The trucking industry has been especially hostile to weight limitation and particularly to differentiations from state to state, which they regard as harassment.

To a great extent, the good roads movement in general and the trucking industry in particular have emerged victorious. A portion of this victory was scored in the interstate highway program with its encouragement of highway spending and its discouragement of further toll road building. Victories have also been scored at the state level with monotonous regularity. Certainly the victory won by the truckers in allegedly railroad-dominated Pennsylvania on the truck weight issue seems to support this.

Currently the liveliest conflict between highways and other modes of transportation is taking place in urban areas where supporters of mass transportation systems have been competing with renewed energy since the passage of the Urban Mass Transportation Act of 1964. In December, 1969, a rapid rail transit system was begun in the Washington, D.C., metropolitan area to be completed in stages over a ten-year period. When completed, the system will be a network of almost 100 miles of transit facilities in the District of Columbia, Maryland, and Virginia. Almost half of the mileage will be below surface.[51]

Other cities have also created rapid transit authorities. In the San Francisco Bay area efforts to follow the Washington plan are well under way but have been delayed by financial difficulties. In general two serious disadvantages plague the supporters of mass transportation. First, subway and rail facilities are extraordinarily expensive and are only economically feasible in those few cities with high concentrations of employment in the central business district. Currently only five cities — New York, Chicago, Philadelphia, Boston, and Cleveland — operate rapid transit systems. Most experts believe that of the remaining large cities in the United States only Washington and San Francisco could support rapid transit systems. A dozen other cities, however, are giving some consideration to rapid transit systems. The second problem plaguing supporters of mass transportation, no matter what form the system takes, is the continued attitudinal bias among users in favor of the private automobile.[52]

Other Social and Economic Interests

The second category of conflict involves groups with secondary interests or those involved in single struggles. These groups include economic and other interests that are not as dependent upon highways as truckers but whose welfare is affected in some measure by highway decisions. It also includes groups of people who experience property loss or gain from highway decisions. A list of such groups would include: (1) Utility companies interested in highways for purposes of industrial attraction; (2) Motel, restaurant, and gasoline operators concerned not only with construction of more highways but also with their location in terms of existing enterprises; (3) Downtown business groups, both in large cities and small towns, fearful of the loss of business resulting from suburban shopping centers that have superior highway access; (4) Neighborhood and downtown theater owners threatened by competition from highway drive-in theaters; (5) Farmers interested in farm-to-market roads; (6) School administrators concerned with satisfactory roads for school buses; (7) Groups concerned with an adequate network of national and civil defense highways; (8) Nature lovers and others concerned with preservation of scenic beauty spots and natural resources; (9) Neighborhood groups disturbed by threats to property values resulting from highway location; (10) Property owners displaced by highway building needs. (In this case not only are some individuals forced to abandon property against their wishes, but some are beneficiaries of large profits from speculation in right-of-way purchase.) [53]

This list is only suggestive and by no means exhaustive, but it does provide some idea of the range of issues about which disputes occur and variations that might exist in their outcomes. The major issues in dispute among these groups include highway classification and emphasis on expenditure within classes, decisions regarding highway location, right-of-way purchase, and the problem of displacement and abandonment of existing property use in favor of highways. Illustrations of disputes in the cities of New York and New Orleans serve as examples of the position held by several categories of groups listed above.

The cancellation of the interstate highway route on the edge of the French Quarter in July, 1969, is an excellent illustration of the activities of groups concerned about aesthetic factors. At the time, it was reported that the controversy was sparked by national groups interested in preserving historic sites and by national conservation groups opposed to urban highways that impair the quality of the environment and add to pollution problems.[54] It is doubtful that these groups could have won without help from other interests such as the groups in New York fighting against encroachment by new highways upon inner-city neighborhoods. In New York the neighborhood groups consisted largely of low-income, predominantly black populations newly activated to make demands of this kind. Specifically the New York case involved the construction of the Cross-Brooklyn and Lower Manhattan expressways. In the struggle support for the neighborhood groups was also forthcoming from a beseiged mayor who was attempting to survive in a difficult three-way election campaign.

The decision announced by Secretary Volpe cancelling the New Orleans project was closely followed by a similar announcement in New York. Groups in other large cities in similar situations could also expect relief.

An interesting additional aspect of the New Orleans decision was the possibility that the outcome was influenced somewhat by a tax controversy that had little if anything to do with highways. President Nixon was in jeopardy of losing a key tax fight in Congress at the time. A crucial member of the House of Representatives in the tax fight, Hale Boggs, lived in the district that included suburban New Orleans, but not the French Quarter. When the abandonment of the interstate highway in the French Quarter was agreed upon the federal counterpart funds were released for other purposes. A decision was made to use those funds to construct a portion of a beltway in suburban New Orleans in Mr. Boggs's district.[55]

The result of all of these events seems to have been that a great many people were made happy without causing very much discomfort to others. Aesthetic and neighborhood groups were victorious in the specific setting and given hope in future controversies and the president of the United States was able to offer his appreciation to a member of Congress who had worked hard for an important piece of legislation without violating the established rules of the game for the distribution of interstate highway funds. This case involved higher level officials and a wider group of participants than most controversies but it serves to illustrate the political interplay so common to highway decision making.

Issues involving social and economic interests have been resolved quite differently from state to state. Possible explanations for these differences may stem from high and low population concentrations, highly competitive two-party systems, and heavy industrial and agricultural concentration.

Patterns of conduct among the states on issues other than expenditures are less discernible because of the absence of systematic data, but variations could be determined by ranking state highway procedures on a continuum with engineering considerations at one end and political considerations at the other. On highway location issues, for example, most states probably would be found in the middle of the continuum. However, on matters of rights-of-way purchase, compensation for property expropriation, and related issues, differences among them would be far greater.

Highway Builders

Competition among various industries supplying material and labor for highway construction and maintenance represent a third source of conflict. The most heated controversies occur over which materials should be used, the maintenance of competitive bidding, and the like. Because of very strict regulations in many states, resulting in part from federal programs, much of the discretion has been removed from matters of highway construction. When industries urge their products upon highway departments because they help solve problems of terrain, freezing, or excess moisture, conflicts arise over granting preferential treatment. Occasionally, preferential treatment is defended on the ground that a home industry ought to be protected against underpricing by out-of-state bidders.

A matter of major importance politically is the distribution of maintenance equipment contracts. Maintenance expenditures are generally rather small in terms of individual outlays. As a result contracts can be broken up in such a way that a system of favoritism and patronage is possible because outlays are smaller than the minimum required for competitive bidding.[56] Highway maintenance crews are also susceptible to patronage manipulation because they consist of much unskilled labor, and employment regulations for highway labor are extremely flexible in some states.[57] Related to this is union hostility to the use of convict labor on highway crews.[58] No convenient measurements are available to facilitate explanation of differences among states in construction and maintenance practices,[59] and it would be an oversimplification to characterize this as a function of the party system.

Partisan and Local Representational Interests

The last of the four conflict areas involves partisan and local service needs. In the American political system with its loose partisan ties, a political party cannot depend upon membership dues as its main source of revenue in conducting campaigns. Therefore, it is essential to solicit money from large donors. What better source can be found than industries and organizations that benefit directly from government activity? In this respect, highway contractors are an especially fruitful source of funds. Presumably, however, donors expect some favor in return. We may hypothesize that states with one-party, highly personalized politics are more susceptible to favoritism in exchange for contributions from the highway industry than two-party states in which other factors tend to downgrade the importance of these contributions.* Bernd reports on contributions in Georgia as follows:

> Figures on receipts by major candidates in recent years (1946–54) indicate that at least 50 per cent of the money handled by central headquarters and auxiliary groups came from highway contractors and liquor dealers. The inordinate contractor position in Georgia stems from the new governor's dominance of the highway board and the legislature, which nominally elects the board, and from the negotiated non-competitive contract, frequently let by the individual county. Rewarding his faithful backers is the quintessence of the governor's loyalty code and he has the power to pay his political debts.[60]

The assumption, however, that the need of officeholders to pay off highway builders stems simply from their desire to repay them for their

---

* This hypothesis is examined on p. 512.

campaign contributions understates the role of highway building in the fulfillment of partisan and representational needs. Public works projects are a splendid device for attaining public recognition without arousing hostilities. Construction of buildings and roads may elicit popular support from the direct beneficiaries, whereas opposition from nonbeneficiaries remains minimal. Subsequently, public officials and political parties of whatever point of view, in both one-party and two-party states, find highway building far more efficacious in attaining partisan ends than support for controversial programs in the health, education, or welfare field. Huey Long built his political dynasty very largely in this way.[61]

This phenomenon, however, not only crosses political party lines and party systems but also serves legislators and elected executives equally well. As a result, there is a never ending struggle between a governor and state highway officials who favor primary statewide highways and the many legislators, whether urban or rural, who are anxious to deliver public works for the benefit of their own constituents. In most states, prior to the passage of the Federal Interstate Highway Act in 1956, localism was victorious. The interstate program, however, has reversed the pattern somewhat. Nevertheless, even on interstate highways successful entreaties are made for exits to local communities with minimal traffic demands, for advertisements of local roadside facilities, and for the construction of additional access routes in urbanized areas. In short, therefore, the fulfillment of partisan and constituency needs by elected officeholders is likely to follow paths of little resistance. Relatively few people see themselves as harmed by new or improved highways and, even if a new highway program helps the other fellow more, everyone can be rewarded with something.

VARIATIONS

Highway politics may be examined in a number of ways for comparison. These include the forms and processes by which decisions are made; the successes and failures of contestants, measured by the quantity and kinds of highways constructed or maintained; and the quality of the outputs of the highway system. Each of these presents analytical problems. Comparison of the form and process of decision making has much to commend it, but unfortunately data are too sketchy to do more than provide impressionistic observations. The optimal approach to an understanding of output variation would be to compare states using a widely accepted measure of the quality of the highway system. Unfortunately, judgment varied widely about what a good highway system should include. In principle, of course, there are criteria for quality measurement. These might include measures of travel time, safety, and travel comfort and convenience. Data are available on some of these, but their value as measures of highway system quality is doubtful. For example, it is possible to express highway safety in terms of deaths per thousand people or per million miles traveled. It is not clear, however, whether variations among states on this dimension are associated more with the highway itself or with the speed limit and the highway safety program. In fact, from the evidence available, the latter may explain more of the variation inasmuch as the lowest death rates are found in the low spending states in the congested corridor from Maine to Maryland. Therefore, until better quantitative measures are developed to compare qualitative differences in output this approach will have limited merit.

The third device for examining variations among states in highway policy is to compare expenditures. For numerous reasons this is at best only a crude measure and in some output areas it is inadequate. For highways, definitions of outputs among states are sufficiently similar and sufficiently related to expenditure level that it is possible to make meaningful comparisons. The following comparisons are based on three expenditure measures. The first is the percentage of highway expenditures to all other expenditures. In other words, this is an indicator of the success of highway support in relation to support for other programs. The second is per capita expenditure, and the third is expenditure per $1,000 individual income. These describe variation by population and wealth. In all three measures we have used state and local expenditures because of the great ambiguity among states regarding what is a state road and what is a local road.

Spending was compared to several political variables and some socioeconomic and other environmental indicators. Two of the political variables examined have a direct connection with highway decision making — the independence of the highway department from the governor and the extent of diversion of highway use revenues to other functions. Three have an indirect connection — the competitiveness of the political party system, partisan control by Democrats rather than Republicans, and voter participation in state politics. The environmental variables included were the area of the states, urbanization as measured by the percentage of population living in standard metropolitan statistical areas, industrialization,[62] per capita income, and persons per motor vehicle.

As the discussion above has already suggested there seems to be no relation between the formal organization of the highway department and comparative success in obtaining support for highway programs. This can be explained in part because formal independence from the governor is not critical to highway supporters. In effect, while independence may be desirable in maximizing highway expenditures, similar results may be achieved in other ways. The same cannot be said for the issue of diversion and earmarking highway revenues. As has been stated earlier, a distinct relation exists between the states that permit diversion of highway user funds and those that spend relatively little for highways. It is hard to tell whether the success of the highway interests has led to anti-diversion measures or whether the reverse is the case. Undoubtedly, however, anti-diversionary practices are a benchmark of success for highway supporters.

One of the political variables that we examined, party competition, has been given wide attention for many years by political scientists as a phenomenon having an important relation to policy outputs. The suggested hypothesis is that in states with low party competition, or more specifically in one-party states, highway interests ought to fare better than in competitive states since highway builder and user groups are among the largest contributors to political campaigns at the state level.[63] In a two-party situation the money goes into the party coffers and is less identifiable. Therefore, it is more difficult for highway groups to commit candidates to specific programs. In contrast, in one-party states campaigns and campaign finances are individualized, enabling highway groups to deal directly with the candidate.[64] We shall see in the quantitative analysis that follows that evidence does not support this hypothesis.

In order to examine the relative importance of the environmental and political variables we first did a simple correlational analysis between each of our spending measures and each of the environmental and political variables. Because of the relations among some of the variables we also did a partial correlational analysis. Such an analysis indicates the degree of relation between one variable and the phenomenon being tested when other variables in the analysis are held constant.

Table 4 lists the correlations between each of the spending measures and the environmental variables. Three somewhat related variables — urbanization, industrialization, and persons per vehicle — each demonstrate a significant negative relation to the percentage of state and local highway expenditures as a percentage of total state and local spending. The more urban, the more industrial, and the lower the incidence of automobile ownership to population, the less will be spent on highways.

When per capita expenditure is substituted urbanization continues to be a significant negative force. In addition, however, great land size seems

TABLE 4
Relationship Between Environmental Indicators and State and Local Highway Expenditures[a]

	Area of states	Percentage of population in standard metropolitan statistical areas, 1960	Industrialization[b]	Per capita income, 1965	Persons per motor vehicle, 1967
Average state and local highway expenditures as a percentage of total state and local expenditures, 1963-1967	.2560	-.7815[a]	-.4544[a]	-.2547	-.3038[a]
Average per capita state and local expenditures, 1963-1967	.6050[a]	-.5103[a]	-.1397	.1693	-.1513
Average state and local highway expenditures per $1,000 personal income, 1963-1967	.4955[a]	-.7058[a]	-.3648[a]	-.2241	-.2320

[a]Figures are simple correlation coefficients for the fifty states; [a]indicates a statistically significant relationship.
[b]The measure used is one minus the percentage of the work force engaged in agriculture, fisheries, and forestry.

to show a positive relationship, which suggests simply that states such as Alaska, Nevada, or Montana must spend more per capita because of vast distances between cities and towns. When wealth is used as the measure for expenditure comparison, again urbanization represents a significant negative force. This time industrialization also seems to be a significant negative factor and area a positive one. Therefore, regardless of the measure used, highway expenditures tend to be higher the smaller the number of people living in standard metropolitan areas.

In Tables 5 and 6 we have introduced the political variables in our analysis. In Table 5 we have examined the effect of party competition in the forty-eight states that have partisan elections for each of the houses of the legislature from 1958 to 1966 and in the election of governors in all states from 1958 to 1966. We also examined voter participation in gubernatorial elections in all states from 1958 to 1966.[65] None of the simple correlations was significant for any of the three spending measures. Furthermore, when we performed a partial correlational analysis controlling all of the environmental variables the political variables still demonstrated no significant correlation.

In Table 6 we examined what difference it makes which political party controls the various state decision making arenas. A small negative relationship appeared between Democratic party control and highway spending both in the simple correlations and when environmental variables were controlled in partial correlational analysis. In no instance, however, was the relationship significant.[66]

This analysis seems to suggest that peculiarities of the political system as measured by the indicators that we have used have little or nothing to do with variations in highway spending. Environmental factors such as geographical area, urbanization, and industrialization have more to do with variation. Undoubtedly the most significant of these is the lack of urbanization.

Explanation of this result is not a simple matter, but speculation may suggest some relevant factors. Support for highway spending has been widespread. In fact, it matters little whether a state is urban or rural, Democratic or Republican, one-party or two-party, wealthy or poor, industrial or agricultural — its people will endorse highway building. It is abetted by the growth of federal grants, which have displayed some partiality to sparsely populated areas inasmuch as the formulae for grants have included mileage and area factors. In states with large population concentrations, highway expenditures must compete with state expenditures for education, welfare, health, and local expenditures for urban services. High-

TABLE 5
Relations Among Environmental Indicators, Party Competition, Voter Participation, and State and Local Highway Expenditures

| | Interparty competition participation | | | | | | | |
| | Lower house | | Upper house | | Governor | | Percentage of electorate voting for governor | |
	Simple correlation	Partial correlation	Simple correlation	Partial correlation	Simple correlation	Partial correlation	Simple correlation	Partial correlation
Average state and local highway expenditure as a percentage of total state and local expenditure, 1963-1967	−.0100	.1356	.0153	.2223	.0600	.1704	.1093	.1744
Average per capita state and local expenditure, 1963-1967	.1911	.1615	.2469	.2572	.2473	.1929	.1823	.1231
Average state and local highway expenditure per $1,000 personal income, 1963-1967	.0308	.1648	.0775	.2707	.0951	.1925	.1147	.1628

Figures are simple and partial correlation coefficients; partial coefficients control for the effect of area, urbanization, industrialization, per capita income, and persons per vehicle.

TABLE 6

Relations Among Environmental Indicators, Partisanship, and State and Local Highway Expenditures

| | Democratic party control | | | | | |
| | Lower house | | Upper house | | Governor | |
	Simple correlation	Partial correlation	Simple correlation	Partial correlation	Simple correlation	Partial correlation
Average state and local highway expenditures as percentage of total state and local expenditures, 1963-1967	−.2510	−.2334	−.2062	−.1928	−.0158	−.1500
Average per capita state and local expenditures, 1963-1967	−.2838	−.1314	−.2744	−.1276	−.1960	−.1538
Average state and local highway expenditures per $1,000 personal income, 1963-1967	−.2080	−.1566	−.1736	−.1310	−.0513	−.1734

Figures are simple and partial correlation coefficients; partial coefficients control for the effect of area, urbanization, industrialization, per capita income, and persons per vehicle.

ways fare reasonably well, but other functions do comparatively better in heavily populated states than in states with little urban concentration. The pervasively felt need for highways, irrespective of political ideology or urbanization, does not exist universally for other major programs of state and local government. As a result, it appears that variations in highway expenditures occur not so much because some states have wanted to do more or less in the highway field, but because other functions have been either emphasized or neglected.

CONCLUSIONS

Extremely rapid expansion of highway systems has taken place in the United States in the twentieth century. This development may be attributed to several factors including an affluent society and a political system friendly to the automotive transportation industry. Increased support from the political system has been directly proportional to the shift of responsibility for decision making regarding highway construction and maintenance from local government to agencies of the state and national government. The increased role of the federal government as a result of highway legislation in 1944 and 1956 has been a prime consideration in the development of a reasonably uniform system of primary highways throughout the United States.

The decision-making process and the issues about which decisions have been made also have developed reasonably uniformly. Generally, controversies in highway politics may be listed under four headings:

1. Disputes involving competition between automotive transportation and other forms of transportation (subsumed under this are conflicts between supporters of private automotive uses and public transportation);
2. Disputes involving other interests (social, economic, aesthetic) aided or hindered by the construction or abandonment of particular roads;
3. Disputes involving producers of highway materials and equipment and builders of highways;
4. Disputes concerning partisan and local needs.

Clashes involving each of these categories have occurred in all states from time to time with similar results. Supporters of the automotive industry and private auto usage generally have emerged victorious over their adversaries. However, some recent inroads have been made in urban areas in support of public transportation, protection of inner-city neighborhoods, and aesthetic character. Until the mid-1960s rural transportation was given priority over urban transportation problems. The pattern has now begun to change. Highway location, purchase of rights-of-way, purchase of equipment and materials, and construction contracts have been subjected to increasingly rigorous standards, although continued flexibility in several aspects of construction and maintenance permits favoritism and, perhaps, corruption.

Despite these uniformities among the states, the total allocation of state and local resources for highway purposes varies. In several states more than one-fourth of all state and local expenditure is devoted to highways, whereas in others less than one-eighth is devoted to this purpose. There is little evidence that the political party system, partisan complexion, or other aspects of the institutional structure for decision making relate to expenditure variation. To be sure, low-spending states tend to be those in which earmarking of funds is less well defined and protected, but this is more symptomatic than explanatory of the low-spending states.

There is also little evidence of a relation between the wealth or industrialization level of states and their emphasis on highway expenditure. There is, however, a significant relation between highway expenditure and metropolitanism in which the states with the highest proportion of their population living in standard metropolitan statistical areas devote the smallest proportion of state and local expenditure to highways. Apparently, this is the result of the commitment in these states to greater expenditure for other programs and is, therefore, not so much antipathy for highway construction as positive support for schools, hospitals, welfare programs, or public housing.

SELECTED BIBLIOGRAPHY

Altshuler, Alan A. *The City Planning Process*. Ithaca: Cornell University Press, 1965, 17–84. A description and analysis of an urban expressway controversy, with special emphasis on the impact of planners and highway engineers.

Burch, Philip H., Jr. *Highway Revenue and Expenditure Policy in the United States*. New Brunswick: Rutgers University Press, 1962. A description of federal, state, and local fiscal policy placed in its political and administrative setting.

Dearing, Charles L. *American Highway Policy*. Washington: The Brookings Institution, 1941. A description of highway policy in the United States from its inception to 1940.

Dye, Thomas R. *Politics, Economics and the Public: Policy Outcomes in the American States*. Chicago: Rand McNally, 1966, 149–177. A multivariate analysis of highway expenditure policy outcomes in the American states.

Friedman, Robert S. *State and Local Relations in Highway Finance in Louisiana*. Baton Rouge: Bureau of Public Administration, Louisiana State University, 1962. A case study dealing with the extent of urban-rural and city-county conflict in state aid to localities in Louisiana.

Hodges, Luther H. *Businessman in the State House*. Chapel Hill: University of North Carolina Press, 1962, 126–149. A discussion by a governor of his relationships with a state highway department and his efforts to reorganize its governing board.

Labatut, Jean, and Wheaton J. Lane (eds.). *Highways in Our National Life*. Princeton: Princeton University Press, 1950. A collection of essays dealing with the history of the development of highways and with sociological, political, economic, and engineering problems related to highways.

Meyer, John R., John F. Kain, and Martin Wohl. *The Urban Transportation Problem*. Cambridge: Harvard University Press, 1965. An economic analysis of urban transportation systems.

Owen, Wilfred. *The Metropolitan Transportation Problem*. Washington: The Brookings Institution, 1966. A discussion of all modes of urban transportation in the United States with a prescription for the future.

United States Bureau of Public Roads, *Highway Statistics,* annual. Washington: United States Government Printing Office. A comprehensive compendium of federal, state, and local highway statistics, including motor fuel use, motor vehicle registration, highway finance, road mileage, and federal aid.

United States Congress, House of Representatives, Special Subcommittee on the Federal Aid Highway Program to the Committee on Public Works, *House Reports,* Nos. 363, 364, 1246, 1285, and 1819, Eighty-Seventh Congress, and *House Report,* No. 617, Eighty-Eighth Congress. Washington: U.S. Government Printing Office, 1961–63. A series of reports based on hearings of a special house subcommittee on the seamier side of the interstate highway program in Oklahoma, Florida, New Mexico, and Massachusetts.

Westin, Alan F. (ed.). *The Uses of Power: Seven Cases in American Politics.* New York: Harcourt, Brace, 1962, 323–376. A case study, "Pressure Politics in Pennsylvania: The Truckers vs. the Railroads," by Andrew Hacker, describes many of the ramifications of a conflict over limitation on weight carried by trucks.

CHAPTER FOURTEEN

The Politics of Taxation

Clara Penniman

Governors can be defeated on the issue of high taxes, but governors also can be elected on issues of program expansion. Political journalists in the last decade or so have often attributed the defeats of state governors to taxes raised while they were in office. But governors have also been re-elected in the last decade, and the journalist's explanation may well be "program expansion," which is never explained by "increased taxes," although the one may have been necessary for the other. Taxes are presumed politically bad, expenditures politically good. Even though revenues arise from federal grants-in-aid, income from governmental enterprises, fees, and special charges, high expenditure states are normally high tax states. And high expenditures states are frequently high service states providing quality programs that may reduce private budget costs.

Although taxes, expenditures and services are often related, the relationship is not an absolute one. Federal grants in aid are not directly tied to taxes and consequently may raise expenditures in some states disproportionate to taxes. Also, states vary in the effectiveness with which they use expenditures so that the quality of services from similar amounts of expenditures will differ. Finally, high expenditures may represent an attempt to meet unusually serious problems and may not significantly improve the quality of life. For example, high taxes in New York are, in part, efforts to meet such difficult problems and do not necessarily provide higher qualities of living.

Citizens frequently find the relation between taxes and expenditures hard to keep in mind. I once listened to a vehement statement in opposition to a proposed tax increase before the Joint Finance Committee of the Wisconsin legislature. As the irate taxpayer came to a pause, a legislator mildly asked him if he had not appeared before them the week before asking for state assistance for the local airport. With hardly a pause in his criticism of the tax proposal, the citizen snapped "yes" to the question. Not necessarily individual irrationality, but different desires and perspectives among citizens may lead to such conduct. Voter A believes in good schools but is willing to do without four-lane highways in various sections of the state. If his desires were generally shared, increased and improved education might be bought with no increase in taxes. Voter B, however, demands many four-lane highways as a convenience for his personal travel and as a requisite for his business. To satisfy the expenditure demands of both A and B, new and increased taxes are needed, yet A and B, who view expenditure priorities differently, may pool their resources politically to oppose the tax increases. Activists, whether officeholders or not, organize to increase particular expenditures or to oppose additional taxes but seldom manage to find the strength to oppose expenditures or to support tax increases. Welfare, urban renewal, and antipollution measures can find many supporters and not too many opponents until the tax bills to raise the necessary funds are proposed.

Which decision is made first, to tax or to spend? Do taxes follow expenditures or are expenditures simply fitted to tax revenues? Since political alignments on these issues vary, the order of decision may determine the magnitude of both. If expenditures are more popular than taxes, then making the decision to spend before deciding what taxes could finance the expenditure should produce larger budgets than making the decisions in reverse order. Or to state it another way, expenditures will be higher in states where governors and legislators emphasize programs rather than how to finance them. Such a hypothesis requires modification. No institutional arrangements to look at expenditures or revenues first and then match the other insures separation. Protagonists within and without the government know the probable magnitudes of present revenues and hence the margin at which further expenditures will demand further taxes. Or conversely, looking initially at taxes may blur but will not obliterate all of the expenditure demands.

If tax decisions are not independent of expenditure decisions, neither are they independent of the past nor of the political, social, and economic environment that influences the complex of attitudes and preferences of the citizenry for each state. In this chapter we will first discuss something of the nature of policy choices made in taxation. We will then bring together information on state tax patterns. Finally, we shall analyze the tax pattern from the point of view of a political scientist. Will political factors help explain the marginally different tax policy decisions made by the fifty states?

ISSUES IN TAXATION

Taxes mean the redistribution of income and wealth in some fashion. They are routinely redistributive in form and as a function of the government services purchased. A progressive income tax takes from the more well-off at a greater rate than from the less well-off. Estate and inheritance taxes place a substantial levy on wealth. Corporate income and other business taxes constitute levies on industry and business. Even sales and property taxes, which are classed as regressive and take more proportionately from lower than higher income groups, may be spent for services that benefit the needs of lower income groups.

Not all governmental revenues come from taxes. The national government raised 10 per cent of its revenue in 1967 from charges such as postal rates; state governments also raised 10 per cent of their revenue from various charges, including higher education tuition; and local governments collectively raised 22 per cent of their revenues from sources other than taxes. State liquor stores not only regulate liquor sales but also increase state revenues through their profits. Similarly, profits from publicly owned water or light and gas utilities are a source of revenue. Charges for the use of a park or tuition charges for education may avoid raising taxes. How much of the cost of public higher education should be borne by the student or his family through higher tuition (including the possibility of full-cost tuition) rather than by the state's taxpayers is likely to be a hotly debated issue in the 1970s.

Lotteries in New Hampshire, New Jersey, and New York are a new means for raising public money in the United States in this century.[1] * Although seemingly low in political cost, they are expensive in their administrative costs and may have expensive long-run system consequences. New Hampshire's administrative costs, including prize money, were greater than the net return to the state in a recent fiscal year (1969), and New York's record is not much better. For the fiscal year ending March, 1969, the New York state lottery grossed $48.98 million, but the net receipts, which are dedicated to education amounted to $26.94 million. This $22 million over-

* [See p. 604 for notes to this chapter. — Eds.]

head cost, or almost 49 per cent of gross collections, contrasts with less than 5 per cent of total revenues as a normal administrative cost for state income taxes! No study has been made of who buys lottery tickets, and on whom the tax impact falls, but probably the lottery is a highly regressive income source with lower- and lower-middle-income individuals buying a disproportionate number of tickets. The chance of large winnings may be especially appealing when you have little, but equity would not be well served if every large winner were in the lower-income groups.*

Economists analyze taxes and charges for determining who eventually pays the tax and what the effect will be of such costs on business and personal decisions as well as on the resulting distribution of income and wealth. Where possible, taxes should be raised to combat inflation and the added revenues used to pay off indebtedness. Conversely, taxes should be lowered and expenditures raised to combat depression. A business, in choosing between essentially similar areas for a location but with a county or urban boundary line between, and with property tax rates higher on one side of the boundary than the other, would rationally choose the lower tax side. Someone purchasing a home would do the same if everything but the tax rates were equal. The specific provisions of a corporate income tax also may affect a business decision if everything else is more or less equal. Sales taxes, by adding to the prices of products, will restrict aggregate purchases of consumers. Liquor and cigarette taxes are justified either to reduce consumption of these undesirable items or as an easy way to raise revenue. Personal income taxes and inheritance-estate taxes may produce investment decisions to legally avoid the full impact of the tax rates. Attempts to discover whether high income tax rates will influence individuals to reduce their work output have so far been indecisive. It has not been proven that the income tax reduces work effort and economic growth.

Tax measures do not pave the road to popularity for politicians. Seldom is politics as "who gets what" more exposed than when a major new tax is adopted or when important amendments are added to existing taxes. Politicians normally avoid such redistributive decisions as often as possible. Interest groups in working with legislators define all tax proposals in the most extreme demands of those they represent. Legislative leaders can only hope to survive by using all their skills as brokers to modify whatever major tax is adopted, at least to avoid the appearance of favoring excessively one group against another in society. Unlike expenditure decisions

---

* Interestingly, neither the Governments Division of the Bureau of the Census nor the Advisory Commission on Intergovernmental Relations has commented on or even identified lottery receipts in their reports and analyses.

for programs in the budget, an increase in taxes brings out little support or even interest from the bureaucracy. Bureaucrats are concerned for the programs of their clientele, and someone else can worry about taxes. Governors and legislators must somehow convince sufficient numbers of citizens that particular program demands can be met only by new or increased taxes. And they must further modify and adjust the taxes chosen, to secure legislative majorities. Agreement may be reached to pass a progressive income tax, for example, if farmers in an agricultural state are given certain allowances in computing net income. In an oil producing state, the *quid pro quo* may be depletion allowances. Similarly agreement may be reached on a general sales tax if the burden is reduced by exempting all food. Lobbyists for education or transportation programs may accept almost any tax that will raise substantial revenue for their program needs.

The political scientist wants to know why states, given the availability of certain resources, have made at least marginally different tax decisions. They try to look at the whole system: the general political and socioeconomic culture in which political institutions operate, the inputs into the political system, the outputs from the political system, and their outcomes, which in turn affect the inputs. We can generally identify the tax policies that are the outputs of the political system, and we can suggest the economist's version of the outcomes of the tax policies on individuals and business. It is much more difficult to develop satisfactory analyses of the conversion processes either from inputs into outputs or from outputs into outcomes with a feedback to inputs. In other words, we can predict outputs with only limited success from our descriptions of either the socioeconomic or political characteristics of the environment.

The American states have many social, economic, and political institutions and characteristics in common. In fact, the differences appear to have grown less in the last fifty years as the economy has become more national than ever with tremendous interstate movements of people and goods. Both Congress and the state legislatures have assumed a larger role in regulating the economy and in providing services as a response to the nationalizing of the economy and society. These political, economic, and social similarities limit the number of possible system characteristics the political scientist must include to explain the differences in tax policies (outputs) among the states. In fact, these common constraints limit both the number of differences in the systems and their outputs. We are looking at the marginally significant tax policy decisions among the states and the marginal differences in political characteristics on the assumption that different tax policy decisions are not merely the result of differences in economic levels or urban-rural characteristics. We presume that the degree of party competition, the extent of citizen participation, perhaps the length of the governor's term and the probability of his reelection, the population apportionment of the legislative body, and the extensiveness and effectiveness of group organization are among the important political characteristics that affect inputs. We also assume, and here our task increases, that these characteristics are significant not only in the present but backwards for possibly decades. We are still isolating political characteristics and political outputs that various states have in common. The scholarly work of the last decade has been most useful, but it is not completed. We should remember this as we examine tax policies of the states and attempt to find common factors that explain them.

Another difficulty hinders the analyst. The legislator, who acts as a broker in tax policy decisions, almost never provides a clean-cut statute that follows the model for a progressive individual income tax or regressive general sales tax. Even if the legislator had provided such a statute, its administration would cause it to vary from the model. Economists classify state income taxes as progressive and state sales taxes as regressive, but they recognize that the content of an income or sales tax statute may affect significantly the degree of regressivity or progressivity. An income tax that permits the deduction of the federal income tax is definitely less progressive than an identical tax without this provision. A sales tax with a credit refund through the income tax for taxpayers in lower-income brackets is not as regressive as many models. The combinations of tax provisions (outputs) for legislative bodies to select that affect the ultimate issue of tax burden (impact or outcome) are almost infinite. Policy decisions in other areas such as formulas for grants to education or local government organization decisions further determine tax burden. These results, which our general models frequently cannot measure, may in turn influence demands on legislators to modify tax policies in new legislative sessions. Tax policy choices, like other policy decisions, are never completed.

PATTERNS IN TAXATION

Most present state taxes were not part of the inputs from which nineteenth-century politicians made state revenue decisions. Until the Wisconsin income tax law of 1911, state income taxes were not accepted as significant sources of state revenue by either economists or politicians; the general sales tax was first adopted for state taxation by Mississippi in 1932, and motor vehicle and gasoline taxes followed the increasing use of the automobile in this century.

Major Decision Outlines

Each way of describing the tax systems of the states serves a purpose. Carefully chosen descriptions can shift the position of a state from a high to a low tax state, or at least from high to medium or medium to low. Some combination of rates or data will support any position. Listen to tax discussions at a party, to a candidate's speech, or to the rhetoric of legislators. Read the governor's revenue message. What facts are left out? What is the reason for the emphasis? Do the conclusions logically follow? Both citizens and their representatives take positions on taxes or foreign policy or environmental pollution that are based on normally incomplete and frequently inaccurate information. Particular analogies may be repeated again and again as if they had substantive meaning. In private conversation with me in Oregon, several people indicated that even with the present use of property and income taxes there was an "eventual need for the sales tax to give the third leg to the stool." *

Tax systems might be analyzed using only state taxes, using state and local taxes, or even state and local taxes and charges to make up total state and local general revenue, as the census bureau measures it. For some purposes we might even add federal grants. The publications of the Advisory Commission on Intergovernmental Relations and many of those of the Governments Division of the Bureau of the Census normally combine state and local taxes for their analyses. This may well be the common way in which the individual taxpayer views his taxes. It also eliminates the difficulty of differentiating among the states in the division of programs and fiscal responsibility between the state capitol and city and town halls. Our initial comparisons will combine state and local taxes according to types, height, and a concept of burden. We will also think historically.

At the beginning of this century, taxes for state governments accounted for less than 20 per cent of state and local taxes. Today state taxes account for 52 per cent of state and local totals. As expenditure demands

---

* The logic of the Advisory Commission on Intergovernmental Relations in arguing that every state needs property, sales, and incomes taxes as major taxes because most states have them is not much more convincing. See for example, Advisory Commission on Intergovernmental Relations, *A Staff Report: Measures of State and Local Fiscal Capacity and Tax Effort* (Washington, D.C.: United States Government Printing Office, 1962).

have grown, the states have assumed more of the costs either by taking over full responsibility for a program or by providing more funds through grants-in-aid or shared taxes. The vaunted fiscal independence of villages, cities, and counties in the nineteenth century no longer exists. Leagues of municipalities, organizations of metropolitan areas, county board associations, and other lobbying groups work to persuade governors, legislators, and political party leaders of their dire needs and of the necessity of distributing grants or sharing taxes to the advantage of their clientele. Such efforts may result in shifting local property tax burdens or making it difficult for the central city to incorporate suburban areas or gain their cooperation in costly programs of special consequence to the city. The metropolitan problem almost without exception includes differential tax burdens and needs among the communities.

In the twentieth century taxes at all levels have increased. The citizen of 1900 would be amazed at the affluence of most individuals today after taxes. The increasing abundance of our economy has meant that citizens can choose to have government do more and still have more left to spend personally than in earlier periods. Figure 1 shows the trends of governmental taxes and the estimated per capita personal income by decades from 1902 to 1967.* Whereas the national government raised 37 per cent of the total tax revenues of the country in 1902 and local governments raised 51 per cent, the relative weights of governmental tax levies in 1967 had shifted to 65.4 per cent of the national government, 18.1 per cent for the states, and 16.5 per cent for local governments. Yet state and local governments collected almost $20 billion more in taxes in 1967 than just five years earlier in 1962, a growth of roughly 50 per cent. The growth of state expenditures and demands for even more state and local programs have raised issues of additional and perhaps new types of national government financial assistance. One frequent argument is that the general affluence of the country indicates that income and wealth are available for taxation without economic hardship, but for several reasons state and local governments either do not have sufficient taxable resources within their boundaries to meet needs or are unable or unwilling to tax sufficiently. Other arguments stress the equity of the income tax, the seeming ability of the national government alone to use it adequately, and the general interdependence of the nation as goods, services, and people ignore state boundary lines in their movements.

* We use 1967 data for most of our state-local analysis since detailed information in state and local revenues is available only through the five-year studies of the Governments Division of the census bureau.

FIGURE 1
Income and Taxes over Selected Years

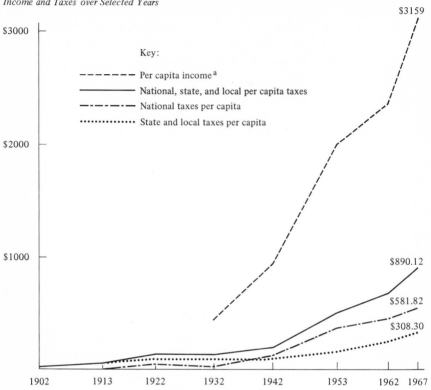

a Reliable per capita income data before 1932 unavailable.
Sources: Personal income statistics from Department of Commerce, Office of Business Economics, *Survey of Current Business.* See Table 2 for sources. For the tax data see United States Department of Commerce, Bureau of the Census, *Census of Governments, 1967,* Vol. 4, No. 5: *Compendium of Government Finances* and preceding volumes. See sources in Table 1.

TAXES CHOSEN.   In taking over an increasing responsibility for raising taxes for direct state services and for funding many local services, legislatures have concentrated on individual and corporate income taxes, sales taxes, and automobile taxes. By 1970 forty-two states had a corporate income tax and all but nine had an individual income tax. Only the five states of Alaska, Delaware, Montana, New Hampshire, and Oregon lacked a general sales tax. Only Hawaii lacked an automobile registration tax; all fifty states had gasoline taxes. All the states had cigarette taxes, and only Nevada was without estate taxes. Finally, all fifty states either taxed liquor or sold it through government-owned stores with the profits returned to the state or, in North Carolina, to the county.

A check of 1967 state revenue statistics indicates that Delaware, Massachusetts, Minnesota, New York, Oregon, and Wisconsin emphasize the income tax. For decades, these states have given personal and corporate income taxes the leading role in their state tax structures by frequently drawing 40 per cent or more of their state tax revenue from this source alone. Arizona, Hawaii, Illinois, Indiana, Michigan, Washington, and West Virginia obtained more than 40 per cent of their revenue from general sales tax in both 1962 and 1967.

COMPARATIVE TAX LEVELS AND STABILITY.   Table 1 lists New York as the state with the highest taxes per capita in the country, $459.40, in 1967. Alabama had the lowest taxes per capita, $191.37, or less than half those of New York. By examining taxes in per capita terms, we assume that population affects both the cost of government and the burden of taxes. Presumably the density of population also affects the cost of government. Regional salary levels may affect both the cost of government and the burden of taxes.

Comparisons over the years from 1902 to 1967 show that state and local governments do not readily change their levels of taxation. Eight states in the upper quartile of per capita taxes in 1967 were also in the upper quartile at least five times out of eight selected time periods in this century: 1902, 1913, 1922, 1932, 1942, 1953, 1962, and 1967. Four states were in the upper quartile all eight years. Washington appeared seven of the eight years. Stability in rank is even stronger on the low tax side where eleven of the twelve states were in the lower quartile at least five of the eight years. Eight of these eleven appeared all eight times; Kentucky and Texas appeared seven times; West Virginia, six.*

Comparisons over the years from 1902 to 1967 show that the gap between the lowest and highest per capita tax states has significantly narrowed. Although New York and Alabama did not have the highest and lowest tax rates in 1902, both were in the upper and lower quartiles — New York, sixth highest, and Alabama, fourth lowest. In 1902 and 1913, the highest taxing states were collecting approximately seven times the revenue of the lowest taxing states. In 1922, the margin was almost ten-to-

---

* This analysis does not establish that the repeating states in the eight-year statistics were also in the upper quartile or lower quartile all or most other years. A quick check of the available census data (and the census does not provide information on local revenues for all of the intervening years) suggests a strong presumption that the same states have been high or low during most of the twentieth century.

TABLE 1

State and Local Per Capita Tax Comparisons, 1967

	Per capita state and local taxes, 1967[a]	Number of times in eight selected years state is upper quartile[b]
Upper quartile		
New York	$459.40	8
California	406.60	8
Hawaii[c]	406.75	—
Nevada	374.31	8
Massachusetts	369.70	8
Wisconsin	362.29	5
Washington	359.11	7
Minnesota	350.74	4
Wyoming	350.20	4
Colorado	343.15	6
Delaware	339.52	2
Connecticut	335.92	6
Iowa	333.77	2
Lower quartile		
Ohio	$249.77	1
Virginia	236.04	8
Texas	227.36	7
Georgia	227.33	8
North Carolina	224.56	8
West Virginia	222.69	6
Kentucky	211.40	7
Tennessee	210.86	8
Arkansas	119.46	8
South Carolina	196.52	8
Mississippi	196.47	8
Alabama	191.37	8

[a]United States Department of Commerce, Bureau of the Census, *Census of Governments* 1967, Vol. 4, No. 5; *Compendium of Government Finances* (Washington, D.C.: United States Government Printing Office, 1969), Table 27.

[b]Identification of number of times state appeared consistently in high or low quartile based on these data and that in Table 1, *Politics in the American States*, Herbert Jacob and Kenneth N. Vines, editors, 1965 edition.

[c]Since Hawaii territorial statistics are not comparable, a thirteenth state is included for quartile.

one. By the depression year of 1932, the difference had dropped to approximately four-to-one; and, as we have already noted, in 1967 the high was only slightly more than twice the lowest per capita state and local tax collections.

How real is this narrowing margin? First, the reliability of the percentage margin as an index of narrowing differences among the states assumes that factors influencing cost have not changed in this century, or, more realistically, that they have changed in the same direction and in the same proportion for all states. We do not have enough data to establish whether base factors, such as "real cost of living" variations, increasing urbanization, shifts in population density, and corruption or efficiency in government operation, have changed relatively in the same degree.* We have statistics for some factors, but we have only general impressions for others. For example, we know that several states adopted measures during the first and second decades of this century to improve the efficiency of their governments and to reduce or eliminate the usual sources of corruption. Other states have not yet taken some of these steps but still may have improved their position in both areas.

Common factors accounting for taxes have changed and that change has been in the same direction across the nation. It appears that the broad influences across the country of increased population, increasing urbanization, and increasing affluence are more important than the differential details. Nevertheless, caution is required in interpreting whether or not the gap between states is narrowing. Beyond and above the general trend may be the fact that the absolute difference between high and low taxing states in 1967 was substantially greater than that difference in 1902. In the early years, services in all the states were fairly minimal and large percentage differences in the level of taxes may have had only a slight differential effect on most citizens. Today, though the percentage difference is smaller, the services require greater sums and alter the quality of living for many citizens. We know, for example, that in 1965 the average monthly aid to families with dependent children in Alabama of $48.23 contrasted with New York's average assistance figure of $203.84 or Wisconsin's figure of $186.03. New York and Wisconsin set no maximum aid, whereas Alabama's maximum was $124.00. Federal funds supplied 79 per cent of Alabama's assistance and less than 50 per cent of New York's and Wisconsin's. Even with a cost of living adjustment, the quality of living in Alabama and New York or Wisconsin must have been different.

TAX BURDEN. The above discussion of levels and stability of per capita taxes says nothing about the tax burden in relation to income. The concept of tax burden refers to taxes as a per cent of an individual's or a family's income, as a per cent of income by income classes, or as a relation of total taxes to total income in a state. The overall level of state and local taxes in a state in relation to overall personal income is usually identified as the total tax burden.

---

* Since neither federal grants-in-aid nor revenue from state or local charges are included, we are not looking at the full amount available for expenditures.

Table 2 contains the ratio of state and local taxes to personal income for five selected years beginning in 1932. A look at this table indicates a bunching of states as high or low tax burden states.* Although the list of high and low per capita states and high and low states in the relation of taxes to income are by no means identical, we again find consistency that confirms our expectation that income levels as well as tax levels do not change rapidly. Six of the twelve states in the upper quartile in 1967 appeared in at least four of the selected years. Three states, Idaho, New York, and South Dakota, from the 1967 list as well as Louisiana and Mississippi from previous lists ranked in the upper quartile three of the selected years.

Consistency for low burden is also strong. Maryland (though not included in 1967) and Pennsylvania report low tax burdens for four of the selected years; Connecticut, Missouri, and Virginia were in the low tax burden group in all five years. An additional five states show low tax burdens in three of the five years: Illinois, Nebraska, New Jersey, and Ohio from the 1967 low quartile and Delaware earlier.

The relation of the mix of tax ingredients to the distribution of income in the states indicates tax burden in a more refined sense by income groups. Neither the total tax, nor the total income, nor their distribution in the states is constant, so that the precise tax burden varies from year to year. Moreover, no centrally gathered statistics tell us with certainty what the distribution of income is, nor do we know without question who finally pays a particular tax.† The burden of some taxes may be almost totally exported by the levying state to users in other states. Thus, Minnesota's taxes on its iron mines are paid by iron and steel users throughout the nation, as are Louisiana's oil taxes. Other states with natural resources may similarly succeed in reducing their own tax burdens.

---

* These burden rankings and the more refined ones that follow require caution in interpretation. Tax burden is a defined term, and the word burden high or low, should not produce a simple emotional reaction. A high tax burden may mean a high level of governmental services and a generally good standard of living, whereas a low tax burden may mean the reverse. Or it may mean simply that incomes are low in the first instance and high in the second instance, and a similar tax system and level of services is present on both occasions. Or the categorization may result from other combinations of decisions and circumstances. Here, as in other instances, value judgments and preferences should include considerations of economic trends.

† Economists almost universally accept some economic assumptions relative to shifting and incidence, but they would widely dispute others. It is usually assumed that personal income taxes are paid by the individual. In the case of rental property, it is usually assumed that the renter pays the property taxes through the increased rentals levied by the landlord. Most retail sales taxes are assumed to be paid by the purchaser on the item. Not only are there refinements even to these assumptions but, in the case of corporation income tax, the assumption divides the taxes among profits, wages, and prices, depending on the precise competitive position of the corporation.

TABLE 2

Gross Tax Burdens, Selected Years^a

	Percentage of per capita income to state and local taxes				
State	1967	1962	1953	1942	1932
Upper quartile					
New York	12.22	10.63	–	10.1	–
Arizona	11.78	10.52	9.53	–	21.4
South Dakota	11.71	–	10.11	–	31.5
Wyoming	11.66	11.40	–	–	–
Wisconsin	11.47	10.62	–	9.4	18.6
Idaho	11.39	–	9.44	–	21.6
Vermont	11.36	11.87	9.82	9.5	–
Minnesota	11.25	11.22	9.87	10.1	17.7
Utah	11.23	–	–	–	–
North Dakota	11.22	–	11.06	10.2	24.3
California	11.09	–	–	–	–
Montana	10.97	10.53	–	9.0	18.6
Louisiana	–	11.39	10.76	9.4	–
Mississippi	–	10.90	9.69	–	18.9
Lower quartile					
Nebraska	8.81	8.24	–	6.6	–
Tennessee	8.80	8.49	–	–	–
Pennsylvania	8.74	8.68	6.19	–	11.5
Kentucky	8.71	–	6.81	–	–
New Jersey	8.71	8.21	6.81	–	–
Missouri	8.70	7.95	6.25	7.1	10.6
Connecticut	8.46	8.43	6.48	7.1	11.7
New Hampshire	8.44	–	–	–	–
Virginia	8.41	7.27	6.62	5.7	11.4
Texas	8.28	–	–	6.9	–
Illinois	7.95	–	6.54	–	11.6
Ohio	7.77	8.24	5.92	–	–
Delaware	–	7.74	4.56	5.7	–
Maryland	–	8.22	6.57	6.0	10.4

^{a}Only those states are included that appeared in the upper or lower quartiles three or more times out of the five years. States omitted are normally in the middle range of taxes in relation to personal income, "gross tax burden." A blank in a column for an individual state means that it was not in the upper (or lower) quartile that year.

Source: Calculations were made from data on per capita taxes in Table 1 and from data on annual personal income reported for calendar year 1953 and reported by Department of Commerce, *Survey of Current Business,* August, 1954; for calendar year 1962, *Survey of Current Business,* August, 1963; and *Survey of Current Business,* August, 1968. Also used were ratios for 1932 and 1942 shown in Table 22, United States Department of Commerce, Bureau of the Census, *Historical Review of State and Local Government Finances,* June, 1948.

Despite the difficulties, scholars from time to time have attempted to make the needed estimates and to analyze the distribution of state and local tax burdens by income groups, although no study makes the distribution state by state. Although economic assumptions, changes in state and local tax laws, and changes in the economy will affect the detailed findings, the

TABLE 3

State and Local Taxes as a Percentage of Income, 1965

Income classes	State and local tax ratio
Under $2,000	25%
$2,000 - 4,000	11
4,000 - 6,000	10
6,000 - 8,000	9
8,000 - 10,000	9
10,000 - 15,000	9
15,000 and over	7
Total	9

Source: Economic Report of the President, 1969 (Washington, D.C.: United States Government Printing Office, 1969.) Income excludes transfer payments, but includes realized capital gains in full and undistributed corporate profits.

general conclusion that state and local tax systems are regressive has been found in every study covering the fifty, or forty-eight, states. In Table 3 are estimates of the overall distribution by income classes of state and local taxes raised in the United States in 1965. The table shows a clear regressive pattern. Taxes fall hardest on the lowest income level and in descending order on incomes as they increase.* If federal taxes are taken by themselves, the pattern of rates is clearly progressive, except for the under $2,000 income class. Even this class no longer shows a regressive rate when transfer payments are considered. In fact, the combination of federal, state, and local taxes has a progressive structure with transfer payments.

Tax burden studies would require statistics beyond any that are normally gathered. Even well-directed and financed studies require estimates and assumptions based at best on limited samples. The economic interdependence of the states brings especially difficult problems into assumptions of tax shifting and incidence. Hence, national aggregate studies usually give the best obtainable view subject to modification by state patterns. If the overall national finding is regressive for a state that has an average income level and distribution, and a tax system that depends largely on the usual ingredients — a general sales tax, low or no income taxes, gasoline, tobacco, and liquor excise taxes, motorist and motor vehicle licenses, and (locally) the property tax — deviations from the average in either the income distribution or the tax system would modify the findings. For example, an analysis of the distribution of Wisconsin's tax burden in

* Standard tax terminology defines *regressive* taxes as taxes that decrease as a ratio of income with increases in income; *progressive* taxes as taxes that increase as a ratio of income with increases in income; *proportional* taxes as taxes that show a constant ratio without regard to changes in income. Both a tax and a tax system may be classified in this basis.

1956 (when Wisconsin had no general sales tax) suggested regression at the bottom of the income scale, approximate proportionality in the middle, and slight progression at the top (see Table 4).

Some differences in the national aggregate findings and the Wisconsin findings result from differing assumptions, but broadly the results are as expected. Wisconsin in 1956 depended heavily on personal and corporate income taxes and traditionally has taxed somewhat higher than the average state. The subsequent adoption of a sales tax with food exemptions probably still would show a progressive effect on the over $10,000 income class. With all the reservations already stated, it is clearly not easy to compare state tax systems on a regressive-progressive tax burden scale with the degree of certainty possible when we were merely comparing reported collections with personal income.

Apart from the general property tax, which is the major ingredient of all local tax systems, what preferences for income or sales taxes do our high and low tax states exhibit? A check of Table 1 tells us that the preferences are not too pronounced. The consistently high per capita tax states of Massachusetts, New York, and Wisconsin have also been heavy users of the income tax. The relation is even stronger if we only check the high per capita states in 1962 and 1967 when five are strong income tax states. Even if tax burden is our measure, New York, Minnesota, and Wisconsin remain high on the list. In per capita terms, only Hawaii and Washington are both high sales tax and high tax states, and only Hawaii remains if tax burden is our measure. Hawaii is a strong income as well as sales tax state that puts small emphasis on the property tax.

TABLE 4
Wisconsin's Effective Tax Rates, 1956

Income class	Adjusted gross income revised
$0 - Under 1,000	29.83%
1,000 - 1,999	14.94
2,000 - 2,999	11.10
3,000 - 3,999	9.67
4,000 - 4,999	8.87
5,000 - 5,999	8.46
6,000 - 6,999	8.34
7,000 - 9,999	8.31
10,000 and over	10.88
All classes	9.76

Source: Adapted from University of Wisconsin Tax Study Committee Report, *Wisconsin State and Local Tax Burden* (Madison: University of Wisconsin Press, 1969), 55, Table 8. The effective rates are based on the 1956 state and local tax structure.

The low tax states, measured per capita by tax burden, exhibit little consistency, except perhaps eclecticism, in their choice of tax. Only Illinois appears as both a high sales tax state and a low tax burden state. About all that we can conclude from this review is that state political systems that place a heavy emphasis on the income tax in their tax policy output seem slightly more apt to levy heavy taxes than state political systems that emphasize the sales tax or a group of taxes without choosing a principal tax.

Summary

In this section, we have described the types of taxes employed today and historically by the states and their local governments. We combined state and local taxes to gain a sense of the level and burden of taxes and to determine the high and low taxing states. We ranked the states according to a gross sense of tax burden, both in total state and local taxes as per capita or in relation to income and in the emphasis that the several states put on the normally progressive income tax or the more regressive sales tax. We also noted that states may levy special charges as well as taxes, but that the inclusion of these charges does not materially change the identification of high and low taxing states. The analysis should have created a sense of some of the issues in tax policies and of a certain amount of stability in types and levels of taxes chosen by the states.

CONSTRAINTS ON TAX POLICY POSED BY CONSTITUTIONALISM AND TRADITION

Since taxes must come out of the income or wealth of residents or citizens of a nation, income and wealth are necessarily constraints on the levels and even types of taxes. A poor country has a different ceiling on taxes than a wealthy country. An agricultural nation, especially one in which barter is common, finds an income tax less feasible than an industrial nation. An authoritarian nation is freer to use the tax power than a nation whose voters regularly elect their representatives, although the income tax has been less popular in authoritarian than in democratic states.

In the United States the federal system of government has affected taxation as it has most other institutions and practices. Written constitutions frequently set detailed constraints on taxes. An examination of the constitutional constraints in the United States may assist in explaining much of the conformity as well as some of the differences in tax patterns.

Constitutional Constraints

The Constitution in Article I, Section 8, provides that the Congress "have power to lay and collect taxes, duties, imposts and excises," but in Section 9 it prohibits "capitation, or other direct, tax . . . unless in proportion to the census." The Sixteenth Amendment in 1913 assured that this provision would not prevent personal and corporate income taxes. Both the states and the national government were prohibited from laying any tax or duty on exports from or among the states. In practice, the Constitution has prevented state taxation only when it taxed interstate commerce or violates due process under the Fourteenth Amendment. Not by the Constitution but by congressional action in certain grants-in-aid legislation, most notably the Hayden-Cartwright Act, are the states required to segregate taxes for specified use. Thus, the Hayden-Cartwright Act of 1934 requires, with a few exceptions, that the states place gasoline tax revenues in special funds for highway purposes only.

Although the Constitution did not establish separate tax paths for the national government and for state and local governments, nineteenth-century practices differed almost as if separate roads had been prescribed. Until the twentieth century, with brief exceptions, the national government depended on customs and excises for revenue; the state and local governments utilized the general property tax. In 1902, state and local governments raised $860 million from taxes, 82 per cent of which was raised by the property tax. Actually, the towns, villages, and cities spent most of the $860 million, or a total of $704 million. In the same year, national governmental taxes totalled only $513 million. The national government subsequently has had to meet recurring crises of war, depression, and threats of war. These, together with increasing demands in a changing and ever more interdependent economic and social system, have magnified the level and choice of taxes by the national government. Sixty-five years after 1902, the national government collected $115,121 million in taxes, with 83 per cent of this amount coming from individual and corporate income taxes unknown in 1902.* The states collected $31,926 million also from an increasing variety of taxes. Local government collections of $29 million are largely drawn from property taxes. The states are gradually breaking out of the limitations they placed on their own taxing powers and especially on those

* The national government, as well as the Confederate government, raised war funds through income taxes in the 1860s. The federal government subsequently let its income tax lapse. When the Supreme Court held a new national income tax act unconstitutional in 1894, efforts were shortly made to amend the Constitution. The Sixteenth Amendment in 1913 permitted national income taxes.

of their local governments. Almost every state constitution, however, continues to ignore the admonition of the National Municipal League that "ideally, a [state] constitution should be silent on the subject of taxation and finance, thus permitting the legislature and the governor freedom to develop fiscal policies for the States to meet the requirements of their time." [2] Fear of future legislative extravagance or legislative favoritism led some states to limit borrowing, to prohibit raising taxes for specific purposes, and to include statements requiring the uniformity and universality of taxes (actually property taxes but often not so identified) that provided the base for later restrictive state court decisions.

The single rate of the sales tax has normally led state courts to approve it, whereas they deny the constitutionality of income taxes under the universality and uniformity clauses of old property tax laws. Even today states without an income tax could only adopt such taxes after the passage of appropriate constitutional amendments. The 1962 Michigan constitution prohibits the levying of a progressive income tax. Nevada would have to amend its constitution to levy an estate or inheritance tax. Illinois finally adopted a proportional income tax in 1969 after almost four decades of struggle over constitutional provisions and their interpretation.

State constitutions may also limit the total permissible height of taxes. These restrictions, where they exist, often apply to local governments only. Finally, by statute or constitutional provision, taxes may be set aside for only one type of expenditure. Most states have not only accepted the restrictions on taxes imposed by some grant-in-aid legislation but have restricted the uses of other taxes in addition. Whether such action helps or hinders the affected program is debatable.[3]

National, state, or local constitutions can be amended, but amendment takes time and unusual majorities. Where constitutional change is required, any new tax, any increase in taxes, or other change in taxation faces barriers that are lifted only under great pressure.

Federalism

More limiting perhaps than formal constitutional barriers and, in fact, helping to bring about constitutional restrictions, is the concern for "what the other fellow does." Federation allows opportunities for freedom and experimentation, but its members often seek the solace of uniformity. States constantly test their tax policies against those of their sister states. Florida in 1924 repealed its inheritance-estate law in an overt appeal to the wealthy of the nation to end their days where fine physical and tax climates would be combined. Nevada followed with similar constitutional action in 1925. Only congressional passage of the 1926 law to permit crediting state inheritance-estate taxes against federal estate taxes probably prevented a rush of other states from copying the Florida tax action, although neither the wishes nor the actions of other state legislators could reproduce Florida's physical climate.

Interstate competition is a constant touchstone for tax decisions in height and type. What the neighboring states are doing regarding taxes is almost a beginning and ending point of discussions in political campaigns, in state legislatures, and among many voters. If neighbor A has a sales tax, it is an argument for state B to adopt it. If neighbor C has low per capita taxes, many in state B will argue that theirs should be at least as low — but without lowering state services!

Volumes of economic analysis and empirical evidence to the contrary have not eliminated the argument in tax discussions that high taxes drive out business and scare new industry away.* We have already pointed out that Congress wrote the 80 per cent state credit against national estate taxes in 1926 at the insistence of states that otherwise might have felt compelled to follow Florida and Nevada in repealing existing estate taxes. The unemployment compensation tax was enacted nationally in part because of the argument that only national action would encourage most states to enact the program.

Practicing federalism may keep states in similar tax paths, but when one or more states pioneer others are likely to follow. The breakthrough in state income taxation by Wisconsin in 1911 brought a rapid succession of adoptions within a few years. Even somewhat peculiar local technical provisions (such as Wisconsin's for deduction of dependency exemption by a fixed dollar figure from the calculated tax total with the effect of increasing progressiveness), reappeared in the Kentucky and Arizona statutes. Adoption of sales taxes also shows a bunched pattern. The creativity of one or two states brought adaptation from many others under the common pressure of the depression. Today the demand is to reduce local property taxes and place a greater fiscal responsibility on the state, almost without regard to how the new funds are raised.

---

* When pressed, the more knowledgeable tax discussant agrees that taxes are important only on the margins when all other desired conditions, i.e., transportation, raw materials, labor force, etc., are equal. Yet the fact that most locational decisions can more readily be explained in these terms than at the margins has not lessened political use of the argument. It is an argument used in highly industrial states such as Illinois as well as in less industrial states such as Iowa. See Glenn W. Fisher, *Taxes and Politics: A Study of Illinois Public Finance* (Urbana: University of Illinois Press, 1969), Chap. 6.

Nebraska adopted both a general sales tax and an income tax in 1967 after twenty years of having an unusually high property tax component in its state-local tax system.* By the 1960s, one simply expected to find each new set of tax tables reporting Nebraska first in its dependence on the property tax. Without either an income tax or a general sales tax, the state as well as its local governments used the property tax and attempted to keep it down by refusing many of the demands for governmental expenditures. As the vehemence of demands for services grew so did demands for a new general purpose state tax. In 1965, Governor Morrison, apparently believing property rates had reached their ceiling and unwilling to recommend a new state tax, slashed state agency budget requests. The legislature, more responsive to program demands, increased many budget items in an attempt to force the governor to support a new tax. With a different governor and some new legislators, the general sales tax and income tax were adopted in 1967.[4] Immediately Nebraska's ranking for dependence on the property tax went down; its ranking for use of the general sales tax and income tax went up. Its local state tax collections jumped 42 per cent from 1967 to 1968 and another 12 per cent between 1968 and 1969. Its ranking for expenditures went up, and its tax policy outputs conformed more closely to the other forty-nine states.

The Nebraska example, as well as many others, suggests that an equilibrium mechanism in our federal system has tended to keep the states within certain tax policy parameters. The founders expected and desired diversity, and diversity exists. We can find leaders and laggards among the states in different rates of policy adoptions, but pressures for conformity also exist.

Other Past Decisions

Apart from the requirements of constitutions and the call of federalism for uniformity, our analysis so far suggests that the tradition of a state can be both descriptive and explanatory. We have noted that high tax states often remain high tax states, and low tax states remain low. States that initially made the income tax or the sales tax a major revenue raiser have continued to do so. No state has revised a preference that was strongly expressed in the past. Even the distribution of tasks between the

---

* Similarly, New Jersey finally adopted a general sales tax in 1966 after unusually heavy dependence on the property tax and with no state income or sales taxes. The adoption of sales taxes in the 1960s by several income tax states also followed pressures in the political system "to do something about high property taxes."

state and its local governments has a tendency to remain constant. Once levels of services and taxes are established, they tend to be cumulative. In other words, states, consciously or not, seldom radically change ranking in tax or expenditure.

Economists discussing national trends in Western nations find that customary levels of taxes continue until dislodged by crisis. They do not consistently define crisis, however, and can identify it by looking backward more easily than by looking forward. The Great Depression of the 1930s appears to have been a crisis for the United States but not for England. Wars have been crises for both.[5]

Ira Sharkansky, among others, has found that available analyses in political, social, and economic terms for expenditures in the American states are less successful predictors than previous years' budgets.[6] Yet explanations of tradition or incrementalism advance us only a short distance. Can we find a definition for crises in state governments that would indicate the points at which a tradition to tax heavily or lightly is made? Is there, for example, a point of balance in agricultural, labor, and industrial interests that is critical for decisions? Do the degree of party competition, the presence of a particular leader, the distribution of income that may affect the degree of voter participation, the manner of legislative apportionment, and other similar characteristics determine the direction of the decision? We lack case studies that would answer these questions.

CONSTRAINTS POSED BY SOCIOECONOMIC
AND POLITICAL ENVIRONMENT

So far we have discussed state taxes as almost all levies not made by the national government. We have included property taxes locally levied as well as the variety of taxes levied by the states. The individual citizen in any of the over 80,000 local governmental units (he is likely to live under the jurisdiction of several — county, city, village, or town, and one or more special districts) and one of the 50 states must pay taxes to all of the units in which he lives and works. But more and more political scientists believe that confining our attention to the state political system and its tax policy decisions in current years is the most profitable area of research. Local property taxes are those that remain after the state political system has determined general levels of taxes, types of taxes, and locally shared tax and grant-in-aid policies.

For the rest of our analysis, we adopt the state viewpoint of this volume that the general ratio local taxes bear to state taxes is one of the outcomes of the tax policy outputs of the state political system conversion process. High local property taxes may indeed activate demands on the state political system for change, but the actual local taxes are policy outputs of the local political system conversion process. We can predict that the political system of any state with unusually high property taxes compared to its neighbors or to other states in the Union will sooner or later be faced with demands to reduce local property taxes through state action.

In a March, 1970, telephone survey, citizens in Wisconsin frequently assumed that their high property taxes could be mitigated by the governor and the legislature. This assumption was a major political issue of the campaign. Leading 1970 Wisconsin legislative and gubernatorial candidates also viewed questions of the height and equity of local property taxes as live state issues. There is evidence that voters in New Jersey, Nebraska, Oregon, and probably most of the other states similarly saw the height of property taxes as largely a state issue. The separate political systems of thousands of local units of government make decisions on property tax rates that result in different rates from community to community, but the most decisive determinant of the individual's local property tax bill since World War II, if not earlier, is the extent to which the state takes responsibility for programs and shares taxes or provides grants-in-aid to cities, towns, and counties. State after state has recognized and increased its fiscal responsibility for total state and local costs.

Environment and Tax Policies

By looking at current tax decisions and attempting to relate them to the socioeconomic and political environments of the several states, we will attempt to relate economic and political traits to tax policy change. Beginning with selected state taxes and charges, Ira Sharkansky and I in a study not yet published, have attempted to examine the high income and high sales tax states in terms of selected economic and political characteristics. Table 5 ranks states with distinctive tax policies, most notably those emphasizing individual income taxes, general sales taxes, or taxes on the withdrawal of natural resources. For measures of tax policy, we have used the amounts collected by each of the forty-eight contiguous states from the major sources listed by the Bureau of the Census for 1968: individual income, corporate income, retail sales, excises and license fees on various commodities, rents and royalties, severance taxes, property taxes, and charges for a variety of service-for-fee programs. We define a state's reliance on each form of revenue by the percentage of total general revenue that it provides. A factor analysis of these percentages identifies the groups of taxes that are used in combination and which taxes tend to be avoided by those states that use others. From these data, we compute summary scores for each state that reflect the clusters of taxes that are used.

Tax Policy and Economic Traits

With any knowledge of the data for industrialization-affluence, one would intuitively associate states such as Massachusetts and New York that emphasize income taxes with states such as Illinois, Ohio, and Pennsylvania that emphasize sales taxes. Maine and Washington seem more related in economic-social characteristics to Vermont and Oregon than to several of the other sales tax states where their tax policy choice placed them. Our statistical testing of industrialization-affluence with the clustering of high income and high sales tax states confirmed our intuition and failed to show any significant correlation between scores on industrialization-affluence and tax policy chosen. Table 6 reports the simple correlations we found. Neither industrialization nor affluence is regularly related to either policy choice. Both income and sales tax groups in Table 5 include states with above and below average per capita incomes, states that are urban-industrial, and states that are rural. Almost all regions of the country are represented in each group. The Rocky Mountain states are in neither, and Maryland is the farthest south of the income tax states. The large urban, industrial states of California, Michigan, and Texas show up in neither cluster. Although California gives some preference to the sales tax, it uses sales, income, and property taxes extensively. Texas gathers significant

TABLE 5
States Making Heavy Use of Specified Taxes, 1968

Sales and excise	Income	Severance, rents, and royalties
Florida	New York	Louisiana
Washington	Delaware	New Mexico
Ohio	Oregon	Texas
Maine	Wisconsin	Wyoming
Tennessee	Maryland	Oklahoma
Illinois	Minnesota	Montana
Nebraska	Vermont	
South Carolina	Massachusetts	
Pennsylvania		

revenue from its oil taxes, so that the sales tax represents a smaller portion of state revenue. Michigan today uses the sales tax heavily, special corporation taxes, and a proportional income tax that in combination make the state neither a high income nor sales tax state.

In addition to separating our income and sales tax states, our clusters also point out three states that stand far above the others in their reliance on rents and royalties plus severance taxes. Louisiana, New Mexico, and Texas tax their natural wealth in oil and minerals. Other oil-producing states or states with other great natural resources do not tax as heavily. These other states have chosen to ignore the tax opportunities presented by a major economic resource since, in fact, much of the tax is exported to citizens elsewhere.

Tax Policy and Political Traits

If our economic variables relate so badly with states' preferences for either income or sales taxes, will political variables serve us any better? The usual assumptions of shifting and incidence of taxes would place the individual income tax in the class of taxes more favorable to the have-nots of society. Other taxes, especially general sales taxes, would appear more favorable to the haves. Some authors suggest that the competitive two-party states provide greater options for the have-not voters to act in their own self-interest. A factor analysis of state political traits produced a competition-turnout dimension measuring aspects of party competition and voter participation. As with the economic environment, we tested the correspondence of the political environment features with the income-sales tax policies of the states, and again found no significant correlations. The coefficients give no indication that the political features operate in any consistent fashion upon the tax policies chosen by the state governments. Both income and sales tax clusters include one-party, low participation states as well as two-party, high participation states.

TABLE 6
Coefficients of Simple Correlation Between State Scores on Tax Factors and on Economic and Political Measures

Tax factors	Economic and political measures		Competition-turnout
	Industrialization	Affluence	
Severance, rents, and royalties	−.25	−.07	−.12
Sales and excise, income	−.08	−.23	−.25

The failure of our statistical measures of economic or political environment traits to show a significant correlation with tax policies may, of course, be due to the inadequacy of the traits used or to the absence of tests in different time periods. Since we are still not satisfied that neither economic nor political environment characteristics are related to tax policies, we must continue to look further for explanations.

Tax Choices and Other Policy Decisions

If tax choices are major policy decisions, we should expect some consistency between the type of tax choice made and other policies that are adopted. The study that Sharkansky and I are conducting provides some support for this expectation. Half of the high income tax states — Massachusetts, Minnesota, New York, and Wisconsin — also rank high on the measures for strong education and welfare policies whereas two of the high sales-excise states — South Carolina and Tennessee — rank low (see Table 7). With one exception the other states ranked as high income or sales-excise tax states did not stand out as high or low spenders for education and welfare. The strong exception to our generalization was Illinois, which has been a nonuser of the income tax until 1969, a high user of sales and excises, and a low tax effort state. However, Illinois scored high in 1968 on welfare-education expenditures.

Before examining the exception, we will look further at the four high income tax states with high welfare-education measures. They are all high expenditure states. Are they liberal in other respects? All four states had adopted workmen's compensation laws before 1915. Massachusetts adopted minimum wage legislation in 1912, Wisconsin in 1913, New York

TABLE 7

States Scoring at Least ± 1.000 on Sales-Income Tax Factor and on Measure of Welfare-Education Programs

	High education-welfare	Low education-welfare
High sales-excise[a]	Illinois	South Carolina Tennessee
High income[b]	Massachusetts Minnesota New York Wisconsin	

[a]Scoring at least +1.000 on sales-income tax factor.
[b]Scoring lower than −1.000 on sales-income tax factor.

in 1933 (still among the first twenty to do so), and Minnesota in 1913. Moreover, all these states have covered an above average proportion of their working population with minimum wage legislation. An index of adoption of major civil rights legislation also shows these four states among the earliest to write statutes asserting the right of all to use public accommodations, to employment, and to rent or buy housing without discrimination as to race or ethnic origin. This last evidence is important to the liberal classification since neither the labor legislation nor the civil rights legislation use funds heavily and therefore, are not simply a concomitant to high taxes.

By any measure, Illinois is an urban, industrial, wealthy state and has been since the turn of the century. Although Chicago is the third largest city in the nation, Illinois has been a conspicuously low spender in comparison to New York. During three of the last four decades, and in 1967, it has ranked low in taxes in relation to personal income. It has had the problems of an ever more urbanizing society with significant movement of people, often disadvantaged, from other areas of the country. It has rural poverty counties in the southern parts of the state. With the extremes of wealth and poverty, the tax system has unquestionably favored business and the economically well off. It may well be that high welfare payments as well as reasonably good education expenditures have been the necessary compromise in the bargaining process.

Bargaining is something Illinois politicians are well acquainted with. Not only is it a competitive two-party state, but there are down-state and up-state Republicans, and the Democratic party is by no means simply a Chicago operation. Pressure groups have also been a major part of the scene. Glenn W. Fisher, in his study of Illinois taxes, details the coming together of the leading pressure groups in the tax area preparatory to the 1965 legislature and the resulting tax referendum.[7] In fact, the agreements between these groups were not sufficient to achieve a minimal income tax at that time. In an unpublished manuscript, Allan Rosenbaum details some of this continued bargaining, especially the bargaining between the Republican governor and Chicago Democratic Mayor Daley in 1969 to pass the income tax bill and to revise aids to education and state sharing of income and sales taxes to benefit Chicago.[8]

At the beginning of this chapter, we commented on possible relationships between taxes and expenditures. We would like to pursue this now by examining states that heavily emphasize income taxes in contrast to sales taxes. Studies consistently suggest a higher elasticity for the income tax than the sales tax, which means that as personal income rises, state income tax revenues, with constant rates, rise faster than state sales taxes, with constant rates.

Do states with heavy emphasis on the income tax, which, therefore, profit more than sales tax states from general prosperity, find it easier to increase expenditures? Where it is unnecessary to change tax rates and still receive increased revenues, do the income tax states raise their expenditures more than the sales tax states? The data in Figure 2 suggest an affirmative answer. We have plotted census-reported state expenditures at two-year intervals for ten years and revenues for the same period for the eight high income and eight sales tax states in Table 5. The revenue gap between income and sales tax states widened more than the expenditure gap during the decade from 1958 to 1968. This decade reflected years of greater prosperity, and the increased revenues from income taxes facilitated higher expenditures. Sales tax states also had increased revenues and ex-

FIGURE 2
1958-1968 Per Capita Revenues and Expenditures of States Scoring at Least ± 1.000 on the Sales-Income Tax Factor

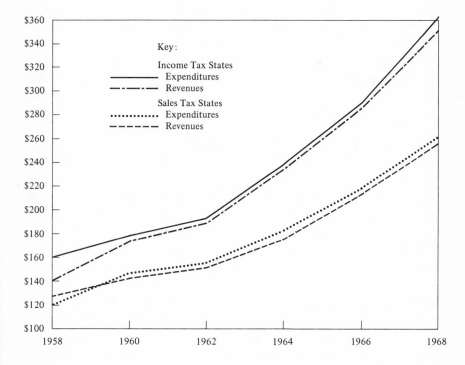

penditures, but it is at least possible that the larger growth in income tax revenues encouraged a corresponding growth in expenditures for the income tax states.

Nothing in our data here, nor in our earlier tables, however, gives us reason to assert that high income tax states are also high expenditure states. Four of our higher income tax states do rate as high expenditure states; but so does Washington, a high sales tax state, and so does California, a state that does not emphasize income rather than sales taxes or the reverse.

Before concluding our analyses, we will look at a recent decision in Oregon to maintain its emphasis on the income tax and its refusal to adopt a general sales tax.

A CASE STUDY:
OREGON KEEPS ITS TRADITION

In a special election of June 3, 1969, Oregon voters refused to approve a general sales tax by a vote of almost 8 to 1! [9] The outcome was not a surprise even though the referendum had provided for some property tax relief from the proposed sales tax revenues. With forty-five states currently using a general sales tax, Oregon is a deviant case in its attachment to the income tax. Like New York and Wisconsin, with which it compares in emphasizing the income tax in its state revenue system, Oregon has often led the way in labor legislation, in civil rights, and in the general quality of its government. It has not led, as New York and Wisconsin have, in the more costly service fields such as education and welfare. Nor has it raised tax revenues on as high a scale as these states or even its neighbors of California and Washington. Washington has no income tax and California has used both a sales tax and an income tax for more than thirty-five years. What makes Oregon different?

Often classified as having a transplanted New England Puritan political culture, Oregon voters rid the state of governmental corruption at the turn of the century.[10] They then passed the initiative, referendum, and recall as weapons against any further failures. The common assertion in the state that Oregon voters are independent, don't like bigness or anything that can be identified as a machine or establishment is believable in this semirural state with its well-educated people. By 1970 only a little over 2 million people lived in its 96,981 square miles. Metropolitan Portland contains more than 25 per cent of this population and only three other cities have over 25,000 inhabitants. Each legislator in the Oregon House of Representatives represents approximately 33,500 people, whereas each representative in California represents approximately 240,000 people, and in New York 120,000 people. Neighbors know each other and know and judge their representatives on an individual rather than party basis.

Unlike in many states the adoption of the closed primary has not encouraged party regularity or generally produced party strength in leadership and programs. The voter changes his party registration with ease and views voting a straight party ticket in general elections as too confining. Democratic registration has been climbing and in 1969 exceeded Republican registration by 535,386 to 424,601. Yet the voters have repeatedly elected Republican governors, and legislative control has shifted back and forth between the two parties. Since the voter sees himself more as an independent than as a party man, candidates try hard to make their own names known to voters but with as little party identification as possible.* Citizens make strong judgments as to commmunity and state needs and communicate these judgments in personal contact as well as by the ballot box.

We earlier noted that Oregonian independence and populist orientation further shows itself in a faith in state regulation more than in extensive services. The state was one of the pioneers in labor legislation. It has passed strong legislation in such civil rights fields as fair employment. It has even prohibited the extension of private ownership of the state's 1,410 miles of magnificent tidal coast line. Its expenditures for education are generous by the standards of its region, but do not place it in the top quartile of states nationally. (It is not uncommon for a rural state to spend for education, highways, and natural resources but proportionately less for other costly services than more urban states.)

Oregon legislators and voters argued throughout the 1920s about an income tax but agreed in 1930 that major state tax revenues would come from that source. Until then the state had used gasoline taxes for highway purposes but otherwise depended on property taxes. Oregon led its neighbors in adopting an individual as well as corporate income tax and has continued to depend upon it far more than California, Utah, Idaho, Colorado, or any of the other mountain states. Washington has never adopted an income tax. Thus, Oregon's decision to use the income tax heavily and to avoid a state sales tax has been maintained in the face of opposite decisions

---

* A well-known incident of Oregonian attachment to the individual more than the party involves former United States Senator Wayne Morse. Morse was elected and reelected to the Senate from Oregon as a Republican. At odds with the Republican party in the 1952 election of Dwight D. Eisenhower, he announced that henceforth he would run as a Democrat. Oregon voters reelected him three times as a Democrat, although he was no more faithful to the Democrats nationally than he had been to the Republicans.

in neighboring states. Opposition to a sales tax has been so intense through most of the years that the state did not adopt a cigarette tax until 1965. In recent campaigns, the income tax has been referred to regularly as the "people's tax." Sales taxes have been identified as in the interest of business and presumably "anti-people." The defeat of the 1969 referendum for a general sales tax with a property tax offset was merely the most recent expression of antipathy.

Oregon's citizens have numerous ways of expressing their tax preferences in addition to the usual opportunity for electing legislators and governors supporting income taxes or opposing sales taxes. All state revenue measures passed by the legislature and approved by the governor become effective only after ninety days. Within this time, any citizen may secure sufficient signatures — 8 per cent of the number of votes cast in the last election for Supreme Court Justice — on a petition to place the proposed legislation on the ballot for voter approval or rejection. Since 1930 voters have consistently supported income taxes and opposed sales taxes, but each referendum has had subtle differences that tested various degrees of support. Increases in income taxes are not necessarily popular with voters who turned them down as recently as 1960 and 1963.

The 1969 Sales Tax Referendum

As indicated by the hours spent in the legislature on tax matters during most of the sessions in the 1960s, Oregon like other states has seen demands for aids and services outstrip predicted revenues. Local complaints of high property taxes and high education costs have brought repeated demands to Salem for additional education aids to hold down property taxes. Whatever the reasonableness of the high property tax claim, the vocal supporters of education believe the quality of the state system will be in danger if the state does not add to local support and reduce the pressure on the property tax.* The campaign for more school aid and the opposition to higher property taxes, added to other state demands, have produced budget crises on several occasions. In an extraordinarily long session in 1967 the legislators were so divided on the issue of higher income taxes or adoption of a sales

---

* We have already noted that by the standards of its neighbors, Oregon is a high expenditure state for education. In 1967, it drew 47.5 per cent of its state and local tax revenue from property taxes — above the average for the nation but not in the top quartile. Whether measures of ratio of property taxes to total taxes, per capita property taxes, or ratio of property taxes to income are used, Oregon's property taxes are above the national average and above the state of Washington but below California's and below the top quartile of states in the nation.

tax to relieve property taxes that they achieved nothing in the area of taxation. A special 1967 fall session succeeded only in cutting back the budget without reaching any new decision on taxes. Confusion was compounded by the fact that Governor McCall's revenue estimate proved to be low and the cuts were unnecessary to balance the budget.

The Republican majority in the Orgeon House in 1969 early determined to pass a sales tax in the apparent belief that the property tax offset provision would sweeten it enough for voter acceptance. Support from the Association of Oregon Industries for the expected referendum campaign was said to have been promised, and those in the know believed this was the year Oregon would accept a sales tax. It is not easy to establish whether the calculation was entirely mistaken from the beginning or, if not, when it became mistaken. Even more confusing is explaining why the plan for pushing through any sales tax was pursued with the growing evidence of almost certain defeat.

We can summarize the bare outlines of what happened. When the legislature convened, the Republican majority on the Tax Committee of the House of Representatives brought to the Republican caucus a sales tax bill with a tax credit provision to reduce the regressivity of a general sales tax and a provision for additional school support to relieve property taxes. The caucus accepted it after some debate. The House passed the bill on a partisan division. It then went to the Senate, which though technically controlled by the Democrats, sixteen to fourteen, actually was controlled by a working coalition of three Conservative Democrats and fourteen Republicans. This coalition had organized the Senate with a Conservative Democrat as president and a Conservative Democrat as chairman of the tax committee. The majority of the Senate Tax Committee was composed of Republicans and Conservative Democrats. Negotiations within the committee, presumably with the governor and with outsiders from Portland, resulted in a sales tax bill without the credit provision that had earlier blunted its regressivity and with a school-property tax relief formula that benefited richer counties more than poorer ones. When the bill came on the floor, two Republicans, reportedly due to mail pressure, bolted the party and a majority was not available to pass it. Later two Democrats opposed to any sales tax decided to vote for the bill to get the issue on the ballot and "settled." The Democrats announced their reasons publicly and asserted their full opposition as they cast affirmative votes. Senate Republican leadership assured the House that this version of the sales tax bill was the only one they could pass and the House must take it or nothing. The House accepted. Governor McCall signed the bill. A petition for a referendum was immediately filed. By election day only the margin of defeat appeared uncertain. No county, rural or urban, supported the sales tax. Multoomah County, with the city of Portland, rejected the proposal better than 10 to 1. The big campaign for a sales tax by the Association of Oregon Industries did not materialize. Newspapers either opposed the sales tax or were at most lukewarm.

The Oregon tax controversy is a classic case in the issues posed: general criticism of the height of local property taxes; general complaint, not always accurate in detail, as to the height of taxes in Oregon; widespread agreement that more money should be spent for schools; vocal political leadership — Democrats generally opposing any sales tax, AFL-CIO unions opposing any sales tax although ready to support an income tax in principle; the farmer's grange opposed to a sales tax; Republicans, business, especially larger businesses, and the Farm Bureau generally sympathetic to the idea of a sales tax. When it came to the specific bill, most Republicans and business and farm leaders put up little defense in the face of the intense opposition of small businessmen and the evidence of general voter opposition. Support continued from Portland, especially the Portland apartment house group that had previously pushed a limitation on the property tax. Educational groups anxious for more state funds for schools were unwilling to support this bill.

No one characteristic of Oregon will explain this staunch refusal over a forty-year period to accept a sales tax. When forty-five other states use a sales tax, one does not find, and could not expect to find, any general classification of economic, social, or political characteristics that would explain Oregon. It certainly does not compare with the other four states of Alaska, Delaware, Montana, and New Hampshire that do not have a sales tax today.

Although subject to all of the usual pressures for conformity within the federal system, Oregon has maintained certain differences: it probably carries its political party apostasy further, though it is a two-party state with neither party regularly controlling the governor's chair and legislature, party discipline is limited; the initiative and referendum in fiscal matters are more easily available than in any other state, the state has frequently preferred government regulation to large expenditures for services other than highways and education. A rural, populist tradition would seem to have influenced the original income tax and supported it and opposed a sales tax since. The income tax is a "people's tax." When there will be a crisis for Oregon voters that will make them break with the past and turn to either increased income tax rates or a sales tax cannot be predicted. They have stood out as different and followed their own tradition.

CONCLUSIONS

We have explored various dimensions of state tax policies and we have inquired into socioeconomic and political characteristics of the states for explanations of different tax emphases. The most important finding is the increasing use by all of the states of the same tax revenue sources although the emphasis may differ. This is certainly in part a reflection of the continually growing interdependence of the fifty states.

The best predictor of types of taxes, tax emphasis, and tax levels for a given state is its own past, but crises may shift the pattern. In this century, only the decade of the 1930s has exceeded the 1960s in the number of new general revenue taxes adopted by the states. Not depression but the population boom and affluence with their demands for more governmental services, may explain this last revenue crisis. Adoption of new taxes, however, has seldom significantly affected a state's general rank as a high or low tax state. Nor does adoption of new taxes necessarily replace the past dominant tax. Strong income tax states may add sales taxes, but the income tax remains the major revenue raiser. Similarly strong sales tax states remain so even with the addition of an individual income tax.

High income or sales tax states show no consistent agreement with patterns of socioeconomic or political traits. This negative finding may be due to our inadequate measures. For example, some of our political theory suggests a relation between tax policy choices and the presence of a competitive two-party system. The differing ability of the state parties to discipline their members is not measured although it may be critical. Furthermore, our measures of pressure group strength are inadequate. Much of our correlation analysis depends for its reasonableness on associating the social, economic, and political environment with the system's outputs on a measure of stability. The numerous new tax adoptions in the 1960s may make the selection of tax revenues in any year unsatisfactory for the year before or the year after. For example, in a state such as Nebraska that adopted both a sales tax and an income tax in 1967 or in Michigan, which had a sales tax but in 1967 adopted both individual and corporate income taxes, statistics reflect sales tax yields much more successfully than income tax yields. Differences in the changing rate of urbanization may be another factor we do not measure adequately.

We did find some of the expected agreement between tax policy choices and expenditures for education and welfare. Four of the strong income tax states had high state expenditures for education and welfare, and only Illinois of the strong sales tax states similarly ranked high on education-welfare expenditures. Similar agreement of state leadership in certain liberal regulatory measures was shown.

We also found that the greater elasticity of the income tax over the sales tax in an expanding economy appears to encourage greater expenditure increases. This could mean that in periods of prosperity strong income tax states permit governors and legislators to respond more readily to service demands. Where no new or increased taxes are required, political costs for increased services should be lower.

Some regional influences appear to be present in tax policies. Most of the southern states were early users of the income tax, and most today also use sales taxes. In such low income states, sales taxes are frequently more productive. Florida and Texas stand out with no income tax. Until the 1960s a belt of heavy industrial states beginning with Pennsylvania and including Ohio, Indiana, Illinois, and Michigan had no individual income taxes, few corporate income taxes, used the general sales tax extensively, and generally were low in tax effort. Indiana, Illinois, and Michigan now have both corporate and individual income taxes. Several of these states however remain low tax burden states and none ranks high.

Our attempt to explain the tax policies adopted by the fifty states has not produced many certain explanations. More precision is probably needed to measure the effect of tax policy on the diverse state economies and peoples and to relate this outcome to more carefully identified political characteristics. The continued finding of the importance of tradition in predicting next year's tax policies ought to suggest the need for more extensive case studies covering the adoption of major new taxes in the 1960s, but perhaps more important, case studies of such adoptions before World War II are especially needed. The political characteristics of the innovative states at the time of innovation may well lead us furthest.

SELECTED BIBLIOGRAPHY

Advisory Commission on Intergovernmental Relations. *A Staff Report: Measures of State and Local Fiscal Capacity and Tax Effort*. Washington, D.C.: United States Government Printing Office, 1962. An excellent analysis of tax systems among the states and the relative use states make of various taxes of their own resources.

————. *State and Local Finances, Significant Features, 1967–1970* (Washington, D.C.: United States Government Printing Office, 1969).

Bureau of the Census. *Reports of the Census of Governments*. Washington,

D.C.: United States Government Printing Office. Made every five years with last one in 1967, especially *Compendium of Government Finances* and individual state reports.

Burkhead, Jesse. *State and Local Taxes for Public Education*. Syracuse: Syracuse University Press, 1963. Although the focus is on all sources of taxes for education, the main emphasis is an analysis of the property tax and its use over a period of time.

Due, John F. *State Sales Tax Administration*. Chicago: Public Administration Service, 1963. Provides a general historical and economic setting for sales taxes in the states as well as detailed analysis of administration.

Ecker-Racz, L. L. *The Politics and Economics of State-Local Finance*. Englewood Cliffs, N.J.: Prentice-Hall, 1970. This is a good general study of state-local finance by a man who, for many years was director of the tax advisory staff of the United States Treasury Department and more recently assistant director of the Advisory Commission on Intergovernmental Relations.

Fabricant, Solomon. *The Trend of Government Activity in the United States Since 1900*. New York: National Bureau of Economic Research, 1952. This is the classic in the area of economic analysis of state and local, as well as national, expenditures in this country.

Governments Division, United States Bureau of the Census, annual reports, especially *State Tax Collections* and *Government Finances*.

National Bureau of Economic Research. *Public Finances: Needs, Sources, and Utilization*. Princeton: Princeton University Press, 1961. This is a fairly technical, economic analysis of expenditure and tax policy at all levels of American government by leading economists.

Peacock, Alan T., and Jack Wiseman. *The Growth of Public Expenditures in the United Kingdom*. Princeton: Princeton University Press, 1961. This is the British companion to the Fabricant United States analysis. Both are worthwhile for insights and methodology, as well as for findings.

Pechman, Joseph. "The Rich, the Poor, and the Taxes They Pay," *The Public Interest*, No. 17 (Fall, 1969): 21ff. Although this article focuses on federal taxes, it is a good description of tax burden and includes discussion of state and local tax systems.

Penniman, Clara, and Walter W. Heller. *State Income Tax Administration*. Chicago: Public Administration Service, 1959. Provides a general historical and economic setting for income taxes in the states, as well as detailed analysis of administration.

Sharkansky, Ira. *Spending in the American States*. Chicago: Rand McNally, 1968. This is a good study using a variety of techniques that attempts to find explanations for different patterns of spending among the states.

Epilogue

Herbert Jacob and Kenneth N. Vines

The preceding chapters document a striking transformation in the study of state politics. Although formerly the study of state politics lagged badly in utilization of sophisticated analysis, it has risen qiuckly to a position of leadership in the discipline. Where the field of state politics once entailed the examination of individual states and single institutions, it now encompasses systematic comparison of all the states and of many processes across state and institutional boundaries. Moreover, state politics has led in the employment of advanced techniques of analysis and the testing of theoretical propositions. In many respects state politics has become a showpiece for comparative political science.

This accomplishment was foreshadowed and urged almost twenty years ago by a special report of the Committee on Political Behavior of the Social Science Research Council.[1] * The Committee argued that a systematic study of comparative state politics would not only benefit our understanding of American politics but would also offer opportunities for significant methodological and theoretical advances in political science. The SSRC report reiterated what thoughtful political scientists had long argued: general theories of politics can be validated only through comparative analysis, substituting the variations of existing conditions for the induced variation of laboratory experiments in the physical sciences. A comparative state politics appeared to have potential that was lacking in comparison of foreign governments. Studies of foreign governments rarely involved cross-national comparisons because of difficulties in obtaining data, establishing

* [See p. 605 for notes to this chapter. — Eds.]

556

valid indicators of important concepts, and determining the equivalency of measures and concepts. As a result of these difficulties cross-national comparison has produced uneven results.

Such difficulties are less disabling in a comparative study of American states. Data are more generally available, reliable indicators are obtained with more facility, and the problems of equivalency are negligible due to the common constitutional framework and political culture of the states. Here, if anywhere, political scientists could find considerable scope for increasing skills in comparative analysis and expanding our knowledge about politics.

The SSRC report was the prelude to the establishment of a program of research support that provided grants in comparative state politics. Some influential studies of state politics developed from research conducted under the auspices of the program and it provided a distinct impetus for the development of comparative state politics.

The publication of this second edition of a book that summarizes advances and explores new frontiers in the study of state politics provides an occasion for assessing the explanatory power of comparative analysis of the American states. The studies in this collection are typical of recent work in the field and many of the leading scholars in the area are included in this volume.

ACCOMPLISHMENTS IN THE COMPARATIVE ANALYSIS OF STATES

The accomplishments of comparative state research have been varied. They range from useful specific findings and descriptions to sophisticated multivariate analyses; they include innovative explorations but have also led to the establishment of a "new orthodoxy" in the study of state politics.

One of the first results of comparative analysis indicated that legislative reapportionment would not drastically change the level of state expenditures for urban programs. It sounded a note of realistic caution to the soaring hopes of the reapportionment reformers of the 1960s. Long before the 1970 census these studies indicated that central cities would have little to gain while suburbs would grow in legislative strength.[2] Another study permitted deeper insight into the variation of political processes in state legislatures.[3] Measures that permitted specification of the level of party competition, the strength of gubernatorial power, and interest group strength also were developed. In addition, powerful support has been gathered for the incremental hypothesis that political changes occur only at the margins, that most expenditure decisions simply reflect past patterns of behavior. Substantial changes occur over a period of years instead of in sudden leaps forward.[4]

Overshadowing these findings, however, was the development of a new orthodoxy that asserted that political processes had little power to explain the level of expenditures and outputs of state governments. If one examined social, economic, and political indicators, most of the attributable variance was accounted for by social and economic indicators. Political indicators are closely associated with socioeconomic variables but by themselves contributed little to the explanation. It is only a slight parody of these findings to assert that politics makes little difference in the governance of the American states. If one knows the level of economic development, one can know as much as is to be known at the moment about the genesis of state outputs.[5] This new orthodoxy is stated precisely enough to indicate its faults and the directions that future research should take to modify or reject it. We believe that this seemingly outrageous description of state politics is an artifact of inadequate measurement of concepts, the utilization of inappropriate techniques of analysis, and overly narrow definitions of what constitutes politically relevant outputs and outcomes.

INADEQUACIES OF CONCEPT MEASUREMENT

Our theoretical statements speak about demands for policy outputs that political institutions convert into authoritative decisions. Data are available on the income and educational levels of the population of the states, the proportions who live in urban, suburban, and rural areas, the proportions who are white collar and blue collar workers, the level of industrial, extractive, and agricultural production in the states, the number of whites and blacks, and the like. None of these are synonymous with demands made on the political system. None are inputs into political structures, but we may infer demands and resources from them. The poor are perhaps more likely to demand a high level of welfare programs. However, if a state has mostly poor people in it, it may not have the resources to meet this demand. Urban populations may demand a higher level of educational expenditures, whereas rural populations may seek greater expenditures on highways. Such inferences are based on little or no systematic information about the behavior of voters in the states. Although many investigations speak of inputs leading to conversion processes leading to outputs, they actually do not measure demand.

Our measures of the political processes in the states are similarly crude and shamefully sparse. We measure the level of inter-party competition in elections, legislatures, or frequency of turnover between parties. We have no measures of the executive, legislative, and judicial processes that capture the political strength of groups in each of these branches. We possess few indicators of the resources that are politically relevant for the many groups populating the fifty states.

Our poverty is ironically due to the wealth of census data available for the fifty states. Census data, because they were readily available, have been used for the preliminary analyses of the last decade. These indicators have now been exploited to their full extent. Having shown that they can use sophisticated data analysis techniques, the students of state politics must now obtain data more relevent to the concepts they are using. They must collect data that are not routinely solicited by government agencies as well as recover data that are collected but not universally published.

INAPPROPRIATE USE OF ANALYTIC MODELS

The statistical models which have been used by most investigators of state politics presume that the variables that are entered into regression equations are conceptually related. That is generally not true of current research. We relate 1970 data on income with 1970 data on expenditures even though we know that there is a lag between the demands generated by the inflation or depression of 1970 and the political decisions made on account of those conditions. In the states, that lag is often considerable because many state legislatures convene only every two years; further, it usually takes many years to convert demands for programs into authoritative decisions to administer them. Few scholars would deny the existence of such time lags. But we do not know their exact dimensions and therefore are hampered in utilizing our hunches about them in formal analysis. We do not know whether it is more appropriate to enter 1967, 1968, or 1969 indicators of demand into a regression equation seeking to explain 1970 levels of expenditures. Moreover, it is likely that the time lags will be different for various demands. An increase in the incidence of bombings at state universities may trigger a quicker legislative response than an increase in enrollments. Increases in the black population of states may take much longer to reflect themselves in states with few other minority groups than in states with many minority groups. Measurement of time lags is essential for more powerful utilization of existing statistical techniques. In order to measure time lags, we need, however, to find better measures of demands.

We do not argue that the models that scholars have been using are inappropriate. Some charge that the models are static, whereas politics is obviously dynamic. That charge is false. The systems framework around which most research is organized is a dynamic framework. It incorporates a sequential perspective and accounts for change through alterations in inputs or outputs through the feedback process. The fault does not lie in the theoretical framework but in the nature of the data applied to it. Most of these data are cross-sectional, representing one point of time rather than longitudinal, representing observations over many points of time. Present findings make the need for the analysis of time series obvious.

OVERLY NARROW CONCEPTUALIZATIONS OF OUTPUTS

Most analysis has concentrated on explaining the level of expenditures in the fifty states and accounting for differences in those levels. These levels are important, and because existing data made such analysis readily possible, it was the first task to which most scholars addressed themselves. But the level of expenditures alone cannot explain the political process in the states. Which counties get highway funds is perhaps more controversial than how much money shall be put in the highway fund; which communities will benefit from state expenditures in education is more controversial than the total amount the state spends on education. Such distributional questions have always been the center of the political scientist's attention. They must be reasserted in the study of state politics.[6] Again the available data often do not lend themselves to the analysis of this question. State governments disguise information about the distribution of state expenditures while publicizing data about the levels of expenditure. Once more, the scholar must strike out on his own to retrieve the data necessary for his analyses.

Moreover, many authoritative outputs cannot be measured financially. Unfortunately, we have been unable to include an analysis of the politics of regulation in the states, even though regulatory decisions are hotly contested in the political arena. We need measures of such decisions, their consequences, and how the states vary in their regulatory approaches. Likewise, the output of the states in regulating private life through statutes on divorce, abortion, occupational licensing, and the work of the courts is not captured by expenditure data but these activities are an important part of the states' political activities.

POLITICAL DEVELOPMENT
AND COMPARATIVE ANALYSIS

Oddly enough, one of the main themes in the study of foreign governments has barely been touched by students of state politics. Studies of foreign governments have made substantial progress both in developing theories of political development and in charting stages of development. As a consequence, studies of political development have quite forcefully shown that nations differ according to stage of political development and that, to a large extent, developing and developed nations should not be compared within the same categories.

Attention to political development in the American states may also lead to more discriminating analysis. There seems little doubt, for example, that states such as Mississippi and Massachusetts differ not only in their state institutions and policies but also in political development. The chapter in this volume that deals with the diffusion of innovation among the states hints at a model of political development. Such a model could well yield new resources for comparative analysis. In a somewhat similar vein, the suggestion has sometimes been made that southern states should be omitted from comparative analysis because these states form a distinct grouping that obscures meaningful analysis for all the states. Construction of a model of state political development and description of the stages of development would identify states that have reached similar stages of development and clarify the variations among the states. It may well be that it is just as inappropriate to compare states with dissimilar political developments as to compare developing and developed nations. Comparative analysis that controls for political development might well clarify analysis that at present is constrained by the use of cruder measurements of state political and social differences.

SYSTEMS THEORY
AND COMPARATIVE ANALYSIS

A final observation on the theory of our comparative state politics criticizes it from the perspective of systems theory. Our studies of state politics have made substantial progress in viewing politics from a systems perspective, particularly when we compare these studies with traditional discrete and case studies of states.

Current studies analyze systemic functions such as inputs according to the institutions with which they are associated. However, that results in an analysis of subsystems rather than the whole system of state politics. We have dealt with subsystems such as the legislature and the executive. These partial glimpses of the political process do not take full advantage of the potential of a systems model. A systems perspective should consider all inputs associated with a decision, rather than dividing them according to the institutions in which they occur. Examining all inputs, conversion processes and outputs that are related to each other would provide us a more general conception of the political system; it would avoid reification of institutions. Such analysis would identify general features of state political processes rather than simply point to institutional variations.

It may well be our task to identify dimensions of the political system, as Chapter Nine of this volume suggests and pioneers in investigating. Certain traits of the political process are similar and cohere on one dimension, whereas others belong to different dimensions. For example, some traits of judicial institutions may have more in common with legislative institutions than they have in common with other judicial features. A really general treatment of state politics would make it possible to identify the dimensions of the political system. Currently we think too much in terms of institutions and of particular states. The task of future studies of state politics must be to identify those functions and dimensions that characterize whole state political systems although this task is hardly possible with the present state of knowledge about the states.

We may pride ourselves in having come a long way from the particularistic description of individual states and institutions in the comparative study of state politics. But the advances we have made do not carry us to the comprehensive understanding of politics in the states that we would like to have. We have exploited the available data. We now need to invest additional resources for collecting relevant data about inputs, about conversion processes, about non-fiscal outputs and develop measures of the time lags that exist in their impact on the political process. The promise that was prophesied in the 1954 SSRC report has been partially fulfilled but much remains to be done to realize the full potential of a comparative state politics.

Notes

CHAPTER ONE

1. United States Bureau of the Census, *State Government Finances in 1969,* Series GF69, No. 3 (Washington, D.C.: United States Government Printing Office, 1969), 28.
2. United States Bureau of the Census, *Summary of State Government Finances in 1963* (Washington, D.C.: United States Government Printing Office, April, 1963), 18.
3. The most recent extensive analysis of regional differences among the states is by Ira Sharkansky, *Regionalism in American Politics* (Indianapolis: Bobbs-Merrill, 1970).
4. The Confederate states were Alabama, Arkansas, Florida, Georgia, Louisiana, Mississippi, North Carolina, South Carolina, Tennessee, Texas, and Virginia.
5. The standard political analysis, although somewhat dated, is by V. O. Key, Jr., *Southern Politics* (New York: Alfred A. Knopf, 1949). More recent is Donald R. Matthews and James W. Prothro, *Negroes and the New Southern Politics* (New York: Harcourt, Brace, & World, 1966).
6. His principal books expounding the systems framework are *The Political System* (New York: Alfred A. Knopf, 1953) and *A Systems Analysis of Political Life* (New York: John Wiley & Sons, 1965).
7. See for example Lewis A. Froman, Jr., *The Congressional Process* (Boston: Little, Brown, 1967); Richard F. Fenno, Jr., *The Power of the Purse* (Boston: Little, Brown, 1966); Clement E. Vose, *Caucasians Only* (Berkeley: University of California Press, 1959).
8. James E. Price, "A Test of the Accuracy of Crime Statistics," *Social Problems,* 14 (1966): 214–221; James Q. Wilson, "Crime in the Streets," *The Public Interest* (Fall, 1966), 26–35.
9. Jacob S. Siegel, "Completeness of Coverage of the Non-White Population in the 1960 Census and Current Estimates and Some Implications," United States Congress, House Committee on the Post Office and Civil Service,

Subcommittee on the Census and Statistics, *1970 Census Plans,* Hearings, 90th Congress, 1st Session, Serial No. 90–16, 135–149; Reynolds Farley, "The Quality of Demographic Data for Non-Whites," *Demography,* 5 (1968): 1–10.

10. A careful though difficult discussion of some of the problems of comparative analysis is in Adam Przeworski and Henry Teune, *The Logic of Comparative Analysis* (New York: Wiley Interscience, 1970).

11. For an extended discussion of this relationship see Ira Sharkansky, *Spending in the American States* (Chicago: Rand McNally, 1967).

12. For a readable but technical introduction to correlation statistics see Hubert M. Blalock, *Social Statistics* (New York: McGraw-Hill, 1960), 273–391.

13. Charles F. Cnudde and Donald J. McCrone, "Party Competition and Welfare Policies in the American States," *American Political Science Review,* 63 (1969): 858–866.

14. Matthews and Prothro, *Negroes and the New Southern Politics,* 46 and 226.

15. See United States Bureau of the Census, *City-County Data Book, State Government Finances,* and *Historical Statistics for the U.S.* (Washington, D.C.: United States Government Printing Office).

CHAPTER TWO

1. David Riesman, *Faces in the Crowd* (New Haven: Yale University Press, 1952), originally alluded to this distinction. It has received its most elaborate statement in Ulf Himmelstrand, *Social Pressures, Attitudes, and Democratic Processes* (Stockholm: Almqvist & Wiksell, 1960) and in Murray Edelman, *Symbolic Uses of Politics* (Urbana: University of Illinois Press, 1964).

2. A thirteen-state study of the 1968 election has been conducted by a group of scholars coordinated by James Prothro of the University of North Carolina. Unfortunately, their data were not available for inclusion here.

3. Data from the 1968 election study were not readily accessible for inclusion here.

4. See Angus Campbell, *et al., The American Voter* (New York: John Wiley & Sons, 1960), 94–96, for a more complete discussion of these factors.

5. From a speech given by Norman Nie at State University of New York at Buffalo on 26 April 1970, based on data drawn from the section on the United States in an eight-nation study of political participation directed by Sidney Verba of the University of Chicago.

6. For a summary of findings on this point consult Lester W. Milbrath, *Political Participation* (Chicago: Rand McNally, 1963), Chap. 4.

7. Richard E. Dawson and James A. Robinson, "Inter-Party Competition, Economic Variables, and Welfare Policies in the American States," *Journal of Politics,* 25 (1963): 265–289.

8. See Milbrath, *Political Participation,* 138–141.

9. Robert A. Dahl, *Who Governs? Democracy and Power in an American City* (New Haven: Yale University Press, 1961); Jack Jensen, "Political Participation: A Survey in Evanston, Illinois" (M.A. thesis, Northwestern University, 1960).

10. See V. O. Key, Jr., *Southern Politics* (New York: Alfred A. Knopf, 1949), Part 5, "Restrictions on Voting."

11. For information on a variety of impediments to voting, see *Hearings of the United States Commission on Civil Rights, New Orleans, Louisiana, 1960–1961* (Washington, D.C.: United States Government Printing Office, 1961).
12. See Milbrath, *Political Participation,* Chap. 5, for a summary of these findings.
13. Harold F. Gosnell, *Why Europe Votes* (Chicago: University of Chicago Press, 1930); Stein Rokkan, "The Comparative Study of Political Participation: Notes Toward a Perspective on Current Research," in Austin Ranney (ed.), *Essays on the Behavioral Study of Politics* (Urbana: University of Illinois Press, 1962), 47–90.
14. The detailed information on states presented in this section is drawn from the *Report of the President's Commission on Registration and Voting Participation* (Washington, D.C.: United States Government Printing Office, November, 1963).
15. "Electing a Canadian Government," in Paul Fox (ed.), *Politics Canada* (Toronto: McGraw-Hill, 1963), 269–270.
16. "That All May Vote," a report of the Freedom to Vote Task Force of the Democratic National Committee (Washington, D.C.: December, 1969).
17. Data and conclusions are from Shelley M. Zoler, "Negro Concentration and Registration Rates in the South: An Examination of Persistence and Change?" (unpubl. paper, Political Science Department, SUNY at Buffalo, 1969).
18. Kelley, Ayres, and Bowen derive essentially the same conclusion from their study of registration in cities for the 1960 presidential election. Stanley Kelley, Jr., Richard E. Ayres, and William G. Bowen, "Registration and Voting: Putting First Things First," *American Political Science Review,* 61 (June, 1967): 373–374.
19. Campbell, *et al., The American Voter,* Chap. 11.
20. See Milbrath, *Political Participation,* Chaps. 2 and 4, for an expanded discussion of these points.
21. Angus Campbell, "Surge and Decline: A Study of Electoral Change," *Public Opinion Quarterly,* 24 (1960): 397–418.
22. The precise wording of all four questions was:
    1. As you know, every citizen has some kind of relationship to government but people differ in what they think their relationships are or ought to be. On these cards we have listed some things people tell us they *do* for the government or the political system. Please sort the cards into *four* piles [HAND GREEN PLACE CARD TO RESPONDENT]: (1) those things you do *regularly;* (2) those things you do *fairly often;* (3) those things you *seldom* do; (4) those things you *never do at all.*
    2. Now, please sort through the cards once again according to what you feel you have a *responsibility* to give to the political system. Please sort the cards into *four* piles [TURN OVER GREEN PLACE CARD]: (1) those things you feel it is *essential* for you to do; (2) those things you feel you have an *important* responsibility to do; (3) those things you feel you have *some* responsibility to do; and (4) those things you feel you have *no responsibility* to do at all.
    3. People differ on how effectively government in general does things for them. On these cards we have listed some of the things people tell us the government does or should do for them. Please sort through the cards and place them into *four* piles [HAND BLUE PLACE CARD TO RESPONDENT]: (1) those things you feel the government does a *very*

effective job of providing; (2) those things you feel the government does a *moderately effective* job of providing; (3) those things you feel the government is *not very effective* in providing; (4) those things you feel the government does *ineffectively or not at all.* If you don't know what the government is doing in this regard, place the card in a pile at the bottom.

4. Now, please sort through the cards once again according to what you feel the government has a responsibility to do for you. Please sort the cards into *four* piles [TURN OVER BLUE CARD]: (1) those things you feel it is *essential* for the government to do; (2) those things the government has an *important* responsibility to do; (3) those things the government has *some* responsibility to do; and (4) those things you believe the government should *not attempt to do at all.*

   The placement board provides boxes for the response categories that are spatially ordered on the board. This facilitates constant awareness of the response categories and indicates where cards should be placed as they are sorted. The spatial layout of the categories on the board indicates the ordered relationship of the categories and thus produces data that are about as close to being equal in intervals as one is likely to get from survey research. One of the special advantages of card sorting is that one can obtain the reactions to a long list of stimuli, first according to one frame of reference and then to another, without making respondents uneasy by asking a long sequence of repetitive closed-ended questions. A full discussion of this method may be found in E. F. Cataldo, R. M. Johnson, L. A. Kellstedt, and L. W. Milbrath, "Card Sorting as a Technique for Survey Interviewing," *Public Opinion Quarterly,* 34 (Summer, 1970): 202–215. The same card sort method dealing with inputs and outtakes was used on both waves of interviews. Ten of the input items and twelve of the outtake items appeared in identical form on both waves. Additional items were used on either the first or the second wave, making a total of thirty-eight input items and forty-two outtake items administered to respondents on both waves of the interviews. Persons desiring more complete information on the method or the findings than can be presented here should correspond with the author.

23. An assumption of equality between intervals on the scales was made in order to calculate a mean score. Admittedly, this assumption is not completely justified for data of this type, but using an interval statistic is less distorting in presentation than using a nonparametric statistic.

24. *Colegrove* v. *Green,* 328 U.S. 549 (1946).

25. *Baker* v. *Carr,* 369 U.S. 186 (1962); *Reynolds* v. *Sims,* 12 Lawyers ed. 2d 506 (June 15, 1964).

26. *NLRB* v. *Jones and Laughlin Steel Corp.,* 301 U.S. 1 (1937).

27. For a development of the point made in this paragraph, see Milbrath, *Political Participation,* Chap. 6.

CHAPTER THREE

1. E. E. Schattschneider, *Party Government* (New York: Holt, Rinehart and Winston, 1942), 1, emphasis added.

2. *Ibid.*

3. The most recent detailed survey is *State Party Structures and Procedures: A State-by-State Compendium* (New York: National Municipal League, 1967).

4. Cf. Arthur W. Macmahon, *Encyclopaedia of the Social Sciences* (New York: Macmillan, 1937), XI, 596; Schattschneider, *Party Government,* 66–67; and Samuel J. Eldersveld, *Political Parties: A Behavioral Analysis* (Chicago: Rand McNally, 1964), Chap. 5.

5. V. O. Key, Jr., *Southern Politics in State and Nation* (New York: Alfred A. Knopf, 1949), Chap. 6.

6. See p. 94.

7. Duane Lockard, *New England State Politics* (Princeton: Princeton University Press, 1959), Chaps. 9, 10.

8. As is recognized by at least one prominent advocate of more disciplined national parties, James MacGregor Burns, *The Deadlock of Democracy* (Englewood Cliffs, N.J.: Prentice-Hall, 1963), 236–241.

9. Cf. V. O. Key, Jr., *American State Politics: An Introduction* (New York: Alfred A. Knopf, 1956), 201; Key, *Southern Politics,* Chap. 14; Lockard, *New England State Politics;* Lockard, "State Party Systems and Policy Outputs," in Oliver Garceau (ed.), *Political Research and Political Theory* (Cambridge, Mass.: Harvard University Press, 1968), 190–220; and John H. Fenton, *Midwest Politics* (New York: Holt, Rinehart and Winston, 1966).

10. The best-known studies are: Richard E. Dawson and James A. Robinson, "Inter-Party Competition, Economic Variables, and Welfare Policies in the American States," *Journal of Politics,* 25 (1963): 265–289; and Thomas R. Dye, *Politics, Economics, and the Public: Policy Outcomes in the American States* (Chicago: Rand McNally, 1966).

11. The principal study is Ira Sharkansky and Richard I. Hofferbert, "Dimensions of State Politics, Economics, and Public Policy," *American Political Science Review,* 63 (1969): 867–879. See also Ira Sharkansky, *Spending in the American States* (Chicago: Rand McNally, 1968).

12. The principal measures are lucidly described and their strengths and weaknesses assessed in David G. Pfeiffer, "The Measurement of Inter-Party Competition and Systemic Stability," *American Political Science Review,* 61 (1967): 457–467.

13. The story is well told in Key, *Southern Politics,* 551 ff; and in Alexander Heard, *A Two-Party South?* (Chapel Hill: University of North Carolina Press, 1952).

14. Warren E. Miller, "One-Party Politics and the Voter," *American Political Science Review,* 50 (1956): 707–725.

15. Cf. Angus Campbell, Philip E. Converse, Warren E. Miller, and Donald E. Stokes, *The American Voter* (New York: John Wiley & Sons, 1960), Chaps. 6, 7, and p. 555; Fred I. Greenstein, *Children and Politics* (New Haven: Yale University Press, 1965); and V. O. Key, Jr., *Public Opinion and American Democracy* (New York: Alfred A. Knopf, 1961), Chaps. 5, 12, 13, 17, 18.

16. For the general pattern, see Campbell, *et al., The American Voter,* Chaps. 15–17; Key, *American State Politics,* Chap. 8; and William H. Flanigan, *Political Behavior of the American Electorate* (Boston: Allyn and Bacon, 1968), 45–46. For instances of the general pattern in particular states, see Leon D. Epstein, *Politics in Wisconsin* (Madison: University of Wisconsin Press, 1958), Chap. 4; Frank J. Sorauf, *Party and Representation: Legis-*

lative Politics in Pennsylvania (New York: Atherton Press, 1963), Chap. 2; and Heinz Eulau, "The Ecological Basis of Party Systems: The Case of Ohio," *Midwest Journal of Political Science,* 1 (1957): 125–135. Iowa is apparently an exception: see David Gold and John R. Schmidhauser, "Urbanization and Party Competition: The Case of Iowa," *Midwest Journal of Political Science,* 4 (1960): 62–75.

17. In *Smith* v. *Allwright,* 321 U.S. 649 (1944) the Court held that when the primary election of one party is, in effect, the final election, the executive committee of the dominant party becomes an agent of the state, and any rules it makes barring blacks from voting in its primaries are just as much violations of the Fifteenth Amendment as if they were laws adopted by the state legislature.

18. Key, *Southern Politics,* 395–396.

19. For more detailed summaries, see *State Party Structures and Procedures: A State-by-State Compendium.*

20. Cf. Austin Ranney, *Illinois Politics* (New York: New York University Press, 1960), 9–11.

21. Daniel M. Ogden, Jr., and Hugh A. Bone, *Washington Politics* (New York: New York University Press, 1960), 26–28.

22. See Key, *Southern Politics,* Chaps. 2, 8; Allan P. Sindler, *Huey Long's Louisiana: State Politics, 1920–1952* (Baltimore: The Johns Hopkins Press, 1956); and William Manchester, "The Byrd Machine," *Harper's Magazine,* 205 (November, 1952): 80–87.

23. See Ralph A. Straetz and Frank J. Munger, *New York Politics* (New York: New York University Press, 1960), 27, 62–63, 65; and G. Theodore Mitau, *Politics in Minnesota* (Minneapolis: University of Minnesota Press, 1960), 24–26.

24. See Justin N. Feldman, "How Tammany Holds Power," *National Civic Review,* 39 (1950): 330–334; James Reichley, *The Art of Government: Reform and Organization Politics in Philadelphia* (New York: Fund for the Republic, 1959); and Edward Banfield, *Political Influence* (Glencoe, Ill.: The Free Press, 1960).

25. Cf. Lockard, *New England State Politics,* Chap. 12; and V. O. Key, Jr., *Politics, Parties, and Pressure Groups,* 5th ed. (New York: Thomas Y. Crowell, 1964), 336.

26. Key, *Politics, Parties, and Pressure Groups,* 316.

27. The best general discussion is James Q. Wilson, *The Amateur Democrats* (Chicago: University of Chicago Press, 1962).

28. See Epstein, *Politics in Wisconsin,* Chap. 5; and Frank J. Sorauf, "Extra-Legal Parties in Wisconsin," *American Political Science Review,* 48 (1954): 692–704.

29. See Francis M. Carney, *The Rise of the Democratic Clubs in California* (New York: Holt, Rinehart and Winston, 1958); and Hugh A. Bone, "New Party Associations in the West," *American Political Science Review,* 45 (1951): 1115–1120.

30. See Donald C. Blaisdell, "The Riverside Democrats," in Paul Tillett (ed.), *Cases on Party Organization* (New York: McGraw-Hill, 1963), 64–92; Robert S. Hirschfield, *et al.,* "A Profile of Political Activists in Manhattan," *Atlantic Monthly,* 206 (October, 1960): 65–70; and Daniel P. Moynihan, " 'Bosses' and 'Reforms': A Profile of New York Democrats," *Commentary,* 31 (June, 1961): 461–470.

31. As, for example, the Democratic Federation of Illinois: see Ranney, *Illi-*

nois Politics, 29–30. For another example, the New Democratic Coalition, established by pro-McCarthy activists after the 1968 Democratic national convention, has made some efforts to win nominations and party offices at the state as well as the national level, but so far it has had relatively little success.

32. For example, under New York's 1970 law candidates for statewide offices are designated by the parties' state central committees. Anyone receiving 25 per cent or more of the committee's votes may require that a primary be held, and primaries may also be required by any candidate who secures 10,000 signatures on a petition. In 1970 the Democratic State Central Committee designated former Supreme Court justice Arthur Goldberg for the gubernatorial nomination, but Goldberg, to avoid the charge of being the "bosses' man," himself demanded a primary, which he won by a narrow margin. For a summary of the systems used in the various states, see *The Book of the States, 1968–69* (Chicago: Council of State Governments, 1968), 23.

33. See the arguments reviewed in Charles E. Merrian and Louise Overacker, *Primary Elections,* rev. ed. (Chicago: University of Chicago Press, 1928).

34. Among the more notable are: Key, *American State Politics,* Chap. 5, pp. 97–118; Cortez A. M. Ewing, *Primary Elections in the South* (Norman, Okla.: University of Oklahoma Press, 1953); Julius Turner, "Primary Elections as the Alternative to Party Competition in 'Safe' Districts," *Journal of Politics,* 15 (1953): 197–210; Allan P. Sindler, "Bifactional Rivalry as an Alternative to Two-Party Competition in Louisiana," *American Political Science Review,* 49 (1955): 641–662; James A. Robinson, "Inter-Party Competition and Primary Contesting: The Case of Indiana," *American Political Science Review,* 52 (1958): 1066–1077; Malcolm E. Jewell, "Party and Primary Competition in Kentucky State Legislative Races," *Kentucky Law Journal,* 48 (1960): 517–535.

35. Key, *Politics, Parties, and Pressure Groups,* 441.

36. See Campbell, *et al., The American Voter,* 96–99.

37. Austin Ranney and Leon D. Epstein, "The Two Electorates: Voters and Non-Voters in a Wisconsin Primary," *Journal of Politics,* 28 (1966): 598–616; and Ranney, "The Representativeness of Primary Electorates," *Midwest Journal of Political Science,* 12 (1968): 224–238.

38. Key, *Politics, Parties, and Pressure Groups,* 381–383.

39. Curtis Martin and Rudolph Gomez, *Colorado Government and Politics* (Boulder, Colo.: Pruett Press, 1964), Chap. 9.

40. Key, *Politics, Parties, and Pressure Groups,* 387–388.

41. Ranney, *Illinois Politics,* 24–26.

42. For Louisiana, see Sindler, *Huey Long's Louisiana;* for Virginia, see Key, *Southern Politics,* Chap. 2.

43. For Georgia, see Key, *Southern Politics,* Chap. 6; and William J. Keefe, "Southern Politics Revisited," *Public Opinion Quarterly,* 20 (1956): 405–412.

44. Ogden and Bone, *Washington Politics,* 47.

45. *The Book of the States, 1968–69,* 24–26.

46. See Stanley Kelley, Jr., *Professional Public Relations and Political Power* (Baltimore: The Johns Hopkins Press, 1956); and Dan Nimmo, *The Political Persuaders: The Techniques of Modern Election Campaigns* (Englewood Cliffs, N.J.: Prentice-Hall, 1970).

47. The classic general study is Alexander Heard, *The Costs of Democracy*

(Chapel Hill: University of North Carolina Press, 1960). The most authoritative study of a single state is David Adamany, *Financing Politics: Recent Wisconsin Elections* (Madison: University of Wisconsin Press, 1969).

48. Heard, *The Costs of Democracy,* Chaps. 5, 7, especially Table 7, 100–102.
49. *Ibid.,* 162–168.
50. Cf. *ibid.,* Chap. 2; and Jasper B. Shannon, *Money and Politics* (New York: Random House, 1959).
51. The states using each form of regulation are given in *The Book of the States, 1968–69,* 32–35.
52. See Heard, *The Costs of Democracy,* Chap. 16; and Herbert Alexander, *Money, Politics, and Public Reporting* (Princeton: Citizens' Research Foundation, 1960).
53. Election calendars for each state are given in *The Book of the States, 1968–69,* 23–26.
54. The figures for 1932 to 1950 in Table 4 are taken from Key, *American State Politics,* 38, Table 2.
55. The argument is summarized and analyzed in Austin Ranney, *The Doctrine of Responsible Party Government* (Urbana: University of Illinois Press, 1954, 1962).
56. See Pendleton Herring, *The Politics of Democracy* (New York: W. W. Norton, 1940, 1965); Herbert Agar, *The Price of Union* (Boston: Houghton Mifflin, 1959); and Austin Ranney and Willmoore Kendall, *Democracy and the American Party System* (New York: Harcourt, Brace & World, 1956).
57. Key, *American State Politics,* Chap. 3.
58. See pp. 171–173.
59. Belle Zeller (ed.), *American State Legislatures* (New York: Thomas Y. Crowell, 1954), 194, and Table 12, 196. No comparable survey has been made since the Zeller study, but her conclusions are generally borne out by later studies: see Malcolm E. Jewell, *The State Legislature: Politics and Practice* (New York: Random House, 1964), 89–92; and William J. Keefe and Morris S. Ogul, *The American Legislative Process: Congress and the States,* 2d ed. (Englewood Cliffs, N.J.: Prentice-Hall, 1968), Chap. 9.
60. Jewell, *The State Legislatures,* 85–89.
61. Keefe and Ogul, *The American Legislative Process,* 293.
62. Jewell, *The State Legislatures,* 77–85.
63. Paul T. David, Ralph M. Goldman, and Richard C. Bain, *The Politics of National Party Conventions* (Washington, D.C.: The Brookings Institution, 1960), Chap. 5.
64. Coleman B. Ransone, Jr., *The Office of Governor in the United States* (University, Ala.: University of Alabama Press, 1956), Chaps. 2, 7. See also Jewell, *The State Legislatures,* Chap. 5.
65. *The Book of the States, 1968–69,* 133. Delaware and Missouri limit their governors to a lifetime total of two terms.
66. Ransone, *The Office of Governor,* 94.
67. *Ibid.,* 193. For a more recent and more quantitative analysis of this question see Sarah P. McCally, "The Governor and His Legislative Party," *American Political Science Review,* 60 (1966): 923–942.
68. For more detailed discussions of southern Republican resurgence, see Virginius Dabney, "What the GOP Is Doing in the South," *Harper's Maga-*

zine (May, 1963): 86–94; Keefe, "Southern Politics Revisited"; Kenneth N. Vines, "Republicanism in New Orleans," *Tulane Studies in Political Science,* 2 (1955): 89–134; and Donald R. Matthews and James W. Prothro, *Negroes and the New Southern Politics,* Chap. 13.

69. An illuminating analysis is given in Campbell, Converse, Miller, and Stokes, *The American Voter,* Chap. 16.

70. *Congressional District Data Book* (Washington, D.C.: Bureau of the Census, 1963), 2.

71. *Statistical Abstract of the United States, 1962* (Washington, D.C.: Bureau of the Census, 1962), 30, Table 24.

72. Key, *Southern Politics,* Chap. 31.

73. Campbell, *et al.,* 446–449.

74. Cf. Key, *Southern Politics,* Chaps. 18–22; and Malcolm B. Parsons, "Quasi-Partisan Conflict in a One-Party Legislative System: The Florida Senate, 1947–1961," *American Political Science Review,* 56 (1962): 605–614.

75. Cf. Samuel C. Patterson, "Dimensions of Voting Behavior in a One-Party State Legislature [Oklahoma]," *Public Opinion Quarterly,* 26 (1962): 185–200.

76. Clinton Rossiter, *Parties and Politics in America* (Ithaca: Cornell University Press, 1960), 188.

CHAPTER FOUR

1. Arthur Bentley, *The Process of Government* (San Antonio: Principia Press of Trinity University, 1949), 176. For a critique of group theory literature, see Robert T. Golembiewski, " 'The Group Basis of Politics': Notes on Analysis and Development," *American Political Science Review,* 54 (1960): 962.

2. Lester Milbrath, *The Washington Lobbyists* (Chicago: Rand McNally, 1963), 241–282.

3. Robert Engler, *The Politics of Oil* (New York: Macmillan, 1961), 380.

4. Milbrath, *Washington Lobbyists,* 302–303.

5. Harmon Zeigler and Michael A. Baer, *Lobbying: Interaction and Influence in American State Legislatures* (Belmont, Calif.: Wadsworth, 1969), 191.

6. Milbrath, *Washington Lobbyists,* 271.

7. Zeigler and Baer, *Lobbying,* 192.

8. *Ibid.*

9. *Ibid.,* 165.

10. *Ibid.,* 105.

11. *Ibid.,* 85.

12. John W. Thibaut and Harold H. Kelley, *The Social Psychology of Groups* (New York: John Wiley & Sons, 1961), 48, and Zeigler and Baer, *Lobbying,* 38–40, 81–82.

13. Zeigler and Baer, *Lobbying,* 82.

14. *Ibid.,* 107.

15. *Ibid.,* 20–21.

16. The classification of states according to strength of interest groups and legislative cohesion is taken from Belle Zeller (ed.), *American State Legislatures* (New York: Thomas Y. Crowell, 1954), 190–191. Because of certain methodological problems, the classification is subject to criticism. To decide whether a state is characterized by strong, moderate, or weak interest groups, questionnaires were sent to political scientists in each state. The

limitations of this method are apparent. However, there is reason to assume that these evaluations are relatively accurate in view of the consistent patterns that appear in the economic and political factors associated with the three groups of states. The measure of legislative cohesion is taken from the same study but is not subject to the same criticism since objective evaluations of cohesion do exist. The extent of party competition, taken from Austin Ranney's classification, is appropriate since it relies only on state elections. One modification has been made in Ranney's classification. Modified one-party Democratic and modified one-party Republican states are merged into a single category since the direction of the partisanship is of no concern.

17. Duane Lockard, *New England State Politics* (Princeton: Princeton University Press, 1959), 79.

18. V. O. Key, Jr., *Southern Politics in State and Nation* (New York: Alfred A. Knopf, 1949), 56.

19. Hywell Evans, *Governmental Regulation of Industrial Relations* (Ithaca: New York State School of Industrial and Labor Relations at Cornell, 1961), 92–93. States having right-to-work laws are Alabama, Arizona, Arkansas, Florida, Georgia, Indiana, Iowa, Kansas, Louisiana, Mississippi, Nebraska, Nevada, North Carolina, North Dakota, South Carolina, South Dakota, Tennessee, Texas, Utah, Virginia, and Wyoming.

20. *Proceedings of the A.F.L.–C.I.O. 4th Constitutional Convention,* 2 (1961): 176–180.

21. Quoted in Joseph R. Gladden, Jr., "A Modern Revolution in Georgia: Organized Labor and the General Assembly," (Senior honors thesis, Emory University, 1963), 28.

22. Thomas Payne, "Under the Copper Dome: Politics in Montana," in Frank H. Jonas (ed.), *Western Politics* (Salt Lake City: University of Utah Press, 1961), 197–198.

23. Burton K. Wheeler with Paul Healy, *Yankee from the West* (Garden City, N.Y.: Doubleday, 1962), 84.

24. Joseph Kinsey Howard, *Montana: High, Wide and Handsome* (New Haven: Yale University Press, 1943), 245.

25. *Ibid.,* 249.

26. Richard T. Ruetten, "Anaconda Journalism: The End of an Era," *Journalism Quarterly,* 37 (1960): 3–12. See also John M. Schiltz, "Montana's Captive Press," *Montana Opinion* (1956): 1–11.

27. Quoted in Engler, *The Politics of Oil,* 354.

28. Clifton McClesky, *The Government and Politics of Texas* (Boston: Little, Brown, 1963), 136–150.

29. Raymond A. Bauer, Ithiel de Sola Pool, and Lewis Anthony Dexter, *American Business and Public Policy* (New York: Atherton Press, 1963), 266.

30. See *The New York Times,* November 9, 1969, 40, and February 6, 1970, 1. Increasing federal support of antipollution measures provided some of the impetus for this legislation.

31. On national interest in the Maine legislation see *ibid.,* January 15, 1970, 44. On changing voter attitudes toward the "oil and timber oligarchy" and the immediate effects of the oil spill in the Santa Barbara Channel on prospective offshore oil developments in Maine see *ibid.,* February 6, 1970, 1.

32. Legislation aimed at curbing pollution passed on February 5, 1970. The tanker *Arrow,* grounded a day earlier, did not begin major breakup until after this date. While not directly affecting the vote, it may be surmised that this event will hamper attempts by oil interests to circumvent the effects of the legislation. On the *Arrow* episode, see *ibid.,* February 8, 1970, 82; February 9, 78; February 12, 74; February 13, 1; February 15, 2.
33. Percentages for 1951 are computed from data contained in United States Bureau of the Census and United States Bureau of Old-Age and Survivors Insurance, cooperative report, *County Business Patterns, First Quarter, 1951,* Part 1, United States Summary (Washington, D.C.: United States Government Printing Office, 1953), 107. Percentages for 1968 computed from data contained in United States Bureau of the Census, *County Business Patterns, 1968,* Michigan CBP–68–24, (Washington, D.C.: United States Government Printing Office, 1969), 4–9.
34. Stephen B. and Vera H. Sarasohn, *Political Party Patterns in Michigan* (Detroit: Wayne State University Press, 1957).
35. Joseph LaPalombara, *Guide to Michigan Politics* (East Lansing: Michigan State University, Bureau of Social and Political Research, 1960), 104.
36. *Ibid.*
37. See John P. White and John R. Owens, *Parties, Group Interests and Campaign Finance: Michigan '56* (Princeton: Citizens' Research Foundation, 1960) for a careful analysis of the role of labor unions and automobile manufacturers in party finance.
38. Robert Lee Sawyer, Jr., *The Democratic State Central Committee in Michigan, The Rise of the New Politics and the New Political Leadership* (Ann Arbor: University of Michigan, Institute of Public Administration, 1960), 261.
39. Wayne L. Francis, *Legislative Issues in the Fifty States: A Comparative Analysis* (Chicago: Rand McNally, 1967), 44–45.
40. See Austin Ranney and Willmoore Kendall, *Democracy and the American Party System* (New York: Harcourt, Brace & World, 1956), 459–533, for a discussion of national parties as moderators of group conflict.
41. Nicholas A. Masters, "Organized Labor as a Base of Support for the Democratic Party," *Law and Contemporary Problems,* 27 (1962): 255.
42. V. O. Key, Jr., *Public Opinion and American Democracy* (New York: Alfred A. Knopf, 1961), 524.
43. Joseph P. Harris and Leonard Rowe, *California Politics,* 2nd ed. (Stanford: Stanford University Press, 1959), 20. The dominance of railroads has been noted in other states. See Dayton David McKean, *Pressures on the Legislature of New Jersey* (New York: Columbia University Press, 1938); and Andrew Hacker, "Pressure Politics in Pennsylvania: The Truckers vs. the Railroads," in Alan F. Westin (ed.), *The Uses of Power* (New York: Harcourt, Brace & World, 1963), 326.
44. See, for example, Lester Velie, "The Secret Boss of California," *Colliers,* August 14 and 20, 1949.
45. William Buchanan, *Legislative Partisanship: The Deviant Case of California,* University of California Publications in Political Science, Vol. 13 (Berkeley and Los Angeles: University of California Press, 1963).
46. *Ibid.,* 22.
47. John C. Wahlke, *et al., The Legislative System* (New York: John Wiley & Sons, 1962), 100.

48. Edwin N. Atherson and Associates, *Legislative Investigative Report* (Sacramento: Premier Publications, 1949). This is a reprint of the report prepared by H. R. Philbrick and printed in the *Senate Journal,* April 4, 1939, and subsequently removed from the record.

49. Buchanan, *Legislative Partisanship,* 143.

50. Nicholas A. Masters, Robert H. Salisbury, and Thomas H. Eliot, *State Politics and the Public Schools* (New York: Alfred A. Knopf, 1964), 37–38.

51. Samuel C. Patterson, "The Role of the Lobbyist: The Case of Oklahoma," *Journal of Politics,* 25 (1963): 79.

52. Zeigler and Baer, *Lobbying,* 61.

53. Walter DeVries, *The Michigan Lobbyist: A Study in the Bases and Perceptions of Effectiveness* (Ph.D. dissertation, Michigan State University, 1960), 36. See also John P. Hackett, "Lobbying in Rhode Island," *Providence Sunday Journal,* August 11, 1963, and Patterson, "The Role of the Lobbyist," 79.

54. Zeigler and Baer, *Lobbying,* 76.

55. DeVries, *The Michigan Lobbyist,* 63; North Carolina Political Studies Program; Thomas J. Moore, "An Analytical Study of Lobbying During the 1962 Session of the General Assembly of Virginia" (unpublished), 36. The last source was made available through the courtesy of Professor Spencer Albright of the University of Richmond. See also Zeigler and Baer, *Lobbying,* 44.

56. Zeigler and Baer, *Lobbying,* 84.

57. See Harmon Zeigler, "The Effects of Lobbying: A Comparative Assessment," *Western Political Quarterly,* 22 (1969): 122–140.

58. Zeigler and Baer, *Lobbying,* 43.

59. Zeller (ed.), *American State Legislatures,* 249; Patterson, "The Role of the Lobbyist," 76; DeVries, *The Michigan Lobbyist,* 78; Leon Epstein, *Politics in Wisconsin* (Madison: University of Wisconsin Press, 1958), 118–119.

60. Zeigler and Baer, *Lobbying,* 46–49.

61. *Ibid.*

62. DeVries, *The Michigan Lobbyist,* 65, 78–79, 222–223.

63. Milbrath, *The Washington Lobbyists,* 77.

64. Patterson, "The Role of the Lobbyist," 78.

65. Zeigler and Baer, *Lobbying,* 50–53.

66. *Ibid.,* 53.

67. Epstein, *Politics in Wisconsin,* 103. DeVries, *The Michigan Lobbyist,* 177. William C. Havard and Loren P. Beth, *The Politics of Misrepresentation* (Baton Rouge: Louisiana State University Press, 1962), 235–236.

68. Zeigler and Baer, *Lobbying,* 169.

69. *Ibid.,* 176–177.

70. Hacker, "Pressure Politics in Pennsylvania," 333.

71. Alexander Heard, *The Costs of Democracy* (Chapel Hill: University of North Carolina Press, 1960), 175.

72. Lockard, *New England State Politics,* 163. See also Joseph LeVow Steinberg, "Labor in Massachusetts Politics: The Internal Organization of the C.I.O. and A.F.L. for Political Action, 1948–1955," (Senior honors thesis, Harvard University, 1956).

73. Joseph L. Bernd, *The Role of Campaign Funds in Georgia Primary Elections, 1936–1958* (Macon: The Georgia Journal, 1958), 3. Another good

example of the explicit expectations that accompany contributions is the case of Ellis Arnall and an oil investor group. The investors agreed to provide strong backing for Arnall in his 1942 gubernatorial race against Eugene Talmadge because Talmadge failed to support statutory authorization for a pipeline project. See *ibid.,* 4–5.

74. Zeigler and Baer, *Lobbying,* 114.
75. Andrew J. Biemiller, "R-T-W Forces Try 'Back Door,'" *American Federationist,* 68 (1961): 5.
76. Zeigler and Baer, *Lobbying,* 117–119.
77. Bauer, de Sola Pool, and Dexter, *American Business and Public Policy,* 422–433. See also Donald R. Matthews, *U. S. Senators and Their World* (Chapel Hill: University of North Carolina Press, 1960), 177–178.
78. Zeigler and Baer, *Lobbying,* 82.
79. Frank Bonilla, "When is Petition 'Pressure'?" *Public Opinion Quarterly,* 20 (1956): 46–48.
80. Zeigler and Baer, *Lobbying,* 112–113.
81. Kenneth Janda, Henry Teune, Melvin Kahn, and Wayne Francis, *Legislative Politics in Indiana* (Indiana University: Bureau of Government Research, n.d.), 18–19. See also Henry Teune, "Occupational Affiliation and Attitudes Towards Interest Groups" (Paper presented to the 1962 meeting of the American Political Science Association).
82. Zeigler and Baer, *Lobbying,* 163.
83. *Ibid.,* 131.
84. *Ibid.,* 130.
85. *Ibid.,* 169.
86. *Ibid.,* 110.
87. J. Leiper Freeman, *The Political Process: Executive Bureau–Legislative Committee Relations* (Garden City, N.Y.: Doubleday, 1955). On state administrative politics see the following: Harmon Zeigler, *The Florida Milk Commission Changes Minimum Prices* (New York: The Inter-University Case Program, 1963); Donald G. Balmer, *Interest Groups in Action: A Case Study of Oregon Milk Control, 1933–1954* (Ph.D. dissertation, University of Washington, 1956); William W. Boyer, "Policy Making by Government Agencies," *Midwest Journal of Political Science,* 4 (1960): 267–288; James W. Fesler, "Independence of State Regulatory Agencies," *American Political Science Review,* 34 (1940): 935–947.
88. Patterson, "The Role of the Lobbyist," 83. See also Patterson, "The Role of the Labor Lobbyist" (Paper presented to the 1962 meeting of the American Political Science Association).
89. DeVries, *The Michigan Lobbyist,* 115–121.
90. Zeigler and Baer, *Lobbying,* 77–78.
91. *Ibid.,* 77, 136.
92. *Ibid.,* 148.
93. Malcolm E. Jewell, *The State Legislature* (New York: Random House, 1962), 93.
94. Buchanan, *Legislative Partisanship,* 102.
95. Zeigler and Baer, *Lobbying,* 130.
96. Wahlke, *et al., The Legislative System,* 334.
97. Harmon Zeigler, "The Florida Milk Commission Changes Minimum Prices," reprinted in Edwin A. Bock (ed.), *State and Local Government: A Case Book* (University, Ala.: University of Alabama Press, 1963), 395–428.

CHAPTER FIVE

1. Council of State Governments, *The Book of the States.* Published biennially by the Council of State Governments, Chicago.
2. Indices of socioeconomic development used throughout this chapter were derived from United States Bureau of the Census, *United States Census of Population 1960,* "United States Summary" PC–1(1)–1C (Washington, D.C.: United States Government Printing Office, 1962). The measure of wealth is the state's median family income; the measure of urbanization is the proportion of the state's population living in urban rather than rural areas; and the measure of education is the median number of school years completed by the population over twenty-five years old.
3. Thomas R. Dye, *Politics, Economics and the Public* (Chicago: Rand McNally, 1966); Richard E. Dawson and James A. Robinson, "Interparty Competition, Economic Variables, and Welfare Politics in the American States." *Journal of Politics,* 25 (May, 1963): 265–289; Richard Hofferbert, "The Relation Between Public Policy and Some Structural and Environmental Variables in the American States," *American Political Science Review,* 60 (March, 1966): 73–82; Ira Sharkansky and Richard Hofferbert, "Dimensions of State Politics, Economics, and Public Policy," *American Political Science Review,* 63 (September, 1969): 867–879; Charles E. Cnudde and Donald J. McCrone, "Party Competition and Welfare Policies in the American States," *American Political Science Review,* 63 (March, 1969): 858–866.
4. Allan P. Sindler, "Bifactional Rivalry as an Alternative to Two-Party Competition in Louisiana," *American Political Science Review,* 49 (1955): 641.
5. V. O. Key, Jr., *Southern Politics in State and Nation* (New York: Alfred A. Knopf, 1949).
6. Paul T. David and Ralph Eisenberg, *Devaluation of the Urban and Suburban Vote* (Charlottesville: Bureau of Public Administration, University of Virginia, 1961). See also Manning J. Dauer and Robert G. Kelsay, "Unrepresentative States," *National Municipal Review,* 44 (1955): 551–575.
7. *Colegrove* v. *Green,* 328 U.S. 549 (1946).
8. *Baker* v. *Carr,* 369 U.S. 186 (1962).
9. *Wesberry* v. *Sanders,* 84 S. Ct. 526 (1964).
10. *Ibid.*
11. *Gray* v. *Sanders,* 83 S. Ct. 801 (1963).
12. *Ibid.,* 809.
13. *Reynolds* v. *Sims,* 84 S. Ct. 1362 (1964).
14. *Ibid.,* 1381.
15. Apparently representational schemes once fair and equitable can grow archaic very rapidly, for as late as 1948 Earl Warren as governor of California, wrote:

> The agricultural counties of California are far more important in the life of our state than the relationship their population bears to the entire population of the state. It is for this reason that I never have been in favor of redistricting their representation in our state senate on a strictly population basis. It is the same reason that the founding fathers of our country gave balanced representation to the states of

the Union, equal representation in one house and proportionate representation based on population in the other. Quoted in *Time*, June 26, 1962, 22.

16. John C. Wahlke, *et al., The Legislative System* (New York: John Wiley & Sons, 1962), 425.

17. See Malcolm Jewell, *The State Legislature* (New York: Random House, 1962), 17–33; Loren P. Beth, *The Politics of Misrepresentation* (Baton Rouge: Louisiana University Press, 1962); Gordon E. Baker, *Rural Versus Urban Political Power* (New York: Doubleday, 1955).

18. Advisory Commission on Intergovernmental Relations, *A Report to the President for Transmittal to Congress* (Washington, D.C.: United States Government Printing Office, 1955), 39.

19. Thomas R. Dye, "Malapportionment and Public Policy in the States," *Journal of Politics,* 27 (August, 1965): 586–601; Herbert Jacob, "The Consequences of Malapportionment: A Note of Caution," *Social Forces* (Winter, 1965): 256–261; David Brady and Douglas Edmonds, *The Effects of Malapportionment on Policy Outputs in the American States* (Iowa City: Laboratory for Political Research, University of Iowa, 1966).

20. David Derge, "Metropolitan and Outstate Alignments in the Illinois and Missouri Legislative Delegations," *American Political Science Review,* 52 (1958): 1052–1065. Richard T. Frost, "On Derge's Metropolitan and Outstate Legislative Delegations," *American Political Science Review,* 53 (1959): 792–795; Robert S. Friedman, "The Urban Rural Conflict Revisited," *Western Political Quarterly,* 14 (1961): 495.

21. *Tallahassee Democrat,* October 26, 1969, B1.

22. Peter Rossi, "Community Decision-Making," in Roland Young (ed.), *Approaches to the Study of Politics* (Evanston: Northwestern University Press, 1958).

23. Gaetano, Mosca, *The Ruling Class* (New York: McGraw-Hill, 1939).

24. Frank Sorauf, *Party and Representation* (New York: Atherton Press, 1963), 89–94.

25. See Congressional Quarterly Service, *Revolution in Civil Rights,* 4th ed., June, 1968 (Washington, D.C.: Congressional Quarterly Services), 113.

26. Sorauf, *Party and Representation,* 74.

27. Wahlke, *et al., The Legislative System,* 488.

28. Sorauf, *Party and Representation,* 67.

29. For an excellent survey of women in state legislatures from 1921 to 1964, see Emmy F. Werner, "Women in State Legislatures," *Western Political Quarterly,* 21 (March, 1968): 40–50.

30. The data on social characteristics of state legislators are voluminous. Useful studies include: Charles S. Hyneman, "Who Makes Our Laws," *Political Science Quarterly,* 55 (1940): 556–581; Paul Beckett and Celeste Sunderland, "Washington State Lawmakers," *Western Political Quarterly,* 10 (1957): 180–202; Joseph A. Schlesinger, "Lawyers and American Politics," *Midwest Journal of Political Science,* 1 (1957): 26–39; David Derge, "The Lawyer as Decision-Maker in the American State Legislature," *Journal of Politics,* 21 (1959): 408–433; Victor S. Hjelm and Joseph P. Pisciotte, "Profiles and Careers of Colorado State Legislators," *Western Political Quarterly,* 21 (December, 1968): 698–722; Wahlke, *et al., The Legislative System,* 489–490; Sorauf, *Party and Representation,* 75–81.

31. Sorauf, *Party and Representation,* 91.

32. *Ibid.*, 75–81.
33. *Ibid.*, 83.
34. Quotations from Wahlke, *et al.*, *The Legislative System*, 95–134.
35. Sorauf, *Party and Representation*, 103.
36. Wahlke, *et al.*, *The Legislative System*, 95.
37. Harmon Zeigler and Michael Baer, "The Recruitment of Lobbyists and Legislators," *Midwest Journal of Political Science*, 12 (November, 1968): 493–513; W. J. M. MacKenzie, "Local Government Experience of Legislators" in John C. Wahlke and Heinz Eulau (eds.), *Legislature Behavior* (Glencoe, Ill.: The Free Press, 1959).
38. Sorauf, *Party and Representation*, 111; Leon D. Epstein, *Politics in Wisconsin* (Madison: University of Wisconsin Press, 1958), 131.
39. V. O. Key, Jr., *American State Politics* (New York: Alfred A. Knopf, 1956), 171–181.
40. Jewell, *The State Legislature*, 36.
41. Sorauf, *Party and Representation*, 117.
42. Duncan MacRae, "The Relations Between Roll Call Votes and Constituencies in the Massachusetts House of Representatives," *American Political Science Review*, 46 (1952): 1046–1055; Robert W. Becker, *et al.*, "Correlates of Legislative Voting: Michigan House of Representatives, 1954–61," *Midwest Journal of Political Science*, 6 (1962): 384–396.
43. *Congressional Record*, February 15, 1967.
44. G. R. Boynton, Samuel C. Patterson, and Ronald D. Hedlund, "The Structure of Public Support for Legislative Institutions," *Midwest Journal of Political Science*, 12 (May, 1968): 163–180.
45. John Grumm, "Structural Determinants of Legislative Output," Mimeo., Department of Political Science, University of Kansas.
46. This section relies heavily upon Wahlke, *et al.*, *The Legislative System*, 146–161; quotations are from the same study.
47. Harmon Zeigler and Michael Baer, *Lobbying: Influence and Interaction in American State Legislatures* (Belmont, Calif.: Wadsworth, 1969), 126.
48. Duane Lockard, *The Politics of State and Local Government* (New York: Macmillan, 1963), 28.
49. Jewell, *The State Legislature*, 93.
50. See Loren P. Beth and William C. Havard, "Committee Stacking and Political Power in Florida," *Journal of Politics*, 23 (1961): 57–83. In contrast, see Gilbert Y. Steiner and Samuel K. Gove, *Legislative Politics in Illinois* (Urbana: University of Illinois Press, 1960), 12–13.
51. This section relies heavily upon Wahlke, *et al.*, *The Legislative System*, 170–190; quotations are from the same study.
52. *Ibid.*, 245–266; quotations are from the same study.
53. Sorauf, *Party and Representation*, 125.
54. Charles G. Bell and Charles E. Price, "Pre-Legislative Sources of Representational Roles," *Midwest Journal of Political Science*, 13 (May, 1969): 254–270.
55. John W. Soule, "Future Political Ambitions and the Behavior of Incumbent State Legislators," *Midwest Journal of Political Science*, 13 (August, 1969): 439–454. These findings are confirmed at the level of city councilmen by Kenneth Prewitt and William Noulin, "Political Ambitions and the Behavior of Incumbent Politicians," *Western Political Quarterly*, 22 (June, 1969): 298–308.
56. William J. Keefe, "Parties, Partisanship and Public Policy in the Pennsyl-

vania Legislature," *American Political Science Review,* 48 (1954): 450–464; Thomas R. Dye, "A Comparison of Constituency Influences in the Upper and Lower Chambers of a State Legislature," *Western Political Quarterly,* 14 (1961): 473–480.

57. Wahlke, *et al., The Legislative System,* 425.
58. Wayne L. Francis, *Legislative Issues in the Fifty States* (Chicago: Rand McNally, 1967).
59. Wahlke, *et al., The Legislative System,* 359.
60. Perhaps the best systematic comparative study of party voting in state legislatures is LeBlanc, "Voting in State Senates: Party and Constituency Influences," 33–57; also, Malcolm Jewell provides useful comparative data on party voting in state legislatures. See Jewell, *The State Legislature,* 52, and "Party Voting in American State Legislatures," *American Political Science Review,* 49 (1955): 773–791. Jewell cites the following published studies as sources of data on roll call votes: Duane Lockard, *New England State Politics* (Princeton: Princeton University Press, 1959); Keefe, "Parties, Partisanship, and Public Policy," 450–464; Thomas A. Flinn, "The Outline of Ohio Politics," *Western Political Quarterly,* 13 (1960): 702–721; Dean R. Cresap, *Party Politics in the Golden State* (Los Angeles: The Haynes Foundation, 1954).
61. LeBlanc, "Voting in State Senates," 45.
62. MacRae, "Relations Between Votes and Constituencies," 1046–1055; Becker, *et al.,* "Correlates of Legislative Voting," 384–396.
63. MacRae, "Relations Between Votes and Constituencies," 1046–1055; Dye, "Comparison of Influences," 473–480; Sorauf, *Party and Representation,* 133–146; Becker, *et al.,* "Correlates of Legislative Voting," 384–396.
64. Thomas A. Flinn, "Party Responsibility in the States: Some Causal Factors," *American Political Science Review,* 58 (1964): 60–71.
65. *Ibid.,* 71.
66. MacRae, "Relations Between Votes and Constituencies," 1046–1055; Dye, "Comparison of Influences," 473–480.
67. For an analysis of the constituency basis of party cohesion in Kansas see John G. Grumm, "A Factor Analysis of Legislative Voting," *Midwest Journal of Political Science,* 7 (1963): 336–356.
68. Daniel M. Ogden, Jr., and Hugh A. Bone, *Washington Politics* (New York: New York University Press, 1960).
69. Wahlke, *et al., The Legislative System,* 351–359.
70. Robert H. Salisbury, *Missouri Politics and State Political Systems* (University of Missouri, Bureau of Governmental Research, 1959).
71. *Ibid.* See also Samuel C. Patterson, "Dimensions of Voting Behavior in a One-Party State Legislature," *Public Opinion Quarterly,* 26 (Summer 1962): 185–200. A study of voting in the one-party Florida senate also shows a division of constituencies; the fast-growing, and socially and economically changing south Florida constituencies aligned against the relatively unchanging, traditional north Florida constituencies. See Malcolm B. Parsons, "Tensions and Conflict in a One-Party Legislative System," *American Political Science Review,* 56 (1962): 605–614.
72. Wahlke, *et al., The Legislative System,* 267–286.
73. Quotation *ibid.,* 253.
74. *Ibid.,* 311–342.
75. Zeigler and Baer, *Lobbying.*
76. Lockard, *The Politics of State and Local Government,* 283–284.

77. For a discussion of the governor's legislative powers, see Jewell, *The State Legislature*, 105–127; and Coleman B. Ransone, Jr., *The Office of Governor in the United States* (University, Ala.: University of Alabama Press, 1956).

78. Frank J. Sorauf, "The Silent Revolution in Patronage," *Public Administration Review*, 20 (1960): 30.

79. Robert B. Highsaw, "The Southern Governor — Challenge to the Strong Executive Theme," *Public Administration Review*, 19 (1959): 7.

80. Ira Sharkansky, "Agency Requests, Gubernatorial Support, and Budget Success in State Legislatures," *American Political Science Review*, 62 (December, 1968): 1220–1231.

81. Sarah P. McCally, "The Governor and His Legislative Party," *American Political Science Review*, 60 (December, 1966): 923–942.

82. Quotations from Wahlke, *et al.*, *The Legislative System*, 255.

CHAPTER SIX

1. See A. E. Buck, *The Reorganization of State Governments in the United States* (New York: Columbia University Press, 1938), for a rundown of state organizational problems in the thirties. A current outline is Earl L. Darrah and Orville F. Poland, *The Fifty State Governments: A Compilation of State Executive Organization Charts* (Berkeley: Bureau of Public Administration, University of California, 1961). See also Council of State Governments, *Reorganizing State Government* (Chicago: Council of State Governments, 1950).

2. *The New York Red Book* (Albany: Williams Press, 1960–61). State manuals contain the most readily available details on administrative structure. For a compilation of the contents of the manuals for each state, see Charles Press and Oliver Williams, *State Manuals, Blue Books and Election Results* (Berkeley: Institute of Governmental Studies, University of California, 1962).

3. Thomas J. Anton, "Roles and Symbols in the Determination of State Expenditures," *Midwest Journal of Political Science*, 11 (1967): 27–43.

4. V. O. Key, Jr., *American State Politics* (New York: Alfred A. Knopf, 1956), 99; Joseph A. Schlesinger, "A Two-Dimensional Scheme for Classifying States According to Degrees of Inter-Party Competition," *American Political Science Review*, 49 (1955): 1120–1128.

5. Table 1 analyzes elective competition for six state executive offices.

6. Lincoln Steffens, *Autobiography* (New York: Harcourt, Brace & World, 1931).

7. Dean E. Mann, "The Selection of Federal Political Executives," *American Political Science Review*, 58 (1964): 97.

8. Joseph A. Schlesinger, *Ambition and Politics: Political Careers in the United States* (Chicago: Rand McNally, 1966), 24.

9. Key, *American State Politics*, Chap. 2.

10. Coleman B. Ransone, Jr., *The Office of Governor in the United States* (University, Ala.: University of Alabama Press, 1956), 123ff.

11. Warren Moscow, *Politics in the Empire State* (New York: Alfred A. Knopf, 1948), 186–187.

12. See Chapter Four of this volume for a fuller treatment of pressure groups in the states.

13. Robert B. Highsaw and Charles N. Fortenberry, *The Government and Ad-*

ministration of Mississippi (New York: Thomas Y. Crowell, 1954), 326.

14. On the relations between the Anaconda Company and the Montana government, see Joseph K. Howard, *Montana, High, Wide and Handsome* (New Haven: Yale University Press, 1943).

15. Council of State Governments, *The Book of the States, 1968–69* (Lexington, Ky.: Council of State Governments, 1968), 182–183.

16. Ralph Smuckler and George Belknap, *Leadership and Participation in Urban Political Affairs* (East Lansing: Governmental Research Bureau, Michigan State University, 1956), 30.

17. See Anthony Downs, *An Economic Theory of Democracy* (New York: Harper & Row, 1957), 96–113, for an elaboration of the relationship between uncertainty and the development of ideology.

18. On the development of various arguments about administration, see Herbert Kaufman, "Emerging Conflicts in the Doctrines of Public Administration," *American Political Science Review,* 50 (1956): 1057–1073.

19. Samuel K. Gove, "Why Strong Governors?" *National Civic Review,* 53 (1964): 131–136.

20. There is a large amount of literature on the subject of administrative reform. For a critical survey see Dwight Waldo, *The Administrative State* (New York: Ronald Press, 1948), as well as his *The Study of Public Administration* (New York: Random House, 1955). A good summary with particular reference to the states is in Duane Lockard, *The Politics of State and Local Government* (New York: Macmillan, 1963), Chap. 12.

21. Paul Dolan, *The Government and Administration of Delaware* (New York: Thomas Y. Crowell, 1956), 94–95.

22. *The New York Times,* January 11, 1961.

23. For a critical discussion of the effects of limitations on succession, as well as other aspects of the governors' powers, see Gove, "Why Strong Governors?"; and Robert B. Highsaw, "The Southern Governor — Challenge to the Strong Executive Theme," *Public Administration Review,* 19 (1959): 7–11.

24. See Leslie Lipson, *The American Governor, from Figurehead to Leader* (Chicago: University of Chicago Press, 1939).

25. Samuel Krislov, "Constituency versus Constitutionalism: The Desegregation Issue and Tensions and Aspirations of Southern Attorneys General," *Midwest Journal of Political Science,* 3 (1959): 75–92.

26. Deil S. Wright, "Executive Leadership in State Administration," *Midwest Journal of Political Science,* 11 (1967): 1–26.

27. E. Nelson Swinerton, "Ambition and American State Executives," *Midwest Journal of Political Science,* 12 (1968): 538–549.

28. For an earlier classification see F. W. Prescott, "The Executive Veto in the American States," *Western Political Quarterly,* 3 (1950): 98–112.

29. On the Mississippi governor, see Highsaw, "The Southern Governor," 9.

30. For a discussion of the difficulties faced by a New York governor in gaining control of that state's administration, see Clark D. Ahlberg and Daniel P. Moynihan, "Changing Governors — and Policies," *Public Administration Review,* 20 (1960): 195–204.

31. Thad L. Beyle, "The Governor's Formal Powers: A View from the Governor's Chair," *Public Administration Review,* 28 (1968): 540–545.

32. Sarah P. McCally, "The Governor and His Legislative Party," *The American Political Science Review,* 60 (1966): 923–942.

33. Thomas R. Dye, "Executive Power and Public Policy in the States," *The Western Political Quarterly,* 22 (1969): 926–939.

34. Brian R. Fry and Richard F. Winters, "The Politics of Redistribution," *The American Political Science Review,* 64 (1970): 508–522.

CHAPTER SEVEN

1. Henry Cabot Lodge (ed.), *The Federalist* (New York: G. P. Putnam's Sons, 1889) No. 68, pp. 423–28.
2. This section relies heavily on Ira Sharkansky, *Public Administration: Policy-Making in Government Agencies* (Chicago: Markham, 1970), Chap. 4.
3. See the categories of organizational theories employed by Herbert Kaufman in *Politics and Policies in State and Local Governments* (Englewood Cliffs, N.J.: Prentice-Hall, 1963), Chap. 2.
4. See Albert Lepawsky, *Administration: The Art and Science of Organization and Management* (New York: Alfred A. Knopf, 1949), Chap. 8.
5. James March and Herbert Simon, *Organizations* (New York: John Wiley & Sons, 1958), Chap. 2.
6. Charles Lindblom, *The Policy-Making Process* (Englewood Cliffs, N.J.: Prentice-Hall, 1968).
7. This section on state administrative units and their control mechanisms relies on tabular materials presented in *The Book of the States, 1964–65* (Chicago: Council of State Governments, 1964); and John G. Grumm and Calvin W. Clark, *Compensation for Legislators in the Fifty States* (Kansas City, Mo.: Citizens Conference on State Legislators, 1966).
8. Thomas J. Anton, *The Politics of State Expenditure in Illinois* (Urbana: University of Illinois Press, 1966), 146.
9. Richard Neustadt, *Presidential Power: The Politics of Leadership* (New York: John Wiley & Sons, 1960).
10. David S. Brown, "The President and the Bureaus: Time for a Renewal of Relationship?" *Public Administration Review,* 26 (September, 1966): 174–182.
11. These are not the only attributes of state administrators that warrant attention. Ideally, this chapter would give equal attention to the incidence of political accountability, separation of powers and checks and balances, and hierarchy apparent in each state's administrative structures. These goals lie beyond our grasp at this time. We are limited by the availability of existing data and scholarship. Perhaps in the near future one of our readers will fill in some of the gaps in what we know about the administrative branches in each of the states.
12. Andrew T. Coward, "Anti-Poverty Expenditures in the American States: A Comparative Analysis," *Midwest Journal of Political Science,* 13 (May, 1969): 219–236.
13. Ira Sharkansky, *The Politics of Taxing and Spending* (Indianapolis: Bobbs-Merrill, 1969), Chap. 4.
14. Allen Schick, "Control Patterns in State Budget Execution," *Public Administration Review,* 24 (June, 1964): 97–108; and Ira Sharkansky, *The Routines of Politics* (New York: Van Nostrand Remhold, 1970).
15. Sharkansky, *Politics of Taxing and Spending,* 109ff.
16. Ira Sharkansky, *Spending in the American States* (Chicago: Rand McNally, 1968), 45.
17. Deil S. Wright, "Executive Leadership in State Administration," *Midwest Journal of Political Science,* 11 (February, 1967): 1–26.
18. For a description of the techniques employed, see Chapter Nine in this

book, Ira Sharkansky and Richard I. Hofferbert, "The Dimensions of State Policy."

19. The variables entered into this factor analysis represent conditions circa 1967 and come from *The Book of the States, 1968–69* (Chicago: Council of State Governments, 1968). In selecting salaries for inclusion in the factor analysis, we excluded those of the governor, attorney general, and other officials who are directly elected in most of the states and seem to be described more accurately as members of the executive rather than the administration.

20. Undoubtedly this feature is highlighted by the use of an orthagonal factor technique.

21. The standard for a "high" or a "low" designation is a factor score of ± .700.

22. The development of these socioeconomic factors is described in Sharkansky and Hofferbert, "Dimensions of State Policy."

23. The data come from the *County-City Data Book, 1967* (Washington: United States Bureau of the Census, 1968). The thirty-six states were chosen for a larger study of policy making in welfare on the basis of their provision of policy data, by counties, for each major public assistance program. See Ira Sharkansky, "Economic Development, Representative Mechanisms, Administrative Professionalism and Public Policies: A Comparative Analysis of Within-State Distributions of Economic and Political Traits, *The Journal of Politics,* 33 (February, 1971).

24. The formula for computing a coefficient of variability is the standard deviation of a variable divided by its mean; thus, states with low coefficients show the most equal distribution of administrators' salaries among their counties. We show juxtapositions of administrators' salaries with economic traits by means of coefficients of simple correlation; those states with high positive correlations have high salaries in counties with high levels of income or industrialization; those states with high negative correlations have high salaries in counties with low levels of income or industrialization; those states with weak correlations show no particular linear pattern between county economic traits and administrators' salaries.

25. The average coefficient of variability for administrators' salaries in the thirty-six states is .097, reflecting greater within-state similarity than the coefficients for the percentage of employees employed in manufacturing (.544), median family income (.219), or a measure of two-party competition (.196). See Sharkansky, "Economic Development."

26. As shown by a positive correlation in Table 9 between the coefficient of variability for salaries and the industrialization factor.

27. Ira Sharkansky, *Policy Analysis in Political Science* (Chicago: Markham, 1970), Chap. 4.

28. Sharkansky, *The Politics of Taxing and Spending,* Chap. 6. The services in different fields are necessarily defined in terms of these fields. Some measurements define the units of service (e.g., miles of highway) in relation to population. Some measures employ the incidence of beneficiaries among people likely to use a service (e.g., the proportion of poor citizens receiving welfare benefits). Others measure the rate at which a program is performed. Others assess services by the frequency with which the population chooses to use a program (e.g., the proportion of a population who attends schools or visits parks). And some assess services indirectly by measuring

the continued existence of phenomena (e.g., disease or crime) that administrative outputs are designed to control. Because there are no indicators of the services that are supported by the spending of state governments alone, it is necessary to test the correspondence between state and local spending and the public services provided within each of the states.

29. For a discussion of these service factors, see Sharkansky and Hofferbert, "Dimensions of State Policy."

CHAPTER EIGHT

1. For examples of exceptional political activity in state courts see Henry Robert Glick, "Judicial Role Perceptions and Behavior: A Study of American State Judges" (unpublished dissertation, Tulane University, 1967).

2. William J. Brennan, Jr., "State Supreme Court Judge Versus United States Supreme Court Justice: A Change in Function and Perspective," *University of Florida Law Review,* 29 (1966): 236.

3. *NAACP* v. *Button,* 9 L Ed. 2nd 416 (1965).

4. American Judicature Society, *Canons of Judicial Ethics* (Chicago: American Judicature Society, 1969), Report No. 8.

5. For example, Stuart Nagel, "Political Party Affiliation and Judges' Decisions," *American Political Science Review,* 55 (1961): 843–851.

6. Wallace S. Sayre and Herbert Kaufman, *Governing New York City* (New York: Russell Sage Foundation, 1960), 538 and Chap. 15 generally.

7. For a historical treatment of selection see William Carpenter, *Judicial Tenure in the United States* (New Haven: Yale University Press, 1918).

8. American Judicature Society, *The Extent of Adoption of the Non-Partisan Appointive-Elective Plan for the Selection of Judges* (Chicago: American Judicature Society, 1967), Report No. 18.

9. James Herndon, "Appointment as a Means of Initial Accession to Elective State Courts of Last Resort," *North Dakota Law Review,* 38 (1962): 60–73.

10. Jack Ladinsky and Alan Silver, "Popular Democracy and Judicial Independence," *Wisconsin Law Review* (1966): 132–133, n. 14.

11. Herbert Jacob, *Justice in America* (Boston: Little, Brown, 1965), 98.

12. Malcolm Moos, "Judicial Elections and Partisan Endorsements of Judicial Candidates in Minnesota," *American Political Science Review,* 35 (1941): 69–75; Sidney Ulmer, "The Political Party Variable on the Michigan Supreme Court," *Journal of Public Law,* 11 (1962): 352–362.

13. Kenneth N. Vines, "The Selection of Judges in Louisiana," *Tulane Studies in Political Science,* 8 (1962): 114–116.

14. Ladinsky and Silver, "Popular Democracy and Judicial Independence," 147–162.

15. *The New Orleans Times Picayune,* August 9, 1934, 1.

16. *Ibid.,* August 30, 1962, Sec. II, 2.

17. Jacob, *Justice in America,* 96–97.

18. John E. Crow, "Subterranean Policies: A Judge Is Chosen," *Journal of Public Law,* 12 (1963): 275–289.

19. *Ibid.,* 288.

20. The following discussion of the Missouri plan operation is from Richard A. Watson and Rondal G. Downing, *The Politics of the Bench and the Bar: Judicial Selection Under the Missouri Nonpartisan Court Plan* (New York: John Wiley & Sons, 1969), especially Chaps. 1 and 10.

21. *Ibid.,* 338–339.
22. Herbert Jacob, "The Effect of Institutional Differences in the Recruitment Process: The Case of State Judges," *Journal of Public Law,* 13 (1964): 104–119.
23. Watson and Downing, *Politics of Bench and Bar,* Chap. 6.
24. *Ibid.,* 319.
25. See James Willard Hurst, *The Growth of American Law* (Boston: Little, Brown, 1950), 147–169.
26. "ABA Model State Judicial Article (1962)," *Task Force Report: The Courts* (Washington, D.C.: United States Government Printing Office, 1967), 92–96.
27. For a listing of state court organizations see *State Court Systems,* (Chicago: Council of State Governments, 1970), Table 1.
28. See especially Jacob, *Justice in America,* Chap. 9.
29. Kenneth Dolbeare, *Trial Court in Urban Politics* (New York: John Wiley & Sons, 1967).
30. See Glick, "Judicial Role Perceptions and Behavior: A Study of American State Judges," Chap. 7.
31. See David W. Adamany, "The Party Variable in Judges' Voting: Conceptual Notes and a Case Study," *American Political Science Review,* 63 (1969): 57–73.
32. Data on decisional processes is drawn from interviews with the justices of four state supreme courts: Pennsylvania, New Jersey, Massachusetts and Louisiana. For a more extended report see Glick, "Judicial Role Perceptions and Behavior."
33. Robert J. Sickels, "The Illusion of Judicial Consensus: Zoning Decisions in the Maryland Court of Appeals," *American Political Science Review,* 59 (1965): 100–104.
34. For example, see Michael A. Musmano, "Dissenting Opinions," *Dickinson Law Review,* 60 (1955–56): 152–153.
35. Nagel, "Political Party Affiliation," and "Ethic Affiliation and Judicial Propensities," *Journal of Politics,* 24 (1962): 92–110.
36. *Ibid.*
37. Don Ramsey Bowen, "The Explanation of Judicial Voting Behavior from Sociological Characteristics of Judges," (Ph.D. dissertation, Yale University, 1965).
38. On the Michigan court see Sidney Ulmer, "Political Party Variable on Michigan Supreme Court," and Glendon Schubert, *Quantitative Analysis of Judicial Behavior* (Glencoe, Ill.: Free Press, 1959), 129–131.
39. Malcolm M. Feeley, "Comparative Analysis of State Supreme Court Behavior," (Ph.D. dissertation, University of Minnesota, 1969).
40. Adamany, "Party Variable in Judges' Voting."

CHAPTER NINE

1. See Charles E. Lindblom, *The Policy-Making Process* (Englewood Cliffs, N.J.: Prentice-Hall, 1968).
2. See David Easton, *A Systems Analysis of Political Life* (New York: John Wiley & Sons, 1965).
3. Celebrated in Massachusetts to mark the "evacuation" by the British of revolutionary Boston.

4. See Morton Grodzins, *The American System,* Daniel J. Elazar (ed.) (Chicago: Rand McNally, 1966).
5. See Daniel J. Elazar, *American Federalism: A View from the States* (New York: Thomas Y. Crowell, 1966); also Ira Sharkansky, "The Utility of Elazar's Political Culture: A Research Note," *Polity,* 2 (September, 1969): 66–83.
6. Thomas R. Dye, *Economics, Politics and the Public: Policy Outcomes in the American States* (Chicago: Rand McNally, 1966). See also Richard E. Dawson and James A. Robinson, "Inter-Party Competition, Economic Variables, and Welfare Policies in the American States," *Journal of Politics,* 25 (May, 1963): 265–289; Richard I. Hofferbert, "The Relation between Public Policy and Some Structural and Environmental Variables in the American States," *American Political Science Review,* 60 (March, 1966): 73–82; and Ira Sharkansky, "Regionalism, Economic Status and the Public Policies of American States," *Social Science Quarterly,* (June, 1968): 9–26.
7. Dye, *Economics, Politics and the Public,* Dawson and Robinson, "Inter-Party Competition," and Hofferbert, "Relation between Public Policy and Some Structural and Environmental Variables."
8. Compare the findings reported in Harvey E. Brazer, *City Expenditures in the United States* (New York: National Bureau of Economic Research, 1959) with those in Ira Sharkansky, *Spending in the American States* (Chicago: Rand McNally, 1968), Chap. 4.
9. See Chapter Fourteen in this volume, "The Politics of Taxation."
10. As suggested by the following coefficients of simple correlation between the per capita receipts by state and local governments from various taxes and per capita personal income, 1962. Note that the property tax receipts vary most directly with economic conditions:

> property tax   .55
> personal income tax   .25
> general sales tax   −.01

See also Sharkansky, *Spending in the American States,* 86–89.
11. Robert L. Lineberry and Edmund P. Fowler, "Reformism and Public Policies in American Cities," *American Political Science Review,* 61 (September, 1967): 701–716.
12. Charles F. Cnudde and Donald J. McCrone, "Party Competition and Welfare Policies in the American States," *American Political Science Review,* 63 (September, 1969): 858–866; and Ira Sharkansky and Richard I. Hofferbert, "Dimensions of State Politics, Economics, and Public Policy," *American Political Science Review,* 63 (September, 1969): 867–879.
13. Thomas R. Dye, "Income Inequality and American State Politics," *American Political Science Review,* 63 (March, 1969): 157–163.
14. Bryan Fry and Richard Winters, "The Politics of Redistribution," *American Political Science Review,* 64 (June, 1970): 508–523.
15. Ira Sharkansky, *The Routines of Politics* (New York: Van Nostrand Reinhold, 1970).
16. Charles Lindblom, "The Science of Muddling Through," *Public Administration Review,* 19 (Spring 1959): 257–264; "Decision Making in Taxation and Expenditure," in *Public Finances: Needs, Sources and Utilization* (Princeton: National Bureau of Economic Research, 1961), 295–336; plus the work cited in note 1 above.
17. Aaron Wildavsky, *The Politics of the Budgetary Process* (Boston: Little, Brown, 1964), Chap. 3.

18. Thomas J. Anton, *The Politics of State Expenditure in Illinois* (Urbana: University of Illinois Press, 1966). See also John P. Crecine, *Governmental Problem-Solving: A Computer Simulation of Municipal Budgeting* (Chicago: Rand McNally, 1969).
19. See Sharkansky, *The Routines of Politics,* Chap. IX.
20. Because of the problems involved in isolating the public services of state from local governments, all of our policy measures pertain to the combined activities of state and local governments within each state.
21. For a lucid critique of single indicator analysis and a discussion of the methodological justification for multiple indicators see Eugene J. Webb, Donald T. Campbell, Richard D. Schwartz, and Lee Sechrest, *Unobtrusive Measures: Nonreactive Research in the Social Sciences* (Chicago: Rand McNally, 1966), 3ff.
22. The technique of factor analysis starts from the basic assumption that interrelations among separate variables signal the existence of underlying traits — factors — that they share in common. A factor analysis manipulates a collection of variables in order to discern the various patterns of relationships among them. The groups of variables that related closely to one another, but only loosely (or not at all) to variables in other groups are extracted as the principal factors. The individual variables that show the strongest relationships with other members of their factor have, in the language of factor analysis, the highest *loadings*. A variable's loading is the coefficient of correlation between that variable and the underlying factor. By knowing the variables with the highest loadings on each factor, it is possible to infer something about the underlying traits that the factor represents. The variables with the highest loadings come closest to representing the underlying trait, although it is unlikely that any single variable represents that trait perfectly.

Writers have been critical of some uses to which factor analysis has been put, particularly with the increased availability of prepackaged programs and sophisticated computing facilities. Two major criticisms are relevant in the present context. First, it is charged that factor analysis has been used in lieu of theory. If one simply feeds the computer all the data at his command, some factors will emerge. Factor analysis is not a substitute for theory. Some prior rationale must justify the particular variables fed into the computer. Second, the technique has been criticized because the factors that emerge often seem to make little sense in terms of the theory with which one is working. Theory is juggled to accommodate the findings about measurements selected in haphazard fashion.

This is not the appropriate context in which to explore the intricacies of factor analysis. But we do recognize the necessity to account for some of the major criticisms and to point out how we have tried to minimize the difficulties in our inquiry. We have attempted to avoid these pitfalls in two ways. First, we chose our variables because of their widespread currency in analyses by other scholars and because of the appealing theoretical rationale these analysts have offered. But we have been sensitive to the possibility of biased results. Certain initial steps were taken to reduce this bias. Factor analysis cannot be relied upon to define the dimensions of a complex phenomenon (e.g., state policy or the state political system), particularly if the collection of variables subject to factor analysis is preloaded with many measures of the same phenomenon, each of which is highly correlated with others. Thus, our first task was to insure that we did not "stack" our deck of variables with highly intercorrelated measures of the same phenomenon. This problem was particularly acute in the case of measures of party competition. Similar screening of the policy variables we examined did not reveal comparable duplications.

Second, the factors we obtained *do* make sense and we have employed a number of checks to insure that the apparent sense they make is not an artifact of the technique. To maintain prima facie relevance, we used factor analysis in "stages" first to select from among a large collection those variables that load highly on principal factors and then to define the loadings of these variables on factors that contain only those highly loaded components. In this way, the factor technique produces relatively pure factors, devoid of large numbers of variables that contribute only weakly to the principal factors. A large number of policy variables load low on two principal factors, and several variables load about equally on each principal factor. In order to simplify these factors for clarity and further analysis, we eliminated all variables loading below .5 on both principal factors and those loading at least .5 on one but above .4 on the other factor in each sector. We then made separate factor analyses of the variables that remained after this culling procedure. The values derived from this final set of analyses constitute the bases for constructing indices for each state's standing on each dimension of the political policy.

To simplify the presentation of our factors, we present, in Tables 4, 6, and 7, the highest loading variables in order of their importance. For the loadings themselves, the reader is referred to Sharkansky and Hofferbert, "Dimensions."

We move from the use of factor analysis to identify principal dimensions of a phenomena (policy, politics, or economics) to its use in constructing state-by-state indices for the strength of each factor. Factor scores show how each state compares with all the others on a particular factor. The computation of factor scores takes account of the loading of individual variables in each factor, and the score of each state on each of the variables. The score for Alabama on the welfare-education factor, for example, is computed from the state scores on the individual variables in the factor (welfare payments and educational indicators), weighted according to their loadings in the factor. Once we have computed scores for each of the states on each of the factors that we introduce in this chapter, we can use their scores for a series of comparative analyses. As we see below, we determine how a state's score on a policy factor corresponds with its scores on political and economic factors. In making these analyses, we use the actual factor scores. For simplicity of illustration, however, Table 7 shows state rankings on each of the factors. For the scores themselves, the reader is referred to Sharkansky and Hofferbert, "Dimensions."

23. Although some research has relied almost exclusively on expenditures as indicators of public policy, it is risky to assume an expenditure-service relationship. The current expenditures of state and local governments are not indicators of the service that is actually provided to the population. (See Ira Sharkansky, *Spending in the American States,* Chap. 7.) But on the other hand, spending may represent the effort that state and local governments are making in order to improve or maintain their services. Therefore it deserves a place on our list of policy variables.

24. Selected for the availability of data from the 1960 census of population and the 1962 census of governments.

25. See Philip H. Burch, Jr., *Highway Revenue and Expenditure Policy in the United States* (New Brunswick, N.J.: Rutgers University Press, 1962), 23.

26. In collecting the data for the measures of outputs and services, the assumption was made that recorded information is a reasonably accurate reflection of fact. The authors recognize considerable controversy about the reliability of the data. Yet the data chosen appear to be the best available, and they enjoy wide use among social scientists. For comments about each item the reader is referred to the sources. The sources of the political variables include: *Census of Governments, 1962* (especially Volumes 1, 3, and 4) (Washington, D. C.: U.S. Government Printing Office); *The Book of the States, 1964–65* (Lexington, Ky: Council of State Governments, 1964); *Statistical Abstract of the United States, 1964* (Washington, D.C.: United States Government Printing Office, 1965). The index of gubernatorial power comes from Chapter Six in this volume; the index of suffrage regulations comes from Chapter Two in this volume; the indices of legislative apportionment come from Paul T. David and Ralph Eisenberg, *Devaluation of the Urban and Suburban Vote* (Charlottesville, Va.: Bureau of Public Administration, University of Virginia, 1961), 5, 15; and Glendon Shubert and Charles Press, "Measuring Malapportionment," *American Political Science Review,* 58 (1964): 969. The sources for service variables include: National Education Association, *Rankings of the States, 1963;* United States Bureau of Public Roads, *Annual Report, 1963;* Social Security Administration, *Social Security Bulletin; Annual Statistical Supplement, 1963; The Book of the States, 1964–65; Statistical Abstract of the United States, 1964.*

27. For a discussion of the politics of old-age assistance in Alabama, see Sharkansky, *Spending in the American States,* 138–141.

28. John G. Grumm, "Structure and Policy in the Legislature," a paper presented at the Southwestern Social Science Association annual meeting, Dallas, March, 1967.

29. See Chapter Six in this volume.

30. Lewis A. Froman, Jr., "Some Effects of Interest Group Strength in State Politics," *American Political Science Review,* 60 (December, 1966): 952–962.

31. See George A. Bishop, "The Tax Burden by Income Class, 1958," *National Tax Journal,* 14 (March, 1961): 41–58.

32. V. O. Key, Jr., *Southern Politics* (New York: Alfred A. Knopf, 1949); Key, *American State Politics: An Introduction* (New York: Alfred A. Knopf, 1956); Duane Lockard, *New England State Politics* (Princeton: Princeton University Press, 1959); John H. Fenton, *Politics in the Border States* (New Orleans: Hauser Press, 1957); and Fenton, *Midwest Politics* (New York: Holt, Rinehart, and Winston, 1966).

33. See W. W. Rostow, *The Stages of Economic Growth* (Cambridge: Cambridge University Press, 1960).

34. See, for an elaboration of this argument, Hofferbert, "Socioeconomic Dimensions of the American States, 1890–1960," *Midwest Journal of Political Science* (August, 1968), and Sharkansky and Hofferbert, "Dimensions."

35. Dye, *Economics, Politics and the Public.*

36. Our confidence in the theoretical potential of these two factors is heightened by some current inquiry that we are doing with comparable data

from several non-American settings. Preliminary analyses of the social structures of subnational units in France, Mexico, India, and Switzerland reveal social multidimensionality, the contents of which are conceptually quite comparable to the factors found in the American states. See Hofferbert and Sharkansky, "Dimensions."

37. Hofferbert, "Socioeconomic Dimensions of the American States, 1890–1960," 401–418.
38. See Ira Sharkansky, *Regionalism in American Politics* (Indianapolis: Bobbs-Merrill, 1970).
39. See the works cited in note 32 above.
40. We define the deviant states on the basis of a regression equation that takes the general form of:
$$Y = a + b_1X_1 + b_2X_2 + b_3X_3 + b_4X_4$$
Y equals the policy score predicted for each state on the basis of its socioeconomic and political scores; X_1 through X_4 represent each state's socioeconomic and political factors; the a and b's are constants, which, when multiplied with the X's and summed as in the equation above equal the predicted policy scores. These constants are defined by a forty-eight-state analysis and are designed to yield policy factor scores that stand in the most typical relationships to the socioeconomic and political factor scores. In order to identify those states whose actual policy scores are out of line with their socioeconomic and political scores, we employ a simple subtraction:
Actual policy score − predicted policy score = Residual
The states with the highest positive and negative residuals are listed in Table 9 as the states that are appreciably above or below the policy scores expected for them on the basis of socioeconomic and political factors. Table 9 lists states whose residuals are at least ± .400.
41. Only states with enough counties to permit sophisticated techniques of intrastate analysis and to provide county-by-county reports of payments made to recipients of each major public assistance program were chosen. The welfare data come from "Recipients of Public Assistance and Total Assistance Payments, by Program, State and County, June, 1966," mimeographed, United States Department of Health, Education, and Welfare, Welfare Administration, Bureau of Family Services, Division of Research.
42. Martha Derthick, "Intercity Differences in Administration of the Public Assistance Program: The Case of Masachusetts," in James Q. Wilson, *City Politics and Public Policy* (New York: John Wiley & Sons, 1968), 243–266.
43. The coefficient of variability is calculated simply by dividing the statewide mean for a county policy (x) into its standard deviation according to the formula:
$$V = \frac{\sigma x}{\bar{x}}$$
44. That is, show the highest negative county correlations between average welfare payments and family income. Such states tend to score low in industrialization and professionalism-local reliance. Correlations between industrialization and the measure of distribution of welfare payments are .43 for AFDC and .45 for general assistance. Correlations between professionalism-local reliance and the measure of distribution of welfare

payments are .31 for AFDC, .36 for aid to the blind, and .41 for general assistance.

45. See T. Harry Williams, *Huey Long* (New York: Alfred A. Knopf, 1970).

46. In a separate piece of research, for example, one of the present authors discovered that professionalism-local reliance is the strongest of a long list of socioeconomic and political variables in explaining the level of state support for Medicaid, a fairly recent program of federal-state-local assistance for medical care of the economically deprived.

CHAPTER TEN

1. Dissenting opinion in *New State Ice Co.* v. *Liebmann,* 285 U.S. 262 (1932), 311.

2. See "The States Have Done Much," in Terry Sanford, *Storm over the States* (New York, 1967), 53–68.

3. Nelson A. Rockefeller, *The Future of Federalism* (New York, 1964), 15–16.

4. Charles Press and Charles R. Adrian, "Why Our State Governments Are Sick," *The Antioch Review* (Summer, 1964): 149–165.

5. For examples see Gary A. Steiner (ed.), *The Creative Organization* (Chicago, 1965); and Tom Burns and G. M. Stalker, *The Management of Innovation* (London, 1961).

6. For an excellent discussion of this important distinction see, Lawrence B. Mohr, "Determinants of Innovation in Organizations," *The American Political Science Review* (March, 1969): 111–126.

7. Before the mistake was discovered, the Arkansas statute, which reproduced a model prepared by the National Association of Retail Druggists, was copied either verbatim or with minor changes by seventeen states. Ewald T. Grether, *Price Control Under Fair Trade Legislation* (New York, 1937), 19–20.

8. Morton Grodzins, *The American System,* Daniel J. Elazar (ed.) (Chicago, 1966), 84.

9. In later work I will report the results of comparisons of the diffusion patterns of issues from different subject matter areas. Preliminary efforts at such comparisons, however, have not revealed significant variations. There does not seem to be much difference in the diffusion patterns of issues of different types.

10. For a discussion of this phenomenon see Murray Edelman, *The Symbolic Uses of Politics* (Urbana, Ill., 1964), Chaps. 2 and 9.

11. Duane Lockard, *Toward Equal Opportunity* (New York: 1968), 23.

12. The beginning point for the existence of each state was the date upon which it was officially organized as a territory. Using this system, Oklahoma is the last state to come into being, having been organized in 1890. If a program began its diffusion before a state came into existence, that issue was not included in figuring the innovation score for the state.

13. *Fortune* (February, 1968), 191.

14. Everett M. Rogers, *Diffusion of Innovations* (New York, 1962), 40, 285–292. Also see S. N. Eisenstadt, *The Political Systems of Empires* (New York, 1963), 27, 33–112.

15. For a discussion of "slack" resources and innovation see Richard M. Cyert

and James G. March, *A Behavioral Theory of the Firm* (Englewood Cliffs, N.J., 1963), 278–279.

16. Rogers, *Diffusion of Innovations;* Mohr, "Determinants of Innovation"; and also: Edwin Mansfield, "The Speed of Response of Firms to New Techniques," *Quarterly Journal of Economics* (1963), 293–304; Jerald Hage and Michael Aiken, "Program Change and Organizational Properties: A Comparative Analysis," *American Journal of Sociology* (1967), 516–517; and Richard J. Hall, S. Eugene Haas, and Norman J. Johnson, "Organizational Size, Complexity and Formalization," *American Sociological Review* (1967), 903–912.

17. Regional effects of this kind appear frequently in analyses of data from the American states. In many studies, especially those involving measures of political participation or party competition, strong relationships appear that are actually only a result of the distinctive nature of the southern states. In order to insure that the correlations in this analysis were not merely a result of the social and political peculiarities of the South, the eleven states of the Confederacy were removed from all distributions. Since the southern states do not cluster at one extreme of the innovation scale, no great changes occurred in correlation coefficients based upon data from the thirty-nine states outside the South. Within the eleven southern states, however, almost all the relationships were substantially reduced in size. Because only eleven states are involved, this fact is difficult to interpret, but will be treated more fully in later work. For an example of this problem discussed in another context see Raymond Wolfinger and John Osgood Field, "Political Ethos and the Structure of City Government," *The American Political Science Review* (March, 1966), 306–326. For a more extensive discussion of the methodological implications see the analysis of "interaction effects" in Hugh Donald Forbes and Edward R. Tufte, "A Note of Caution in Causal Modelling," *ibid.,* (December, 1968), 1261–1262; and the communication from Dennis D. Riley and Jack L. Walker, *ibid.,* (September, 1969), 890–892. Noel G. Butlin in "A New Plea for the Separation of Ireland," *The Journal of Economic History* (June, 1968), 274–291, makes a similar point about regional peculiarities within the United Kingdom.

18. Theodore Lowi, "Toward Functionalism in Political Science: The Case of Innovation in Party Systems," *The American Political Science Review* (1963), 570–583. Evidence that seems to confirm Lowi's theory may be found in Charles W. Wiggens, "Party Politics in the Iowa Legislature," *Midwest Journal of Political Science* (1967), 60–69; and Frank M. Bryan, "The Metamorphosis of a Rural Legislature," *Polity* (1968), 191–212.

19. Joseph A. Schlesinger has developed an index of the "general opportunity level" in each state. The index measures the relative number of chances that exist in each state to achieve major political office. See *Ambition and Politics: Political Careers in the United States* (Chicago, 1966), 37–56.

20. James D. Barber, *The Lawmakers: Recruitment and Adaptation to Legislative Life* (New Haven, 1965). For testimony from legislators about the importance of reapportionment see Frank M. Bryan, "Who Is Legislating," *National Civic Review* (December, 1967), 627–633; Allan Dines, "A Reapportioned State," *ibid.,* (February, 1966), 70–74, 99.

21. Rogers, *Diffusion of Innovations.* Also see Mansfield, "Speed of Response"; James S. Coleman, Elihu Katz, and Herbert Menzel, *Medical Innovation:*

A Diffusion Study (Indianapolis, 1966); and John W. Loy, Jr., "Social Psychological Characteristics of Innovators," *American Sociological Review* (1969), 73–82.

22. For a somewhat different view see Norman Meller, "Legislative Staff Services: Toxin, Specific, or Placebo for the Legislature's Ills," *The Western Political Quarterly* (June, 1967), 381–389.

23. One other index deals with political phenomenon: Rodney Mott's index of judicial prestige. The Mott index measures the degree to which state supreme courts were used as models by the legal profession. It is based on a study of citations in federal Supreme Court decisions and all state supreme court decisions, the number of cases reprinted in standard textbooks, and the opinion of a panel of prominent legal scholars; it covers the period 1900 to 1930. The Mott index and the innovation score from the same time period are correlated at .62. This finding might be interpreted to mean that emulative behavior in the judicial arena is not much different from that in the legislative arena. For details of the Judicial Prestige Index see Rodney L. Mott, "Judicial Influence," *The American Political Science Review* (March, 1936), 295–315.

24. Data for this table was derived from Richard Hofferbert's collection, "American State Socioeconomic, Electoral, and Policy Data: 1890–1960," which he has graciously allowed me to use.

25. The sources are Richard Hofferbert, "Classification of American State Party Systems," *Journal of Politics* (1964), 550–567; David and Eisenberg, *Devaluation of Urban and Suburban Vote;* Schlesinger, *Ambition and Politics;* and John Grumm, "Structure and Policy in the Legislature," (Paper presented at the Southwestern Social Science Association Meetings, 1967).

26. Herbert Jacob, "The Consequences of Malapportionment: A Note of Caution," *Social Forces* (1964), 260–266; Thomas R. Dye, "Malapportionment and Public Policy in the States," *Journal of Politics* (1965), 586–601; Richard I. Hofferbert, "The Relation Between Public Policy and Some Structural and Environmental Variables in the American States," *The American Political Science Review* (March, 1966), 73–82; David Brady and Douglas Edmonds, "One Man, One Vote — So What?" *Trans-Action* (March, 1967), 41–46. A recent article questions some of the conclusions of this research: Alan G. Pulsipher and James L. Weatherby, Jr., "Malapportionment, Party Competition, and the Functional Distribution of Governmental Expenditures," *The American Political Science Review* (December, 1968), 1207–1219.

27. See Herbert Simon, *Administrative Behavior,* 2nd ed. (New York, 1957); Cyert and March, *Behavioral Theory of the Firm;* and Charles E. Lindblom, *The Intelligence of Democracy* (New York, 1965).

28. For a comprehensive review of the literature on decision making see Donald W. Taylor, "Decision Making and Problem Solving," and Julia Feldman and Herschel E. Kanter, "Organizational Decision Making," in James G. March (ed.), *Handbook of Organizations* (Chicago, 1965), 48–86, 614–649. Also see W. Richard Scott, "Theory of Organizations," in Robert E. L. Faris (ed.), *Handbook of Modern Sociology* (Chicago, 1964), 485–529.

29. Decision rules of this kind are mentioned in both Taylor, "Decision Making and Problem Solving," 73–74; and Cyert and March, *Behavioral Theory of the Firm,* especially 34–43.

30. William M. Evan, "The Organization-Set: Toward a Theory of Inter-Organizational Relations," in James D. Thompson (ed.), *Approaches to Organizational Design* (Pittsburgh, 1966), 173–191.

31. Some recent examples are William Anderson, *The Nation and the States, Rivals or Partners?* (Minneapolis, 1955); M. J. C. Vile, *The Structure of American Federalism* (London, 1961); William Riker, *Federalism: Origin, Operation, Significance* (Boston, 1964); Daniel J. Elazar, *American Federalism: A View from the States* (New York, 1966); Grodzins, *The American System*. For a general critique see A. H. Birch, "Approaches to the Study of Federalism," *Political Studies* (1966), 15–33.

32. This is not the first study to discover the important role of emulation and competition in the development of public policy. Richard Hofferbert in "Ecological Development and Policy Change in the American States," *Midwest Journal of Political Science* (1966), 485; and Ira Sharkansky in "Regionalism, Economic Status and the Public Policies of American States," *Southwestern Social Science Quarterly* (1968), both mention the influence of other states in the calculations of state decision makers. Several earlier students of local government complained that sparsely populated, arid western states had blindly copied from the heavily populated eastern states forms of local government that were inappropriately suited for the conditions prevailing in the Great Plains. See A. Bristol Goodman, "Westward Movement of Local Government," *The Journal of Land and Public Utility Economics* (1944), 20–34; Herman Walker, Jr. and Peter L. Hansen, "Local Government and Rainfall," *The American Political Science Review* (September, 1946), 1113–1123. Robert L. Crain has recently used emulation as a principal explanatory variable in his study of the spread of water fluoridation programs among American cities, "Fluoridation: The Diffusion of an Innovation Among Cities," *Social Forces* (1966), 467–476; as did Thomas M. Scott in "The Diffusion of Urban Governmental Forms as a Case of Social Learning." *The Journal of Politics* (1968), 1091–1108.

33. This set of hypotheses is consistent with more general theories concerning the manner in which human beings formulate judgments and establish expectations in all areas of life. See Leon Festinger, "A Theory of Social Comparison Processes," *Human Relations* (1954), 117–140; and Robert Merton, *Social Theory and Social Structure,* rev. ed. (Glencoe, Ill., 1957), 225–420.

34. John C. Harsanyi, "Rational Choice Models v. Functionalistic and Conformistic Models of Political Behavior," (Paper delivered at the American Political Science Association Meetings, 1967), 17.

35. Lockard, *Toward Equal Opportunity,* 20–21.

36. Allan Spitz, "The Transplantation of American Democratic Institutions," *Political Science Quarterly* (1967), 386–398.

37. Duane Lockard, *Connecticut's Challenge Primary: A Study in Legislative Politics,* (New York, 1959), Eagleton Case #7.

38. *Ibid.,* 2.

39. *Ibid.,* 22.

40. R. J. May, *Federalism and Fiscal Adjustment* (Oxford, 1969), 44.

41. For a somewhat similar argument concerning government spending see Anthony Downs, "Why the Government Budget Is Too Small in a Democracy," *World Politics* (July, 1960), 541–563.

42. Alvin H. Hansen, *The Postwar American Economy: Performance and Problems* (New York, 1964), 30–31.

43. For evidence of this perspective, see Thomas J. Anton, *The Politics of State Expenditure in Illinois* (Urbana, Ill., 1966), 263.

44. *The New York Times,* February 15, 1968, 1, 12.

45. An earlier version of this chapter, "The Diffusion of Innovations Among the American States," *The American Political Science Review* (September, 1969), 880–899, came to the attention of the majority leader of the senate in New York, Senator Earl W. Brydges. He expressed no surprise and stated, "We plan to continue to have New York state lead the nation. At the 1970 session we shall be adopting new programs, including a new mental hygiene law, a new criminal code, a new education formula, and a host of other pioneering legislation." *Niagara Falls Gazette,* October 22, 1969, 1.

46. Nicholas A. Masters, Robert Salisbury, and Thomas H. Eliot, *State Politics and the Public* (New York, 1964), 12.

47. *Ibid.,* 25.

48. *Ibid.,* 21. For a similar discussion of the importance of aspirations in determining the speed with which innovations are adopted see Rufus P. Browning, "Innovative and Noninnovative Decision Processes in Government Budgeting," in Robert T. Golembiewski (ed.), *Public Budgeting and Finance* (Itasca, Ill., 1968), 128–145.

49. State programs often have been adopted and developed before being accepted by the pioneers and diffusing among the states. The federal government, for example, frequently has been taken as a model for change, as with the diffusion of state research commissions modeled on the National Science Foundation. For a description see Harvey M. Sapolsky, "Science Advice for State and Local Government," *Science* (April, 1968), 280–284. Foreign governments have also been employed as models. For an example, see Donald C. Rowat, "The Spread of the Ombudsman Idea," in Stanley V. Anderson (ed.), *Ombudsman for American Government?* (Englewood Cliffs, N.J., 1968), 7–36. For fascinating insights into the foreign origins of portions of La Follette's Progressive program in Wisconson see John R. Common, *Myself* (New York, 1934), 107–110; and Charles McCarthy, *The Wisconsin Idea* (New York, 1912), 10–11, 19–33.

50. This demarcation has often been used in research on regionalism. See Ira Sharkansky, *Regionalism in American Politics* (Indianapolis, 1970), 26–32.

51. For a more detailed description of the methods and results of this analysis see my article "The Diffusion of Innovations Among the American States," 892–896.

52. Unpublished memo from The Council of State Governments, Chicago, Illinois.

53. Mail survey of presidents and executive secretaries of professional societies of state officials (N = 72) conducted during 1968 at the Institute of Public Policy Studies, The University of Michigan, Ann Arbor.

54. For a discussion of the role of professional organizations in determining career lines see Fred E. Katz, "Occupational Contact Networks," *Social Forces* (1958), 52–58. Also see Jack Ladinsky, "Occupational Determinants of Geographic Mobility Among Professional Workers," *American Sociological Review* (1967), 253–264.

55. Merton, *Social Theory and Social Structure.* Also see Alvin W. Gouldner,

"Cosmopolitans and Locals: Toward an Analysis of Latent Social Roles," *Administrative Science Quarterly* (1957), 281–306; and Harold L. Wilensky, *Intellectuals in Labor Unions* (Glencoe, Ill., 1956).

56. A small portion of the difference between the two columns in Table 6 is an artifact of measurement. Since not all the programs in this analysis have been adopted by all forty-eight states, laggard states sometimes remain. As time passes and programs receive widespread acceptance these laggard states slowly fall into line and adopt the programs. Since the programs in the first two time periods have been around longer, they have more likely completed their spread among the states and thus, given our scoring procedure, are also more likely to have a longer period of diffusion.

57. United States Advisory Commission on Intergovernmental Relations, *1970 State Legislative Program* (Washington, D.C., 1969).

58. The best recent analysis of long-term changes in the American political system is Donald Stokes, "Parties and the Nationalization of Electoral Forces," in William N. Chambers and Walter Dean Burnham (eds.), *The American Party Systems* (New York, 1967), 182–202. Also see Norval D. Glenn and J. Simmons, "Are Regional Cultural Differences Diminishing?" *Public Opinion Quarterly* (1967), 196–205; and Sharkansky, *Regionalism in American Politics*.

59. The following data are taken from interviews conducted in ten states during 1968 and 1969. The project was supervised by Jack L. Walker and financed by a grant from the Carnegie Corporation.

60. The interviews in Iowa were conducted by Mr. Dale H. Poel of Dalhousie University in connection with his doctoral dissertation. The requirements of his project led him to eliminate the welfare department, take only one interview in mental health, and add the conservation commission and the development commission to his sample.

61. The exact wording of the questions and the method used to construct the index are described in the footnotes to Table 9.

62. It is possible that this was caused, in part, by the differences in the sample of administrators interviewed in Iowa. For the differences, see note 60 above.

63. This consensus is shared by the presidents and executive secretaries of professional societies of state administrators. An index of approval built from answers to similar questions by our seventy-two respondents on the 1968 mail survey mentioned in note 53 above results in California, New York, Michigan, Wisconsin, and Connecticut, in that order, being ranked as the most pioneering states. This index of approval correlated at (Spearman rank order) .68 with the innovation index in Table 1.

64. For an analysis of differences in regional patterns derived from the innovation score over time, see my article "The Diffusion of Innovations Among the American States," 895–896.

65. For a provocative study of the importance of the professional community in both facilitating, and, at times, resisting innovation see Marshall H. Becker, "Sociometric Location and Innovativeness: Reformulation and Extension of the Diffusion Model," *American Sociological Review* (April, 1970), 267–282.

66. These new information networks are spreading into all the states, but even today the isolation of some state capitals is a major obstacle to the adoption of new ideas. See Alan L. Clem's description of the isolation of Pierre,

the capital of South Dakota, in *Prairie State Politics: Popular Democracy in South Dakota* (Washington, D.C.; 1967), 137; and Norton E. Long's emphasis on the importance of information sources in "After the Voting Is Over," *Midwest Journal of Political Science* (1962), 183–200. For a general review of communications theory and its application to politics see Richard R. Fagen, *Politics and Communication* (Boston, 1966), especially 34–69, 88–106. Also see Karl W. Deutsch, *The Nerves of Government*, 2nd ed. (New York, 1966), especially 145–256.

CHAPTER ELEVEN

1. These statistics are taken from the extremely useful compendium, *Rankings of the States, 1963,* Research Report 1963-R1 (Washington, D.C.: Research Division, National Education Association, 1963).
2. The history of American education is treated in detail by several authors. Especially relied upon are R. Freeman Butts and Lawrence A. Cremin, *A History of Education in the United States* (New York: Henry Holt, 1953) and H. G. Good, *A History of American Education* (New York: Macmillan, 1956).
3. For a convenient discussion of the politics of federal aid to education, past and present, see Frank J. Munger and Richard F. Fenno, *National Politics and Federal Aid to Education* (Syracuse: Syracuse University Press, 1962).
4. *The Book of the States* (Chicago: Council of State Governments, biennial) contains useful data summarizing state governmental structures affecting education.
5. Stephen K. Bailey, Richard T. Frost, Paul E. Marsh, and Robert C. Wood, *Schoolmen and Politics: A Study of State Aid to Education in the Northeast* (Syracuse: Syracuse University Press, 1962), 27.
6. See, for example, Arthur E. Bestor, *Educational Wastelands* (Urbana: University of Illinois Press, 1953).
7. A recent and judicious discussion of the pros and cons of present certification practices is in James B. Conant, *The Education of American Teachers* (New York: McGraw-Hill, 1963). See also James D. Koerner, *The Miseducation of American Teachers* (Boston: Houghton Mifflin, 1963).
8. New York: Teachers College, Columbia University, 1905.
9. The most important statements are contained in George Strayer and Robert Haig, *The Financing of Education in the State of New York* (New York: Macmillan, 1923); and Paul Mort, *State Support for Public Schools* (New York: Teachers College, Columbia University, 1926).
10. Paul Mort, Walter Reusser, and John Polby, *Public School Finance,* 3rd ed. (New York: McGraw-Hill, 1960), 218.
11. A pioneering discussion of group interests in education is Thomas H. Eliot, "Toward an Understanding of Public School Politics," *American Political Science Review,* 53 (1959): 1032–1052. For expressions of the "educationalist" argument, see Arthur E. Bestor, *The Restoration of Learning* (New York: Alfred A. Knopf, 1955), and *Educational Wastelands;* Hyman Rickover, *Education and Freedom* (New York: E. P. Dutton, 1959).
12. Bailey, *et. al., Schoolmen and Politics,* 23–26. Much of the discussion that follows is drawn from the Bailey study and from Nicholas A. Masters, Robert H. Salisbury, and Thomas H. Eliot, *State Politics and the Public Schools* (New York: Alfred A. Knopf, 1964).

13. See *NEA Handbook,* 1963–64 (Washington, D.C.: National Education Association, 1963), 347–350.
14. For a convenient summary of the development of the NEA, see Edgar B. Wesley, *NEA: The First Hundred Years* (New York: Harper, 1957).
15. Bailey, *et al., Schoolmen and Politics,* 46.
16. Masters, *et al., State Politics and the Public School,* 141, n. 2.
17. The issues involved in race and education are examined in Albert Blaustein and Clarence Ferguson, *Desegregation and the Law* (New Brunswick: Rutgers Univerity Press, 1957); Don Schoemaker (ed.), *With All Deliberate Speed* (New York: Harper and Bros., 1957); and the annual reports of the U.S. Civil Rights Commission. A summary of several of these can be found in Wallace Mendelson, *Discrimination* (Englewood Cliffs, N.J.: Prentice-Hall, 1962). The most comprehensive work on religion and the public schools is Leo Pfeffer, *Church, State, and Freedom* (Boston: Beacon, 1953). Also see David Fellman, *The Supreme Court and Education* (New York: Teachers College, Columbia University, 1960); and Theodore Powell, *The School Bus Law* (Middletown, Conn.: Wesleyan University Press, 1960).
18. See, for example, the discussion of Missouri in Masters, *et al., State Politics and the Public Schools,* 12–99. Less adaptive school leaders apparently were found by John Wahlke, Heinz Eulau, William Buchanan, and Leroy Ferguson in their study of state legislators in Tennessee, Ohio, California, and New Jersey; see *The Legislative System* (New York: John Wiley & Sons, 1962), especially 335.
19. Wahlke, *et al., The Legislative System,* 337, found that among major types of interest groups education associations were least likely to be regarded as unselfish or public spirited but most able to mobilize votes to affect the outcome of elections.
20. *Ibid.,* 200.
21. *Ibid.,* 212–213.
22. Mort, *et al., Public School Finance,* 80–87, report a number of studies that have attempted to correlate the educational outputs, measured in terms of both educational achievement and kind of school program, with expenditure levels. The findings are quite consistent for different periods of time and different school systems, showing a correlation of about .6.
23. Charles S. Benson reports that per pupil spending and per capita income showed a correlation of .79 in 1929–30, and .84 in 1959–60, suggesting the durability of the relationship. See *The Economics of Public Education* (Boston: Houghton Mifflin, 1961), 62–63.
24. Richard E. Dawson and James A. Robinson, "Inter-Party Competition, Economic Variables, and Welfare Policies in the American States," *Journal of Politics,* 25 (1963): 286–289.
25. Mort, *et al., Public School Finance,* 197.
26. Much of the following discussion is based upon Frederick Rudolph, *The American College and University* (New York: Alfred A. Knopf, 1962).
27. *The Dartmouth College Case,* 4 Wheaton 518.
28. Rudolph, *The American College and University,* 211.
29. *Ibid.,* 185.
30. *Ibid.,* 261–262.
31. No single summary of the formal governmental structures affecting higher education is presently available. Even if it were, it would soon be out of date for the systems are changing rapidly in many states. Works that discuss

the questions of governmental structure include Malcolm Moos and Francis Rourke, *The Campus and the State* (Baltimore: The Johns Hopkins Press, 1959); Lyman A. Glenny, *Autonomy of Public Colleges* (New York: Mc-Graw-Hill, 1959); John J. Corson, *Governance of Colleges and Universities* (New York: McGraw-Hill, 1960); and T. R. McConnell, *A General Pattern for American Public Higher Education* (New York: McGraw-Hill, 1962).

32. Glenny, *Autonomy of Public Colleges,* is a particularly thorough discussion of the problems of coordination as well as an illustration of the variety now existing in institutional forms.

33. 347 U.S. 483 (1954).

34. A summary of reorganization developments may be found in C. O. Fitz-water, *School District Reorganization* (Washington, D.C.: United States Department of Health, Education, and Welfare, 1957).

CHAPTER TWELVE

1. Council of State Governments, *Book of the States, 1970–71* (Chicago: The Council of State Governments, 1970), 196–197.

2. U.S. Department of Health, Education and Welfare, *Health, Education and Welfare Trends: 1966–67,* Part I (Washington, D.C.: United States Government Printing Office, 1968), S.151.

3. William Blackstone, *Commentaries on the Laws of England,* 12th ed. (London, 1793), Book I, Chap. i, 131, quoted in Edith Abbott, *Public Assistance,* I (Chicago: University of Chicago Press, 1940), 3–4.

4. Hilary M. Leyendecker, *Problems and Policy in Public Assistance* (New York: Harper and Bros., 1955), 21–23.

5. *Shapiro* v. *Thompson,* 394 U.S. 618 (1969).

6. Leyendecker, *Problems and Policy,* 30.

7. Josephine Brown, *Public Relief: 1929–1939* (New York: Henry Holt, 1958), 5–6.

8. Lucy W. Brown, "Poor Relief Laws: A Digest," (American Public Welfare Association, 1934), taken from *ibid.,* 18.

9. Brown, *Public Relief: 1929–1939,* 20.

10. *Ibid.,* 22–25.

11. *Ibid.,* 26–28.

12. Leyendecker, *Problems and Policy,* 54.

13. Brown, *Public Relief: 1929–1939,* 27.

14. *Ibid.,* 427–428.

15. *Ibid.,* 33.

16. Quoted in *ibid.,* 34.

17. Leyendecker, *Problems and Policy,* 67.

18. *Ibid.,* 69–70.

19. Brown, *Public Relief: 1929–1939,* 306–312.

20. *Ibid.*

21. Data concerning these various programs will be presented in the following section and used in the analysis relating state efforts in welfare to social, economic, and political conditions.

22. United States Department of Health, Education and Welfare, *Social Security Programs in the United States* (Washington, D.C.: United States Government Printing Office, 1968), 86.

23. *Shapiro* v. *Thompson* 394 U.S. 618 (1969).

24. Department of Health, Education and Welfare, *Social Security Programs in the United States*, 94–95.

25. Computed from data presented in Table 3, p. 452.

26. The six indices employed here do not exhaust the types of measures or dimensions of state welfare effort that could be significant in comparing welfare effort. They pertain solely to amounts of money spent and numbers of persons receiving aid. They are the aspects of state welfare effort for which comparable data for all the states are readily available. One important aspect of state welfare policies that it would be useful to investigate would be the ease or lack of ease with which various welfare benefits are available to potential recipients. This aspect of welfare policy is not necessarily discernible from expenditure figures or data pertaining to numbers of recipients. We were unable to find sufficient data to allow us to develop good measures of the restrictiveness of eligibility requirements. We can, however, suggest one study that developed such a measure for one welfare program, AFDC. This study found a fairly strong relationship between the amount of money allowed by the state per recipient (AFDC) and the leniency of eligibility requirements. Those states allowing higher payments per recipient tended to be more lenient in eligibility requirements. This would suggest that state welfare eligibility requirements, or ease of access to welfare benefits, are probably most highly related to the same factors as our measure of average payment per recipient, which we discuss below and use in subsequent analysis. See Department of Health, Education and Welfare, Social and Rehabilitation Service, Office of Research, Demonstration and Training, Division of Intramural Research, *Welfare Policy and Its Consequences for the Recipient Population: A Study of the AFDC Program* (Washington, D.C.: United States Government Printing Office, 1969), especially 12–18.

27. Duane Lockard, *New England State Politics* (Princeton: Princeton University Press, 1959), 337.

28. V. O. Key, Jr., *Southern Politics in State and Nation* (New York: Alfred A. Knopf, 1949), 298–314.

29. Richard E. Dawson and James A. Robinson, "Inter-Party Competition, Economic Variables, and Welfare Policies in the American States," *Journal of Politics*, 25 (May, 1963): 265–289; Thomas R. Dye, *Politics, Economics, and the Public* (Chicago: Rand McNally, 1966), 293; and Richard E. Dawson, "Social Development, Party Competition, and Policy," in William Nisbet Chambers and Walter Dean Burnham, *The American Party Systems: Stages of Political Development* (New York: Oxford University Press, 1967), 203–237.

30. See, for example, Charles Cnudde and Donald J. McCrone, "Party Competition and Welfare Policies in the American States," *American Political Science Review*, 58 (September, 1969): 858–866; and Ira Sharkansky, *Spending in the American States* (Chicago: Rand McNally, 1968).

31. In all three instances the major party is the party that held the highest number of seats or received the largest percentage of votes over the particular time period. Competition scores were calculated for those long periods preceding 1941, 1951, and 1966 (for the long periods election data for the ten years preceding the three welfare years were used); and two short periods that included data from the two elections just prior to 1941, 1951, and 1966. The inclusion of both long and short terms allows the comparison of long-term competition with short-term competition.

32. The correlations of the remaining variables generally run in the same direction as those presented in the tables.

33. For OA, AB, and APTD, however, the strength of the correlation decreases over the years.

34. John H. Fenton, *People and Parties in Politics* (Glenview, Ill.: Scott, Foresman, 1966), 45.

CHAPTER THIRTEEN

1. United States Department of Commerce, Bureau of the Census, *Historical Statistics of the United States, 1789–1945* (Washington, D.C.: United States Government Printing Office, 1949), 220–223; and United States Department of Transportation, Bureau of Public Roads, *Highway Statistics 1967* (Washington, D.C.: United States Government Printing Office, 1969), 167.

2. The highway director in one large industrial state was asked confidentially to list the very best and very worst highway systems in the United States in terms of technical and administrative quality. He answered without equivocation. A few years later a similar official in another industrial state was asked the same question. He did not equivocate either. However, his list was significantly different. One can assume from this that highway officials do indeed have somewhat different standards for measuring quality despite their common professionalism.

3. For background on the development of American highways prior to World War II, see Charles L. Dearing, *American Highway Policy* (Washington, D.C.: The Brookings Institution, 1941).

4. *Ibid.*, 226–227.

5. The first two of these are discussed separately on pp. 493–495, 499–500.

6. David Levin, "The Highway and Land Use," in Jean Labatut and Wheaton J. Lane (eds.), *Highways in Our National Life* (Princeton: Princeton University Press, 1960), 268.

7. Much of the discussion of the politics of highway classification is based on Philip H. Burch, *Highway Revenue and Expenditure Policy in the United States* (New Brunswick, N.J.: Rutgers University Press, 1962), 140–160.

8. *Ibid.*, 140.

9. *Ibid.*, 144.

10. United States Department of Transportation, Bureau of Public Roads, *Highway Statistics 1967*, 157.

11. Of the eighteen states fitting this category ten have highway departments that are administratively independent of the governor, five have departments that are semi-dependent, and three have departments that are dependent. This distribution is very similar to that found in the other thirty-two states. For a discussion of the administrative relationships between highway departments and governors see pp. 486–487.

12. Of the eighteen states fitting this category approximately one-third were states in the highest quartile of gubernatorial power and one-third in the lowest quarter. For a discussion of the powers of the governor see pp. 230–234.

13. Burch, *Highway Revenue and Expenditure Policy,* 20–33.

14. For a discussion of the early federal aid programs, see Dearing, *American Highway Policy,* 78–99, and Burch, *Highway Revenue and Expenditure Policy,* 211–242.

15. Federal Aid Road Act of 1916, 39 Stat. 355 (1916).

16. Dearing, *American Highway Policy,* 89.

17. Federal Aid Highway Act of 1944, 58 Stat. 838 (1944).

18. Glenn Fisher, *The Federal Highway Program* (unpublished manuscript, Institute of Public Administration, University of Michigan, 1961), 7.

19. Burch, *Highway Revenue and Expenditure Policy,* 250–251.

20. The Federal Aid Highway Act of 1956, 70 Stat. 374 (1956).

21. Burch, *Highway Revenue and Expenditure Policy,* 250–251.

22. Congressional Quarterly, *Weekly Report,* Vol. 37, No. 41 (October 10, 1969), 1946–1949.

23. *Forbes,* October 1, 1968, 41.

24. Robert S. Friedman, *State and Local Relations in Highway Finance in Louisiana* (Baton Rouge: Bureau of Public Administration, Louisiana State University, 1962).

25. Robert S. Friedman, *The Michigan Constitutional Convention and Administrative Organization: A Case Study in the Politics of Constitution-Making* (Ann Arbor: Institute of Public Administration, University of Michigan, 1963), 52.

26. Edward L. Pinney and Robert S. Friedman, *Political Leadership and the School Desegregation Crisis in Louisiana,* Eagleton Institute, Cases in Practical Politics, No. 31, 6.

27. Data on formal highway administrative organizations were derived from Highway Research Board, National Academy of Sciences — National Research Council, *State Highway Administrative Organizations: An Analysis,* Special Report 51 (Washington, D.C.: Highway Research Board, 1959). These data were updated by correspondence with the fifty state highway departments. It is interesting that despite reorganization activities in a number of states in the decade following the Highway Research Board publication only three states changed their position substantially in relation to the governor.

28. *Ibid.,* 20.

29. Luther Hodges has described vividly his efforts to create an at-large highway commission while serving as governor of North Carolina in *Businessman in the Statehouse* (Chapel Hill: University of North Carolina Press, 1962), 126–149.

30. Highway Research Board, *State Highway Administrative Organizations,* 22.

31. *State Government News* (Lexington, Ky.: Council of State Governments, May, 1970) 2–3.

32. Alan Altshuler, *The City Planning Process* (Ithaca: Cornell University Press, 1965), 17–83.

33. *Ibid.,* 77.

34. "Pressures in the Process of Administrative Decision: A Study of Highway Location," *University of Pennsylvania Law Review,* 108 (1960): 534ff.

35. See particularly Eighty-Seventh Congress, *House Reports,* No. 363, 364, 1246, 1285, 1819, and Eighty-Eighth Congress, *House Report,* No. 617.

36. Eighty-Seventh Congress, *House Report,* No. 1285, 65–66.

37. Anthony Lewis in *The New York Times,* June 19, 1961, 1.

38. Paul Ylvisaker, "The Natural Cement Issues," in Harold Stein (ed.), *Public Administration and Policy Development: A Case Book* (New York: Harcourt, Brace, 1952), 107–141.

39. The material regarding this conflict is taken from Andrew Hacker, "Pres-

sure Politics in Pennsylvania," in Alan Westin (ed.), *The Uses of Power* (New York: Harcourt, Brace, 1962), 324–370.

40. This section is based in part upon the findings of Burch in *Highway Revenue and Expenditure Policy.*

41. Data on highway finances are derived from two annual publications: United States Department of Commerce, Bureau of the Census, *Governmental Finances in the United States;* and United States Department of Transportation, Bureau of Public Roads, *Highway Statistics.*

42. Burch, *Highway Revenue and Expenditure Policy,* 161–163.

43. See, for example, *ibid.,* 127.

44. Paul T. David and Ralph Eisenberg, *Devaluation of the Urban and Suburban Vote* (Charlottesville: Bureau of Public Administration, University of Virginia, 1961), 5.

45. Friedman, *State and Local Relations in Highway Finance in Louisiana,* 48–60.

46. *Ibid.,* 24–30.

47. *Ibid.,* 75–76.

48. Simple product moment correlations were as follows: percentage of total expenditure and per capita expenditure, .77; percentage of total expenditure and per $1,000 per income expenditure, .90; and per capita expenditure and per $1,000 income expenditure, .92.

49. Dearing, *American Highway Policy,* 226–228.

50. For a general treatment of the railroad position on highway policy, see American Association of Railroads, *Highways* (Washington, D.C.: American Association of Railroads, 1955).

51. For a description of the Washington rapid transit system see Washington Metropolitan Area Transit Authority, *Metro* (Washington, D.C.: Washington Metropolitan Area Transit Authority, 1969).

52. See John Lansing and Dwight Blood, *The Changing Travel Market* (Ann Arbor: Survey Research Center, University of Michigan, 1964).

53. An excellent discussion of group interests in highway politics may be found in Daniel P. Moynihan, "New Roads and Urban Chaos," *The Reporter,* 22 (April 14, 1960). See also generally Burch, *Highway Revenue and Expenditure Policy;* Murray Levin, *The Compleat Politician* (Indianapolis: Bobbs-Merrill, 1962); Rosendo A. Gomez, *Intergovernmental Relations in Highways* (Minneapolis: University of Minnesota Press, 1950), 63–65; and Robert S. Allen (ed.), *Our Sovereign State* (New York: Vanguard, 1949), 100–101.

54. *The New York Times,* July 13, 1969.

55. *Ibid.*

56. Anthony Lewis in *The New York Times,* June 19, 1961, 1.

57. Frank J. Sorauf, "State Patronage in a Rural County," *American Political Science Review,* 50 (December, 1956): 1046–1056.

58. Gomez, *Intergovernmental Relations in Highways,* 64.

59. See especially Eighty-Seventh Congress, *House Reports,* Nos. 363, 364, 1285, 1918, and Eighty-Eighth Congress, *House Report,* No. 617.

60. Joseph L. Bernd, *The Role of Campaign Funds in Georgia Primary Elections, 1936–1958* (Macon: The Georgia Journal, 1958).

61. See Allan P. Sindler, *Huey Long's Louisiana: State Politics, 1920–1952* (Baltimore: The Johns Hopkins Press, 1956).

62. Industrialization of the states is measured as one minus the percentage of employment in agriculture, forestry, or fisheries.
63. Alexander Heard, *The Costs of Democracy,* (Chapel Hill: University of North Carolina Press, 1960), 144; and Bernd, *The Role of Campaign Funds,* 3.
64. Burch, *Highway Revenue and Expenditure Policy,* 189.
65. The measures used for party competition, partisanship, and voter participation are those found in Thomas R. Dye, *Politics in States and Communities* (Englewood Cliffs, N.J.: Prentice-Hall, 1969).
66. Thomas R. Dye in *Economics, Politics and the Public: Policy Outcomes in the American States,* (Chicago: Rand McNally, 1966) found a significant negative relationship between Democratic partisan control and highway expenditures. There are two possible explanations for the differences in these findings which come to mind. First, Dye used state expenditures rather than state and local expenditures. Second, the period of his study was 1958 to 1962 and our data cover 1963 to 1967.

CHAPTER FOURTEEN

1. R. Clay Sprowls, "On the Terms of the New York State Lottery," *National Tax Journal,* 23 (1970): 74ff.
2. National Municipal League, *Salient Issues of Constitutional Revision* (1961), 136, quoted by Advisory Commission on Intergovernmental Relations, *State Constitutional and Statutory Restrictions on Local Taxing Powers* (Washington, D.C.: United States Government Printing Office, 1962), p. 7.
3. The assumption both of scholars and interest groups has been generally that segregated, decidated, or earmarked funds advantaged the program selected. An important modification is suggested by James M. Buchanan, "The Economics of Ear-Marked Taxes," *Journal of Political Economy,* 71 (October, 1963); and *Earmarked State Taxes* (New York: Tax Foundation, 1965).
4. Ira Sharkansky, *The Routines of Politics* (Chicago: Van Nostrand Reinhold, 1970).
5. Alan T. Peacock and Jack Wiseman, *The Growth of Public Expenditures in the United Kingdom* (Princeton: Princeton University Press, 1961), see especially Chap. 2, 12–34.
6. Ira Sharkansky, *Spending in the American States* (Chicago: Rand McNally, 1968), 146.
7. Glenn W. Fisher, *Taxes and Politics, A Study of Illinois Public Finance* (Urbana: University of Illinois Press, 1969).
8. Allen Rosenbaum, "Republicans, Reformers, and Richard J. Daley," mimeo., University of Wisconsin, 1969.
9. I want to acknowledge the financial support of Ford Foundation funds from the Center for Public Policy and Administration, University of Wisconsin, for travel costs to Oregon. I also want to thank, unfortunately anonymously in this context, all those state legislators, state officials, newspapermen, and University of Oregon faculty members who assisted in my understanding of the Oregon sales tax referendum.
10. Frank H. Jonas (ed.), *Politics in the American West* (Salt Lake City: University of Utah Press, 1969). See John M. Swarthout and Kenneth R. Gervais, "Oregon: Political Experiment Station," 296.

EPILOGUE

1. Social Science Research Council, Committee on Political Behavior, *Research in State Politics,* December 1954, mimeo., 24 pp.
2. One of the editors wrote in an article published in 1964: "Our data demonstrate that malapportionment in and of itself is not associated with some of the major ailments of state politics. . . . The practical impact (of reapportionment) may be quite different than currently expected. Many of the new seats will go to suburban areas which are often more conservative than the rural areas which will lose seats. In the North, the Republican party will not lose nearly as many seats as some Democrats hope, for most of the new suburbs are almost as Republican as the rural areas. Moreover, many of the issues which concern the cores of metropolitan areas divide them from the suburbs. Increasing the voice of suburban voters may not bring additional state aid to the central cities; it is perhaps more likely that a new stalemate will develop on those issues which deeply divide the core cities from suburban areas." Herbert Jacob, "The Consequences of Malapportionment: A Note of Caution," *Social Forces* 43 (1964): 260.
3. John C. Wahlke, Heinz Eulau, William Buchanan, and Leroy C. Ferguson, *The Legislative System* (New York: John Wiley & Sons, 1962).
4. Empirical support for this proposition is one of the central foci of Ira Sharkansky's work. See his Chapter Seven in this volume and *The Politics of Taxing and Spending* (Indianapolis: Bobbs-Merrill, 1969).
5. One of the boldest assertions of this position is by Thomas R. Dye, *Politics, Economics and the Public* (Chicago: Rand McNally, 1966). See also Ira Sharkansky, *Spending in the American States* (Chicago: Rand McNally, 1968). In contrast, note the treatment of political variables in Chapter Nine of this volume by Ira Sharkansky and Richard Hofferbert.
6. A beginning has been made by Ira Sharkansky in Chapter Seven of this book. See also Thomas R. Dye, "Income Inequality and American State Politics," *American Political Science Review* 64 (1970): 157–163, and Brian R. Fry and Richard F. Winters, "The Politics of Redistribution," *American Political Science Review,* 64 (1970): 508–522.

Appendixes to Chapter Nine

Appendix 1

Education

* *1. Percentage of ninth grade students (1959) graduating three years later.
* *2. Percentage of candidates passing selective service mental examination.
* 3. State and local government expenditures for education per capita.

Highways

* 4. Total road mileage per capita.
* *5. Rural road mileage per rural resident.
* 6. Municipal road mileage per urban resident.
* 7. Percentage of designated interstate mileage completed.
* 8. Population per highway fatality.
* *9. State and local government expenditures for highways per capita.

Welfare

* *10. Average payment, aid to families of dependent children.
* *11. Average payment, old age assistance.
* *12. Average payment, aid to the blind.
* *13. Average payment, aid to the permanently and totally disabled.

  The data all pertain to 1962.
  * Variables surviving test for high loading on a single factor.

607

14. Incidence of AFDC recipients among population with incomes of less than $2,000.

*15. Incidence of OAA recipients among population with incomes of less than $2,000 and over 65 years of age.

16. Incidence of AB recipients among population with incomes of less than $2,000.

17. Incidence of APTD recipients among population with incomes of less than $2,000.

18. State and local government expenditures for public welfare per capita.

Health

19. Proportion of white infants surviving their first year of life.

20. Proportion of nonwhite infants surviving their first year of life.

21. State and local government expenditures for health, hospitals, and sanitation per capita.

Natural Resources

22. Visits per 10,000 population to state parks.

*23. Fishing licenses sold per 10,000 population.

*24. Hunting licenses sold per 10,000 population.

*25. State and local government expenditures for natural resources per capita.

General

26. Total state and local government general expenditures per capita.

Appendix 2

Participation and Party Competition

*1. Percentage voting age population voting for governor.
2. Percentage voting age population voting for United States Representative.
*3. Number of items on Milbrath's list of suffrage regulations on which a state scores as a "facilitator."
*4. Percentage of gubernatorial vote won by major party.
5. Percentage of Congressional vote won by major party.
*6. Percentage of seats in lower house of state legislature held by major party.
7. Percentage of seats in upper house of state legislature held by major party.
**8. Number of years during 1953–1963 when major party controlled governor's office.
*9. Number of years during 1954–1962 when major party controlled lower house of legislature.
**10. Number of years during 1954–1962 when major party controlled upper house of legislature.

Institutions and Personnel

**11. Dauer-Kelsey index of legislative apportionment.
**12. David-Eisenberg index of legislative apportionment.
**13. Shubert-Press index of legislative apportionment.
**14. Number of state legislators.
*15. Legislator's compensation.
*16. Total expenditures on legislative services per legislator (minus compensation).
**17. Number of legislative committees.
*18. Number of bills introduced into the legislature.
19. Number of bills passed by the legislature.

Unless indicated otherwise, the data pertain to 1962.
* Variables surviving tests for high loading on a single factor and for high correlation among substantively similar variables.
** Variables surviving test for high correlation among substantively similar variables.

**20. Proportion of bills introduced that were passed.

**21. Number of days in the legislative session.

**22. Term of judges on state court of last resort.

**23. Minimum age requirement for judges on appeals courts.

**24. Minimum age requirement for judges on trial courts.

*25. Compensation for judges on court of last resort.

**26. Minimum term that will make state judges eligible for pension.

27. Number of state employees per 10,000 population.

28. Average salary of state employees.

**29. Percentage of state employees covered by state personnel system.

**30. Schlesinger index of gubernatorial formal power.

**31. Number of separately elected executive officials in the state government.

**32. Number of state plus local government employees per 10,000 population.

**33. Average salary of state plus local government employees.

**34. Percentage of state and local government employees covered by government supported health and hospital insurance.

**35. Percentage of state and local government employees covered by government supported life insurance.

36. Number of words in state constitution.

**37. Number of amendments in state constitution.

**38. Date of state constitution's ratification.

**39. Population per local governmental unit.

Fiscal Structure

**40. Percentage of state and local government revenues collected from real property taxes.

**41. Percentage of state and local government revenues collected from individual income taxes.

**42. Percentage of state and local government revenues collected from general sales taxes.

43. Percentage of state and local government revenues collected from excise taxes.

**44. Percentage of state and local government revenues collected from current service charges.

45. Percentage of state government revenue received as federal aid.

*46. Percentage of state and local government revenue received as federal aid.

47. Percentage of state and local government revenue raised by state government.

*48. Percentage of state and local government revenue spent by state agencies.

49. Percentage of state and local government revenue raised by local governments.

50. Percentage of local revenue received from the state government.

**51. Percentage of state aid to localities allocated on the basis of fixed criteria of population or the amount of certain taxes collected locally.

52. Percentage of state aid to localities allocated on the basis of need.

**53. State aid to localities per capita.

Appendix to Chapter Ten

Following are eighty-eight programs upon which the innovation score is based.

1. Accountants licensing
2. Advertising commissions
3. Agricultural experiment stations
4. Aid for roads and highways
5. Aid to the blind (Social security)
6. Aid to dependent children (Social security)
7. Aid to permanently and totally disabled (Social security)
8. Air pollution control
9. Alcoholic beverage control
10. Alcoholic treatment agencies
11. Antiage discrimination
12. Antiinjunction laws
13. Architects licensing
14. Australian ballot
15. Automobile registration
16. Automobile safety compact
17. Beauticians licensing
18. Board of health
19. Budgeting standards
20. Child labor standards
21. Chiropractors licensing
22. Cigarette tax
23. Committee on the aged
24. Compulsory school attendance
25. Conservation of oil and gas
26. Controlled access highways
27. Council on the arts
28. Court administrators
29. Debt limitations
30. Dentists licensing
31. Direct primary
32. Education agencies
33. Education television
34. Engineers licensing
35. Equal pay for females
36. Fair housing — private
37. Fair housing — public
38. Fair housing — urban renewal areas
39. Fair trade laws
40. Fish agency
41. Forest agency
42. Gasoline tax
43. Geological survey
44. Highway agency
45. Home rule — cities
46. Human relations commissions
47. Initiative and referendum
48. Integrated bar
49. Junior college — enabling legislation
50. Juveniles supervision compact

51. Labor agencies
52. Legislative preplanning agencies
53. Legislative research agencies
54. Library extension system
55. Mental health standards committee
56. Merit system
57. Migratory labor committee
58. Minimum wage law
59. Normal school — enabling act
60. Nurses licensing
61. Old age assistance (Social security)
62. Parking agencies — enabling act for cities
63. Park system
64. Parolees and probationers supervision company
65. Pharmacists licensing
66. Planning board — state level
67. Development agency
68. Police or highway patrol
69. Probation law
70. Public housing — enabling legislation
71. Real estate brokers — licensing
72. Reciprocal support law
73. Retainers agreement
74. Retirement system for state employees
75. Right to work law
76. School for the deaf
77. Seasonal agricultural labor standards
78. Slaughterhouse inspection
79. Soil conservation districts — enabling legislation
80. Superintendent of public instruction
81. Tax commission
82. Teacher certification — elementary
83. Teacher certification — secondary
84. Urban renewal — enabling legislation
85. Utility regulation commission
86. Welfare agency
87. Workmen's compensation
88. Zoning in cities — enabling legislation

Glossary

Coefficient of determination: The square of the simple or multiple correlation coefficient. It indicates the amount of variation accounted for by the variables included in the correlation. A correlation coefficient of .6 is equal to a coefficient of determination of .36 and indicates that 36 per cent of the variance is accounted for.

Coefficient of variation: A standardized measure of the amount of dispersion in a distribution. It ranges from 0 to 100; the higher the coefficient, the more dispersion there is around the mean of the distribution.

Correlation coefficient: A statistic that indicates how closely two phenomena are associated with each other. The coefficient ranges from −1 to 0 to + 1. When it is near zero, the association is negligible; as it approaches −1 or +1, the relationship is closer. A relationship of −1 or +1 indicates that the two phenomena always occur together. When the coefficient has a negative (−) sign, the two phenomena are inversely related to each other: a coefficient of −.58 between rioting and income would indicate that rioting occurred more frequently as income dropped. A coefficient with a positive (+) sign indicates a direct relationship: a coefficient of .68 between income and education indicates that as income rises, education also is higher.

Dependent variables: The phenomenon that is explained in a relationship of analysis. If one wishes to account for expenditure levels by analyzing the availability of economic resources, expenditure level is the dependent variable.

Dimension: In factor analysis, the geometric axis along which an underlying factor stands. When several dimensions exist, they are generally independent of one another. Sharkansky identifies two dimensions of administrative professionalism. The first is composed of salary variables; the second is composed of fringe benefit variables. The two dimensions are independent of each other.

Factor analysis: A statistical technique to delineate clusters of related variables on independent dimensions. Many political phenomena may be factor ana-

613

lyzed to produce two clusters or factors: one centers around elections and the other relates to institutional characteristics.

Factor loading: In factor analysis an indication of the degree to which a particular variable is associated with one of the underlying dimensions or factors discovered by the analysis. The factor loading is interpreted as a correlation coefficient between the variable and the factor. In a factor analysis of socioeconomic variables in the states, per capita income is assigned a particular factor loading that indicates the degree to which per capita income is associated with the underlying dimension of industrialization.

Factor scores: In factor analysis weights are assigned to each observation that indicate the degree to which that observation is associated with one of the factors or dimensions discovered in the factor analysis. A factor analysis of socioeconomic variables in the states produces a dimension called industrialization. The industrialization factor score for each state shows the degree to which each state is industrialized.

Independent variables: The phenomena used to explain some other occurrence in a relationship of analysis. If one wishes to explain voting behavior by race and age, voting behavior is the dependent variable; race and age are the independent variables.

Index numbers: A composite of several variables used to construct an indicator of a phenomenon not easily captured by a single variable. The Cost-of-Living Index is a composite of the prices of many goods used by American consumers. No single price (such as for housing, or lamb chops, or shoes) would, in general, be as reliable as a composite of many prices.

Log bars: A graphic technique to portray changes in phenomena. In comparing change in a small ($1 million) program and in a large ($100 million) one, a log bar graph makes the amount of change directly comparable. If the amount of dollar change were graphed, a doubling of the smaller program would be dwarfed by a relatively small change in the larger program.

Mean: A measure of the most typical case for the interval scale data. It is the arithmetic center of a distribution, most commonly referred to as "the average." The mean is calculated by dividing the sum of the values in a distribution by the number of observations in the distribution. The mean tax revenues of the states equal the sum of all the tax revenues for the states divided by 50.

Median: The middle point of a distribution so that half the observations fall below it and half fall above it. A measure of the most typical case for the ordinal scale data. A median family income of $3,278 for a state means that half the incomes of the states' families are more than $3,278 and half are less.

Multiple correlation coefficient: The degree of relationship between more than two phenomena. It ranges from 0 to +1 and is interpreted in the same way as a simple correlation coefficient.

Partial correlation coefficient: Indicates the relationship between two phenomena when other variables are being held constant. One may wish to know the relationship between income and education holding race and urbanism constant. The coefficient ranges from −1 to 0 to +1. It is interpreted in the same way as the correlation coefficient.

Pearsonian correlation: See *correlation coefficient.*

Per capita: A calculation holding population constant. Per capita income is the income per person thus making the income figures of large and small states directly comparable because population is being held constant.

Product moment correlation: See *correlation coefficient.*

Range: An indication of the difference between the highest and lowest value found for a variable.

Rank-order correlation: A statistic that indicates how closely two phenomena are associated with one another. Its calculation is based on prior calculation of rankings of the two distributions that are being examined. If one wishes to examine the association between interest group activity and party competition in the fifty states, one first ranks the states from most active to least active on the interest group variable and then ranks the states from most competitive to least competitive on the party competition variable. The rankings of the states are then used to calculate the correlation coefficient. The coefficient ranges from -1 to 0 to $+1$. For its interpretation, see *correlation coefficient,* above.

Regression equation: Indicates the amount of change produced in a dependent variable by one unit change in the independent variables. A regression equation might indicate how many units of agricultural production, manufacturing and retail sales are required to produce one unit of personal income.

Residual: In regression and correlation analysis, an indication of the amount of variation left unexplained by the variables used in the analysis. An examination of the residuals reveals the deviant or exceptional cases that are left unexplained by the association found to hold for the other observations.

Scale: A composite of several variables that meets rigorous statistical standards. Scales are most frequently used in measuring attitudes; unlike indices they must be replicable for other observations and their components must be related to each other in specified ways.

Simple correlation: See *correlation coefficient.*

Standard deviation: A standardized measure of dispersion around the mean of a distribution. One standard deviation on either side of the mean in a normally distributed phenomena (a bell-shaped curve) equals 68.3 per cent of the cases, two standard deviations equal 95.4 per cent of the cases, and three standard deviations equal 99 per cent of the cases.

Statistical significance: A statement that the particular measurement could not have occurred by chance except in the specified proportion of cases. When a correlation coefficient is statistically significant at the .05 level, it cannot have occurred by chance more frequently than 5 times in a hundred. Such a statement of statistical significance can be interpreted as the likelihood that an error is being made in attributing a relationship when in fact it doesn't occur. In this case, such an error is likely only 5 times in a hundred.

Variance: The square of the standard deviation. It is also a measure of dispersion, but most easily understood when converted into standard deviations. See *standard deviation.*

Zero-order correlation: See *correlation coefficient.*

Index